Kingston New Hampshire

Early Families, Patriots and Soldiers

Kathleen E. Hosier

HERITAGE BOOKS
2015

HERITAGE BOOKS

AN IMPRINT OF HERITAGE BOOKS, INC.

Books, CDs, and more—Worldwide

For our listing of thousands of titles see our website
at
www.HeritageBooks.com

Published 2015 by
HERITAGE BOOKS, INC.
Publishing Division
5810 Ruatan Street
Berwyn Heights, Md. 20740

Heritage Books by the author:

Kingston, New Hampshire Early Families, Patriots, and Soldiers

Vital Records of Rye, New Hampshire: A Transcript of the Births, Baptisms, Marriages, and Deaths in This Town to the Year 1890

International Standard Book Numbers
Paperbound: 978-1-55613-909-3
Clothbound: 978-0-7884-6125-5

TABLE OF CONTENTS

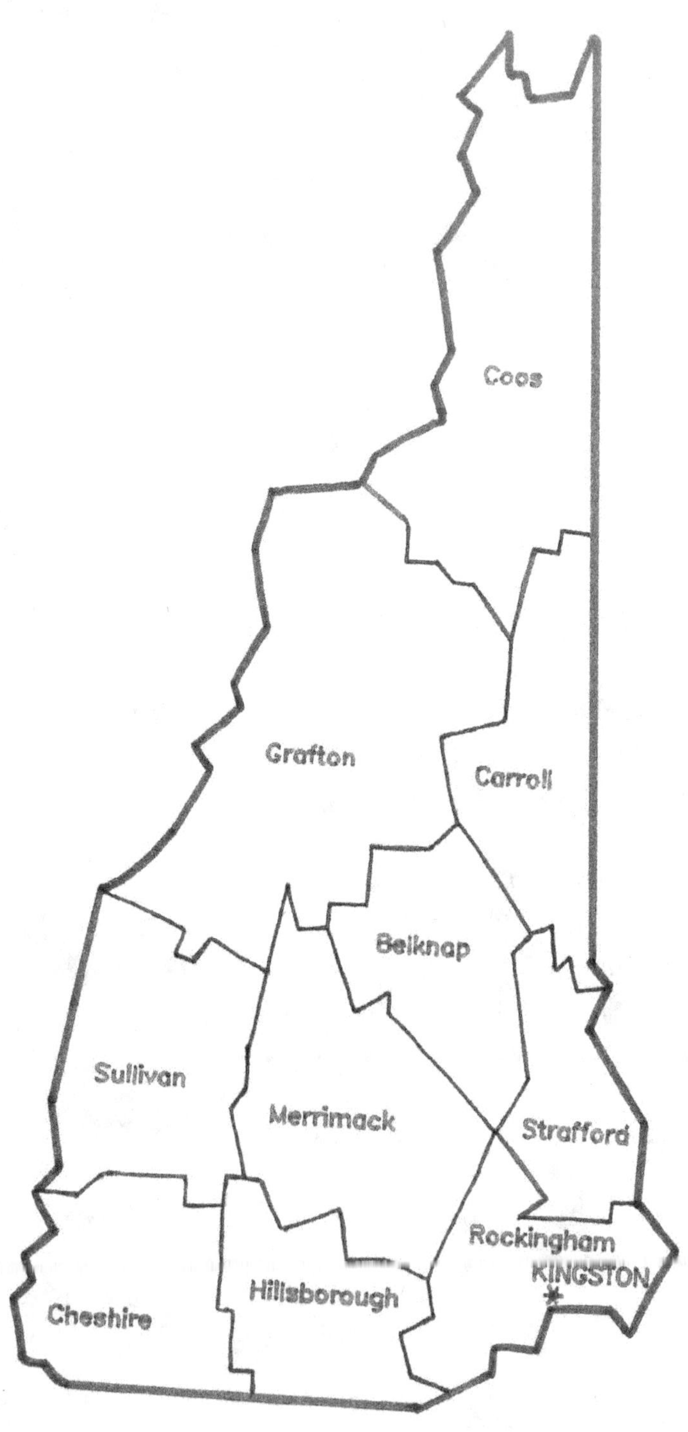
Coos
Grafton
Carroll
Belknap
Sullivan
Merrimack
Strafford
Rockingham
KINGSTON
Cheshire
Hillsborough

PREFACE

Three hundred years have passed since the town of Kingston was granted a Charter in 1694.

The early settlers of Kingston were made up mostly of inhabitants from Hampton, NH. Although the town had been established in 1694, it often had to be abandoned because of Indian attacks and wolves. Eventually Kingston was resettled and the town began to grow. By 1740 many families had moved into town from Amesbury, Salisbury, and Newbury, MA, and as the population became larger, petitions were directed to the colonial government to incorporate new towns. After the Revolutionary War, bounty lands were granted to those who had fought for independence and the migration of Kingston families can be found from Maine to Ohio.

Section I of this book covers the genealogies of Early Families living in Kingston, including the original grantees, from its founding to the period when new towns were incorporated within the original boundaries.

Section II contains the Patriots and Soldiers of Kingston who contributed to the cause of American Independence in the Revolutionary War. Included are those who signed the Association Test in Kingston, as well as those who resided, enlisted, were mustered or served for the town of Kingston. Some of the men are listed as Kingston men for one enlistment, but can be found as listed for a different town in another muster roll.

The families are arranged alphabetically by heads of families and include pertinent information, when available, on births, deaths and marriages.

The statistics for the births, deaths and marriages have been abstracted from microfilmed copies of original town records as well as transcripts, printed vital records, probate records, family genealogies and town histories.

I wish to thank Martha Long of Kingston for furnishing unpublished and printed materials relating to Kingston and George Harmon for his notes on Kingston families. Their interest and support are greatly appreciated.

Kathleen Hosier
6 Aug 1993

KINGSTOWN CHARTER

WILLIAM & MARY By the Grace of God of England Scotland france & Ireland King
~~~~~~ & Queen Defender of the faith &ca To
< > all People to whom these Presents Shall
< P-S > come Greeting KNOW YE That We of our
< > Special Grace Certain knowledge & mere
~~~~~~ motion for the Due Encouragement of Settling a New Plantation by & with the Advise & Consent of our Council Have given & granted & by these Presents as far as in us lyes do give & Grant unto our beloved Subjects James Prescot Senr Isaac Godfrey Thomas Philbrook Junr Gersham Elkins Samuel Colcott Thomas Webster Samuel Derbon William Godfrey Jacob Garland John Mason Ebenezr Webster Nathll Sandburn Benja Sandburn John Moulton Daniel Moulton and frances Toale & Several others of their Majestys Loveing Subjects that inhabit or Shall Inhabit within the Said Grant within our Province of New Hampshire all that Tract of Land to begin Seven Miles Westward of the meeting House now Standing in Hampton from thence to run A Due Course West & B: North Ten Miles into the Country for its Breadth four miles Notherly from the head Point of the West Line from the Sd Meeting House & Southerly within three Miles of the Nothermost Side of Merrimack River and that the Same be A Town Corporate by the name of Kingstown to the Persons above named or other of their majestys Subjects that do & Shall Inhabit Forever And we do by these Presents give & Grant unto the sd men & inhabitants of our Sd Town of Kingstown and to Such Others that Shall hereafter inhabit all & Every the Streets & Lanes & high ways within the sd Town for the Publick use & Service of the men & Inhabitants thereof & Travellers there togeather with full Power Lycence & Authority to the Said men & Inhabitants & Such as Shall inhabit within the Sd Town FOREVER to Establish Appoint Order & Direct the Establishing makeing Laying

out ordering Amending & Repairing of all Streets Lanes High ways ferry Places & bridges in & thro out the Sd Town necessary needfull & Convenient for the men & Inhabitants of the Sd Town and for all Travellers & Passengers there PROVIDED always that our sd Lycence So as above granted for the Establishing makeing & Laying out of Such Lanes Highways Fences Places & Bridges be not Extended nor Construed to Extend to the takeing away of Any Person or Persons Right or Property with out his her or their Consent or by Some Law of our sd Province, TO HAVE & TO HOLD & Enjoy all & singular the Premisses as aforesd to the Sd Kingstown and their Successors for ever rendring & paying therefor to us our heirs & Successors or to Such other officer or officers as Shall be Appointed to receive the Same yearly the annual Quit rent or Acknowledgmt of one Peppercorn in the Sd Towm on the five & Twentieth of October yearly forever & for the better order rule & Government of the Sd Town We do by these Presents Grant for us our heirs & Successors unto the sd men & Inhabitants or those that Shall Inhabit the sd Town That Yearly & every year upon the first Tuesday in March for ever they the Sd men & Inhabitants and Such as Shall Inhabitt the Sd Town Shall Ellect & Chuse by the Major part of them Two Sufficient & Able men householders of Sd Town to be Constables for the year Ensueing which sd men So Chosen & Ellected Shall be Presented to the next Quarter Sessions of the Peace to be held for the sd Province there to take the Accustomed Oaths Appointed by Law for the Execution of their offices under Such Penalties as the Law in our Sd Province Shall Direct upon refusal or neglect therein And we Do by these Presents Grant for us our heirs & Successors unto the sd Persons & Inhabitants And Such as Shall Inhabit in Sd Town that Yearly & every year upon the first Tuesday In March forever they the sd men & Inhabitants or the Majr Part of them Shall Ellect & Chuse three Inhabitants & Householders within our Sd Town to be overseers of the Poor & highways or Select men for our sd Town for the year Ensueing with Such Powers Previledges & Authoritys as any overseers or Select men within our sd Province HAVE & ENJOY or Ought to Have & Enjoy In Testimony whereof we have Caused the Seal of Our Sd Province to be here-unto affixed Wittness John Usher Esq our Lieu-tentant Governour & Coma'nder in Chieff of our Sd Province at our Town of New Castle the Sixth Day of August in the Sixth year of our reigne Annoq Domini 1694

John Usher Lt Governour

William Redford Dept Secry

(New Hampshire State Papers vol.25 p180-81)

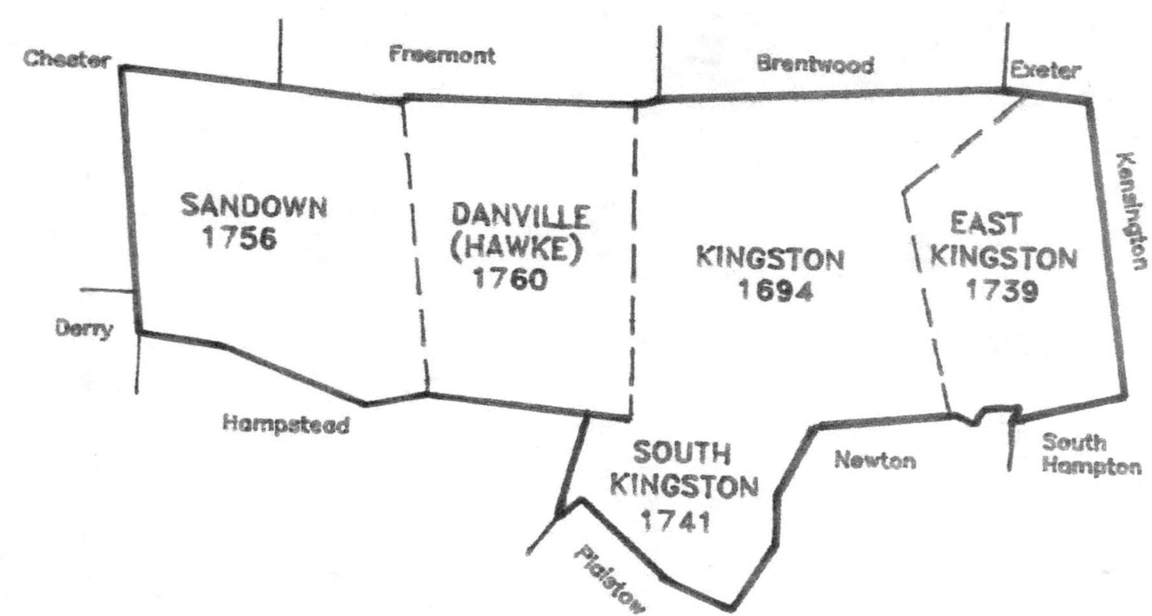
Chester
Freemont
Brentwood
Exeter
Kensington
SANDOWN
1756
DANVILLE
(HAWKE)
1760
KINGSTON
1694
EAST
KINGSTON
1739
Derry
Hampstead
SOUTH
KINGSTON
1741
Newton
South
Hampton
Plaistow

HISTORICAL BACKGROUND

Kingston, NH is located in Rockingham County in the southeast corner of the state. It is bounded on the north by Brentwood, east by East Kingston, south by Newton and Plaistow and west by Danville and Hampstead. It consists of 12,188 acres, 800 of which are covered with water. There are several ponds in the town, the largest being Great Pond which covers 300 acres. Near the center of town is a large plain where the principal town is situated.

Kingston was originally a part of Hampton, NH. In early 1694, several inhabitants of Hampton petitioned the governor for a grant of a township to be formed mainly from the unimproved land in the western part of Hampton.

On 6 Aug 1694 Kingston was incorporated under the administration of Lieutenant-Governor John Usher. It was originally granted as KINGS-TOWN and was so called until about 1800 when the present spelling came into general use.

The original grant included the present towns of Kingston, East Kingston, Danville (Hawke), and Sandown, NH.

In the early days, the people living in the town of Kingston had to abandon their homes because of wolves and Indian attacks. In 1705, it was re-settled and the proprietors built a garrison in the center of town and scouts were sent out to keep an eye on lurking Indians.

Although discouraged by the dangers and difficulties of Indian hostilities, the colonials began to cultivate the lands and the town began to grow.

In colonial times, no town was considered truly settled until a church was established.

The problem then arose in finding a minister willing to locate to a frontier community.

On 29 Sep 1725, the First Church of Kingston was organized with Reverend Ward Clark as the first ordained minister. At that time eighty-one families belonged to Kingston.

The rapid growth of New Hampshire was reflected in the number of taverns in each town. These taverns not only provided refreshments and entertainment for travelers, but served as a gathering place for friends and strangers where local news and politics could be discussed. Kingston had more than most towns because of its location on the post road leading from Boston to Portsmouth. The first tavern in Kingston was licensed to Captain Jonathan Sanborn in 1706.

By 1735, Kingston was a thriving town on the western frontier. It had erected sawmills to replace hand hewing and gristmills for finer grinding of wheat flour. At this time there were no schoolhouses in the town. However, the interest in learning is reflected in the Town Records where fees are listed as being paid to schoolmasters for keeping schools.

The first cemetery in town was laid out in 1725 and is known as the Kingston Plains Cemetery. In the oldest section, occasionally inscriptions can be read today that identify the graves of many children who died during one of the worst epidemics in colonial times. The epidemic known as "throat distemper" (Diphtheria) started in Kingston in the spring of 1735 and struck mainly young children. By the end of 1736 over one hundred deaths of children were recorded in the church records. The epidemic lasted until the end of 1738 by which time many families had lost all of their younger members.

On 2 May 1738 a petition was signed by fifty-three inhabitants living in the easterly part of Kingston for a new parish. This area was set off and incorporated as Kingston, East Parish on 17 Nov 1738. A meetinghouse was built in this east parish and on Lord's Day 18 Nov 1739, twenty-five members were admitted into the 2nd Church of Christ in Kingston. The boundries of East Kingston were established 7 Aug 1740.

In 1741, the boundry was established of what is now South Kingston.

The western part of Kingston as originally granted was set off 6 Apr 1756 by the Governor and Council and incorporated into the town of Sandown.

On 22 Feb 1760, another portion in the western part of Kingston was set off and incorporated into the town of Hawke (now known as Danville).

In 1767, Hampstead paid the town of Kingston 1000 pounds in settlement for any claims Kingston might have had on land which became part of Hampstead.

Most societies for the descendants of American Revolutionary soldiers accept service for the period falling between 19 Apr 1775 (Battle of Lexington) and 26 Nov 1783 (withdrawal of British troops from New York), but in New Hampshire, the American Revolution may be said to have started with an armed raid upon Fort William and Mary at Newcastle, NH in Dec 1774. Although this was really an uprising of the people, the act itself demonstrates the intensity of the feelings men had against the Mother Country.

The Revolutionary War officially began with the Battle of Lexington 19 Apr 1775 and a certain quota of men were demanded from each town. The quotas were determined according to the male population of militaty age, that is sixteen to sixty years. However, before the close of the war the demand for troops was so great that regiments were compelled to enroll many boys and old men who were considerably outside the age limits.

The Seventh Militia Regiment of NH was commonly called the KINGSTOWN REGIMENT and when the news of the Battle of Lexington reached Kingston the men, both young and old, quickly responded.

Josiah Bartlett, a signer of the Declaration of Independence, served as Colonel of the Seventh Militia 1777-1779; therefore, the men who enlisted came to Kingston where they were mustered and reviewed. Some who came were too young or because of age and infirmities could not pass muster.

Those who were incapable of the physical rigors of army life rendered support for the cause of Independence in other capacities such as supplying materials or serving in a Civil office.

In Kingston, the Association Test was signed 23 Sep 1776 and all but twelve men signed. Of those who did not sign, three later went into the army. The other men were either conscientious of taking up arms or felt some measure of infringement on their rights, but all appeared friendly to their country and the American Cause.

In reading the Muster Rolls and Pension Records at the National Archives in Washington, D.C., one can see that the men of Kingston exemplified the motto "LIVE FREE or DIE."

....

SECTION I

EARLY FAMILIES

ORLANDO BAGLEY, b Amesbury, MA 21 Feb 1706/7 son of Orlando & Dorothy (Harvey) Bagley (AVR): d Kingston, NH (Est Adm) 23 Feb 1770 (PRNH 9: 371): m Amesbury, MA 23 Jul 1728 Mary Kendrick (AVR), b Ipswich, MA 11 Oct 1704 dau of John & Frances (Burnham) Kendrick (IpVR).

Orlando signed a petition in 1738 for a new parish in the easterly part of Kingston. Mary Bagley was admitted to the 2nd Church of Christ in Kingston 20 Jan 1740.

Children: 1st 6 born Amesbury, MA (AVR)

1. **JOHN**, b 16 Jul 1729
2. **ANN**, bpt 24 Jan 1730/1: m Kingston, NH 24 Aug 1749 Jonathan French (KChR)
3. **ORLANDO**, b 27 Jun 1732: m Salisbury, MA 27 Apr 1757 Rebecca French (SVR)
4. **JOHN**, bpt Feb 1733/4
5. **SETH**, b 18 Jun 1735: d (prob) Kingston, NH 26 Sep 1738 (NHVR)
6. **PHINEAS**, b 31 Mar 1737: m Kingston, NH 27 Dec 1757 Mary Hobbs (NHGR 3:89)
7. **MERAH**, bpt Kingston, NH 8 Oct 1738 (NHGR 5:104): d Kingston, NH 14 Nov 1738 (NHVR)
8. **SETH**, b Kingston, NH 27 Oct 1739 (KTR): d Salisbury, MA 24 Sep 1804 (SVR): m bef 1775 Abigail Greeley (Greeley Gen p113)
9. **MARY**, b Kingston, NH 11 Sep 1740 (KTR)
10. **DOROTHY**, b Kingston, NH 6 Jul 1743 (KTR)
11. **SARAH**, bpt Kingston, NH 2 Sep 1744 (KChR)
12. **JOHN**, bpt Kingston, NH 30 Mar 1746 (KC hR): d bef 16 May 1812 of Waterborough, ME (ME Fam 1:7): m Kingston, NH 24 Apr 1769 Hannah French (KChR)

ROBERT BARBER, m(1) Kingston, NH 23 Mar 1743 Penelope Hunt (KTR), b abt 1726, bpt Kingston, NH 1 Apr 1730 dau of Charles & Hannah (Welch) Hunt (NHGR 2:65): m(2) Kingston, NH 9 Oct 1759

Abigail Bean (KTR).
Robert was admitted to the Kingston Church 29 Apr 1744 & dismissed to New Salisbury 8 Aug 1773.

Children: born Kingston, NH (KTR)
(by 1st wife)
1. **HANNAH**, b 28 Dec 1743
2. **MARY**, b 10 Oct 1745
3. **ELIZABETH**, b 8 Oct 1750
4. **ESTHER**, bpt 1 Apr 1753 (NHGR 6:29): d Kingston, NH 16 Apr 1753 (NHVR)

(by 2nd wife)
5. **PETER**, b 5 Dec 1760
6. **JETHRO**, b 4 Mar 1762
7. **ESTHER**, b 12 Mar 1764

JOHN BARNARD, b Amesbury, MA 30 Nov 1703 son of Thomas & Elizabeth (Price) Barnard (OF p874): d (Est Adm) 24 Oct 1748 (EA 6:122): m Amesbury, MA 16 Apr 1724 Mary Stanwood (AVR), b Amesbury, MA 18 May 1698 dau of Samuel & Hannah (Pressey) Stanwood (AVR), d Amesbury, MA 26 Jun 1747 (AVR).

Children:
1. **(SON)**, d Kingston, NH 4 Nov 1730 (NHGR)
2. **SAMUEL**, over a.14yrs in 1748
3. **(CHILD)**, d Kingston, NH 21 Sep 1735 (NHGR 3:37)
4. **MARY**, living 1748
5. **RACHEL**, living 1748

STEPHEN BARNARD, b Amesbury, MA 7 Nov 1719 son of Thomas & Elizabeth (Price) Barnard (AVR): d 1797 (DAR 1:36): m Kingston, NH 6 Sep 1743 Mary Collins (KTR), b Salisbury, MA (prob) 31 Mar 1725 dau of Ephraim & Ester (_) Collins (SVR).

Children:
1. **EASTER**, b Kingston, NH 21 APR 1744 (KTR)
2. **ABIGAIL**, b Amesbury, MA 27 Aug 1750 (AVR)
3. **MARY**, b Kingston, NH 17 Apr 1753 (KTR): m Danville, NH 9 Nov 1780 Henry Judkins (NE

HGR 58:125)
4. **ALES**, b Kingston, NH 15 Apr 1756 (KTR)
5. **SARAH**, b Kingston, NH 9 Jan 1759 (KTR)

NATHAN BARTLETT, b Newbury, MA 30 May 1717 son of John & Mary (Ordway) Bartlett (NVR): d Kingston, NH 31 May 1801 a.84yrs (GI p2): m Salisbury, MA 5 Mar 1740/1 Joanna Flanders (SVR), b Salisbury, MA 20 May 1719 dau of Philip & Joanna (Smith) Flanders (SVR), d Kingston, NH 19 May 1804 (GI p2).

Nathan & Joanna, his wife, were admitted to the 2nd Church of Christ in Kingston 5 Feb 1743.

Children: last 8 born Kingston, NH (KTR)
1. **JOANNA**, b Salisbury, MA 4 Jan 1741/2 (SVR)
2. **JOHN**, b 31 Jul 1743: d Kingston, NH 17 Nov 1747 (KTR)
3. **MARY**, b 5 Sep 1745
4. **JOHN**, b 31 Dec 1747
5. **EBENEZER**, b 23 Apr 1750: d Kingston, NH 12 Mar 1838 (NHVR): m ___
6. **NATHAN**, b 25 Feb 1752: m Kingston, NH 9 Sep 1772 Mary Blaisdell (HA p18)
7. **ZIPPORAH**, b 6 Mar 1754
8. **JEREMIAH**, b 6 Dec 1757: living 1833
9. **SARAH**, b 19 Apr 1761

EBENEZER BATCHELDER, b Hampton, NH 10 Dec 1710 son of Nathaniel & Elizabeth (Foss) Batchelder (HH p591): d E. Kingston, NH 1784: m Kingston, NH 1 Feb 1733 Dorothy Boynton (KTR), b Newbury, MA 12 Dec 1715 dau of William & Joanna (Stevens) Boynton (NVR).

Ebenezer & his wife were admitted to the Kingston Church 18 Jul 1736. In 1738 Ebenezer signed a petition for a new parish in the easterly part of Kingston.

Children:
1. **NATHAN**, b Kingston, NH 23 Oct 1734 (KTR): d 1801 (DAR 1:43): m Kingston, NH 8 Apr

1756 Margaret Bean (KChR)

2. **RICHARD**, bpt Kingston, NH 28 Nov 1736 (NH GR 2:71): d E. Kingston, NH 18 May 1753 (CR)
3. **WILLIAM**, b 2 Nov 1738
4. **NATHANIEL**, bpt Kingston, NH 22 Feb 1741 (KChR)
5. **BETTY**, bpt Kingston, NH 5 Aug 1744 (KChR)
6. **EBENEZER**, bpt Kingston, NH 15 Feb 1747 (KChR)
7. **JOSIAH**, bpt Kingston, NH 31 Dec 1749 (KC hR): m 22 Oct 1778 Sarah Blake (Batchelder Gen p148)
8. **DOROTHY**, bpt Kingston, NH 27 May 1753 (KChR)
9. **ANN**, bpt Kingston, NH 12 Feb 1758 (KChR)
10. **JOANNA**, bpt Kingston, NH 12 Oct 1760 (KChR)

FRANCIS BATCHELDER, bpt Hampton, NH 24 Dec 1710 son of Benjamin & Susanna (Page) Batchelder (HH p591): m Hampton Falls, NH 20 Jan 1732 Mary Blake (HFTR), b Hampton, NH 7 Sep 1712 dau of Moses & Abigail (Smith) Blake (HmVR p44).

Francis & his wife, from Hampton Falls, were admitted to the Kingston Church 26 Dec 1737. In 1738 Francis signed a petition for a grant of land in Kingston.

Children: bpt Kingston, NH (KChR & NHGR)

1. **ANNA**, b 26 Jun 1733
2. **ENOCH**, b 10 Jun 1735
3. **ELIJAH**, bpt 7 Jun 1741: d Kingston, NH 30 Oct 1753 (NHVR)
4. **EUNICE**, bpt 23 Jul 1744: d (prob) Kingston, NH 2 May 1749 (NHVR)
5. **EUNICE**, bpt 2 Apr 1749
6. **MOLLY**, bpt 22 Apr 1750

JOSIAH BATCHELDER, b Hampton, NH 28 Oct 1700 son of Benjamin & Susanna (Page) Batchelder (HmVR p71): d Kingston, NH (WP) 16 Dec 1769 (PRNH 7:38): m(1) Kingston, NH 7 Feb 1728 Abigail Lamphrey (KTR), b Hampton, NH 3 May

1705 dau of Benjamin & Jane (Batchelder) Lamphrey (HmVR p32), d Kingston, NH 14 Dec 1736 (NHGR 3:39): m(2) Sarah ____ (PRNH 7:38). A Josiah Batchelder of Kingston m Newbury, MA 18 Jan 1737/8 Sarah Morse (NVR).

Josiah own'd ye Covenant & had his own child baptized named Abigail & a child he had taken which was named Hannah which was a bastard child of Magoons 5 Aug 1733. His wife was admitted to the Kingston Church 6 Jun 1736. In 1738 Josiah signed a petition for a new parish in the easterly part of Kingston.

Children: born Kingston, NH (KTR)

1. **ABIGAIL**, b 6 Jun 1732: d Kingston, NH (prob) 21 Nov 1735 (NHGR 3:38)
2. **DEBORAH**, b 1 Feb 1734: d Kingston, NH 5 Jun 1735 (NHGR 2:133)
3. **BENJAMIN**, b 11 Sep 1736

NATHAN BATCHELDER, b Hampton, NH 2 Jul 1700 son of Nathaniel & Elizabeth (Foss) Batchelder (Hm VR p70): d E. Kingston, NH (WP) 28 May 1755 (PR NH 5:249): m Hampton Falls, NH 25 Feb 1724 Mary (Mercy) Tilton (HFTR), b Hampton, NH 3 Mar 1703/4 dau of Joseph & Margaret (Sherburne) Tilton (HmVR p30), d aft 1755.

Nathan's family belonged to Kingston when Rev Ward Clark took charge of the church on 29 Sep 1725. In 1738 he signed a petition for a new parish in the easterly part of Kingston.

Children: 1st 5 born Kingston, NH (KTR)

1. **NATHANIEL**, b 4 Jan 1725: d Kingston, NH 11 Oct 1735 (KTR)
2. **ELIZABETH**, b 3 May 1728: m Kingston, NH 30 Jan 1752 Rev James Hobbs (KChR)
3. **ANNA**, b 29 Jan 1731/2: living 1755
4. **MARY**, b 26 May 1733: d Kingston, NH 12 Oct 1735 (KTR)
5. **NATHANIEL**, b 13 Aug 1735: d E. Kingston, NH Apr 1809 (CR): m So Hampton, NH 5 Jan 1757 Susanna Gale (SHVR)
6. **JOSEPH**, b 20 Oct 1738: d 15 Dec 1738

7. **MOLLY**, b 3 Jul 1740: living 1755
8. **NATHAN**, b 31 May 1743: d Loudon, NH 9 Dec 1815: m So Hampton, NH 19 Oct 1769 Mary Greeley (SHVR)
9. **SARAH**, b 20 Jan 1748: d 1 Jan 1786: m 27 Aug 1765 Obediah Clement (Batchelder Gen)

PHINEAS BATCHELDER, b Hampton, NH 1 Nov 1701 son of Nathaniel & Elizabeth (Foss) Batchelder (HmVR p27): d E. Kingston, NH 16 Jan 1793 (LND p81): m Kingston, NH 17 Jan 1727 Elizabeth Gilman (KTR), b Kingston, NH 22 Mar 1709 dau of Jacob & Mary (Ladd) Gilman (KTR), d E. Kingston, NH 27 May 1773 (LND p81).

In 1730 Phineas signed a petition regarding the township of Kingston. His wife was admitted to the Kingston Church 14 Mar 1736 & in 1738 he signed a petition for a new parish in the easterly part of Kingston.

Children: 1st 4 born Kingston, NH (KTR)

1. **STEPHEN**, b 21 Apr 1727
2. **MARY**, b 13 Apr 1729: m (prob) Kingston, NH 15 Nov 1749 Jacob Hook (KTR)
3. **JOHN**, b 28 Feb 1730/1: d E. Kingston, NH 18 May 1797: m 1 Jan 1760 Mrs Mercy Batchelder (Batchelder Gen p147)
4. **DANIEL**, b 26 Oct 1733: d Kingston, NH 16 Jan 1733/4 (KTR)
5. **ELIZABETH**, bpt 22 Dec 1734 (NHGR 2:69): d Kingston, NH 4 Feb 1735 (NHGR 2:133)
6. **ELIZABETH**, b 5 Sep 1736: d Kingston, NH (prob) 5 Dec 1736 (NHGR 3:39)
7. **ELIZABETH**, b 20 Dec 1739: d 5 Nov 1746
8. **NATHANIEL GILMAN**, b 20 Dec 1741: d Fayette, ME 10 Oct 1817 (Batchelder Gen): m (1) So Hampton, NH 5 Jul 1764 Dorothy Currier (SHVR): m(2) E. Kingston, NH 2 May 1775 Sarah Davis (OF p739)
9. **DOLLY**, b 20 Dec 1742: d 9 Oct 1743
10. **DOLLY**, b 14 Dec 1744: d 8 Nov 1746
11. **HANNAH**, b 8 Oct 1746

BENJAMIN BEAN, b Kingston, NH 5 May 1699 son of

James & Sarah (Bradley) Bean (KTR): d 1738: m Eastham, MA 5 Aug 1725 Mehitable Mayo (Bean Gen p133), b abt 1705 dau of Nathaniel & Mary (Brown) Mayo. Mehitable m(2) Jeremiah Bean.

Children: bpt Kingston, NH (NHGR 2:68)

1. **SARAH**, b 14 May 1727: bpt 4 Nov 1733
2. **BENJAMIN**, b 9 May 1729: bpt 4 Nov 1733
3. **MEHITABLE**, bpt 4 Nov 1733
4. **DAVID**, bpt 4 Nov 1733
5. **JONATHAN**, bpt 4 Nov 1733

DANIEL BEAN, b Exeter, NH 23 Mar 1662/3 son of John & Margaret (_) Bean (HE p4g): d Kingston, NH (Est Adm) 7 May 1718 (PRNH 2:36): m (prob) Mary Fifield (TAG 15:222), b Hampton, NH 3 May 1676 dau of Benjamin & Mary (Colcord) Fifield (HmVR p107).

Daniel left Kingston in 1707 & went to live in Exeter.

Children:

1. **DANIEL**, b abt 1685: d (W) 1745: m (prob) Ann Sanborn (TAG 16:168)
2. **JOHN**, d abt 1732: m Martha Sinkler (TAG 16:169)
3. **SAMUEL**, d Kingston, NH 9 Apr 1737 (KTR): m Sarah ____
4. **MARY**, m John Quimby (TAG 16:170)

DANIEL BEAN, b abt 1685 son of Daniel & Mary (Fifield) Bean: d abt 1745: m Ann Sanborn dau of Joseph & Mary (Gove) Sanborn (TAG 16:168).

Daniel & his family belonged to Kingston when Rev Ward Clark took charge of the church on 29 Sep 1725.

Children: (TAG 16:168)

1. **JOSEPH**, m (prob) Kingston, NH 13 Nov 1734 Miriam Folsom (KTR)
2. **JONATHAN**, b (prob) abt 1720: d E. Bethel ME 1800 (RG 1:43): m Kingston 14 Sep 1744/5 Abigail Gordon (NHGR 3:42)
3. **DAVID**, b 10 Feb 1725: d Candia, NH 10 Apr

1793 (CG p29): m Kingston, NH 2 May 1748 Mary Judkins (NHGR 3:43)
4. **BENJAMIN**, b abt 1726

DANIEL BEAN, bpt Kingston, NH 21 Apr 1728 son of Samuel & Sarah (_) Bean (NHGR 2:48): m (prob) Kingston, NH 4 Mar 1745 Abigail Clifford (KTR).

Children: born Kingston, NH (KTR)
1. **BATHSHEBA**, b 3 Jul 1746
2. **MARY**, b 3 Sep 1747: d Kingston, NH 18 Dec 1749 (KTR)
3. **SAMUEL**, b 22 Apr 1749
4. **SARAH**, b 23 Apr 1751
5. **MARY**, b 26 Jun 1753
6. **DANIEL**, b (no date)

JAMES BEAN, b Exeter, NH 17 Dec 1672 son of John & Margaret (_) Bean (HE p4g): d Kingston, NH 6 Jan 1753 (NHVR): m(1) ___ Coleman (NEM p56): m(2) Kingston, NH Dec 1697 Sarah Bradley (KTR), b Haverhill, MA 16 Aug 1673 dau of Daniel & Mary (Williams) Bradley (HvVR), d Kingston, NH 17 Jul 1738 (NHVR): m(3) Kingston, NH 2 Nov 1738 Mary (Prescott-Coleman) Crosby (NHGR 3:40), b Hampton, NH 11 Jun 1677 dau of James & Mary (Boulter) Prescott (HmVR p109), d Kingston, NH 3 Jan 1741 (NHVR).

James was granted lot no. 15 in Kingston 10 Jul 1702. His family belonged to Kingston in 1725 when Rev Clark took charge of the church.

Children: last 6 born Kingston, NH (KTR)
(by 1st wife)
1. **JOHN**, b abt 1693: d 1747: m Sarah ___
2. **EDWARD**, b abt 1695

(by 2nd wife)
3. **BENJAMIN**, b 5 May 1699: d 1738: m 5 Aug 1725 Mehitable Mayo (Bean Gen p133)
4. **MARGARET**, b 16 Apr 1702
5. **JOSEPH**, b 17 Oct 1704: d Kingston, NH (WP) 12 Jan 1767: m Kingston, NH 16 Mar 1725 Hannah Davis (KTR)

6. **JEREMIAH**, b 9 Apr 1707: d Dec 1796: m Hampton, NH 13 Nov 1729 Sarah Blake
7. **SAMUEL**, b 11 Jan 1710/11: m Kingston, NH 8 Sep 1731 Mary Buswell (NHGR 2:45)
8. **CATHERINE**, b 22 Aug 1714: m Kingston, NH 21 Jan 1741 Simmons Buzzell (KTR)

JEREMIAH BEAN, b Kingston, NH 9 Apr 1707 son of James & Sarah (Bradley) Bean (KTR): d Dec 1796 (DAR 1:46): m Hampton, NH 13 Nov 1729 Sarah Blake (HH p603), b Hampton, NH 24 Feb 1707 dau of Philemon & Sarah (Dearborn) Blake (HmVR p39), d aft 1788.

Jeremiah was admitted to the Kingston Church 6 Jul 1729 & his wife was admitted 12 Apr 1730. They were dimissed to Brentwood Jan 1751.

Children: (BtTR)

1. **JEMIMA**, b 3 Dec 1730: m(1) Kingston, NH 15 Jan 1751/2 Jacob Smith (NHGR 3:45): m (2) Kingston, NH 28 Dec 1756 Joseph Eastman (NHGR 3:89): m(3) Abel Webster
2. **JEREMIAH**, b 19 Nov 1732
3. **JONATHAN**, b 21 Feb 1735: d 10 Aug 1735
4. **JONATHAN**, b 10 Sep 1736: m(1) Mary Leavitt: m(2) Lydia Sleeper (DAR 1:47)
5. **ELISHA**, b 4 Feb 1740
6. **JOSEPH**, b 4 Apr 1742: d Jun 1744
7. **JOSEPH**, b 7 Jun 1745
8. **BENJAMIN**, b 29 Mar 1747: d 20 Feb 1750
9. **BENJAMIN**, b 24 Feb 1750

JOSEPH BEAN, b Kingston, NH 17 Oct 1704 son of James & Sarah (Bradley) Bean (KTR): d Kingston, NH (WP) 12 Jan 1767 (PRNH 8:370): m Kingston, NH 16 Mar 1725 Hannah (Joanna) Davis (KTR), b Amesbury, MA 27 May 1702 dau of Jeremiah & Mary (Huntington) Davis (AVR), d 17 Nov 1785 (Bean Gen p134).

Joseph belonged to Kingston when Rev Ward Clark took charge of the church 29 Sep 1725. In 1730 he signed a petition regarding the township of Kingston.

Children: born Kingston, NH (KTR & NHGR)

1. **COLMAN**, bpt 6 Feb 1725: d Kingston, NH 9 Jul 1731 (NHGR 2:132)
2. **MARGARET**, bpt 26 Nov 1727: d Kingston, NH 28 Jun 1735 (NHGR 2:134)
3. **MIRIAM**, bpt 21 Jun 1730: m Kingston, NH 20 Nov 1748 Jacob French (NHGR 3:44)
4. **NAOMI**, b 19 Feb 1730: d (prob) bef 1767
5. **JOSEPH**, bpt 7 Jan 1733: d Kingston, NH Jun 1735 (NHGR 2:133)
6. **SETH**, bpt 12 May 1734: d Kingston, NH Jun 1735 (NHGR 2:133)
7. **SETH**, b 8 Apr 1736: d Kingston, NH 31 Mar 1738 (NHVR)
8. **MARGARET**, b 12 Aug 1738: m Kingston, NH 8 Apr 1756 Nathan Batchelder (KChR)
9. **SARAH**, b 19 Apr 1740: m ____ Smith
10. **JOSEPH**, b 30 Sep 1743
11. **PETER**, b 28 Jan 1744/5

JOSEPH BEAN, son of Daniel & Ann (Sanborn) Bean: d Kingston, NH 24 Mar 1753 (KTR); (Est Adm) 25 Apr 1753 (PRNH 4:371): m (prob) Kingston, NH 13 Nov 1734 Miriam Folsom (KTR), dau of Nathaniel & Susanna (Jackson) Folsom: d Kingston, NH (WP) 29 Feb 1754 (PRNH 8:5).

He is probably the Joseph Bean Jr who signed a petition in 1738 for a grant of land in Kingston.

Children: born Kingston, NH (KTR)

1. **JOSEPH**, b 3 Apr 1738
2. **NATHANIEL**, b 10 Nov 1739
3. **MARY**, b 8 Aug 1741: m Kingston, NH 12 Sep 1759 William Eastman (NHGR 3:91)
4. **JONATHAN**, b 31 Aug 1743: d bef 1764
5. **DANIEL**, b 30 Sep 1745
6. **FOLSOM**, b 22 Aug 1747
7. **MIRIAM**, b 1 Jul 1749: living 1764
8. **JEREMIAH**, b abt 1750 (PRNH 4:371): d Kingston, NH 29 Sep 1756 (NHVR)

SAMUEL BEAN, b Exeter, NH son of Daniel & Mary (Fifield) Bean (LND p84): d Kingston, NH 9 Apr

1737 (KTR): m Sarah ___ (TAG 16:169), d Kingston, NH 18 Sep 1750 (KTR).

Administration on the estate of Samuel Bean of Kingston was granted to his widow 3 Jun 1737 (PRNH 2:640). Samuel belonged to Kingston when Rev Clark took charge of the church in 1725.

Children: bpt Kingston, NH (NHGR 2:48)

1. **MARY**, bpt 21 Apr 1728: m Kingston, NH 23 Nov 1737 Benjamin Sawyer (NHGR 3:39)
2. **HANNAH**, bpt 21 Apr 1728: m Kingston, NH 8 Sep 1743 John Griffin (KTR)
3. **DANIEL**, bpt 21 Apr 1728: m (prob) 4 Mar 1745 Abigail Clifford (KTR)
4. **ALICE**, bpt 21 Apr 1728: d (prob) 29 Nov 1730 (NHGR 2:132)
5. **SARAH**, bpt 21 Apr 1728: d (prob) 11 Aug 1735 (NHGR 2:134)
6. **(DAU)**, d 31 Aug 1735 (NHGR 3:37)
7. **ALICE**, b 9 Nov 1736 (KTR): bpt 21 Mar 1736/7: d aft 1788: m Hampstead, NH 13 Nov 1755 Samuel Watts (HmstR)

SAMUEL BEAN JR, b Kingston, NH 11 Jan 1710/11 son of James & Sarah (Bradley) Bean (KTR): d bef 27 Feb 1779: m Kingston, NH 8 Sep 1731 Mary Buswell (NHGR 2:45), b Kingston, NH 19 Mar 1714 dau of William & Judith (Davis) Buswell (KTR), d Sutton, NH Aug 1811 (HSt p607).

Samuel signed a petition regarding the township of Kingston in 1730 & in 1738 he signed a petition for a grant of land in Kingston.

Children: bpt Kingston, NH (NHGR)

1. **(CHILD)**, d Kingston, NH 8 Oct 1735
2. **JUDITH**, bpt Jan 1736: d Sutton, NH 9 Nov 1817: m Kingston, NH 5 Jun 1754 Moses Quimby (KTR)
3. **JOSEPH**, bpt 28 Aug 1737: killed at Quebec Sep 1759
4. **CORNELIUS**, bpt 3 Aug 1739/40
5. **SARAH**, bpt 16 Jan 1742/3: d 20 Jul 1820: m 13 Mar 1768 Samuel Peaslee
6. **MARY**, bpt 29 Dec 1745: d 1832: m 1767

Benjamin Wells
7. **SAMUEL**, bpt 14 Feb 1747/8
8. **JEAN**, bpt 3 Jun 1750
9. **WILLIAM**, bpt 26 Apr 1753: d Hatley, Canada 15 Jan 1833: m 1 Jan 1773 Sarah Griffin (HSt p608)
10. **ELIZABETH**, b 6 May 1755: d 20 Sep 1821 (HSt p608)
11. **ISAAC**, bpt 2 Oct 1757 (Bean Gen p139)

ELI BEEDE, b Isle of Jersey abt 1699 (NEHGR 109:242): d Kingston, NH May 1789: m Mehitable Sleeper (NEHGR 109:242), b Kingston, NH 25 Apr 1701 dau of Aaron & Elizabeth (Shaw) Sleeper (KTR).

Eli was admitted to the Kingston Church 14 Mar 1742.

Children: (Boston & East. MA by Cutter 4:1697)
1. **HEZEKIAH**, d Kingston, NH (bur) 1 Jun 1789 (NHVR): m(1) Kingston, NH 9 Jul 1747 Hepsibah Smith (KTR): m(2) Kingston, NH 12 Nov 1772 Judith Gove (KTR)
2. **DANIEL**, b Kingston, NH 21 Jul 1729 (NEHGR 5:214): d 7 Apr 1799 (DAR 1:49): m(1) Kingston, NH 22 Jan 1749/50 Patience Prescott (NHGR 3:44): m(2) 27 Feb 1795 wid Dorothy Eldridge
3. **THOMAS**, b Kingston, NH 1 Jun 1732 (KTR): d 6 Mar 1806: m Elizabeth Ewing (DAR 1: 49)
4. **JONATHAN**, b Kingston, NH 17 Sep 1734 (KTR): d Amesbury, MA 14 Aug 1825 (AVR): m(1) abt 1754 Ann Sleeper: m(2) Amesbury, MA 23 Aug 1786 Susanna Hoeg (AVR)
5. **ELIZABETH**, b Feb 1739: m Kingston, NH 7 Dec 1754 John Huntoon Jr (KTR)
6. **JOANNA**, d bef 17 Jun 1789: m Samuel Davis

HEZEKIAH BEEDE, son of Eli & Mehitable (Sleeper) Beede (NEHGR 109:242): d Kingston, NH (bur) 1 Jun 1789 (NHVR): m(1) Kingston, NH 9 Jul 1747 Hepsibah Smith (KTR), d Kingston, NH 12 Mar 1772 (KTR): m(2) Kingston, NH 12 Nov 1772

Judith Gove (KTR), b 1734? dau of Jeremiah & Sarah (Cram) Gove (Gove Gen p65).

Children: last 6 born Kingston, NH (KTR)
(by 1st wife)

1. **PHINEAS**, b Kingston, NH 24 Sep 1749: d 1 Jan 1806: m Sarah Batchelder
2. **HEPSIBAH**, b Brentwood, NH 24 Apr 1751 (Bt TR): bpt Kingston, NH 26 May 1751 (NHGR 6:26)
3. **MEHITABLE**, b Brentwood, NH 25 Dec 1752 (BtTR)
4. **KEZIAH**, b Brentwood, NH 27 Nov 1754: d Brentwood, NH 26 Mar 1756 (BtTR)
5. **KEZIAH**, b Brentwood, NH 17 Apr 1757
6. **BEZABEEL**, b 22 Aug 1759: m Kingston, NH 18 Dec 1782 Judith Morgan (NHGR 3:131)
7. **JEHOSHEBA**, b 15 Jan 1762: m Kingston, NH 14 Aug 1782 Edward Magoon (NHGR 3:131)
8. **REZIAH**, b 6 Jul 1764: d Keene, NY 24 Nov 1841: m 11 Apr 1785 Mary Ann Stroud
9. **DEBORAH**, b 26 Sep 1766
10. **AZARIAH**, b 29 Nov 1768: m Exeter, NH 8 Jul 1786 Elizabeth Lord (HE p79g)

(by 2nd wife)

11. **JEREMIAH**, b 19 Dec 1774

JOHN BISHOP, m Kittery, ME 8 Jan 1712/3 Eleanor Frye (KitVR p47), b abt 1668 dau of Adrian & Hannah (White) Frye (LND p248). Eleanor m(1) bef 1692 John Brooks.

John had land laid out to him in Kingston 9 Sep 1715.

DANIEL BLAISDELL, b Amesbury, MA 5 Mar 1701/2 son of Jonathan & Hannah (Jameson) Blaisdell (AVR): d Kingston, NH 20 Dec 1732 (NHGR 2:132): m Amesbury, MA (int) 2 Sep 1721 Naomi Tuxbury (AVR), b Amesbury, MA 6 Aug 1702 dau of Henry & Hannah (_) Tuxbury (AVR). Naomi m(2) Salisbury, MA (int) 4 Oct 1735 Israel Morrill (SVR).

Daniel signed a petition regarding the township of Kingston 1730. His wife, Naomi, was admitted to the Kingston Church 20 Aug 1732.

Children: 1st 4 born Amesbury, MA (AVR)

1. **CHRISTOPHER**, b 22 Mar 1721/2: m(1) Amesbury, MA 23 Nov 1742 Sarah Nichols (AVR) m(2) Frances ___ (ExA 9:55)
2. **DANIEL**, b 10 Apr 1724: d Salisbury, MA 8 Apr 1793 (SVR): m Salisbury, MA (int) 13 Jun 1747 Rachel Edwards (SVR)
3. **JACOB**, b abt 1726: d Salisbury, MA 21 Nov 1760 (SVR): m Mary ___ (ExA 9:55)
4. **MOSES**, b 28 Sep 1728: d 1790 (DAR 2:18): m (int) 27 Oct 1750 Anna Sanborn
5. **ELEANOR**, b 1729: d Kingston, NH 2 Aug 1732? (OF p624)
6. **PHEBE**, b abt 1730: d Kingston, NH 23 Oct 1732 a.2yrs (NHGR 2:132)
7. **ELEANOR**, b (posth) 1733: d Candia, NH 1817 a.85yrs: m ____ Neal

EBENEZER BLAISDELL, b Amesbury, MA 14 Aug 1711 son of Ralph & Mary (Davis) Blaisdell (AVR): m Kingston, NH 29 Oct 1739 Sarah Stockman (KTR), dau of Robert & Lydia (Folsom) Stockman (PRNH 3:95).

Ebenezer was admitted to the Kingston Church 8 Apr 1739.

Children: born Kingston, NH (KTR)

1. **SARAH**, b 8 Nov 1740: d Kingston, NH 28 Jul 1744 (KTR)
2. **MARY**, b 17 May 1743
3. **SARAH**, b 6 May 1745
4. **EBENEZER**, b 7 Jan 1747/8
5. **SUSANNAH**, b 20 Mar 1749/50
6. **MARTHA**, bpt 5 Jul 1752 (KChR): m 25 Sep 1786 Thomas Weeks

ENOCH BLAISDELL, b Amesbury, MA 9 Jul 1714 son of Jonathan & Hannah (Jameson) Blaisdell (AVR): d 12 Feb 1790 (DAR 1:64): m Salisbury, MA 6 Feb 1735/6 Mary Satterlee (SVR), dau of Jacob & Flower (Norton) Satterlee (Hartford Times 8-8-42).

Enoch signed a petition in 1738 for a new parish in the easterly part of Kingston.

Children: born Amesbury, MA (AVR)

1. **SUSANNA**, b 4 Sep 1737
2. **ELIJAH**, b 5 Sep 1739: d Amesbury, MA 22 Jan 1739 (AVR)
3. **ELIJAH**, b 31 Dec 1740: m Amesbury, MA 14 Mar 1759 Mary Sargent (AVR)
4. **JUDITH**, b 17 Mar 1742/3: m Amesbury, MA 2 Dec 1762 Pasky Pressy (AVR)
5. **BETTY**, b 6 Aug 1746: m So Hampton, NH 26 Sep 1772 Joshua Mitchell (SHVR)
6. **MARY**, b 19 Jul 1751
7. **JACOB**, b 8 Apr 1754: d 25 Apr 1831 (DAR 1:64): m Brentwood, NH 26 Mar 1778 Ruth Morse (BtTR)
8. **ENOCH**, b 16 Oct 1759: d Amesbury, MA 30 Oct 1759 (AVR)
9. **JOSEPH**, b 16 Oct 1759

JONATHAN BLAISDELL, b Amesbury, MA 15 Aug 1709 son of Jonathan & Hannah (Jameson) Blaisdell (AVR): d E. Kingston, NH (WP) 29 Jan 1782 (ExA 9:50): m Amesbury, MA 5 Aug 1731 Hannah Jones (AVR), b Amesbury, MA 22 Jun 1710 dau of John & Hannah (Hoeg) Jones (AVR).

Jonathan signed a petition in 1738 for a new parish in the easterly part of Kingston.

Children: last 7 bpt Kingston, NH (KChR)

1. **HENRY**, b Kingston, NH 12 Jan 1732 (KTR): d Kingston, NH Oct 1735 (NHGR 3:38)
2. **(CHILD)**, d Kingston, NH Oct 1735 (NHGR 3:38)
3. **HENRY**, bpt (prob) 31 Oct 1736 (NHGR 2: 71): d Aug 1828 (DAR 1:64): m(1) Kingston, NH 22 Nov 1758 Mary Currier (KChR): m(2) Danville, NH 4 Mar 1772 Sarah Dolloff (NEHGR 58:122): m(3) Kingston, NH 20 Dec 1778 Hannah Ross (NHGR 3:130): m(4) 29 Sep 1792 Hannah Nicholson
4. **(CHILD)**, d Kingston, NH 11 Mar 1739 (NH VR)
5. **MARY**, bpt 23 Nov 1740: d Brentwood, NH 8 Jul 1825 (CG p27): m 26 Aug 1762 Isaac Whittier

6. **JONATHAN**, bpt 24 Jul 1743: m Kingston, NH 23 Sep 1762 Miriam Blaisdell (NHGR 3:91)
7. **ABNER**, bpt 6 Apr 1746: d.y.
8. **EBENEZER**, bpt 27 Nov 1748
9. **HANNAH**, bpt 16 Jun 1751
10. **ELIZABETH**, bpt 29 Jul 1753
11. **HANNAH**, bpt 28 Mar 1756: m So Hampton, NH 13 May 1779 Daniel Eastman (SHVR)

RALPH BLAISDELL, b Amesbury, MA 21 Apr 1692 son of Ebenezer & Sarah (Colby) Blaisdell (AVR): m abt abt 1711 Mary Davis (OF p620), b Amesbury, MA 6 Jan 1689 dau of Jeremiah & Mary (Huntington) Davis (AVR).

Children: born Amesbury, MA (AVR)

1. **EBENEZER**, b 14 Aug 1711: m Kingston, NH 29 Oct 1739 Sarah Stockman (KTR)
2. **TIMOTHY**, b 16 Jul 1713: d Amesbury, MA Sep 171? (AVR)
3. **HUMPHREY**, b 4 Sep 1714: d Amesbury, MA 19 Jul 1726 (AVR)
4. **RALPH**, b 6 Jan 1717/8: d Kingston, NH 13 Apr 1806 (NHVR): m Kingston, NH 18 Oct 1748 Miriam Rowell (KTR)
5. **TIMOTHY**, b 8 May 1720: m Kingston, NH 3 Jan 1744/5 Joanna Stockman (KTR)
6. **JOHN**, b 5 Mar 1725/6: d Amesbury, MA 10 Aug 1735 (AVR)
7. **SARAH**, b 17 Jul 1730: d Amesbury, MA 14 Jul 1733 (AVR)
8. **DOROTHY**, b abt 1732: bpt Kingston, NH 22 Apr 1744 (KChR): m Kingston, NH Nov 1752 Stephen Tongue (KTR)

RALPH BLAISDELL, b Amesbury, MA 10 Apr 1698 son John & Elizabeth (Challis) Blaisdell (AVR): d abt 1780: m Amesbury, MA 10 Apr 1718 Mary Nichols (AVR), b Amesbury, MA 11 Oct 1701 dau of Thomas & Jane (Jameson) Nichols (AVR).

Ralph's family belonged to Kingston in 1725 when Rev Clark took charge of the church.

Children: (ExA 9:52)

1. **MOSES**, b Amesbury, MA 17 Jul 1720 (AVR): m Kingston, NH 16 Jul 1745/6 Mary Prescott (NHGR 3:42)
2. **ELIZABETH**, b abt 1722: m Kingston, NH 6 Mar 1745/6 John Fellows (NHGR 3:42)
3. **MARY**, b Kingston, NH 4 Feb 1724/5: m Kingston, NH 16 Jan 1745 Timothy Eastman (KTR)
4. **THOMAS**, m Kingston, NH 25 Oct 1750 Dorothy Clough (KChR)
5. **DANIEL**, lived E. Kingston, NH
6. **HANNAH** (Lydia ? Blaisdell Papers 2:7), m Kingston, NH 10 Nov 1748 William Runnels (NHGR 3:44)
7. **JOHN**, b abt 1733: d 28 Nov 1799 (DAR 1: 64): m So Hampton, NH 10 May 1759 Judith Shephard (SHVR)
8. **MIRIAM**, m Kingston, NH 23 Sep 1762 Jonathan Blaisdell (NHGR 3:91)

JONATHAN BLAKE, b Hampton, NH 10 Apr 1715 son of Moses & Abigail (Smith) Blake (HmVR p50): d Danville, NH 15 Mar 1794 (DnTR): m (prob Hampton Falls, NH) 2 Jun 1737 Mary Sanborn (DnTR), b 5 Sep 1719 dau of John & Mehitable (Fifield) Sanborn (DnTR), d Danville, NH 5 May 1808 (DnTR).

Jonathan, from Hampton Falls, was admitted to the Kingston Church 3 Apr 1739.

Children: 1st 8 bpt Kingston, NH (NHGR & NHVR)

1. **TIMOTHY**, bpt 19 Jul 1741: d Strafford, VT 25 Jul 1821: m Danville, NH 22 Dec 1763 Susanna Morrill (NEHGR 58:47)
2. **MARY**, bpt 15 Jul 1744
3. **HEZEKIAH**, bpt 25 Jan 1746/7: d Kingston, NH 25 Oct 1747 (NHVR)
4. **SARAH**, bpt 9 Oct 1748
5. **HEZEKIAH**, bpt 25 Jun 1751: d Danville, NH 19 May 1821 (DnTR): m abt 1776 Hannah Dimond
6. **JONATHAN**, bpt 9 Dec 1753: m Kingston, NH 18 Feb 1777 Lucy Robinson (NHGR 3:130)
7. **ELIJAH**, bpt 12 Oct 1755: d Chelsea, VT 17

Nov 1839 (NHPR 4:117): m Strafford, VT 4 Nov 1784 Sarah Preston

8. **TRISTRAM SANBORN**, bpt 8 Oct 1758
9. **SARAH**, b Danville, NH 5 May 1761 (DnTR): m Kingston, NH Apr 1804 Joseph Williams (NHGR 4:173)
10. **TRISTRAM SANBORN**, b Danville, NH 31 May 1764 (DnTR): m Miriam Brown

WILLIAM BOYNTON, b Newbury, MA 26 May 1690 son of Joshua & Hannah (Barnet) Boynton (NVR): d E. Kingston, NH 29 Apr __ a.73y (CR): m Salisbury, MA Nov 1713 Joanna Stevens (SVR), b Salisbury, MA 15 Oct 1692 dau of John & Dorothy (Hubbard) Stevens (SVR), d E. Kingston, NH.

William & his wife were dismissed from Salisbury & admitted to the Kingston Church 20 Aug 1732. In 1738 William signed a petition for a new parish in the easterly part of Kingston.

Children:

1. **DOROTHY**, b Newbury, MA 12 Dec 1715 (NVR): m Kingston, NH 1 Feb 1733 Ebenezer Batchelder (KTR)
2. **HANNAH**, b Salisbury, MA 26 Sep 1717 (SVR) m Kingston, NH 15 Dec 1737 Obediah French (NHGR 3:39)
3. **WILLIAM**, b Salisbury, MA 5 Jul 1719 (SVR) d E. Kingston, NH 31 Jan 1744 (CR)
4. **RICHARD**, b Salisbury, MA 28 May 1721 (SVR)
5. **JOHN**, b Salisbury, MA 31 Aug 1724 (SVR): m Kingston, NH 14 Jul 1748 Anna Smith (KChR)
6. **JOSHUA**, b Salisbury, MA 16 Aug 1725 (SVR)
7. **MARTHA**, b Salisbury, MA 2 Sep 1726 (SVR): m (prob) 25 Dec 1746 Timothy Tilton (KTR)
8. **BETTE**, b Salisbury, MA 6 Mar 1727/8 (SVR): d E. Kingston, NH 15 Jan 1744 (CR)
9. **BARZILLAI**, bpt Kingston, NH 10 Jan 1730/1 (NHGR 2:65): d Kingston, NH 2 Sep 1735 (NHGR 3:37)
10. **JOANNA**, bpt (prob) Kingston, NH 22 Oct 1732 (NHGR 2:67): d E. Kingston, NH 17

Jan 1744 a.13yrs (CR)

JOHN BROOKS, b 27 Feb 1703/4 son of John & Eleanor (Frye) Brooks (LND p112): d aft 1786: m probably 2nd (int) Aug 1740 Eleanor (Meader) Libby (LND p433), b Dover, NH 3 Jun 1704 dau of Nathaniel & Eleanor (_) Meader (DvVR p18). Eleanor m(1) 13 Jan 1724/5 Daniel Libby.

John lived in Kingston in 1725, but sold out by 1729 & moved to Biddeford, ME.

MICHAEL BROOKS, d Kingston, NH (bur) 20 Jun 1781 (NHVR): m Kingston, NH 8 Nov 1739 Lydia (Robie) Dow (NHGR 3:40), b 23 May 1703 dau of Ichabod & Lucy (Page) Robie (LND p590), d Kingston, NH 15 Dec 1781 (NHVR). Lydia m(1) Kingston, NH 14 Aug 1729 Amassa Dow (KTR).

Lydia was admitted to the Kingston Church 29 Apr 1742.

DANIEL BROWN, b Salisbury, MA 12 Dec 1720 son of Ephraim & Lydia (Eastman) Brown (SVR): m Kingston, NH 18 Mar 1740 Ruth Morrill (KTR), b (prob) Salisbury, MA 9 Nov 1721 dau of Ezekiel & Abigail (Wadleigh) Morrill (SVR).

Children: born Kingston, NH (KTR)

1. **LYDIA**, b 29 Aug 1744
2. **ABIGAIL**, b 13 Aug 1746
3. **RUTH**, b 1 Nov 1748
4. **DANIEL**, b 10 Dec 1750: d 14 Sep 1818 (DAR 1:91): m Margaret Elliot
5. **EZEKIEL**, bpt Kingston, NH 7 Sep 1755 (NH GR 6:32)
6. **EZEKIEL**, b 10 Aug 1756: d Brunswick, ME 4 Jun 1798 (RG 1:85): m 3 Feb 1780 Eliza beth Mallet
7. **MIRIAM**, b 23 Mar 1753
8. **SARAH**, b 13 Feb 1758

JOSHUA BROWN, b Newbury, MA 11 Jul 1704 son of Joseph & Sarah (Treadwell) Brown (NVR): d Kingston, NH 23 Apr 1756 (KTR): m Salisbury, MA 8 Dec 1726 Joanna Morrill (SVR), b Salisbury, MA

17 Feb 1707 dau of Jacob & Elizabeth (Stevens) Morrill (SVR). Joanna m(2) Kingston, NH 30 Nov 1758 Jonathan Brown (NHGR 3:90).

Children: 1st 6 born Salisbury, MA (SVR)
1. **SARAH**, b 12 Aug 1727
2. **ELIZABETH**, b 12 Aug 1729
3. **JOSEPH**, b 28 Aug 1733: d Andover, NH 6 Apr 1812 (ExA 13:170): m Kingston, NH 29 Dec 1757 Elizabeth Sawyer (KTR)
4. **JOANNA**, b 10 Dec 1736
5. **RUTH**, b 22 Mar 1739/40
6. **JACOB**, b 21 Jan 1741/2
7. **NATHANIEL TREDWELL**, b Kingston, NH May 1744 (KTR): d Kingston, NH 21 Feb 1746 (NHVR)
8. **ABIGAIL**, b Kingston, NH 18 Sep 1746 (KTR): bpt 21 Sep 1746 (NHGR 5:154)
9. **NATHANIEL**, b Kingston, NH 29 Oct 1748 (KTR): m 17 Nov 1771 Mary Clifford

SAMUEL BROWN, b Salisbury, MA 27 Mar 1716 son of Abraham & Hannah (Morrill) Brown (SVR): d 1774 (ExA 12:100): m(1) Mary ___: m(2) Rachel ___.

Samuel was dismissed from the 2nd Church of Christ in Salisbury to the 2nd Church of Christ in Kingston 4 Aug 1745.

Children: bpt Kingston, NH (KChR)
1. **MARY**, b So Hampton, NH 6 Apr 1744 (SHVR): m Kingston, NH 5 May 1763 William Rowell (KChR)
2. **ABRAHAM**, bpt 20 Oct 1745: m So Hampton, NH 3 Dec 1770 Mary Emmons (SHVR)
3. **ELIZABETH**, bpt 11 Jan 1747
4. **MOSES**, bpt 25 Dec 1748
5. **RUTH**, bpt 16 Dec 1750: m Samuel Fifield (TAG 19:102)
6. **HANNAH**, bpt 2 Sep 1753
7. **REBECCA**, bpt 28 May 1758
8. **MIRIAM**, bpt 20 Apr 1760
9. **THOMAS**, bpt 23 Jun 1765

SIMEON BROWN (Dr), b Newbury, MA 16 May 1708 son of Joseph & Sarah (Treadwell) Brown (NVR): d Haverhill, MA (WP) 7 Apr 1760 (ExA 13:171): m Kingston, NH 13 Mar 1729 Hannah Young (KTR), b Salisbury, MA 31 Mar 1713 dau of Henry & Ruth (Morrill) Young (SVR). Hannah m(2) bef 1773 Benjamin French (ExA 13:171).

Simeon was admitted to the Kingston Church 14 Sep 1735 & his wife was admitted 25 Apr 1736. In 1738 he signed a petition for a grant of land in Kingston.

Children: 1st 6 born Kingston, NH (KTR)

1. **HENRY YOUNG**, b 19 Oct 1730: m Andover, MA 19 Oct 1752 Elizabeth Lovejoy (AndVR)
2. **SUSANNAH**, b 23 Sep 1732: d Kingston, NH 11 Aug 1735 (KTR)
3. **JOSEPH**, b 1 Jul 1735: d (Est Adm) 22 Jan 1759 (ExA 13:171): m (prob) Haverhill, MA 30 Jan 1755 Priscilla Gage (HvVR)
4. **SARAH**, b 31 Jul 1737: d Kingston, NH 29 Aug 1739 (NHVR)
5. **SIMEON**, bpt 1 Jul 1739 (NHGR 5:105)
6. **HANNAH**, bpt 27 Sep 1741 (NHGR 5:107)
7. **HANNAH**, b Haverhill, MA 25 Dec 1743 (Hv VR): d Haverhill, MA 21 Oct 1752 (HvVR)
8. **SIMEON**, b Haverhill, MA 17 Apr 1746 (Hv VR)
9. **ANNE**, b Haverhill, MA 11 Aug 1748 (HvVR)
10. **RUTH**, b Haverhill, MA 19 Sep 1750 (HvVR): unmd in 1773
11. **BENAIAH**, b Haverhill, MA 14 Jun 1754 (HvVR)

THOMAS BROWN, b Newbury, MA 8 Dec 1705 son of Thomas & Elizabeth (Berry) Brown (NVR): m Newbury, MA 14 Nov 1727 Deborah Merrill (NVR), b Newbury, MA 12 Jul 1709 dau of John & Deborah (Hazeltine) Merrill (NVR).

Thomas & his wife, from Newbury, were admitted to the 1st Kingston Church 14 Sep 1735. In 1738 Thomas signed a petition for a new parish in the easterly part of Kingston.

Children:
1. **ELIZABETH**, b Newbury, MA 8 Nov 1728 (NVR)
2. **MOSES**, b Newbury, MA 1731 (NVR)
3. **(CHILD)**, d Kingston, NH 11 Nov 1736 (NHGR 3:39)
4. **(CHILD)** d Kingston, NH 23 Feb 1738 (NHVR)

SAMUEL BUSWELL (BUZZELL), b Salisbury, MA 25 May 1662 son of Samuel & Sarah (Keyes) Buswell (SVR): d Kingston, NH 8 Mar 1747 over 90yrs (NHVR): m abt 1689 Jane Simmons (NEM p126), b Rowley, MA 15 Mar 1668 dau of John & Elizabeth (Boynton) Simmons (RwVR).

Children: 1st 6 born Bradford, MA (BdVR)
1. **JANE**, b 7 May 1690
2. **SARAH**, bpt 10 May 1691
3. **WILLIAM**, b 23 Jul 1692: m Salisbury, MA (int) 30 Oct 1713 Judith Davis (SVR)
4. **MEHITABLE**, b 15 Jan 1694/5
5. **JANE**, b 11 Aug 1697: d 18 Aug 1699
6. **JOSEPH**, b 17 Mar 1699/1700
7. **JANE**, b Amesbury, MA 24 Oct 1702 (AVR)
8. **SAMUEL**, b Salisbury, MA 18 Dec 1705 (SVR): d Kingston, NH (Est Adm) 31 Aug 1757 (PRNH 6:130)
9. **SIMMONS**, b Salisbury, MA 22 Nov 1709 (SVR): m(1) Salisbury, MA (int) 4 Nov 1738 Abigail Stockman (SVR): m(2) Kingston, NH 21 Jan 1741 Catherine Bean (KTR)
10. **NATHANIEL**, b Salisbury, MA 6 Nov 1712 (SVR): m (prob) Joanna ___

SAMUEL BUSWELL, b Salisbury, MA 14 Jun 1702 son of Isaac & Anna (Ordway) Buswell (SVR): d (WP) 1795: m(1) Salisbury, MA 3 Jan 1726/7 Mary Worthen (SVR), b Amesbury, MA 17 Mar 1701/2 dau of Samuel & Deliverance (Heath) Worthen (AVR). Mary's father mentions her children in his will (PRNH 6:19): Samuel m(2) Salisbury, MA Aug 1748 Sarah Thorn (SVR).

Children: 1st 4 born Kingston, NH (KTR)
(by 1st wife)

1. **ANNA**, b 7 Nov 1727: m(1) Kingston, NH 26 Nov 1750 John Brown Jr (KChR): m(2) Thomas Critchett
2. **DELIVERANCE**, b 28 Dec 1729: m Kingston, NH 18 Dec 1751 Israel Clifford (NHGR)
3. **MARY**, b 17 Jun 1736: d prob bef 1760
4. **ISAAC**, b 31 Aug 1738
5. **JUDITH**, b 11 Dec 1740: m aft 1760 Andrew Glidden

(by 2nd wife)

6. **SAMUEL**, b 22 Oct 1749: d bef 1781
7. **JOHN**, b 26 Jan 1752: m 29 Aug 1774 Mary Smith (HCnt p48)
8. **JAMES**, b 19 Feb 1757: d Gilmanton, NH: m 7 Dec 1780 Ruth Lord

SIMMONS BUSWELL (BUZZELL), b Salisbury, MA 22 Nov 1709 son of Samuel & Jane (Simmons) Buswell (SVR): m(1) Salisbury, MA (int) 4 Nov 1738 Abigail Stockman of Kensington (SVR): m(2) Kingston, NH 21 Jan 1741 Catherine Bean (KTR), b Kingston, NH 22 Aug 1714 dau of James & Sarah (Bradley) Bean (KTR).

Children: born Kingston, NH (KTR)

1. **JOSEPH**, b 25 Dec 1742
2. **SARAH**, b 17 Mar 1743/4
3. **HANNAH**, b 27 Apr 1746
4. **MEHITABLE**, b 15 Jan 1748/9: m (prob) John Hughes of Windham
5. **JEAN** (Jane), b 11 Mar 1750/1
6. **DAVID**, b 28 May 1753: d Kingston, NH 2 Mar 1755 (KTR)
7. **JONATHAN**, b 28 May 1753: d Kingston, NH 26 Sep 1753 (KTR)

WILLIAM BUSWELL (BUZZELL), b Bradford, MA 23 Jul 1692 son of Samuel & Jane (Simmons) Buswell (BdVR): d Kingston, NH 21 Feb 1779 (NHVR): m Salisbury, MA (int) 30 Oct 1713 Judith Davis (SVR), b Newbury, MA 2 Jun 1691 dau of Cornelius & Sarah (_) Davis (NVR), d Kingston, NH 1 Sep 1775 (KTR).

William belonged to Kingston when Rev Clark

took charge of the church in 1725. He lived in that part of Kingston that is now Danville.

Children: born Kingston, NH (KTR)

1. **MARY**, b 19 Mar 1714: m Kingston, NH 8 Sep 1731 Samuel Bean (NHGR 2:45)
2. **SARAH**, b 17 Apr 1718: d Kingston, NH 29 Sep 1735 (KTR)
3. **WILLIAM**, b 8 Dec 1720: d 1792: m Kingston, NH 27 Feb 1745/6 Elizabeth Winsley
4. **MEHITABLE**, b 10 Mar 1723: m(1) Kingston, NH 31 Oct 1745 Isaac Smith (KTR): m(2) Amesbury, MA (int) 7 Nov 1761 Caleb Pilsbury (AVR)
5. **JOSEPH**, b 8 Jul 1725: d Kingston, NH 14 Aug 1735 (KTR)
6. **SAMUEL**, b 14 Apr 1729: d Loudon, NH 26 Oct 1781: m Kingston, NH 14 Jan 1755 Mary Winsley (KTR)
7. **CORNELIUS**, b 17 Jul 1731: d Kingston, NH 11 Aug 1735 (KTR)

WILLIAM BUSWELL, b Salisbury, MA 3 Apr 1697 son of Isaac & Anna (Ordway) Buswell (OF p81): d Kingston, NH (prob bur) 1 Jan 1778 (NHVR): m Salisbury, MA 14 Jul 1731 Abigail Thorn (SVR), b Salisbury, MA 3 Sep 1707 dau of James & Hannah (Brown) Thorn (SVR), d Kingston, NH (prob bur) 10 Jan 1783 (NHVR).

Abigail, wife of William, was admitted to the Kingston Church from Salisbury 26 Oct 1735.

Children: born Kingston, NH (KTR)

1. **HANNAH**, b 16 May 1732: m Kingston, NH 16 May 1750 Amassa Dow (KTR)
2. **PHEBE**, b 16 Jun 1736: m Kingston, NH 9 Jun 1763 Samuel Winslow Jr (KTR)
3. **JAMES**, b 10 Apr 1740: m Kingston, NH 3 Feb 1761 Elizabeth Clough (KTR)
4. **JOHN**, b 1 May 1743: d Kingston, NH 11 Feb 1747 (KTR)
5. **DANIEL**, b 3 May 1746: m 4 Jul 1776 Hannah Runnels (Buswell 1:25)
6. **ABIGAIL**, b 3 Sep 1749

7. **SARAH**, b 20 Mar 1752: d Kingston, NH 6 Apr 1752 (KTR)

WILLIAM BUSWELL 3rd, b Kingston, NH 8 Dec 1720 son of William & Judith (Davis) Buswell (KTR): d 1792 (DAR 1:108): m Kingston, NH 27 Feb 1745/6 Elizabeth Winsley (KTR), b Kingston, NH 8 Feb 1724/5 dau of Samuel & Hulda (Swett) Winsley (KTR).

William & his wife were admitted to the Kingston Church 3 Oct 1747.

Children: born Kingston, NH (KTR)

1. **HULDAH**, b 19 Aug 1747
2. **SARAH**, b 3 Dec 1749: d Kingston, NH 14 May 1752 (KTR)
3. **MARTHA**, b 25 May 1752
4. **JUDITH**, b 7 Feb 1755
5. **HANNAH**, b 28 Jan 1758
6. **ELIZABETH**, b 12 Jul 1760
7. **WILLIAM**, b 15 Feb 1763: m 9 Mar 1786 Lucy Flanders
8. **SARAH**, b 6 Mar 1766
9. **MOSES**, b 13 Jul 1768
10. **JOSEPH**, b 30 Aug 1770

SILAS CAMMET, b Salisbury, MA 25 Apr 1725 son of Thomas & Margaret (Hallowell) Cammett (SVR): m Kingston, NH 27 Nov 1746 Catherine Judkins (KTR), b Kingston, NH 17 Nov 1721 dau of Samuel & Abigail (Harriman) Judkins (KTR).

Catherine was dismissed from the Kingston Church to Sandown in 1760.

Children: 1st 4 born Kingston, NH (KTR)

1. **JONATHAN**, b 29 Feb 1747/8
2. **JOHN**, b 30 Dec 1749
3. **SILAS**, b 24 Dec 1751
4. **ANNE**, b 10 Dec 1753
5. **SAMUEL**, b Sandown, NH 11 May 1756 (SdTR): d 11 Jun 1825: m Elizabeth Sleeper
6. **MIRIAM**, b Sandown, NH 3 Sep 1758 (SdTR)
7. **THOMAS**, b Sandown, NH 17 Aug 1760 (SdTR): d Cortland, NY 3 Aug 1835 (NHPR 8:35)

8. **MARY**, b Sandown, NH 22 Sep 1762 (SdTR)

ANNIS CAMPBELL, possibly son of Alexander & Jeanet Campbell (PRNH 3:724): d Danville, NH 12 Mar 1808: m Abigail ___.

The wife of Annis Campbell was admitted to the Kingston Church 5 Aug 1758.

Children: bpt Kingston, NH (NHVR)

1. **ANNIS**, b Dec 1744 (DnTR): bpt 5 Aug 1758: m Danville, NH 12 Dec 1765 Elizabeth Webster (NEHGR 58:47)
2. **DAVID**, b 19 Feb 1746 (DnTR): d 4 Feb 1803 (DAR 1:111): m Sarah Patterson
3. **ABIGAIL**, b May 1748 (DnTR): bpt 6 Sep 1758
4. **ROBERT**, b 2 Dec 1750 (DnTR)
5. **ALEXANDER**, b 3 Feb 1752 (DnTR): bpt 6 Sep 1758
6. **HANNAH**, b 23 Mar 1754 (DnTR): bpt 6 Sep 1758
7. **SARAH**, b 16 May 1755 (DnTR): bpt 6 Sep 1758
8. **JOHN**, b 21 Dec 1757 (DnTR): bpt 6 Sep 1758
9. **JESSE**, b Nov 1759 (DnTR): bpt 4 Nov 1759
10. **PHINEAS**, b Nov 1762 (DnTR): bpt 20 Jun 1762

JOHN CARTER, b Salisbury, MA 8 Jun 1688 son of John & Martha (Brown) Carter (SVR): m Amesbury, MA 25 Apr 1711 Judith Bagley (AVR), b Amesbury, MA 13 Nov 1690 dau of Orlando & Sarah (Sargent) Bagley (AVR).

John signed a petition regarding the township of Kingston in 1730. He & his wife were admitted to the 2nd Church of Christ in Kingston 2 May 1742.

Children: 1st 7 born Salisbury, MA (SVR)

1. **ABIGAIL**, b 21 May 1712
2. **THOMAS**, b 29 Oct 1713: d bef 1782: m Kingston, NH 25 Jan 1738/9 Mary Webster (NHGR 3:40)

3. **JOHN**, b 14 Sep 1715: d Newton, NH (WP) 24 Dec 1798: m Kingston, NH 2 Feb 1737/8 Elizabeth Webster (NHGR 3:40)
4. **SAMUEL**, b 14 Jan 1717/8
5. **EPHRAIM**, b 30 Mar 1719
6. **BENJAMIN**, b 5 Feb 1722/3
7. **ORLANDO**, b 30 Aug 1724: m (prob) Kingston, NH Apr 1744/5 Margaret Locke (NHGR 3:42)
8. **MOSES**, b Amesbury, MA 14 Apr 1734 (AVR)
9. **SAMUEL**, bpt Kingston, NH 24 Jan 1742 (KChR)
10. **JACOB**, bpt Kingston, NH 24 Jan 1742 (KChR)

PAUL CHASE, b Amesbury, MA 27 Mar 1721 son of Charles & Hepzibah (Carr) Chase (AVR): d 1756 in the French & Indian War; Est Adm 26 Dec 1756 (PRNH 5:507): m Salisbury, MA 27 Mar 1746 Sarah Pike (SVR), b Salisbury, MA 16 Feb 1725 dau of Joseph & Jemima (Morrill) Pike (SVR), d aft 1771. Sarah m(2) Moses Sawyer.

Paul lived in the westerly section of Kingston.

Children:

1. **CARR**, b Amesbury, MA 25 Nov 1746 (AVR): d Campton, NH 23 Dec 1808: m Newburyport, MA 15 Apr 1779 Sarah (Remick) Rowe
2. **ENOCH**, b Amesbury, MA 8 Oct 1748 (AVR)
3. **SAMUEL**, bpt Kingston, NH 28 Aug 1751
4. **ANNA** (Nanny), bpt Kingston, NH 28 Aug 1751 (NHGR 6:26): m 1774 Timothy Darling
5. **JOSEPH**, b 25 Apr 1753: d 17 Jun 1844 (DAR 1:126): m(1) Nov 1772 Judith Cooper: m(2) 29 Mar 1785 Sarah Doolittle: m(3) 10 Nov 1812 Mary Whitman (Chase Gen p146)

DANIEL CHENEY, b Haverhill, MA 10 Jan 1728/9 son of Thomas & Hannah (Stevens) Cheney (HvVR): m Elizabeth Hadley (Cheney Gen p257).

Children: (Cheney Gen p258)

1. **NATHANIEL**, bpt Kingston, NH 3 Jun 1755

(NHGR 6:32): d 6 Mar 1847 (DAR 1:128): m Hampstead, NH 28 Jul 1777 Mary Stevens (HmstR)

2. **JOSEPH**, bpt Kingston, NH 2 Dec 1755 (NH VR): m Elizabeth ___
3. **ENOCH**, bpt Sandown, NH 29 Oct 1757 (NH VR): m Goffstown, NH 28 Dec 1780 Susanna Pattee
4. **JONATHAN DUSTIN**, b abt 1759: m Lavinea Ward
5. **MARY**, b abt 1761: m 2 Feb 1786 Stephen Hadley
6. **ELIZABETH**, bpt Hampstead, NH 13 Jun 1762: m 30 May 1786 Joseph Sargent
7. **MARY**, b abt 1763: m 24 Oct 1786 Caleb Mills
8. **HANNAH**, bpt Salem, NH 23 Jul 1777: m 23 Nov 1786 Timothy Sargent
9. **SARAH**, bpt Salem, NH 23 Jul 1777: m 26 Nov 1789 Aaron Quimby
10. **DANIEL**, bpt Salem, NH 23 Jul 1777: m 30 Apr 1789 Patty Wheeler
11. **THOMAS**, b 23 Nov 1774: bpt 23 Jul 1777: m 10 Nov 1801 Charlotte Ewell
12. **NANNE WEST**, bpt 23 Jul 1777

BENJAMIN CHOATE, b Ipswich, MA abt 1680 son of John & Ann (_) Choate: d Kingston, NH 26 Nov 1753 a.73yrs (KTR): m Kingston, NH 12 Jun 1707 Abigail Burnum (KTR), b Ipswich, MA 1691, d 9 Jan 1776 (Choate Gen p19).

Benjamin had land laid out to him in Kingston 21 Feb 1705. His family belonged to Kingston in 1725 when Rev Clark took charge of the church.

Children: born Kingston, NH (KTR)

1. **JONATHAN**, b 31 May 1708: d Kingston, NH 9 Jan 1752 (KTR): m Kingston, NH 2 May 1738 Elizabeth Moody (KTR)
2. **ABIGAIL**, b 2 Jun 1710: d Kingston, NH 19 Nov 1710 (KTR)
3. **ABIGAIL**, b 16 Sep 1711: d Kingston, NH 15 Apr 1717 (KTR)
4. **BENJAMIN**, b 30 Dec 1713: d Kingston, NH

7 Dec 1714 (KTR)
5. **BENJAMIN**, b 7 Aug 1715: d Kingston, NH (Est Adm) 28 Aug 1758 (PRNH 6:297): m Kingston, NH 22 Dec 1741 Ruth Edwards (KTR)
6. **LUSE**, b 23 Dec 1717 (stillborn)
7. **RUHUMAH**, b 22 Dec 1718: d Kingston, NH 4 Jan 1808 (NHVR): m Kingston, NH 15 Sep 1747 David French (KTR)
8. **JEREMIAH**, b 12 Aug 1721: d Kingston, NH 25 May 1722 (KTR)
9. **ABIGAIL**, b 27 Mar 1723: d Kingston, NH 20 Mar 1736 (KTR)
10. **JOSEPH**, m Susanna ____ (Choate Gen p44)

BENJAMIN CHOATE JR, b Kingston, NH 7 Aug 1715 son of Benjamin & Abigail (Burnum) Choate (KTR): d Kingston, NH 28 Jul 1758 (KTR): m Kingston, NH 22 Dec 1741 Ruth Edwards (KTR), b Salisbury, MA 18 Oct 1721 dau of Rice & Sarah (Long) Edwards (SVR). Ruth m(2) William Sleeper (PRNH 6:300).

In 1738 Benjamin signed a petition for a land grant in Kingston.

Children: born Kingston, NH (KTR)
1. **AMMI**, b 15 Sep 1742
2. **BENJAMIN**, b 19 Oct 1744: d Kingston, NH 19 Jan 1749 (KTR)
3. **JOSEPH**, b 17 Jan 1747: d Kingston, NH 18 Jan 1747 (KTR)
4. **SIMEON**, b 14 Jan 1748: d 22 Sep 1829: m (1) 29 May 1770 Ruth Thompson: m(2) Salisbury, MA 9 Apr 1797 Hannah Norton (SVR)
5. **RUTH**, b 1 Aug 1750: d 7 Mar 1814: m Brentwood, NH 15 Oct 1771 Benjamin Judkins (BtTR)
6. **BENJAMIN**, b 8 Aug 1754: m Kingston, NH 15 Oct 1777 Jane Bradbury (NHGR 3:130)

JONATHAN CHOATE, b Kingston, NH 31 May 1708 son of Benjamin & Abigail (Burnum) Choate (KTR): d Kingston, NH 9 Jan 1752 (KTR): m Kingston, NH 2 May 1738 Elizabeth Moody (KTR), b abt 1719 dau of Clement & Elizabeth (Scribner) Moody (TAG 61:226). Elizabeth m(2) bef 1757 Jacob Bridgham (PRNH 6:39).

Jonathan was admitted to Kingston 1st Church 2 Jun 1728. He signed a petition in 1738 for a grant of land in Kingston.

Children: born Kingston, NH (KTR)

1. **JEREMIAH**, b 19 Aug 1739
2. **JONATHAN**, b 4 Nov 1741: d Kingston, NH 3 Aug 1742 (KTR)
3. **JONATHAN**, b 6 Nov 1743: d Tamworth, NH 25 Apr 1837: m Mary Bean (Choate Gen p70)
4. **ABIGAIL**, b 26 May 1747
5. **ELIZABETH**, b 11 Dec 1749
6. **ANNE**, b 20 Dec 1751: d Sandwich, NH 5 Oct 1848: m Moultonboro, NH 1770 Stephen Webster (MGFH 1:209)

BENJAMIN CILLEY, b abt 1713 son of Benoni & Eleanor (Getchell) Cilley (ME Gen & Bio 2:124): d Danville, NH (Est Adm) 29 Oct 1765 (PRNH 8: 228): m Kingston, NH 4 Mar 1736 Judith Darling (NHGR 2:46), b Salisbury, MA 15 Jun 1714 dau of John & Mary (Page) Darling (SVR).

Children: bpt Kingston, NH (NHGR)

1. **WILLIAM**, d Brooks, ME 1818 (ME Fam 2:45): m Kingston, NH 29 Nov 1754 Ann Clark (NH GR 3:87)
2. **JOHN**, bpt 22 Apr 1739: d aft 1790 (DAR 1: 131): m Danville, NH 15 Jul 1761 Abigail Clark (DnTR)
3. **BENJAMIN**, bpt 23 May 1742: d Andover, NH 9 Mar 1804: m Ossipee, NH 8 Oct 1763 Apphia Kennison (IGI)
4. **MOSES**, bpt 12 Aug 1744: m (prob) Danville, NH 5 Dec 1771 Elizabeth Thorn (NEHGR 58:122)
5. **AARON**, bpt 23 Nov 1746: d 11 Mar 1805: m Elizabeth Dodge (DAR 1:131)
6. **ELIZABETH**, m Nathan Rowe
7. **MARY**, bpt 16 Dec 1750: m Danville, NH 22 Dec 1768 Ebenezer Tucker (NEHGR 58:121)

8. **SAMUEL**, bpt 13 May 1753: d 10 Dec 1842: m Elizabeth Eastman (DAR 1:131)

JOHN CLARK, b Stratham, NH 26 Feb 1705 son of John & Mary (Rundlett) Clark (NHGR 1:188): d Kingston, NH (Est Adm) 15 Dec 1753 (PRNH 4: 488): m Kingston, NH May 1731 Elizabeth Clifford (KTR), possibly dau of Jacob & Elizabeth (Mayhew) Clifford, bpt Hampton, NH 14 May 1710 - but see HH p640.

John & his wife Elizabeth were admitted to the Kingston Church 26 Nov 1738. John signed a petition for a grant of land in Kingston in 1738.

Children: born Kingston, NH (KTR)

1. **ANNE**, b 1 Sep 1733: m Kingston, NH 29 Nov 1754 William Cilley (NHGR 3:87)
2. **JOHN**, b 25 Jan 1735: living 1758
3. **SATCHEL**, b 15 Mar 1737: d 4 May 1809: m Rachel Cate (DAR 1:135)
4. **HANNAH**, b 4 Jul 1739: m Kingston, NH 8 Mar 1758 Benjamin Darling (KTR)
5. **ABIGAIL**, b 3 Jul 1741: m Danville, NH 15 Jul 1761 John Cilley (DnTR)
6. **ELIZABETH**, b 8 Dec 1743: living 1758
7. **BENJAMIN**, b 9 Oct 1745: living 1758
8. **MAURICE**, b 14 Apr 1747: living 1758
9. **JACOB**, b 15 Apr 1749: d 4 Jul 1830: m Mary Ricker (DAR 1:134)
10. **MAYHEU**, b 28 May 1752: living 1758

WARD CLARK (Rev), b Exeter, NH 12 Dec 1703 son of Rev John & Elizabeth (Woodbridge) Clark (HE p6g): d Kingston, NH 5 May 1737 (KTR): m Kingston, NH 21 Nov 1727 Mary Frost (KTR), b Kittery, ME 18 Sep 1702 dau of Charles & Sarah (Wainwright) Frost (KitVR p15), d Kingston, NH 27 Jul 1735 (KTR).

Rev Clark was the first ordained minister of Kingston 29 Sep 1725 & during his pastorate 130 persons were received into the church & 471 were baptized.

Children: born Kingston, NH
1. **JOHN**, b 22 Jul 1730 (KTR): d Kingston, NH 23 Aug 1735 (NHGR 3:37)
2. **TYLER**, d (prob) Kingston, NH 27 Jul 1735 (NHGR 2:134)
3. **BENJAMIN**, d Kingston, NH 26 Aug 1735 (NHGR 3:37)
4. **ELIZABETH**, d Kingston, NH 29 Aug 1736 (NHGR 3:39)

OBEDIAH CLEMENT, b Haverhill, MA 22 May 1707 son of Job & Mehitable (Ayer) Clement (HvVR): m (1) Haverhill, MA 18 Dec 1729/30 Priscilla Heath (HvVR), b (prob) Haverhill, MA 15 Dec 1712 dau of Joseph & Hannah (Bradley) Heath (HvVR): m(2) Haverhill, MA 20 Dec 1733 Sarah Flanders (HvVR) b Amesbury, MA 29 Mar 1714 dau of Daniel & Sarah (Colby) Flanders (AVR).

Children: last 9 born Kingston, NH (KTR)
1. **JOB**, b Haverhill, MA 25 Sep 1734 (HvVR)
2. **DANIEL**, b Haverhill, MA 20 Oct 1736 (HvVR)
3. **ABRAHAM**, b 6 Aug 1738: d Kingston, NH 11 Aug 1738 (KTR)
4. **EZEKIEL**, b 22 Jun 1739
5. **ABIGAIL**, b 21 Nov 1741
6. **OBEDIAH**, b 19 Feb 1743: d 27 Jul 1829 (DAR 1:137): m(1) 27 Aug 1765 Sarah Batchelder: m(2) Sarah Baker
7. **PHILIP**, b 29 Apr 1745: d Kingston, NH 1 May 1745 (KTR)
8. **REUBEN**, b 9 Jul 1746: d Kingston, NH 6 Sep 1749 (KTR)
9. **SARAH**, b 23 Aug 1748
10. **REUBEN**, b 25 Jan 1749/50
11. **JONATHAN**, b 14 Jan 1753

ISAAC CLIFFORD, b Hampton, NH 24 May 1696 son of Israel & Ann (Smith) Clifford (HmVR p64): d Kingston, NH 11 Sep 1745 (KTR): m Sarah Taylor dau of William & Margaret (Bean) Taylor (LND p676), d Kingston, NH 10 Nov 1741 (NHVR).

Isaac's family belonged to Kingston when Rev

Clark took charge of the church in 1725. In 1738 he signed a petition for a grant of land in Kingston.

Children: born Kingston, NH (KTR)

1. **JOSEPH**, b 17 Jun 1718: d Kingston, NH 3 Feb 1783 (NHVR): m Kingston, NH 28 Dec 1737 Mary Healey (KTR)
2. **ISAAC**, b 1 May 1721: d aft 1790 (DAR 1: 138): m Sarah Healey (LND p151)
3. **SARAH**, b 13 Feb 1723: m Kingston, NH 12 Aug 1741 Nathaniel Ladd (KTR)
4. **DAVID**, b 17 Dec 1725: m Kingston, NH Apr 1744/5 Joanna Moody (NHGR 3:42)
5. **WILLIAM**, b 31 Oct 1727: m Kingston, NH 21 Apr 1746 Abigail Gove (KTR)
6. **ISRAEL**, b 21 Feb 1728/9: m Kingston, NH 18 Dec 1751 Deliverance Buswell (NHGR)
7. **ZACHARIAH**, b 21 May 1730: d Kingston, NH 23 May 1752 (KTR)
8. **ABIGAIL**, b 3 Aug 1733
9. **ELIZABETH**, b 21 Aug 1735: m (prob) Kingston, NH 7 Nov 1754 Moses Thurston (NHGR 3:87)
10. **JOHN**, b 18 Mar 1737: d Kingston, NH 26 Apr 1741 (NHVR)
11. **TRISTRAM**, b 4 Mar 1738/9: living 1750

JOHN CLIFFORD, b Hampton, NH 6 Feb 1686 son of John & Sarah (Godfrey) Clifford (HmVR p10): d Kingston, NH 17 Feb 1782 (NHVR): m Ann ____, d Kingston, NH 20 Nov 1781 a.92yrs (NHVR).

John signed a petition in 1738 for a new parish in the easterly part of Kingston. Ann Clifford wife of John was admitted to the 2nd Church of Christ in Kingston 28 Nov 1742.

Children:

1. **JOHN JR**, m Kingston, NH 23 Aug 1744 Elizabeth Sleeper (KChR)
2. **(SON)**, b abt 1721: d Kingston, NH 19 Aug 1735 a.14yrs (NHGR 3:37)
3. **(CHILD)**, d Kingston, NH 9 Aug 1735 (NHGR)
4. **(CHILD)**, d Kingston, NH 27 Aug 1735

5. **(CHILD)**, d Kingston, NH 3 Sep 1735

JOSEPH CLIFFORD, son of John & Sarah (Godfrey) Clifford (LND p151): d Kingston, NH (WP) 4 Mar 1723/4 (PRNH 2:203): m(1) Kingston, NH 13 Apr 1710 Sarah French (KTR), b Salisbury, MA 18 Mar 1685/6 dau of Simon & Joanna (Jackman) French (SVR), d Kingston, NH 6 Dec 1714 (KTR): m(2) Kingston, NH 2 Jan 1715/6 Lydia Perkins (KTR), b 30 Jan 1689 dau of James & Leah (Cox) Perkins (LND p542), d Kingston, NH 8 Sep 1723 (KTR).

Joseph was taken in & made a freeholder of Kingston 30 Apr 1705. He was granted 200 acres of land in Kingston 30 Oct 1706.

Children: born Kingston, NH (KTR)
(by 1st wife)

1. **JOANNA**, b 12 Nov 1711: m Kingston, NH 28 Aug 1728 Samuel Fifield (KTR)
2. **ABIGAIL**, b 18 Aug 1713: m Kingston, NH 6 Jan 1736/7 Abraham Sanborn (KTR)

(by 2nd wife)

3. **JOHN**, b 23 Aug 1719: d Kingston, NH 3 Nov 1735 (KTR)
4. **JOSEPH**, b 9 Dec 1721: d Kingston, NH 11 Oct 1735 (KTR)

RICHARD CLIFFORD, b Hampton, NH 27 Mar 1698 son of Israel & Ann (Smith) Clifford (HmVR p67): d aft 1762: m(1) Hampton, NH 26 Dec 1721 Hephzibah Basford (LND p151), b Hampton, NH 28 Jun 1699 dau of Jacob & Elizabeth (Clifford) Basford (HmVR p69): m(2) Kingston, NH 1 Jan 1742 Judith Woodman (KChR), b Newbury, MA 21 Sep 1705 dau of Archelaus & Hannah (_) Woodman (NVR).

Richard belonged to Kingston when Rev Clark took charge of the church in 1725. In 1738 he signed a petition for a new parish in the easterly part of Kingston.

Children: (New Eng Fam by Quimby 4:701)
(by 1st wife)

1. **ELIZABETH**, b Kingston, NH 7 Jun 1731

(KTR): bpt 12 Oct 1735 (NHGR 2:70)

2. **JONATHAN**, bpt Kingston, NH 12 Oct 1735 (NHGR 2:70)

(by 2nd wife)

3. **RICHARD**, b 9 Jan 1742/3: bpt Kingston, NH 13 Feb 1743 (KChR): m Abigail ___
4. **HANNAH**, b 17 Aug 1744: bpt Kingston, NH 19 Aug 1744 (KChR)
5. **ISRAEL**, b 9 Mar 1746: bpt Kingston, NH 23 Mar 1746 (KChR): d Dunbarton, NH 1834: m Achiah ___
6. **TIRZAH**, b 30 Dec 1747: bpt Kingston, NH 10 Jan 1748 (KChR)

WILLIAM CLIFFORD, b 22 Jan 1711 son of Zachariah & Mehitable (Smith) Clifford (HH p640): d abt 1776: m 22 Jan 1734 Sarah Towle (LND p688), b Hampton, NH 2 May 1709 dau of Benjamin & Sarrah (Bowden) Towle (HmVR p39), d 1803.

William & his wife Sarah were admitted to the Kingston Church 14 Mar 1742.

Children: born Kingston, NH (KTR)

1. **ZACHARIAH**, b 31 Oct 1734: m (prob) Kingston, NH 13 Jan 1757 Else Scribner (NHGR 3:89)
2. **JOSEPH**, b 4 Jun 1736
3. **BENJAMIN**, b 26 Apr 1738
4. **RICHARD**, b 12 Mar 1740
5. **JOHN**, b 1 Jan 1741/2
6. **ANTHONY**, b 13 Oct 1743
7. **SARAH**, b 22 Sep 1745
8. **MARGARET**, b 27 Dec 1747
9. **JACOB**, b 14 Apr 1749: m 7 Jan 1773 Abigail ___
10. **MEHITABLE**, b 10 Apr 1752

WILLIAM CLIFFORD, b Kingston, NH 31 Oct 1727 son of Isaac & Sarah (Taylor) Clifford (KTR): m Kingston, NH 21 Apr 1746 Abigail Gove (KTR), b 9 Mar 1729 dau of Ebenezer & Elizabeth (Stewart) Gove (Gove Gen p66). Abigail m(2) 14 Sep 1758 Benjamin Prescott.

Children: born Kingston, NH (KTR)
1. **ABIGAIL**, b 14 Feb 1746/7
2. **WILLIAM**, b 4 May 1748
3. **ISAAC**, b 3 Dec 1750
4. **SAMUEL**, b 12 Nov 1752

CALEB CLOUGH, b Salisbury, MA 26 Oct 1682 son of John & Mercy (Page) Clough (SVR): m(1) Salisbury, MA (int) 29 Mar 1707 Mary Mason (SVR), dau of John & Elizabeth (Ward) Mason (LND p465): m(2) Salisbury, MA 27 Dec 1722 Lydia Perkins (SVR), dau of (prob) Humphrey & Martha (Moulton) Perkins (LND p541).

Caleb was taken in with grants & priviledges in Kingston 30 Apr 1705 & had 40 acres of land laid out to him in his 1st division 19 Dec 1705. In 1738 he signed a petition for a new parish in the easterly part of Kingston.

Children: born Salisbury, MA (SVR)
(by 1st wife)
1. **CALEB**, b 23 Jun 1708: m Salisbury, MA 27 Nov 1728 Abi Thompson (SVR)
2. **JOSHUA**, b 16 Jan 1709: m Salisbury, MA (int) 26 Mar 1731 Hannah Flanders (SVR)

(by 2nd wife)
3. **HUMPHREY**, b 16 Nov 1723: m Salisbury, MA 9 Mar 1748 Hannah Daniels (SVR)
4. **MARY**, b 18 May 1726: m Salisbury, MA 26 Mar 1747 Ebenezer Currier (SVR)

CORNEILIUS CLOUGH, b Salisbury, MA 7 May 1680 son of John & Mercy (Page) Clough (SVR): m(1) Kingston, NH 13 Jan 1714 Joanna Sanborn (KTR), b Hampton, NH 1 Dec 1692 dau of Benjamin & Sarah (Worcester) Sanborn (HmVR p87), d 1717 (NEHGR 10:274): m(2) Kingston, NH 3 Sep 1718 Ann Evans (KTR), b Salisbury, MA 5 Nov 1687 dau of Thomas & Hannah (Brown) Evans (SVR).

Corneilius was granted 200 acres of land in Kingston at a meeting of the freeholders 30 Oct 1706. His family belonged to Kingston when Rev Clark took charge of the church in 1725. In 1738 he signed a petition for a grant of land in Kingston.

Children: born Kingston, NH (KTR)
(by 1st wife)
1. **BENJAMIN**, b 26 Jan 1715
2. **BENJAMIN**, b 23 Apr 1716: d Kingston, NH 4 Apr 1792 (GI p6): m(1) Kingston, NH 20 Mar 1747 Elizabeth Smith (KTR): m(2) Kingston, NH 1 May 1753 Mary Sanborn (KTR)

(by 2nd wife)
3. **THOMAS**, b Salisbury, MA 6 Feb 1719/20 (SVR)
4. **ANN**, b 3 Jan 1723/4: m Kingston, NH 15 Sep 1746 Edward Sleeper (KTR)
5. **ABIGAIL**, b 15 Sep 1726: d Kingston, NH (prob) 29 Sep 1735 (NHGR 3:37)
6. **JOHN**, b 6 Oct 1730: d Kingston, NH (prob) 27 Oct 1730 (NHGR 2:132)

DANIEL CLOUGH, b Salisbury, MA 19 Jul 1718 son of Samuel & Sarah (Robie) Clough (SVR): d (WP) Kingston, NH 25 Apr 1753 (PRNH 4:327): m Salisbury, MA 18 Dec 1740 Sarah Baker (SVR), b Salisbury, MA 25 Jan 1720/1 dau of William & Sarah (Heard) Baker (SVR), d 19 Jul 1765. Sarah m(2) Kingston, NH 26 Mar 1755 Stephen Webster (NHGR 3:88).

Daniel & his wife were admitted to the 2nd Church of Christ in Kingston 7 Mar 1742.

Children: bpt Kingston, NH (KChR)
1. **MIRIAM**, bpt 28 Mar 1742
2. **ELIZABETH**, bpt 3 Nov 1745: m 20 Apr 1761 David Webster
3. **SARAH**, bpt 28 Feb 1749: d 10 Nov 1776: m Samuel Dearborn
4. **DANIEL**, bpt 26 Apr 1752: d 20 Jul 1814: m Weare, NH 28 Jul 1789 Ruth Annis
5. **OLIVER** (Clough Gen p109), b 1753: d 25 Sep 1847: m Sarah Hurvey (DAR 1:139)

ELISHA CLOUGH, b Salisbury, MA 14 May 1717 son of John & Elizabeth (Long) Clough (SVR): m

Kingston, NH 2 Oct 1740 Mary Welch (KTR), b Kingston, NH 20 Jan 1717/8 dau of Samuel & Mary (Judkins) Welch (KTR).

Elisha was admitted to the Kingston Church 14 Mar 1742.

Children: 1st 9 born Kingston, NH

1. **ELIZABETH**, b 18 Sep 1741 (KTR): m Kingston, NH 3 Feb 1761 James Buswell (KTR)
2. **MARY**, b 13 Jun 1743 (KTR): m Kingston, NH 7 May 1765 Benjamin Winslow (KTR)
3. **ELISHA JR**, bpt 12 May 1745 (NHGR 5:112)
4. **RICHARD**, b 1 Sep 1747 (KTR): m(1) Mary Clough: m(2) Elizabeth __: m(3) Concord, NH 19 Nov 1776 Sarah Dow (NHGR 6:51)
5. **JONATHAN**, bpt 8 Oct 1749 (NHGR 5:158): d 11 Oct 1805: m(1) So Hampton, NH 3 Feb 1774 Abigail Buswell (SHVR): m(2) Atkinson, NH 6 Feb 1787 Ann West
6. **LEVI**, b abt 1750
7. **MARTHA**, bpt 21 Jul 1751 (NHGR 6:26)
8. **ANN**, bpt 24 Feb 1754 (NHGR 6:30)
9. **DAVID**, b abt 1756: d Bow, NH 1815: m 25 Aug 1783 Hannah Winslow
10. **TABITHA**, b Danville, NH 27 Mar 1760 (Dn TR): m 27 May 1784 Samuel Hoyt

EZRA CLOUGH, b Kingston, NH 24 Jun 1709 son of Joseph & Mary (Jenness) Clough (KTR): m(1) Rowley, MA 26 Dec 1734 Mary (Mercy) Stewart (Rw VR), b Rowley, MA 26 Oct 1715 dau of Ebenezer & Elizabeth (Johnson) Stewart (RwVR), d Byfield, MA 10 Mar 1756: m(2) 15 Mar 1759 Bethia Doty.

Children: last 8 bpt Byfield, MA (EA vol 2)

1. **ELIZABETH**, bpt Kingston, NH 2 May 1736 (NHGR 2:70): d Kingston, NH 4 Nov 1737 (NHVR)
2. **MERCY**, bpt Kingston, NH 11 Sep 1737 (NHGR 5:103): d Kingston, NH 8 Nov 1737 (NHVR)
3. **EBENEZER**, bpt 10 Dec 1738: d 24 Mar 1740
4. **NATHANIEL**, bpt 31 Aug 1740
5. **EZRA**, b abt 1741
6. **ELIZABETH**, bpt 3 Jul 1748: d 15 Mar 1749

7. **EBENEZER**, bpt 5 Apr 1752
8. **MERCY**, bpt 18 Aug 1754
9. **SAMUEL**, bpt 8 Mar 1761
10. **AMOS**, bpt 9 May 1762

ICHABOD CLOUGH, b Salisbury, MA 29 Jun 1697 son of Benoni & Hannah (Merrill) Clough (SVR): d Kingston, NH (WP) 29 Jan 1745/6 (PRNH 3:321): m Salisbury, MA 20 Dec 1722 Rebecca Clough (SVR), b Salisbury, MA 3 Jun 1696 dau of Thomas & Ruth (Connor) Clough (SVR), d Kingston, NH (Est Adm) 25 Oct 1749 (PRNH 3:736).

Ichabod belonged to Kingston in 1725 when Rev Clark took charge of the church. In 1730 he signed a petition regarding the township of Kingston & in 1738 he signed a petition for a new parish in the easterly part of Kingston.

Children: last 7 bpt Kingston, NH (NHGR)

1. **ELIJAH**, b Salisbury, MA 5 Jun 1724 (SVR): m Kingston, NH 18 Jun 1746 Sarah Noyes (KChR)
2. **ZACHEUS**, b 6 Mar 1725: d 1810 (DAR 1: 139): m abt 1752 Love Meader
3. **EZEKIEL**, bpt 5 Nov 1727: d 1743
4. **ELISHA**, bpt 5 Nov 1727
5. **DAVID**, bpt 10 May 1730: d Kingston, NH 14 Feb 1731 (NHGR 2:132)
6. **JONATHAN**, bpt 2 Jan 1732: living 1749/50
7. **RUTH**, bpt 4 Nov 1733: d 1745
8. **HANNAH**, bpt 16 Nov 1735: d 1744
9. **MARTHA**, bpt 13 Aug 1738: d 1762: m Elijah Webster

JOSEPH CLOUGH, b Salisbury, MA 14 Oct 1684 son of John & Mercy (Page) Clough (SVR): d Kingston, NH 13 Oct 1732 (NHGR 2:132): m Kingston, NH 11 Aug 1708 Mary Jenness (KTR), d Kingston, NH 12 Oct 1732 (NHGR 2:132).

Joseph was granted 200 acres of land in Kingston at a meeting of the freeholders 30 Oct 1706. His family belonged to Kingston when Rev Clark took charge of the church in 1725.

Children: born Kingston, NH (KTR)

1. **EZRA**, 24 Jun 1709: m Rowley, MA 26 Dec 1734 Mercy Stewart: m(2) Bethia Doty
2. **MERCY**, b 15 Apr 1711: m Kingston, NH 25 Nov 1731 Andrew Webster (NHGR 2:45)
3. **JOSEPH**, b 17 May 1713: d Kingston, NH 25 Feb 1716 (KTR)
4. **MOSES**, b 13 Feb 1714/5: d Kingston, NH 5 Apr 1716 (KTR)
5. **MARY**, b Apr 1716: d Kingston, NH Apr 1716 (KTR)
6. **JOSEPH**, b 4 Jul 1717: m Salisbury, MA (int) 17 Jul 1742 Mary Blake (SVR)
7. **MARY**, b 3 Jul 1719: living in 1732
8. **MOSES**, b 30 Sep 1720: d Kingston, NH 30 Nov 1720 (KTR)
9. **REUBEN**, b Nov 1721/2: m(1) Kingston, NH 5 Dec 1744 Love Sanborn (NHGR 3:41): m(2) Sandown, NH 19 Oct 1767 Mrs Mary Huse (SdTR)
10. **OBEDIAH**, b 1 Feb 1722/3: d Kingston, NH (Est Adm) 6 Mar 1756 (PRNH 5:402): m Kingston, NH 17 Feb 1746/7 Sarah Wadleigh (NHGR 3:43)
11. **TABITHA**, a.9yrs in 1733 (PRNH 2:452)
12. **ELIZABETH**, a.4yrs in 1733 (PRNH 2:451)
13. **LOVE**, a.4yrs in 1733 (PRNH 2:451): m Salisbury, MA 9 Aug 1749 John Ring (SVR)

REUBEN CLOUGH, b Kingston, NH Nov 1721/2 son of Joseph & Mary (Jenness) Clough (KTR): m(1) Kingston, NH 5 Dec 1744 Love Sanborn (NHGR 3:41), b Kingston, NH 10 Jun 1726 dau of Jonathan & Theodate (Sanborn) Sanborn (KTR), d Sandown, NH 10 Aug 1767 (SdTR): m(2) Sandown, NH 19 Oct 1767 Mary (Ferrin) Huse (SdTR), b Amesbury, MA 1 Aug 1722 dau of Jonathan & Sarah (Wells) Ferrin (AVR). Mary m(1) Amesbury, MA 13 Nov 1740 Israel Huse (AVR).

Children: (SdTR)

1. **MARY**, b 17 May 1745: bpt Kingston, NH 4 Aug 1745 (NHGR 5:112)
2. **THEODATE**, b 27 May 1747: bpt Kingston, NH

31 May 1747 (NHGR 5:155)
3. **JONATHAN**, b 21 Jan 1749: bpt Kingston, NH 5 Mar 1748/9 (NHGR 5:157)
4. **JOANNA**, b 15 Apr 1751: bpt Kingston, NH 28 Apr 1751 (NHGR 5:160)
5. **LOVE**, b 6 Apr 1753: bpt Kingston, NH 21 Feb 1754 (NHGR 6:30)
6. **REUBEN**, b 17 Mar 1755: d Sandown, NH 11 Jun 1755 (SdTR)
7. **REUBEN**, b 10 Mar 1756: m Hannah Sargent
8. **DOLLE**, b 23 Apr 1758: d Sandown, NH 22 Apr 1764 a.6yrs (SdTR)
9. **JOSEPH**, b 6 Apr 1760: d Sandown, NH 28 May 1764 a.4yrs (SdTR)
10 **BETTE**, b 5 Mar 1762

THEOPHILUS CLOUGH, b Salisbury, MA 28 Nov 1703 son of Samuel & Sarah (Robie) Clough (SVR): d Kingston, NH (Est Adm) 3 Jan 1753 (PRNH 4:297): m Salisbury, MA 4 Jan 1727/8 Sarah French (SVR), b Salisbury, MA 18 Mar 1708 dau of Timothy & Mary (Harriman) French (SVR).

Theophilus signed a petition regarding the township of Kingston in 1730 & in 1738 signed a petition for a new parish in the easterly part of Kingston.

Children: bpt Kingston, NH (NHGR & KChR)
1. **MARY**, b 5 Oct 1728: m Kingston, NH 26 Apr 1750 Chellis Currier (KChR)
2. **ABIGAIL**, b 26 Nov 1730: living 1754
3. **SARAH**, bpt 21 Oct 1733: m So Hampton, NH 13 Dec 1753 Jonathan Currier (SHVR)
4. **THEOPHILUS**, bpt 9 May 1736: d Enfield, NH 14 Feb 1801: m So Hampton, NH 19 Jan 1758 Elizabeth Currier (SHVR)
5. **SAMUEL**, bpt 2 Jul 1738: d 31 Dec 1811 (DAR 1:139): m Kingston, NH 19 Feb 1760 Miriam Satterly (NHGR 3:91)
6. **TIMOTHY**, bpt 19 Oct 1740: m Miriam ___
7. **ANNA**, bpt 27 Mar 1743: m Ichabod Roby
8. **MARTHA**, bpt 20 Apr 1746: d Westmoreland, NH 6 Oct 1822 (Hoyt Gen): m Eastman Hoyt
9. **RICHARD**, bpt 22 May 1748: m Elizabeth

Currier

PETER COFFIN (Rev), b Exeter, NH 8 Dec 1713 son of Eliphalet & Judith (Noyes) Coffin (HE p7g): m Hampton, NH 29 Jan 1739/40 Dorothy Gookin (Hm VR p134), b Hampton, NH 2 Apr 1722 dau of Nathaniel & Dorothy (Cotton) Gookin (HmVR p151), d E. Kingston, NH 18 Jun 1749 (CR).

Peter was the 1st minister of the 2nd Church of Christ in Kingston.

Children: bpt Kingston, NH (KChR)
1. **PETER**, bpt 11 Jan 1741
2. **ELIPHALET**, bpt 23 Jan 1743
3. **DOROTHY**, bpt 24 Mar 1745
4. **JUDITH**, bpt 19 Apr 1747
5. **NATHANIEL**, bpt 11 Jun 1749

DAVID COLBY, b Amesbury, MA 15 Oct 1711 son of Isaac & Hannah (Getchell) Colby (AVR): d aft 1780 (DAR 1:143): m(1) Elizabeth ___, d Kingston, NH abt 1755/6: m(2) Kingston, NH 13 Oct 1757 Maria (Norton) Emmons (NHGR 3:89), b Salisbury, MA 9 Nov 1704 dau of Solomon & Sarah (_) Norton (SVR). Maria m(1) Salisbury, MA 16 Jul 1723 Samuel Emmons (SVR).

Children: 1st 2 born Amesbury, MA (AVR)
1. **HANNAH**, b 27 Sep 1736
2. **MOLLY**, b 18 Dec 1738
3. **ELIZABETH**, b 13 Mar 1740 (SdTR)
4. **DAVID**, b 15 Oct 1745: d Aug 1821 (DAR 1:143): m(1) abt 1770 Polly Randall: m(2) bef 1798 Margaret Craig (Colby Gen p80)

JONATHAN COLBY, b Amesbury, MA 26 Sep 1703 son of John & Mary (Frame) Colby (AVR): m Amesbury, MA 19 Mar 1722/3 Dorothy Tuxbury (AVR), b Amesbury 26 Jan 1703/4 dau of John & Hannah (Colby) Tuxbury (AVR).

Jonathan lived in the westerly section of Kingston.

Children: born Amesbury, MA (AVR)

1. **JOHN**, bpt 23 Apr 1727
2. **BENJAMIN**, bpt 7 Sep 1729: m Salisbury, MA 12 Nov 1755 Bette Carr (SVR)
3. **ELIZABETH**, b 31 May 1732
4. **JOHN**, b 26 Feb 1734/5
5. **DOROTHY**, bpt 14 Mar 1739

ORLANDO COLBY, b Amesbury, MA 3 Feb 1705/6 son of Thomas & Frances (_) Colby (AVR): d (W) Sandown, NH 19 Sep 1781: m Salisbury, MA 12 Sep 1728 Keziah Rowell (SVR), b Salisbury, MA 14 Feb 1707 dau of Job & Bethia (Brown) Rowell (SVR), d Sandown, NH 16 Feb 1775: m(2) Danville, NH 25 Jul 1775 Judith Quimby (NEHGR 58: 123).

Orlando lived in the westerly section of Kingston.

Children: 1st 6 born Amesbury, MA (AVR)
1. **RUTH**, b 10 Aug 1729: m ___ Davis
2. **MOSES**, b 30 Oct 1731: d Danville, NH 7 Apr 1777 (DnTR): m Amesbury, MA 22 Jun 1754 Anna Tuxbury (AVR)
3. **JEMIMA**, b 3 Jan 1734: d bef 1781: m Kingston, NH 29 Jan 1756 David Straw (NHGR 3:88)
4. **JONATHAN**, b 24 Feb 1735/6: d Sandown, NH 14 Jun 1774 (SdTR): m Mary ___
5. **KEZIAH**, b 23 Jul 1738: d Sandown, NH Sep 1773 (SdTR)
6. **ROWELL**, b 5 Feb 1740: d Sandown, NH 26 Dec 1761 (SdTR)
7. **ENOS**, b Kingston, NH 16 Apr 1746 (KTR)
8. **THOMAS**, b Kingston, NH 16 Apr 1746 (KTR): d Kingston, NH 2 May 1746 (KTR)
9. **THOMAS** (Colby Gen p75), m Hampstead, NH 19 Nov 1767 Alice Davis (HmstR)
10. **DOROTHY**, b Kingston, NH 17 May 1749 (KTR): d Kingston, NH 29 Jan 1753 (KTR)

PHILIP COLBY, b Amesbury, MA 2 May 1707 son of Philip & Anne (Webster) Colby (AVR): d abt 1746 (PRNH 3:412): m Amesbury, MA 4 Sep 1729 Tabitha Weed (AVR), b Amesbury, MA 2 Apr 1711 dau of

Ephraim & Hannah (Annis-Worthen) Weed (AVR).
Administration on the estate of Philip Colby of Kingston was granted to Tabitha Colby his widow 26 Nov 1746 (PRNH 3:412).

Children: born Amesbury, MA (AVR)
1. **TABITHA**, b 4 Feb 1731/2
2. **MARY**, b 8 Jan 1733/4
3. **PHILIP**, bpt 12 Sep 1736
4. **HANNAH**, b 12 Mar 1738
5. **NICHOLAS**, b 9 Aug 1740: m(1) Amesbury, MA 4 Dec 1764 Susanna Pressy: m(2) Amesbury, MA 8 Oct 1775 Judith Wells (AVR)
6. **ELIZABETH**, b 19 Feb 1742/3
7. **ANN**, b 3 Jul 1745

EBENEZER COLCORD, b Hampton, NH 20 May 1695 son of Samuel & Mary (Ayers) Colcord (HmVR p63): d Brentwood, NH (Est Adm) 28 May 1766 (PRNH 8: 297): m Kingston, NH 10 Dec 1720 Hannah Fellows (KTR), b Salisbury, MA 20 Jul 1697 dau of Samuel & Abigail (Barnard) Fellows (SVR).
Ebenezer signed a petition for a grant of land in Kingston in 1738.

Children: born Kingston, NH (KTR)
1. **SAMUEL**, b 5 Feb 1721/2: d Candia, NH 1787 (TAG 17:219): m Kingston, NH 9 Jan 1745/6 Mehitable Stevens (NHGR 3:42)
2. **EBENEZER**, b 1 May 1724: d Kingston, NH 1 May 1724 (KTR)
3. **EBENEZER**, b 5 Jan 1726: d Brentwood, NH 4 Jan 1824 (CG p23): m Kingston, NH 22 Jan 1749/50 Patience Stevens (NHGR 3:44)
4. **PETER**, b 19 Mar 1727/8: d Kingston, NH 19 Mar 1727/8 (KTR)
5. **HANNAH**, b 26 Aug 1730: d Kingston, NH 25 Sep 1735 (KTR)
6. **PETER**, b 22 Apr 1732: d Kingston, NH 7 May 1732 (KTR)
7. **ABIGAIL**, b 18 May 1733: d Kingston, NH 20 Oct 1735 (KTR)
8. **MARY**, b 1 Aug 1735: d Kingston, NH 2 Nov 1735 (KTR)

EDWARD COLCORD, b Hampton, NH 1 Apr 1692 son of Samuel & Mary (Ayers) Colcord (HmVR p18): d Kingston, NH (WP) 27 Oct 1756 (PRNH 5:482): m Kingston, NH 24 Nov 1714 Mary Gordon (KTR), dau of Nicholas & Sarah (Hale-Sewall) Gordon (LND p273), d bef 1767.

Edward had 28 acres of land laid out to him in Kingston 5 Mar 1712.

Children: (TAG 17:219)

1. **EDWARD**, b Kingston, NH 2 Jan 1715/6 (KTR): d Exeter, NH 13 Nov 1793 (CG p50): m abt 1743 Hannah Veasey
2. **SARAH**, b abt 1718: d unmd 1783
3. **MARY**, b abt 1721: d 15 Dec 1795: m Peter Hersey
4. **ELIZABETH**, b abt 1725: d Kingston, NH 3 Dec 1791 (GI p8)
5. **HANNAH**, b abt 1727: m Kingston, NH 27 Mar 1753 Ephraim Winslow (KTR)
6. **LYDIA**, b abt 1729: m(1) Kingston, NH 25 Dec 1747 Benjamin Philbrick (NHGR 3:43): m(2) abt 1770 Joseph Philbrick
7. **MERIAH**, b 1731: unmd 1756
8. **DEBORAH**, b 1733: m abt 1756 Zebulon Edgerly
9. **ANN**, b abt 1735: m Kingston, NH 15 Sep 1760 Benjamin Stevens Jr (KTR)

JONATHAN COLCORD, b Hampton, NH 4 Mar 1683/4 son of Samuel & Mary (Ayers) Colcord (HmVR p10): d Newmarket, NH 31 Dec 1773 (LND p155): m ______, prob d bef 6 Sep 1743 (TAG 17:218).

Jonathan left Kingston abt 1707 & removed to what is now Newmarket, NH.

Children: (TAG 17:218)

1. **HANNAH**, b 21 Dec 1708: d Kingston, NH 13 May 1795 (NHVR): m Kingston, NH 22 Apr 1730 Daniel Gilman (KTR)
2. **JONATHAN**, b abt 1715: m(1) Sarah Burleigh: m(2) Jerusha ____
3. **SUSANNAH**, m Benjamin Dearborn
4. **EDWARD**, b abt 1719: d (WP) 16 Jan 1797: m

Jane Coffin of Dover

5. **GIDEON**, b abt 1721: d 21 Sep 1773: m Rachel Parsons

SAMUEL COLCORD, b abt 1656 son of Edward & Ann (Ward) Colcord (TAG 17:216): d Kingston, NH 5 Oct 1736 (KTR): m abt 1681 Mary Ayers (NEM p168), b Haverhill, MA 22 Mar 1660 dau of Thomas & Elizabeth (Hutchins) Ayers (HvVR), d Kingston, NH 29 May 1739 (KTR)

Samuel was an original grantee of Kingston in 1694. He was granted 200 acres of land at a meeting of the freeholders of Kingston 19 Dec 1700. He belonged to Kingston in 1725 when Rev Clark took charge of the church.

Children: born Hampton, NH (HmVR)

1. **SAMUEL**, b 11 Mar 1681/2: d Kingston, NH (Est Adm) 4 Jun 1718 (PRNH 2:36): m Kingston, NH 13 Sep 1704 Elizabeth Folsom (KTR)
2. **JONATHAN**, b 4 Mar 1683/4: d Newmarket, NH 31 Dec 1773 (LND p155): m ___
3. **ELIZABETH**, b 26 Dec 1686: m Kingston, NH 5 Dec 1710 Ebenezer Stevens (KTR)
4. **HANNAH**, b 17 Apr 1689: m 24 Jul 1709 Samuel Dudley (TAG 17:217)
5. **EDWARD**, b 1 Apr 1692: d (WP) 27 Oct 1756: m Kingston, NH 24 Nov 1714 Mary Gordon (KTR)
6. **EBENEZER**, b 20 May 1695: d Brentwood, NH (Est Adm) 28 May 1766: m Kingston, NH 10 Dec 1720 Hannah Fellows (KTR)
7. **MARY**, b 24 Mar 1697/8: m(1) Kingston, NH 6 Dec 1714 Thomas Sleeper (KTR): m(2) Kingston, NH 5 May 1725 Ebenezer Eastman (KTR)

SAMUEL COLCORD JR, b Hampton, NH 11 Mar 1681/2 son of Samuel & Mary (Ayers) Colcord (HmVR p83): d Kingston, NH (Est Adm) 4 Jun 1718 (PRNH 2:36): m Kingston, NH 13 Sep 1704 Elizabeth Folsom (KTR), dau of Peter & Susanna (Mills) Folsom (LND p238), d Kingston, NH 8 Apr 1756

(KTR). Elizabeth m(2) Kingston, NH 19 Aug 1718 Samuel Sanborn (KTR).
Samuel Jr had land laid out to him in Kingston 19 Jul 1702.

Children: born Kingston, NH (KTR)
1. **PETER**, b 27 Jun 1705
2. **ELIZABETH**, b 15 Jun 1708
3. **SAMUEL**, b 22 Aug 1710: d Kingston, NH 23 Jan 1783 (GI p8): m Kingston, NH 28 Dec 1732 Mehitable Ladd (KTR)
4. **BENJAMIN**, b 10 Jan 1713/4: d Kingston, NH 30 Jan 1713/4 (KTR)
5. **MARY**, b 1 Jan 1714/5: m Kingston, NH 21 Oct 1736 Ebenezer Stevens (KTR)

JABEZ COLEMAN, b Rowley, MA 27 Mar 1668 son of Tobias & Lydia (Jackson) Coleman (RwVR): d Kingston, NH (killed by Indians) 7 Sep 1724 (KTR): m Hampton, NH 2 Nov 1699 Mary Prescott (HmVR p56), b Hampton, NH 11 Jun 1677 dau of James & Mary (Boulter) Prescott (HmVR p109). Mary m(2) Kingston, NH 9 Nov 1730 Thomas Crosby (KTR). She m(3) Kingston, NH 2 Nov 1738 James Bean (NHGR 3:40).
Jabez was granted 200 acres of land at the legal meeting of freeholders of Kingston 19 Dec 1700. Widow Coleman belonged to Kingston in 1725 when Rev Clark took charge of the church.

Children:
1. **JOSEPH**, b Kingston, NH 23 Sep 1701 (KTR): d Kingston, NH 7 Sep 1724 with his father (KTR): m ____

JOSEPH COLEMAN, b Kingston, NH 23 Sep 1701 son of Jabez & Mary (Prescott) Coleman (KTR): d Kingston, NH 24 Sep 1724 (KTR): m ____

Children: (PRNH 2:239)
1. **PHEBE**, b abt 1722: m Kingston, NH 6 Feb 1738/9 Abraham Colby (NHGR 3:40)
2. **MARGARET**, b (posth) 1724-5

EBENEZER COLLINS, b Amesbury, MA 21 Jan 1704 son of John & Elizabeth (Barnard) Collins (AVR): m Kingston, NH Mar 1726 Apphia Merrill (KTR), b Salisbury, MA 25 Feb 1704 dau of Moses & Mary (Clough) Merrill (SVR).

In 1730 Ebenezer signed a petition regarding the township of Kingston & in 1738 he signed a petition for a new parish in the easterly part of Kingston.

Children: 1st 6 born Kingston, NH (KTR)

1. **SARAH**, b 28 Jun 1726: m Kingston, NH 15 Nov 1749 Joseph Hoit (KChR)
2. **JONATHAN**, b 28 Apr 1728: d aft 1790: m 19 Aug 1751 Elizabeth Prescott (DAR #107290)
3. **MARY**, b 3 Apr 1730: m Moses Stevens
4. **ELIZABETH**, 2 Jul 1731
5. **ROBERT**, b 12 Mar 1733: d 1777 (DAR 1:146)
6. **MARCY**, b 17 Mar 1733: m Kensington, NH 9 Jul 1760 Daniel Sanborn (NHVR)
7. **BENJAMIN**, bpt 18 Oct 1741 (KChR)
8. **APPHIA**, bpt 25 Dec 1743 (KChR): m Kensington, NH 25 Nov 1762 James Fogg (NHVR)
9. **EBENEZER**, bpt 3 Mar 1746 (KChR)

JONATHAN COLLINS, b Amesbury, MA 11 Sep 1695 son of John & Elizabeth (Barnard) Collins (AVR): d Kingston, NH 15 Oct 1725 (NHGR 2:131): m Salisbury, MA 21 Jan 1720/1 Mary Green (SVR), b Hampton, NH 15 Apr 1701 dau of John & Abiel (Marston) Green (HmVR p72). Mary m(2) Newbury, MA 28 Dec 1727/8 Benjamin Brown (NVR).

Probably the Jonathan who was a Quaker and had land laid out to him at a meeting of the freeholders of Kingston 4 Mar 1717/8. He belonged to Kingston in 1725 when Rev Clark took charge of the church.

THOMAS CORBIN'S name appears on a list of Kingston men who swore allegiance to the King in 1727.

Children: (poss)

1. **ELIZABETH**, bpt Kingston, NH 25 Jun 1727

(NHGR 2:47): m Kingston, NH 29 Dec 1745/6 Samuel Huntoon Jr (NHGR 3:42)

JOHN CORSER (COSER), b abt 1718 son of John & Tabitha (Kenney) Corser (Virkus 4:125): d 1791 (DAR 1:155): m Kingston, NH Sep 1742 Jean (Jane) Nichols (KTR), b (poss) Amesbury, MA 3 Sep 1721 dau of Jonathan & Mary (Challis) Nichols (AVR).

Children: born Kingston, NH (KTR)

1. **THOMAS**, b 1 May 1743: d 11 Dec 1829 (DAR 1:155): m(1) Ann Dunlap: m(2) Mary (Carter) Downing (NHPR 15:123)
2. **SAMUEL**, b 3 May 1745
3. **JONATHAN**, b 13 Oct 1747
4. **JOHN**, b 2 May 1751
5. **DAVID**, b 27 Jan 1754: d 23 Aug 1827 (DAR 1:155): m Salisbury, MA 17 Mar 1776 Ruth Blaisdell (SVR)
6. **JEAN** (Jane), b 18 Jan 1756
7. **WILLIAM**, b 12 Apr 1758
8. **ALEEN**, b 24 Aug 1760

THOMAS CRITCHETT, m Kingston, NH 9 May 1739 Mary Roberts (NHGR 3:40), dau of John & Elizabeth (_) Roberts (PRNH 3:413).

Thomas & his wife were admitted to the Kingston Church 28 Feb 1742. They were dismissed to Brentwood Jan 1751.

Children: bpt Kingston, NH (NHGR)

1. **EDWARD**, bpt 28 Feb 1741/2: m Abigail Gordon
2. **SARAH**, bpt 28 Feb 1741/2
3. **JOHN**, bpt 2 Oct 1743
4. **ELIAS**, bpt 1 Jun 1746
5. **MARY** (twin), bpt 19 Jun 1748
6. **THOMAS** (twin), bpt 19 Jun 1748

THOMAS CROSBY, b Roxbury, MA 4 Mar 1660 son of Anthony & Prudence (Wade) Crosby (LND p173): d Kingston, NH 30 Mar 1735 (NHGR 2:133): m(1) 29 Oct 1685 Deborah Fifield (LND p173), b Hampton,

NH 6 Feb 1660 dau of William & Mary (_) Fifield (HmVR p93): m(2) Kingston, NH 9 Nov 1730 Mary (Prescott) Coleman (KTR), b Hampton, NH 11 Jun 1677 dau of James & Mary (Boulter) Prescott (HmVR p109).

Mary Crosby was admitted to the Kingston Church 31 Mar 1734.

Children: 1st 8 born Hampton, NH (HmVR)

1. **HANNAH**, b 27 Dec 1687
2. **ABIGAIL**, b 2 Jun 1689
3. **PRUDENCE**, b 8 Mar 1691/2: m 24 Mar 1715 John Johnson (TAG 16:165)
4. **JONATHAN**, b 8 May 1694
5. **MEHITABLE**, b 5 Jan 1695/6: m Greenland, NH 21 Jan 1720 Samuel Haines (NEHGR 65: 352)
6. **ELIZABETH**, b 26 Apr 1699
7. **JONATHAN**, b 24 Jan 1700/01
8. **SAMUEL**, b 22 Nov 1703
9. **ANTHONY** (TAG 15:221)

JEREMIAH CURRIER, b Amesbury, MA 8 Aug 1706 son of John & Judith (Stevens) Currier (AVR): d Kingston, NH (Est Adm) 26 Aug 1761 (PRNH 7: 194): m Amesbury, MA 1 May 1729 Anna Bagley (AVR), b Amesbury, MA 18 May 1709 dau of John & Hannah (Fowler) Bagley (AVR), d abt 1770.

Children:

1. **JOHN**, b Amesbury, MA 31 Jan 1729/30 (AVR) d Kingston, NH 30 Oct or 18 Nov 1735 (NH GR 3:38)
2. **HANNAH**, b Amesbury, MA 3 Dec 1731 (AVR): d Kingston, NH 30 Oct or 18 Nov 1735 (NH GR 3:38)
3. **HANNAH**, b Kingston, NH 25 Aug 1736 (KTR): living 1770
4. **JEREMIAH**, b Kingston, NH 19 Dec 1738 (KTR): m Brentwood, NH 10 May 1769 Sarah Greeley (BtTR)
5. **JUDITH**, b Kingston, NH 14 Oct 1741 (KTR)
6. **MOSES**, bpt Kingston, NH 5 Aug 1744 (KC hR): d Kingston, NH (WP) 24 Apr 1770 (PR

NH 9:396): m Elizabeth Eastman
7. **ELIPHALET**, bpt Kingston, NH 31 May 1747 (KChR): d Kingston, NH (WP) 27 Jun 1770 (PRNH 9:383)
8. **ANN**, bpt Kingston, NH 3 Jun 1750 (KChR): m bef 1770 William Graves of So Hampton

JOHN CURRIER, b Amesbury, MA 16 Jan 1713 son of John & Judith (Stevens) Currier (AVR): d (WP) Kingston, NH 1 Mar 1758 (PRNH 6:191): m Salisbury, MA 29 Apr 1736 Ruth French (SVR), b Salisbury, MA 9 Dec 1713 dau of Timothy & Mary (Harriman) French (SVR).

Children: last 6 bpt Kingston, NH (KChR)
1. **JUDITH**, bpt Amesbury, MA 10 Apr 1737 (AVR)
2. **EZRA**, b 2 Apr 1739: d E. Kingston, NH 30 Aug 1745 (OF p915)
3. **MARY**, bpt 31 May 1741: m Kingston, NH 22 Nov 1758 Henry Blaisdell (KChR)
4. **RHODA**, bpt 27 Mar 1743
5. **EZRA**, bpt 21 Apr 1745: d E. Kingston, NH 27 Apr 1813 (CG p46): m Mehitable Eaton
6. **JUDITH**, bpt 4 Sep 1748: d E. Kingston, NH 16 Jul 1830 a.82yrs (CR): m 6 Apr 1769 Jonathan Ladd Webster
7. **JOHN**, bpt 15 Mar 1752: d E. Kingston, NH 12 May 1809 (CG p46): m 28 Mar 1777 Phebe Whicher
8. **TIMOTHY**, bpt 3 Mar 1754: prob d bef 1757

RICHARD CURRIER, b Amesbury, MA 12 Apr 1673 son of Thomas & Mary (Osgood) Currier (AVR): d Amesbury, MA 8 Feb 1747/8 (AVR): m Salisbury, MA 29 Aug 1695 Dorothy Barnard (SVR), b abt 1677 dau of John & Frances (Hoyt) Barnard (ExA 6:121), d Amesbury, MA 2 Mar 1765 (AVR).
Richard received land in Kingston from the selectmen in 1711.

Children: 1st 10 born Amesbury, MA (AVR)
1. **DAVID**, b 17 Feb 1695/6: m Amesbury, MA 11 Dec 1718 Keziah Colby (AVR)

2. **JONATHAN**, b 7 Feb 1698/9: m Amesbury, MA 25 Jan 1721/2 Anne Challis (AVR)
3. **HANNAH**, b 31 Jul 1701: m Amesbury, MA 26 Oct 1721 Samuel Lowell (AVR)
4. **JOHN**, b 5 Apr 1704: m Newbury, MA 23 Jan 1728/9 Mary Johnson (AVR)
5. **DOROTHY**, b 5 Nov 1706: m (prob) Amesbury, MA 18 Nov 1725 James Crocker (AVR)
6. **RICHARD**, b 12 Feb 1708/9: m Salisbury, MA 25 Nov 1731 Sarah Merrill (SVR)
7. **MERRIAM**, b 10 Apr 1711: m Amesbury, MA 19 Dec 1728 Moses Titcomb (AVR)
8. **AARON**, b 2 Jan 1716/7
9. **BARNARD**, b 15 Apr 1719: d 14 Jun 1793 (DAR 1:169): m Amesbury, MA 23 Oct 1739 Mrs Mary Emery (AVR)
10. **MARY**, b 2 Aug 1722: m Amesbury, MA 1 Sep 1743 Peter Coffin (AVR)
11. **MOSES**, m Amesbury, MA 24 Oct 1734 Rhoda Wells (AVR)

DANIEL DARLING, b Salisbury, MA 27 Nov 1711 son of John & Mary (Page) Darling (SVR): d Kingston, NH 13 Nov 1760 (KTR): m Kingston, NH 27 Dec 1733 Susanna Webster (KTR), b Kingston, NH 9 Jul 1712 dau of Ebenezer & Hannah (Judkins) Webster (KTR).

Daniel & his wife were admitted to the Kingston Church 16 Mar 1735.

Children: born Kingston, NH (KTR)

1. **JOHN**, b 27 Jul 1735: m Kingston, NH 2 Mar 1758 Mary Sawyer (NHGR 3:90)
2. **BENJAMIN**, b 30 Mar 1738: m Kingston, NH 8 Mar 1758 Hannah Clark (KTR)
3. **DANIEL**, b 10 Aug 1741: d Kingston, NH 22 Jan 1767 (KTR)
4. **RUTH**, b 19 Sep 1744: d Kingston, NH 15 Jan 1760 (KTR)
5. **ABRAHAM**, b 26 Dec 1746
6. **MOLLIE**, b 24 Oct 1748

JOHN DARLING, b Salisbury, MA 21 Feb 1683 (SVR) son of Naomi Flanders (In 1684 Naomi Flanders was summoned to court at Ipswich & acknowledged that the child was illegitimate): d (WP) Kingston, NH 31 Oct 1753 (PRNH 4:461): m Salisbury, MA (int) 6 Nov 1708 Mary Page (SVR), b Salisbury, MA 29 Sep 1686 dau of Onesipherous & Mary (Hauxworth) Page (SVR).

John & his wife were received into the Church of Christ in Kingston 13 Apr 1729, by dismission from the church in Salisbury. He signed a petition for a new parish in the easterly part of Kingston in 1738.

Children: born Salisbury, MA (SVR)

1. **ABIGAIL**, b 4 Oct 1709: m Kingston, NH 20 Feb 1728/9 Benjamin Swett (KTR)
2. **DANIEL**, b 27 Nov 1711: d 13 Nov 1760: m Kingston, NH 27 Dec 1733 Susanna Webster (KTR)
3. **JUDITH**, b 15 Jun 1714: m Kingston, NH 4 Mar 1736 Benjamin Cilley (NHGR 2:46)
4. **JOHN**, b 27 Sep 1716: d 1795: m Newbury, MA 18 Oct 1738 Hannah Morse (NVR)
5. **NAOMI**, b 12 Jul 1719: m Kingston, NH 7 Jul 1741 Jacob Flanders Jr (KTR)
6. **ONESIPHEROUS**, b 12 Jan 1721: m Kingston, NH 17 Nov 1748 Elizabeth Norton (NHGR 3:44)
7. **PHILIP**, b 24 Feb 1722/3
8. **PHILIP**, b 29 Aug 1724
9. **MARY**, b 8 Dec 1725
10. **RUTH**, bpt Kingston, NH 3 Aug 1729 (NHGR 2:48): d Kingston, NH 20 Jan 1730 a.6mos (NHGR 2:131)

JOHN DARLING JR, b Salisbury, MA 27 Sep 1716 son of John & Mary (Page) Darling (SVR): d 1795: m Newbury, MA 18 Oct 1738 Hannah Morse (NVR), b 1719 dau of William & Sarah (Merrill) Morse (Virkus 7:752).

John was admitted to the Kingston Church 26 Oct 1735. In 1738 he signed a petition for a new parish in the easterly part of Kingston.

Children: bpt Kingston, NH (KChR)

1. **WILLIAM**, bpt 21 Mar 1742
2. **JOHN**, bpt 5 Feb 1744
3. **MARY**, bpt 15 Jun 1746
4. **BENJAMIN BACHELLER**, bpt 8 May 1748
5. **TIMOTHY**, bpt 9 Dec 1750: m 1774 Anna Chase (Virkus 7:752)
6. **PETER**, bpt 19 Aug 1753
7. **MOSES**, bpt 18 Jan 1756
8. **JOSIAH**, bpt 29 Apr 1759
9. **SARAH**, bpt 21 Jun 1761
10. **LYDIA**, bpt 15 Nov 1761

JOHN DAVIS, b Amesbury, MA 7 Feb 1725/6 son of Jonathan & Martha (Dow) Davis (AVR): d Kingston, NH Dec 1760 (KTR); (Est Adm) 4 Apr 1761 (PRNH 7:123): m Kingston, NH 7 Apr 1748 Hannah Wadleigh (KTR).

Children: born Kingston, NH (KTR)
1. **ELEANOR**, b 30 Jun 1749
2. **JONATHAN**, b 20 Mar 1751: d Kingston, NH Mar 1751 (KTR)
3. **JUDITH**, b 7 Apr 1752
4. **PHINEAS**, b 25 Mar 1754
5. **JOHN**, b 16 Jul 1759: d Kingston, NH 22 Dec 1841 (NHVR)

SAMUEL DAVIS, b Amesbury, MA 25 Mar 1721 son of Samuel & Mary (Fowler) Davis (AVR): d abt 1797 (DAR 1:180): m Kingston, NH 19 Nov 1746 Dorothy Hadley (KTR), d aft 1797 living Corinth, VT (OF p732,1063).

Samuel had land granted to him in Kingston 8 Mar 1748.

Children: 1st 2 born Kingston, NH (KTR)
1. **DAVID**, b 21 Jun 1748
2. **MARY**, b 28 Oct 1749
3. **JUDITH**, bpt Kingston, NH 1 Jan 1752 (NHGR 6:27)
4. **SIMEON**, b Corinth, VT 1 Mar 1767
5. **SARAH**, b Corinth, VT 20 Jul 1769
6. **TIMOTHY**, b Corinth, VT 16 Nov 1772
7. **HANNAH**, b Corinth, VT 10 sep 1775

SAMUEL DEARBORN, b Hampton, NH 27 Jan 1669 son of Henry & Elizabeth (Marian) Dearborn (HmVR p101): d aft 1746 (LND p189): m Hampton, NH 12 Jul 1694 Mercy Batchelder (HmVR p79), b Hampton, NH 11 Dec 1677 dau of Nathaniel & Mary (Carter) Batchelder (HmVR p109).

Samuel was an original grantee of Kingston in 1694, but evidently never lived there.

Children: born Hampton, NH (HmVR)

1. **MARY**, b 23 Apr 1695: m Hampton, NH 30 Dec 1714 John Blake (HmVR p60)
2. **MERCY** (twin), b 21 Feb 1696/7
3. **MEHITABLE** (twin), b 21 Feb 1696/7: m 15 Jan 1719 Thomas Berry (HH p661)
4. **SARAH**, b 17 Jun 1699: m 24 Nov 1720 Edward Tuck (LND p695)
5. **MERCY**, b 18 Jan 1701/2
6. **JEREMIAH**, b 1 Apr 1704: d 1751: m Hampton, NH 23 Dec 1725 Sarah Taylor (HmVR)
7. **ELIZABETH**, b 9 Nov 1706: d Hampton, NH 30 Nov 1706 (HmVR p34)
8. **NATHANIEL**, b 21 Jan 1709/10: m Hampton, NH 2 Dec 1731 Mary Batchelder (HH p661)
9. **HENRY**, b 21 Nov 1712: m 19 Jan 1738 Margaret Sherburne (HH p661)
10. **SAMUEL**, b 1 Nov 1715: d 5 Feb 1736
11. **ELIZABETH**, b 11 Oct 1717
12. **ABIGAIL**, b 19 Oct 1720: m 25 Nov 1742 Col Abraham Drake

THOMAS DENT, m Kingston, NH 10 Oct 1714 Achaicus ____ (poss) Sanborn (KTR), bpt 9 May 1697 dau of Jonathan & Elizabeth (Sherburne) Sanborn (LND p604). A Thomas Dent of Kingston m Amesbury, MA 13 Apr 1742 Mary Challis (AVR). Perhaps this was a 2nd marriage.

Thomas had land laid out to him in Kingston 5 Mar 1712. His family belonged to Kingston in 1725. In 1730 he signed a petition regarding the township of Kingston.

Children: born Kingston, NH (KTR & NHGR)

1. **ABRAHAM**, b 9 May 1715: d Kingston, NH 24

May 1715 (KTR)

2. **JOHN**, b 16 Aug 1719: d Kingston, NH Mar 1798 (NHVR): m Kingston, NH 27 Aug 1741 Sarah Sanborn (KTR)
3. **ACHAICUS**, d Kingston, NH 3 Dec 1730
4. **THOMAS**, d Kingston, NH 7 Dec 1730
5. **DANIEL**, bpt 29 Oct 1732: d Kingston, NH 25 Mar 1738 (NHVR)
6. **(CHILD)**, d Kingston, NH 19 Jun 1736
7. **MARTHA**, bpt 23 Oct 1737: d Kingston, NH 31 Mar 1748 (NHVR)
8. **MARY**, bpt 13 Apr 1739/40: m (prob) Kingston, NH 27 Dec 1757 John Wadley (KTR)

ISRAEL DIMOND, b abt 1724 possibly son of Reuben & Dorothy (Worthen) Dimond: m(1) Kingston, NH 6 Dec 1748 Mary Chandler (KTR), d Kingston, NH 27 Sep 1754 (KTR): m(2) Kingston, NH 4 Mar 1756 Mary (Stevens) Philbrick (KTR). Mary m(1) Kingston, NH 20 Sep 1744 Jeremiah Philbrick (KTR).

Israel was admitted to the Kingston Church 8 Nov 1756.

Children: born Kingston, NH (KTR)
(by 1st wife)

1. **MARY**, b 15 Aug 1749
2. **EPHRAIM**, b 22 Apr 1751

(by 2nd wife)

3. **ISRAEL**, b 8 May 1757: m Danville, NH 27 Jan 1778 Abigail Eastman (NEHGR 58:124)
4. **HANNAH**, b 1 Mar 1760: m abt 1776 Hezekiah Blake (Blake Gen p50)
5. **JOHN**, b 18 Sep 1762: d Kingston, NH 18 Sep 1763 (KTR)
6. **DOROTHY**, b 31st ? Feb 1765

JOHN DODGE, probably d bef 1760: m Hannah ____ (possibly Webster at Ipswich, MA 3 Feb 1734/5)

John was admitted to the Kingston Church 14 Mar 1742.

Children: bpt Kingston, NH (NHGR 5:109,112)

1. **JOHN**, b 28 Feb 1742 (KTR): bpt 6 Jun 1742

2. **SIMON**, bpt 24 Mar 1744/5: d Kingston, NH 6 Dec 1745 (NHVR)
3. **RUTH** (poss), d Kingston, NH 28 Mar 1753 (NHVR)

BENJAMIN DOLE (Dr), b Newbury, MA 16 Nov 1679 son of John & Mary (Gerrish) Dole (NVR): d Hampton, NH 8 May 1707 (HmVR p127); Est Adm 3 Jun 1707 (PRNH 1:589): m Hampton, NH 11 Dec 1700 Frances Sherburne (HmVR p57), b Hampton, NH 29 Sep 1676 dau of Samuel & Love (Hutchins) Sherburne (HmVR p84). Frances m(2) Hampton, NH 18 Jan 1710/11 William Stanford of Ipswich, MA (HmVR p60).

Land was laid out in Kingston to Dr Benjamin Dole 3 Jan 1705.

Children: born Hampton, NH (HmVR)
1. **JONATHAN**, b 14 Apr 1703
2. **MARY**, b 30 Mar 1705: m Hampton, NH 26 Nov 1724 Rev John Tuck (HmVR p61)
3. **LOVE**, b 22 Nov 1706: d Hampton, NH 12 Jan 1711/12 (HmVR p127)

AMASSA DOW, b abt 1704 son of David Dow (Dow Book p390): d Salisbury, MA (Est Adm) 2 Dec 1730 (Essex Probate Index 1:271): m Kingston, NH 14 Aug 1729 Lydia Robie (KTR), b Hampton, NH 23 May 1703 dau of Ichabod & Lucy (Page) Robie (LND p590). Lydia m(2) Kingston, NH 8 Nov 1739 Michael Brooks of Biddeford (NHGR 3:40).

Children: Kingston, NH (KTR)
1. **AMASSA**, b 17 Jan 1729/30: m Kingston, NH 16 May 1750 Hannah Buswell (KTR)

AMASSA DOW, b Kingston, NH 17 Jan 1729/30 son of Amassa & Lydia (Robie) Dow (KTR): m Kingston, NH 16 May 1750 Hannah Buswell (KTR), b Kingston, NH 16 May 1732 dau of William & Abigail (Thorn) Buswell (KTR).

Amassa & his wife were admitted to the Kingston Church 6 Jun 1752.

Children: born Kingston, NH (KTR)

1. **SARAH**, b 21 Mar 1752: m Bow, NH 19 Nov 1776 Richard Clough (Dow Book p390)
2. **SAMUEL**, b 22 Mar 1755
3. **JOHN**, bpt 5 Mar 1758 (NHVR)
4. **MERIBAH**, bpt 16 Aug 1760 (NHVR)
5. **HANNAH**, bpt 28 Nov 1762 (NHVR)

CHALLIS DOW, b Salisbury, MA 22 Dec 1721 son of John & Dinah (Severance) Dow (SVR): m(1) Sarah ___ ? : m(2) Ipswich, MA 30 Dec 1746 Sarah Coleman (IpVR).

Children:

(by 1st wife)

1. **REBECCA**, b 24 Aug 1739 (SdTR)
2. **MARY**, b 5 Jun 1742 (SdTR)

(by 2nd wife)

3. **LYDIA**, b 4 Feb 1747: bpt So Hampton, NH 15 Jul 1750 (NEHGR 53:168)
4. **MARY**, bpt Kingston, NH 26 Jul 1752 (NHGR 6:28)
5. **REBECCA**, bpt So Hampton, NH 19 Oct 1755 (NEHGR 53:276)

ISAAC DOW, b 13 Mar 1716 son of John & Mary (_) Dow (Dow Book p396): d Sandown, NH Jul 1784 (SdTR): m Amesbury, MA 9 Dec 1742 Martha Hannaford (AVR), probably dau of John Hannaford.

Children: (SdTR)

1. **THOMAS**, b 9 Sep 1743: d 18 Mar 1822 (DAR 1:200): m 28 Feb 1767 Mary Barker
2. **ELIZABETH**, bpt Amesbury, MA 30 Dec 1744 (AVR): m 30 May 1764 Abner Whitcher
3. **MARTHA**, b 18 Dec 1744: d 12 Feb 1753
4. **ISAAC**, b 1 Oct 1746: d Sandown, NH 8 Feb 1768 (SdTR)
5. **ELA**, b 24 Apr 1748: m Sandown, NH 23 Mar 1780 Abigail Hoyt (SdTR)
6. **ANNA**, b 1 Mar 1750: m 1776 John Barker
7. **JESSE**, b 8 Aug 1753: m 12 Mar 1778 Phebe Palmer
8. **MARTHA**, b 28 Aug 1755

9. **ABIGAIL**, b 25 May 1758

PHILLIP DOW, b Salisbury, MA 26 Apr 1695 son of Joseph & Mary (Challis) Dow (SVR): d aft 1756: m(1) Salisbury, MA 2 Jan 1723/4 Hannah Griffin (SVR), b Salisbury, MA 25 Mar 1702 dau of John & Susanna (Brown) Griffin (SVR), d Kensington, NH 23 Jul 1753 (NHVR): m(2) Sarah (Ayers) Freese (LND p202), bpt (prob) Portsmouth, NH 8 Sep 1718 dau of George & Abigail (Perkins) Ayers (Newington Fam by Hardon p16). Sarah m(1) Hampton, NH 1 Jul 1736 Jonathan Freese (HmVR p134).
The wife of Phillip Dow was admitted to the Kingston First Church 14 Jul 1728.

Children: last 5 born Kensington, NH (NHVR)
1. **BONINIAH**, b Salisbury, MA 8 Oct 1724 (SVR): m So Hampton, NH 24 Sep 1751 Miriam French (NEHGR 52:429)
2. **(CHILD)**, d Kingston, NH 19 Sep 1728 (NHGR 2:131)
3. **EZEKIEL**, b Hampton, NH 1 May 1731 (HmVR p168): bpt Kingston, NH 8 Jul 1731 (NHGR 2:66): d Kensington, NH 21 Jun 1736 (NHVR)
4. **EPHRAIM**, b Hampton, NH 25 Aug 1732 (HmVR p168): d Kensington, NH 22 Jun 1736 (NH VR)
5. **JEMIMA**, b Hampton, NH 30 Jan 1733/4 (HmVR p169): bpt Kingston, NH 26 May 1734 (NHGR 2:68)
6. **HANNAH**, b 13 Aug 1736: d Kensington, NH 30 Apr 1738 (NHVR)
7. **PHINEAS**, b 2 Jan 1738: d Kensington, NH 12 Jun 1748 a.11yrs (NHVR)
8. **EBENEZER**, b 5 Nov 1739: d 11 Mar 1814 (DAR 1:200): m(1) So Hampton, NH 19 May 1761 Sarah French (SHVR): m(2) Mary Sanborn
9. **JONATHAN**, b 26 Mar 1741
10. **HANNAH**, b 20 Jun 1743: d Kensington, NH 22 Jun 1749 a.6yrs (NHVR)

JONATHAN DOWNING, d Kingston, NH (Est Adm) 25

Nov 1760 (PRNH 7:55): possibly m Gloucester, MA 30 Jan 1728/9 Sarah Day (GlVR).

Children:

1. **SARAH**, b Gloucester, MA 11 Dec 1729 (GlVR): m Kingston, NH 29 Dec 1747 Isaac Webster (NHGR 3:43)
2. **PRISILA**, b Rowley, MA 22 Dec 1731 (RwVR)
3. **JONATHAN**, b Rowley, MA 6 Jan 1733/4 (RwVR)
4. **JONATHAN**, b Newbury, MA 13 Sep 1738 (NVR)
5. **JOHN**, bpt Kingston, NH 14 Mar 1741/2 (NH GR 5:108)
6. **JOHN**, b Kingston, NH Mar 1743 (KTR): d (prob) Kingston, NH 19 Feb 1744 (NHVR)
7. **JOSEPH**, bpt Kingston, NH 7 Jul 1745 (NHGR 5:112): d Kingston, NH 8 Aug 1747 (NHVR)
8. **SAMUEL**, b Kingston, NH 2 Dec 1748 (KTR): d Jul 1777: m Sandown, NH abt 1764 Mary Carter (NHPR 15:127)

DAVIDSON DUDLEY, b abt 1708 son of Stephen & Sarah (Davidson) Dudley: d Brentwood, NH 1787 (Dudley Gen p290): m Anna Ladd (DAR 1:204).

Davidson was admitted to the Kingston Church 24 Jan 1742 & dismissed to Brentwood Jan 1751.

Children:

1. **DAVIDSON**, d 1757
2. **STEPHEN**, d Waterborough, ME 1814: m Phebe Webster
3. **TIMOTHY**, bpt Kingston, NH 7 Feb 1741/2 (NHGR 5:108): d 1778 (DAR 1:204): m Mary Leavitt
4. **SARAH**, bpt Kingston, NH 16 Sep 1744 (NHGR 5:111)
5. **ANNA**, bpt Kingston, NH 10 May 1747 (NHGR 5:155): m Waldron Webster
6. **PETER COFFIN**, bpt Kingston, NH 24 Sep 1749 (NHGR 5:158): d York, ME: m Polly Perry
7. **TRUEWORTHY**, bpt Kingston, NH 5 Aug 1753 (NHGR 6:30): d in Rev War
8. **PEGGY**, bpt Kingston, NH 28 Sep 1755 (NH

VR): m Nathaniel Chase

JAMES DUDLEY, b 1715 son of James & Mercy (Folsom) Dudley (Dudley Gen p283): d Brentwood, NH 1761; WP 24 May 1761 (PRNH 7:157): m Deborah (poss) Bean, d Andover, NH 1810.

James Jr was admitted to the Kingston Church 10 Jan 1742 & dismissed to Brentwood Jan 1751.

Children:

1. **STEPHEN**, bpt Kingston, NH 31 Aug 1739/40 (NHGR 5:106): m ___ Sleeper
2. **HANNAH**, bpt Kingston, NH 28 Feb 1741/2 (NHGR 5:108): m Kingston, NH 18 Nov 1762 Nathaniel Gilman (NHGR 3:129)
3. **JAMES**, b abt 1745: d aft 1817 (DAR 1:204): m ___ Glidden
4. **ELIPHALET**
5. **JONATHAN**, b 1752: d 1776
6. **JOHN**, d 1815: m Danville, NH 4 Mar 1779 Abigail Dudley (NEHGR 58:124)

SAMUEL DUDLEY, b 18 Mar 1720 (DAR 1:204) son of James & Mercy (Folsom) Dudley: d 30 Aug 1797 a.77yrs (Dudley Gen p283): m(1) Kingston, NH 24 Apr 1740 Mary Ladd (NHGR 3:40), b Kingston, NH 3 Jan 1722/3 dau of Daniel & Mehitable (Philbrick) Ladd (KTR): m(2) ___ Sleeper: m(3) ____ Clark.

Samuel & his wife Mary were admitted to the Kingston Church 14 Feb 1742.

Children:

1. **DANIEL**, bpt Kingston, NH 19 Jul 1741 (NHGR 5:107)
2. **DANIEL**, bpt Kingston, NH 6 Mar 1742/3 (NHGR 5:109): d 20 Jun 1811 (DAR 1:204): m Susy Dinsmore
3. **MEHITABLE**, m Daniel Stevens
4. **LYDIA**, m ___ Ingraham
5. **MARY**, b abt 1746: m John Haines
6. **SAMUEL**, b abt 1747: d 1795: m Sarah Young
7. **MICAJAH**, b Brentwood, NH 27 Nov 1751: d Durham, ME May 1798: m Susanna Foster

8. **JEREMIAH**, b 27 Aug 1753: d 10 Nov 1838 (DAR 1:204): m 10 Dec 1780 Elizabeth Turner (Dudley Gen p432)
9. **MOSES**, b 1755: d Mainesville, OH: m 29 Nov 1776 Apphia Sleeper
10. **ELIPHALET**, b 1759: m ____ Gilman
11. **JAMES**, b 1761: d Hampden, ME 5 Nov 1805: m Pittston, ME 1785 Sibyl Cheney

BENJAMIN EASTMAN, b Salisbury, MA 13 Jul 1710 son of Samuel & Elizabeth (Scribner) Eastman (SVR): d Kingston, NH 11 Sep 1751 (NHVR): m Kingston, NH 16 Aug 1733 Margaret Graves (KTR), dau of William & Margaret (Redman) Graves (LND p283).

Benjamin signed a petition regarding the township of Kingston in 1730 & in 1738 he signed a petition for a land grant.

Children: born Kingston, NH (KTR)

1. **EDWARD**, b 23 Feb 1734
2. **MARY**, b 3 Apr 1736
3. **MARGARET**, bpt 10 Dec 1738 (NHGR 5:104): m Kingston, NH 27 Oct 1762 Israel Graves (NHGR 3:129)
4. **JOHN**, b 24 Feb 1741: d Kingston, NH 11 Sep 1804 (GI p10): m Danville, NH 17 Feb 1774 Joannah French (NEHGR 58:123)
5. **SARAH**, b 27 Jun 1743
6. **BENJAMIN**, bpt 13 Oct 1745 (NHGR 5:153): d Kingston, NH 25 Sep 1746 (NHVR)
7. **ELIZABETH**, 6 Jul 1747
8. **ANNE**, b 6 Jun 1750

DAVID EASTMAN, b Salisbury, MA 11 Jun 1720 son of John & Hulda (Kingsbury) Eastman (SVR): m Salisbury, MA 17 Aug 1742 Susanna Flanders (SVR), b Salisbury, MA 24 Apr 1725 dau of John & Sarah (Prince) Flanders (SVR).

Children: (SdTR)

1. **SUSANNA**, b 12 Nov 1744
2. **MOLLE**, b 5 Nov 1745
3. **JOHN**, b 11 Mar 1748

4. **KINGSBURY**, b 22 Jun 1750
5. **SARAH**, b 4 Aug 1752
6. **DAVID**, b 13 Jan 1755

EBENEZER EASTMAN, b Salisbury, MA 11 Jan 1701/2 son of Samuel & Elizabeth (Scribner) Eastman (SVR): d Kingston, NH (WP) 9 Apr 1746 (PRNH 3: 352): m Kingston, NH 5 May 1725 Mary (Colcord) Sleeper (KTR), b Hampton, NH 24 Mar 1697/8 dau of Samuel & Mary (Ayers) Colcord (HmVR p67). Mary m(1) Kingston, NH 6 Dec 1714 Thomas Sleeper (KTR).

Ebenezer signed a petition for a grant of land in Kingston 1738.

Children: born Kingston, NH (KTR)

1. **SAMUEL**, 26 Mar 1727: d 1799: m Kingston, NH 8 Sep 1748 Abigail Hubbard (NHGR 3:43)
2. **EBENEZER**, b 14 Jul 1729: d Kingston, NH 4 Dec 1799 (KTR): m Kingston, NH 19 Jun 1758 Sarah Fifield (KTR)
3. **EDWARD**, b 14 Jan 1731/2: m Kingston, NH 6 May 1759 Hannah (Anna) Judkins (KTR)
4. **MARY**, b 24 Aug 1734
5. **JONATHAN**, b 28 Jun 1737: d Kingston, NH 7 Mar 1740 (KTR)
6. **HANNAH**, b 29 Apr 1741

EDWARD EASTMAN, b Salisbury, MA 30 Mar 1708 son of Samuel & Elizabeth (Scribner) Eastman (SVR): d bef 1744: m Kingston, NH 25 Jan 1730 Deliverance Graves (NHGR 2:45), dau of William & Margaret (Redman) Graves (LND p283).

Edward's name is on a list of Kingston men who swore allegiance to the King in 1727.

JOSEPH EASTMAN, b Salisbury, MA 6 Jan 1697 son of Samuel & Elizabeth (Scribner) Eastman (SVR): d E. Kingston, NH 18 Nov 1768 a.71yrs (CR); (WP) 9 Dec 1768 (PRNH 8:392): m Kingston, NH 9 Feb 1728/9 Patience Smith (KTR), dau of Nicholas & Mary (Gordon) Smith (LND p646).

Joseph signed a petition for a new parish in the easterly part of Kingston in 1738.

Children: born Kingston, NH (KTR)

1. **ELIZABETH**, b 27 Oct 1729: m Kingston, NH 13 Nov 1755 Joseph Weare (KChR)
2. **SHUAH**, b 23 May 1731: unmd in 1768
3. **JOSEPH**, b 3 Jun 1735: d E. Kingston, NH 10 Feb 1770 a.36yrs (CR): m Kingston, NH 22 Nov 1756 Sarah Smith (KChR)
4. **TIMOTHY**, b 25 Feb 1736/7
5. **PATIENCE**, b 14 Dec 1738: d Gilmanton, NH May 1804: m 29 May 1760 Daniel Gale
6. **MARY**, b 18 Apr 1741: m Richard Smith (PR NH 8:394)
7. **PHILIP**, b 23 Sep 1742 (not in will)

JOSEPH EASTMAN, d Kingston, NH 2 Sep 1774 (KTR): m(1) Kingston, NH 10 Mar 1751 Hannah Calef (KTR), d Kingston, NH 5 Dec 1754 (KTR): m(2) Kingston, NH 30 Jan 1756 Jemima (Bean) Smith (KTR), b 3 Dec 1730 dau of Jeremiah & Sarah (Blake) Bean (BtTR). Jemima m(1) Kingston, NH 15 Jan 1751/2 Jacob Smith (NHGR 3:45), m(3) Danville, NH 4 Jun 1777 Abel Webster (NEH GR 58:124).

Children: 1st 6 born Kingston, NH (KTR)
(by 1st wife)

1. **SARAH**, b 14 Jul 1751: m Danville, NH 15 Sep 1771 Benjamin Bean (NEHGR 58:122)
2. **HANNAH**, b 14 Nov 1754: d Kingston, NH 20 Nov 1755 (NHVR)

(by 2nd wife)

3. **HANNAH**, b 6 Nov 1757: m Danville, NH 14 Nov 1775 Samuel Bean (NEHGR 58:123)
4. **SHUAH**, b 27 Oct 1760
5. **HENRY**, b 4 Jul 1763: m Sarah Bean
6. **JEMIMA**, b 22 May 1766: m Levi Bean
7. **JOSEPH** (Bean Gen p137)
8. **ELIZABETH**, bpt 21 Jun 1772 (NHVR)

SAMUEL EASTMAN, b Salisbury, MA 20 Nov 1657 son of Roger & Sarah (?Smith) Eastman (SVR): d Kingston, NH 27 Feb 1725 (NHGR 2:131): m Salisbury, MA 4 Nov 1686 Elizabeth Scribner (SVR), b abt 1658 dau of John & Mary (_) Scribner (LND

p615).

Samuel was granted 40 acres of land in Kingston at a meeting of the freeholders 5 Nov 1702.

Children: born Salisbury, MA (SVR)

1. **RUTH**, b 5 Mar 1687/8: d Kingston, NH 6 Apr 1718 (KTR): m Kingston, NH 1 Jan 1714 William Long (KTR)
2. **ELIZABETH**, b 1 Dec 1689: m Salisbury, MA 10 Dec 1713 Thomas Fellows (SVR)
3. **MARY**, b 4 Jan 1691: m Salisbury, MA 24 Nov 1714 John Burley (SVR)
4. **SARAH**, b 3 Apr 1694
5. **SAMUEL**, b 5 Jan 1695/6: d Kingston, NH 20 Dec 1753 (NHVR): m(1) Kingston, NH 17 Sep 1719 Shuah Fifield (KTR): m(2) Kingston, NH 7 Nov 1728 Sarah (Brown) Clough (KTR)
6. **JOSEPH**, b 6 Jan 1697: d E. Kingston, NH 18 Nov 1768 (CR): m Kingston, NH 9 Feb 1728/9 Patience Smith (KTR)
7. **ANN**, b 22 May 1700: m Kingston, NH 22 Dec 1720 Philip Huntoon (KTR)
8. **EBENEZER**, b 11 Jan 1701/2: d Kingston, NH (WP) 9 Apr 1746: m Kingston, NH 5 May 1725 Mary (Colcord) Sleeper (KTR)
9. **THOMAS**, b 21 Jan 1703/4: m(1) Kingston, NH Jan 1729 Abigail French (KTR): m(2) 16 Jan 1744 Mary Fifield: m(3) So Hampton, NH 24 Jan 1751 wid Elizabeth French (SHVR)
10. **TIMOTHY**, b 29 Mar 1706: (not in father's will)
11. **EDWARD**, b 30 Mar 1708: m Kingston, NH 25 Jan 1730 Deliverance Graves (NHGR 2:45)
12. **BENJAMIN**, b 13 Jul 1710: m Kingston, NH 16 Aug 1733 Margaret Graves (KTR)

SAMUEL EASTMAN JR, b Salisbury, MA 5 Jan 1695/6 son of Samuel & Elizabeth (Scribner) Eastman (SVR): d Kingston, NH 20 Dec 1753 (NHVR): m(1) Kingston, NH 17 Sep 1719 Shuah Fifield (KTR), b Kingston, NH 13 Mar 1702/3 dau of Joseph & Sarah (Sherburne) Fifield (KTR), d Kingston, NH

3 Aug 1726 (NHGR 2:131): m(2) Kingston, NH 7 Nov 1728 Sarah (Brown) Clough (KTR), b Hampton, NH 15 Mar 1705/6 dau of William & Ann (Heath) Brown (HmVR p36).

Samuel belonged to Kingston when Rev Clark took charge of the church 29 Sep 1725. In 1738 he signed a petition for a grant of land.

Children: born Kingston, NH (KTR)
(by 1st wife)

1. **TIMOTHY**, b 6 Jan 1720/1: m Kingston, NH 16 Jan 1745 Mary Blaisdell (KTR)
2. **ELIZABETH**, b 31 Mar 1725
3. **JOSEPH**, living 1757 (PRNH 6:104)
4. **SAMUEL**, living 1757(PRNH 6:104): m Kingston, NH 1 Aug 1754 Mary Eastman (NHGR 3:87)

(by 2nd wife)

5. **SHUAH**, b 5 Dec 1731: m Chase Osgood (DAR 1:507)
6. **WILLIAM**, b 31 Jan 1734/5: d 3 May 1807 (DAR 1:212): m(1) Kingston, NH 12 Sep 1759 Mary Bean (NHGR 3:91): m(2) Jane Knight
7. **EZEKIEL**, d Kingston, NH 10 Dec 1735 (NHGR 3:38)
8. **EZEKIEL**, b 21 Oct 1736: living 1753 (PRNH 4:495)
9. **ELIZABETH**, b 26 Apr 1739: m Samuel French
10. **EBENEZER**, b 24 Apr 1746: d 27 Oct 1794 (DAR 1:211): m 15 Nov 1773 Mary Butler
11. **NEHEMIAH**, b 20 Jan 1747/8

THOMAS EASTMAN, b Salisbury, MA 21 Jan 1703/4 son of Samuel & Elizabeth (Scribner) Eastman (SVR): d (WP) Kingston, NH 25 Mar 1752 (PRNH 4:187): m(1) Kingston, NH Jan 1729 Abigail French (KTR), b Salisbury, MA 22 Sep 1710 dau of Joseph & Abigail (Brown) French (SVR), d Kingston, NH 8 Feb 1742/3 (KTR): m(2) 16 Jan 1744 Mary Fifield (TAG 16:17?), b Stratham, NH 10 Oct 1705 dau of Edward & Elizabeth (Leavitt) Fifield (NHGR 1:190): probably m(3) So Hampton, NH 24 Jan 1751 wid Elizabeth French (SHVR).

Abigail wife of Thomas Eastman was admitted to the Kingston Church 13 Apr 1729. In 1738 Thomas signed a petition for a new parish in the easterly part of Kingston.

Children: born Kingston, NH (KTR)
(by 1st wife)

1. **OBEDIAH**, b 21 Oct 1729: d Kingston, NH (Est Adm) 27 May 1765 (PRNH 8:171): m So Hampton, NH 28 Dec 1752 Judith Currier (SHVR)
2. **EDWARD**, b 25 Feb 1732/3: d Danville, NH 7 Nov 1815 (CG p39): m(1) Kingston, NH 5 Jan 1757 Sarah (Wadley) Clough (NHGR 3: 89): m(2) aft 1782 Prudence (Stevens) Bryant: m(3) Hannah (Hoyt) Hazelton (DAR 2:65)
3. **THOMAS**, b 23 Apr 1735: d Danville, NH (WP) 23 Dec 1760 (PRNH 6:556)
4. **ABIGAIL**, b 10 Jul 1737
5. **SARAH**, b 27 Mar 1738
6. **PHEBE**, b 2 Jan 1740/1

(by 2nd wife - TAG 16:172)

7. **SARAH**, b 13 Oct 1744: d Sanbornton, NH
8. **EBENEZER**, b 9 Feb 1746: d 14 Sep 1810: m Abigail Barker (DAR 1:211)
9. **MARY**, b 25 Jun 1750: m Eliphalet Gordon: lived New Hampton, NH

TIMOTHY EASTMAN, b Kingston, NH 6 Jan 1720/1 son of Samuel & Shuah (Fifield) Eastman (KTR): m Kingston, NH 16 Jan 1745 Mary Blaisdell (KTR), b Kingston, NH 4 Feb 1724/5 dau of Ralph & Mary (Nichols) Blaisdell (KTR).
Timothy was admitted to the Kingston Church 17 Feb 1742 & Mary was admitted 19 Aug 1753.

Children: born Kingston, NH (KTR)

1. **JACOB**, b 31 Jul 1745
2. **STEPHEN**, b 17 May 1747
3. **SAMUEL**, b 16 Oct 1749
4. **BENJAMIN**, b 12 Feb 1752

THEOPHILUS EATON, b Salisbury, MA 3 Jul 1721

son of Jonathan & Judith (Ash) Eaton (SVR): m Kingston, NH 23 Feb 1743 Abigail Fellows (KC hR), b Kingston, NH 6 Nov 1721 dau of Ebenezer & Elizabeth (Brooks) Fellows (KTR).

Children: born Kingston, NH (KTR)
1. **JUDITH**, b 29 Feb 1743/4
2. **MOSES**, b 8 Feb 1745/6
3. **ELIZABETH**, b 20 Jul 1749
4. **JONATHAN**, b 24 Feb 1752
5. **EBENEZER**, b 22 Aug 1756
6. **SARAH**, b 28 Apr 1759
7. **JAMES**, b 27 Jan 1762
8. **ABIGAIL**, b Jul 1763

EPHRAIM ELKINS, b Kingston, NH 30 Aug 1710 son of Moses & Ann (Shaw) Elkins (KTR): m Mary ___ who d Kingston, NH 28 May 1739 (NHVR).
Ephraim's name appears on a list of Kingston men who swore allegiance to the King in 1727. His wife, Mary, was admitted to the Kingston Church 7 Jan 1733.

GERSHOM ELKINS, b abt 1641 son of Henry & Mary (_) Elkins (LND p218): d Hampton, NH 12 Jan 1717/8 (HmVR p125): m Hampton, NH 15 May 1667 Mary Sleeper (HmVR p75), dau of Thomas & Joanna (Lee?) Sleeper (LND p638).
Gershom was an original grantee of Kingston in 1694. He was granted 200 acres of land at a meeting of the freeholders of Kingston 19 Dec 1700.

Children: born Hampton, NH (HmVR)
1. **JONATHAN**, b 24 Jan 1668: d Hampton, NH 12 Feb 1745 (HmVR p208): m Hampton, NH 24 Dec 1703 Joanna Robie (HmVR p58)
2. **MOSES**, b 4 Dec 1670: d Kingston, NH 9 May 1737 (KTR): m Kingston, NH 17 Nov 1701 Ann Shaw (KTR)
3. **JOSEPH**, not in father's will 1714
4. **MARY**, b 2 Sep 1674: d Hampton, NH 9 Feb 9 Feb 1702/3 (HmVR p120): unmd
5. **JOANNA**, b 14 Mar 1677: d 12 Jan 1762:

unmd (LND p217)

6. **HENRY**, d Kingston, NH (killed by Indians) 17 Sep 1707 (KTR)
7. **THOMAS**, b abt 1682: d Hampton, NH 25 May 1760 (LND p217): m Hampton, NH 8 Feb 1710/11 Hannah Fogg (HmVR p61)

HENRY ELKINS, b Hampton, NH son of Gershom & Mary (Sleeper) Elkins (LND p217): d Kingston, NH (killed by Indians) 17 Sep 1707 (KTR).

Henry was granted 200 acres of land in Kingston 30 Oct 1706. Administration on the estate of Henry Elkins of Kingston was granted 4 Nov 1707 to Thomas Elkins of Hampton (PRNH 1:608).

JOSEPH ELKINS, b Kingston, NH 1 Feb 1702/3 son of Moses & Ann (Shaw) Elkins (KTR): m Kingston, NH 2 Dec 1725 Elizabeth Huntoon (NHGR 2:44), dau of Philip & Hannah (_) Huntoon (LND p363).

Joseph & his wife were admitted to the Kingston Church 3 Mar 1728.

Children: born Kingston, NH (KTR)

1. **MARGARET**, b 2 Dec 1725
2. **ANNA**, b 10 Oct 1726: d Kingston, NH 11 Aug 1735 (KTR)
3. **ELIZABETH**, b 30 Apr 1730: d Kingston, NH 14 Aug 1735 (KTR)
4. **DOROTHY**, b 17 May 1732: d Kingston, NH 15 Aug 1735 (KTR)
5. **MARY**, b 1 Jun 1734: d Kingston, NH 22 Aug 1735 (KTR)

MOSES ELKINS, b Hampton, NH 4 Dec 1670 son of Gershom & Mary (Sleeper) Elkins (HmVR p102): d Kingston, NH 9 May 1737 (KTR): m Kingston, NH 17 Nov 1701 Ann Shaw (KTR), b Hampton, NH 20 Oct 1681 dau of Joseph & Elizabeth (Partridge) Shaw (HmVR p82).

Moses was granted 200 acres of land at a meeting of the freeholders of Kingston 19 Dec 1700. His family belonged to Kingston when Rev Clark took charge of the church in 1725.

Children: born Kingston, NH (KTR)

1. **JOSEPH**, b 1 Feb 1702/3: m Kingston, NH 2 Dec 1725 Elizabeth Huntoon (NHGR 2:44)
2. **MARY**, b 5 Aug 1704: m Kingston, NH 26 Dec 1723 Samuel Tucker (KTR)
3. **MEHITABLE**, b 20 Jul 1706: d Kingston, NH 9 Dec 1711 (KTR)
4. **OBEDIAH**, b 19 Jul 1708: d Danville, NH (WP) 29 Oct 1766 (PRNH 8:81) m Kingston, NH 1 Dec 1730 Abigail French (KTR)
5. **EPHRAIM**, b 30 Aug 1710: m Mary ___
6. **MEHITABLE**, b 13 Jun 1713: m Kingston, NH 1 Jan 1734/5 Joel Judkins (KTR)
7. **JOANNA**, b 15 Jul 1715: d Danville, NH 4 Jan 1801 (CG p39): m Kingston, NH 7 Nov 1736 Jonathan French (KTR)
8. **MOSES**, b 20 Jul 1717
9. **HENRY**, b 22 Mar 1720: d Kingston, NH 27 Mar 1720 (KTR)

OBEDIAH ELKINS, b Kingston, NH 19 Jul 1708 son of Moses & Ann (Shaw) Elkins (KTR): d Danville, NH (WP) 29 Oct 1766 (PRNH 8:81): m Kingston, NH 1 Dec 1730 Abigail French (KTR), b Kingston, NH 7 Apr 1713 dau of Simon & Sarah (Heard) French (KTR).

Obediah was admitted to the Kingston Church 21 Apr 1728 & his wife Abigail was admitted 15 Apr 1733.

Children: born Kingston, NH (KTR)

1. **SARAH**, b 31 Aug 1731
2. **JACOB**, b 8 Feb 1732/3: d Kingston, NH 28 Mar 1733 (KTR)
3. **JACOB**, b 25 May 1734
4. **ABIGAIL**, b 26 May 1736
5. **SARAH**, b 3 Sep 1738
6. **OBEDIAH**, b 23 Jun 1741
7. **PETER**, b 8 Apr 1746: d 24 Feb 1798 (DAR 1:217): m Danville, NH 11 Jun 1767 Huldah Buswell (DnTR)
8. **RACHEL**, b 16 Nov 1749
9. **JOSEPH**, b 6 Oct 1751

SAMUEL EMMONS, b Hampton, NH 12 Nov 1700 son of Joseph & Mary (Webster) Emmons (HmVR p71): d Kingston, NH (Est Adm) 27 Apr 1757 (PRNH 6:49): m Salisbury, MA 16 Jul 1723 Maria Norton (SVR), b Salisbury, MA 9 Nov 1704 dau of Solomon & Sarah (_) Norton (SVR). Maria m(2) Kingston, NH 13 Oct 1757 David Colby (NHGR 3:89).

Samuel signed a petition regarding the township of Kingston in 1730 & in 1738 he signed a petition for a new parish in the easterly part of Kingston.

Children:
1. **JOSEPH**, living 1757
2. **(DAU)**, d Kingston, 19 Jun 1735 (NHGR 2:133)
3. **(CHILD)**, d Kingston, NH 23 Jun 1735 (NHGR 2:133)
4. **(CHILD)**, d Kingston, NH 30 Jun 1735 (NHGR 2:134)

EBENEZER FELLOWS, b Salisbury, MA 10 Nov 1692 son of Samuel & Abigail (Barnard) Fellows (SVR): d Kingston, NH 5 Feb 1741/2 (KTR): m Kingston, NH 12 Nov 1718 Elizabeth Brooks (KTR), b 24 Jan 1695 dau of John & Eleanor (Frye) Brooks (LND p112).

Ebenezer belonged to Kingston in 1725 when Rev Clark took charge of the church. In 1738 he signed a petition for a new parish in the easterly part of Kingston.

Children: born Kingston, NH (KTR)
1. **JOHN**, b 27 Apr 1720: d 1812 (DAR 1:232): m(1) Kingston, NH 6 Mar 1745/6 Elizabeth Blaisdell (NHGR 3:42): m(2) Kingston, NH 4 Dec 1766 Mary (Tucker) Keniston (KChR)
2. **ABIGAIL**, b 6 Nov 1721: m Kingston, NH 23 Feb 1743 Theophilus Eaton (KChR)
3. **MARY**, b 31 Dec 1723: unmd in 1776
4. **EBENEZER**, b 19 Aug 1727
5. **JOSEPH**, b 10 Jun 1729: d 14 Mar 1811 (DAR 1:232): m(1) Kingston, NH 2 Jan 1754 Margaret Webster (KTR): m(2) Seabrook, NH 16

Jul 1776 Deborah Pevier
6. **BENJAMIN**, b 16 Mar 1730/1: d bef 13 May 1776: lived Newbury, MA
7. **ANNE**, b 15 Mar 1733/4: m __ Swain
8. **ELIZABETH**, b 22 Jun 1738

JOHN FELLOWS, b Hampton, NH 23 May 1701 son of Samuel & Deborah (Sanborn) Fellows (HmVR p72): d Kingston, NH (Est Adm) 4 Dec 1723 (PRNH 2: 187).

Administration on the estate of John Fellows of Kingston was granted to his brother Isaac Fellows of Hampton 4 Dec 1723.

SAMUEL FELLOWS, b Salisbury, MA 13 Jan 1646 son of Samuel & Ann (_) Fellows (SVR): d 5 Dec 1729: m Salisbury, MA 2 Jun 1681 Abigail Barnard (SVR), b Salisbury, MA (prob) 20 Jan 1656 dau of Thomas & Eleanor (_) Barnard (SVR).

Samuel was granted 200 acres of land in Kingston at a meeting of the freeholders 30 Oct 1706.

Children: born Salisbury, MA (SVR)
1. **SAMUEL**, b 1683: d Kingston, NH 12 Oct 1714 (KTR): m Kingston, NH 14 Nov 1710 Sarah Webster (KTR)
2. **THOMAS**, b 29 Jan 1685: m Salisbury, MA 10 Dec 1713 Elizabeth Eastman (SVR)
3. **JOSEPH**, b 23 Apr 1688
4. **ANN**, b 28 Apr 1690
5. **EBENEZER**, b 10 Nov 1692: d Kingston, NH 5 Feb 1741/2 (KTR): m Kingston, NH 12 Nov 1718 Elizabeth Brooks (KTR)
6. **HANNAH**, b 20 Jul 1697: m Kingston, NH 10 Dec 1720 Ebenezer Colcord (SVR)
7. **ELEANOR**, b Dec 1699

SAMUEL FELLOWS JR, b Salisbury, MA 1683 son of Samuel & Abigail (Barnard) Fellows (SVR): d Kingston, NH 12 Oct 1714 (KTR): m Kingston, NH 14 Nov 1710 Sarah Webster (KTR), b Hampton, NH 19 Sep 1690 dau of Thomas & Sarah (?Godfrey) Webster (HmVR p12).

Samuel Jr was granted 200 acres of land in Kingston at a meeting of the freeholders 30 Oct 1706.

Children: born Kingston, NH (KTR)
1. **SAMUEL**, b 15 Jun 1712: living 1736 of Chelmsford, MA (PRNH 2:572)
2. **JOSEPH**, b 27 Feb 1714: d 1795: m(1) Kingston, NH 1 Jan 1737/8 Elizabeth Young (KTR): m(2) Kingston, NH 7 Mar 1757 Mrs Sarah Green (KTR)

THOMAS FELLOWS, b Salisbury, MA 24 Jan 1718/9 son of Thomas & Elizabeth (Eastman) Fellows (SVR): m Kingston, NH 4 Dec 1744 Sarah Muchmore (KTR), b (prob) Gosport, NH 26 Jun 1726 dau of William & Sarah (_) Muchmore (NEHGR 67:243).

Children: born Kingston, NH (KTR)
1. **SARAH**, b 20 Oct 1746
2. **TIMOTHY**, b 5 Sep 1748
3. **WILLIAM**, b 7 Sep 1750
4. **SAMUEL**, b 5 May 1753
5. **HANNAH**, b 21 May 1755
6. **ELIZABETH**, b 22 Jun 1757
7. **RACHEL**, b 6 Dec 1759
8. **JACOB**, b 4 Apr 1764
9. **RUTH**, b 14 Jul 1766
10. **ELEANOR**, b 15 Sep 1768

EDWARD FIFIELD, b Hampton, NH 27 Mar 1679 son of Benjamin & Mary (Colcord) Fifield (HmVR p111): d Stratham, NH (WP) 30 Apr 1766 (PRNH 8:203): m Elizabeth Leavitt, dau of Moses & Dorothy (Dudley) Leavitt (LND p424).

Edward was granted 200 acres of land at a meeting of the freeholders of Kingston 19 Dec 1700. He withdrew from Kingston & went to Stratham, NH before 1707.

Children: born Stratham, NH (NHGR 1:190-1)
1. **EDWARD**, b 11 Feb 1704: m Stratham, NH 9 Nov 1727 Elizabeth Veasy (NHGR 1:183)
2. **MARY**, b 10 Oct 1705: d bef 1760: m 16 Jan

1744 Thomas Eastman (TAG 16:172)

3. **BENJAMIN**, b 10 Oct 1707: d (WP) 30 May 1771: m(1) Sarah ___: m(2) Mary ____
4. **MOSES**, b 30 Jul 1709: d bef 1765: m Hampton Falls, NH 1 Mar 1733 Abigail Fifield (TAG 16:173)
5. **JONATHAN**, b 25 Mar 1711: d (WP) 28 Jul 1779: m Miriam Veasey (TAG 16:173)
6. **DOROTHY**, b 23 Aug 1713: m Kingston, NH 23 Nov 1732 John Fifield Jr (KTR)
7. **ELIZABETH**, b 4 May 1716: m David Lyford of Epping (children listed NHGR 5:72)
8. **JOHN**, b 5 Nov 1718: m(1) Kingston, NH 1 Feb 1739 Elizabeth Greeley (KTR): m(2) 11 Jul 1757 Mary Brown (TAG 16:174)
9. **JOSEPH**, b 15 Mar 1721: d 1 Apr 1792: m Hannah ____ (TAG 16:174)

EDWARD FIFIELD, b Stratham, NH 11 Feb 1704 son of Edward & Elizabeth (Leavitt) Fifield (NHGR 1:190): d (W) 25 Mar 1782 (TAG 16:172): m Stratham, NH 9 Nov 1727 Elizabeth Veasey (NHGR 1:183).

Edward & his wife were admitted to the Kingston Church 12 Apr 1730. In 1738 he signed a petition for a new parish in the easterly part of Kingston.

Children: bpt Kingston, NH

1. **WILLIAM**, b 14 Aug 1730 (TAG 16:172): m Kingston, NH 14 Feb 1755 Anne Sinkler (NHGR 3:88)
2. **ELIZABETH**, bpt 21 Mar 1734 (NHGR 2:68): d Kingston, NH 22 Mar 1734 (NHGR 2:133)
3. **EDWARD** (?), bpt 14 Mar 1735 (TAG 16:172)
4. **SAMUEL**, bpt 13 Jul 1735 (NHGR 2:69): d 3 Sep 1812 (DAR 1:235): m Ruth Brown
5. **ELIZABETH**, bpt 25 May 1740 (KChR)
6. **MARY**, bpt 3 Feb 1745 (KChR)

JOHN FIFIELD, b Hampton, NH 21 Nov 1671 son of Benjamin & Mary (Colcord) Fifield (HmVR p103): d Kingston, NH abt 1750 (TAG 15:221): m(1) Abigail Weare (TAG 55:19), b Hampton, NH 13 Sep

1676 dau of Nathaniel & Elizabeth (Swaine) Weare (HmVR p108): m(2) abt 1709 Martha Andrews, b 25 Dec 1673 dau of Thomas & Martha (Baker-Antrim) Andrews (TAG 15:221), d Kingston, NH 12 May 1716 (KTR): m(3) Kingston, NH 16 Aug 1716 Mary Webster (KTR), b Hampton, NH 19 May 1696 dau of Thomas & Sarah (?Godfrey) Webster (HmVR p64).

John was granted 200 acres of land in Kingston 19 Dec 1700. His family belonged to Kingston in 1725 when Rev Clark took charge of the church.

Children: last 10 born Kingston, NH (KTR)
(by 1st wife)
1. **SHUAH**, d.y. (TAG 55:19)
2. **ELIZABETH**, b Hampton, NH 25 Nov 1698 (HmVR p68): m(1) Hezekiah Sleeper: m(2) Kingston, NH abt 1725 Jonathan Webster (TAG 16:165)
3. **JOHN**, d.y. (TAG 55:19)
4. **JOHN**, b Hampton, NH 31 Aug 1701 (HmVR p73): d.y. (TAG 55:19)

(by 2nd wife)
5. **ABIGAIL**, b 23 Aug 1711: m Hampton Falls, NH 1 Mar 1733 Moses Fifield (TAG 16:173)
6. **MARY**, b 8 Aug 1713: d bef 1746: m 14 Dec 1737 Paul Sanborn (TAG 16:166)

(by 3rd wife)
7. **MARTHA**, b 4 May 1718: m Kingston, NH 28 Dec 1738 Samuel Cilley (NHGR 3:40)
8. **SHUAH**, b 7 May 1720: m Kingston, NH 19 Jul 1739 Sinkler Bean (NHGR 3:40)
9. **BENJAMIN**, b 2 Feb 1721/2: d Concord, NH 8 Mar 1794: m 1747 Hannah Peters
10. **WILLIAM**, b 8 Jan 1724/5
11. **ALICE**, b 3 Jun 1727: m Kingston, NH 10 Apr 1749 Ebenezer Towle (NHGR 3:44)
12. **MEHITABLE**, b 29 Nov 1729: d Kingston, NH 17 Oct 1730 (NHGR 2:132)
13. **JONATHAN**, b 24 Feb 1731/2
14. **PAUL**, b 23 Sep 1735

JOHN FIFIELD, b Stratham, NH 5 Nov 1718 son of

Edward & Elizabeth (Leavitt) Fifield (NHGR 1: 190): m(1) Kingston, NH 1 Feb 1739 Elizabeth Greeley (KTR), b Kingston, NH 14 Sep 1721 dau of Joseph & Elizabeth (Young) Greeley (KTR): m (2) Kensington, NH 11 Jul 1757 Mary Brown (NH VR), b Kensingston, NH 4 Mar 1737 dau of Benjamin & Mary (_) Brown (NHVR).

Children:
(by 1st wife) - born Kingston, NH (KTR & KChR)

1. **NATHANIEL**, b 11 May 1739: d 2 Apr 1813 (DAR 1:235): m Janet Cilley (TAG 19:101)
2. **ELIZABETH**, b 1 Nov 1741
3. **MARY**, b 25 Oct 1743
4. **BATHSHEBA**, bpt 8 Dec 1745
5. **JOSEPH**, bpt 14 Feb 1748
6. **DAVID**, bpt 17 Mar 1751: d 5 Jan 1806 (DAR 1:235): m Abigail Larey
7. **JOHN** (twin), bpt 24 Feb 1754
8. **MARY** (twin), bpt 24 Feb 1754

(by 2nd wife) - born Kensington, NH (NHVR)

9. **MOSES**, b abt 1758: d 19 Nov 1759
10. **MOSES**, b 29 Feb 1760: d 3 Jul 1832 (DAR 1:235) m 7 Nov 1785 Lucy Levistone (TAG 19:106)
11. **LYDIA**, b 19 Aug 1761
12. **HANNAH**, b 1 Oct 1762: m 23 Feb 1794 Joseph Smith (TAG 19:106)
13. **DOROTHY**, b 7 Oct 1765: m Bennet Hall
14. **PHEBE**, b 14 Feb 1768: m Daniel Folsom
15. **MOLLY**, b 31 May 1770: m Jacob Folsom
16. **ABIGAIL**, b 18 Jul 1772: m Gilmanton, NH 21 Apr 1793 Stephen Folsom
17. **JUDITH**, b 14 Mar 1775: d 30 Jul 1780
18. **ANNA**, b 10 Dec 1776: m John Folsom

JOHN FIFIELD JR, b (prob) Kingston, NH 3 Jan 1709/10 son of Joseph & Sarah (Sherburne) Fifield (KTR): d Kingston, NH (WP) 27 Dec 1769 (PRNH 9:231): m(1) Kingston, NH 23 Nov 1732 Dorothy Fifield (KTR), b Stratham, NH 23 Aug 1713 dau of Edward & Elizabeth (Leavitt) Fifield (NHGR 1:190), d Kingston, NH 22 Mar 1765 (KTR): m(2) Haverhill, MA 25 Jul 1765 Mrs

Hannah Brown (HvVR).

John Jr & Dorothy his wife were admitted to the Kingston Church 15 Apr 1733. In 1738 John signed a petition for a grant of land in Kingston.

Children: born Kingston, NH (KTR)

1. **JOHN**, b 1 Oct 1733: m Kingston, NH 13 Oct 1757 Anna Snow (NHGR 3:89)
2. **EDWARD**, b 6 Apr 1735: d Kingston, NH 19 Dec 1735 (KTR)
3. **SARAH**, b 28 Aug 1736: m Jacob Bohonon (TAG 29:126)
4. **DOROTHY**, b 9 Apr 1738: living 1769
5. **JOSEPH**, b 22 Mar 1740: d 29 Sep 1813 (DAR 1:235): m Kingston, NH 10 May 1760 Anna Badger (KTR)
6. **ELIZABETH**, b 8 Jan 1742: m Kingston, NH 2 Sep 1762 Joseph Bean (NHGR 3:91)
7. **MARTHA** (twin), b 16 Jan 1744: d 16 Oct 1802: m Kingston, NH 21 Oct 1762 Daniel Huntoon (NHGR 3:129)
8. **MARY** (twin), b 16 Jan 1744: d Kingston, NH 29 Feb 1744 (NHVR)
9. **JONATHAN**, b 19 Mar 1746: d 15 Jan 1828 (DAR 1:235): m Danville, NH 4 Jun 1772 Dorcas Pearson (NEHGR 58:122)
10. **EDWARD**, b 22 Jan 1748: d 19 Aug 1834: m Dorothy Sleeper (DAR 1:235)
11. **SHUAH**, b 17 Jan 1749/50: m aft 20 Mar 1769 Ananiah Bohonon (TAG 29:126)
12. **ABRAHAM**, b 21 Aug 1752: d 9 Jun 1840 (DAR 1:235): m Abigail Silloway (TAG 19:94)
13. **SAMUEL**, b 28 Apr 1754: d Kingston, NH 9 May 1754 (NHVR)

JOSEPH FIFIELD, b Hampton, NH 7 Mar 1676/7 son of Benjamin & Mary (Colcord) Fifield (HmVR p108): d Kingston, NH 7 Jun 1761 (KTR): m Hampton, NH 24 Apr 1701 Sarah Sherburne (HmVR p57), b Hampton, NH 14 Jan 1681 dau of Samuel & Love (Hutchins) Sherburne (HmVR p83), d Kingston, NH 3 Apr 1765 (KTR).

Joseph received lot no. 3 at a meeting of the

freeholders of Kingston 18 Jul 1701. He was granted full rights in the 1st & 2nd division of land in 1705. His family belonged to Kingston in 1725 when Rev Clark took charge of the church.

Children: born Kingston, NH (KTR)

1. **SHUAH**, b 13 Mar 1702/3: d Kingston, NH 3 Aug 1726 (NHGR 2:131): m Kingston, NH 17 Sep 1719 Samuel Eastman (KTR)
2. **SAMUEL**, b 28 Oct 1704: m Kingston, NH 28 Aug 1728 Joanna Clifford (KTR)
3. **JOHN**, b 3 Jan 1709/10: m (prob) Kingston, NH 23 Nov 1732 Dorothy Fifield (KTR)
4. **SARAH**, b 17 Dec 1712: d Kingston, NH 6 Aug 1764 (KTR): m Kingston, NH 24 Dec 1736 Benjamin Stevens (KTR)
5. **MARGARET**, b 6 Jul 1716: m Kingston, NH Dec 1736 Peter Dearborn (NHGR 2:46)

SAMUEL FIFIELD, b Kingston, NH 28 Oct 1704 son of Joseph & Sarah (Sherburne) Fifield (KTR): d (WP) 1 Jan 1775 (TAG 16:171): m Kingston, NH 28 Aug 1728 Joanna Clifford (KTR), b Kingston, NH 12 Nov 1711 dau of Joseph & Sarah (French) Clifford (KTR).

Samuel signed a petition regarding the township of Kingston in 1730 & in 1738 he signed a petition for a grant of land in Kingston.

Children: born Kingston, NH (KTR)

1. **SHUAH**, b 30 Jan 1728/9: d Kingston, NH 13 Feb 1751 (KTR): m Kingston, NH 15 Dec 1748 Samuel Stevens (KTR)
2. **SARAH**, b 9 Apr 1730: d Kingston, NH 21 May 1736 (KTR)
3. **JOSEPH**, b 12 Sep 1731: d Kingston, NH 31 Oct 1742 (KTR)
4. **SAMUEL**, b 25 Jul 1733: d Kingston, NH 16 Jul 1811 (GI p11): m Kingston, NH 21 Feb 1757 Mary Eastman (KTR)
5. **JOHN CLIFFORD**, b 7 Apr 1736: d Kingston, NH 24 Jul 1800 (GI p11): m So Hampton, NH 4 Jun 1765 Hannah Sanborn (SHVR)

6. **HANNAH**, b 5 Oct 1737: d 30 Jul 1769: m John Sanborn (TAG 19:99)
7. **SARAH**, b 5 Jan 1739: d Kingston, NH 5 May 1794 (KTR): m Kingston, NH 19 Jun 1758 Ebenezer Eastman (KTR)
8. **PETER**, b 7 Aug 1740: d Kingston, NH (bur) 31 May 1807 (NHVR): m Danville, NH 5 Jul 1773 Sarah French (NEHGR 58:123)
9. **JOSEPH**, b 29 Jul 1743: d (WP) 27 Sep 1804 (TAG 19:100): m abt 1770 Elizabeth Sanborn
10. **JOANNA**, b 17 Feb 1744/5: d Kingston, NH 7 Mar 1829 (GI p11): m Kingston, NH 21 Mar 1769 Thomas Elkins Jr (KChR)
11. **STEPHEN**, b 10 Dec 1746: m Hampton Falls, NH 15 Mar 1768 Margaret Sanborn
12. **EBENEZER**, b 10 Dec 1751: d Readfield, ME 3 Jun 1834 (RG 1:235): m Hampton Falls, NH 8 Apr 1773 Mary Sanborn
13. **ELIZABETH**, b 17 Jan 1754

ASA FLANDERS, b Amesbury, MA 7 Feb 1707/8 son of Stephen & Sarah (Blaisdell) Flanders (AVR): m Salisbury, MA 16 Mar 1731/2 Mehitable Dow (SVR), b Hampton, NH 13 Jan 1705/6 dau of Simon & Mehitable (Green) Dow (HmVR p33).

Children: last 3 born So Hampton, NH (SHVR)

1. **SARAH**, b Salisbury, MA 24 Dec 1732 (SVR)
2. **ISAAC**, b Salisbury, MA 13 Nov 1735 (SVR): m Judith ___
3. **DAVID**, b Salisbury, MA 15 Jan 1737? (SVR)
4. **ASA**, b 16 Jun 1743
5. **STEPHEN**, b 23 Dec 1747: bpt Kingston, NH 26 Apr 1753 (NHGR 6:29)
6. **SIMON**, b 15 Feb 1750: bpt Kingston, NH 26 Apr 1753 (NHGR 6:29)

JACOB FLANDERS, b Salisbury, MA 5 Aug 1689 son of John & Elizabeth (Sargent) Flanders (SVR): m Salisbury, MA (int) 27 Sep 1710 Mercy Clough (SVR), bpt Salisbury, MA 20 Sep 1691 dau of John & Mercy (Page) Clough (SVR).

Jacob's family belonged to Kingston in 1725

when Rev Clark took charge of the church.

Children:

1. **TABITHA**, b Salisbury, MA 7 Apr 1711 (SVR): d Salisbury, NH 18 Feb 1810: m Concord NH 26 Sep 1736 Andrew Bohonon (NHGR 6:50)
2. **ELIZABETH**, m Concord, NH 22 Mar 1737 Daniel Rolf Jr (NHGR 6:50)
3. **JACOB**, b Kingston, NH 14 Aug 1715 (KTR): m Kingston, NH 7 Jul 1741 Naomi Darling (KTR)
4. **RUTH**, bpt Kingston, NH 31 Dec 1727 (NHGR 2:47): m 8 Aug 1740 John Elliot
5. **MERCY**, bpt Kingston, NH 31 Dec 1727 (NHGR 2:47)
6. **EZEKIEL**, b Kingston, NH 21 May 1721: m Concord, NH (int) 8 Aug 1742 Sarah Bishop
7. **JOHN**, b 10 Jan 1724 (DAR 1:240): d (WP) 23 Oct 1792: m Concord, NH 5 Nov 1749 Eunice Jackman
8. **(CHILD)**, d Kingston, NH 16 May 1726 (NHGR 2:131)
9. **JESSE**, bpt Kingston, NH 31 Dec 1727 (NHGR 2:47): d aft 1790 (DAR 1:240): m(1) Kingston, NH 9 Nov 1748 Ruth Webster (KChR): m(2) 8 Dec 1770 Elizabeth Blanchard
10. **PHILIP**, m at Amesbury, MA 23 Oct 1753 wid Mary Martin (SVR)
11. **(CHILD)**, d Kingston, NH 15 Aug 1735 (NHGR 3:37)
12. **HANNAH**, d 1786: m John Knowlton
13. **MEHITABLE**, b Boscawen, NH 30 Aug 1740

JACOB FLANDERS, b Kingston, NH 14 Aug 1715 son of Jacob & Mercy (Clough) Flanders (KTR): m Kingston, NH 7 Jul 1741 Naomi Darling (KTR), b Salisbury, MA 12 Jul 1719 dau of John & Mary (Page) Darling (SVR).

Children:

1. **MERCY**, b Kingston, NH 27 May 1745 (KTR): m Boscawen, NH (int) 21 Mar 1767 Samuel Danforth

2. **ABIGAIL**
3. **ANDREW**, m(1) Abigail ___: m(2) 4 Feb 1793 Sally Jackman
4. **JOSEPH**, b Kingston, NH 27 Jul 1753 (KTR)
5. **MARY**, b Boscawen, NH 13 May 1755: m (int) 12 Jan 1777 Elkanah Danforth
6. **ONESIPHORUS**, b Boscawen, NH 20 Dec 1761: d Haverhill, NH 10 Nov 1839: m 20 Apr 1778 Sally Foster

PHILIP FLANDERS, b Salisbury, MA 8 Jan 1681 son of Stephen & Abigail (Carter) Flanders (SVR): m Salisbury, MA 2 Feb 1709/10 Joanna Smith (SVR), b Salisbury, MA 22 May 1686 dau of Richard & Elizabeth (_) Smith (SVR).

Philip forfeited his rights in Kingston in 1715.

Children: born Salisbury, MA (SVR)

1. **SARAH**, b 16 Nov 1710
2. **PHILIP**, b 13 Mar 1712/3: d Chester, NH (Est Adm) 21 Mar 1758 (PRNH 6:221): m Salisbury, MA 2 Oct 1735 Hannah Morrill (SVR)
3. **ZIPPORAH**, b 4 Mar 1715/6: m Salisbury, MA 17 Jan 1733/4 John Bartlett (SVR)
4. **JOANNA**, b 20 May 1719: m Salisbury, MA 5 Mar 1740/1 Nathan Bartlett (SVR)
5. **ABIGAIL**, b 15 Aug 1722: m Salisbury, MA 17 Jan 1743/4 Joseph Jones (SVR)
6. **RICHARD**, b 6 Apr 1725
7. **ABIAH**, b 25 Jan 1727/8

STEPHEN FLANDERS, b Amesbury, MA 6 Mar 1705 son of Stephen & Sarah (Blaisdell) Flanders (AVR): m(1) Salisbury, MA 27 Jun 1726 Sarah Perkins (SVR), dau of Humphrey & Martha (Moulton) Perkins (NEHGR 12:80): m(2) Salisbury, MA (int) 7 Jul 1733 Elizabeth Stevens (SVR).

Stephen Flanders, from Salisbury, was admitted to the Kingston Church 6 May 1738.

Children:

1. **MIRIAM**, b Salisbury, MA 27 Nov 1726

(SVR): m Kingston, NH 5 Dec 1750 Jacob Quimby (NHGR 3:44)

2. **DAVID** (prob), b abt 1728: m(1) ____: m(2) Kingston, NH 18 Apr 1759 Ebenezer Nichols (NHGR 3:90): m(3) Haverhill, MA 21 Oct 1796 Charity (Fowler) Chase (HvVR)
3. **EZEKIEL**, b Salisbury, MA 24 Oct 1730 (SVR): m Kingston, NH 10 Jul 1750 Ann Nichols (NHGR 3:44)
4. **NATHANIEL**, bpt Salisbury, MA 21 May 1732: d Kingston, NH 16 Oct 1745 (NHVR)
5. **SARAH**, bpt Kingston, NH 14 Feb 1741/2 (NHGR 5:108)

JOHN FOLSOM, b Stratham, NH abt 1718 son of Nathaniel & Susanna (Jackson) Folsom (Folsom Gen p127): d 1790 (DAR 1:243): m Kingston, NH 16 Oct 1741 Abiah Carr (NHGR 3:41):

John was admitted to the Kingston Church 28 Dec 1740 & his wife was admitted 14 Mar 1742. They were dismissed to Brentwood Jan 1751.

Children: bpt Kingston, NH (NHGR & NHVR)

1. **SUSANNA**, bpt 16 Jan 1742/3
2. **MARY**, bpt 23 Sep 1744
3. **SARAH**, bpt 22 Jun 1746
4. **NICHOLAS CARR**, bpt 12 Jul 1747: d abt 1827: m bef 1767 Mehitable Flanders
5. **NATHANIEL**, bpt 2 Jul 1749
6. **NATHANIEL**, bpt 21 Apr 1751: m 7 May 1796 Susanna Pinkham
7. **JOHN**, bpt 8 Apr 1753
8. **ABIAH**, bpt 12 Oct 1755
9. **ELIZABETH**, bpt 1 May 1757
10. **JOSEPH SECOMB**, bpt 28 Sep 1760

JOSIAH FOWLER, b Amesbury, MA 28 Mar 1704 son of William & Hannah (Bagley) Fowler (AVR): m(1) Kingston, NH 20 Apr 1730 Elizabeth Webster (NH GR 2:45), b Kingston, NH 11 Jan 1710/11 dau of Thomas & Sarah (?Godfrey) Webster (KTR), d Kingston, NH 5 Apr 1746 (NHVR): m(2) Kingston, NH 28 Nov 1745/6 Catherine Hoyt (NHGR 3:42).

Children: 1st 3 born Amesbury, MA (AVR)

1. **SARAH**, bpt Amesbury, MA 16 Sep 1733 (AVR): d Kingston, NH 28 Oct 1747 (NHVR)
2. **HANNAH**, b 13 Mar 1735/6
3. **JOSIAH**, b 30 Mar 1739
4. **WILLIAM**, bpt Kingston, NH 30 Dec 1744 (NHGR 5:112)

WILLIAM FOWLER, b Amesbury, MA 8 Jun 1668 son of Thomas & Hannah (Jordan) Fowler (AVR): d (W) 18 Oct 1735 (PRNH 2:549): m Hannah Dow (LND p242), b Hampton, NH 25 Aug 1672 dau of Joseph & Mary (Sanborn) Dow (HmVR p103).

"Endorsed a will of William Fowler late of Kingston Dec'd exhib'd by the Exec'r who refused 30th Oct 1745 Not proved." (PRNH 2:549).

Children: last 6 born Amesbury, MA (AVR)

1. **HANNAH**, b Hampton, NH 4 Apr 1692 (HmVR p85): m Amesbury, MA 7 Apr 1708 John Bagley (AVR)
2. **MARY**, b 3 Dec 1694: m Amesbury, MA 18 Sep 1718 Samuel Davis (AVR)
3. **THOMAS**, b 1 Apr 1698: d (WP) Newton, NH 28 Jan 1752 (PRNH 4:40)
4. **JOSIAH**, b 28 Mar 1704: m(1) Kingston, NH 20 Apr 1730 Elizabeth Webster: prob m(2) Kingston, NH 28 Nov 1745/6 Catherine Hoyt
5. **WILLIAM**, b 14 Oct 1706: m Kingston, NH 8 Oct 1730 Lydia Severance (NHGR 2:45)
6. **PHILIP**, b 12 Oct 1709: d (WP) Newmarket, NH 26 Aug 1767 (PRNH 5:106)
7. **JOSEPH**, b 28 Apr 1715

BENJAMIN FRENCH, b Salisbury, MA 6 Oct 1696 son of Henry & Elizabeth (Collins) French (SVR): m (1) Salisbury, MA 20 Mar 1718 Margaret Allen (SVR), b Salisbury, MA 20 Dec 1697 dau of Stillson & Margaret (_) Allen (SVR), d Salisbury, MA 31 Oct 1719 (SVR): m(2) Salisbury, MA 5 Apr 1720 Judith Greeley (SVR), b Salisbury, MA 13 Jun 1696 dau of Andrew & Sarah (Brown) Greeley (SVR).

Benjamin signed a petition for a new parish

in the easterly part of Kingston in 1738.

Children: 1st 5 born Salisbury, MA (SVR)
(by 1st wife)
1. **BENJAMIN**, b 11 Oct 1719
(by 2nd wife)
2. **JABEZ**, b 7 Mar 1720/1: d 9 Oct 1806: m 5 Jan 1743 Hannah Hills (HC p526)
3. **ZEPHANIAH**, b 23 Mar 1722/3: d (Est Adm) 20 Jul 1764 (PRNH 8:82): m Kingston, NH 18 Mar 1746 Mary Greeley (KChR)
4. **BENJAMIN**, b 3 Dec 1724: d Salisbury, MA 14 May 1804 (SVR): m Joanna ___
5. **MARGARET**, b 2 Jan 1726/7: d Kingston, NH 30 Oct 1730 (NHGR 2:132)
6. **JUDITH**, b Kingston, NH 16 Jan 1729/30 (KTR): d Gilmanton, NH 1814: m Kingston, NH 25 Jan 1750 Moses Page (KChR)
7. **(DAU)**, d Kingston, NH 14 Jul 1735 (NHGR 2:134)
8. **HANNAH**, b Kingston, NH 24 Feb 1736 (KTR)

BENJAMIN FRENCH, b Kingston, NH 25 Feb 1717 son of Nathaniel & Sarah (Judkins) French (KTR): m Kingston, NH 12 Aug 1741 Ruth Huntoon (KTR), b Kingston, NH 11 Feb 1723 dau of Philip & Ann (Eastman) Huntoon (KTR).

Benjamin & his wife were admitted to the Kingston Church 30 Apr 1742.

Children: born Kingston, NH
1. **ELIZABETH**, b 28 Mar 1742 (KTR)
2. **SARAH**, b 24 Sep 1743 (KTR): d Kingston, NH 20 Nov 1744 (NHVR)
3. **NATHANIEL**, bpt 20 Oct 1745 (NHGR 5:153): d Kingston, NH 13 Oct 1746 (NHVR)
4. **SARAH**, bpt 22 Nov 1747 (NHGR 5:155)
5. **ANN**, bpt 15 Oct 1752 (NHGR 6:28)
6. **HANNAH**, bpt 2 Nov 1755 (NHVR)

JONATHAN FRENCH, b Kingston, NH 19 Apr 1713 son of Nathaniel & Sarah (Judkins) French (KTR): d Danville, NH 13 Sep 1785 (CG p39): m Kingston, NH 7 Nov 1736 Joanna Elkins (KTR), b Kingston,

NH 15 Jul 1715 dau of Moses & Ann (Shaw) Elkins (KTR), d Danville, NH 4 Jan 1801 (CG p39).

Jonathan signed a petition in 1738 for a grant of land in Kingston.

Children: 1st 11 born Kingston, NH (KTR)

1. **JOANNA**, b 18 Aug 1737: d Kingston, NH 16 Aug 1737 (KTR)
2. **HENRY**, b 26 Oct 1738: d Kingston, NH 30 Sep 1746 (KTR)
3. **ELIZABETH**, b 11 Apr 1740
4. **JONATHAN**, b 1 Jun 1741: d Kingston, NH 14 Jun 1741 (KTR)
5. **JONATHAN**, b 15 Apr 1744: d Kingston, NH 29 May 1744 (KTR)
6. **JOSEPH** (twin), b 29 May 1745: d Kingston, NH 27 Aug 174_ (KTR)
7. **MARY** (twin), b 29 May 1745: d Kingston, NH 5 Sep 1746 (KTR)
8. **HENRY**, b 25 Jan 1747: m(1) 21 Dec 1769 Judith Sanborn: m(2) Anna Shephard
9. **MARY**, b 18 Feb 1750: m Danville, NH 25 Apr 1776 Henry Judkins (NEHGR 58:124)
10. **JOANNA**, b 14 Jan 1752: m Danville, NH 17 Feb 1774 John Eastman (NEHGR 58:123)
11. **MEHITABLE**, b 23 Nov 1754
12. **JONATHAN**, b 28 Apr 1757: m Kingston, NH 27 Feb 1783 Mehitable Batchelder (NHGR 3:132)

NATHANIEL FRENCH, b Salisbury, MA 8 Dec 1678 son of Samuel & Abigail (Brown) French (SVR): d Kingston, NH (WP) 25 Apr 1750 (PRNH 3:434): m Kingston, NH 24 Jun 1704 Sarah Judkins (KTR), b Exeter, NH 13 Nov 1676 dau of Joel & Mary (Bean) Judkins (LND p393).

At a meeting of the freeholders of Kingston 30 Oct 1706, Nathaniel was granted 200 acres of land. His family belonged to Kingston when Rev Clark took charge of the church in 1725.

Children: born Kingston, NH (KTR)

1. **SAMUEL**, b 24 Oct 1705: d Kingston, NH 20 Sep 1790 (NHVR): m Kingston, NH 1 Apr

1736 Abigail Godfrey (KTR)
2. **NATHANIEL**, b 2 Apr 1707: d Kingston, NH 7 Apr 1775 (GI p12): m Kingston, NH 12 Oct 1729 Abigail Eastman (KTR)
3. **ELIZABETH**, b 1 Apr 1709: m Kingston, NH 17 Jan 1726/7 Isaac Godfrey (NHGR 2:44)
4. **SARAH**, b 20 Feb 1710/11
5. **JONATHAN**, b 19 Apr 1713: d Danville, NH 13 Sep 1785 (CG p39): m Kingston, NH 7 Nov 1736 Joanna Elkins (KTR)
6. **SARAH**, b 25 Sep 1715: m Kingston, NH 27 Dec 1738 Samuel Sleeper (KTR)
7. **BENJAMIN**, b 25 Feb 1717: m Kingston, NH 12 Aug 1741 Ruth Huntoon (KTR)
8. **MARY**, b 9 Sep 1720: m Kingston, NH 2 Jul 1742 Stephen Gilman (KTR)
9. **THOMAS GILBERT** (adopted), son of Mary Gilbert; bpt Kingston, NH 6 Jul 1739/40 (NHGR 5:106)

NATHANIEL FRENCH JR, b Kingston, NH 2 Apr 1707 son of Nathaniel & Sarah (Judkins) French (KTR): d Kingston, NH 7 Apr 1775 (GI p12): m Kingston, NH 12 Oct 1729 Abigail Eastman (KTR), d Kingston, NH 2 Sep 1798 a.90yrs (GI p13).

Children: born Kingston, NH (KTR)
1. **ELIZABETH**, b 4 Mar 1731
2. **ABRAHAM**, b 22 Apr 1733: d Kingston, NH 12 May 1800 (GI p12): m Kingston, NH 15 Jan 1756 Sarah Smith (KTR)
3. **NATHANIEL**, b 10 Feb 1735/6
4. **WILLIAM**, b 23 May 1738: d Kingston, NH 23 Sep 1743 (KTR)
5. **SECOMB**, b 31 Oct 1740: d Kingston, NH 21 Sep 1743 (KTR)
6. **ABIGAIL**, b 17 Jan 1744
7. **MARY**, b 22 Nov 1746
8. **MARTHA**, b 5 Mar 1749

SIMON FRENCH, b Salisbury, MA 26 Aug 1683 son of Joseph & Sarah (Eastman) French (SVR): d Kingston, NH (WP) 26 Sep 1764 (PRNH 8:46): m Kingston, NH 24 Nov 1709 Sarah Heard (KTR), dau

of Benjamin & Ruth (Eastman) Heard (LND p321).
Simon was taken in & made a freeholder of Kingston Apr 1705. He was granted 200 acres of land at a meeting of the freeholders 30 Oct 1706. His family belonged to Kingston in 1725 when Rev Clark took charge of the church.

Children: born Kingston, NH (KTR)
1. **RUTH**, b 29 May 1711: d Kingston, NH 12 Aug 1735 (NHGR 2:134)
2. **ABIGAIL**, b 7 Apr 1713: m Kingston, NH 1 Dec 1730 Obediah Elkins (KTR)
3. **JACOB**, b 12 Aug 1715
4. **RACHEL**, b 12 Apr 1717: d Kingston, NH 28 Sep 1717 (KTR)
5. **DAVID**, b 20 Aug 1719: d Kingston, NH 20 Oct 1792 (NHVR): m Kingston, NH 15 Sep 1747 Ruhamah Choate (KTR)

JACOB GALE, b Newbury, MA 30 Nov 1708 son of Daniel & Rebecca (Swett) Gale (NVR): d E. Kingston, NH 6 May 1760 (CR): m Newbury, MA 20 Oct 1735 Susannah (Morrill) Collins (NVR), b Salisbury, MA 5 Aug 1714 dau of Jacob & Mary (Webster) Morrill (SVR). Susannah m(1) Salisbury, MA 10 Feb 1731/2 John Collins (SVR).
Jacob signed a petition for a new parish in the easterly part of Kingston in 1738.

Children: last 12 born Kingston, NH (KTR)
1. **JACOB**, b Newbury, MA 20 Jun 1736 (NVR): d 22 Jan 1784 (DAR 1:257): m Kingston, NH 9 Nov 1758 Abigail Tappan (NHGR 3:90)
2. **SUSANNA**, b 28 Nov 1737: m So Hampton, NH 5 Jan 1757 Nathaniel Batchelder (SHVR)
3. **DANIEL**, b 2 Sep 1739: d Nov 1801 (DAR 1:257): m 29 May 1760 Patience Eastman
4. **ELIPHALET**, b 5 Sep 1741
5. **AMOS**, 21 Apr 1743: d Kingston, NH 29 Apr 1743 (KTR)
6. **AMOS**, b 9 Apr 1744: d Kingston, NH Jun 1813 (NHVR): m Kingston, NH 12 Nov 1765 Hannah Gilman (NHGR 3:130)
7. **ELI**, b 23 Feb 1745: d 1810 (DAR 1:257): m

Dorothy Blaisdell

8. **MARY**, b 22 Nov 1747
9. **BENJAMIN**, b 6 Mar 1748/9
10. **JOHN COLLINS**, b 26 Nov 1750: d Franklin, NH 29 Aug 1812 (CG p53)): m 1772 Rebecca Webster
11. **STEPHEN**, b 12 Oct 1752: d Kingston, NH 23 Oct 1754 (KTR)
12. **HENRY**, b 2 Oct 1754: d Kingston, NH 19 Oct 1754 (KTR)
13. **STEPHEN**, b 5 Jan 1756

JACOB GARLAND, b Hampton, NH 20 Dec 1656 son of John & Elizabeth (Philbrick) Garland (HmVR p90): d aft 1731: m Newbury, MA 17 Jan 1681 Rebecca Sears (NVR), b Newbury, MA 15 Nov 1661 dau of Thomas & Mary (Hilton) Sears (NVR).

Jacob was an original grantee of Kingston in 1694.

Children: (NVR, HmVR & LND p254)

1. **JACOB**, b Newbury, MA 26 Oct 1682: d Newbury, MA 19 Nov 1682 (NVR)
2. **REBECCA**, b Newbury, MA 3 Dec 1683: d.y.
3. **JACOB**, b Hampton, NH 3 Jul 1686: d Hampton, NH (Est Adm) 25 Dec 1735 (PRNH 2: 559): m(1) 26 Apr 1708 Hannah Sanborn: m (2) 24 Oct 1723 Sarah Drake (LND p254)
4. **MARY**, b abt 1688: d Hampton, NH 1 Feb 1749: m 4 Dec 1707 Thomas Dearborn (HH p662)
5. **SARAH**, b Hampton, NH 24 Feb 1689
6. **THOMAS**, b Hampton, NH 9 Mar 1691/2: bpt 11 Dec 1698: d bef 1703
7. **TABITHA**, bpt 11 Dec 1698
8. **JOSEPH**, b Hampton, NH 29 Dec 1697: bpt 11 Dec 1698
9. **JOHN** (twin), b Hampton, NH 28 Sep 1700: m Elizabeth Philbrick (HH p721)
10. **ELIZABETH** (twin), b Hampton, NH 28 Sep 1700
11. **THOMAS**, bpt 3 Jan 1703: m 23 May 1726 Elizabeth Moulton (HH p721)

THOMAS GEORGE, b Amesbury, MA 25 Mar 1699 son of Samuel & Elizabeth (Freame) George (AVR): m Sarah Swett (PRNH 3:569), b Hampton, NH 23 Dec 1700 dau of John & Bethia (Page) Swett (HmVR p72), d Kingston, NH (prob) 29 Aug 1797 a.92yrs (NHVR).

Thomas belonged to Kingston when Rev Clark took charge of the church in 1725. In 1730 he signed a petition regarding the township of Kingston.

Children: bpt Kingston, NH (NHGR 2:47)

1. **MARY**, bpt 31 Dec 1727
2. **MOSES**, bpt 31 Dec 1727
3. **JOSEPH**, bpt 31 Dec 1727

DANIEL GILES, b abt 1682 son of Mark Giles: m Eunice ____ (LND p260), d aft 1769.

Daniel's name appears on a list of Kingston men who swore allegiance to the King in 1727.

Children:

1. **DANIEL JR**, m Kingston, NH 5 Jan 1743 Sarah Magoon (KChR)
2. **ABIGAIL**, m Kingston, NH 16 Jun 1735 John Leavitt (NHGR 2:46)
3. **MARY**, m Kingston, NH 10 Dec 1740 William Gilman (NHGR 3:41)
4. **JOSEPH**, m Kingston, NH 26 Jun 1742 Joanna Akers (NHGR 3:41)

JACOB GILMAN, probably son of John & Grace (York) Gilman (LND p264): d Kingston, NH 11 Mar 1743 (NHVR): m Kingston, NH 1 Sep 1704 Mary Ladd (KTR), b Exeter, NH 28 Dec 1682 dau of Nathaniel & Elizabeth (Gilman) Ladd (HE p27g).

Jacob was granted 200 acres of Land at a meeting of the freeholders of Kingston 30 Oct 1706. His family belonged to Kingston in 1725 when Rev Clark took charge of the church.

Children: born Kingston, NH (KTR)

1. **DANIEL**, b 7 Aug 1705: d Kingston, NH 14 Mar 1797 (NHVR): m Kingston, NH 22 Apr

1730 Hannah Colcord (KTR)
2. **JOHN**, b 15 Mar 1707: m Kingston, NH 18 Dec 1735 Sarah Stevens (NHGR 2:46)
3. **ELIZABETH**, b 22 Mar 1709: d 27 May 1773 (LND p81): m Kingston, NH 17 Jan 1727 Phineas Batchelder (KTR)
4. **STEPHEN**, b 9 Aug 1713: d Kingston, NH (Est Adm) 28 Jun 1758 (PRNH 6:278): m Kingston, NH 2 Jul 1742 Mary French (KTR)
5. **JACOB**, d Kingston, NH 7 Jul 1757 (KTR): m Kingston, NH 4 May 1741 Abigail Moody (KTR)
6. **MARY**, b 19 Dec 1715: m Kingston, NH 21 Jun 1733 David Moody (NHGR 2:45)
7. **ABIGAIL**, b 7 Oct 1720: m Kingston, NH 26 Apr 1739 Samuel Stevens (NHGR 3:40)
8. **NATHANIEL**, b 25 May 1726
9. **DOROTHY**, d Kingston, NH 7 Jun 1735 (NHGR 2:133)

JACOB GILMAN, son of Jacob & Mary (Ladd) Gilman (PRNH 2:801): d Kingston, NH 7 Jul 1757 (KTR); Est Adm 27 Jul 1757 (PRNH 6:105): m Kingston, NH 4 May 1741 Abigail Moody (KTR), b abt 1724 dau of John & Abigail (_) Moody (TAG 61:229), d Kingston, NH (WP) 31 Jul 1765 (PRNH 7:278).

Children: born Kingston, NH (KTR)
1. **JOHN MOODY**, b 1 Feb 1742/3
2. **NATHANIEL**, b 3 Sep 1745: d Kingston, NH 22 Jan 1762 (KTR)
3. **JACOB**, b 14 Oct 1747
4. **SAMUEL**, b 3 Oct 1749
5. **PETER**, b 25 Jan 1751
6. **JONATHAN**, b 6 Aug 1754
7. **STEPHEN**, b 24 Aug 1757: d 17 Mar 1830 (DAR 1:269): m(1) Anne Huntoon: m(2) Sep 1793 Dorothy Clough
8. **JEREMIAH**, under 7yrs in 1762 (PRNH 7:278)

JOHN GILMAN, b Kingston, NH 15 Mar 1707 son of Jacob & Mary (Ladd) Gilman (KTR): d Kingston, NH (Est Adm) 30 Oct 1765 (PRNH 8:233): m Kingston, NH 18 Dec 1735 Sarah Stevens (NHGR 2:46), dau of Samuel & Patience (Gordon) Stevens (LND p659).

John signed a petition regarding the township of Kingston in 1730.

Children: bpt Kingston, NH (NHGR)

1. **NICHOLAS**, bpt 31 Oct 1736: d 30 Apr 1786 (DAR 1:269): m Elizabeth Thing
2. **SARAH**, bpt 10 Sep 1738: d Kingston, NH 26 Aug 1748 (NHVR)
3. **NATHANIEL**, bpt 5 Apr 1741: m Kingston, NH 18 Nov 1762 Hannah Dudley (NHGR 3:129): lived Mt Vernon, ME
4. **DANIEL**, bpt 23 Jan 1742/3
5. **JOHN**, bpt 12 May 1745
6. **DOLLY**, bpt 14 Aug 1748: d Kingston, NH 8 Sep 1750 (NHVR)
7. **SAMUEL STEVENS**, bpt 9 Dec 1750: m Elizabeth Dudley (ME FAM 3:87)
8. **SARAH**, bpt 21 Jun 1752
9. **PHINEAS** (twin), bpt 24 Aug 1755: d Kingston, NH 21 Nov 1756 (NHVR)
10. **DOLLY** (twin), bpt 24 Aug 1755: d 21 Oct 1849: m Kingston, NH 25 Mar 1779 David Sanborn (NHGR 3:130)

STEPHEN GILMAN, probably son of John & Grace (York) Gilman (LND p264): d Kingston, NH 1712 (killed by Indians).

Stephen was granted 200 acres of land at a meeting of the freeholders of Kingston 30 Oct 1706. Administration on his estate was granted to his brother Cartee Gilman Jul 1712 (PRNH 1:689).

STEPHEN GILMAN, b Kingston, NH 9 Aug 1713 son of Jacob & Mary (Ladd) Gilman (KTR): d Kingston, NH (Est Adm) 28 Jun 1758 (PRNH 6:278): m Kingston, NH 2 Jul 1742 Mary French (KTR), b Kingston, NH 9 Sep 1720 dau of Nathaniel & Sarah (Judkins) French (KTR).

Stephen was admitted to the Kingston Church 24 Jan 1742.

Children: born Kingston, NH (KTR)
1. **JACOB**, b 9 Mar 1743
2. **DOROTHY**, bpt 16 Sep 1744 (NHGR 5:111): d Kingston, NH 22 Nov 1747 (NHVR)
3. **STEPHEN**, bpt 25 May 1746 (NHGR 5:153): d Kingston, NH 11 Dec 1747 (NHVR)
4. **DANIEL**, b 22 Nov 1747
5. **DOROTHY**, b 25 Oct 1749
6. **MARY**, b 18 Jun 1752
7. **ELIZABETH**, b 3 Sep 1756

WILLIAM GILMAN, son of Cartee & Hannah (Towle) Gilman (LND p264): d bef 1752 (Gilman Gen p39): m Kingston, NH 10 Dec 1740 Mary Giles (NHGR 3:41), dau of Daniel & Eunice (_) Giles (LND p261).

William received land in Kingston where he lived from his father in 1748.

Children:
1. **(DAU)**, d Kingston, NH 16 Oct 1745 (NHVR)
2. **DOLLE**, b Kingston, NH 12 Jul 1746 (KTR)
3. **HANNAH**, b Brentwood, NH 21 Nov 1748 (Bt TR) bpt Kingston, NH 4 Dec 1748 (NHGR 5: 157)

ISAAC GODFREY, b Watertown, MA 15 Apr 1639 son of William & Margery (_) Godfrey (LND p269): d Hampton, NH 27 Dec 1717 (HmVR p124): m Hampton, NH 15 Jul 1670 Hannah Marian (HmVR p76), dau of John & Sarah (Eddy) Marian (LND p458).

Isaac was an original grantee of Kingston in 1694.

Children: born Hampton, NH (HmVR & LND p268)
1. **HANNAH**, b 24 Apr 1671:
2. **WILLIAM**, b 9 Nov 1672: d (WP) 25 May 1743: m Hampton, NH 17 Jan 1699/1700 Priscilla Annis (HmVR p56)
3. **SARAH**, b 29 Aug 1674
4. **ISAAC**, b Jan 1676: d 4 Nov 1680 (LND p268)
5. **MARY**, b 7 Sep 1678: d Hampton, NH 25 Mar 1702 (HmVR p120)

6. **JAMES**, b 26 Feb 1681
7. **ABIGAIL**, unmd 1710
8. **ELIZABETH**, unmd 1710
9. **HANNAH**, bpt 7 Mar 1696/7: m 12 Aug 1736 Ephraim Hoyt (LND p268)
10. **JONATHAN**, b 19 Apr 1691: bpt 7 Mar 1696/7: d 3 Mar 1733/4: m 3 Dec 1719 Mehitable Blake (LND p268)

ISAAC GODFREY, b Hampton, NH 4 Dec 1700 son of William & Priscilla (Annis) Godfrey (HmVR p71): d E. Kingston, NH (Est Adm) 26 Feb 1768 (PRNH 9:111): m Kingston, NH 17 Jan 1726/7 Elizabeth French (NHGR 2:44), b Kingston, NH 1 Apr 1709 dau of Nathaniel & Sarah (Judkins) French (KTR).

Isaac & his wife were admitted to the Kingston Church 18 Nov 1733. In 1738 Isaac signed a petition for a new parish in the easterly part of Kingston.

Children: bpt Kingston, NH

1. **ISAAC**, bpt 4 Jun 1732: d Kingston, NH 8 Jul 1735 (NHGR 2:134)
2. **NATHANIEL**, bpt 11 Aug 1734 (NHGR 2:69): d Kingston, NH 11 Jul 1735 (NHGR 2:134)
3. **WILLIAM**, d Kingston, NH 10 Jul 1735 (NHGR 2:134)
4. **(INFANT)**, d Kingston, NH 2 May 1736 (NHGR 3:39)
5. **SARAH**, bpt 11 Mar 1738/9 (NHGR 5:105): d Kingston, NH 6 Aug 1738 (NHVR)
6. **WILLIAM**, bpt 16 Nov 1740 (KChR)
7. **ELIZABETH**, bpt 6 Feb 1743 (KChR)
8. **ISAAC**, bpt 25 Nov 1744 (KChR)
9. **PRISCILLA**, bpt 30 Nov 1746 (KChR)

WILLIAM GODFREY, b Hampton, NH 9 Nov 1672 son of Isaac & Hannah (Marian) Godfrey (HmVR p104): d Hampton, NH (WP) 25 May 1743 (PRNH 3:52): m Hampton, NH 17 Jan 1699/1700 Priscilla Annis (HmVR p56), b Newbury, MA 10 Nov 1677 dau of Charles & Sarah (Chase) Annis (NVR), d No Hampton, NH 31 Aug 1768 (HH p729).

Wiliiam was an original grantee of Kingston in 1694.

Children: born Hampton, NH (HmVR)
1. **ISAAC**, b 4 Dec 1700: m Kingston, NH 17 Jan 1726/7 Elizabeth French (NHGR 2:44)
2. **MARY**, b 29 Jul 1703: d 20 Dec 1738
3. **ANNE**, b 14 Apr 1706: m Hampton, NH 15 May 1728 Zachariah Towle (HH p1004)
4. **JAMES**, b 22 Mar 1710 (HH p729): m(1) Rye, NH 4 Feb 1740 Patience ___ (Rye VR): m(2) Sarah Marston

BENONI GORDON, b Exeter, NH 1709 son of Thomas & Elizabeth (Harriman) Gordon (HE p22g): d Fremont, NH (WP) 27 Dec 1769 (PRNH 9:320): m Abigail Smith (LND p645), dau of Ithiel & Mary (_) Smith.

Abigail, wife of Benoni, was admitted to the Kingston Church 29 Apr 1742.

Children: last 5 bpt Kingston, NH (NHGR)
1. **ALEXANDER**, living 1769
2. **ELIZABETH**, m Kingston, NH 1 Nov 1753 Jeremiah Bean (NHGR 3:86)
3. **MARY**, b abt 1739: d Fairfax, VT 24 Aug 1822: m Kensington, NH 16 Oct 1760 Thomas Blake (NHVR)
4. **ABIGAIL**, m Edward Critchett (PRNH 9:321)
5. **TABITHA**, bpt Kingston, NH 20 Nov 1743: m William Mudgett (PRNH 9:321)
6. **THOMAS**, living 1769
7. **ENOCH**, bpt Kingston, NH 25 May 1746
8. **JOSIAH**, bpt Kingston, NH 28 Aug 1748: m 1775 Hannah Gordon (NEHGR 134:233)
9. **BENONI**, bpt Kingston, NH 5 May 1751: m Danville, NH 25 Mar 1773 Mary Gordon (NEH GR 58:123)

DANIEL GORDON, b Exeter, NH 1682 son of Alexander & Hannah (Lissen) Gordon (HE p22g): d bef 1736: m Haverhill, MA 15 Sep 1708 Margaret Harriman (HvVR), b Haverhill, MA 6 Oct 1681 dau of Mathew & Elizabeth (Swan) Harriman (HvVR).

Daniel had land laid out to him in Kingston 30 Nov 1709. He forfeited his rights in Kingston 5 Mar 1715.

Children: born Kingston, NH (KTR)
1. **ELIZABETH**, b 28 Jun 1709
2. **MARY**, b 20 Feb 1711: d Haverhill, MA 21 May 1738 (HvVR): m Haverhill, MA 8 Apr 1728 Nathan Merrill (HvVR)
3. **ABNER**, b 24 Nov 1712: m So Hampton, NH 14 Aug 1745 Elizabeth Straw (SHVR)
4. **MARGARET**, b 27 Oct 1714: d Kingston, NH 21 Jan 1714/5 (KTR)
5. **ALEXANDER**, b 29 Jan 1715/6: d Salem, NH 7 Jan 1793 (NEHGR 146:323): m(1) Haverhill, MA 22 Jun 1742 Susanna Pattee (HvVR): m (2) abt 1758 Hannah Stanley

THOMAS GORDON, b Haverhill, MA 24 Aug 1701 son of Thomas & Elizabeth (Harriman) Gordon (HvVR): d 27 Aug 1772: m(1) Mary Scribner (LND p615), dau of John & Elizabeth (Cloyes) Scribner (PRNH 2:565), d 16 Oct 1756: m(2) Deliverance Eastman (Gordon Gen p7), d 12 Jul 1791.

Mary, wife of Thomas Gordon, was admitted to the Kingston Church 18 Apr 1742.

Children:
1. **DANIEL**, b 1732
2. **LOVE**, b 1734: m Brentwood, NH 11 Jul 1756 Enoch Bean (BtTR)
3. **ELIZABETH**, b 1738
4. **MARY**, bpt Kingston, NH 5 Jul 1741 (NHGR 5:107): m James Bean
5. **THOMAS**, bpt Kingston, NH 31 Jan 1741/2 (NHGR 5:108): d Brentwood, NH 28 Jul 1819 (CG p24): m(1) Brentwood, NH 26 Aug 1765 Dorothy Gilman (BtTR): m(2) 28 Jul 181_ Mary Swain
6. **SCRIBNER**, bpt Kingston, NH 4 Nov 1744 (NH GR 5:112): d Brentwood, NH 12 Mar 1817 (CG p24): m 17 Mar 1768 Hannah Marston

JOSEPH GOSS, bpt Greenland, NH 1716 son of Robert & Jane (Berry) Goss (NEHGR 28:417): m bef 1736 Hannah Smith (LND p277), dau of Israel & Hannah (_) Smith.

Joseph & his wife Hannah were admitted to the Kingston Church 31 Jan 1742 & were dismissed to Brentwood Jan 1751.

Children: bpt Kingston, NH (NHGR)

1. **DELIVERANCE**, bpt 16 Sep 1744
2. **RACHEL**, bpt 3 Apr 1748

DANIEL GOULD, Inventory of the estate of Daniel Gould of Kingston 9 Dec 1745 (PRNH 3:320).

JOSEPH GOULD, b Amesbury, MA 1 Jul 1700 son of Samuel & Sarah (Rowell) Gould (AVR): d So Hampton, NH (Est Adm) 27 Dec 1752 (PRNH 4:294): m Amesbury, MA 2 Jun 1726 Abigail Hoyt (AVR), b Amesbury, MA 13 May 1705 dau of Robert & Martha (Stearns) Hoyt (AVR). Abigail m(2) So Hampton, NH 10 Jun 1756 Maj Thomas Pike (SHVR).

Joseph signed a petition for a new parish in the easterly part of Kingston in 1738.

Children: 1st 5 born Amesbury, MA (AVR)

1. **STEPHEN**, b 17 Feb 1726/7
2. **MARTHA**, b 28 May 1728
3. **JOSEPH**, b 12 Jan 1729/30
4. **CHRISTOPHER**, b 2 Jan 1731/2: m So Hampton, NH 11 Oct 1756 Abigail Shephard (SHVR)
5. **MOSES**, b 2 Apr 1735
6. **JOHN**, b So Hampton, NH 17 Mar 1738 (SH VR): bpt Amesbury, MA 6 Jan 1739/40 (AVR)
7. **EBENEZER**, b So Hampton, NH 5 Dec 1743 (SHVR)

JOHN GRAHAM, b Edinburgh, Scotland 1694 son of Andrew Graham (Virkus 6:256): d CT 1774: m(1) Kingston, NH 8 Jan 1719/20 Love Sanborn (KTR), b Kingston, NH 30 Aug 1702 dau of Jonathan & Elizabeth (Sherburne) Sanborn (KTR), d Stafford Springs, CT 1725 (LND p604): m(2) 1726 Abigail Chauncey (Virkus 6:256), b 1701 dau of Isaac &

Sarah (Blackleach) Chauncey.

Children:
(by 1st wife)
1. **ELIZABETH**, b Kingston, NH 2 Sep 1720 (KTR)

(by 2nd wife)
2. **ANDREW**, b 28 Jan 1729: d 15 Jun 1785 (DAR 1:279): m Martha Curtis
3. **SARAH**, m Gideon Hurd

JAMES GRAVES, b 22 Apr 1714 son of Samuel & Sarah (Perkins) Graves (LndVR p69): d So Hampton, NH 7 May 1765 (SHVR); WP 26 Jun 1765 (PRNH 8:163): m Haverhill, MA 1 Sep 1741 Sarah Roberts (HvVR), b Haverhill, MA 19 Apr 1722 dau of David & Mary (Dow) Roberts (HvVR).

Children:
1. **DAVID**, b Kingston, NH 1 Jun 1742 (KTR): m 5 May 1768 Ruth Wadleigh
2. **OLIVE**, b Kingston, NH 10 Sep 1743 (KTR): m bef 1765 Benjamin Clough (PRNH 8:164)
3. **SAMUEL**, b Kingston, NH 27 Mar 1745 (KTR)
4. **WILLIAM**, living 1773
5. **JAMES**, b abt 1748: d So Hampton, NH 15 Jun 1765 a.17yrs (SHVR)
6. **HANNAH**, m bef 1773 ___ Gooding
7. **PHINEAS**, living 1773
8. **SARAH**, (PRNH 8:164)
9. **ABIGAIL**, (PRNH 8:165)
10. **MARTHA**, (PRNH 8:165)
11. **LYDIA**, (PRNH 8:165)
12. **LUCY**, bpt So Hampton, NH 22 Aug 1762 (NEHGR 53:279)
13. **MOLLY**, bpt So Hampton, NH 16 Oct 1762

SAMUEL GRAVES, b Andover, MA 23 Dec 1682 son of Abraham & Anna (Hayward) Graves (AndVR): d (Est Adm) Haverhill, MA 28 Oct 1747 (PRNH 3:500): m (1) bef 1709 Sarah Perkins (LND p283), b Hampton, NH 3 Oct 1782 dau of James & Leah (Coxe) Perkins (HmVR p84), d 16 Jun 1724 (LND p283): m (2) Londonderry, NH 29 Jan 1724/5 Martha (Hale)

Bond (LndVR p214). Martha (prob) m(1) Bradford, MA 8 Dec 1715 John Bond (BdVR).

Samuel Graves of Kingston gave bond for the administration of the estate of his son Samuel Graves of Kingston 15 Nov 1734 (PRNH 2:519).

Children: (LndVR)
(by 1st wife)

1. **SARA**, b 17 Dec 1709
2. **SAMUEL**, b 16 Apr 1711: d Kingston, NH (Est Adm) 15 Nov 1734 (PRNH 2:519)
3. **JAMES**, b 22 Apr 1714: d So Hampton, NH 7 May 1765 (SHVR): m Haverhill, MA 1 Sep Sep 1741 Sarah Roberts (HvVR)
4. **ANNA**, b 26 Jul 1716
5. **EBENEZER**, b 2 Jul 172_: d Londonderry, NH 10 Dec 1724 a.1yr 2mo
6. **SARA** (prob), d Londonderry, NH 16 Jul 1724 a.1yr 2mo
7. **LYDIA**, b 9 Jul 1724

(by 2nd wife)

8. **MARTHA**, b 16 Jul 1726
9. **MARY**, b 21 Jul 1729

ANDREW GREELEY, b Gloucester, MA 17 Mar 1713/4 son of Joseph & Elizabeth (Young) Greeley (GlVR): d E. Kingston, NH 21 Dec 1801 (CR): m(1) Kingston, NH 5 Nov 1741 Mary Webster (KTR), b Kingston, NH 15 Sep 1724 dau of Ebenezer & Hannah (Judkins) Webster (KTR), d E. Kingston, NH 26 Sep 1791 (CR): m(2) Kingston, NH 22 Sep 1794 Elizabeth Flanders (NHGR 3:135).

Children:

1. **DAVID**, b Kingston, NH 19 Sep 1742 (KTR)
2. **ENOCH**, b Salisbury, MA 22 Sep 1745 (SVR): d Salisbury, MA 30 Nov 1749 (SVR)
3. **MARY**, b Salisbury, MA 15 Jan 1747/8 (SVR): m 29 Oct 1769 Nathan Batchelder
4. **SUSANNA**, b Salisbury, MA 17 Nov 1750 (SVR): m 8 Aug 1771 Joseph Tilton
5. **ENOCH**, b Salisbury, MA 1 Aug 1754 (SVR): m Kingston, NH Mar 1780 Dorothy Batchelder (NHPR 24:120)

6. **ANNE**, bpt Kingston, NH 23 Apr 1758 (KChR): m Kingston, NH 28 Jun 1785 Reuben Greeley (NHGR 3:132)
7. **BETTY**, b Salisbury, MA 25 Jan 1766 (SVR)

JONATHAN GREELEY, b Salisbury, MA 2 Jan 1705/6 son of Jonathan & Jane (Walker) Greeley (SVR): d E. Kingston, NH 1 Jun 1755 (CR): m Salisbury, MA 13 Mar 1735 Martha French (SVR), b Salisbury, MA 7 Jul 1709 dau of Edward & Mary (Winsley) French (SVR), d E. Kingston, NH 22 Aug 1781 a.76yrs (CR).

Jonathan signed a petition for a new parish in the easterly part of Kingston in 1738.

Children: last 5 bpt Kingston, NH (KChR)

1. **MOSES**, b Kingston, NH 10 Oct 1736 (KTR): d E. Kingston, NH 5 Mar 1814 (CR): m Salisbury, MA 7 Dec 1775 Hannah Kenney (SVR)
2. **JANE**, b 16 Mar 1739: d E. Kingston, NH 8 Mar 1811 (CR): m E. Kingston, NH 26 Mar 1760 David Tilton (Greeley Gen p98)
3. **JONATHAN**, bpt 24 Jan 1742: d E. Kingston, NH 3 Dec 1789 (CR): m(1) Kingston, NH 1 Oct 1767 Martha Noyes (KChR): m(2) Kingston, NH 12 Mar 1780 Mary Bartlett (NHGR 3:131)
4. **AARON**, bpt 7 Apr 1745: d 12 Sep 1813 (DAR 1:282): m 25 Oct 1772 Susanna Burnham
5. **MARTHA**, bpt 14 Feb 1748: m Kingston, NH 16 Sep 1789 James Flanders (NHGR 3:134)
6. **PHILIP**, bpt 12 Aug 1750: d 22 Oct 1832 (DAR 1:282): m 2 Feb 1774 Dolly Tilton
7. **EDWARD**, bpt 14 Apr 1754: d E. Kingston, NH 5 Nov 1817 (CR)

JOSEPH GREELEY, b Salisbury, MA 24 Nov 1683 son of Andrew & Sarah (Brown) Greeley (SVR): d (WP) Kingston, NH 28 Jan 1761 (PRNH 5:194): m Ipswich, MA (int) 18 Feb 1709/10 Elizabeth Young (IpVR), dau of Samuel & Elizabeth (Masterson) Young (LND p777).

Joseph was granted 11 acres of land in Kingston 6 Jun 1719. His family belonged to Kingston in 1725 when Rev Clark took charge of the church. In 1738 Joseph signed a petition for a new parish in the easterly part of Kingston.

Children:
1. **SAMUEL**, b Salisbury, MA 3 Sep 1712 (SVR)
2. **ANDREW**, b Gloucester, MA 17 Mar 1713/4 (GlVR): m(1) Kingston, NH 5 Nov 1741 Mary Webster (KTR): m(2) Kingston, NH 22 Sep 1794 Elizabeth Flanders (NHGR 3:135)
3. **JOSEPH**, b Gloucester, MA 8 Oct 1715 (Gl VR): d Gilmanton, NH 5 Jun 1792: m Kingston, NH 2 Dec 1741 Elizabeth Dudley (KTR)
4. **JONATHAN**, b Salisbury, MA 20 Sep 1718 (SVR): m 28 Nov 1743 Esther Nowell
5. **ELIZABETH**, b Kingston, NH 14 Sep 1721 (KTR): m Kingston, NH 1 Feb 1739 John Fifield (KTR)
6. **MARY**, b Kingston, NH 9 Apr 1723 (KTR): m Kingston, NH 18 Mar 1746 Zephaniah French (KChR)
7. **DAVID**, d Kingston, NH 21 Jun 1735 (NHGR)
8. **NATHANIEL**, d Kingston, NH 1 Jul 1735 (NHGR 2:134)

JOSEPH GREELEY JR, b Gloucester, MA 8 Oct 1715 son of Joseph & Elizabeth (Young) Greeley (Gl VR): d Gilmanton, NH 5 Jun 1792 (Greeley Gen p65): m Kingston, NH 2 Dec 1741 Elizabeth Dudley (KTR), b Brentwood, NH 20 Oct 1722 dau of Jonathan & Dinah (Bean) Dudley, d Gilmanton, NH 1809 (CG p56).

Joseph Jr signed a petition for a new parish in the easterly part of Kingston in 1738.

Children: born Kingston, NH (KTR)
1. **SARAH**, b 7 May 1743: m Brentwood, NH 10 May 1769 Jeremiah Currier (BtTR)
2. **SAMUEL**, b 27 Aug 1745: d Kingston, NH 26 Oct 1746 (KTR)
3. **SAMUEL**, b 16 Sep 1747: m Brentwood, NH 12 Jun 1773 Mary Leavitt (BtTR)
4. **ELIZABETH**, b 8 Aug 1749: m Brentwood, NH

11 Feb 1770 Edward Robinson Gilman (BtTR)
5. **ELEANOR**, b 11 Oct 1752: m Brentwood, NH 27 Sep 1778 Joseph Wiggin (BtTR)
6. **MARY**, b 28 Apr 1755: d Kingston, NH 28 Aug 1760 (KTR)
7. **JOSEPH**, b 22 Feb 1758: d Kingston, NH 1 Sep 1760 (KTR)
8. **NOAH**, b 29 Jul 1760: m Kingston, NH 7 Jan 1783 Hannah Morrill (NHGR 3:131)
9. **MARY**, b 31 Dec 1762: m Brentwood, NH 15 Sep 1781 Timothy Smith (BtTR)
10. **JOSEPH**, b 22 May 1762: m Mary Wyman

ABRAHAM GREEN, b Hampton, NH 28 Aug 1707 son of John & Abial (Marston) Green (HmVR p36): d Kingston, NH 6 Apr 1751 (NHVR): m(1) Hampton, NH 12 Nov 1730 Comfort Dow (HmVR p133), b Hampton, NH 28 Oct 1708 dau of Jabez & Esther (Shaw) Dow (HmVR p38), d Hampton Falls, NH 20 Jun 1736 (HFTR): m(2) Hampton Falls, NH 29 Sep 1737 Sarah Treadwell (HFTR). Sarah m(2) Kingston, NH 7 Mar 1757 Joseph Fellows (KTR).

The estate of Abraham Green of Kingston was administered 24 Apr 1751 (PRNH 4:118).

Children: 1st 5 born Hampton Falls, NH (HFTR)
(by 1st wife)
1. **ESTHER**, b 22 Aug 1731: d Hampton Falls, NH 3 Jun 1736 (HFTR)
2. **ASCHEL**, b 9 Sep 1733: d Hampton Falls, NH 8 Jun 1736 (HFTR)
3. **COMFORT**, b 9 Jan 1734: m Hampton, NH 2 Nov 1752 John Marston (HH p845)

(by 2nd wife)
4. **PETER**, b 30 Jun 1739
5. **SARAH**, b 9 Jun 1741: d Kingston, NH 6 Feb 1745/6 (KTR)
6. **JOHN**, b Kingston, NH 3 Feb 1742/3 (KTR): d Kingston, NH 23 Jan 1745/6 (KTR)
7. **MARTHA**, b Kingston, NH 24 Sep 1744 (KTR): d Kingston, NH 3 Feb 1745/6 (KTR)
8. **SARAH**, b Kingston, NH 1 Sep 1746 (KTR): m Ephraim Jones
9. **MARTHA**, b Kingston, NH 13 Jul 1748 (KTR):

m Silas Peaslee
10. **ANNA**, b Kingston, NH 1 Apr 1750: living 1770
11. **ESTHER**, d Kingston, NH 30 Jan 1755 (KTR)

EPHRAIM GRIFFIN, b Salisbury, MA 22 Apr 1713 son of John & Hannah (Davis) Griffin (SVR): m Hampton, NH 3 Jun 1736 Mary Elkins (HmVR p134), b Hampton, NH 5 May 1714 dau of Thomas & Hannah (Fogg) Elkins (HmVR p55).

Mary Griffin was admitted to the Kingston Church 3 Apr 1742 & was dismissed to No Yarmouth 1749.

Children:
1. **JOHN**, b 18 Jul 1738: m 21 Nov 1765 Deborah Tucker (ME Fam 3:102)
2. **EPHRAIM**, b 13 Jun 1740: m No Yarmouth, ME 24 Jun 1762 Judith Blaisdell (ME Fam 1:18)
3. **SAMUEL**, b Kingston, NH 10 Aug 1742 (KTR): m (int) 23 Aug 1766 Priscilla Royal
4. **MARY**, b Kingston, NH 14 Sep 1744 (KTR): d Kingston, NH 17 Feb 1747/8 (KTR)
5. **JONATHAN**, b Kingston, NH 26 Feb 1746/7 (KTR): m (prob) Cumberland, ME 3 Dec 1772 Mary Blaisdell (ME Fam 3:102)
6. **HENRY**, b 1 Jun 1751: d 23 Sep 1753
7. **SETH**, b 29 Jan 1754: m 15 Jul 1776 Judith Mitchell (ME Fam 3:102)

ISAAC GRIFFIN, b Salisbury, MA 21 Dec 1699 son of John & Susanna (Brown) Griffin (SVR): d Kingston, NH (WP) 25 Feb 1756 (PRNH 5:231): m (1) Salisbury, MA 7 Jan 1724/5 Susanna Clough (SVR), b Salisbury, MA 19 Dec 1704 dau of John & Elizabeth (Long) Clough (SVR): m(2) Kingston, NH 4 Oct 1754 Hannah (Clifford) Judkins (NHGR 3:87), dau of Jacob & Elizabeth (Mayhew) Clifford (LND p393). Hannah m(1) bef 1728 Benjamin Judkins.

Isaac signed a petition regarding the township of Kingston in 1730 & in 1738 he signed a petition for a new parish in the easterly part of Kingston.

Children: born Kingston, NH (KTR)
1. **PHEBE**, b 28 Dec 1725
2. **ELIZABETH**, b 8 Nov 1728: m Kingston, NH 27 Oct 1754 John Page (KChR)
3. **ISAAC**, b 5 Aug 1731: m Kingston, NH 14 Aug 1752 Mary Rowen (NHGR 3:86)
4. **MARY**, b 23 Jun 1734: m Kingston, NH 23 Aug 1750 Moses Blake Jr (KChR)

JOHN GRIFFIN, b Amesbury, MA 30 May 1713 son of Theophilus & Hannah (Fowler) Griffin (AVR): m Kingston, NH 8 Sep 1743 Hannah Bean (KTR), bpt Kingston, NH 21 Apr 1728 dau of Samuel & Sarah (_) Bean (NHGR 2:48).

Children: born Kingston, NH
1. **HANNAH**, b 16 Sep 1744 (KTR)
2. **ANNE**, b 16 Mar 1746/7 (KTR)
3. **SARAH**, b 29 May 1749: d Kingston, NH 9 Sep 1750 (KTR)
4. **JOHN**, b 8 Sep 1751 (KTR)
5. **THEOPHILUS**, bpt 3 Nov 1754 (KChR): d 23 Sep 1814 (DAR 1:286): m Sarah Martin
6. **MARY** (twin), bpt 30 Apr 1758 (KChR)
7. **SARAH** (twin), bpt 30 Apr 1758 (KChR)

THEOPHILIUS GRIFFIN, b Amesbury, MA 22 Oct 1689 son of Theophilius & Mary (Colby) Griffin (AVR): d Deerfield, NH: m Amesbury, MA 18 Dec 1710 Hannah Fowler (AVR)

Theophilius belonged to Kingston in 1725 when Rev Clark took charge of the church. In 1738 he signed a petition for a new parish in the easterly part of Kingston.

Children: 1st 4 born Amesbury, MA (AVR)
1. **THEOPHILUS**, b 17 Jun 1711
2. **JOHN**, b 30 May 1713: m Kingston, NH 8 Sep 1743 Hannah Bean (KChR)
3. **LYDIA**, b 21 Oct 1715: m Kingston, NH 18 Mar 1736 David Osgood (NHGR 2:46)
4. **MARY**, b 23 Oct 1717

5. **ELIPHALET**, b Kingston, NH 24 May 1720 (KTR): d Deerfield, NH 1792: m Salisbury, MA 21 May 1745 Anne Eaton (SVR)
6. **ANN**, b Kingston, NH 18 Aug 1722 (KTR)
7. **THOMAS**, b Kingston, NH 4 Sep 1725 (KTR)
8. **JOSEPH**, b Kingston, NH 28 Jun 1728 (KTR)
9. **BENJAMIN**, b Kingston, NH 8 Nov 1730 (KTR)

GEORGE GURDY, m Amesbury, MA 4 Apr 1709 Hannah Martin (AVR), b abt 1680 dau of John & Mary (Weed) Martin (TAG 59:15). Hannah d (W) Kingston 4 Dec 1752 (PRNH 4:282). Hannah m(2) Amesbury, MA 15 Feb 1727/8 Richard Gent (AVR).

George forfeited his rights in Kingston 27 Mar 1715.

Children: born Amesbury, MA (AVR)

1. **SARAH**, b 20 Nov 1709
2. **JOHN**, b 20 May 1711
3. **JACOB**, b 22 Sep 1713: d (W) Chester, NH 10 Apr 1755 (PRNH 5:262)
4. **MESHECH**, b 11 Aug 1717: m Kingston, NH 31 Jul 1751 Patience Eaton (NHGR 3:45)
5. **HANNAH**, b 7 Oct 1719

MESHECH GURDY, b Amesbury, MA 11 Aug 1717 son of George & Hannah (Martin) Gurdy (AVR): d aft 1776: m Kingston, NH 31 Jul 1751 Patience Eaton (NHGR 3:45).

Meshech lived in the westerly section of Kingston.

Children: (SdTR)

1. **MARY**, b 7 Apr 1752: bpt Kingston, NH 12 Apr 1752 (NHGR 6:27)
2. **JUDITH**, bpt Kingston, NH 27 Oct 1754 (NH GR 6:31)
3. **JACOB**, b 17 Feb 1759: m 1782 Mary Favor (Virkus 5:185)
4. **SAMUEL**, b 20 Feb 1764
5. **SARAH**, b 7 Apr 1766

JAMES HEATH, b Haverhill, MA 25 Mar 1683 son of Josiah & Mary (Davis) Heath (HvVR): d (WP) 30

Jan 1744/5 (PRNH 3:229): m(1) bef 1706 Mary (Bradley) Heath (HvVR), b Haverhill, MA 16 Apr 1671 dau of Daniel & Mary (Williams) Bradley (HvVR). Mary m(1) Haverhill, MA 23 Jan 1690/1 Bartholomew Heath (HvVR): James m(2) bef 1731 Dinah (Davis) Mudgett (HvVR), b Haverhill, MA 24 Mar 1706/7 dau of Stephen & Mary (Tucker) Davis (HvVR). Dinah m(1) bef 1726 William Mudgett (HvVR). She m(3) ____ Robinson (PRNH 4:358).

James, of Kingston, was granted guardianship of Ebenezer Mudgett 24 Nov 1742 (PRNH 3:136).

Children: 1st 6 born Haverhill, MA (HvVR)
(by 1st wife)
1. **DAVID**, b 14 Apr 1706
2. **NATHANIEL**, b 12 Jan 1707/8
3. **JUDITH**, b 25 Aug 1709: m Haverhill, MA 23 Sep 1730 John Kezar (HvVR)
4. **JAMES**, b 28 May 1711
5. **Mary**, b 30 Mar 1713: d aft 1713 (HvVR)

(by 2nd wife)

6. **JOSHUA** (alias **ELIJAH**), b 12 Jan 1730/1: d 1776 (DAR 1:319): m Hampstead, NH (int) 2 Feb 1754 Hannah Dearborn (HmstR)
7. **MARY**, b Hampstead, NH 27 Jan 1734: d 25 May 1748 (HmstR)
8. **MIRIAM**, b Hampstead, NH 30 Mar 1736 (HmstR): m John Pell (PRNH 4:359)
9. **SUSANNA**, b Hampstead, NH 27 Jul 1738 (HmstR): living 1758
10. **ASA**, b Hampstead. NH 29 Jan 1740 (HmstR)
11. **ENOCH**, b Hampstead, NH 27 Feb 1744

JOHN HERSEY, m Kingston, NH 21 May 1741 Elizabeth Judkins (KTR), b Kingston, NH 27 May 1715 dau of Samuel & Abigail (Harriman) Judkins (KTR).

Children: born Kingston, NH (KTR)
1. **PETER**, b 16 Jul 1742
2. **ELIZABETH**, b 18 Mar 1744/5: d Kingston, NH 18 Jul 1745 (KTR)
3. **SAMUEL**, b 8 Sep 1746

4. **JOHN**, b 26 Mar 1749
5. **ICHABOD**, b 2 Aug 1752
6. **MARY**, b 29 Aug 1754: bpt 27 Oct 1754 (NHGR 6:31)

JAMES HEULET (HELAT), belonged to Kingston in 1725 when Rev Clark took charge of the church.

DANIEL HIBBARD, b Methuen, MA 1728 son of John & Dorothy (Graves) Hibbard (Hibbard Gen p29) m Kingston, NH 23 Feb 1743/4 Ruth Huse (KTR).

Daniel settled in the westerly section of Kingston.

Children:

1. **RUTH**, b Kingston, NH 9 Jan 1744/5 (KTR)
2. **DANIEL**, b Haverhill, MA 18 Nov 1750 (Hv VR): d Edgecomb, ME 27 Jun 1823: m 16 Feb 1775 Sarah Wadlin (ME FAM 2:135)
3. **JOSEPH**, b Sandown, NH 17 Nov 1757 (SdTR)
4. **LYDIA**, b Sandown, NH 21 Jun 1760 (SdTR)
5. **HANNAH**, b Haverhill, MA 19 Feb 1762 (HvVR)

JONATHAN HOBBS, b Hampton, NH 18 Nov 1717 son of Morris & Theodate (Batchelder) Hobbs (HmVR p55): m Falmouth, ME (int) 4 Oct 1741 Ann Blake (Blake Gen p266), bpt Hampton, NH 19 Aug 1722 dau of Jasper & Susanna (Brackett) Blake (HH p604).

Jonathan & his wife Ann were admitted to the Kingston Church 19 Jun 1743 & dismissed to Falmouth 19 Apr 1750.

Children: 1st 3 bpt Kingston, NH (NHGR)

1. **SUSANNA**, bpt 19 Jun 1743: m Falmouth, ME (int) 20 Sep 1764 Stephen Staples (ME Fam 2:274)
2. **MORRIS**, bpt 22 Sep 1745
3. **ANNE**, bpt 8 Feb 1746/7
4. **JONATHAN**, bpt Falmouth, ME 1750: d Falmouth, ME 19 Mar 1838: m(1) Topsham, ME (int) 6 Sep 1779 Mary Staples: m(2) Freeport, ME 21 Dec 1809 Eleanor (Morrill)

Porter (ME Fam 2:141)

DYER HOOK, b Salisbury, MA 1 Sep 1720 son of Jacob & Elizabeth (French) Hook (SVR): d Danville, NH 11 Mar 1776 (CG p39): m Kingston, NH 21 Nov 1744 Hannah Brown (KTR), b (prob) Salisbury, MA 3 Nov 1722 dau of Abraham & Hannah (Morrill) Brown (SVR), d Danville, NH 20 Sep 1800 (CG p39).

Dyer & his wife were admitted to the Kingston Church 27 Feb 1746.

Children: 1st 5 born Kingston, NH (KTR)

1. **ABRAHAM**, b 17 Nov 1745: m Danville, NH 22 Nov 1768 Rachel Elkins (DnTR)
2. **ELISHA**, b 18 Nov 1747: d Danville, NH 22 Feb 1831: m 1 Mar 1773 Sarah Clark
3. **DYER**, b 21 Jan 1749/50: m Sarah Sleeper
4. **ISRAEL**, b 17 Jan 1754: d Danville, NH 23 Mar 1813 (CG p39): m Danville, NH 12 Jan 1780 Dorothy Griffin (NEHGR 58:125)
5. **HANNAH**, b 24 Oct 1757: d Brentwood, NH 9 Jul 1796 (BtTR): m Brentwood, NH 23 Feb 1780 Dr Thomas Stowe Ranney (BtTR)
6. **PETER**, b Danville, NH 17 Dec 1763 (DnTR)

HUMPHREY HOOK, b Salisbury, MA 27 Jul 1722 son of Jacob & Elizabeth (French) Hook (SVR): d Danville, NH 8 Jan 1801 (DnTR): m(1) Kingston, NH 24 Nov 1747 Hannah Philbrick (KTR), b Kingston, NH 6 Feb 1724 dau of Jedediah & Mary (Taylor) Philbrick (KTR), d Danville, NH 28 Aug 1771 (DnTR): m(2) Sarah Reddington (DAR 1:341).

Humphrey lived in the westerly section of Kingston.

Children: 1st 6 born Kingston, NH (KTR)
(by 1st wife)

1. **MARY**, b 13 Jul 1748
2. **MARTHA**, b 9 Aug 1750: m Jabez Smith
3. **JACOB**, b 30 Jul 1752: d Kingston, NH 9 May 1757 (KTR)
4. **HANNAH**, b 12 Dec 1754: d Kingston, NH

5 Feb 1755 (KTR)

5. **JEDEDIAH**, b 2 Mar 1756: d Kingston, NH 9 Apr 1757 (KTR)
6. **JACOB**, b 13 Feb 1758
7. **ELIZABETH**, b Danville, NH 30 Mar 1760 (Dn TR): m Reuben Hall
8. **HANNAH**, b Danville, NH 9 Aug 1762 (DnTR)
9. **JACOB**, b Danville, NH 10 Jul 1764: d 10 Jul 1764 (DnTR)
10. **HUMPHREY**, b Danville, NH 28 May 1765
11. **REUBEN**, b Danville, NH 22 Jul 1768: d 24 Dec 1768 (DnTR)

(by 2nd wife)

12. **LUCY**, bpt Danville, NH 30 Apr 1775 (NEHGR 58:45)
13. **ANNA**, b Danville, NH 9 Jan 1777 (DnTR)
14. **REUBEN**, b Danville, NH 16 Nov 1778 (DnTR)

PHILIP HOYT, b Amesbury, MA 1 Apr 1697 son of William & Dorothy (Colby) Hoyt (AVR): m Metheun, MA 5 Aug 1736 Mary Lowell (MthVR), b Haverhill, MA 2 Feb 1712/13 dau of John & Mary (Davis) Lowell (HvVR).

Philip signed a petition in 1730 regarding the township of Kingston (see OF p207).

JEREMIAH HUBBARD, b Salisbury, MA 27 Aug 1692 son of John & Jane (Follinsby) Hubbard (SVR): d Kingston, NH (Est Adm) 27 Oct 1762 (PRNH 7: 357): m Haverhill, MA 28 Feb 1722/3 Mercy Johnson (HvVR), d aft 1762.

Jeremiah had land laid out to him in Kingston 14 Feb 1714/5. His family belonged to Kingston when Rev Ward Clark took charge of the church on 29 Sep 1725.

Children: born Kingston, NH (KTR)

1. **JOSEPH**, b 11 Mar 1723/4: d Kingston, NH 18 Mar 1750 (KTR)
2. **JANE**, b 5 Feb 1725/6
3. **RICHARD**, b 11 Aug 1728: d Kingston, NH 21 Apr 1755 a.27yrs (KTR)
4. **MARCY**, b 26 Mar 1732

JOHN HUBBARD, b Salisbury, MA 12 Apr 1669 son of Richard & Martha (Allen) Hubbard (SVR): d Kingston, NH (WP) 4 Mar 1723/4 (PRNH 2:174): m Salisbury, MA Jane Follinsby (SVR), dau of Thomas & Mary (_) Follinsby (LND p236).

John had 30 acres of land laid out to him in Kingston 25 Feb 1702/3 & was granted 200 acres at a meeting of the freeholders 30 Oct 1706. In 1725 his widow is listed as belonging to Kingston when Rev Clark took charge of the church.

Children: 1st 8 born Salisbury, MA (SVR)

1. **RICHARD**, b 17 Jan 1690
2. **JEREMIAH**, b 27 Aug 1692: d Kingston, NH 22 Sep 1762 (NHVR): m Haverhill, MA 28 Feb 1722/3 Mercy Johnson (HvVR)
3. **MARY**, b 29 Nov 1694
4. **RICHARD**, b 27 Dec 1696: d Kingston, NH 26 Dec 1782 (GI p15): m(1) Haverhill, MA 27 Dec 1722 Abigail Davis (HvVR): m(2) Kingston, NH 16 Oct 1734 Abigail Taylor (KTR): m(3) Dorcas ___
5. **MARTHA**, b 8 Oct 1698: d (WP) 11 Jan 1776: m 26 Oct 1725 Noah Champney (LND p353)
6. **JANE**, b 10 Jun 1700
7. **ANNA**, b 22 Jul 1702: m Kingston, NH 3 Oct 1728 Rev William Thompson (NHGR 2:44)
8. **KEZIAH**, b 10 Jul 1704: m Scarboro, ME 1 Jan 1734 John Libby (LND p434)
9. **JOHN**, b Kingston, NH 21 Jul 1706: d Kingston, NH 6 Sep 1706 (KTR)
10. **DOROTHY**, b Kingston, NH 8 Jan 1708 (KTR)
11. **JEMIMAH**, b Kingston, NH 3 Mar 1711 (KTR): m Kingston, NH 27 Dec 1732 John Meserve (NHGR 2:45)
12. **JOHN**, b Kingston, NH 28 Jan 1715 (KTR): living 1753 (LND p353)

JOHN HUBBARD, b Kingston, NH 28 Jan 1715 son of John & Jane (Follinsby) Hubbard (KTR).

In 1738 John signed a petition for a grant of land in Kingston.

RICHARD HUBBARD, b Salisbury, MA 27 Dec 1696

son of John & Jane (Follinsby) Hubbard (SVR): d Kingston, NH 26 Dec 1782 (GI p15): m(1) Haverhill, MA 27 Dec 1722 Abigail Davis (HvVR), b Haverhill, MA 11 Mar 1702/3 dau of Elisha & Grace (Shaw) Davis (HvVR), d Kingston, NH 25 Sep 1733 (KTR): m(2) Kingston, NH 16 Oct 1734 Abigail Taylor (KTR), dau of William & Margaret (Bean) Taylor (LND p676), d Kingston, NH 9 Dec 1768 (KTR): m(3) Dorcas ____, b abt 1712, d Kingston, NH 28 Jan 1774 a.62yrs (GI p15).

Richard & his family belonged to Kingston in 1725 when Rev Clark took charge of the church.

Children: born Kingston, NH (KTR)
(by 1st wife)

1. **DOROTHY**, b 25 Jul 1722: m 1741 Samuel Small
2. **ELIZABETH**, b 25 Dec 1724: m 25 Dec 1745 Samuel Libby
3. **MARTHA**, b 6 Nov 1726: m Cambridge, MA 25 Dec 1758 Thomas Durant (LND p353)
4. **ABIGAIL**, b 22 Nov 1728
5. **GRACE**, b 22 Dec 1730
6. **JOHN**, b 12 Apr 1733: d Readfield, ME: m Kingston, NH 30 Apr 1754 Joanna Davis (KTR)

(by 2nd wife)

7. **MARY**, b 21 May 1735: m Kingston, NH 15 Apr 1756 John Stevens (KTR)
8. **GRACE**, b 8 Jan 1736/7: m Kingston, NH 13 Jul 1758 Samuel Stewart (KTR)
9. **ANNE**, b 17 Oct 1738: d Kingston, NH 19 Aug 1747 (NHVR)
10. **MARGARET**, b 30 Aug 1740
11. **RICHARD**, b 3 Dec 1742: d Kingston, NH 11 Nov 1780 (KTR): m Kingston, NH 21 Dec 1762 Elizabeth Webster (KTR)
12. **BENJAMIN**, b 12 Nov 1744: d Kingston, NH 16 Aug 1747 (NHVR)
13. **ANNA**, d Kingston, NH 30 Sep 1748 (NHVR)
14. **SARAH**, b 16 Feb 1751
15. **JEDEDIAH**, b 16 Jul 1755

CHARLES HUNT, m Hannah Welch (LND p363), b abt

1680 (prob) dau of Philip & Hannah (Haggert) Welch (LND p734). Hannah m(1) Kingston, NH 4 Feb 1707/8 Thomas Scribner (KTR).

Hannah was admitted to the Kingston Church 2 Jan 1742.

Children: bpt Kingston, NH (NHGR 2:65)

1. **MARGARET**, b Amesbury, MA 27 Aug 1721 (AVR): bpt 1 Apr 1730
2. **SARAH**, bpt 1 Apr 1730
3. **PENELOPE**, bpt 1 Apr 1730: m Kingston, NH 23 Mar 1743 Robert Barber (KTR)

CHARLES HUNTOON, b Kingston, NH 12 Oct 1725 son of John & Mary (Rundlett) Huntoon) (KTR): d 27 May 1818 (DAR 1:357): m Kingston, NH 14 Nov 1749 Meriah Smith (KTR), b Exeter, NH 20 May 1729 (UR p44).

Children: born Kingston, NH (KTR)

1. **MARIAH**, b 13 Oct 1750: d May 1778: m Unity, NH 19 Apr 1770 Elijah Weed (UR p48)
2. **JOHN**, b 4 Jan 1753: d 1838: m Susanna Chase (DAR LB 12:241)
3. **CHARLES**, b 15 Dec 1755: m Unity, NH 16 Oct 1778 Meriah Smith (UR p46)
4. **JOSIAH**, b 1 May 1758: d Lowell, MA 28 Feb 1794: m Hannah Glidden (DAR 1:357)
5. **REUBEN**, b 7 Sep 1761: d 30 Jan 1764
6. **NATHANIEL**, b 21 Jun 1764: m Unity, NH 1 Jan 1789 Dorothy Thurston (UR p47)
7. **REUBEN**, b 3 Dec 1768

JOHN HUNTOON, b abt 1696 son of Philip & Betsey (Hall) Huntoon (LND p363): d Kingston, NH (bur) 8 Dec 1778 (NHVR): m abt 1717 Mary Rundlett (LND p600), dau of Charles & Lydia (Ladd) Rundlett.

John belonged to Kingston in 1725 when Rev Clark took charge of the church. In 1738 he signed a petition for a grant of land in Kingston.

Children: born Kingston, NH (KTR & NHGR)

1. **SAMUEL**, 18 Jun 1718: d May 1796 (DAR 1: 357): m(1) Kingston, NH 6 May 1742 Hannah Ladd (KTR): m(2) 1768 wid Margaret Newley
2. **NATHANIEL**, b 18 Jun 1721 (DAR 1:357): m (1) Kingston, NH 7 Jun 1742 Anne Dearborn (KTR): m(2) Kingston, NH 26 Aug 1789 Martha Judkins (NHGR 3:134)
3. **LYDIA**, b 1723: bpt Kingston, NH 8 May 1726: m Kingston, NH 4 Nov 1740 Jonathan Sleeper (NHGR 3:40)
4. **CHARLES**, b 12 Oct 1725: d 27 May 1818 (DAR 1:357): m Kingston, NH 14 Nov 1749 Meriah Smith (KTR)
5. **JOHN**, bpt 1 Oct 1727: d Canterbury, NH 14 Nov 1821: m Kingston, NH 7 Dec 1754 Elizabeth Beede (KTR)
6. **JOSIAH**, bpt 7 Sep 1729: m Kingston, NH 11 Dec 1755 Joanna Ladd (NHGR 3:88)
7. **DANIEL**, bpt 7 Nov 1731: d Kingston, NH 4 Jul 1735 (NHGR 2:134)
8. **MARY**, bpt 26 May 1734: d Kingston, NH 22 Jul 1735 (NHGR 2:134)
9. **MARY**, bpt 4 Jul 1736: d Kingston, NH 30 Sep 1747 (NHVR)
10. **DANIEL**, bpt 9 Jul 1738: d 16 Oct 1802 (DAR 1:357): m Kingston, NH 21 Oct 1762 Martha Fifield (NHGR 3:129)
11. **JOSEPH**, bpt 1 Nov 1741: d Stanstead, Canada 8 Mar 1813: m Sarah Davis (DAR 1:357)
12. **BENJAMIN**, bpt 15 Jul 1744: d aft 1790 (DAR 1:357): m 29 Aug 1764 Deliverance Goss (UR p45)

NATHANIEL HUNTOON, b 18 Jun 1721 (DAR 1:357) son of John & Mary (Rundlett) Huntoon: d Unity, NH 7 Jan 1793 (UR p48): m(1) Kingston, NH 7 Jun 1742 Anne Dearborn (KTR), d Unity, NH 28 Oct 1788: m(2) Kingston, NH 26 Aug 1789 Martha Judkins (NHGR 3:134), b Kingston, NH 1 Aug 1751 dau of John & Esther (Swett) Judkins (KTR).

Children: born Kingston, NH (KTR)

1. **SARAH**, b 11 Jun 1745
2. **CALEB**, b 4 Feb 1748: m Kingston, NH 29

Dec 1773 Judith Carter (UR p50)

3. **PHILIP**, b 18 Jun 1749: d aft 1790 (DAR 1: 357): m Polly Willard
4. **MARY**, b 5 Apr 1753
5. **HANNAH**, b 24 Feb 1756: d Unity, NH 21 Jun 1781 (UR p48): m Joseph Glidden
6. **MARY**, b 14 Nov 1761

PHILIP HUNTOON, b abt 1664 (LND p363): d Kingston, NH 10 May 1752 (NHVR): m(1) Betsey Hall: m(2) by 1702 Hannah ___ (LND p363), d Kingston, NH 22 Dec 1741 (NHVR).

Philip had land laid out to him in Kingston in 1702. His family belonged to Kingston in 1725 when Rev Clark took charge of the church.

Children:
(by 1st wife)

1. **SAMUEL**, d Kingston, NH (killed by Indians) 22 Jul 1710 (KTR)
2. **PHILIP**, d Salisbury, NH May 1780 (LND p363): m(1) Kingston, NH 22 Dec 1720 Ann Eastman (KTR): m(2) ____ Calliot
3. **JOHN**, b abt 1696: d Kingston, NH (bur) 8 Dec 1778 (NHVR): m abt 1717 Mary Rundlett (LND p600)

(by 2nd wife)

4. **SARAH**, b Kingston, NH 21 Apr 1703 (KTR): d Kingston, NH 15 May 1703 (KTR)
5. **ELIZABETH**, m Kingston, NH 2 Dec 1725 Joseph Elkins (NHGR 2:44)
6. **SARAH**, m Kingston, NH 1 Jan 1729 Darby Kelly (KTR)

PHILIP HUNTOON JR, son of Philip & Betsey (Hall) Huntoon (LND p363): d Salisbury, NH May 1780 (LND p363): m(1) Kingston, NH 22 Dec 1720 Ann Eastman (KTR), b Salisbury, MA 22 May 1700 dau of Samuel & Elizabeth (Scribner) Eastman (SVR), d Kingston, NH 15 Jul 1750 (NHVR): m(2) ____ Calliot.

Philip belonged to Kingston in 1725 when Rev Ward Clark took charge of the church.

Children: born Kingston, NH (KTR)

1. **HANNAH**, b 19 Jun 1721: m Kingston, NH Apr 1743 Josiah Judkins (KTR)
2. **RUTH**, b 11 Feb 1723: m Kingston, NH 12 Aug 1741 Benjamin French (KTR)
3. **SCRIBNER**, b 9 Jan 1724/5: d Kingston, NH 27 Aug 1730 (NHGR 2:131)
4. **SAMUEL**, b 27 Jul 1727: m Kingston, NH 29 Dec 1745/6 Elizabeth Corbin (NHGR 3:42)
5. **BENJAMIN**, b 12 Sep 1729: d Franklin, NH 6 Dec 1815 (CG p53): m(1) Kingston, NH 7 Feb 1751 Judith Clough (KTR): m(2) Kingston, NH Jan 1757 Abigail Page (KTR): m (3) Kingston, NH 17 Jul 1758 Mercy (Dearborn) Quimby (KTR): m(4) 21 Jun 1772 Hannah (James) Dearborn
6. **SCRIBNER**, b 8 May 1731: d Kingston, NH 19 Sep 1744 (NHVR)
7. **PHILIP**, b 8 May 1737: d Kingston, NH 20 Sep 1744 (NHVR)
8. **JONATHAN**, b 2 Oct 1740: d Kingston, NH 30 Sep 1744 (NHVR)

ISRAEL HUSE JR, b Newbury, MA 5 Mar 1719 son of Israel & Ruth (Bodwell) Huse (NVR): d Sandown, NH (Est Adm) 26 Nov 1756 (PRNH 5:532): m Amesbury, MA 13 Nov 1740 Mary Ferrin (AVR), b Amesbury, MA 1 Aug 1721 dau of Jonathan & Sarah (Wells) Ferrin (AVR). Mary m(2) Sandown, NH 19 Oct 1767 Reuben Clough (SdTR).

Children: born Kingston, NH (KTR)

1. **ABIGAIL**, b 3 Nov 1741: m Kingston, NH 25 Sep 1759 Nathaniel Ingalls (NHGR 3:91)
2. **HANNAH**, b 23 Oct 1744: m Sandown, NH 26 Aug 1761 Moses Hook (SdTR)
3. **JONATHAN**, b 19 Aug 1745: d Strafford, VT 25 Feb 1819: m Judith ___
4. **JOSEPH**, b 4 Jan 1751
5. **MARY**, b 18 Nov 1754: d Kingston, NH 3 Jul in the 15th month of her age (KTR)
6. **SARAH** (PRNH 5:535)
7. **ISRAEL**, b Sandown, NH 14 Feb 1757: d Sandown, NH a.5mos (SdTR)

JAMES HUSE, b Newbury, MA 29 Jun 1698 son of Thomas & Hannah (Webster) Huse (NVR): d Hampstead, NH 11 Apr 1753: Est Adm 29 Aug 1753 (PRNH 4:454): m Gloucester, MA 30 Oct 1727 Elizabeth Gilbord (GlVR)

James settled in the westerly section of Kingston.

Children: 1st 5 born Newbury, MA (NVR)

1. **MARTHA**, b 14 Sep 1729: d Newbury, MA 27 Mar 1736 (NVR)
2. **JAMES**, b 16 Dec 1730: d Newbury, MA 7 Apr 1736 (NVR)
3. **ELIZABETH**, b 27 Oct 1732: d Newbury, MA 5 Apr 1736 (NVR)
4. **THOMAS**, b 21 Oct 1734: d Newbury, MA 5 Apr 1736 (NVR)
5. **MARTHA**, b 1 Apr 1737: m Hampstead, NH 27 Mar 1759 Simon Follinsby (HmstR)
6. **ELIZABETH**, bpt 23 Nov 1738: d.y.
7. **ELIZABETH**, b Hampstead, NH 26 Dec 1740: d 21 Feb 1830: m Hampstead, NH 27 Mar 1759 Timothy Stevens (HmstR)
8. **JAMES**, b Hampstead, NH 11 Sep 1744: d Enfield, NH 6 May 1829: m 28 Apr 1768 Abigail Ayer

EBENEZER HUTCHINSON, b Hampton Falls, NH 11 Aug 1711 son of Timothy & Hannah (_) Hutchinson: d 11 Aug 1788: m Elizabeth Marsh, b abt 1708, d 21 Aug 1804 (MGFH 4:1718).

Children: bpt Kingston, NH

1. **HENRY**, bpt 12 Oct 1746 (NHGR 5:154)
2. **JOHN**, bpt 12 Oct 1746 (NHGR 5:154)
3. **THEOPHILUS**, bpt 12 Oct 1746 (NHGR 5:154)
4. **JOSEPH**, bpt 7 Aug 1748 (NHGR 5:156): d Readfield, ME 17 Aug 1828: m 6 Dec 1785 Ann Whittier
5. **ELIZABETH**, bpt 15 Oct 1752 (NHGR 6:28)

PETER JOHNSON, b Hampton, NH 25 Nov 1674 son of Peter & Ruth (Moulton) Johnson (HmVR p106): m 1 Apr 1708 Esther Hobbs (LND p383), b Hampton, NH

12 Apr 1679 dau of Morris & Sarah (Swett) Hobbs (HmVR p111).

Peter was granted 200 acres of land at a meeting of the freeholders of Kingston 19 Dec 1700.

Children: born Hampton, NH
1. **RUTH**, b 3 Feb 1712 (HH p771): m Hampton, NH 29 Oct 1730 Samuel Leavitt (HmVR p135)
2. **PETER**, b 11 Jul 1714 (HmVR p52): m 19 Apr 1737 Sarah Dow (HH p771)

JOHN JONES, b Amesbury, MA 1 May 1724 son of John & Susannah (Fowler) Jones (AVR): m Kingston, NH 13 Oct 1748 Hannah Dow (KTR), b Salisbury, MA 24 Nov 1728 dau of Elihu & Mehitable (Cilley-Eaton) Dow (SVR).

Children: born Kingston, NH (KTR)
1. **JACOB**, b 30 Dec 1749
2. **MEHITABLE**, b 23 Mar 1751: d Kingston, NH 24 Sep 1751 (KTR)
3. **JOHN**, b 27 Apr 1753
4. **MIRIAM**, b 24 Sep 1755

JOSEPH JONES, b (prob) Amesbury, MA 14 Jun 1722 son of John & Susannah (Fowler) Jones (AVR): m Kingston, NH 11 Jan 1744 Abigail Flanders (KTR), b Salisbury, MA 15 Aug 1722 dau of Philip & Joanna (Smith) Flanders (SVR).

Children: born Kingston, NH (KTR)
1. **PHILIP**, b 9 Oct 1745
2. **SUSANNA**, b 1 Apr 1748
3. **RICHARD**, b 19 Nov 1750
4. **JOHANA**, b 16 Apr 1753
5. **JOSEPH**, b 16 Feb 1757
6. **JAMES**, b 10 Jul 1759
7. **ABIGAIL**, b 19 Jun 1762

NATHAN JONES, b Amesbury, MA 14 Feb 1717/8 son of John & Susanna (Fowler) Jones (AVR): m Salisbury, MA 23 Feb 1737/8 Alice Collins (SVR), b (prob) Salisbury, MA 17 Dec 1715 dau of Ephraim

& Esther (_) Collins (SVR).

Children: last 4 born Kingston, NH (KTR)
1. **EZRA**, b Amesbury, MA 28 Oct 1738 (AVR): m Danville, NH 8 Nov 1764 Mehitable Bean (NEHGR 58:47)
2. **EPHRAIM**, b Amesbury, MA 8 Jun 1745 (AVR)
3. **MERIAM**, b 9 Aug 1747
4. **JOHN**, b 21 Jan 1750/1
5. **NATHAN**, b 13 Dec 1753: m Danville, NH 21 Nov 1771 Mary Collins (NEHGR 58:122)
6. **JONATHAN**, b 2 Sep 1756

BENJAMIN JUDKINS, b Exeter, NH son of Joel & Mary (Bean) Judkins (LND p393): d Kingston, NH (WP) 27 Nov 1745 (PRNH 3:246): m bef 1728 Hannah Clifford (LND p393), b Hampton, NH 1 Aug 1701 dau of Jacob & Elizabeth (Mayhew) Clifford (HmVR p73). Hannah m(2) Kingston, NH 4 Oct 1754 Isaac Griffin (NHGR 3:87).

Benjamin belonged to Kingston in 1725 when Rev Clark took charge of the church. In 1738 he signed a petition for a grant of land.

Children: (PRNH 3:246)
1. **(SON)**, adopted

JOEL JUDKINS, b Kingston, NH 25 Sep 1712 son of Samuel & Abigail (Harriman) Judkins (KTR): d Kingston, NH 5 Jun 1754 (NHVR): m Kingston, NH 1 Jan 1734/5 Mehitable Elkins (KTR), b Kingston, NH 13 Jun 1713 dau of Moses & Ann (Shaw) Elkins (KTR).

Children: born Kingston, NH (KTR)
1. **SAMUEL**, b 8 Jun 1736: d 1809 (DAR 1:377): m Kingston, NH 11 Dec 1755 Sarah Bohonon (KTR)
2. **MOSES**, b 5 Feb 1737/8: m 16 Feb 1773 Ruhamah French (Judkin Gen p11)
3. **ANNA** (Hannah), b 11 Sep 1739: m Kingston, NH 6 May 1759 Edward Eastman (NHGR 3:90)
4. **LEONARD**, b 11 Sep 1741: m Kingston, NH 13 Jan 1763 Sarah Cram (KTR)

5. **JOSEPH**, b 23 Aug 1743: d Kingston, NH 10 Jan 1804 (GI p16): m 20 Apr 1766 Rebecca Sanborn (Judkin Gen p12)
6. **ABIGAIL**, b 9 Aug 1745
7. **MEHITABLE**, b 22 May 1747: d Kingston, NH 13 Jan 1749/50 (KTR)
8. **BENJAMIN**, b 18 Apr 1749: d Brentwood, NH 18 May 1790 (CG p23): m Brentwood, NH 15 Oct 1771 Ruth Choate (BtTR)
9. **HENRY**, b 5 Dec 1750: d Kingston, NH 27 Sep 1825 (GI p16): m(1) Danville, NH 25 Apr 1776 Mary French (NEHGR 58:124): m(2) Danville, NH 9 Nov 1780 Mary Barnard (NEH GR 58:125)
10. **CALEB**, b 16 Jan 1753: d Salisbury, NH 25 Aug 1816: m 13 Jan 1777 Mary Huntoon (HS p645)

JOSIAH JUDKINS, b Exeter, NH abt 1717 son of Job & Elizabeth (York) Judkins (Judkins Gen p5): m Kingston, NH Apr 1743 Hannah Huntoon (KTR), b Kingston, NH 19 Ju 1721 dau of Philip & Ann (Eastman) Huntoon (KTR), d Hopkinton, NH 18 Jul 1778.

Children: born Kingston, NH

1. **ANNE**, bpt 11 Mar 1743/4 (NHGR 5:111): d Kingston, NH 7 Dec 1748 (NHVR)
2. **PHILIP**, bpt 30 Mar 1746 (NHGR 5:153): d Kingston, NH 5 Dec 1748 (NHVR)
3. **JONATHAN**, bpt 30 Oct 1748 (NHGR 5:157)
4. **ANNE**, b 19 Feb 1751 (KTR): m 7 May 1772 Abraham Batchelder
5. **PHILIP**, b 29 Aug 1754 (KTR): m Hopkinton, NH 25 Nov 1773 Miriam Hunt
6. **JUDAH**, b 17 Mar 1756 (KTR): m 22 Sep 1774 Daniel Batchelder
7. **JONATHAN**, b 20 Dec 1759 (KTR)
8. **JOSIAH**, b 25 Aug 1762 (KTR): m 25 Mar 1788 Sarah Allen

SAMUEL JUDKINS, b Exeter, NH son of Joel & Mary (Bean) Judkins (LND p393): d Kingston, NH 23 Feb 1741/2 (KTR): m Kingston, NH 30 Nov 1710

Abigail Harriman (KTR), b Haverhill, MA 7 Nov 1683 dau of Mathew & Elizabeth (Swan) Harriman (HvVR), d Kingston, NH 8 Oct 1756 (NHVR).
  Samuel was granted 200 acres of land in Kingston at a meeting of the freeholders 30 Oct 1706. His family belonged to Kingston in 1725 when Rev Clark took charge of the church.

Children: born Kingston, NH (KTR)
1. **JOEL**, b 25 Sep 1712: d Kingston, NH 5 Jun 1754 (NHVR); m Kingston, NH 1 Jan 1734/5 Mehitable Elkins (KTR)
2. **ELIZABETH**, b 27 May 1715: m Kingston, NH 21 May 1741 John Hersey (KTR)
3. **JOHN**, b 8 Feb 1719: d Kingston, NH 29 May 1788 (NHVR): m(1) Kingston, NH 21 Nov 1744 Martha Hook (KTR): m(2) Kingston, NH 7 Nov 1750 Esther Swett (KTR)
4. **CATHERINE**, b 17 Nov 1721: m Kingston, NH 27 Nov 1746 Silas Cammet (KTR)
5. **ABIGAIL**, b 14 Jul 1725: m Kingston, NH 29 Nov 1743 David Weed (KTR)
6. **MARY**, b 8 Apr 1727: d Candia, NH 22 Nov 1808 (CG p29): m Kingston, NH 2 May 1748 David Bean (NHGR 3:43)

DANIEL KELLY, of Hampton & Kingston 1721-1740: m Catherine ____ (LND p395).
  Catherine was admitted to the Kingston Church 19 Oct 1735.

Children: 1st 2 born Hampton, NH (HmVR p168)
1. **DANIEL**, b 27 Aug 1727
2. **MARY**, b 29 Jun 1729
3. **CATHERINE**, bpt Kingston, NH 28 May 1738 (NHGR 5:104)

DARBY KELLY, b abt 1705: d 1788 (DAR 1:380): m (1) Kingston, NH 1 Jan 1729 Sarah Huntoon (KTR), dau of Philip & Hannah (_) Huntoon (LND p363): m(2) Brentwood, NH 3 Dec 1761 Sarah Dudley (BtTR), b 1721 dau of Jonathan & Dinah (Bean) Dudley (Dudley Gen p285), d New Hampton, NH 27 Mar 1825 a.105yrs.

Children:
(by 1st wife) born Kingston, NH (KTR)
1. **EDWARD**, b 18 Jul 1731
2. **SAMUEL**, b 25 Aug 1733: d 28 Jun 1813 (DAR 1:381): m Brentwood, NH 1 Oct 1756 Elizabeth Bowdoin (BtTR)
3. **PHILIP**, b 12 Jun 1735
4. **HANNAH**, bpt Exeter, NH 9 Mar 1740 (KChR)

(by 2nd wife) born Brentwood, NH (BtTR)
5. **DUDLEY**, b 11 Jan 1763: d 1836 (DAR 1:380): m Ruth Dow
6. **DANIEL**, b 10 Aug 1765

RICHARD KENISTON, d Kingston, NH 28 Jun 1759 (KTR): m Kingston, NH 13 Dec 1750 Mary Tucker (KTR). Mary m(2) Kingston, NH 4 Dec 1766 John Fellows (KChR).

A widow Mary Keniston was admitted to the Kingston Church 26 Sep 1762.

Children: born Kingston, NH (KTR)
1. **REUBEN**, b 2 Aug 1751
2. **SARAH**, b 2 Mar 1754
3. **RACHEL**, b 22 Dec 1756
4. **MARY**, b 28 Mar 1759

DANIEL KIDD, Administration on the estate of Daniel Kidd of Kingston was granted to Mary Kidd 29 Aug 1753 (PRNH 4:454).

Children: (PRNH 4:455-7)
1. **AGNES**, m ____ Alexander
2. **MARY**, m ____ Cochran
3. **MARGARET**, m ____ Dunisen
4. **SARAH**, m ____ Garven
5. **SUSANNAH**, m ____ Watts
6. **Elizabeth**, m ____ Garven

DANIEL LADD, b Exeter, NH 18 Mar 1686/7 son of Nathaniel & Elizabeth (Gilman) Ladd (HE p27g): d Brentwood, NH (Est Adm) 31 Oct 1770 (PRNH 9:439): m Kingston, NH 29 Apr 1712 Mehitable Philbrick (KTR), b Hampton, NH 26 Mar 1693 dau of Thomas & Mehitable (Ayers) Philbrick (HmVR

p14), d Kingston, NH 23 Jan 1779 (KTR).
Daniel & his family belonged to Kingston in 1725 when Rev Clark took charge of the church.

Children: born Kingston, NH (KTR)
1. **MEHITABLE**, b 30 Jun 1713: m Kingston, NH 28 Dec 1732 Samuel Colcord (KTR)
2. **ELIZABETH**, b 11 Feb 1716/7: m 21 Dec 1731 John Nay (LND p407)
3. **ANNA**, b 25 Jun 1718
4. **HANNAH**, b 17 Apr 1720: m Kingston, NH 6 May 1742 Samuel Huntoon (KTR)
5. **MARY**, b 3 Jan 1722/3: m Kingston, NH 24 Apr 1740 Samuel Dudley (NHGR 3:40)
6. **DANIEL**, b 25 Apr 1725/6: d Apr 1809 (DAR 1:397): m(1) abt 1748 Joanna Dudley: m(2) Susannah Dow: m(3) Ruth Bradley (LND p407)
7. **STEPHEN**, b 30 Aug 1728: m(1) Kingston, NH 28 Nov 1754 Abigail Webster (NHGR 3:87): m(2) Bethia Swett
8. **JOHN**, bpt 24 May 1730 (NHGR 2:65): d Kingston, NH 8 Jan 1731 (NHGR 2:132)
9. **JOANNA**, b 27 Jul 1735: m Kingston, NH 11 Dec 1755 Josiah Huntoon (NHGR 3:88)
10. **JOHN**, b 21 Oct 1737: d 15 Mar 1784 (DAR 1:397): m Mary Moody (LND p407)

JOHN LADD, b Exeter, NH 6 Jul 1689 son of Nathaniel & Elizabeth (Gilman) Ladd (HE p27g): d abt 1750: m Kingston, NH 14 Apr 1713 Elizabeth Sanborn (KTR), b Hampton, NH 27 Dec 1692 dau of Jonathan & Elizabeth (Sherburne) Sanborn (HmVR p14).
John belonged to Kingston in 1725 when Rev Clark took charge of the church. In 1730 he signed a petition regarding the township of Kingston.

Children: born Kingston, NH (KTR)
1. **ELIZABETH**, b 22 May 1714: m Kingston, NH 19 Jun 1729 Jeremiah Webster (KTR)
2. **LOVE**, b 25 Mar 1716: d Kingston, NH 19 Jun 1720 (KTR)

3. **BENJAMIN**, b 25 Apr 1718: m Kingston, NH 11 Feb 1746 Mary French (KTR)
4. **JOHN**, b 7 May 1720: d Kingston, NH (bur) 21 Oct 1802 a.82yrs (NHVR): m bef 1748 Alice Thing (LND p407)
5. **NATHANIEL**, b 17 Jun 1722: m Kingston, NH 12 Aug 1741 Sarah Clifford (KTR)
6. **JONATHAN**, b 25 Aug 1724
7. **TRUEWORTHY**, b 1 May 1726: d Goffstown, NH 26 Apr 1778 (LND p407): m Kingston, NH 1 Nov 1750 Lydia Harriman (KTR)
8. **LOVE**, b 1 Feb 1728: d Kingston, NH 18 Jun 1736 (NHGR 3:39)
9. **DOROTHY**, b 2 Nov 1730: m Kingston, NH 3 Apr 1746 Benjamin Sanborn (KTR)

NATHANIEL LADD, b Kingston, NH 17 Jun 1722 son of John & Elizabeth (Sanborn) Ladd (KTR): d 1790 (DAR 1:397): m Kingston, NH 12 Aug 1741 Sarah Clifford (KTR), b Kingston, NH 13 Feb 1723 dau of Isaac & Sarah (Taylor) Clifford (KTR).

Nathaniel & his wife Sarah were admitted to the Kingston Church 22 Nov 1741.

Children: born Kingston, NH (KTR)

1. **JEREMIAH**, b 3 Oct 1742: m(1) Priscilla Sanborn: m(2) Meribah Simmons
2. **NATHANIEL**, b 28 Sep 1744: m(1) ____: m(2) Miriam (Ladd) Proctor
3. **LOVE**, b 27 Sep 1746: m Danville, NH 1 Jun 1772 Timothy Simonds (NEHGR 58:122)
4. **ISAAC**, b 2 Jun 1749: m Dolly Blaisdell
5. **JOHN**, b 26 Sep 1751
6. **BENJAMIN**, b 25 Sep 1753: m(1) Deborah Allen: m(2) Deborah ___ (DAR 1:397)
7. **ELIZABETH**, b 6 Jan 1756: m Jacob Draper
8. **SARAH**, b 13 Dec 1757: m 12 Jun 1777 Samuel Thompson

TREWORTHY LADD, b Kingston, NH 1 May 1726 son of John & Elizabeth (Sanborn) Ladd (KTR): d Goffstown, NH 26 Apr 1778 (Ladd Gen p31): m Kingston, NH 1 Nov 1750 Lydia Harriman (KTR), d

8 Apr 1819.
Treworthy was admitted to the Kingston Church 3 Apr 1742.

Children: 1st 6 born Kingston, NH (KTR)
1. **JONATHAN**, b 7 Aug 1751
2. **MEHITABLE**, b 26 Jan 1753: m ___ Heath
3. **JOHN**, b 6 Jan 1755: m 6 Jun 1775 Jerusha Lovejoy
4. **BETSEY**, b 3 Sep 1756: m Aaron Noyes
5. **LYDIA**, b 4 Jan 1759: m Samuel Eaton
6. **LOVE**, b 29 Jan 1761: m Joel Emery
7. **KEZIAH**, bpt Kingston, NH 13 Feb 1763 (NH VR): m Moses Hacket
8. **LOIS**, b 4 Jan 1767: m 29 Jul 1788 David Morgan
9. **LUCY**, b 1769: m 26 Jun 1778 Stephen Clement

JONATHAN LAWRENCE, son of David Lawrence (LND p419). Probably the Jonathan whose name appears on a list of Kingston men who swore allegiance to the King 1727.

NEHEMIAH LEAVITT, b abt 1690 son of Nehemiah & Alice (Cartee?-Gilman) Leavitt (LND p424): d bef 1740: m J___.
Nehemiah & his wife J___ owned the covenant at the Kingston 1st Church 21 Sep 1729.

Children: bpt Kingston, NH (NHGR 2:65)
1. **JOHN**, b 16 Oct 1712: bpt 21 Sep 1729: m (prob) Kingston, NH 16 Jun 1735 Abigail Giles (NHGR 2:46)
2. **NEHEMIAH**, abt 1714: bpt 21 Sep 1729
3. **ELIZABETH**, bpt 21 Sep 1729
4. **SARAH**, bpt 21 Sep 1729
5. **M____**, bpt 21 Sep 1729
6. **ANNA**, b abt 1722: bpt 21 Sep 1729

EDWARD LINKFIELD, d Kingston, NH 9 May 1737 (NHVR): m Londonderry, NH 9 Sep 1723 Hannah Goffe (LndVR p226), b Londonderry, NH 4 Feb 1705/6 dau of John & Hannah (_) Goffe (LndVR

p68).

Children:
1. **BENJAMIN**, over 14yrs in 1748 (PRNH 3:617)

SAMUEL LOCKE, b Hampton, NH 4 Sep 1698 son of Edward & Hannah (Jenness) Locke (HmVR p68): m 11 Feb 1725 Margaret Ward (LND p441), b Hampton, NH 2 Jul 1705 dau of Thomas & Sarah (_) Ward (HmVR p32).

Samuel & his wife were admitted to the Kingston 1st Church 12 Apr 1730. In 1738 he signed a petition for a new parish in the easterly part of Kingston.

Children: born Kingston, NH (KTR)
1. **MARGARET**, b 7 Oct 1725: m Kingston, NH Apr 1744/5 Orlando Carter (NHGR 3:42)
2. **SAMUEL**, b 22 Apr 1728: d Kingston, NH 26 May 1729 (KTR)
3. **ABIGAIL**, b 12 Dec 1730: d Kingston, NH 14 Mar 1731 (KTR)
4. **HANNAH**, b 31 Jan 1731/2: d Kingston, NH 17 Jun 1735 (KTR)
5. **WARD**, b 9 Jun 1734
6. **SARAH**, b 15 Aug 1736: d Kingston, NH 17 Oct 1745 (KTR)
7. **EDWARD**, b 18 Dec 1741: d Feb 1824: m Abigail Haines (Locke Gen p44)
8. **SAMUEL**, b 18 Feb 1744
9. **THOMAS**, b 1 Jan 1746/7: d Seabrook, NH 15 Mar 1835 (CG p126): m Elizabeth Collins
10. **SARAH**, b 7 Apr 1750: d Kingston, NH abt 5 May 1753 (NHVR)

WILLIAM LONG, b Salisbury, MA 25 Jun 1682 son of Richard & Ann (French) Long (SVR): d Kingston, NH (Est Adm) 31 Jan 1754 (PRNH 5:21): m (1) Kingston, NH 1 Jan 1714 Ruth Eastman (KTR), b Salisbury, MA 5 Mar 1687/8 dau of Samuel & Elizabeth (Scribner) Eastman (SVR), d Kingston, NH 6 Apr 1718 (KTR): m(2) Kingston, NH 21 Dec 1719 Sarah Shephard (KTR), b Salisbury, MA 25 Jun 1686 dau of Solomon & Sarah (Eastman)

Shephard (SVR), d Kingston, NH (Town Record reads 7 Mar 1720/1 - obviously an error in this date or with the date of the third marriage): m(3) Kingston, NH 11 Jan 1720/1 Deborah Tongue (KTR), b Salisbury, MA 8 Jul 1687 dau of Stephen & Mary (Payne) Tongue (SVR).

William was taken in in a full right in the 1st & 2nd division at Kingston Apr 1705. He was granted 200 acres of land at a meeting of the freeholders 30 Oct 1706. His family belonged to Kingston in 1725 when Rev Clark took charge of the church.

Children: born Kingston, NH (KTR)
(by 1st wife)

1. **ANN**, b 1 Oct 1716: d Kingston, NH 7 Nov 1716 (KTR)
2. **RICHARD**, b 3 Dec 1717: m Kingston, NH 18 Aug 1743 Elles Moody (KTR)

(by 3rd wife)

3. **JOSEPH**, b 21 Feb 1720/1: d Kingston, NH 9 May 1721 (KTR)
4. **RUTH**, b 15 Apr 1725: m Kingston, NH 12 Feb 1744/5 Benjamin Severance (NHGR 3:42)
5. **EBENEZER**, b 23 Oct 1727: d Kingston, NH 2 Apr 1808 (NHVR): m Kingston, NH 12 Mar 1752 Anna Towle (NHGR 3:86)
6. **STEPHEN**, b 10 Sep 1731: m Kingston, NH 3 Jun 1755 Judith Rowell (NHGR 3:88)

SAMUEL LOVERING, d abt 1759: m Kingston, NH 19 Oct 1748 Mary Gooden (KTR).

Administration on the estate of Samuel Lovering of Kingston was granted to William Lovering of Kingston 11 Feb 1760 (PRNH 6:518).

Children: born Kingston, NH (KTR)

1. **JOSEPH**, b 1 Jan 1749: m Sarah ___
2. **MOSES**, b 10 Jun 1751
3. **SAMUEL**, b 14 Mar 1754
4. **(CHILD)**, d Kingston, NH 11 Aug 1756 (NH VR) - possibly Moses or Samuel
5. **ABIGAIL**, b 14 Dec 1757

WILLIAM LOVERING, d Kingston, NH 10 May 1785 (NHVR): m Comfort Smith (LND p646), dau of Nicholas & Mary (Gordon) Smith, d Kingston, NH 12 Jan 1783 (NHVR).

Comfort, wife of William, was admitted to the Kingston Church 3 Jun 1739.

Children:

1. **BENJAMIN**, d Kingston, NH 11 Apr 1737 (NHVR)
2. **BENJAMIN**, bpt Kingston, NH 16 Apr 1738 (NHGR 5:103): m Kingston, NH Dec 1759 Jemima Thorn (KTR)
3. **ABIGAIL**, bpt Kingston, NH 4 Jan 1740/1 (NHGR 5:107): d Kingston, NH 19 Nov 1745 (NHVR)
4. **MARY**, d Kingston, NH 13 Jan 1746 (NHVR)

JAMES LOWELL, b Hampton Falls, NH 22 Oct 1725 son of Joseph & Sarah (Prescott) Lowell (HFTR): d abt 1830 m abt 1747 Mary Clark (Lowell Gen p25).

Children: bpt Kingston, NH

1. **OLIVER**, b 1747: d bef 11 Jun 1811: m Elizabeth ___ (Lowell Gen p41)
2. **DANIEL**, bpt 26 Jun 1748 (NHGR 5:156)
3. **SARAH**, bpt 14 Oct 1750 (NHGR 5:159): d Seabrook, NH 29 Dec 1825: m 1769 John Brown
4. **MARY**, bpt 16 Nov 1755 (NHVR)
5. **JOSEPH**, bpt 3 Aug 1760 (NHVR)

EDWARD LUFKIN, b Kingston, NH 5 Sep 1730 son of John & Elizabeth (Pride) Lufkin (KTR): m Kingston, NH 6 Dec 1750 Sarah Moody (KTR), b abt 1731, (prob) bpt Kingston, NH 31 Aug 1735 dau of Philip Moody (NHGR 2:70).

Children: born Kingston, NH (KTR)

1. **HANNAH**, b 5 May 1751
2. **JOHN**, b 3 Mar 1753
3. **(CHILD)**, d Kingston, NH 2 Jul 1756 (NHVR)
4. **PHILIP MOODY**, bpt 19 Nov 1757 (NHVR)

JOHN LUFKIN, b Chebacco, MA 11 Jan 1700 son of Thomas & Sarah (Downing) Lufkin (IpVR): m Gloucester, MA 5 Nov 1724 Elizabeth Pride (IpVR), b Beverly, MA 25 Feb 1703/4 dau of Joseph & Elizabeth (Bond) Pride (BvVR).

Children: 1st 4 bpt Ipswich, MA (IpVR)

1. **JOHN**, bpt 12 Dec 1725
2. **HENRY**, bpt 12 Mar 1726/7
3. **ELIZABETH**, bpt 9 Jun 1728
4. **EDWARD**, b Kingston, NH 5 Sep 1730 (KTR): bpt 31 Oct 1731: m Kingston, NH 6 Dec 1750 Sarah Moody (KTR)
5. **BETTE**, b Kingston, NH 5 Apr 1738 (KTR)
6. **SARAH**, bpt Kingston, NH 26 Oct 1739/40 (NHGR 5:106): d 29 Nov 1745 (NHVR)
7. **HANNAH**, bpt Kingston, NH 29 Sep 1743 (NHGR 5:110): d 9 Dec 1745 (NHVR)

HENRY LUNT, b Newbury, MA 2 Apr 1714 son of Skiper & Elizabeth (Browne) Lunt (NVR): d Chester, NH (Est Adm) 19 Feb 1761 (PRNH 7:101): m Kingston, NH 11 Feb 1741/2 Abigail Morrill (KTR), b Salisbury, MA 27 Jan 1719 dau of Ezekiel & Abigail (Wadleigh) Morrill (SVR).

Henry was admitted to the 2nd Church of Christ in Kingston 15 Aug 1742 & his wife was admitted 3 Apr 1743. They were later dismissed to Chester.

Children: born Kingston, NH (KTR)

1. **RUTH**, b 9 Feb 1742/3
2. **ELIZABETH**, b 12 May 1745
3. **EZEKIEL**, b 4 May 1748

JOSEPH MACREST (MACREASE), b Salisbury, MA 28 Aug 1683 son of Benoni & Lydia (Fifield) Macrest (SVR): m(1) Hampton, NH 12 Feb 1708 Sarah Dole (LND p451), b Newbury, MA 11 Dec 1683 dau of John & Mary (Gerrish) Dole (NVR): m(2) Salisbury, MA 27 Aug 1733 Mary (Green) Longfellow (SVR), b Hampton, NH 17 Apr 1693 dau of Jacob & Sarah (Downer) Green (HmVR p85). Mary m(1) Hampton, NH 28 May 1713 Nathan Longfellow (HmVR

p61).

Joseph was granted 200 acres of land by the freeholders of Kingston 30 Oct 1706.

Children: born Salisbury, MA (SVR)

1. **MARY**, b 19 Nov 1710
2. **LYDIA**, b 15 Jul 1712: m Salisbury, MA 27 Aug 1730 Sylvanus Carr (SVR)

BENJAMIN MAGOON, son of Alexander & Sarah (Blake) Magoon (LND p452): m Dinah Gordon (Gordon Gen p4), b Haverhill, MA 26 Jan 1702/3 dau of Thomas & Elizabeth (Harriman) Gordon (HvVR), d aft 1757 (PRNH 6:188).

Benjamin, of Kingston, administered the estate of his brother John in 1731.

Children:

1. **(CHILD)**, d Kingston, NH Oct 1735 (NHGR 3:38)

JOHN MAGOON, possibly son of Alexander & Sarah (Blake) Magoon (LND p452): d Kingston, NH 14 Jul 1730 (NHGR 2:131): m Hampton Falls 5 Dec 1723 Sarah Magoon (LND p452), possibly dau of John & Martha (Ash) Magoon (LND p452).

John & his family belonged to Kingston in 1725 when Rev Clark took charge of the church.

Children: bpt Kingston, NH (NHGR 2:47)

1. **JOHN**, bpt 12 Nov 1727
2. **MOSES**, bpt 12 Nov 1727: m Kingston, NH Feb 1748/9 Ann Clatterday (NHGR 3:44)

JOHN MARCH, m Kingston, NH 10 Jun 1732 Margaret Bean (KTR), dau of Samuel & Mary (Severance) Bean (PRNH 2:691).

Margaret wife of John March was admitted to the Kingston Church 14 Nov 1736.

Children: born Kingston, NH (KTR)

1. **MARY**, b 9 Aug 1732: d Kingston, NH 7 Dec 1735 (KTR)
2. **SAMUEL**, b 15 Oct 1734: m (prob) Kingston,

NH 17 Feb 1756 Mary Derby (NHGR 3:88)

4. **MARY**, b 1 Dec 1736
5. **JOHN**, b 1 Apr 1739
6. **STEVEN**, b 27 Jul 1741: d 1813 (DAR 1: 437): m Hampstead, NH 27 Nov 1766 Miriam Bean (HmstR)
7. **HITTIE**, b 1 Apr 1744
8. **MYARIAH**, b 27 Apr 1746: d Kingston, NH 31 May 1747 (KTR)
9. **(CHILD)**, d Kingston, NH 1 May 1751 (NHVR)
10. **URIAH**, b 5 Apr 1752
11. **MYARIAH**, b 5 Apr 1754

FRANCIS MASON, son of John & Elizabeth (Ward) Mason (LND p465): d Kingston, NH 7 Apr 1718 (PRNH 2:45): m Greenland, NH 26 Jan 1717/8 Mary Edmons (NEHGR 65:352), (prob) dau of Thomas Edmons of Portsmouth, NH. Mary m(2) Portsmouth, NH 27 Nov 1718 John Jenness (NEHGR 23:395).

Francis was taken in & made a freeholder with grants & priviledges in Kingston 30 Apr 1705. At a meeting of the freeholders on 30 Oct 1706, he was granted 200 acres of land.

JOHN MASON, d Hampton, NH 29 Feb 169_ (HmVR p118) - 1696 (LND p465): m Hampton, NH 11 Jul 1672 Elizabeth Ward (HmVR p76), b Hampton, NH 10 Dec 1651 dau of Thomas & Margaret (Shaw) Ward (HmVR p544): d 21 May 1697 (LND p465).

John was an orignal grantee of Kingston in 1694.

Children: born Hampton, NH (HmVR & LND p465)

1. **ELIZABETH**, b 5 May 1674: m Hampton, NH 10 Nov 1698 James Johnson (HmVR p81)
2. **MARGARET**, b 28 Apr 1676: d Hampton, NH 29 Oct 1694 (HmVR p118)
3. **JOHN**, b 30 Jan 1678: d 1718: m Mercy ___
4. **FRANCIS**, d 7 Apr 1717/8: m Greenland, NH 26 Jan 1718 Mary Edmons (NEHGR 65:352)
5. **MARY**, m Salisbury, MA (int) 29 Mar 1707 Caleb Clough (SVR)
6. **HANNAH**
7. **CATHERINE**, b 19 Sep 1687: m Hampton, NH

10 Jun 1713 John Edmonds (HH p854)

8. **ESTHER**
9. **JOSEPH**, b abt 1693: m bef 1724 Mary Drisco (LND p465)
10. **BENJAMIN**, b abt 1696: d Stratham, NH 18 Mar 1770: m Jean Massury (LND p465)

STEPHEN MERRILL, b Newbury, MA 6 Jun 1711 son of Nathan & Hannah (Kent) Merrill (NVR): d "in ye service at Fort William Henry 1756" (TwkVR): m Newbury, MA 4 Nov 1731 Elizabeth Bailey (NVR), b Newbury, MA 12 Jan 1714 dau of David & Experience (Putnam) Bailey (NVR), d Tewksbury, MA 9 Nov 1796 a.82yrs (TwkVR).

Stephen signed a petition in 1738 for a new parish in the easterly part of Kingston. He was dismissed from the Kingston church to ye church in Tewksbury 5 Jun 1743.

Children: last 6 born Tewksbury, MA (TwkVR)

1. **HANNAH**, b Newbury, MA 27 Sep 1732 (NVR)
2. **DAVID**, b Newbury, MA 2 Apr 1735 (NVR): d 11 Aug 1811 (DAR 1:464): m Tewksbury, MA 18 Nov 1756 Mary Watson (TwkVR)
3. **ELIZABETH**, b Kingston, NH 3 Dec 1737 (KTR): d Tewksbury, MA 21 Dec 1764 (Twk VR)
4. **EXPERIENCE**, bpt Kingston, NH 1 Jun 1740 (KChR)
5. **NATHAN**, b 20 Feb 1743
6. **STEPHEN**, b 3 Jul 1745: d Tewksbury, MA 19 Feb 1761 (TwkVR)
7. **MOLLY**, b 14 Feb 1747: m Tewksbury, MA 24 May 1776 Newman Scarlett (TwkVR)
8. **SUSANNA**, b 15 May 1750: m 9 May 1771 Jonathan Frost Jr
9. **JOSEPH**, b 18 Apr 1752: d Tewksbury, MA 15 Apr 1753 (TwkVR)
10. **SARAH**, b 14 Feb 1754

DAVID MOODY, b Exeter, NH abt 1710 son of Clement & Sarah (Clark) Moody (TAG 61:232): d aft 1754: m Kingston, NH 21 Jun 1733 Mary Gilman (NHGR 2:45), b Kingston, NH 19 Dec 1715 dau of

Jacob & Mary (Ladd) Gilman (KTR).

Children: bpt Kingston, NH (NHGR)
1. **JOHN**, bpt 12 Oct 1735: d (prob) Kingston, NH 22 Dec 1735 (NHGR 3:38)
2. **DANIEL**, bpt 12 Oct 1735: m Kingston, NH 3 Aug 1758 Esther Moody (NHGR 3:90)
3. **JOHN**, bpt 4 Feb 1738/9: m Gilmanton, NH 1 Nov 1764 Abigail Swett
4. **SARAH**, bpt 5 Apr 1741
5. **MARY**, bpt 7 Aug 1743
6. **DAVID**, bpt 20 Oct 1745
7. **GILMAN** (TAG 61:233), b Exeter, NH abt 1753: m Gilmanton, NH 21 Aug 1778 Anne James

PHILLIP MOODY, b Exeter, NH abt 1697 son of Clement & Sarah (Clark) Moody (TAG 61:227): d bef 9 Jun 1769: m ____.

Phillip received land in Kingston from his father in 1718. He belonged to Kingston in 1725 when Rev Clark took charge of the church.

Children: bpt Kingston, NH (NHGR 2:47,70)
1. **JOHN**, bpt 12 Nov 1727: m Kingston, NH 25 May 1749 Abigail Glidden (NHGR 3:44)
2. **ALICE**, bpt 12 Nov 1727
3. **DANIEL**, bpt 12 Nov 1727: m(1) Kingston, NH 30 Apr 1752 Mary Glidden (NHGR 3:86): m(2) Unity, NH 17 Feb 1791 Elizabeth Jackson
4. **MARY**, bpt 31 Aug 1735
5. **SARAH**, bpt 31 Aug 1735: m (poss) Kingston, NH 6 Dec 1750 Edward Lufkin (KTR)
6. **ABIGAIL**, bpt 31 Aug 1735: m Kingston, NH 30 Mar 1756 Thomas Gordon (NHGR 3:88)
7. **LYDIA**, bpt 31 Aug 1735

WILLIAM MOREY, b Newbury, MA 1 Sep 1722 son of William & Alice (Williams) Morey (NVR): d 30 Oct 1804 (DAR 1:479): m Kingston, NH 11 Sep 1745/6 Dorcas Cilley (NHGR 3:42), b abt 1728 dau of Benoni & Eleanor (Getchell) Cilley (Virkus 4:126).

Children: bpt Kingston, NH
1. **JOSEPH**, bpt 25 Oct 1747 (NHGR 5:155): d Kingston, NH 19 Oct 1750 (NHVR)
2. **BETTY**, bpt 4 Jun 1749 (NHGR 5:157)
3. **JOSEPH**, bpt 11 Aug 1751 (NHGR 6:26): d Kingston, NH 29 Aug 1751 (NHVR)
4. **ELEANOR**, bpt 28 Jan 1753 (NHGR 6:29)
5. **SARAH**, bpt 15 Jun 1755 (NHGR 6:32)

JOHN MORGAN, son of Richard & Rebecca (Holdridge) Morgan: d Stratham, NH 29 Sep 1745 (LND p491): m(1) Hampton, NH 18 Jul 1700 Deborah Blake (HmVR p57), b Hampton, NH 27 Jun 1679 dau of Timothy & Naomi (Sleeper) Blake (HH p602): m (2) Hampton, NH 31 Dec 1724 Mary Dearborn (LND p491).

Children:
(by 1st wife) born Hampton, NH (HmVR)
1. **LUTHER**, b 1 May 1701: m 1 Aug 1723 Abigail Sanborn (NEHGR 10:274)
2. **JOANNA**, b 4 Aug 1703
3. **JOHN**, b 24 Sep 1707
4. **TIMOTHY**, b 24 Oct 1710: m Hampton Falls, NH 16 Jan 1735 Betty Massey (HFTR)
5. **DEBORAH**, b 27 Aug 1713
6. **ANNA**, b 8 Sep 1721

(by 2nd wife)
7. **MARY**, b Hampton Falls, NH 15 Nov 1725 (HFTR): m Kingston, NH 29 May 1746 William Tandy (KTR)
8. **PAUL**, b Hampton Falls, NH 8 Jul 1727 (HF TR): m So Hampton, NH 4 Dec 1746 Margery Maxfield (SHVR)
9. **PARKER**, b Hampton Falls, NH 2 Oct 1731 (HFTR): d Kingston, NH 20 May 1735 (NHGR 2:133)
10. **REBECCA**, bpt Kingston, NH 9 Mar 1735 (NH GR 2:69): m (prob) Kingston, NH 5 Feb 1756 John Atkinson (NHGR 3:88)
11. **PARKER**, b Kingston, NH 26 Oct 1738 (KTR)
12. **JOSEPH**, b Kingston, NH 15 May 1740 (KTR)
13. **RHODA**, b Kingston, NH 31 Oct 1741 (KTR)

LUTHER MORGAN, b Hampton, NH 1 May 1701 son of John & Deborah (Blake) Morgan (HmVR p72): m 1 Aug 1723 Abigail Sanborn (NEHGR 10:274), b Hampton, NH 22 Feb 1702/3 dau of Nathaniel & Rebecca (Prescott) Sanborn (HmVR p28).

Children: born Hampton Falls (HFTR)

1. **ABIGAIL**, b 2 Jul 1725
2. **RACHEL**, b 23 Oct 1729
3. **NATHANIEL**, b 11 May 1731: bpt Kingston, NH 17 Oct 1731 (NHGR 2:66)
4. **DEBORAH**, b 12 Feb 1735: d Kensington, NH 12 May 1750 a.16yrs (NHVR)
5. **EDWARD**, b 23 Jan 1737
6. **JEREMIAH**, b 18 Aug 1740: d Pembroke, NH 21 Jul 1819: m Pembroke, NH 12 Jan 1764 Elizabeth Lovejoy

PAUL MORGAN, b Hampton Falls, NH 8 Jul 1727 son of John & Mary (Dearborn) Morgan (HFTR): m So Hampton, NH 4 Dec 1746 Margery Maxfield (SHVR).

Children:

1. **JOHN**, b So Hampton, NH 3 Nov 1747 (SHVR): bpt Kingston, NH 6 Nov 1748 (NHGR 5:157)
2. **(CHILD)**, d Kingston, NH 8 Mar 1750 (NHVR)
3. **JONATHAN TYLER**, bpt Kingston, NH 18 Aug 1751 (NHGR 6:26)

BENJAMIN MORRILL, b Salisbury, MA 18 Feb 1707/8 son of John & Mary (Stevens) Morrill (SVR): d E. Kingston, NH 21 Oct 1754 a.47yrs (CR): m Salisbury, MA 26 Nov 1730 Abigail Clough (SVR), b Salisbury, MA 22 Nov 1711 dau of Samuel & Sarah (Robie) Clough (SVR), d E. Kingston, NH 3 Jul 1754 a.43yrs (CR).

Benjamin's wife was admitted to the Kingston Church 7 Oct 1733. In 1738 Benjamin signed a petition for a new parish in the easterly part of Kingston.

Children: bpt Kingston, NH

1. **HANNAH**, bpt 28 Nov 1731 (NHGR 2:66): m Kingston, NH 29 Jan 1752 Samuel Stevens

(KTR)

2. **MOSES**, b 12 Dec 1733: bpt 28 Mar 1734 (NHGR 2:68): d E. Kingston, NH 13 Sep 1765 (CR): m So Hampton, NH 18 Feb 1755 Miriam Currier (SHVR)
3. **SARAH**, bpt 21 May 1738 (NHGR 5:103)
4. **BENJAMIN**, bpt 10 May 1741 (KChR): d Biddeford, ME (Est Adm) 13 May 1763 (PRNH 7: 415)
5. **JOHN**, bpt 19 Feb 1744 (KChR): living 1760
6. **SAMUEL**, bpt 9 Feb 1746 (KChR)
7. **SAMUEL**, bpt 2 Jul 1749 (KChR)

EPHRAIM MORRILL, b Salisbury, MA 9 Dec 1717 son of Ezekiel & Abigail (Wadleigh) Morrill (SVR): probably m Kingston, NH 6 Jan 1746/7 Dorothy Hoyt (NHGR 3:43), b Amesbury, MA 23 Aug 1718 dau of Joseph & Dorothy (Worthen) Hoyt (AVR).

Dorothy was admitted to the 2nd Church of Christ in Kingston from So Hampton 4 Jul 1742.

Children: last 4 (OF p779)

1. **DOROTHY**, bpt Kingston, NH 20 Mar 1748 (KChR)
2. **JOSEPH**, b 9 Feb 1752: m Gilmanton, NH 17 Aug 1784 Martha Bean
3. **JEREMIAH**
4. **NATHAN**
5. **EPHRAIM**

HENRY MORRILL, b Kingston, NH 14 Aug 1717 son of Jacob & Mary (Webster) Morrill (KTR): d 9 Oct 1799 (DAR 2:151): m(1) Kingston, NH 30 Jan 1740/1 Susanna Folsom (KTR), b abt 1721 dau of Nathaniel & Susanna (Jackson) Folsom (Folsom Gen p86), d 17 Nov 1778: m(2) Danville, NH 18 Mar 1779 Anna (Tuxbury) Colby (NEHGR 58:124), b abt 1726, d Danville, NH 1804 a.78yrs (CG p39). Anna m(1) Amesbury, MA 22 Jun 1754 Moses Colby (AVR).

Henry & his wife Susanna were admitted to the Kingston Church 27 Dec 1741.

Children: 1st 7 born Kingston, NH (KTR)

1. **MARY**, b 24 May 1742
2. **SUSANNAH**, b 10 Apr 1744: m Danville, NH 22 Dec 1773 Timothy Blake (NEHGR 58:47)
3. **MIRIAM**, b 14 Jul 1746: d Kingston, NH Jul 1754 (KTR)
4. **HENRY**, b 22 Apr 1749
5. **APPHIA**, b 22 Jun 1752: m Danville, NH 6 Dec 1770 Nehemiah Sleeper (NEHGR 58:122)
6. **MIRIAM**, b 17 May 1755: m Danville, NH 23 Dec 1777 Simeon Hoyt (NEHGR 58:124)
7. **SARAH**, b 28 Sep 1757
8. **NATHANIEL**, b 1 Nov 1762: d 20 Jan 1844 (DAR 1:480): m(1) Jun 1783 Elizabeth Eastman: m(2) Sally (Johnson) Flanders
9. **HENRY**, b 13 Mar 1768

JACOB MORRILL, b Salisbury, MA 2 May 1689 son of Jacob & Susanna (Whittier) Morrill (SVR): m (1) Salisbury, MA 28 Oct 1712 Mary Webster (SVR), dau of John & Bridget (Huggins) Webster (OF p345), d Kingston, NH 20 Aug 1727 (NHGR 2: 131): m(2) Kingston, NH 10 Oct 1728 Mehitable (Fifield) Sanborn (NHGR 2:44), b Hampton, NH 9 Apr 1687 dau of Benjamin & Mary (Colcord) Fifield (HmVR p10), d Kingston, NH 2 Jan 1748 (NHVR). Mehitable m(1) Kingston, NH 1 Jan 1706/7 John Sanborn (KTR).

Jacob signed a petition in 1738 for a grant of land in Kingston.

Children:
(by 1st wife)

1. **SUSANNA**, b Salisbury, MA 5 Aug 1714 (SVR): m(1) Salisbury, MA 10 Feb 1731/2 John Collins (SVR): m(2) Newbury, MA 20 Oct 1735 Jacob Gale (NVR)
2. **APPHIA**, m Newbury, MA 15 Dec 1735 Joseph Swasey (NVR)
3. **HENRY**, b Kingston, NH 14 Aug 1717 (KTR): d 9 Oct 1799: m(1) Kingston, NH 30 Jan 1740/1 Susanna Folsom (KTR): m(2) Danville, NH 18 Mar 1779 Anna Colby
4. **JACOB**, b ? 1728: d Brentwood, NH 11 Jan 1811 ?

(by 2nd wife)
5. **JOHN**, b Kingston, NH 23 Feb 1730 (KTR): m Kingston, NH 8 Nov 1750 Bethia Swett (KTR)

JOHN MORRILL, b Salisbury, MA 28 Mar 1713 son of Ezekiel & Abigail (Wadleigh) Morrill (SVR): m(1) Salisbury, MA (int) 6 Nov 1736 Abigail Flanders (SVR): m(2) Kingston, NH 19 Aug 1740 Edith Turrill (KChR), b Abington, MA 29 Aug 1720 dau of Gideon & Edith (Ayer) Turrill (AbVR).

Edith Morrill, wife of John, was admitted to the 2nd Church of Christ in Kingston 4 Jul 1742.

Children: 1st 2 born So Hampton, NH (SHVR)
(by 1st wife)
1. **JONATHAN**, b 28 Oct 1737

(by 2nd wife)
2. **MICAJAH**, b 28 Apr 1741: bpt Kingston, NH 12 Jul 1741 (KChR)
3. **HANNAH**, bpt Kingston, NH 30 Oct 1743 (KChR)

JOHN MORRILL, b Kingston, NH 23 Feb 1730 son of Jacob & Mehitable (Fifield-Sanborn) Morrill (KTR): d bef 10 Feb 1760: m Kingston, NH 8 Nov 1750 Bethia Swett (KTR), b Kingston, NH 27 Sep 1731 dau of Nathan & Mary (Dearborn) Swett (KTR). Bethia m(2) Stephen Ladd.

John & his wife were admitted to the Kingston Church 12 Jan 1752.

Children: born Kingston, NH (KTR)
1. **MEHITABLE**, b 31 Oct 1751
2. **MARY**, b 9 Oct 1754
3. **JACOB**, b 24 Dec 1756
4. **JOHN**, bpt 10 Feb 1760 (NHVR)

DANIEL MOULTON, b Hampton, NH 16 Mar 1673 son of John & Lydia (Taylor) Moulton (HmVR p104): d Hampton, NH 14 Jan 1717/8 (HmVR p125); Est Adm 4 Jun 1718 (PRNH 2:52): m Mary __

Daniel was an original grantee of Kingston in 1694.

Children: born Hampton, NH (HmVR & HH p865)

1. **JUDITH**, b 17 Feb 1700/1; bpt 13 Jun 1708
2. **DANIEL**, bpt 13 Jun 1708: m 27 Dec 1721 Phebe Philbrick (HH p865)
3. **SARAH**, bpt 13 Jun 1708
4. **LYDIA**, bpt 13 Jun 1708: m Newbury, MA 11 Jan 1726/7 Daniel Coffin (NVR)
5. **NOAH**, b 23 Feb 1704/5: m Rye, NH 16 Nov 1749 Patience Locke (Rye VR)
6. **MARY**, b 16 Dec 1706
7. **JOB**, b 23 Oct 1709
8. **RACHEL**, b 23 Jan 1712
9. **ELIZABETH**, bpt 21 Aug 1715
10. **MARTHA**, bpt 21 Apr 1717

HENRY MOULTON, b Hampton, NH 1 Mar 1697/8 son of Josiah & Elizabeth (Worthington) Moulton (HmVR p71): m Hampton, NH 20 Nov 1722 Mary Garland (HH p868), b Hampton, NH 7 Sep 1699 dau of Peter & Sarah (Taylor) Garland (HmVR p69).

Henry lived in the westerly section of Kingston.

Children: (HH p868)

1. **MICAH**, b 1723: d 27 Feb 1736
2. **MARY**, b abt 1725: d 2 Mar 1736
3. **PETER**, b abt 1727: d 1 Mar 1736
4. **JOSIAH**, bpt 6 Jun 1731: d 9 Mar 1736
5. **JONATHAN**, bpt 25 Feb 1733: d 15 Mar 1736
6. **HENRY**, bpt 27 Apr 1735: d 1817: m Betsey Mace
7. **SARAH**, bpt 10 Jun 1737
8. **JAMES**, bpt 25 Nov 1739
9. **DAVID**, bpt 25 Apr 1742: lived in Hampstead, NH

JOHN MOULTON, bpt Newbury, MA Mar 1638 son of John & Anne (Green) Moulton (HmVR p3): d 1705 (NEHGR 141:328): m Hampton, NH 23 Mar 1665/6 Lydia Taylor (HmVR p75), dau of Anthony & Phillippa (_) Taylor (LND p673), d 1729.

John was an original grantee of Kingston in 1694.

Children: born Hampton, NH (HmVR)
1. **MARTHA**, b 16 Nov 1666: m Humphrey Perkins (LND p541)
2. **JOHN**, b 30 May 1669: d 1 Apr 1740: m 11 Dec 1713 Rebecca Smith (LND p498)
3. **LYDIA**, b 13 Jul 1671: d Hampton, NH 13 Jul 1678 (HmVR p117)
4. **DANIEL**, b 16 Mar 1673: d Hampton, NH 14 Jan 1717/8 (HmVR p125): m Mary ___
5. **JAMES**, b 29 Jul 1675: m Hampton, NH 15 Oct 1702 Dorothy Clements (HmVR p58)
6. **NATHAN** (LND p498), m Hampton, NH 26 Apr 1705 Sarah Reaser (HmVR p58)
7. **DAVID**, d 15 Feb 1732/3 (LND p498): m 2 Jan 1710 Sarah Leavitt
8. **ANNA**, b 2 Mar 1678: m Hampton, NH 12 Nov 1695 Caleb Marston (HmVR p80)
9. **LYDIA**, b 19 Jul 1681 (LND p498): m Hampton, NH 1 Jul 1702 Thomas Marston (HmVR p58)
10. **JACOB**, b 21 Jun 1686: d 7 Mar 1751: m Hampton, NH 10 Dec 1714 Sarah Smith (HmVR p60)
11. **RACHEL**, b 4 Oct 1690: d 8 Jun 1758 (HH p863): m Hampton, NH 21 May 1718 Capt Jabez Smith (HmVR p61)

JOHN MUZZEY (MUSSEY), b abt 1689 son of John & Elizabeth (_) Mussey (OF p264): d Kingston, NH 26 Oct 1723 (KTR): m Amesbury, MA 17 Dec 1713 Hannah Dimond (AVR), b Amesbury, MA 4 Sep 1693 dau of Israel & Abiell (Prowse) Dimond (AVR), d 29 Nov 1748. Hannah m(2) Kingston, NH 5 Nov 1730 Philip Morse (KTR).

Widow Mussey belonged to Kingston in 1725 when Rev Clark took charge of the church.

Children: born Kingston, NH (KTR)
1. **JOHN**, b 5 Nov 1714: d Hampstead, NH 15 Jan 1786 (HmstR): m Haverhill, MA 29 Nov 1739 Abiah Hunkins (HvVR)

2. **ELIZABETH**, b 22 Apr 1716
3. **HANNAH**, b 22 Aug 1718
4. **REUBEN**, b 28 Nov 1720: m Andover, MA 10 May 1743 Sarah Phelps (AndVR)
5. **BENJAMIN**, b 12 May 1722: m abt 1750 Abigail Weeks

REUBEN MUZZEY, b Kingston, NH 28 Nov 1720 son of John & Hannah (Dimond) Muzzey (KTR): d Amherst, NH 20 Nov 1788: m Andover, MA 10 May 1743 Sarah Phelps (AndVR), b Andover, MA 20 Jul 1715 dau of John & Sarah (Andrews) Phelps (And VR).

Reuben was admitted to the 2nd Church of Christ in Kingston 28 May 1742 & Sarah was admitted 6 Nov 1743 by dismission from the 2nd Church in Andover.

Children: bpt Kingston, NH (KChR)

1. **JONATHAN**, bpt 26 Feb 1744: d 1761
2. **JOHN**, bpt 1 Sep 1745: d 17 Jan 1831 (DAR 1:489): m(1) Beulah Butler: m(2) Rhoda Bartlett
3. **SARAH**, bpt 1 May 1748: m 1775 William Stewart
4. **REUBEN DIMOND**, bpt 19 Nov 1749: d 25 Sep 1819 (DAR 2:153): m Sarah Straw

THOMAS NEWMAN, m(1) Chebacco, MA 18 Oct 1739 Abigail Young (IpVR), b Gloucester, MA 24 Oct 1718 dau of Ichabod & Abigail (Elwell) Young (GlVR): m(2) Kingston, NH 25 Dec 1755 Mary Webster (KChR).

Children: bpt Kingston, NH (KChR)
(by 1st wife)

1. **ELIZABETH**, bpt 20 Jul 1740
2. **ABIGAIL**, bpt 30 May 1742
3. **THOMAS**, bpt 13 May 1744
4. **SARAH**, bpt 27 Jul 1745
5. **WILLIAM**, bpt 20 Nov 1748

(by 2nd wife)

6. **JOHN**, bpt 24 Oct 1756
7. **ABIGAIL**, bpt 27 Aug 1758

8. **EBENEZER**, bpt 1 Feb 1761

JOHN NEWTON, d Kingston, NH 7 Sep 1756 (NHVR): m Judith ____, d Kingston, NH 5 Oct 1756 (NHVR).

John signed a petition in 1738 for a grant of land in Kingston. Administration on the estate of John Newton of Kingston was granted 26 Jan 1757 to his son John Newton (PRNH 6:17).

Children:
1. **JOHN**, living 1776

MARGARET NEWTON (widow), d Kingston, NH 16 Sep 1756 (NHVR). She is probably the Widow Newton who belonged to Kingston in 1725 when Rev Clark took charge of the church.

Children: (prob)
1. **JOHN**, d Kingston, NH 7 Sep 1756 (NHVR): m Judith ___
2. **MARGARET**, m (prob) Kingston, NH 1 Sep 1735 Jonas Clay (NHGR 2:46)

JONATHAN ORDWAY, d Kingston, NH (prob) 7 Nov 1753 (NHVR); Est Adm 21 Mar 1754 (PRNH 5:77): m Kingston, NH 2 Jul 1746 Hannah Morrill (KTR). Hannah m(2) Kingston, NH 23 Dec 1755 Samuel Robie (KTR).

Children: 1st 2 born Kingston, NH (KTR)
1. **HANNAH**, b 6 Jul 1747
2. **NEHEMIAH**, b 25 Nov 1749
3. **JAMES**, b Newton, NH 19 Dec 1751 (NwtTR)

JOSEPH ORDWAY, Administration on the estate of Joseph Ordway of Kingston was granted to his widow Susanna Ordway 24 Nov 1755 (PRNH 5:354).

Children: born Framingham, MA (IGI)
1. **ABIGAIL**, b 13 Mar 1751
2. **SAMUEL**, b 17 Jun 1753: bpt Kingston, NH 3 Jun 1755 (NHGR 6:32)

EBENEZER PAGE, b Salisbury, MA 19 Jul 1720 son of John & Mary (Winsley) Page (SVR): d Gilmanton, NH 27 Sep 1805 (Greeley Gen p141): m Kingston, NH 29 Dec 1743 Hannah Shepard (KTR), d Gilmanton, NH 16 Jun 1797.

Ebenezer & his wife Hannah were admitted to the Kingston Church from Salisbury 31 Mar 1744 & dismissed to Nottingham East Feb 1762.

Children: 1st 5 born Kingston, NH (KTR)

1. **MARY**, b 5 Jul 1745
2. **EBENEZER**, b 1 Jun 1747: m(1) Mary___: m (2) 13 Mar 1783 Molly Tucker
3. **BENJAMIN**, b 23 Aug 1749: d (Est Adm) Gilmanton, NH 11 Jan 1786 (Straf Prob p197)
4. **ISRAEL**, b 17 May 1752: d Kingston, NH 28 Jul 1759 (KTR)
5. **BETTE**, b 24 Dec 1755: m Gilmanton, NH 27 Mar 1776 John Shepard
6. **HANNAH**, b Gilmanton, NH 14 Mar 1758
7. **WINSLOW**, b Gilmanton, NH 13 Jul 1760: m Salisbury, MA 13 Jan 1784 Martha True (SVR)
8. **TRUE**, b Gilmanton, NH 21 Apr 1764: d So Monteville, ME 6 Mar 1817: m(1) Gilmanton, NH 1 May 1791 Jemima Carr: m(2) 14 Jul 1805 Abigail (Edgerly) Dockham

JABEZ PAGE, bpt Salisbury, MA 4 Feb 1710/11 son of Onesiphorus & Ruth (Merrill) Page (SVR): d Danville, NH 4 May 1782 a.71yrs (CG p39): m Salisbury, MA 30 Jan 1735 Abigail Flanders (SVR), bpt Salisbury, MA 10 Dec 1721 dau of Thomas & Katherine (Hackett) Flanders (Page Gen p30), d Danville, NH 15 Oct 1791 a.79yrs (CG p39).

Jabez & his wife, from Salisbury, were admitted to the Kingston Church 3 Apr 1742.

Children:

1. **RUTH**, b Salisbury, MA 2 Sep 1738 (SVR): m (prob) Kingston, NH 13 Dec 1759 Caleb Towle (NHGR 3:91)
2. **THOMAS**, b Kingston, NH 30 Apr 1743 (KTR):

d Danville, NH 26 Jun 1829 (CG p39): m Kingston, NH 11 Jul 1763 Mary Elkins (NH GR 3:129)

3. **HENRY**, b Kingston, NH 17 Jul 1750 (KTR): d Sandown, NH 30 Dec 1836: m Danville, NH 21 May 1778 Sarah Page (NEHGR 58:124)
4. **ELIZABETH**, b 14 Jul 1754: m Andrew Page

JOHN PAGE, b Salisbury, MA 11 Nov 1728 son of John & Mary (Winsley) Page (SVR): d Danville, NH 8 Jul 1767 a.39yrs (CG p39); Est Adm 30 Sep 1767 (PRNH 9:51): m Kingston, NH 19 Sep 1749 Anne Webster (KTR), bpt Kingston, NH 15 Jun 1735 dau of Benjamin & Elizabeth (Stuart) Webster (NHGR 2:69): d Danville, NH 29 Apr 1822 (CG p39).

John was admitted to the Kingston Church 3 Aug 1754.

Children: 1st 5 born Kingston, NH (KTR)

1. **BENJAMIN**, b 1 Sep 1750: d Kingston, NH 29 Sep 1753 (KTR)
2. **ELIZABETH**, b 10 Oct 1752: d Kingston, NH 9 Oct 1753 (KTR)
3. **ELIZABETH**, b 14 Sep 1754
4. **SARAH**, b 18 Jan 1757: d 24 Feb 1834: m Danville, NH 21 May 1778 Henry Page (NE HGR 58:124)
5. **MARY**, b 28 Jan 1760
6. **BENJAMIN**, b Danville, NH 10 Mar 1762 (Dn TR): bpt Kingston, NH 9 May 1762 (NHVR)
7. **MARY**, b Danville, NH 4 May 1764: d 15 Aug 1764 (DnTR)

ONESIPHORUS PAGE, b Salisbury, MA 18 Sep 1708 son of Joseph & Elizabeth (_) Page (SVR): d (Est Adm) Kingston, NH 9 Dec 1758 (PRNH 6:354): m Salisbury, MA 28 Oct 1731 Patience Dow (SVR), b Salisbury, MA 19 Jan 1712 dau of Jeremiah & Elizabeth (Perkins) Dow (SVR).

Children: bpt Kingston, NH (KChR)

1. **SARAH**, b Salisbury, MA 10 Mar 1732 (SVR)
2. **WINTHROP**, b Salisbury, MA 28 Jan 1733/4

(SVR)
3. **BENJAMIN**, bpt 5 Sep 1742
4. **SARAH**, bpt 5 Sep 1742
5. **RUTH**, bpt 5 Sep 1742
6. **WINTHROP**, bpt 5 Sep 1742
7. **ONESIPHORUS**, bpt 16 Oct 1743: m Newbury, MA 28 Apr 1767 Mehitable Doty (NVR)
8. **BETTY**, bpt 22 Sep 1745
9. **PATIENCE**, bpt 16 Jun 1751
10. **DAVID**, b abt 1756: bpt 24 May 1761

DAVID PEASLEE, b Haverhill, MA 2 Apr 1713 son of John & Mary (Martin) Peaslee (HvVR): d Sutton, NH abt 1800 (HSt p863): m Amesbury, MA 9 Feb 1742 Rachel Straw (AVR), bpt Amesbury, MA 2 Jun 1728 dau of John & Lydia (Sargent) Straw (AVR).

David lived in the area of Kingston now known as Sandown.

Children: (SdTR)
1. **DOROTHY**, b 12 Nov 1744
2. **SAMUEL**, b 5 Jun 1746: d Sutton, NH 12 Sep 1821: m 13 Mar 1768 Sarah Bean
3. **PETER**, b 8 Mar 1749
4. **DAVID**, b 6 Mar 1751
5. **RACHEL**, b 12 May 1754
6. **ABRAHAM**, b 20 Jul 1756: d 1815 (DAR 1: 523): m 24 Dec 1778 Martha Bean
7. **ISAAC** (twin), b 3 May 1760: m Danville, NH 15 Oct 1781 Mary Collins (NEHGR 58: 125)
8. **JACOB** (twin), b 3 May 1760
9. **TIMOTHY**, b 5 Oct 1763: m Mary Andrew
10. **SARAH**, b 12 Apr 1766: m 8 Jul 1785 Ephraim Hildreth
11. **JOHN**, b 11 Nov 1768: m 25 Jun 1789 Olive Bailey

JACOB PEASLEE, b Haverhill, MA 11 May 1710 son of John & Mary (Martin) Peaslee (HvVR): d Kingston, NH 29 Jul 1744 (KTR): m Amesbury, MA 25 Dec 1735 Huldah Brown (AVR), b Hampton, NH 3 Nov 1715 dau of John & Abigail (Johnson) Brown

(HmVR p50).

Children:
1. **ELIJAH**, b Kingston, NH 15 Jul 1741 (KTR): m 1766 Esther Goodell (Virkus 7:490)

JEDEDIAH PHILBRICK, b Kingston, NH 9 Aug 1700 son of Thomas & Mehitable (Ayers) Philbrick (KTR): d Kingston, NH 20 Mar 1754 (KTR): m Kingston, NH 25 Aug 1721 Mary Taylor (KTR), dau of William & Margaret (Bean) Taylor (LND p676).
Jedediah belonged to Kingston when Rev Clark took charge of the church in 1725. In 1738 he signed a petition for a grant of land in Kingston.

Children: born Kingston, NH (KTR)
1. **JEREMIAH**, b 2 Jan 1722: d Kingston, NH 9 Mar 1754 (KTR): m Kingston, NH 20 Sep 1744 Mary Stevens (KTR)
2. **HANNAH**, b 6 Feb 1724: d Danville, NH 28 Aug 1771 (CG p39): m Kingston, NH 24 Nov 1747 Humphrey Hook (KTR)
3. **THOMAS**, b 11 Jan 1726: d Kingston, NH 8 Sep 1730 (KTR)
4. **BENJAMIN**, b 4 Jul 1728: d Kingston, NH 10 Sep 1730 (KTR)
5. **THOMAS**, b 23 Oct 1730: d Kingston, NH 16 Aug 1735 (KTR)
6. **BENJAMIN**, b 6 Mar 1734: d Kingston, NH 27 Jan 1735/6 (KTR)
7. **THOMAS**, b 1 Jan 1737/8: d Kingston, NH 5 May 1739 (KTR)
8. **SAMUEL**, b 11 Feb 1739/40: d Kingston, NH 4 Apr 1779 (NHVR): m 9 Feb 1767 Sarah Sanborn
9. **JEDEDIAH**, b 17 Aug 1742: d Kingston, NH 3 Dec 1743 (KTR)
10. **JOSEPH**, b 4 Nov 1748: d 1822 (NEHGR 38: 284): m Mehitable ____

JEREMIAH PHILBRICK, b Kingston, NH 21 Sep 1684 son of Thomas & Mehitable (Ayers) Philbrick (KTR): d bef 1715: m (poss) Boston, MA 25 Dec

1712 Mary McCartly (LND p546).

Jeremiah received a lot in Kingston 17 Jul 1702. Administration on the estate Jeremiah Philbrick of Kingston, was granted to Daniel Ladd of Kingston 6 Dec 1721 (PRNH 2:141).

JEREMIAH PHILBRICK, b Kingston, NH 2 Jan 1722 son of Jedediah & Mary (Taylor) Philbrick (KTR): d Kingston, NH 9 Mar 1754 (KTR): m Kingston, NH 20 Sep 1744 Mary Stevens (KTR). Mary m(2) Israel Dimond (PRNH 5:117).

Jeremiah was admitted to the Kingston Church 31 Oct 1741 & his wife was admitted 6 Jun 1751.

Children: born Kingston, NH (KTR)

1. **JEDEDIAH**, b 4 Feb 1744/5
2. **JOHN**, b 22 Apr 1747: d Kingston, NH 16 May 1751 (NHVR)
3. **ELIZABETH**, b 15 Dec 1749

THOMAS PHILBRICK JR, b Hampton, NH 14 Mar 1659 son of James & Ann (Roberts) Philbrick (HmVR p549): d Kingston, NH 1 Jan 1711/12 (KTR): m Kingston, NH 14 Apr 1681 Mehitable Ayers (KTR), b (prob) Haverhill, MA 14 Sep 1656 dau of Robert & Elizabeth (Palmer) Ayers (HvVR), d Kingston, NH 14 Sep 1727 (NHGR 2:131). Mehitable m(2) Timothy Hillard (LND p331).

Thomas Jr was an original grantee of Kingston in 1694. He was granted 200 acres of land at a meeting of the freeholders 19 Dec 1700.

Children: (KTR & HmVR)

1. **(DAU)**, b 13 Jan 1681/2
2. **(SON)**, b 30 May 1683
3. **JEREMIAH**, b 21 Sep 1684: d bef 1715: m (poss) Boston, MA 25 Dec 1712 Mary McCartly (LND p546)
4. **ELIZABETH**, b 17 Oct 1686: m Haverhill, MA 18 Oct 1705 Abraham Bradley (HvVR)
5. **TIMOTHY**, b 14 May 1689: d Kingston, NH 17 Nov 1711 (KTR)
6. **ANN**, b 14 Mar 1691: m Kingston, NH 5 Jun 1712 John Sleeper (KTR)

7. **MEHITABLE**, b 26 Mar 1693: m Kingston, NH 29 Apr 1712 Daniel Ladd (KTR)
8. **HANNAH**, b 19 Dec 1695: d Kingston, NH 18 Jan 1696/7 (KTR)
9. **SAMUEL**, b 13 May 1698: d Kingston, NH 21 Nov 1711 (KTR)
10. **JEDEDIAH**, b 9 Aug 1700: d Kingston, NH 20 Mar 1754 (KTR): m Kingston, NH 25 Aug 1721 Mary Taylor (KTR)
11. **THOMAS**, b 9 Jun 1704: d Kingston, NH 24 Jun 1704 (KTR)

TIMOTHY PHILBRICK, b Hampton, NH 14 May 1689 son of Thomas & Mehitable (Ayers) Philbrick (HmVR p11): d Kingston, NH 17 Nov 1711 (KTR).

Timothy had land laid out to him in Kingston Mar 1706/7. His estate was administered 2 Mar 1713/4 (PRNH 1:722).

JAMES PRESCOTT, b abt 1643: d Kingston, NH 23 Nov 1728 (NHGR 2:131): m abt 1667 Mary Boulter (NEM p602), b Hampton, NH 15 May 1648 dau of Nathaniel & Grace (Swain) Boulter (HH p613), d Kingston, NH 4 Oct 1735 (NHGR 3:37).

James was an original grantee of Kingston in 1694 & was granted 200 acres of land 19 Dec 1700. His family belonged to Kingston in 1725 when Rev Clark took charge of the church.

Children: born Hampton, NH (HmVR)

1. **JOSHUA**, b 1 Mar 1669 (HH p928): m 1710 Sarah Clifford (LND p568)
2. **JAMES**, b 1 Sep 1671: m(1) Hampton, NH 1 Mar 1694/5 Maria Marston (HmVR p79): m(2) 17 Jun 1746 Abigail (Gove-Dalton) Sanborn (LND p568)
3. **REBECCA**, b 15 Apr 1673: m Hampton, NH 3 Dec 1691 Nathaniel Sanborn (HmVR p78)
4. **JONATHAN**, b 6 May 1675: d 6 Jan 1755: m Elizabeth (Pulsifer) Clifford (LND p568)
5. **MARY**, b 11 Jun 1677: m(1) Hampton, NH 2 Nov 1699 Jabez Coleman (HmVR p56): m(2) Kingston, NH 9 Nov 1730 Thomas Crosby (KTR): m(3) Kingston, NH 2 Nov 1738 James

Bean (NHGR 3:40)

6. **ABIGAIL** (twin), b 1 Sep 1679: m 2 Nov 1699 Richard Bounds (LND p568)
7. **TEMPERANCE (PRUDENCE)** (twin), b 1 Sep 1679: d.y.
8. **JOHN**, b 19 Nov 1681: d 1761: m Hampton, NH 8 Aug 1701 Abigail Marston (HmVR p57)
9. **NATHANIEL**, b 19 Nov 1683 (HH p928): m 30 Dec 1703 Ann Marston (LND p568)

JEREMIAH PRESCOTT, b Hampton, NH 8 Dec 1695 son of James & Maria (Marston) Prescott (HmVR p64): m 14 Jan 1720 Hannah Philbrick (LND p568).

Jeremiah's wife was admitted to the Kingston Church 9 Jul 1732 by dismission from ye church of Hampton. In 1738 Jeremiah signed a petition for a new parish in the easterly part of Kingston.

Children: born Kingston, NH

1. **WILLIAM**, b 24 May 1724
2. **MARY**, b 26 May 1727
3. **SARAH**, b 1730: d Tunbridge, VT Feb 1832: m Kingston, NH 28 Nov 1758 Nathaniel Thompson (KTR)
4. **ELIZABETH**, b 14 Mar 1733: m 19 Aug 1751 Jonathan Collins
5. **HANNAH**, bpt Kingston, NH 20 Jul 1735 (NHGR 2:69)
6. **ABIGAIL**, bpt Kingston, NH 31 May 1741 (KChR)

JOSHUA PRESCOTT, b Hampton, NH 1 Mar 1669 son of James & Mary (Boulter) Prescott (HH p928): m 1710 Sarah Clifford (LND p568), b Hampton, NH 10 May 1691 dau of Israel & Ann (Smith) Clifford (HmVR p21).

Joshua belonged to Kingston in 1725 when Rev Clark took charge of the church. In 1738 he signed a petition for a new parish in the easterly part of Kingston.

Children: (HH p929)

1. **NATHAN**, b 1710: m 30 Mar 1736 Ursley Ward

2. **JOSHUA**, b abt 1713: d 12 Jul 1785: m(1) Abigail Ambrose: m(2) abt 1763 Mary Moulton (DAR 1:547)
3. **MARY**, b 1715: m Kingston, NH 25 Mar 1742 Moses Shaw (KChR)
4. **EDWARD**, b 1717: d 1804 (DAR 1:547): m Kingston, NH 9 Jul 1741 Elizabeth Prescott (KChR)
5. **ANNE**, b abt 1719: m Kingston, NH 27 Nov 1746 John Wells (KChR)
6. **REUBEN**, b 1721: m 15 Nov 1749 Alice Daniels
7. **PATIENCE**, b 1724: m Kingston, NH 22 Jan 1749/50 Daniel Beede (NHGR 3:44)
8. **JOHN**, b 1726
9. **ABRAM**, b 1728
10. **(INFANT)**, d Kingston, NH Jul 1733 (NHGR)
11. **(DAU)**, d Kingston, NH 19 Aug 1735 (NHGR 3:37)
12. **(CHILD)**, d Kingston, NH 21 Aug 1735 (NHGR 3:37)
13. **ANN**, bpt Kingston, NH 5 Feb 1737/8 (NHGR 5:103)
14. **MARY**, bpt Kingston, NH 5 Feb 1737/8 (NHGR 5:103)

NATHAN (NATHANIEL) PRESCOTT, b Hampton, NH 19 Nov 1683 son of James & Mary (Boulter) Prescott (HH p928): d 26 Feb 1771: m Hampton, NH 30 Dec 1703 Ann Marston (LND p568), b Hampton, NH 16 Feb 1680 dau of James & Dinah (Sanborn) Marston (HmVR p82), d 10 Dec 1761.

Nathan's name appears on a list of Kingston men who swore allegiance to the King in 1727.

JOHN PRESSEY, b Amesbury, MA 10 Apr 1714 son of John & Elizabeth (Weed) Pressey (AVR): d aft 1766 of Deer Isle, ME: m Newbury, MA 16 Aug 1733 Mercy Chase (NVR), b Newbury, MA 16 Oct 1715 dau of Charles & Hepzibah (Carr) Chase (NVR).

John lived in the westerly section of Kingston.

Children: last 8 born Sandown, NH (SdTR)
1. **THOMAS**, b Amesbury, MA 10 Feb 1733/4
2. **CHARLES**, bpt Amesbury, MA 3 Jul 1737 (AVR): m Newbury, MA 5 Apr 1764 Molle Huse (NVR)
3. **BETTEY**, b Amesbury, MA 14 Mar 1737/8 (AVR): m (prob) Kingston, NH 8 Mar 1759 Cornelius Bean (NHGR 3:90)
4. **MERCY**, b 12 Oct 1743
5. **PAUL**, b 2 May 1745: bpt as **PAIN** in Amesbury, MA 8 Sep 1745 (AVR)
6. **THOMAS COLBY**, b 2 May 1747
7. **JONATHAN**, b 20 Dec 1749
8. **MOLLEY**, b 28 Dec 1752
9. **JOANNA**, b 26 Feb 1753
10. **ELIPHALET CHASE**, b 8 Mar 1755
11. **SARAH**, b 18 Dec 1758

PAUL PRESSEY, b Amesbury, MA 11 Jun 1729 son of John & Elizabeth (Weed) Pressey (AVR): d Danville, NH (Est Adm) 26 Nov 1760 (PRNH 7:57): m (1) Kingston, NH 1 Jan 1751 Hannah Felch (KTR), b Hampton Falls, NH 24 Oct 1731 dau of Daniel & Hepsibeth (_) Felch (HFTR): d Kingston, NH 10 Aug 1757 (KTR): m(2) Kingston, NH 26 Mar 1758 Marcy Hubbard (KTR).

Children: born Kingston, NH
(by 1st wife)
1. **BETTE**, b 26 Apr 1752 (KTR)
2. **JOHN**, bpt Hampstead, NH Jan 1755
3. **MOLLY**, b 27 Jan 1756 (KTR)

(by 2nd wife)
4. **HANNAH**, b 11 Jun 1759 (KTR)

DAVID QUIMBY, b Salisbury, MA 19 Jul 1693 son of John & Mary (Mudgett) Quimby (SVR): m Kingston, NH 25 Dec 1724 Abigail Webster (KTR), b Kingston, NH 15 Apr 1706 dau of Thomas & Sarah (?Godfrey) Webster (KTR)

David & his family belonged to Kingston in 1725 when Rev Clark took charge of the church.

Children: born Kingston, NH (KTR)

1. **ELS (ALICE)**, b 17 Nov 1726: m Kingston, NH 8 May 1745/6 Timothy Sanborn (NHGR 3:42)
2. **SAMUEL**, b 10 Apr 1729: m Kingston, NH May 1757 Ann Young (KTR)
3. **DAVID**, b 4 Dec 1731: d Danville, NH 19 Dec 1794 (CG p40): m Kingston, NH 19 Nov 1755 Mary Wadleigh (KTR)
4. **(CHILD)**, d Kingston, NH 10 May 1736 (NHGR 3:39)
5. **JOHN**, b 16 May 1737
6. **ELIZABETH**, b 12 Nov 1740
7. **MARY**, b 30 Jan 1743/4
8. **SARAH**, b 21 Apr 1746
9. **TIMOTHY**, b 16 Apr 1750

ELIPHALET QUIMBY, b abt 1720 son of Jeremiah & Hannah (George) Quimby: d Kingston, NH Jun 1757 (KTR): m Kingston, NH 1 May 1744 Mary Jewell (KTR).

Children: born Kingston, NH (KTR)

1. **MARY**, b 3 Dec 1747: d Kingston, NH 27 Nov 1750 (KTR)
2. **ANDREW**, b 4 Oct 1750
3. **JONATHAN**, b 15 Aug 1753
4. **DANIEL**, b 9 Sep 1755

JEREMIAH QUIMBY, b Salisbury, MA 24 Aug 1689 son of John & Mary (Mudgett) Quimby (SVR): m Amesbury, MA 14 Jun 1716 Hannah George (AVR), b Amesbury, MA 13 Apr 1694 dau of Samuel & Elizabeth (Freame) George (AVR).

Jeremiah belonged to Kingston in 1725 when Rev Clark took charge of the church. In 1730 he signed a petition regarding the township of Kingston.

Children:

1. **ELIPHALET**, d Kingston, NH Jun 1757 (KTR): m (prob) Kingston, NH 1 May 1744 Mary Jewell (KTR)
2. **MOSES**, b Kingston, NH 13 Apr 1725 (KTR): m Kingston, NH 5 Jun 1754 Juda Bean (KTR)

3. **AARON**, b 1727
4. **JACOB**, b 1728
5. **JEREMIAH**, b 1730
6. **TRISTRAM** (prob), m Kingston, NH 26 Nov 1753 Susanna Blaisdell (KTR)

JOHN QUIMBY JR, b Salisbury, MA 8 Jul 1688 son of John & Mary (Mudgett) Quimby (SVR): d Kingston, NH (WP) 28 May 1755 (PRNH 5:293): m Marcy ____ (Mary Bean - TAG 16:170).

Children: (TAG 16:170)
1. **JOHN**, b abt 1710
2. **DANIEL**, b 1712-20

ELIAS RANO (RENO), m Kingston, NH 5 Apr 1742 Mary Severance (NHGR 3:41), b Kingston, NH 19 Dec 1715 dau of Ephraim & Mary (Burnham) Severance (KTR).

An Elias Rano signed a petition in 1730 regarding the township of Kingston.

Children: born Kingston, NH (KTR)
1. **SAMUEL**, b 23 Apr 1743
2. **ELIZABETH**, b 24 Jan 1744/5
3. **MARY**, b 28 Feb 1746/7
4. **HANNAH**, b 30 Mar 1749
5. **JOHN**, b 27 Apr 1752
6. **JOSEPH** (triplet), bpt 17 Jul 1755 (NHGR)
7. **SARAH** (triplet), bpt 17 Jul 1755 (NHGR)
8. **(CHILD** - triplet), d bef 17 Jul 1755 (NH GR 6:32)

GEORGE ROBERTS, son of John & Elizabeth (_) Roberts of Brentwood (PRNH 3:413): m Kingston, NH 15 Nov 1733 Judith Keniston (NHGR 2:45).

Children: bpt Kingston, NH (NHGR)
1. **JUDAH**, bpt 25 Jan 1740/1
2. **JONATHAN**, bpt 11 Oct 1741
3. **SARAH**, bpt 18 Sep 1743
4. **ELIZABETH**, bpt 7 Apr 1745
5. **ELIPHALET**, bpt 15 Apr 1750
6. **GEORGE**, bpt 15 Apr 1750

ICHABOD ROBIE, b Hampton, NH 26 Nov 1664 son of Henry & Ruth (Moore) Robie (HmVR p97): d Kingston, NH 15 May 1757 a.93yrs (KTR): m(1) Hampton, NH 4 Jan 1693/4 Lucy Page (HmVR p79), b Hampton, NH 22 Sep 1672 dau of Francis & Meribah (Smith) Page (HmVR p103): m(2) aft 1717 wid Lydia Spendlow (LND p590), d Kingston, NH 21 May 1731 (NHGR 2:132).

At a meeting of the freeholders of Kingston, 19 Dec 1700, Ichabod was granted 200 acres of land. His family belonged to Kingston in 1725 when Rev Clark took charge of the church.

Children: 1st 5 born Hampton, NH

1. **MERIAH**, b 6 Oct 1694 (HmVR p88): d Kingston, NH (WP) 30 Nov 1757 (PRNH 6:138): m __ Connor
2. **LUCY**, bpt 13 Mar 1698 (HH p935)
3. **DOROTHY**, bpt 3 Mar 1700 (HH p935): m(1) 25 Nov 1718 Edward Sanborn: m(2) 17 Sep 1729 Benjamin Prescott (LND p590)
4. **LYDIA**, b 23 May 1703 (LND p590): m(1) Kingston, NH 14 Aug 1729 Amassa Dow (KTR): m(2) Kingston, NH 8 Nov 1739 Michael Brooks (NHGR 3:40)
5. **SAMUEL**, b 12 May 1705 (HmVR p32): m Anna (Spendlow) Morrison (LND p652)
6. **RUTH**, b Kingston, NH 3 Sep 1707 (KTR)
7. **WILLIAM**, b Kingston, NH 6 Nov 1709 (KTR): d 1744
8. **SUSANNA**, b Kingston, NH 2 Aug 1713 (KTR): m Kensington, NH 16 Jun 1741 Hezekiah Swaine (NHVR)

SAMUEL ROBIE, b Hampton, NH 12 May 1705 son of Ichabod & Lucy (Page) Robie (HmVR p32): d Sutton, NH 1790 a.86yrs (HSt p931): m(1) Anna (Spendlow) Morrison (LND p652), dau of Philip & Lydia (_) Spendlow, d Kingston, NH 22 Oct 1755 (NHVR): m(2) Kingston, NH 23 Dec 1755 Hannah (Morrill) Ordway (KTR). Hannah m(1) Kingston, NH 2 Jul 1746 Jonathan Ordway (KTR).

Samuel was admitted to the Church of Christ in Kingston 31 Dec 1727. In 1730 he signed a petition regarding the township of Kingston & in 1738 he signed a petition for a grant of land in Kingston.

Children: last 4 born Danville, NH (DnTR) (by 2nd wife)

1. **JONATHAN**, b Kingston, NH 15 Oct 1756 (KTR): d 14 May 1824: m Sarah Nelson (HSt p931)
2. **LUCY**, b 6 Mar 1760: m Mar 1777 Plummer Wheeler
3. **ICHABOD**, b 15 Apr 1762: d 1834: m(1) Miriam Putney: m(2) 1826 Mrs Betsey Chandler
4. **SAMUEL**, b 25 Mar 1765
5. **JAMES**, b 25 Oct 1767

PHILIP ROW's name appears on a list of Kingston men who swore allegiance to the King in 1727.

DANIEL ROWELL, b Amesbury, MA 25 Nov 1705 son of Jacob & Hannah (Barnard) Rowell (AVR): d (Est Adm) 25 Mar 1778 (OF p1082): m Amesbury, MA 14 Mar 1728 Anne Currier (AVR), b Amesbury, MA 3 Mar 1708 dau of John & Judith (Stevens) Currier (AVR).

Daniel signed a petition in 1738 for a new parish in the easterly part of Kingston.

Children: bpt Kingston, NH (KChR)

1. **JONATHAN**, b abt 1730: bpt 23 Oct 1743
2. **JUDITH**, b Kingston, NH 8 Oct 1733 (KTR): m Kingston, NH 3 Jun 1755 Stephen Long (NHGR 3:88)
3. **JACOB**, b Kingston, NH 1 Oct 1735 (KTR): m (prob) Hampstead, NH 8 Aug 1760 Abigail Prescott (HmstR)
4. **HANNAH**, b Kingston, NH 24 Dec 1737 (KTR)
5. **MIRIAM**, bpt 23 Oct 1743: m Joseph Jewell
6. **RHODA**, bpt 23 Oct 1743
7. **NANNY**, bpt 15 Jul 1744
8. **DANIEL**, bpt 1 Dec 1745: d Nov 1831 (DAR 1:584): m Kingston, NH 9 Oct 1768 Judith French (KChR)
9. **ELIZABETH**, bpt 29 Apr 1750: m Adonijah

Fellows
10. **MOSES**, bpt 15 Oct 1752

MOSES ROWELL, b Amesbury, MA 29 Nov 1699 son of Jacob & Hannah (Barnard) Rowell (AVR): d Kingston, NH 20 Jan 1732/3 (NHGR 2:132): m Salisbury, MA 28 Nov 1723 Jemima Chandler (AVR), b Andover, MA 2 May 1701 dau of Joseph & Sarah (Abbott) Chandler (AndVR). Jemima m(2) Kingston, NH Oct 1737 Jacob Brown (NHGR 3:39).

Administration on the estate of Moses Rowell of Kingston was granted to Jemima Rowell of Kingston, widow, 22 May 1733 (PRNH 2:476). His family belonged to Kingston in 1725 when Rev Clark took charge of the church.

Children: bpt Kingston, NH (NHGR 2:70)
1. **HANNAH**, b 18 Mar 1724/5: bpt 19 Nov 1735
2. **SARAH**, bpt 19 Nov 1735
3. **PHEBE**, bpt 19 Nov 1735
4. **SUSANNA**, bpt 19 Nov 1735
5. **JEMIMA**, b 17 Jan 1732/3: bpt 19 Nov 1735

NATHANIEL RUNDLETT, b abt 1710 son of Charles & Lydia (Ladd) Rundlett: m Falmouth, ME 13 May 1737 Mary Mitchell (LND p600).

Probably the Nathaniel of Kingston who swore allegiance to the King in 1727.

Children:
1. **CHARLES**
2. **NATHANIEL**

BENJAMIN SANBORN, b Hampton, NH 20 Dec 1668 son of John & Mary (Tuck) Sanborn (HmVR p100): d 15 Dec 1740: m(1) Sarah Worcester (LND p603), b Salisbury, MA 15 Aug 1667 dau of Timothy & Susanna (_) Worcester (SVR), d Hampton, NH 29 Jan 1720 (HmVR p127): m(2) Hampton, NH 7 Nov 1721 Meribah (Page) Tilton (HH p947), b Hampton, NH 17 Mar 1678/9 dau of Francis & Meribah (Smith) Page (HmVR p111), d Hampton, NH 14 ___ 1723 (HmVR p127): m(3) Hampton, NH 24 Nov 1724 Abigail (Gove) Dalton (HH p947), b Hampton, NH

17 Apr 1670 dau of Edward & Hannah (Partridge) Gove (HmVR p101).

Benjamin was an original grantee of Kingston in 1694, but evidently did not live there.

Children: born Hampton, NH (HmVR)
(by 1st wife)

1. **MARY**, b 27 Oct 1690: m 12 Jan 1715/6 William Healey (LND p321)
2. **JOANNA**, b 1 Dec 1692: d 1717: m Kingston, NH 13 Jan 1714 Cornelius Clough (KTR)
3. **SARAH**, b 30 Sep 1694: d Hampton Falls, NH 26 Apr 1756 (NEHGR 10:274): m 28 Dec 1714 Reuben Sanborn (LND p604)
4. **THEODATE**, b 1696 (LND p603): d Kingston, NH 10 Oct 1756 (NHVR): m Kingston, NH 31 Dec 1719 Jonathan Sanborn (LND p604)
5. **DOROTHY**, b 27 Oct 1698: d 10 Sep 1757 (LND p793): m(1) 15 May 1721 Jethro Batchelder: m(2) 13 Oct 1736 Abraham Moulton
6. **ABIAL**, b 22 Jul 1700: m Hampton Falls, NH 16 Dec 1725 Enoch Colby (LND 603)
7. **JEMIMA**, b 17 May 1702: m(1) Ipswich, MA (int) 15 Oct 1720 John Stacy Jr (IpVR): m (2) Ipswich, MA (int) 11 Nov 1743 Samuel Lord Jr (IpVR)
8. **SUSANNA**, b 20 Sep 1704: d Hampton Falls, NH 21 Jul 1776: m 19 Jul 1750 Joshua Blake (NEHGR 10:274)
9. **BENJAMIN**, b 1 Jun 1706: d.y.
10. **JUDITH**, b 26 Oct 1708: m Hampton Falls, NH 16 Dec 1725 Robert Quimby (LND p603)
11. **BENJAMIN**, b 7 Nov 1712: d (WP) 27 Dec 1752 (PRNH 3:516): m(1) 23 Dec 1733 Hannah Tilton: m(2) Hampton Falls, NH 1 Oct 1737 Dorothy (Tilton) Prescott (HFTR)

(by 2nd wife)

12. **EBENEZER**, b 10 Oct 1723: d (WP) 26 Mar 1746 Hampton, NH (PRNH 3:249)

JOHN SANBORN, b Hampton, NH 1683 son of John & Judith (Coffin) Sanborn (LND p604): d Kingston, NH (Est Adm) 4 Mar 1723/4 (PRNH 2:211): m Kingston, NH 1 Jan 1706/7 Mehitable Fifield (KTR), b Hampton, NH 9 Apr 1687 dau of Benjamin & Mary (Colcord) Fifield (HmVR p10). Mehitable m(2) Kingston, NH 10 Oct 1728 Jacob Morrill (NHGR 2:44).

John was granted 200 acres of land at a meeting of the freeholders of Kingston 30 Oct 1706.

Children: 1st 3 born Kingston, NH (KTR)

1. **TRISTRAM**, b 1 Oct 1710: m Kingston, NH 17 Dec 1730 Abigail Blake (KTR)
2. **ABIGAIL**, b 6 May 1713: d Kingston, NH 10 Mar 1802 (NHVR): m Kingston, NH 10 Feb 1735/6 Elisha Swett (NHGR 2:46)
3. **PAUL**, b 21 Feb 1713/4: m(1) Kingston, NH 14 Dec 1737 Mary Fifield (TAG 16:166): m (2) Kingston, NH 9 Dec 1746 Betsey Currier (KTR)
4. **MARY**, b 5 Sep 1719: m 2 Jun 1737 Jonathan Blake (DnTR)
5. **SARAH**, b 3 Dec 1721: d Kingston, NH 7 Feb 1812 (NHVR): m Kingston, NH 27 Aug 1741 John Dent (KTR)

JONATHAN SANBORN, b Hampton, NH 25 May 1672 son of John & Margaret (Page) Sanborn (HmVR p103): d Kingston, NH 20 Jun 1741 (KTR): m 4 Feb 1691/2 Elizabeth Sherburne (LND p604), b Portsmouth, NH 5 Feb 1671 dau of Samuel & Love (Hutchins) Sherburne (HmVR p84), d Kingston, NH 25 Apr 1755 a.83yrs (GI p24).

Jonathan was granted 200 acres of land at a meeting of the freeholders of Kingston 19 Dec 1700. His family belonged to Kingston in 1725 when Rev Clark took charge of the church.

Children: last 6 born Kingston, NH (KTR)

1. **ELIZABETH**, b Hampton, NH 27 Dec 1692 (HmVR p14): m Kingston, NH 14 Apr 1713 John Ladd (KTR)
2. **SAMUEL**, b Hampton, NH 7 Sep 1694 (HmVR p62): d 8 Apr 1765 (LND p604): m(1) Kingston, NH 19 Aug 1718 Elizabeth (Folsom) Colcord (KTR): m(2) Kingston, NH 4 Aug 1757 wid Elizabeth Pettengill (KTR)

3. **ACHAICUS**, bpt 9 May 1697 (LND p604): m (poss) Kingston, NH 10 Oct 1714 Thomas Dent (KTR)
4. **MARGARET**, b 20 Mar 1698 (HH p947): m Kingston, NH 9 Jan 1714 Moses Sleeper (KTR)
5. **JONATHAN**, b 28 Apr 1700 (HH p947): d (WP) 25 Jun 1760: m(1) Kingston, NH 31 Dec 1719 Theodate Sanborn (LND p604): m(2) Kingston, NH 8 Nov 1757 Mrs Hannah Griffin (NHGR 3:89)
6. **LOVE**, b 30 Aug 1702: d Stafford Springs, CT Mar 1725 (LND p604): m Kingston, NH 8 Jan 1719/20 Rev John Graham (KTR)
7. **DOROTHY**, b 30 Aug 1705: d Kingston, NH Nov 1706 (KTR)
8. **DOROTHY**, b 22 Aug 1706:
9. **SARAH**, b 18 Apr 1708: m Thomas Rollins (LND p604)
10. **JOHN**, b 19 Dec 1710: d Kingston, NH Feb 1710 (KTR)
11. **BENJAMIN**, b 22 Jan 1711: d Kingston, NH 7 Apr 1718 (KTR)
12. **MARY**, b 7 Dec 1713: m Kingston, NH 14 Dec 1732 Peter Sanborn (KTR)

JONATHAN SANBORN, b 28 Apr 1700 son of Jonathan & Elizabeth (Sherburne) Sanborn (HH p947): d Kingston, NH (WP) 25 Jun 1760 (PRNH 6:563): m (1) Kingston, NH 31 Dec 1719 Theodate Sanborn (LND p604), b 1696 dau of Benjamin & Sarah (Worcester) Sanborn (LND p603), d Kingston, NH 10 Oct 1756 (NHVR): m(2) Kingston, NH 8 Nov 1757 Mrs Hannah Griffin (NHGR 3:89).

Jonathan & his family belonged to Kingston in 1725 when Rev Clark took charge of the church.

Children: born Kingston, NH (KTR)

1. **TIMOTHY**, b 15 Aug 1720: d Kingston, NH (bur) 22 Mar 1794 (NHVR): m Kingston, NH 8 May 1745/6 Alice Quimby (NHGR 3:42)
2. **SARAH**, bpt 20 Jan 1723: d Kingston, NH (prob) 9 Oct 1728 (NHGR 2:131)
3. **LOVE**, b 10 Jun 1726: d Sandown, NH 10 Aug

1767 (SdTR): m Kingston, NH 5 Dec 1744 Reuben Clough (NHGR 3:41)
4. **SAMUEL**, b 12 Mar 1730: m(1) Kingston, NH 7 Feb 1751 Hannah Tucker (KTR): m(2) 18 Mar 1767 Mary Barnes
5. **JONATHAN**, b 1732: d Kingston, NH 23 Aug 1735 (NHGR 3:37)
6. **WORCESTER**, b 3 Jun 1734: d 20 Apr 1794: m Kingston, NH 26 Oct 1756 Hannah Fowler (NHGR 3:89)
7. **(CHILD)**, d Kingston, NH 30 Nov 1735 a.2 hrs old (NHGR 3:38)
8. **JOANNA**, b 3 Jul 1736: m Kingston, NH 10 Apr 1755 Robert Crawford (NHGR 3:88)
9. **JONATHAN**, b 23 Nov 1738: d Kingston, NH Mar 1782 (NHVR): m(1) Kingston, NH 15 Dec 1761 Sarah James (KTR): m(2) Kingston, NH 26 Jan 1768 Mary Swett (KTR)

JONATHAN SANBORN, b Hampton Falls, NH 18 Feb 1714 son of Richard & Elizabeth (Batchelder) Sanborn (HFTR): d 20 May 1790 (Sanborn Gen p124): m Kingston, NH 13 Feb 1735 Mary Batchelder (KTR), b Hampton Falls, NH 20 Dec 1715 dau of John & Abigail (Cram) Batchelder (HFTR), d 18 May 1790.

In 1738 Jonathan signed a petition for a grant of land in Kingston.

Children: 1st 6 born Kingston, NH (KTR)
1. **JOHN**, b 8 Sep 1736: m Kingston, NH 17 Jan 1760 Sarah Elkins (NHGR 3:91)
2. **JETHRO**, b 20 Nov 1738: m Kingston, NH 27 Sep 1763 Abigail Elkins (NHGR 3:129)
3. **REBECCA**, b 10 Jun 1744: d Kingston, NH 12 Jul 1746 (KTR)
4. **PHINEAS**, b 17 Mar 1747: d Danville, NH 11 Jul 1773 (DnTR): m Danville, NH 2 Mar 1767 Mary Adams (DnTR)
5. **JOSIAH**, b 17 Oct 1750
6. **MARY**, b 29 Dec 1754: m Danville, NH 7 Dec 1769 Jedediah Philbrick (DNTR)
7. **JONATHAN**, b Danville, NH 4 Mar 1760 (Dn TR): m Danville, NH Dec 1784 Anne Batch-

elder (DnTR)

NATHANIEL SANBORN, b Hampton, NH 27 Jan 1665 son of John & Mary (Tuck) Sanborn (HmVR p98): d Hampton Falls, NH 9 Nov 1723 (NEHGR 10:273): m (1) Hampton, NH 3 Dec 1691 Rebecca Prescott (Hm VR p78), b Hampton, NH 15 Apr 1673 dau of James & Mary (Boulter) Prescott (HmVR p104), d Hampton, NH 10 Aug 170_ (HmVR p121): m(2) bef 1709 Sarah Nason (LND p604), b abt 1663 dau of Richard & Shuah (Colcord) Nason, d 1 Sep 1748 (Sanborn Gen p85).

Nathaniel was an original grantee of Kingston in 1694.

Children: born Hampton, NH (HmVR)
(by 1st wife)
1. **RICHARD**, b 27 Feb 1692/3: d 14 Sep 1773: m(1) 21 Jan 1713 Elizabeth Batchelder: m (2) 13 Jul 1753 Judith (Gove) Prescott
2. **JAMES**, b 6 Aug 1696: d 30 Oct 1784: m 18 Jan 1720 Elizabeth Leavitt (NEHGR 10:274)
3. **RACHEL**, b 4 Oct 1698: m 4 Dec 1718 Thomas Ward (NEHGR 10:274)
4. **JEREMIAH**, b 10 Feb 1700/1
5. **ABIGAIL**, b 22 Feb 1702/3: m 1 Aug 1723 Luther Morgan (NEHGR 10:274)

(by 2nd wife)
6. **NATHAN**, b 27 Jun 17__: m 1733 Catherine Sattalee (Sanborn Gen p100)
7. **JACOB**, b 7 May 1711: m 29 Dec 1731 Amy Sanborn (NEHGR 10:274)
8. **ELIPHAZ**, b 10 Dec 1712
9. **NATHANIEL**, b 10 Nov 1714
10. **JEDEDIAH**, b 10 Jun 1717: m Hampton Falls, NH 28 Jun 1737 Mary Rogers
11. **DANIEL**, b 31 Dec 1719

SAMUEL SANBORN, b Hampton, NH 7 Sep 1694 son of Jonathan & Elizabeth (Sherburne) Sanborn (HmVR p62): d 8 Apr 1765 (LND p604): m(1) Kingston, NH 19 Aug 1718 Elizabeth (Folsom) Colcord (KTR), dau of Peter & Susanna (Mills) Folsom (LND p238), d Kingston, NH 8 Apr 1756 (KTR): m

(2) Kingston, NH 4 Aug 1757 Elizabeth Pettengill (KTR), d Kingston, NH 16 Oct 1765 (KTR).

Samuel & his family belonged to Kingston in 1725 when Rev Clark took charge of the church.

Children: born Kingston, NH (KTR)

1. **BENJAMIN**, b 20 May 1719: d Salisbury, NH 7 Jan 1806: m(1) Kingston, NH 3 Apr 1746 Dorothy Ladd (KTR): m(2) Rebecca ____
2. **DOROTHY**, b 3 May 1721: m(1) Kingston, NH 10 Aug 1741 Thomas Dearborn (NHGR 3:41): m(2) Samuel Emerson (DAR 1:221)
3. **ELIZABETH**, b 7 Apr 1723: m Kingston, NH 7 Apr 1748 John Mudget (NHGR 3:43)

TRISTRAM SANBORN, b son of John & Judith (Coffin) Sanborn (LND p604): d Kingston, NH (WP) 8 Mar 1771 (PRNH 5:264,566): m Kingston, NH 25 Apr 1711 Margaret Taylor (KTR), dau of William & Margaret (Bean) Taylor (LND p676), d Kingston, NH 1771 (GI p27).

Tristram was taken in & made a freeholder in Kingston 30 Apr 1705. He was granted 200 acres of land at a meeting of the freeholders 30 Oct 1706.

Children: born Kingston, NH (KTR)

1. **PETER**, b 25 May 1713: d Kingston, NH 15 Jan 1810 (NHVR): m Kingston, NH 14 Dec 1732 Mary Sanborn (KTR)
2. **JETHRO**, b 20 Dec 1715: d Kingston, NH 30 May 1717 (KTR)
3. **ABRAHAM**, b 2 Mar 1716/7: d Kingston, NH 21 Feb 1780 (NHVR): m Kingston, NH 6 Jan 1736/7 Abigail Clifford (KTR)
4. **TRISTRAM**, b 2 Feb 1718: d Kingston, NH (bur) 19 Oct 1789 (NHVR): m Kingston, NH 28 Sep 1742 Hannah Stevens (KTR)
5. **JETHRO**, b 2 Mar 1720: m Kingston, NH 14 Sep 1744/5 Elizabeth Sanborn (NHGR 3:42)
6. **WILLIAM**, b 1 May 1723: d Kingston, NH (bur) 25 May 1810 (NHVR): m(1) Kingston, NH 6 Oct 1750 Mary Sleeper (KTR): m(2) Kingston, NH 3 Jun 1774 Mrs Elizabeth

Weare (KTR): m(3) Kingston, NH Oct 1788 wid Elizabeth Chase (NHGR 3:133)
7. **(CHILD)**, d Kingston, NH 23 Sep 1727 (NHGR 2:131)
8. **JUDITH**, d Kingston, NH 8 Oct 1730 (NHGR 2:131)
9. **(DAU)**, d Kingston, NH 17 Jun 1733 (NHGR 2:133)

TRISTRAM SANBORN, b Kingston, NH 1 Oct 1710 son of John & Mehitable (Fifield) Sanborn (KTR): m Kingston, NH 17 Dec 1730 Abigail Blake (KTR), bpt Hampton, NH 16 Oct 1709 dau of Moses & Abigail (Smith) Blake (HH p603).

Children: born Kingston, NH (KTR)
1. **JOHN**, b 25 Nov 1731: m(1) Kingston, NH 11 Jan 1753 Elizabeth Clifford (KChR): m(2) Kingston, NH 25 Oct 1759 Elizabeth Snow (NHGR 3:91)
2. **DEBORAH**, b 27 Jan 1733/4: m Kingston, NH 8 Nov 1753 John Tucker (NHGR 3:86)
3. **LYDIA**, b 15 Aug 1736: d Kingston, NH 27 Nov 1757 (NHVR)
4. **HANNAH**, b 12 Aug 1740: d Kingston, NH 9 Oct 1743 (KTR)
5. **MOSES**, b 17 Jul 1742: d 27 Jun 1821 (NHPR 73:29): m Deliverance ____
6. **SIMON**, b 20 Dec 1744: d Kingston, NH 28 Nov 1749 (KTR)
7. **ELISHA**, b 8 Dec 1748: d Kingston, NH 20 Nov 1749 (KTR)
8. **SIMON**, b 2 Feb 1752: d 1812 (DAR 1:591): m(1) ___: m(2) 27 Apr 1795 Anna Randall

BENJAMIN SAWYER, b (poss) Newbury, MA 2 Mar 1716 son of Benjamin & Elizabeth (Jameson) Sawyer (NVR): d bef 28 Oct 1757 (Bean Gen p117): m Kingston, NH 23 Nov 1737 Mary Bean (KTR), bpt Kingston, NH 21 Apr 1728 dau of Samuel & Sarah (_) Bean (NHGR 2:48).

Children: born Kingston, NH (KTR)
1. **BENJAMIN**, b 27 Aug 1738: d Kingston, NH

17 Sep 1738 (NHVR)

2. **MARY**, b 25 Sep 1739
3. **BENJAMIN**, b 29 Apr 1742
4. **JOHN**, b 27 Aug 1751: d Kingston, NH 28 Oct 1757 (NHVR)

GIDEON SAWYER, b Newbury, MA 15 Dec 1719 son of Josiah & Tirzah (Bartlett) Sawyer (NVR): d Danville, NH 26 Dec 1806 (CG p40): m Newbury, MA 25 Dec 1746 Sarah Bartlett (NVR), b Amesbury, MA 19 Aug 1724 dau of Joseph & Sarah (Hoyt) Bartlett (AVR), d Danville, NH 3 Mar 1797 (CG p40).

Children: born Kingston, NH (KTR)

1. **SARAH**, b 12 Jun 1748: bpt Newbury, MA 7 Aug 1748 (NVR): d Kingston, NH 24 May 1765 (KTR)
2. **GIDEON**, b 13 Oct 1751: bpt Newbury, MA 27 Nov 1751 (NVR)
3. **JAMES**, b 30 Jan 1755: bpt Newbury, MA 4 May 1755 (NVR)
4. **JOTHAM**, b 15 May 1757
5. **HANNAH**, b 16 May 1760: bpt Newbury, MA 6 Jul 1760 (NVR): d Danville, NH 4 May 1820 (CG p40)
6. **TAMAR**, b 8 Oct 1762: bpt Newbury, MA 7 Nov 1762 (NVR)
7. **REUBEN**, b 8 Sep 1765

JOSEPH SAWYER, b Newbury, MA 19 Nov 1706 son of Joshua & Elizabeth (_) Sawyer (NVR): d Kingston, NH 15 Jul 1748 (NHVR); WP 31 Aug 1748 (PRNH 3:563): m Newbury, MA 1 Dec 1729 Dorothy Brown (NVR), b Newbury, MA 10 Aug 1712 dau of Thomas & Elizabeth (Berry) Brown (NVR). Dorothy m(2) Kingston, NH 25 May 1749 John Young (NHGR 3:44). She m(3) Kingston, NH 12 Feb 1760 Thomas Thompson (NHGR 3:91).

Joseph & his wife Dorothy were admitted to the Kingston Church 4 Aug 1739.

Children: 1st 3 born Salisbury, MA (SVR)

1. **(SON)**, b 3 Dec 1733

2. **MIRIAM**, b 5 Nov 1735
3. **ELIZABETH**, b 27 Jul 1738: m Kingston, NH 30 Dec 1757 Joseph Brown (NHGR 3:89)
4. **DOROTHY**, b Kingston, NH 14 Dec 1740 (KTR)
5. **JOSEPH**, bpt Kingston, NH 5 Jun 1743 (KC hR): d Kingston, NH 31 Oct 1745 (NHVR)
6. **JUDITH**, b Kingston, NH 6 Oct 1745 (KTR): bpt 1 Dec 1745 (NHGR 5:153)
7. **SARAH**, b Kingston, NH 13 Oct 1748 (KTR)

EDWARD SCRIBNER, b Kingston, NH 27 Apr 1711 son of Thomas & Hannah (Welch) Scribner (KTR): m Kingston, NH 8 May 1735 Rachel Webster (KTR), b Kingston, NH 17 Mar 1710 dau of Ebenezer & Hannah (Judkins) Webster (KTR).

Children: born Kingston, NH (KTR)

1. **HANNAH**, b 23 Nov 1735
2. **THOMAS**, b 1 Jan 1737/8
3. **JOHN**, b 8 Sep 1740
4. **EDWARD**, b 16 Dec 1742: d aft 1791: m(1) 31 Oct 1763 Shuah Bean (TAG 19:94): m(2) Eunice Stevens (DAR 1:600)
5. **BENJAMIN**, b 14 Nov 1745
6. **EBENEZER**, b 21 Jul 1748: d Kingston, NH 10 Aug 1750 (KTR)

SAMUEL SCRIBNER, b Kingston, NH 29 Apr 1716 son of Thomas & Hannah (Welch) Scribner (KTR): d 5 Feb 1794 (DAR 1:600): m Kingston, NH 4 Nov 1740 Hannah Webster (KTR), b Kingston, NH 1721/2 dau of Ebenezer & Hannah (Judkins) Webster (NEHGR 9:160).

Samuel & his wife were admitted to the Kingston Church 18 Apr 1742.

Children: born Kingston, NH (KTR)

1. **SUSANNA**, b 29 Oct 1741
2. **SAMUEL**, b 28 Dec 1743: d aft 1810: m Mary Rayno (DAR 1:600)
3. **JOSEPH**, b 12 Feb 1746: d Kingston, NH 12 Feb 1746 (KTR)
4. **IDDO**, b 12 Feb 1746: d Kingston, NH 9 Mar 1746/7 (KTR)

5. **HANNAH**, b 1 Feb 1747/8
6. **JOSIAH**, b 11 Jul 1750
7. **IDDO**, b 11 Nov 1752: d 5 Feb 1831 (DAR 1: 600): m(1) 30 Dec 1773 Judith Brown: m(2) Mrs Huldah Jewett
8. **EBENEZER**, b 28 Mar 1755
9. **MARY**, b 5 Oct 1759: d Kingston, NH 12 Aug 1764 (KTR)
10. **ELIZABETH**, b 14 Aug 1762

THOMAS SCRIBNER, son of John & Mary (_) Scribner (LND p615): d Kingston, NH 30 Mar 1718; (WP) 4 Jun 1718 (PRNH 2:31): m(1) Kingston, NH 25 Dec 1702 Sarah Clifford (KTR), b Hampton, NH 30 Oct 1673 dau of John & Sarah (Godfrey) Clifford (HmVR p105), d Kingston, NH 5 Jan 1706/7 (KTR): m(2) Kingston, NH 4 Feb 1707/8 Hannah Welch (KTR), b abt 1680 (prob) dau of Philip & Hannah (Haggert) Welch (LND p734). Hannah m(2) Charles Hunt (LND p363).

Thomas was granted a lot in Kingston 10 Jul 1702. He also was granted 200 acres of land at a meeting of the freeholders 30 Oct 1706.

Children: born Kingston, NH (KTR)
(by 1st wife)
1. **JOHN**, b 6 Dec 1703
2. **DEBORAH**, b 7 Sep 1705: m Kingston, NH 29 Dec 1726 Joseph Welch (KTR)

(by 2nd wife)
3. **SARAH**, b 18 Nov 1707/8: d Kingston, NH 9 Mar 1709 (KTR)
4. **ELIZABETH**, b 1 May 1709: m Kingston, NH 13 Nov 1729 Peter Pattee (NHGR 2:45)
5. **EDWARD**, b 27 Apr 1711: m Kingston, NH 8 May 1735 Rachel Webster (KTR)
6. **SAMUEL**, b 29 Mar 1713: d Kingston, NH 31 Mar 1715 (KTR)
7. **SAMUEL**, b 29 Apr 1716: d 5 Feb 1794: m Kingston, NH 4 Nov 1740 Hannah Webster (KTR)
8. **(CHILD)**, b Sep 1718 (PRNH 2:32) - **MARY** dau of Thomas Scribner of Kingston, deceased, m Amesbury, MA 27 Jul 1738 Ben-

jamin Hoeg (AVR)

JOSEPH SECOMBE, son of Peter & Hannah (Willis) Secombe (LND p616): d Kingston, NH 15 Sep 1760 (KTR): m Kingston, NH 16 Jan 1737/8 Mary Thuriel (KTR).

Joseph was a worthy minister of the Gospel in Kingston for more then 20 years according to the Town Records.

EPHRAIM SEVERANCE, b Salisbury, MA 8 Apr 1656 son of John & Abigail (Kimball) Severance (SVR): d Kingston, NH (prob) 24 Oct 1734 (NHGR 2:133): m Salisbury, MA 9 Nov 1682 Lydia Morrill (SVR), b Salisbury, MA 8 Mar 1660 dau of Abraham & Sarah (Clement) Morrill (SVR), d Kingston, NH (prob) 6 Feb 1727/8 (NHGR 2:131).

Ephraim had land laid out to him in Kingston 17 Aug 1714. He belonged to Kingston in 1725 when Rev Clark took charge of the church.

Children: born Salisbury, MA (SVR)

1. **ABIGAIL**, b 29 Aug 1683: m(1) Salisbury, MA 30 Nov 1705 Joseph Abbey (SVR): m(2) Salisbury, MA 11 Dec 1707 Philip Greeley (SVR)
2. **MARY**, b 2 Jul 1685: m Salisbury, MA 14 Mar 1711/2 Abraham Watson (SVR)
3. **LYDIA**, b 15 Jan 1687
4. **EPHRAIM**, b 2 Dec 1689: m Kingston, NH 25 Nov 1714 Mary Burnham (KTR)
5. **DINAH**, b 3 Sep 1692: m Salisbury, MA 6 Jan 1713/4 John Dow (SVR)
6. **EBENEZER**, b 29 Nov 1694: m Kingston, NH 8 Jan 1716/7 Anna Footes (KTR) Fitts?
7. **SARAH**, b 7 Feb 1697/8
8. **JONATHAN**, b 21 Apr 1700: m Salisbury, MA 24 Feb 1725/6 Catherine Tucker (SVR)
9. **HANNAH**, b 13 Dec 1702
10. **LYDIA**, b 9 Sep 1705

EPHRAIM SEVERANCE JR, b Salisbury, MA 2 Dec 1689 son of Ephraim & Lydia (Morrill) Severance (SVR): d Kingston, NH 31 May 1759 (NHVR): m

Kingston, NH 25 Nov 1714 Mary Burnham (KTR). Ephraim's family belonged to Kingston in 1725 when Rev Clark took charge of the church.

Children: born Kingston, NH (KTR & NHGR)

1. **MARY**, b 19 Dec 1715: m Kingston, NH 5 Apr 1742 Elias Rano (NHGR 3:41)
2. **BENJAMIN**, bpt 11 Sep 1726: m Kingston, NH 12 Feb 1744/5 Ruth Long (NHGR 3:42)
3. **ELIZABETH**, bpt 11 Sep 1726
4. **JOSEPH**, bpt 11 Sep 1726
5. **JOHN**, bpt 11 Sep 1726
6. **EPHRAIM**, bpt 23 Jul 1727: d Kingston, NH 20 May 1757 (NHVR): m Kingston, NH 25 Oct 1749 Elizabeth Swett (KTR)
7. **JACOB**, bpt 27 Jul 1729: m Kingston, NH 22 Aug 1753 Sarah George (NHGR 3:86)
8. **SAMUEL**, bpt 9 May 1731

EPHRAIM SEVERANCE JR, bpt Kingston, NH 23 Jul 1727 son of Ephraim & Mary (Burnham) Severance (NHGR 2:47): d Kingston, NH 20 May 1757 (NHVR): m Kingston, NH 25 Oct 1749 Elizabeth Swett (KTR), b Kingston, NH 24 Dec 1724 dau of John & Judith (Young) Swett (KTR). Elizabeth m(2) Kingston, NH 25 Jul 1758 Ebenezer Watson (KTR).

Children: born Kingston, NH (KTR)

1. **JOHN**, b 3 Sep ____; bpt 9 Sep 1750 (NHGR 5:159)
2. **MOSES**, b 19 Mar 1752
3. **PETER**, b 6 Mar 1754: d 31 Jul 1835: m 20 Sep 1779 Abigail (Greeley) Pettengill
4. **JUDITH**, b 25 Mar 1756: m Israel Clifford (NHPR 75:94)

JONATHAN SEVERANCE, b Salisbury, MA 21 Apr 1700 son of Ephraim & Lydia (Morrill) Severance (SVR): d Kingston, NH (prob) 14 May 1786 a.86 yrs (NHVR): m Salisbury, MA 24 Feb 1725/6 Catherine Tucker (SVR), dau of Benoni & Ebenezer (Nichols) Tucker (Putnam's Mag 3:2), d Kingston, NH (bur) 8 Nov 1791 a.90yrs (NHVR).

Children:
1. **BENJAMIN**, b Kingston, NH 22 Jan 1731 (KTR): m Kingston, NH 5 Jun 1755 Judith Nichols (KTR)
2. **LYDIA**, d Kingston, NH 6 Sep 1737 (NHVR)
3. **JONATHAN** (prob), m Kingston, NH 5 Sep 1754 Tryphena Nichols (KTR)
4. **LYDIA**, b abt 1739: bpt (as adult) Kingston, NH 5 Aug 1758: m Kingston, NH 19 Sep 1758 Jonathan Sanborn (NHGR 3:90)

BENJAMIN SHAW, b Hampton, NH 15 Mar 1727 son of Edward & Mary (Johnson) Shaw (HmVR p146): m Kingston, NH 4 Aug 1747 Rebecca Follinsby (KTR).

Children: last 9 born Sandown, NH (SdTR)
1. **MARY**, b Kingston, NH 13 Jan 1748/9 (KTR)
2. **FOLLINSBY**, b Kingston, NH 17 Dec 1750 (KTR): m Mary Edmonds
3. **ANNA**, b 6 Jan 1753
4. **EDWARD**, b 17 Oct 1755: bpt Kingston, NH 26 Nov 1755 (NHVR)
5. **JOSHUA**, b 6 Dec 1757: bpt Sandown, NH 29 Oct 1758 (NHVR)
6. **BENJAMIN**, b 6 Sep 1759: bpt Kingston, NH 23 Sep 1759 (NHVR): m Sarah Sanborn
7. **THOMAS**, b 4 Apr 1762
8. **NATHANIEL**, b 12 Mar 1764
9. **HANNAH**, b 9 Apr 1766: m ___ Sanborn
10. **ABIGAIL**, b 6 Oct 1768
11. **JOSEPH**, b 3 May 1772

ICHABOD SHAW, b Hampton, NH 27 Feb 1722 son of Edward & Mary (Johnson) Shaw (HmVR p146): m Kingston, NH 15 Dec 1742 Sarah Moulton (KTR), b (prob) Hampton, NH 24 Mar 1721/2 dau of Robert & Sarah (Lamphrey) Moulton (HmVR p151).

Ichabod was admitted to the Kingston Church 17 Apr 1743 & dismissed to Sandown 25 Nov 1759.

Children: born Kingston, NH (KTR)
1. **SARAH**, b 21 May 1757
2. **ABIGAIL**, b 14 Apr 1759: d Kingston, NH 27

Apr 1759 (KTR)
3. **MOLLY**, b 21 May 1763: d Kingston, NH 4 Jun 1763 (KTR)
4. **DANIEL** (adopted), bpt Kingston, NH 25 Jan 1753 (NHGR 6:29)

JACOB SILLOWAY, b Amesbury, MA 2 Dec 1725 son of John & Mary (Pressy) Silloway (AVR): m Kingston, NH 3 Jun 1748 Alice Webster (KTR), b Kingston, NH 10 Jan 1724/5 dau of Thomas & Mary (Greeley) Webster (KTR).
 Jacob was admitted to the Kingston Church 3 Apr 1742.

Children: born Kingston, NH (KTR)
1. **(CHILD)**, d Kingston, NH 8 Mar 1749 (NHVR)
2. **JOHN**, b 23 Jun 1750
3. **BENJAMIN WEBSTER**, b 21 Sep 1752: d aft 1800: m Mary Severance
4. **JACOB**, b 11 Dec 1755
5. **GREELEY**, b 11 Aug 1759

JOHN SILLOWAY (OSILLAWAY), probably son of Daniel Silloway: d Kingston, NH 21 Mar 1741 (NHVR): m Amesbury, MA 30 Mar 1715 Mary Pressy (AVR), b Amesbury, MA 7 Feb 1693/4 dau of William & Susanna (Jameson) Pressy (AVR).
 In 1730 John signed a petition regarding the township of Kingston.

Children: born Amesbury, MA (AVR)
1. **WILLIAM**, b 29 Apr 1717: m Kingston, NH 11 Nov 1740 Abigail Sleeper (NHGR 3:40)
2. **MARY**, b 7 Mar 1720/1
3. **JOHN**, b 22 Feb 1722/3
4. **JACOB**, b 2 Dec 1725: m Kingston, NH 3 Jun 1748 Alice Webster (KTR)

WILLIAM SILLOWAY, b Amesbury, MA 29 Apr 1717 son of John & Mary (Pressy) Silloway (AVR): d Kingston, NH 15 Dec 1764 (KTR): m Kingston, NH Sep 1740 Abigail Sleeper (KTR), b Kingston, NH 29 Apr 1720 dau of Hezekiah & Elizabeth (Fifield) Sleeper (KTR).

In 1738 William signed a petition for a grant of land in Kingston.

Children: born Kingston, NH (KTR & NHGR)
1. **HEZEKIAH**, b 10 Oct 1741: bpt 22 Nov 1741
2. **MARY**, bpt 18 Mar 1743/4
3. **JOHN**, bpt 5 Jul 1747: d Kingston, NH 27 Sep 1747 (NHVR)
4. **MARY**, d Kingston, NH 7 Oct 1747 (NHVR)
5. **WILLIAM**, bpt 26 May 1751: d Kingston, NH 10 Sep 1752 (NHVR)
6. **ABIGAIL**, b 11 Jun 1753: d 9 May 1838: m Abraham Fifield (TAG 19:94)
7. **WILLIAM**, b 29 Sep 1756: d Kingston, NH 10 Mar 1764 (KTR)
8. **JOHN**, b 13 Jul 1759
9. **MARY**, b 13 Jul 1759
10. **BETTY**, b 11 Jan 1763: d Kingston, NH 18 Mar 1764 (KTR)
11. **WILLIAM**, b 17 Mar 1765

AARON SLEEPER, b Hampton, NH 20 Feb 1660 son of Thomas & Joanna (?Lee) Sleeper (HmVR p93): d Kingston, NH 9 May 1732 (NHGR 2:132): m Hampton, NH 23 May 1682 Elizabeth Shaw (HmVR p78), b Hampton, NH 23 Oct 1664 dau of Joseph & Elizabeth (Partridge) Shaw (HmVR p96), d Kingston, NH 27 Oct 1708 (KTR).

Aaron was granted 200 acres of land in Kingston at a meeting of the freeholders 19 Dec 1700. His family belonged to Kingston in 1725 when Rev Clark took charge of the church.

Children: 1st 12 born Hampton, NH (HmVR)
1. **ELIZABETH** (prob), b abt 1683: m Joseph Young (Hartford Times 7-19-41)
2. **MOSES**, b 22 Jan 1684/5: d Kingston, NH 13 Jan 1754 (NHVR): m Kingston, NH 9 Jan 1714 Margaret Sanborn (KTR)
3. **THOMAS**, b 3 Nov 1686: m Kingston, NH 6 Dec 1714 Mary Colcord (KTR)
4. **AARON**, b 23 Jul 1688: m Sarah ____
5. **JOSEPH** (twin), b 14 Jun 1690: d Kingston, NH 5 Apr 1753 (NHVR): m Kingston, NH 31

Dec 1713 Sarah Hutchins (KTR)

6. **JOHN** (twin), b 14 Jun 1690: d bef 1727: m(1) Kingston, NH 5 Jun 1712 Ann Philbrick (KTR): m(2) 18 Jul 1717 Mary Towle (LND p638)
7. **SAMUEL**, b 1 Dec 1692
8. **ELISHA**, b 9 May 1694
9. **HEZEKIAH**, b 11 May 1696: d Kingston, NH 30 Sep 1722 (KTR): m Elizabeth Fifield (TAG 16:165)
10. **EBENEZER**, b 18 May 1697: d Hampton, NH 21 May 1698 (HmVR p119)
11. **JONATHAN**, b 17 Mar 1698/9
12. **ABIGAIL**, b 17 Apr 1700: m Hampton, NH 9 Nov 1721 Isaac Fellows (HH p707)
13. **MEHITABLE**, b Kingston, NH 25 Apr 1701 (KTR): m Eli Beede
14. **EBENEZER**, b Kingston, NH 24 Apr 1702 (KTR): d Brentwood, NH (WP) 26 Oct 1768 (PRNH 7:90): m Sarah Ward (LND p719)
15. **(DAU)**, b Kingston, NH 7 Jul 1704: d Kingston, NH 8 Aug 1704 (KTR)
16. **MARY**, b Kingston, NH 21 Feb 1705/6 (KTR): m Kingston, NH 4 Jan 1725 Elisha Winsley (KTR)
17. **ITHAMAR**, b Kingston, NH 15 Sep 1708: d Kingston, NH 10 Nov 1708 (KTR)

AARON SLEEPER JR, b Hampton, NH 23 Jul 1688 son of Aaron & Elizabeth (Shaw) Sleeper (HmVR p18): d Kingston, NH (Est Adm) 25 Apr 1753 (PRNH 4:368): m Sarah ___ (LND p637).

Aaron Jr had land laid out to him in Kingston 26 Jun 1721. In 1730 he signed a petition regarding the township of Kingston.

Children: born Kingston, NH (KTR)

1. **DANIEL**, b 9 May 1715
2. **EDWARD**, b 26 Oct 1719: d Kingston, NH 16 Mar 1811 a.91yrs (GI p29): m Kingston, NH 15 Sep 1746 Ann Clough (KTR)

BENJAMIN SLEEPER, b Kingston, NH 1 Mar 1716/7 son of Thomas & Mary (Colcord) Sleeper (KTR): d

Kingston, NH 3 Nov 1755 (NHVR): m Kingston, NH 30 Jun 1743 Abigail Coffin (KTR), b Dover, NH 16 Jul 1720 dau of Tristram & Jane (Heard) Coffin (DvVR p11). Abigail m(2) Kingston, NH 16 Nov 1758 Richard Jenness (NHGR 3:90).

Benjamin signed a petition in 1738 for a grant of land in Kingston.

Children: born Kingston, NH (KTR)

1. **TRISTRAM**, b 26 Jun 1744: d Rye, NH 26 Jan 1811 (Rye VR): m Rye, NH 18 Dec 1766 Ruth Tarlton (Rye VR)
2. **MARY**, b 25 Aug 1745: d Kingston, NH 19 Jul 1755 (NHVR)
3. **ABIGAIL**, b 24 Dec 1746: d Kingston, NH 18 Jul 1747 (KTR)
4. **THOMAS**, d Kingston, NH 26 Dec 1746 (NHVR)
5. **THOMAS**, b 11 Feb 1747/8: d Kingston, NH 24 Sep 1748 (KTR)
6. **BENJAMIN**, d Kingston, NH 7 Apr 1756 (NHVR)

DAVID SLEEPER, b Kingston, NH 18 Nov 1721 son of Moses & Margaret (Sanborn) Sleeper (KTR): d 18 Oct 1780 (DAR 1:621): m(1) Kingston, NH 24 Nov 1743 Margaret Scribner (KTR), dau of Samuel & Anna (Taylor) Scribner (LND p615): d Kingston, NH 8 Jan 1751/2 (KTR): m(2) Sandown, NH 31 Mar 1752 Ruth James (SdTR), b 29 Mar 1735 dau of Edmund & Priscilla (_) James, d 6 Jul 1823 (Hist of Bristol, NH p389).

Children: nos.4-17 born Sandown, NH (SdTR)

(by 1st wife)

1. **GIDEON**, b Kingston, NH 25 Jul 1744: d 27 Feb 1829 (DAR 2:193): m(1) Danville, NH 28 Feb 1769 Elizabeth Hoyt (NEGHR 58: 121): m(2) Sarah Phillips
2. **DAVID**, b Kingston, NH 8 Sep 1748 (KTR): m Rachel Tilton
3. **PETER**, b Kingston, NH 23 May 1749 (KTR)

(by 2nd wife)

4. **EDMUND**, b 17 Mar 1753: d 1 Jun 1838: m (1) 11 Mar 1779 Lydia Colby: m(2) 7 May

1803 Elizabeth Worthen (HC p592)
5. **NATHAN**, b 12 Apr 1754
6. **MOSES**, b 4 Sep 1755: d 14 May 1838 (DAR 1:621): m Betty Colby
7. **MARGARET**, b 5 Feb 1757: d 13 Jan 1777
8. **MARY**, b 29 Sep 1758: m Theophilus Sanborn
9. **JOHN**, b 15 Apr 1760: d 4 Feb 1818: m 9 May 1785 Elizabeth Tilton
10. **DANIEL**, b 22 Feb 1762: m Dec 1790 Anna Tilton
11. **SAMUEL**, b 14 Feb 1764
12. **DAVID**, b 23 Nov 1765
13. **JETHRO**, b 18 Sep 1767
14. **JONATHAN**, b 6 Feb 1769: d 20 Nov 1775
15. **BENJAMIN**, b 17 Jan 1771: m 1796 Betsey Hill (HC p592)
16. **JOSIAH**, b 14 Jul 1772
17. **RUTH**, b 4 Mar 1774: m James Ingalls
18. **NATHAN**, b 13 Aug 1777
19. **JONATHAN**, b 8 Aug 1780: d 29 May 1805

EBENEZER SLEEPER, b Kingston, NH 24 Apr 1702 son of Aaron & Elizabeth (Shaw) Sleeper (KTR): d Brentwood, NH (WP) 26 Oct 1768 (PRNH 7:90): m Sarah Ward (LND p719), b Hampton, NH 20 May 1702 dau of Thomas & Rachel (Sanborn) Ward (HmVR p26).

Ebenezer belonged to Kingston in 1725 when Rev Clark took charge of the church.

Children: (NHGR)
1. **STEPHEN**, (PRNH 7:91)
2. **ELIZABETH**, m Kingston, NH 23 Aug 1744 John Clifford Jr (KChR)
3. **MEHITABLE**, m John Sanborn (PRNH 7:91)
4. **ANNE**, d Kingston, NH 10 Apr 1728
5. **SARAH**, d Kingston, NH Jul 1731
6. **THOMAS**, bpt Kingston, NH 6 Aug 1732
7. **MARY**, bpt Kingston, NH 13 Oct 1734
8. **ABIGAIL**, bpt Kingston, NH 8 Aug 1736

HEZEKIAH SLEEPER, b Hampton, NH 11 May 1696 son of Aaron & Elizabeth (Shaw) Sleeper (HmVR p15): d Kingston, NH 30 Sep 1722 (KTR): m Elizabeth

Fifield (TAG 16:165), b Hampton, NH 25 Nov 1698 dau of John & Abigail (Weare) Fifield (HmVR p 68). Elizabeth m(2) Kingston, NH abt 1725 Jonathan Webster (LND p787).

Children: born Kingston, NH (KTR)
1. **ELIZABETH**, b 28 Jun 1717
2. **ABIGAIL**, b 29 Apr 1720: m Kingston, NH Sep 1740 William Silloway (KTR)

HEZEKIAH SLEEPER, b Kingston, NH 17 Jan 1724/5 son of Joseph & Sarah (Hutchins) Sleeper (KTR): m Kingston, NH 7 May 1747 Martha Wood (KTR).

Children: born Kingston, NH (KTR)
1. **NEHEMIAH**, b 24 Jan 1747/8
2. **JOSEPH**, b 29 Dec 1750
3. **JONAS**, b 11 Feb 1754
4. **LUSE**, b 3 Apr 1757: d Kingston, NH 4 May 1759 (KTR)
5. **LUSE**, b 29 Dec 1759
6. **HEZEKIAH**, b Oct 1762: d Kingston, NH Oct 1762 (KTR)
7. **LOIS**, b 27 Aug 1763
8. **MARTHA**, b 26 Mar 1766
9. **HEZEKIAH**, b 7 May 1770

JOHN SLEEPER, b Hampton, NH 14 Jun 1690 son of Aaron & Elizabeth (Shaw) Sleeper (HmVR p12): d Kingston, NH (Est Adm) 6 Sep 1720 (PRNH 2:121): m(1) Kingston, NH 5 Jun 1712 Ann Philbrick (KTR), b Hampton, NH 12 Mar 1690/1 dau of Thomas & Mehitable (Ayers) Philbrick (HmVR p13), d Kingston, NH 30 Aug 1716 (KTR): m(2) 18 Jul 1717 Mary Towle (LND p638), b Hampton, NH 20 May 1695 dau of Benjamin & Sarah (Boaden) Towle (HmVR p63), d 1783. Mary m(2) Hampton, NH 29 Mar 1727 Thomas Page (HmVR p131).

John belonged to Kingston in 1725 when Rev Clark took charge of the church.

Children: born Kingston, NH (KTR)
1. **SAMUEL**, b 8 Apr 1713: m Kingston, NH 27 Dec 1738 Sarah French (KTR)

2. **JEDEDIAH**, b 7 Aug 1714
3. **JOHN**, b 5 May 1716: living 1758

JOSEPH SLEEPER, b Hampton, NH 14 Jun 1690 son of Aaron & Elizabeth (Shaw) Sleeper (HmVR p12): d Kingston, NH 5 Apr 1753 (NHVR); m Kingston, NH 31 Dec 1713 Sarah Hutchins (KTR), b Bradford, MA 2 Oct 1694 dau of John & Elizabeth (Hazeltine) Hutchins (BdVR).

Joseph had land laid out to him in Kingston 9 Mar 1711. He belonged to Kingston in 1725 when Rev Clark took charge of the church. In 1730 he signed a petition regarding the township of Kingston.

Children: born Kingston, NH (KTR)

1. **NEHEMIAH**, b 11 Nov 1714: d Kingston, NH 6 May 1730 (NHGR 2:131)
2. **LOVE**, b 20 Jun 1717: m Kingston, NH 29 Nov 1739 Joseph Haggit (NHGR 3:40)
3. **(SON**-eldest), d Kingston, NH 9 May 1732 (NHGR 2:132 - cannot be Hezekiah as he is mentioned in his father's will)
4. **HEZEKIAH**, b 17 Jan 1724/5: m Kingston, NH 7 May 1747 Martha Wood (KTR)
5. **WILLIAM**, bpt 11 Sep 1726 (NHGR 2:47): m (1) Kingston, NH 14 Mar 1745 Dorothy (Rowell) Blaisdell (KTR): m(2) Ruth Choate ? (PRNH 6:300)
6. **ANNE**, m Kingston, NH 31 Oct 1751 John Pearson (NHGR 3:45)

MOSES SLEEPER, b Hampton, NH 22 Jan 1684/5 son of Aaron & Elizabeth (Shaw) Sleeper (HmVR p16): d Kingston, NH 13 Jan 1754 (NHVR): m Kingston, NH 9 Jan 1714 Margaret Sanborn (KTR), b 20 Mar 1698 dau of Jonathan & Elizabeth (Sherburne) Sanborn (LND p604).

Moses was granted 200 acres of land in Kingston at a meeting of the freeholders 30 Oct 1706. He belonged to Kingston in 1725 when Rev Clark took charge of the church.

Children: born Kingston, NH (KTR)

1. **JOHN**, b 28 Jul 1715: d Brentwood, NH (WP) 27 May 1761 (PRNH 7:76): m Kingston, NH 11 Jan 1738/9 Apphia Sanborn (KTR)
2. **JONATHAN**, b 6 Dec 1716: m Kingston, NH 4 Nov 1740 Lydia Huntoon (NHGR 3:40)
3. **MOSES**, b 19 Nov 1719: m Kingston, NH 9 May 1744 Priscilla Smith (KChR)
4. **DAVID**, b 18 Nov 1721: d 18 Oct 1780 (DAR 1:621): m(1) Kingston, NH 24 Nov 1743 Margaret Scribner (KTR): m(2) Sandown, NH 31 Mar 1752 Ruth James (SdTR)
5. **ELIZABETH**, b 30 Aug 1723: m Kingston, NH 22 Nov 1744 Reuben Sanborn (NHGR 3:41)
6. **HENRY**, b 17 Feb 1725: d 16 Dec 1781: m Newbury, MA 29 Mar 1749 Sarah Morse (NVR)
7. **SAMUEL**, b 17 Apr 1727: m 31 Oct 1749 Hannah Batchelder
8. **MARY**, b 9 Mar 1729: m Kingston, NH 6 Oct 1750 William Sanborn (KTR)
9. **BENJAMIN**, b 25 Mar 1731: d Kingston, NH 18 Apr 1731 (NHGR 2:132)
10. **BENJAMIN**, b 14 Feb 1733: m(1) 9 Apr 1750 Hannah Hersey: m(2) Kingston, NH 9 Apr 1759 Hannah Lovering (NHGR 3:90)
11. **SHERBURNE**, b 16 Mar 1734: m Kingston, NH 7 Dec 1758 Hannah Clough (KTR)
12. **ANN**, b 7 Feb 1736: m abt 1754 Jonathan Beede
13. **RICHARD**, b 17 Apr 1738: d Kingston, NH 1 Apr 1813 (NHVR): m Kingston, NH 22 Apr 1762 Martha Fifield (KTR)
14. **LOVE**, b 22 Oct 1739: m Kingston, NH 22 Jun 1759 John Blake (NHGR 3:91)
15. **HEPZIBAH**, b 24 Mar 1742: m 1760 Samuel Lane

SAMUEL SLEEPER, b Kingston, NH 8 Apr 1713 son of John & Ann (Philbrick) Sleeper (KTR): d Sandown, NH 6 Dec 1802 a.89yrs (SdTR): m Kingston, NH 27 Dec 1738 Sarah French (KTR), b Kingston, NH 25 Sep 1715 dau of Nathaniel & Sarah (Judkins) French (KTR), d Sandown, NH 12 Aug 1794 (SdTR).

Samuel signed a petition in 1738 for a grant

of land in Kingston. He & his wife were admitted to the Kingston Church 2 Jan 1742.

Children: born Kingston, NH (KTR)
1. **JOHN**, bpt 7 Oct 1739 (NHGR 5:105)
2. **JOHN**, b 17 Apr 1741: m Sandown, NH 15 Apr 1761 Hannah Tucker (SdTR)
3. **ANN**, b 18 Jul 1743
4. **BENJAMIN**, b 18 Apr 1746: d 15 Oct 1820: m Judith Clough (DAR 1:621)
5. **SAMUEL** (twin), b 13 Apr 1749: d Kingston, NH 10 Jul 1749 (KTR)
6. **SARAH** (twin), b 13 Apr 1749: d Kingston, NH 1 May 1749 (KTR)
7. **NATHANIEL**, b 11 Nov 1750

THOMAS SLEEPER, b Hampton, NH 3 Nov 1686 son of Aaron & Elizabeth (Shaw) Sleeper (HmVR p16): d Kingston, NH (Est Adm) 30 Dec 1723 (PRNH 2: 202): m Kingston, NH 6 Dec 1714 Mary Colcord (KTR), b Hampton, NH 24 Mar 1697/8 dau of Samuel & Mary (Ayer) Colcord (HmVR p67). Mary m(2) Kingston, NH 5 May 1725 Ebenezer Eastman (KTR).

Thomas was taken in & made a freeholder of Kingston 30 Apr 1705. He was granted 200 acres of land at a meeting of the freeholders 30 Oct 1706. His widow belonged to the Kingston Church in 1725.

Children: born Kingston, NH (KTR)
1. **SAMUEL**, b 15 Jan 1715: d Kingston, NH 6 Mar 1715/6 (KTR)
2. **BENJAMIN**, b 1 Mar 1716/7: m Kingston, NH 30 Jun 1743 Abigail Coffin (KTR)
3. **THOMAS**, b 7 Apr 1720: d Kingston, NH 26 Dec 1746 (KTR)
4. **ELIZABETH**, b 8 Sep 1723

ABRAHAM SMITH, b Salisbury, MA 20 Nov 1705 son of Robert & Anne (Brown) Smith (SVR): d Gilmanton, NH Apr 1795 a 89yrs (GG p56): m(1) Salisbury, MA 22 Jan 1729/30 Mary Page (SVR), b Salisbury, MA 26 May 1706 dau of Joseph & Elizabeth (_) Page (SVR): m(2) Kingston, NH 2

Jun 1748 Dorothy Rowell (NHGR 3:43).
Abraham signed a petition in 1738 for a new parish in the easterly part of Kingston.

Children: bpt Kingston, NH (NHGR & KChR)
(by 1st wife)
1. **ANN**, b Kingston, NH 1 Dec 1729 (KTR): bpt 11 Apr 1731
2. **BENJAMIN**, bpt 8 Dec 1734: d 21 Feb 1825 (DAR 1:624): m Kingston, NH 11 Oct 1757 Meribah Tilton (KChR)

(by 2nd wife)
3. **ABRAHAM**, bpt Kingston, NH 16 Sep 1750

EZEKIEL SMITH, m Kingston, NH 11 Mar 1734 Elizabeth Roberts (NHGR 2:45), dau of John & Elizabeth (_) Roberts (PRNH 3:413).

Children: bpt Kingston, NH (NHGR)
1. **ALEXANDER**, bpt 28 May 1738
2. **HANNAH**, bpt 5 Jul 1741
3. **MERCY**, bpt 11 Nov 1744
4. **SARAH**, bpt 12 Oct 1746

ISAAC SMITH, d Kingston, NH 20 Aug 1756 (KTR); Est Adm 29 Dec 1756 (PRNH 5:561): m Kingston, NH 31 Oct 1745 Mehitable Buswell (KTR).
Isaac was admitted to the Kingston Church 13 Dec 1741.

Children: born Kingston, NH (KTR)
1. **JOSEPH**, b 2 Aug 1746
2. **JONATHAN**, b 24 Nov 1748
3. **MEHITABLE**, b 26 Feb 1750/1
4. **ELIZABETH**, b 11 Oct 1755: d Kingston, NH 8 Mar 1756 (KTR)

ITHIEL SMITH, probably son of Ithiel & Mary (_) Smith: d Brentwood, NH (Est Adm) 29 Sep 1756 (PRNH 5:495): m Catherine ___
Ithiel was admitted to the Kingston Church 28 Feb 1741. He was dismissed to Brentwood Jan 1751.

Children: bpt Kingston, NH (NHGR)
1. **ITHIEL**, bpt 22 Mar 1740/1: d Newry, ME 18 Jun 1821: m(1) Bathsheba Foot: m(2) Gorham, ME (int) 17 Jul 1779 Anna Bean
2. **PETER**, bpt 10 Jul 1743
3. **MOLLY**, bpt 22 Feb 1746/7
4. **ANNA**, bpt 23 Apr 1749
5. **HANNAH**, bpt 5 May 1751
6. **SUSANNAH**, (PRNH 5:497)

JOHN SMITH was admitted to the Kingston Church 17 May 1741 & dismissed to Hampton 1751.

Children: bpt Kingston, NH (NHGR)
1. **OLIVER**, bpt 22 Dec 1728
2. **THOMAS**, bpt 28 May 1732
3. **JOHN**, bpt 7 Apr 1734
4. **MARY**, bpt 30 Dec 1739
5. **DEBORAH**, bpt 30 Dec 1739
6. **SIMEON**, bpt 25 Apr 1742

JONATHAN SMITH, b Exeter, NH 9 Jan 1714/5 son of Jonathan & Mary (Ames) Smith (HE p43g): m Brentwood, NH 12 Apr 1739 Sarah Pearson (BtTR)
Jonathan & his wife Sarah were admitted to the Kingston Church 28 Dec 1740.

Children: 1st 6 bpt Kingston, NH (NHGR)
1. **SARAH**, bpt 4 Oct 1741
2. **LYDIA**, bpt 26 Aug 1744
3. **MARY**, bpt 24 May 1747
4. **JONATHAN**, bpt 16 Jul 1749
5. **BETTY**, bpt 13 Jul 1752
6. **PEARSON**, bpt 1 Jun 1755
7. **APPHIA**, b Brentwood, NH 20 May 1759 (BtTR)

NATHANIEL SMITH, b Exeter, NH 15 Sep 1695 son of Nicholas & Mary (Gordon) Smith (HE p43g): d Kingston, NH 6 Aug 1757 (PRNH 4:431): m Berwick, ME 16 Nov 1720 Elizabeth Stone (NEHGR 55: 311), b Kittery, ME 13 May 1694 dau of Daniel & Patience (Goodwin) Stone (KitVR p24), d Kingston, NH (Est Adm) 26 Sep 1757 (PRNH 6:145).

Nathaniel signed a petition in 1738 for a grant of land in Kingston.

Children: born Exeter, NH (HE p43g)

1. **MARY**, b 7 Dec 1721
2. **NATHANIEL**, b 17 Apr 1725
3. **PATIENCE**, b 24 Nov 1727: m Joseph Weare
4. **DANIEL**, b 13 Apr 1730: m Kingston, NH 30 Aug 1757 Hannah Colby (NHGR 3:89)
5. **ELIZABETH**, b 24 Feb 1731/2: m Nathaniel Gordon
6. **SARAH**, b 1 Mar 1733/4
7. **ANNA**, b 7 May 1740: bpt Kingston, NH 11 May 1739/40 (NHGR 5:106)

WILLIAM SMITH, b Salisbury, MA 6 May 1703 son of Robert & Anne (Brown) Smith (SVR): m Salisbury, MA 4 Jan 1727/8 Elizabeth Cilley (SVR), b Salisbury, MA 4 Aug 1705 dau of Benoni & Eleanor (Getchell) Cilley (SVR).

Elizabeth Smith wife of William was admitted to the 2nd Church of Christ in Kingston 13 Apr 1729 by dismission from the church at Salisbury. In 1738 William signed a petition for a new parish in the easterly part of Kingston.

Children: born Kingston, NH

1. **WILLIAM**, b 29 Sep 1729 (KTR): d Kingston, NH 19 Jul 1735 (NHGR 2:134)
2. **RICHARD**, b 3 Sep 1732 (KTR): bpt 15 Oct 1732 (NHGR 2:67)
3. **SARAH**, bpt 1 Jun 1735 (NHGR 2:69): m Kingston, NH 15 Jan 1756 Abraham French (KTR)
4. **(CHILD)**, d Kingston, NH 29 Jul 1735 (NHGR 2:134) - possibly Richard
5. **WILLIAM**, bpt 4 Sep 1737 (NHGR 5:103): d 27 Mar 1830 a.93yrs: m 2 Dec 1761 Betsey Batchelder (Hist of Gilmanton, NH p289)

JOSHUA SNOW, b Woburn, MA 16 Jan 1711 son of Richard & Elizabeth (Reed) Snow (WoVR): d Kingston, NH 28 Aug 1774 (KTR): m Kingston, NH 17 Oct 1739 Anna Bean (KTR), b Exeter, NH dau of Samuel & Mary (_) Bean.

Children: born Kingston, NH (KTR)

1. **ANNA**, b 17 Jun 1740: d 21 Oct 1824: m Kingston, NH 13 Oct 1757 John Fifield Jr (NHGR 3:89)
2. **ELIZABETH**, b 6 Jan 1742: d Kingston, NH 6 Oct 1743 (NHVR)
3. **ELIZABETH**, b 3 Sep 1744: m (prob) Kingston, NH 25 Oct 1759 John Sanborn (NHGR 3:91)
4. **MARY**, b 19 May 1747
5. **JUDA**, b 13 Sep 1749: d 25 Feb 1825: m Kingston, NH 11 Dec 1770 Phineas Bean (KChR)
6. **SUSANA**, b 6 May 1758
7. **JOSHUA**, b 5 Aug 1761

BENJAMIN STEVENS, b Kingston, NH 3 Feb 1712/3 son of Ebenezer & Elizabeth (Colcord) Stevens (KTR): d Kingston, NH 23 Mar 1776 (KTR): m Kingston, NH 24 Dec 1736 Sarah Fifield (KTR), b Kingston, NH 17 Dec 1712 dau of Joseph & Sarah (Sherburne) Fifield (KTR), d Kingston, NH 6 Aug 1764 (KTR).

Benjamin signed a petition in 1738 for a grant of land in Kingston.

Children: born Kingston, NH (KTR)

1. **BENJAMIN**, b 2 Oct 1737: m Kingston, NH 15 Sep 1760 Ann Colcord (KTR)
2. **SAMUEL**, b 29 Jan 1740: d Kingston, NH 30 Sep 1747 (KTR)
3. **ELIZABETH**, b 25 Mar 1742: d Kingston, NH 30 Sep 1747 (KTR)
4. **EBENEZER**, b 21 May 1745

EBENEZER STEVENS, b (prob) Salisbury, MA 29 Jun 1684 son of Benjamin & Hannah (Barnard) Stevens (SVR): d Kingston, NH 1 Nov 1749 (KTR): m Kingston, NH 5 Dec 1710 Elizabeth Colcord (KTR), b Hampton, NH 26 Dec 1686 dau of Samuel & Mary (Ayers) Colcord (HmVR p10), d Kingston, NH 20 Nov 1769 (KTR).

Ebenezer was granted 200 acres of land in Kingston at a meeting of the freeholders 30 Oct 1706. He belonged to Kingston in 1725 when Rev Clark took charge of the church.

Children: born Kingston, NH (KTR)

1. **BENJAMIN**, b 3 Feb 1712/3: d Kingston, NH 23 Mar 1776 (KTR): m Kingston, NH 24 Dec 1736 Sarah Fifield (KTR)
2. **EBENEZER**, b 14 Jun 1715: m(1) Kingston, NH 21 Oct 1736 Mary Colcord (KTR): m(2) Kingston, NH 19 Dec 1768 Mrs Dolly Stevens (KTR)
3. **HANNAH**, b 25 Jun 1718: m Kingston, NH 28 Sep 1742 Tristram Sanborn (KTR)
4. **MARY**, b 23 Mar 1721
5. **SAMUEL**, b 31 May 1724: m(1) Kingston, NH 15 Dec 1748 Shuah Fifield: m(2) Kingston, NH 29 Jan 1752 Hannah Morrill (KTR)
6. **JOHN**, b 9 Mar 1729: m Kingston, NH 15 Apr 1756 Mary Hubbard (KTR)

SAMUEL STEVENS, b 18 Jan 1680 son of Nathaniel & Mehitable (Colcord) Stevens (LND p659): d (WP) Exeter, NH 30 Aug 1738 (PRNH 2:546): m Patience Gordon (LND p659), dau of Nicholas & Maria (Hersey) Gordon (LND p273), d aft 1738.

Samuel's family belonged to Kingston in 1725 when Rev Clark took charge of the church.

Children: (PRNH 2:546-7)

1. **SAMUEL**, m Kingston, NH 26 Apr 1739 Abigail Gilman (NHGR 3:40)
2. **HEALY**, d bef 1758
3. **EDWARD**
4. **NATHANIEL**, b 12 Nov 1723: d Brentwood, NH 16 Apr 1773 (BtTR): m Brentwood, NH 24 Jan 1751 Sarah Blake (BtTR)
5. **SARAH**, m Kingston, NH 18 Dec 1735 John Gilman (NHGR 2:46)
6. **MEHITABLE**, m Kingston, NH 9 Jan 1745/6 Samuel Colcord (NHGR 3:42)
7. **PATIENCE**, bpt 18 Jul 1731 (NHGR 2:66): d Brentwood, NH 17 Jul 1819 (CG p23): m

Kingston, NH 22 Jan 1749/50 Ebenezer Colcord (NHGR 3:44)

SAMUEL STEVENS, b Kingston, NH 31 May 1724 son of Ebenezer & Elizabeth (Colcord) Stevens (KTR): m(1) Kingston, NH 15 Dec 1748 Shuah Fifield (KTR), b Kingston, NH 30 Jan 1728/9 dau of Samuel & Joanna (Clifford) Fifield (KTR), d Kingston, NH 13 Feb 1751 (KTR): m(2) Kingston, NH 29 Jan 1752 Hannah Morrill (KTR), bpt Kingston, NH 28 Nov 1731 dau of Benjamin & Abigail (Clough) Morrill (NHGR 2:66).

Children: born Kingston, NH (KTR)
(by 1st wife)
1. **SAMUEL**, b 30 Jan 1751

(by 2nd wife)

2. **EBENEZER**, b 4 Dec 1753
3. **BENJAMIN**, b 10 Jan 1754
4. **MOSES**, b 26 Apr 1756
5. **SARAH**, b 13 Nov 1757
6. **SARAH**, b 27 Mar 1759
7. **SHUAH**, b 27 Mar 1759
8. **JOHN**, b 3 Nov 1761
9. **DANIEL**, b (no date)
10. **HANNAH**, b 6 Jul 1764
11. **PETER**, b Mar 1766
12. **EDWARD**, b 8 Feb 1768

ROBERT STEWART (STUART), b Rowley, MA 26 Nov 1701 son of Ebenezer & Elizabeth (Johnson) Stewart (RwVR): d Newton, NH (WP) 4 Apr 1782 (Early Settlers of Rowley by Blodget p362): m Newbury, MA 11 Dec 1727 Ann Adams (NVR), b Newbury, MA 29 Apr 1705 dau of Abraham & Ann (Longfellow) Adams (NVR).

Robert & his wife were received into the Church of Christ in Kingston 11 Oct 1730 by dismission from the church of Byfield.

Children:

1. **SAMUEL**, bpt Newbury, MA 10 Nov 1728 (NVR): d Kingston, NH (Est Adm) 2 Dec 1767 (PRNH 9:78): m Kingston, NH 13 Jul

Hubbard (KTR)

2. **ANNA**, bpt Kingston, NH 27 Sep 1730 (NHGR)
3. **SARAH**, bpt Kingston, NH 22 Oct 1732 (NHGR 2:67): d 15 Jan 1813: m(1) Kingston, NH 24 Dec 1751 Samuel Chase (NHGR 3:45): m (2) Newbury, MA 9 Dec 1798 Maj Thomas Noyes (NVR)
4. **(DAU)**, bpt Kingston, NH 28 Nov 1736: d 30 Nov 1736 (NHGR 3:39)
5. **ANNA**, bpt Kingston, NH 12 Dec 1736 (NHGR 2:71: m Kingston, NH 3 Nov 1757 Barnard Hoyt (NHGR 3:89)
6. **MARY**, bpt Kingston, NH 25 Mar 1739 (NHGR 5:105): d 27 Apr 1816: m Nov 1760 Col Samuel Chase (Early Set of Rowley p362)
7. **ELIZABETH**, bpt Kingston, NH 19 Mar 1740/1 (NHGR 5:107): m So Hampton, NH 4 Jun 1767 Reuben Currier (SHVR)
8. **ROBERT**, bpt Kingston, NH 9 Oct 1743 (NHGR 5:110): d 27 Jun 1819 (DAR 1:648): m So Hampton, NH 1 Mar 1770 Ruth Currier (SHVR)
9. **STEPHEN**, b 25 Dec 1745: bpt Amesbury, MA 5 Jan 1745/6 (AVR): m Kingston, NH 5 Apr 1775 Sarah Peaslee
10. **AB**, b 1748: d.y.

ROBERT STOCKMAN, b Salisbury, MA 8 Aug 1683 son of John & Sarah (Pike) Stockman (SVR): d Kingston, NH 6 Apr 1742 (NHVR): m Lydia Folsom (LND p238), dau of John & Abigail (Perkins) Folsom, d aft 19 Feb 1741/2.

Robert & his family belonged to Kingston in 1725 when Rev Clark took charge of the church.

Children: (PRNH 3:95)

1. **ABIGAIL**, d E. Candia, NH 1804 (CG p31): m bef 1741/2 Daniel Rowe
2. **SARAH**, m Kingston, NH 29 Oct 1739 Ebenezer Blaisdell (KTR)
3. **MARY**, b Kingston, NH 27 Dec 1722 (KTR)
4. **JOANNA**, b Kingston, NH 5 Aug 1726 (KTR): m Kingston, NH 3 Jan 1744/5 Timothy Blaisdell (KTR)

5. **(INFANT)**, d Kingston, NH 28 Oct 1729 (NH GR 2:131)
6. **(INFANT)**, d Kingston, NH 7 Aug 1731 (NH GR 2:132)
7. **(CHILD)**, d Kingston, NH 27 Aug 1735 (NHGR 3:37)
8. **JOHN**, living 1742

DAVID STRAW, bpt Amesbury, MA 2 Jun 1728 son of John & Lydia (Sargent) Straw (AVR): m(1) Mary ___: m(2) Kingston, NH 29 Jan 1756 Jemima Colby (NHGR 3:88), b Amesbury, MA 3 Jan 1734 dau of Orlando & Keziah (Rowell) Colby (AVR): m(3) ? Mary ____

David settled in the westerly section of Kingston.

Children: 1st 3 born Kingston, NH (KTR)
(by 1st wife)
1. **JONATHAN**, b 3 Jan 1744/5
2. **JONATHAN**, b 11 Jul 1748
3. **JUDITH**, b 10 Jan 1750/1
4. **BENJAMIN**, bpt Kingston, NH 31 Jan 1753 (KChR)

(by 2nd wife) - born Sandown, NH (SdTR)
5. **BENJAMIN**, b 6 Jun 1756
6. **ROWELL COLBY**, b 9 May 1762
7. **MARY**, b 6 Oct 1765
8. **RHODA**, b 12 Mar 1768

(by 3rd wife)
9. **JUDITH**, b 26 Feb 1776 (SdTR)
10. **SARAH**, b 24 Dec 1779 (SdTR)

JOHN STRAW, b Amesbury, MA 1 Jul 1688 son of William & Mehitable (?Hoyt) Straw (AVR): d (WP) Kingston, NH 28 Nov 1750 (PRNH 4:76): m Amesbury, MA 20 Apr 1710 Lydia Sargent (AVR).

John lived in the westerly section of Kingston.

Children: born Amesbury, MA (AVR)
1. **MEHITABLE**, b 8 Jun 1711: m Amesbury, MA 25 May 1732 David Colby (AVR)
2. **MARY**, b 19 Feb 1712/3: m Amesbury, MA 26

Aug 1730 Peter Colby (AVR)
3. **WILLIAM**, b 23 Jan 1714/15
4. **DAVID**, bpt 2 Jun 1728: m(1) Mary ___: m (2) Kingston, NH 29 Jan 1756 Jemima Colby
5. **JOHN**, bpt 2 Jun 1728
6. **RACHEL**, bpt 2 Jun 1728: m Amesbury, MA 9 Feb 1742 David Peasley (AVR)
7. **ELIZABETH**, bpt 2 Jun 1728: unm 1750

JOHN SWETT, b Hampton, NH 17 May 1670 son of Benjamin & Hester (Weare) Swett (HmVR p101): d Kingston, NH 3 Sep 1753 (KTR): m(1) Hampton, NH 3 Dec 1696 Bethia Page (HmVR p80), b Hampton, NH 23 May 1679 dau of Thomas & Mary (Hussey) Page (HmVR p111), d 16 Apr 1736 (LND p670): m (2) Kingston, NH 10 Nov 1736 Sarah (Treadwell) Brown (NHGR 2:46), b Ipswich, MA 15 Aug 1674 dau of Nathaniel & Abigail (Wells) Treadwell (IpVR), d Kingston, NH 14 Apr 1756 (NHVR). Sarah m(1) abt 1694 Joseph Brown.

John was granted 200 acres at a meeting of the freeholders of Kingston 30 Oct 1706. His family belonged to Kingston in 1725 when Rev Clark took charge of the church.

Children: 1st 5 born Hampton, NH (HmVR)
1. **HULDA**, b 16 Jul 1699: m Kingston, NH 2 Jan 1723/4 Samuel Winsley (KTR)
2. **SARAH**, b 23 Dec 1700: m Thomas George (PRNH 3:569)
3. **JOHN**, b 4 Dec 1702: d Kingston, NH 27 May 1748 (KTR): m Kingston, NH 17 Sep 1724 Judith Young (KTR)
4. **ELISHA**, b 13 Aug 1705: d Kingston, NH 1 Apr 1788 (NHVR): m(1) Kingston, NH 11 Nov 1729 Sarah Tilton (KTR): m(2) Kingston, NH 10 Feb 1735/6 Abigail Sanborn (KTR)
5. **BENJAMIN**, b 17 Oct 1707: d Kingston, NH (bur) 26 Jun 1787 (NHVR): m Kingston, NH 20 Feb 1728/9 Abigail Darling (KTR)
6. **NATHAN**, b Kingston, NH 9 Jun 1711 (KTR): d (WP) 3 Feb 1796: m(1) Kingston, NH 6 Jan 1731 Mary Dearborn (KTR): m(2) Mrs Jane Garland (PRNH 3:364)

7. **MOSES**, b Kingston, NH 28 Nov 1714 (KTR): d Kingston, NH 11 Feb 1714/5 (KTR)

JOHN SWETT JR, b Hampton, NH 4 Dec 1702 son of John & Bethia (Page) Swett (HmVR p28): d Kingston, NH 27 May 1748 (KTR): m Kingston, NH 17 Sep 1724 Judith Young (KTR), d Kingston, NH 5 Dec 1747 (KTR).

Administration on the estate of John Swett Jr of Kingston was granted to Benjamin Swett 29 Jun 1748 (PRNH 3:577). John belonged to Kingston in 1725 when Rev Clark took charge of the church.

Children: born Kingston, NH (KTR)

1. **ELIZABETH**, b 24 Dec 1724: m(1) Kingston, NH 25 Oct 1749 Ephraim Severance (KTR): m (2) Kingston, NH 25 Jul 1758 Ebenezer Watson (KTR)
2. **ANNE**, b 17 Dec 1726
3. **ROBERT**, b 1 Mar 1729: d Kingston, NH 31 May 1749 (KTR)
4. **JOHN**, b 5 Oct 1731
5. **ANNA**, b 17 Jul 1736
6. **HULDAH**, 20 Sep 1737: living 1748
7. **MOSES**, b 28 Mar 1740: m Wells, ME 15 Mar 1770 Priscilla Hatch (Swett Gen p33)
8. **JUDITH**, b 7 Jun 1743: living 1748

ABEL TANDY, bpt Gloucester, MA 18 Jul 1731 son of Richard & Rachel (Allen) Tandy (GlVR): m Kingston, NH 5 Nov 1751 Rachel Smith (KTR).

Abel & his wife were admitted to the Kingston Church 19 Oct 1752 & were dismissed to New Salisbury 8 Aug 1773.

Children: 1st 4 born Kingston, NH (KTR)

1. **RACHEL**, b 2 Sep 1752
2. **ANNE**, b 5 Oct 1754
3. **MEHITABLE**, b 10 Apr 1757
4. **SAMUEL**, b 12 Mar 1759
5. **ABEL**, bpt 19 Jul 1761 (NHVR)
6. **SAMUEL**, b Salisbury, NH 10 Sep 1766
7. **RACHEL**, b Salisbury, NH 7 Oct 1768

8. **PRISCILLA**, b Salisbury, NH 28 Dec 1770

RICHARD TANDY, d Kingston, NH 19 Oct 1777 (NHVR): m Gloucester, MA 17 Mar 1723/4 Rachel Allen (GlVR), d Kingston, NH Jan 1754 (NHVR): possibly m(2) Kingston, NH 17 May 1754 Mary Fifield (NHGR 3:87).

Richard was admitted to the Kingston Church 6 Jun 1736.

Children: 1st 4 born Gloucester, MA (GlVR)

1. **WILLIAM**, b 6 Aug 1725: d Kingston, NH 1 Jan 1800 (NHVR): m Kingston, NH 29 May 1746 Mary Morgan (KTR)
2. **RACHEL**, b 21 Apr 1727: d Kingston, NH 16 Jul 1735 (NHGR 2:134)
3. **SAMUEL**, b 27 May 1729: m Kingston, NH 14 Nov 1751 Hannah Lovering (NHGR 3:45)
4. **ABEL**, bpt 18 Jul 1731: m Kingston, NH 5 Nov 1751 Rachel Smith (KTR)
5. **RICHARD**, d Kingston, NH 17 Jul 1735 (NHGR 2:134)
6. **RACHEL**, bpt Kingston, NH 9 Sep 1739 (NHGR 5:105): d Kingston, NH 26 Jun 1746 (NHVR)
7. **ABIGAIL**, bpt Kingston, NH 31 Jan 1741/2 (NHGR 5:108): d Kingston, NH 17 Jun 1746 (NHVR)
8. **ELIZABETH**, d Kingston, NH 27 Jun 1746 (NH VR)

SAMUEL TANDY, b Gloucester, MA 27 May 1729 son of Richard & Rachel (Allen) Tandy (GlVR): m Kingston, NH 14 Nov 1751 Hannah Lovering (NHGR 3:45).

Children:

1. **RICHARD**, b Kingston, NH 18 Dec 1752 (KTR)

NATHAN TAYLOR, b Exeter, NH 5 Feb 1674 son of William & Ann (Wyeth) Taylor (HE p45g): d ME 1703 (LND p676): m Mar 1699/1700 Sarah Drisco (NEM p730), dau of Timothy & Sarah (Pitman?) Drisco (LND p208).

Nathan was granted lot no. 7 in Kingston 10

Jul 1702. He also had land laid out to him, 60 acres more or less, 9 Feb 1705/6.

SAMUEL THOMPSON, bpt Salisbury, MA 26 Jan 1706/7 son of John & Elizabeth (Brewer) Thompson (SVR): m Newbury, MA 7 Sep 1727 Mary Bartlett (NVR), b Newbury, MA 31 Aug 1703 dau of John & Mary (Ordway) Bartlett (NVR).

Samuel signed a petition for a new parish in the easterly part of Kingston in 1738.

Children: last 5 born Kingston, NH

1. **SAMUEL**, b Amesbury, MA 5 Jun 1729 (AVR): m Kingston, NH 26 May 1757 Catherine Tucker (KTR)
2. **NATHAN (NATHANIEL)**, b Amesbury, MA 12 Nov 1731 (AVR): d aft 1800: m Kingston, NH 28 Nov 1758 Sarah Prescott (KTR)
3. **MOSES**, b 16 Oct 1734 (KTR)
4. **MARY**, b 8 May 1737 (KTR)
5. **HANNAH**, bpt 4 Jan 1741 (KChR)
6. **THOMAS**, bpt 26 Dec 1742 (KChR): d aft 1796: m 1776 Judith Blaisdell
7. **HANNAH**, bpt 2 Jun 1745 (KChR)

WILLIAM THOMPSON (Rev), b Marshfield, MA 26 Apr 1697 son of Edward & Sarah (Webster) Thompson (LND p680): d Scarborough, ME (WP) 1 Oct 1759 (ME Wills by Sargent p868): m Kingston, NH Oct 1728 Anna Hubbard (NHGR 2:44), b Salisbury, MA 22 Jul 1702 dau of John & Jane (Follinsby) Hubbard (SVR).

William was granted 12 acres of land in Kingston 5 Apr 1721.

Children: born Scarborough, ME (Saco Valley by Ridlon p1175)

1. **WILLIAM**, b 25 May 1730: d 1 Feb 1807
2. **ANNA**, b 9 Nov 1733: d 11 Aug 1772: m 28 Feb 1764 Joseph Gerrish (Old Kit p446)
3. **JOHN**, b 3 Oct 1740: d Berwick, ME 21 Dec 1828: m(1) 22 Nov 1768 Sarah Small: m(2) Feb 1784 Sarah (Allen) Morrill

DAVID TILTON, b Hampton Falls 14 Mar 1725/6 son of David & Deborah (Batchelder) Tilton (HFTR): d New Hampton, NH Mar 1808 (Essex Gen 9:143): m Kingston, NH 8 Feb 1749/50 Rebecca Green (KTR), b Hampton Falls, NH 8 Nov 1730 dau of Jacob & Mary (Eaton) Green (HFTR), d New Hampton, NH 6 Jan 1804.

David & his wife were admitted to the Kingston Church 1 Jun 1760.

Children: 1st 6 born Kingston, NH (KTR)

1. **MARY**, b 25 Oct 1750: m Danville, NH 3 Jun 1772 Jacob Ordway (NEHGR 58:122)
2. **RACHEL**, b 17 Feb 1752: d (W) 8 Nov 1831
3. **JEMIMA**, b 19 Jun 1753: d (W) 1841
4. **DAVID**, b 27 Jan 1755: m Danville, NH 16 Dec 1777 Eunice Quimby (NEHGR 58:124)
5. **ELIZABETH**, b 10 Jun 1756: m Kingston, NH 7 Sep 1779 Elijah Sanborn (NHGR 3:131)
6. **LOIS**, b 2 Jan 1758: d Bridgewater, NH 8 Nov 1857: m Kingston, NH Oct 1785 John Fellows (NHGR 3:132)
7. **GREEN**, b Danville, NH 9 Sep 1759 (DnTR): d 8 Mar 1810 (DAR 1:680): m Judith Favor
8. **DEBORAH**, b Danville, NH 29 May 1761: m Danville, NH 15 Mar 1787 Moses Fellows (DnTR)
9. **REBECCA**, b Danville, NH 4 Jan 1763 (Dn TR): m(1) Epping, NH 12 Aug 1779 John Prescott (NHGR 4:91): m(2) Daniel Batchelder
10. **HULDA**, b Danville, NH 18 Mar 1765 (DNTR): m Reuben Huse
11. **JOSIAH**, b Danville, NH 23 Feb 1768: d 7 Jan 1772 (DnTR)
12. **JOHN**, b Danville, NH 8 May 1770 (DnTR): m Phebe Emerson
13. **HANNAH**, b Danville, NH 9 Sep 1772 (DnTR): d 13 Jun 1776

JOSIAH TILTON, b Hampton, NH 1 Apr 1709 son of Samuel & Meribah (Page-Shaw) Tilton (HmVR p39): d E. Kingston 15 Oct 1796 (CR): m Kingston, NH 8 Feb 1732/3 Sarah Flanders (KTR), b Salisbury,

MA 16 Nov 1710 dau of Philip & Joanna (Smith) Flanders (SVR), d E. Kingston, NH 20 Feb 1795 a.83yrs (CR).

Josiah was admitted to the Kingston Church 7 Dec 1735 & his wife was admitted 19 Mar 1734 by dismission from ye church of Salisbury. In 1738 Josiah signed a petition for a new parish in the easterly part of Kingston.

Children: born Kingston, NH (KTR)

1. **SAMUEL**, b 1 Dec 1733: d Deerfield, NH abt 1778: m Kingston, NH 26 Jan 1758 Rebecca Prescott (KChR)
2. **DAVID**, b 27 Oct 1735: d E. Kingston, NH 27 Aug 1825 (CR): m E. Kingston, NH 26 Mar 1760 Jane Greeley (Essex Gen 9:94)
3. **MERIBAH**, b 9 Mar 1738: m Kingston, NH 11 Oct 1757 Benjamin Smith (KChR)
4. **PHILIP**, b 10 Apr 1741: d 26 Jan 1835 (DAR 1:680): m(1) So Hampton, NH 11 Sep 1766 Mary Batchelder (SHVR): m(2) 4 Oct 1809 Eunice Dodge
5. **JOSIAH**, b 22 Oct 1743: d Cornville, ME 13 Feb 1820 (RG 2:693): m(1) 1768 Sarah True: m(2) Kensington, NH 25 Aug 1788 Abigail Nudd (NHVR)
6. **SARAH**, b 27 Mar 1750: m Kensington, NH 5 Nov 1771 Elisha Blake (NHVR)
7. **EBENEZER**, b 3 Oct 1754 (Essex Gen 9:96): m Kensington, NH 23 Jan 1777 Lucy Prescott (NHVR)

TIMOTHY TILTON, b Hampton Falls, NH 4 Oct 1718 son of Joseph & Elizabeth (Hilliard-Shaw) Tilton (HFTR): d 1 Oct 1785 (DAR 1:680): m Kingston, NH 25 Dec 1746 Martha Boynton (KTR), d Loudon, NH 25 Nov 1822 (Essex Gen 9:94).

Children: born Kingston, NH (KTR)

1. **JOSEPH**, b 7 Sep 1748
2. **JOANNAH**, b 13 Sep 1751: m Kensington, NH 4 Apr 1771 Benjamin Rowe (NHVR)
3. **WILLIAM**, b 13 Dec 1753: m Abigail Page
4. **NATHAN**, b 3 Feb 1757: m Susanna Gale

5. **ELIZABETH**, b 7 May 1761: m Belmont, NH 12 Jun 1788 Eliphabet Wood
6. **DAVID**, b 10 Sep 1765: d 8 Sep 1778: m 10 Sep 1787 Sarah Foster

EDMUND TITCOMB, b Newbury, MA 26 Mar 1710 son of Edmund & Elizabeth (Greenleaf) Titcomb (NVR): m(1) Newbury, MA 29 Jul 1730 Sarah Merrill (NVR), dau of Nathan & Hannah (Kent) Merrill (Merrill Memorial p204): m(2) Falmouth, ME (int) 20 Jan 1769 Mehitable (Blake) Sawyer (Titcomb Gen p30).

Possibly the Edmund who signed a petition for a new parish in the easterly part of Kingston in 1738.

Children: born Newbury, MA (NVR)

1. **EDMUND**, b 24 May 1731: m(1) No Yarmouth, ME 3 Dec 1752 Martha Swett: m(2) Mary Whittier
2. **NATHAN**, b 11 Jul 1732: m(1) Falmouth, ME 18 Oct 1755 Deborah Bucknam: m(2) 22 Jan 1763 Olive Phipps
3. **ELIZABETH**, b 27 Oct 1739 (Titcomb Gen p 31): m Falmouth, ME (int) 19 Nov 1757 Adams Merrill
4. **SARAH**, bpt 7 Feb 1741/2
5. **BENAIAH**, bpt 10 Aug 1745: m No Yarmouth, ME (int) 26 Nov 1766 Sarah Carey
6. **DOROTHY**, bpt 2 Nov 1746
7. **JOSEPH**, bpt 6 Nov 1748: m No Yarmouth, ME 12 May 1773 Hannah Sawyer

JAMES TONGUE, d Kingston, NH 3 Feb 1746 (NHVR): m Amesbury, MA 7 Feb 1722/3 Elizabeth Davis (AVR), b Amesbury, MA 9 Jul 1694 dau of Jeremiah & Mary (Huntington) Davis (AVR).

Children: 1st 3 born Amesbury, MA (AVR)

1. **STEPHEN**, b 18 Jan 1725/6: d Kingston, NH 1785: m Kingston, NH Nov 1752 Dorothy Blaisdell (KTR)
2. **ELIZABETH**, b 22 Aug 1732
3. **MARY**, b 7 Jan 1736/7

4. **(CHILD)**, d Kingston, NH 19 Nov 1738 (NH VR)

JAMES TOPPAN (TAPPAN), b Newbury, MA 15 Mar 1701/2 son of John & Martha (Brown) Toppan (NVR): d Kingston, NH (WP) 24 Apr 1765 (PRNH 8: 132): m(1) Salisbury, MA 10 Jun 1725 Mary Allen (SVR), b Salisbury, MA 20 Oct 1706 dau of Stillson & Margaret (_) Allen (SVR), d 4 Nov 1728: m(2) Salisbury, MA (int) 12 Nov 1731 Abigail Morrill (SVR), b Salisbury, MA 6 May 1699 dau of Isaac & Abigail (Brown) Morrill (SVR).
James signed a petition for a new parish in the easterly part of Kingston in 1738.

Children:
(by 1st wife)
1. **MARTHA**, b Salisbury, MA 1 Nov 1726 (SVR): m Kingston, NH Nov 1743 Simon Noyes (NHGR 3:41)

(by 2nd wife) born E. Kingston, NH (SVR)
2. **ABIGAIL**, b 28 Oct 173_: m Kingston, NH 9 Nov 1758 Jacob Gale (NHGR 3:90)
3. **JOHN**, b 23 Nov 173_
4. **JAMES**, b 23 Jun 1736: d E. Kingston, NH 20 May 1755 (CR)
5. **JOHN**, bpt Kingston, NH 19 Dec 1742 (KChR)

CALEB TOWLE, b Hampton, NH 9 May 1701 son of Caleb & Zipporah (Brackett) Towle (HmVR p54): m Hampton, NH 1 Jan 1728/9 Rebecca Prescott (HmVR p132), b Hampton, NH 27 Sep 1711 dau of James & Maria (Marston) Prescott (HmVR p43).

Children: born Kingston, NH (KTR)
1. **ANNA**, b 28 May 1728: d Kingston, NH 26 Apr 1796 (GI p18): m Kingston, NH 12 Mar 1752 Ebenezer Long (NHGR 3:86)
2. **ELISHA**, b 12 Jan 1730/1
3. **MARY**, b 4 Nov 1732
4. **JAMES**, bpt 1736 (HH p1001): d Kingston, NH 5 Jun 1746 (NHVR)
5. **CALEB**, b 28 Dec 1737: d Danville, NH 9 Aug 1765 a.27yrs (CG p40): m Kingston, NH

13 Dec 1759 Ruth Page (NHGR 3:91)

6. **DANIEL**, bpt 12 Oct 1739/40 (NHGR 5:106): d Kingston, NH 30 May 1746 (NHVR)
7. **JEREMIAH**, b 19 Jun 1745
8. **WILLIAM**, d Kingston, NH 29 May 1746 (NHVR)
9. **JAMES**, b 31 Dec 1747: d Danville, NH 31 Dec 1825 a.78yrs (CG p40): m Danville, NH 13 Sep 1768 Abigail Quimby (DnTR)
10. **MARIAH** (twin), bpt 25 Apr 1752 (NHGR 6: 27): d Kingston, NH 12 May 1752 (NHVR)
11. **ZIPPORAH** (Twin), bpt 25 Apr 1752 (NHGR 6: 27): d Kingston, NH 6 May 1752 (NHVR)

FRANCIS TOWLE, b Hampton, NH 1 Aug 1672 son of Philip & Isabella (Austin) Towle (HmVR p103). He changed his name to **FRANCIS DOWLE**: d (Est Adm) 25 Feb 1705/6: m Charlestown, MA 26 Jul 1698 Prudence Russell (LND p689).

Francis was an original grantee of Kingston in 1694.

Children:

1. **FRANCIS**, bpt 6 Apr 1701

BENJAMIN TUCKER, m Amesbury, MA 16 Jan 1745/6 Betty Sargent (AVR), b Amesbury, MA 18 Jun 1717 dau of Philip & Mary (Tewksbury) Sargent (AVR).

Benjamin lived in the westerly section of Kingston.

Children: (SdTR)

1. **SARAH**, b 24 Jun 1749
2. **EBENEZER**, b 17 Mar 1751: bpt Kingston, NH 28 Jul 1751 (NHGR 6:26)
3. **BETTE**, b 16 Jun 1754: bpt Kingston, NH 27 Oct 1754 (NHGR 6:31)
4. **ELIS (ALICE)**, b Sandown, NH 29 Oct 1758
5. **MARY**, b Sandown, NH 28 Mar 1762

EZRA TUCKER, b Amesbury, MA 27 Mar 1706 son of Benoni & Ebenezer (Nichols) Tucker (AVR): d Kingston, NH (Putnam's Mag 3:3): m(1) Amesbury, MA 26 Jan 1726/7 Barsheba Sargent (AVR), b

Amesbury, MA 10 Oct 1709 dau of Charles & Hannah (Foot) Sargent (AVR): probably m(2) Kingston, NH 24 Jan 1745/6 Lydia Hobbs (NHGR 3:42).

Children:
(by 1st wife)- born Amesbury, MA (AVR)
1. **ELIZABETH**, bpt 30 Mar 1729 (OF p511)
2. **HANNAH**, bpt 30 Aug 1730 (OF p512)
3. **MARY**, b 19 Mar 1731/2
4. **CALLAIN**, b 15 May 1734
5. **MEHITABLE**, b 23 Oct 1736
6. **EZRA**, b 3 May 1738 (DAR 1:690): d Henniker, NH 26 Oct 1807: m Kingston, NH 3 May 1759 Hepzibah Pressey (KTR)
7. **SARAH**, b 11 May 1741
8. **BENONI**, b 15 Jun 1743

(by 2nd wife) - born Kingston, NH (KTR)
9. **BARSHEBA**, b 15 Mar 1747
10. **LYDIA**, b 22 Jan 1749
11. **EBENEZER**, b 16 Mar 1752
12. **MERIAM**, b 11 Apr 1754
13. **MEHITABLE**, b 6 May 1756
14. **JACOB**, b 6 Apr 1769
15. **NATHANIEL**, b (no date)

JACOB TUCKER, b Amesbury, MA 22 Sep 1717 son of Benjamin & Alice (Davis) Tucker (AVR): d 27 Jul 1804 (DAR 1:690): m Amesbury, MA 4 Sep 1739 Lydia Hoyt (AVR), b Amesbury, MA 15 Mar 1718/9 dau of Daniel & Sarah (Rowell) Hoyt (AVR).

Jacob lived in the westerly section of Kingston.

Children: 1st 3 born Amesbury, MA (AVR)
1. **SARAH**, b 15 Apr 1740
2. **ALICE**, b 2 Jan 1742
3. **LYDIA**, b 7 Jun 1744
4. **JACOB**, b 22 May 1746 (SdTR)
5. **JUDITH**, bpt Kingston, NH 26 Mar 1751 (KChR)
6. **JOHN**, b 2 Oct 1752 (SdTR)
7. **SARAH**, b Sandown, NH 13 Jan 1755 (SdTR): m Hampstead, NH 21 Dec 1780 Joshua East-

man (HmstR)
8. **MARY**, b Sandown, NH 23 Apr 1761 (SdTR)
9. **JUDITH**, b Sandown, NH 12 May 1763 (SdTR)

MOSES TUCKER, b Salisbury, MA 28 Mar 1704/5 son of Joseph & Phebe (Page) Tucker (SVR): d Sandown, NH 6 Jan 1769 a.64yrs (SdTR): m Haverhill, MA 20 Sep 1727 Joanna Dow (HvVR), b Haverhill, MA 26 Sep 1709 dau of Stephen & Mary (Hutchins) Dow (HvVR), d Sandown, NH 29 Jun 1800 a.90yrs (SdTR).

Children: last 6 born Kingston, NH (KTR)
1. **MARY**, b Salisbury, MA 3 Jan 1728/9 (SVR): d Hampstead, NH 10 Jun 1748: m Hampstead, NH 24 Nov 1744 William Stevens (HmstR)
2. **PARKER**, b Salisbury, MA 11 Jan 1730/1 (SVR): d Salisbury, MA 7 May 1736 (SVR)
3. **PHEBE**, b at Kingston, NH 26 Mar 1735 (SVR): m Chester, NH 21 Dec 1752 Ephraim Webster
4. **MOSES**, b Salisbury, MA 16 Mar 1736/7 (SVR)
5. **SARAH**, b 13 Mar 1739: m Hampstead, NH 5 Jun 1755 Ichabod Rowell (HmstR)
6. **ELIZABETH**, b 8 Apr 1741: m Benjamin Colby
7. **HANNAH**, b 22 Sep 1743: d Sandown, NH 11 Jan 1817 (SdTR): m Sandown, NH 15 Apr 1761 John Sleeper (SdTR)
8. **REUBEN**, b 19 Jun 1747
9. **JOSEPH**, b 22 Oct 1748: d aft 1791 (DAR 1:690): m Abigail Hurd
10. **MARY**, b 5 Oct 1751: m• George Start (DAR 1:643)

SAMUEL TUCKER, b Salisbury, MA 16 Apr 1699 son of Joseph & Phebe (Page) Tucker (SVR): m Kingston, NH 26 Dec 1723 Mary Elkins (KTR), b Kingston, NH 5 Aug 1704 dau of Moses & Ann (Shaw) Elkins (KTR), d Kingston, NH 25 Mar 1756 (NHVR).

Samuel belonged to Kingston in 1725 when Rev Clark took charge of the church. In 1738 he signed a petition for a grant of land in Kingston.

Children: born Kingston, NH (KTR & NHGR)
1. **JONATHAN**, b 2 Jan 1724/5: d Kingston, NH 17 May 1736 (NHGR 3:39)
2. **BENJAMIN**, b 25 Sep 1727: d Kingston, NH 13 Jul 1791 (KTR): m Kingston, NH Sep 1748 Judith Thuriel (KTR)
3. **(CHILD)**, d Kingston, NH 25 Mar 1730 a.9mo
4. **(SON)**, d Kingston, NH 15 Nov 1730
5. **(DAU)**, d Kingston, NH 28 Aug 1731
6. **JOHN**, b 5 Sep 1732: m Kingston, NH 8 Nov 1753 Deborah Sanborn (NHGR 3:86)

GIDEON TURRILL (TIRRELL), b Weymouth, MA 14 Jun 1694 son of William & Mary (Pratt) Turrill (Hist of Weymouth, MA p656): d abt 1750: m Abington, MA (int) 4 Apr 1719 Edith Ayer (AbVR), b Newbury, MA 8 Apr 1702 dau of John & Ruth (Brown) Ayer (NVR). Edith m(2) Newbury, MA 12 Aug 1754 Joseph Jackman (NVR).

Gideon & his wife Edith, from Newbury, were admitted to the 2nd Church of Christ in Kingston Mar 1741.

Children:
1. **EDITH**, b Abington, MA 29 Aug 1720 (AbVR): m Kingston, NH 19 Aug 1740 John Morrill (KChR)
2. **JOHN**, b Abington, MA 29 Aug 1722 (AbVR): d Weymouth, MA 30 Sep 1730
3. **GIDEON**, b Newbury, MA 2 Feb 1724 (NVR)
4. **WILLIAM**, b Newbury, MA 17 Mar 1727 (NVR): d Canterbury, NH 18 Dec 1796: m Kingston, NH 26 Jan 1749 Sarah Stevens (KChR)
5. **MARY**, b Weymouth, MA 28 Aug 1729
6. **ELIZABETH**, bpt Newbury, MA 5 Mar 1731/2 (NVR)
7. **RUTH**, b Newbury, MA 27 May 1734 (NVR): m Hampstead, NH (int) 4 Jan 1755 John Kezer (HmstR)
8. **MYCHAJAH**, b Newbury, MA 29 Nov 1736 (NVR)
9. **JESSE**, b Newbury, MA 11 Aug 1739 (NVR): d Hampstead, NH 31 May 1769: m Hampstead,

NH 24 Nov 1763 Mary Johnson (HmstR)
10. **ABIGAIL**, bpt Kingston, NH 4 Apr 1742 (KChR): m William Rogers
11. **SETH** (Tirrell Gen p42), b Newbury, MA 20 May 1744: m 28 Oct 1788 Esther Corliss

BENJAMIN WADLEIGH, b Exeter, NH abt 1695 son of Robert & Sarah (Nelson) Wadleigh: d Kingston, NH bef 6 Jun 1756 (Pillsbury Anc by M. Holman 1:235): m Salisbury, MA 24 Dec 1722 Judith Clough (SVR), b Salisbury, MA 1 Oct 1700 dau of Thomas & Ruth (Conner) Clough (SVR), d Kingston, NH 19 Dec 1745 (NHVR).

Benjamin & his family belonged to Kingston in 1725 when Rev Clark took charge of the church. In 1738 Benjamin signed a petition for a grant of land in Kingston.

Children: born Kingston, NH (Pillsbury Anc by Mary Holman 1:235)

1. **ANNA**, b abt 1724: bpt 5 Nov 1727 (NHGR)
2. **THOMAS**, b abt 1726: bpt 5 Nov 1727 (NHGR 2:47): d 9 Oct 1787: m(1) Kingston, NH 22 Sep 1748 Margaret Rowen: m(2) Hampstead, NH (int) 1783 Miriam (Jones) Plummer
3. **SARAH**, bpt 30 Mar 1729 (NHGR 2:48): m Kingston, NH 17 Feb 1746/7 Obediah Clough (NHGR 3:43)
4. **JOHN**, b 22 Oct 1730 (KTR): d Kingston, NH 18 May 1734 (NHGR 2:133)
5. **MARY**, b abt 1732: d Danville, NH 31 Oct 1814 a.82yrs (CG p40): m Kingston, NH 19 Nov 1755 David Quimby Jr (NHGR 3:88)
6. **LOVE**, bpt 1 Sep 1734 (NHGR 2:69)
7. **JOHN**, bpt 16 May 1736 (NHGR): m Kingston, NH 27 Dec 1757 Mary Dent (NHGR 3:89)
8. **JUDAH**, bpt 20 Aug 1738 (NHGR 5:104): m (prob) ____ Bean
9. **RUTH**, bpt 2 Mar 1739/40 (NHGR 5:106)

HENRY WADLEIGH, b Exeter, NH 16 May 1666 (IGI) son of Robert & Sarah (_) Wadleigh (LND p707): d Exeter, NH (Est Adm) 20 Feb 1732/3 (PRNH 2:463): m Exeter, NH 3 Dec 1693 Elizabeth

(Gilman) Ladd (HE p48g), b Exeter, NH 16 Aug 1661 dau of John & Elizabeth (Treworgy) Gilman (HE p16g). Elizabeth m(1) 12 Jul 1678 Nathaniel Ladd (LND p263).

Henry was granted land in Kingston as early as 1705. He forfeited his rights 6 May 1715.

Children: born Exeter, NH (HE p48g)

1. **SARAH**, b 3 Sep 1694: m bef 1713 John Scribner
2. **ABIGAIL**, b 2 Sep 1696: m Samuel Magoon
3. **JOSEPH**, b Sep 1698
4. **MARTHA**, b Jan 1700/1: m Ephraim Philbrick
5. **BENJAMIN**, b 1703: d 1716

JOHN WADLEIGH (Capt), b abt 1663 son of Robert & Sarah (_) Wadleigh (LND p707): d 7 Nov 1727 (Pillsbury Anc 1:233): m abt 1683 Abigail Marston (NEM p769), dau of John Marston of Salem (LND p707).

John had land laid out to him in Kingston 3 Jan 1709/10. He also had 40 acres of land laid out in full of his 2nd division 17 Jun 1720.

Children: born Salisbury, MA (SVR)

1. **ABIGAIL**, b 30 Mar 1684: m Salisbury, MA 22 Jan 1704/5 Ezekiel Morrill (SVR)
2. **JOSEPH**, b 7 Mar 1686: m Salisbury, MA 9 Jan 1711/2 Abigail Allen (SVR)
3. **JOHN**, b 14 Aug 1691
4. **ALICE**, b 27 Aug 1693: m Salisbury, MA 10 Dec 1718 William Daniels (SVR)
5. **EPHRAIM**, b 25 Nov 1697
6. **RUTH** ?, b 4 May 1700 (SVR - dau of John & Ruth Wadleigh)

THOMAS WADLEIGH, b Kingston, NH abt 1726: bpt 5 Nov 1727 son of Benjamin & Judith (Clough) Wadleigh (NHGR 2:47): d Hampstead, NH 9 Sep 1787 (HmstR): m(1) Kingston, NH 22 Sep 1748 Margaret Rowen (NHGR 3:43), bpt Amesbury, MA 17 Feb 1727/8 dau of Andrew & Elizabeth (Dow) Rowen (AVR): m(2) Hampstead, NH (int) 1783 Merriam (Jones) Plummer (HmstR). Merriam m(1) Apr 1767

Samuel Plummer.
Thomas received land in Kingston from his father in 1745. He removed to Hampstead abt 1761.

Children: 1st 5 bpt Kingston, NH (NHGR & NHVR)
1. **BENJAMIN**, b 26 Mar 1749: bpt 6 Feb 1752: d Sutton, NH 9 Aug 1817: m abt 1769 Hannah Kezar (HSt p967)
2. **JONATHAN**, b 26 Mar 1751: bpt 6 Feb 1752: m(1) ___ Miles: m(2) 1795 Susanna (Russell) Little
3. **JOSEPH**, b 27 Mar 1753: bpt 26 Apr 1753: m Betsey Ingalls
4. **THOMAS**, b 29 Mar 1755: bpt 29 Jun 1755: d 26 Feb 1827: m Hampstead, NH (int) 9 Dec 1783 Merriam Atwood (HmstR)
5. **JOHN**, bpt 7 Jul 1757
6. **JOHN**, b 14 Mar 1759
7. **JUDITH**, b 31 Mar 1761: m Hampstead, NH (int) 29 Dec 1782 Moses Atwood (HmstR)
8. **MOSES**, b 1 Mar 1763: d 1839: m Hampstead, NH (int) 20 Feb 1790 Elizabeth Dow (Hm stR)
9. **BETSEY**, b 14 May 1766: m(1) Salem, NH 18 Aug 1791 John Kent (HSlm): m (2) ___ Lovering
10. **EPHRAIM**, b 8 Mar 1770: d Hatley, Canada 30 Jan 1852: m 30 Aug 1793 Alice Little
11. **AARON**, bpt 31 Jul 1768: d Starksborough, VT 1848
12. **SUSANNA**, bpt Apr 1774: d 20 Apr 1848: m Benjamin Evans (HSt p968)
13. **HENRY**, b 25 Aug 1778: m ___ Stevens

ABRAHAM WATSON, b Salisbury, MA 13 Dec 1688 son of John & Ruth (Griffin) Watson (SVR): m (prob) Salisbury, MA 14 Mar 1711/12 Mary Severance (SVR), b Salisbury, MA 2 Jul 1685 dau of Ephraim & Lydia (Morrill) Severance (SVR).
Abraham belonged to Kingston in 1725 when Rev Clark took charge of the church. His name is on a list of Kingston men who swore allegiance to the King in 1727.

ANDREW WEBSTER, b Salisbury, MA 12 Nov 1710 son of John & Sarah (Greeley) Webster (SVR): m(1) Kingston, NH 25 Nov 1731 Mercy Clough (NHGR 2:45), b Kingston, NH 15 Apr 1711 dau of Joseph & Mary (Jenness) Clough (KTR): m(2) Hampton Falls, NH 29 Dec 1743 Prudence (Locke) Weare (HFTR), b Hampton, NH 30 May 1707 dau of Edward & Hannah (Jenness) Locke (HmVR p35). Prudence m(1) Ebenezer Weare (PRNH 3:99).

In 1730 Andrew signed a petition regarding the township of Kingston & in 1738 he signed a petition for a new parish in the easterly part of Kingston.

Children: last 4 born Hampton Falls, NH (HFTR)
(by 1st wife)

1. **(CHILD)**, d Kingston, NH 15 Jul 1732 (NHGR 2:132)
2. **JOSEPH**, bpt Kingston, NH 28 Oct 1733 (NH GR 2:68): d Kingston, NH (prob) 25 Jun 1735 (NHGR 2:133)
3. **(CHILD)**, d Kingston, NH 14 Apr 1736 (NHGR 3:39)
4. **JOSEPH**, bpt Kingston, NH 2 Oct 1737 (NHGR 5:103)
5. **MARY**, b Salisbury, MA 7 Sep 1740 (SVR): bpt Kingston, NH 12 Oct 1740 (KChR)

(by 2nd wife)

6. **PRUDENCE**, b 25 Dec 1744
7. **ANDREW**, b 8 Oct 1746: d Orono, ME 1 Nov 1807: m abt 1766 Martha Crane (ME Fam 1:283)
8. **EBENEZER**, b 22 Oct 1749: d Cape Elizabeth, ME 9 Oct 1833: m(1) abt 1767/8 Anna Wescott: m(2) int 2 Aug 1794 Deborah Elder (ME Fam 2:295)
9. **DANIEL**, b 12 Feb 1751

EBENEZER WEBSTER, b Hampton, NH 1 Aug 1667 son of Thomas & Sarah (Brewer) Webster (HmVR p99): d Kingston, NH (WP) 16 Mar 1735/6 (PRNH 2:559): m Kingston, NH 25 Jul 1709 Hannah Judkins (KTR), b Exeter, NH 13 Nov 1676 dau of Joel & Mary (Bean) Judkins (LND p393).

Ebenezer was an original grantee of Kingston in 1694 & was granted 200 acres of land at a meeting of the freeholders 19 Dec 1700. His family belonged to Kingston in 1725 when Rev Clark took charge of the church.

Children: born Kingston, NH (KTR)
1. **RACHEL**, b 17 Mar 1710: m Kingston, NH 8 May 1735 Edward Scribner (KTR)
2. **SUSANNAH**, b 9 Jul 1712: m Kingston, NH 27 Dec 1733 Daniel Darling (KTR)
3. **EBENEZER**, b 10 Oct 1714: m 20 Jul 1738 Susanna Batchelder (NEHGR 7:102)
4. **WILLIAM**, b 26 Aug 1716: d Kingston, NH 6 Nov 1728 (NHGR 2:131)
5. **JOHN**, b 4 Aug 1719: d Kingston, NH 4 Nov 1730 (NHGR 2:132)
6. **HANNAH**, b 1721/2: m Kingston, NH 4 Nov 1740 Samuel Scribner (KTR)
7. **JOSEPH** (twin), b 15 Sep 1724: m Kingston, NH 26 Nov 1747 Maria Goss (NHGR 3:43)
8. **MARY** (twin), b 15 Sep 1724: m Kingston, NH 5 Nov 1741 Andrew Greeley (KTR)
9. **IDDO**, b 9 Feb 1727/8: m Kingston, NH 12 Mar 1746 Jena Goss (KTR)

EBENEZER WEBSTER, b Kingston, NH 10 Oct 1714 son of Ebenezer & Hannah (Judkins) Webster (KTR): d 1792 (DAR 1:724): m 20 Jul 1738 Susanna Batchelder (NEHGR 7:102), b Hampton Falls, NH 28 May 1713 dau of Benjamin & Susanna (Page) Batchelder (HFTR).

Ebenezer signed a petition for a new parish in the easterly part of Kingston in 1738.

Children: last 7 bpt Kingston, NH (KChR)
1. **EBENEZER**, b 22 Apr 1739: d Franklin, NH 22 Apr 1806 (CG p55): m(1) 18 Jan 1761 Mehitable Smith: m(2) Salisbury, MA 13 Oct 1774 Abigail Eastman (SVR)
2. **MERIAH**, bpt Kingston, NH 31 Aug 1740
3. **SUSANNA**, bpt 31 Jan 1742
4. **BENJAMIN**, bpt 22 Apr 1744: d 19 Oct 1827 (DAR 1:724): m(1) Susan Webster: m(2)

Judith Heath

5. **HANNAH**, bpt 6 Oct 1745
6. **MARY**, bpt 25 Jan 1747
7. **WILLIAM**, bpt 13 Aug 1749: d Salisbury, NH 24 Apr 1824: m 17 Nov 1773 Ruth Greeley (Greeley Gen p102)
8. **ESTHER**, bpt 23 Aug 1752

IDDO WEBSTER, b Kingston, NH 9 Feb 1727/8 son of Ebenezer & Hannah (Judkins) Webster (KTR): m Kingston, NH 12 Mar 1746 Jena Goss (KTR), probably dau of Joseph & Hannah (Smith) Goss.

Children: born Kingston, NH

1. **JENA**, b 12 Feb 1747 (KTR)
2. **JENNY**, bpt 4 Sep 1748 (NHGR 5:156)
3. **MARIAH**, bpt 12 Nov 1749 (NHGR 5:158)
4. **HANNAH**, bpt 13 Jul 1752 (NHGR 6:28): d Kingston, NH 9 Jan 1756 (NHVR)
5. **POLLY**, bpt 21 Sep 1755 (NHVR)
6. **JOSEPH GOSS**, bpt 25 Jan 1756: d Kingston, NH 22 Feb 1757 (NHVR)
7. **JENNY**, bpt 14 May 1758 (NHVR)

ISAAC WEBSTER, b Hampton, NH 12 Apr 1670 son of Thomas & Sarah (Brewer) Webster (HmVR p562): d Kingston, NH 21 Feb 1717/8 (PRNH 2:63): m(1) 1 Apr 1697 Mary Hutchins (NEM p789), b Bradford, MA 15 Apr 1676 dau of William & Sarah (Hardy) Hutchins (BdVR): m(2) Sarah ____.

Isaac had land laid out to him in Kingston 5 Apr 1709. Administration on the estate of Isaac Webster of Kingston was granted to his son John Webster of Kingston 4 Jun 1718 (PRNH 2:63).

Children:
(by 1st wife) 1st 4 bpt Hampton, NH (HH p1033)

1. **JOHN**, bpt 27 Jun 1697: d Kingston, NH (WP) 27 Aug 1766 (PRNH 7:388): m Rowley, MA (int) 1 Dec 1719 Sarah Stewart (RwVR)
2. **JONATHAN**, bpt 21 May 1699: m Kingston, NH abt 1725 Elizabeth (Fifield) Sleeper (TAG 16:165)
3. **HANNAH**, bpt 22 Feb 1702

4. **ELIZABETH**, bpt 16 Apr 1704
5. **JOSEPH**, b Newbury, MA 27 Jan 1705 (NVR)
6. **ISAAC**, b Newbury, MA 22 Dec 1707 (NVR)
7. **SARAH**, b Newbury, MA 2 Nov 1709 (NVR): d Kingston, NH 28 Jan 1714/15 (KTR)

(by 2nd wife) born Kingston, NH (KTR)

8. **SAMUEL**, b 26 Mar 1714: d Kingston, NH 4 Mar 1714/15 (KTR)
9. **SAMUEL**, b 25 Aug 1715
10. **GIDEON**, b 20 Dec 1716

JEREMIAH WEBSTER, b Hampton, NH 21 Dec 1703 son of John & Abiah (Shaw) Webster (HmVR p30): d Kingston, NH (WP) 30 Jun 1773 (NEHGR 9:160): m Kingston, NH 19 Jun 1729 Elizabeth Ladd (KTR), b Kingston, NH 22 May 1714 dau of John & Elizabeth (Sanborn) Ladd (KTR).

Jeremiah signed a petition in 1738 for a new parish in the easterly part of Kingston.

Children: born Kingston, NH (KTR & KChR)

1. **ELIZABETH**, b 2 Nov 1730: d Kingston, NH 28 May 1735 (KTR)
2. **JOHN**, b 5 Feb 1732/3: d Kingston, NH 27 May 1735 (KTR)
3. **NATHANIEL**, b 3 May 1735: d Kingston, NH 26 May 1735 (KTR)
4. **JOHN**, b 30 May 1736
5. **ELIZABETH**, b 28 Oct 1738: m Kingston, NH 22 Sep 1758 Joseph Bartlett (NHGR 3:90)
6. **DOROTHY**, bpt 22 Mar 1741
7. **JEREMIAH**, bpt 8 May 1743: d 4 Mar 1817 (DAR 2:221): m Danville, NH 9 Jun 1774 Anne Sleeper (NEHGR 58:123)
8. **JONATHAN LADD**, bpt 22 Sep 1745: d E. Kingston, NH 19 May 1830 (CR): m 6 Apr 1769 Judith Currier
9. **NATHANIEL**, bpt 13 Nov 1748
10. **ELIPHALET**, bpt 12 Apr 1752: d E. Kingston, NH 11 Aug 1818 (CR): m 27 Jan 1774 Hannah Prescott
11. **DOLLEY**, bpt 19 May 1754
12. **JOSIAH**, bpt 5 Dec 1756

JOHN WEBSTER, b Hampton, NH 16 Feb 1673 son of Thomas & Sarah (Brewer) Webster (HmVR p105): d Rye, NH 1734 (PRNH 2:515): m(1) Hampton, NH 21 Sep 1703 Abiah Shaw (HmVR p58), dau of Joseph & Elizabeth (Partridge) Shaw (LND p626): m(2) Sarah ___ NEHGR 9:160).

Bond of Jeremy Webster & Josiah Webster 8 July 1734 for the administration of the estate of their father John Webster of Rye, NH (PRNH 2:515).

Children: born Hampton, NH (HmVR)

1. **JEREMIAH**, b 21 Dec 1703: d (WP) 30 Jun 1773: m Kingston, NH 19 Jun 1729 Elizabeth Ladd (KTR)
2. **CHARITY** (twin), b 2 Apr 1706: m Rye, NH 23 Oct 1734 Zachariah Berry (Rye VR)
3. **JOSIAH** (twin), b 2 Apr 1706: m Rye, NH 21 Sep 1738 Martha Goss (Rye VR)
4. **JOHN**, b 10 Feb 1711: m 29 Nov 1738 Hannah Hobbs
5. **THOMAS**, b 1 Jul 1715: m Kingston, NH 12 Oct 1738 Judith Noyes (KTR)
6. **CALEB**, b 19 Mar 1718/9: d Kingston, NH 17 Jul 1735 (NHGR 2:134)
7. **ABIAH**, b 20 Jan 1721/2: d Rye, NH 2 Jul 1736 (NEHGR 9:160)
8. **ELIZABETH**, b 27 Sep 1724: m Rye, NH 19 Aug 1747 William Kingman (Rye VR)

JOHN WEBSTER, b Newbury, MA 2 Nov 1683 son of John & Bridget (Huggins) Webster (NVR): d (Est Adm) Hampton, NH 11 Nov 1754 (PRNH 5:182): m Salisbury, MA (int) 13 Mar 1707/8 Sarah Greeley (SVR), b Salisbury, MA 21 Oct 1685 dau of Andrew & Sarah (Brown) Greeley (SVR).

John Webster of Salisbury was taken in & made a freeholder of Kingston 30 Apr 1705. He was granted 200 acres of land at a meeting of the freeholders 30 Oct 1706.

Children: born Salisbury, MA (SVR)

1. **JOHN**, b 28 Apr 1709: m(1) Kingston, NH 17 Nov 1730 Ruth Clough (KTR): m(2) Susanna

(Snow) Gale (DAR 1:724)
2. **ANDREW**, b 12 Nov 1710: m(1) Kingston, NH 25 Nov 1731 Mercy Clough (NHGR 2:45): m (2) Hampton Falls, NH 29 Dec 1743 Prudence (Locke) Weare (HFTR)
3. **STEPHEN**, b 5 Oct 1712: m Salisbury, MA (int) 1 Nov 1734 Hannah Swett (SVR)
4. **MARY**, b 30 Sep 1714
5. **NATHAN**, b Jan 1719: m(1) Kingston, NH 5 Dec 1739 Mary Clifford (NHGR 3:40): m(2) Salisbury, MA 26 Jun 1770 Sarah Ring (SVR)
6. **NATHANIEL**, b 25 Mar 1724: d Salisbury, MA 6 May 1784: m Salisbury, MA 15 Nov 1769 Ann Currier (SVR)
7. **ANNE**, b Kingston, NH 2 May 1726 (SVR): m Salisbury, MA Oct 1748 Jacob True (SVR)

JOHN WEBSTER, bpt Hampton, NH 27 Jun 1697 son of Isaac & Mary (Hutchins) Webster (HH p1033): d Kingston, NH (WP) 27 Aug 1766 (PRNH 7:388): m Rowley, MA (int) 1 Dec 1719 Sarah Stewart (Rw VR), b Rowley, MA 19 May 1699 dau of Ebenezer & Elizabeth (Johnson) Stewart (RwVR).

John & his family belonged to Kingston in 1725 when Rev Clark took charge of the church.

Children: bpt Kingston, NH (NHGR)
1. **SARAH**, bpt 11 Dec 1725: m Kingston, NH 6 Sep 1747 Francis Pollard (KTR)
2. **ELIZABETH**, bpt 11 Sep 1725: m Kingston, NH 13 Sep 1742/3 Jacob Carter (NHGR 3:41)
3. **ANNE**, bpt 5 Jun 1726: d Kingston, NH (prob) 26 Jul 1735 (NHGR 2:134)
4. **ISAAC**, bpt 23 Apr 1727: m Kingston, NH 29 Dec 1747 Sarah Downing (NHGR 3:43)
5. **HANNAH**, bpt 27 Oct 1728: living 1763
7. **GIDEON**, bpt 25 May 1735: d Kingston, NH (Est Adm) 29 Dec 1756 (PRNH 5:561)
8. **MARY**, bpt 24 Dec 1738: m ___ Peabody

JOHN WEBSTER JR, b Salisbury, MA 28 Apr 1709 son of John & Sarah (Greeley) Webster (SVR): d 29 Apr 1788 (DAR 1:724): m(1) Kingston, NH 17

Nov 1730 Ruth Clough (KTR), b Salisbury, MA 7 Sep 1711 dau of Thomas & Ruth (Conner) Clough (SVR): m(2) Susannah (Snow) Gale (DAR 1:724), b abt 1713 d Franklin, NH 20 Mar 1804 a.91yrs (CG p54).

John signed a petition in 1730 regarding the township of Kingston & in 1738 he signed a petition for a new parish in the easterly part of Kingston.

Children: born Kingston, NH (KTR)

1. **MARGARET**, b 17 Jan 1732: d Kingston, NH 26 Jul 1735 (KTR)
2. **RUTH**, b 28 Aug 1733: m Kingston, NH 9 Nov 1748 Jesse Flanders (KChR)
3. **MARGARET**, b 1 Dec 1735: m Kingston, NH 2 Jan 1754 Joseph Fellows (KTR)
4. **MARTHA**, b 20 Nov 1737
5. **HUMPHREY**, b 20 Mar 1740: d Kingston, NH 13 Sep 1763 (KTR)
6. **SARAH**, b 17 Jan 1742: m ____ Fowler
7. **JOHN**, b 10 Sep 1744: d Salisbury, NH 3 Feb 1824: m Rebecca Dearborn (HS p845)
8. **HANNAH**, b 28 Aug 1746
9. **REBECCA**, b 10 Aug 1750: d Salisbury, NH 26 Sep 1811: m John Collins Gale (DAR 1: 257)
10. **ISRAEL**, b Jul 1753: d 11 Sep 1835: m 25 Oct 1772 Elizabeth Rolf (NHPR 91:7)
11. **STEPHEN**, b 1 Jan 1754: d aft 1808 (DAR 1: 725): m(1) Susanna Pettingill: m(2) Sarah (Ellison) Parsons
12. **HANNAH**, b 3 Sep 1756

JONATHAN WEBSTER, bpt Hampton, NH 21 May 1699 son of Isaac & Mary (Hutchins) Webster (HH p1033): m Kingston, NH abt 1725 Elizabeth (Fifield) Sleeper (TAG 16:165), b Hampton, NH 25 Nov 1698 dau of John & Abigail (Weare) Fifield (HmVR p68). Elizabeth m(1) Hezekiah Sleeper.

Children: born Kingston, NH (KTR & NHGR)

1. **SHUAH**, bpt 20 Nov 1726: d Kingston, NH 18 Oct 1734 (NHGR 2:133)

2. **JOSEPH**, b 7 Mar 1729
3. **JOHN**, bpt 9 Apr 1732: (poss) d Kingston, NH 22 Jun 1736 NHGR 3:39)
4. **JONATHAN**, bpt 18 Aug 1734
5. **ABRAHAM**, b 22 Aug 1737: m Kingston, NH 30 Mar 1763 Martha Emmons (KTR)
6. **JOHN**, b 9 Mar 1740

JOSHUA WEBSTER, b Kingston, NH 2 Sep 1703 son of Thomas & Sarah (?Godfrey) Webster (KTR): m Abigail ?Waldron (NEHGR 9:160). A Joshua Webster m Greenland, NH 2 Mar 1727 Abigail Kenniston (NEHGR 65:353).

In 1738 Joshua signed a petition for a grant of land in Kingston. Abigail, his wife was admitted to the Kingston Church 21 May 1738.

Children: bpt Kingston, NH

1. **SAMUEL**, bpt 28 Jan 1728 (NHGR 2:48): d Kingston, NH (Est Adm) 26 Dec 1753 (PRNH 4:499)
2. **JOSHUA**, b Kingston, NH 3 May 1729 (KTR): bpt 18 May 1729 (NHGR 2:48)
3. **ABIGAIL**, bpt 30 Feb 1734 (NHGR 2:68)
4. **PHEBE**, bpt 28 Sep 1739/40 (NHGR 5:106)
5. **WALDRON**, bpt 17 Apr 1743 (NHGR 5:109)
6. **JOHN**, bpt 9 Jun 1745 (NHGR 5:112)
7. **WILLIAM**, bpt 11 Jun 1749 (NHGR 5:157): d Kingston, NH 20 Oct 1753 (NHVR)
8. **JOSEPH**, bpt 7 Jun 1752 (NHGR 6:27)
9. **THOMAS**, d Kingston, NH 18 Oct 1753 (NHVR)

SAMUEL WEBSTER, b Kingston, NH 3 Apr 1708 son of Thomas & Sarah (?Godfrey) Webster (KTR): d Allenstown, NH bef 17 Nov 1790: m(1) Ipswich, MA 6 Feb 1732/3 Elizabeth Burnum (IpVR), b Ipswich, MA 3 Jun 1712 dau of David & Elizabeth (Perkins) Burnum (IpVR), d Kingston, NH 20 Oct 1738 (KTR): m(2) Kingston, NH 10 May 1740 Dorothy Stanyan (KTR), b Hampton, NH 27 Jan 1721 dau of Jacob & Dorothy (_) Stanyan (HH p984), d Allenstown, NH 17 Nov 1790 (DAR #330433A461).

Samuel signed a petition in 1738 for a grant of land in Kingston.

Children: born Kingston, NH (KTR)
(by 1st wife)

1. **SARAH**, b 20 Nov 1734: d Kingston, NH 1737
2. **DOROTHY**, b 10 Sep 1735
3. **DAVID**, b 30 Sep 1738: d Kingston, NH Sep 1757 (KTR)

(by 2nd wife)

4. **BURNUM**, b 18 Oct 1740: d Kingston, NH 8 Nov 1758 (KTR)
5. **SARAH**, b 1 Jan 1742/3
6. **ELIZABETH**, b 11 Jan 1745
7. **RACHEL**, b 17 Feb 1747: d Kingston, NH 27 Nov 1751 (KTR)
8. **SAMUEL**, b 1 Jun 1749
9. **RACHEL**, b 7 Dec 1751
10. **JOSEPH STANIEL**, b 2 Apr 1754
11. **ELIZABETH**, b 8 Mar 1756: d 24 Sep 1819: m abt 1776 John Bunten (DAR #330433A461)
12. **DAVID**, b 12 Aug 1758: d 1 Sep 1847: m Sarah Carr (DAR 1:724)
13. **BURNUM**, b 8 May 1761

THOMAS WEBSTER, b Hampton, NH 20 Jan 1664 son of Thomas & Sarah (Brewer) Webster (HmVR p553): d Kingston, NH 7 Mar 1733 (NHGR 2:133): m abt 1689 Sarah ?Godfrey (NEM p790), d Kingston, NH 15 Feb 1717/8 (KTR).

Thomas had land laid out to him in Kingston 18 Jul 1701. He belonged to Kingston in 1725 when Rev Clark took charge of the church.

Children: last 5 born Kingston, NH (KTR)

1. **SARAH**, b Hampton, NH 19 Sep 1690 (HmVR p12): m Kingston, NH 14 Nov 1710 Samuel Fellows Jr (KTR)
2. **THOMAS**, b abt 1693: d Kingston, NH 13 May 1772 (KTR): m Kingston, NH 19 Jun 1717 Mary Greeley (KTR)
3. **MARY**, b Hampton, NH 19 May 1696 (HmVR p64): m Kingston, NH 16 Aug 1716 John Fifield (KTR)
4. **ALICE**, b Hampton, NH 5 Aug 1698 (HmVR p68): d Kingston, NH 30 Oct 1722 (KTR)
5. **BENJAMIN**, b 24 Aug 1701: m(1) Kingston,

NH Feb 1725 Elizabeth Stewart (KTR): m(2) Kingston, NH 1 Dec 1737 Mary Stanyan (KTR)

6. **JOSHUA**, b 2 Sep 1703: m Abigail ?Waldron (NEHGR 9:160)
7. **ABIGAIL**, b 15 Apr 1706: m Kingston, NH 25 Dec 1724 David Quimby (KTR)
8. **SAMUEL**, b 3 Apr 1708: m(1) Ipswich, MA 6 Feb 1732/3 Elizabeth Burnum (IpVR): m(2) Kingston, NH 10 May 1740 Dorothy Stanyan (KTR)
9. **ELIZABETH**, b 11 Jan 1710/11: m Kingston, NH 20 Apr 1730 Josiah Fowler (NHGR 2:45)

THOMAS WEBSTER JR, b abt 1693 son of Thomas & Sarah (?Godfrey) Webster (NEHGR 9:160); d Kingston, NH 13 May 1772 (KTR): m Kingston, NH 19 Jun 1717 Mary Greeley (KTR), b Haverhill, MA 30 Mar 1691 dau of Benjamin & Elizabeth (Smith) Greeley (HvVR).

Thomas Jr belonged to Kingston in 1725 when Rev Clark took charge of the church. In 1738 he signed a petition for a new parish in the easterly part of Kingston.

Children: born Kingston, NH (KTR)

1. **ELIZABETH**, b 27 Mar 1718: m Kingston, NH 2 Feb 1737/8 John Carter (NHGR 3:40)
2. **MARY** (twin), b 31 Mar 1719: m Kingston, NH 25 Jan 1738/9 Thomas Carter (NHGR 3:40)
3. **SARAH** (twin), b 31 Mar 1719: m Kingston, NH 11 Jul 1745 Amos Bootman (KTR)
4. **MARTHA**, b 16 Jun 1722: m Kingston, NH 10 Dec 1745 Thomas Sever (KTR)
5. **ALICE**, b 10 Jan 1724/5: m Kingston, NH 3 Jun 1748 Jacob Silloway (KTR)
6. **MIRIAM**, b 8 Aug 1729: m Kingston, NH 19 Feb 1749/50 Philip Davis (NHGR 3:44)

THOMAS WEBSTER, b Hampton, NH 1 Jul 1715 son of John & Abiah (Shaw) Webster (HmVR p49): m Kingston, NH 12 Oct 1738 Judith Noyes (KTR), dau of James & Sarah (Coffin) Noyes (Noyes Gen p304).

Judith possibly m(2) Newbury, MA 9 Nov 1756 Joseph Couch (NVR).

Children: 1st 3 born Kingston, NH (KTR)
1. **SARAH**, b 12 Oct 1739
2. **JUDITH**, b 7 Jun 1741
3. **LEVI**, b 20 Feb 1742/3
4. **ENOCH**, bpt Kingston, NH 21 Jun 1747 (KChR)
5. **JOANNA**, bpt Kingston, NH 24 Sep 1749 (KChR): d 14 Feb 1794: m 27 Apr 1772 Trueworthy Palmer (NEHGR 68:260)
6. **CALEB**, bpt Kingston, NH 28 Jul 1751 (KChR): d E. Kingston, NH 21 Mar 1809 (CR): m(1) 23 Oct 1773 Mary Tilton: m(2) Kensington, NH 9 Oct 1778 Abigail French (NHVR)

DAVID WEED, b (prob) Amesbury, MA 28 Jun 1722 son of Jonathan & Patience (Martin) Weed (AVR): d 18 Oct 1801 (DAR 1:725): m Kingston, NH 29 Nov 1743 Abigail Judkins (KTR), b Kingston, NH 14 Jul 1725 dau of Samuel & Abigail (Harriman) Judkins (KTR).

Children: born Kingston, NH (KTR)
1. **ELIJAH**, b 30 Jul 1744: m Unity, NH 19 Apr 1770 Meriah Huntoon (UR p48)
2. **SAMUEL**, b 24 Jul 1746
3. **DAVID**, b 24 Jun 1748: d Unity, NH 1 Sep 1778: m Unity, NH 6 Jul 1775 Elizabeth Batchelder (UR p47)
4. **ABIGAIL**, b 23 Sep 1750
5. **JONATHAN**, b 18 May 1753
6. **BENJAMIN**, b 3 Nov 1756
7. **JOSEPH**, b 23 Mar 1760
8. **ANNA**, b 15 Aug 1762
9. **WILLIAM**, b 14 Apr 1765

ORLANDO WEED, b Amesbury, MA 23 Mar 1715 son of Elisha & Sarah (Bagley) Weed (AVR): m Kingston, NH 27 Nov 1740 Sarah Webster (KChR), b Salisbury, MA 6 Jul 1721 dau of John & Mary (_) Webster (SVR).

Orlando & his wife Sarah were admitted to the 2nd Church of Christ in Kingston 13 Dec 1741.

Children:
1. **SARAH**, bpt Kingston, NH 13 Dec 1741 (KChR)
2. **HENRY**, b So Hampton, NH 15 Apr 1743 (SHVR)
3. **MOSES**, b So Hampton, NH 10 Oct 174_

BENJAMIN WELCH, b Kingston, NH 13 Jan 1706/7 son of Samuel & Mary (Judkins) Welch (KTR): m (1) Yarmouth, ME 22 Sep 1735 Maragret Larabee (Saco Valley by Ridlon p827), b 22 Feb 1709 dau of Stephen & Margaret (Pain) Larabee, d 1 Dec 1737: m(2) Elizabeth ___.

Benjamin's name appears on a list of Kingston men who swore allegiance to the King in 1727. He received a deed of land in Kingston from his father Samuel Welch Sr 5 Nov 1729.

Children:
(by 1st wife)
1. **BENJAMIN**, b 9 Sep 1736: d (W) 9 May 1758 (Maine Wills by Sargent p843)

(by 2nd wife)
2. **ELIZABETH**, b 24 Mar 1738: m Cumberland, ME 10 Nov 1760 Roger Googin
3. **THOMAS**, b 14 Feb 1741: m 1764 Mary Clough
4. **MARGARET**, b 26 Feb 1742: m Cumberland, ME 29 Sep 1760 Samuel Moore
5. **MARY**, b 13 May 1745
6. **JOANNA**, b 5 May 1748: m 1764 John Griffin
7. **SUSANNA**, m Jeremiah Mason

DAVID WELCH, b Kingston, NH 30 Jun 1720 son of Samuel & Mary (Judkins) Welch (KTR): d Kingston, NH (Est Adm) 29 Jun 1757 (PRNH 6:96): m (prob) Abigail ____.

David was admitted to the Kingston Church 3 Apr 1742. Abigail Welch was admitted 14 Mar 1742.

Children:

1. **JONATHAN**, bpt Kingston, NH 25 Aug 1751 (NHGR 6:26)
2. **SAMUEL**?, bpt Kingston, NH 3 Sep 1758 son of Abigail now wife of Hoit (NHVR)

JOHN WELCH, b Kingston, NH 7 Aug 1729 son of Joseph & Deborah (Scribner) Welch (KTR): d Sanbornton, NH 1811 (NEHGR 23:419): m So Hampton, NH 5 Dec 1751 Abra Flanders (SHVR), b Salisbury, MA 19 Jun 1729 dau of Jonathan & Judith (Merrill) Flanders (SVR).

John & his wife renew'd their Baptismal Covenant in the Kingston Church 31 Dec 1752.

Children:

1. **BENJAMIN**, bpt Kingston, NH 31 Dec 1752 (NHGR 6:28): m ? wid Cotton
2. **HANNAH**, bpt Kingston, NH 25 May 1755 (NH GR 6:32)
3. **ABRA (EBERY)**, bpt Kingston, NH 8 Jul 1760 (NHVR): m Kingston, NH 13 Nov 1785 George Dutch (NHGR 3:132)
4. **JOSEPH**, b E. Kingston, NH 20 Oct 1761: m Unity, NH 25 Feb 1784 Elizabeth Huntoon
5. **DEBORAH**, b 22 Feb 1764: m 22 Aug 1785 William Prescott (NEHGR 27:174)
6. **JUDITH**, b 1766: m Simeon Brown
7. **JONATHAN**, b 1768: m(1) Abigail Brown: m (2) Hannah Merrill
8. **ELIZABETH**, b 19 May 1770: m 13 Aug 1795 Jonathan Smith (NEHGR 27:174)
9. **SALLY**, b 1772

PHILIP WELCH, b Kingston, NH 8 Jul 1715 son of Samuel & Mary (Judkins) Welch (KTR): m Kingston, NH 5 Jun 1738 Sarah Walsford (KTR).

Children: bpt Kingston, NH (NHGR)

1. **SARAH**, b Kingston, NH 13 Mar 1739 (KTR): bpt 9 Sep 1739
2. **HANNAH**, bpt 4 Oct 1741

SAMUEL WELCH, b Topsfield, MA 1675 son of Philip & Hannah (Haggett) Welch (NEHGR 23:418): d

Kingston, NH 6 Oct 1745 (NHVR): m Haverhill, MA bef 1703 Mary Judkins (HvVR), b Exeter, NH 7 Nov 1678 dau of Joel & Mary (Bean) Judkins (LND p393).

Samuel was granted 200 acres of land in Kingston at a meeting of the freeholders 30 Oct 1706. His family belonged to Kingston in 1725 when Rev Clark took charge of the church.

Children: last 8 born Kingston, NH (KTR)

1. **JOSEPH**, b Haverhill, MA 28 Feb 1702/3 (HvVR): m Kingston, NH 29 Dec 1726 Deborah Scribner (KTR)
2. **HANNAH**, b Haverhill, MA 19 Mar 1704/5 (HvVR)
3. **BENJAMIN**, b 13 Jan 1706/7: m Yarmouth, ME 22 Sep 1735 Margaret Larabee
4. **TABITHA**, b 10 Mar 1708/9: m Kingston, NH 14 Feb 1734 John Clough (NHGR 2:45)
5. **SAMUEL**, b 13 Feb 1711: d Bow, NH Apr 1823 (KTR): m(1) Kingston, NH 22 Jan 1732 Eleanor Clough (KTR): m(2) ? 18 Feb 1746/7 Eleanor Clough: m(3) at a.84yrs 1794 Rachel (Sargent) Elliot (NEHGR 23:418)
6. **MARTHA**, b Feb 1712/3
7. **PHILIP**, b 8 Jul 1715: m Kingston, NH 5 Jun 1738 Sarah Walsford (KTR)
8. **MARY**, b 20 Jan 1717/8: m Kingston, NH 2 Oct 1740 Elisha Clough (KTR)
9. **DAVID**, b 30 Jun 1720
10. **ABIGAIL**, b Mar 1724/5

NOTE: A Samuel Welch m Kingston, NH 24 Jan 1727/8 Hannah Welch (NHGR 2:44). Perhaps this was a 2nd marriage.

SAMUEL WELCH, b Kingston, NH 13 Feb 1711 son of Samuel & Mary (Judkins) Welch (KTR): d Bow, NH Apr 1823 (KTR): m(1) Kingston, NH 22 Jan 1732 Eleanor Clough (KTR), b Salisbury, MA 25 Oct 1712 dau of John & Elizabeth (Long) Clough (SVR): m(2) ? Kingston, NH 18 Feb 1746/7 Eleanor Clough (KTR): m(3) 1794 Rachel (Sargent) Elliot (NEHGR 23:418), b Amesbury, MA 23 Jan

1738 dau of William & Anne (_) Sargent (AVR).

Children: born Kingston, NH
(by 1st wife)
1. **ELEANOR**, b 1733 (NEHGR 23:420)
2. **JONATHAN**, bpt 18 May 1735 (NHGR 2:69)
3. **SAMUEL**, bpt 29 Jun 1738 (NEHGR 23:420)
4. **REUBEN**, b 15 Feb 1740 (KTR)

(by 2nd) wife)
5. **SAMUEL**, b 13 Dec 1748 (KTR)
6. **REUBEN**, b 3 Sep 1750 (KTR)
7. **ELEANOR**, b 30 Nov 1752 (KTR)

THOMAS WELCH, b Kingston, NH 13 Oct 1727 son of Joseph & Deborah (Scribner) Welch (KTR): m Kingston, NH 26 Jun 1752 Elizabeth Pressey (KTR).

Children: born Kingston, NH (KTR)
1. **MOSES**, b 11 Jan 1754
2. **(CHILD)**, d Kingston, NH 15 Nov 1756 (NHVR)
3. **THOMAS**, b 8 Mar 1758: d Kingston, NH 28 Apr 1769 (KTR)
4. **DEBORAH**, b 22 Jun 1762
5. **ARKLOS (ARCHELAUS)**, b 5 Jun 1764: m Molly Morrison
6. **AMOS**, b 28 Feb 1767

JACOB WELLS, b Amesbury, MA 28 Aug 1710 son of Titus & Joanna (Rowell) Wells (AVR): m Amesbury, MA 12 Jul 1732 Ruth Sargent (AVR), b Amesbury, MA 26 Jul 1712 dau of Philip & Mary (Tewksbury) Sargent (AVR).

Jacob settled on the westerly section of Kingston.

Children: last 10 (SdTR)
1. **MARTHA**, bpt Amesbury, MA 2 Mar 1734/5 (AVR)
2. **JOSEPH** (twin), b 27 Feb 1739
3. **BENJAMIN** (twin), b 27 Feb 1739
4. **PHILIP** (twin), b 14 Mar 1741
5. **TITUS** (twin), b 14 Mar 1741

6. **SARGENT**, b 7 Oct 1744: m Danville, NH 22 Oct 1763 Theodate Clough (NEHGR 58:47)
7. **RUTH**, b 3 Oct 1746
8. **JACOB**, b 23 Jan 1749: m Danville, NH 22 Oct 1772 Jemima Williams (NEHGR 58:122)
9. **DOROTHY**, b 6 Feb 1751
10. **MOLEY**, b 6 Jun 1753
11. **TIMOTHY**, b 2 Dec 1755: m Danville, NH 14 Jul 1774 Sarah Williams (NEHGR 58:123)

PHILEMON WELLS, b Amesbury, MA 3 Sep 1708 son of Titus & Joanna (Rowell) Wells (AVR): d bef Jun 1741: m (int) 29 Nov 1729 Ruth Ayers (OF p1021).

Philemon signed a petition in 1738 for a new parish in the easterly part of Kingston.

Children: born Newbury, MA (NVR)

1. **SARAH**, b 20 Dec 1730
2. **TIMOTHY**, b (prob) 15 Oct 1732: bpt 12 Nov 1732: m wid Rebecca Wilson
4. **RUTH**, b 2 Dec 1734
5. **MARY**, bpt 6 Feb 1736/7
6. **ELIZABETH**, bpt 20 May 1739
7. **PHILEMON**, bpt 28 Jun 1741

PHILIP WELLS, b Amesbury, MA 3 Sep 1721 son of Thomas & Sarah (Hadley) Wells (AVR): d bef 1768 (PRNH 9:203): m Amesbury, MA 16 Jul 1741 Mary Jewell (AVR).

Children: last 4 (SdTR)

1. **DOROTHY**, b Kingston, NH 28 Jul 1742 (KTR)
2. **MOLLE**, b Kingston, NH 22 Mar 1744 (KTR)
3. **DAVID**, b 12 Jan 1745
4. **HITE**, b 3 Oct 1747
5. **SARAH**, b 13 Sep 1749
6. **STEPHEN**, b 2 Aug 1751: bpt Kingston, NH 28 Aug 1751 (NHGR 6:26): d 1834: m Mehitable Worthly (DAR 1:728)

DANIEL WEST, b (prob) Hampton Falls, NH 8 Apr 1721 son of Edward & Alice (Leavitt) West (HFTR): m Kingston, NH 6 Dec 1744 Elizabeth

Gordon (NHGR 2:45).

Children: bpt Kingston, NH (NHGR)
1. **ELIZABETH**, bpt 1 Sep 1745
2. **DANIEL**, bpt 19 Jul 1747

WILLIAM WHITTIER (WHICHER), b Salisbury, MA 20 Nov 1714 son of Reuben & Deborah (Pilsbury) Whicher (SVR): d Kingston, NH abt 1771 (Whittier Gen p31): m(1) Kingston, NH 17 Feb 1736/7 Phebe Morrill (KTR), bpt Salisbury, MA 7 Aug 1715 dau of Isaac & Abigail (Brown) Morrill (SVR): m(2) Kingston, NH 29 Apr 1755 Sarah Huntington (KChR).

William signed a petition for a new parish in the easterly part of Kingston in 1738.

Children: born Kingston, NH (KTR)
1. **ISAAC**, b 3 Feb 1737/8: d Brentwood, NH 6 Sep 1807 (CG p27): m Brentwood, NH 26 Aug 1762 Mary Blaisdell (BtTR)
2. **REUBEN**, b 15 May 1740: d Kingston, NH 29 Jan 1740 (KTR)
3. **REUBEN**, b 29 Nov 1741
4. **ABIGAIL**, b 30 Jul 1745: m Salisbury, MA (int) 13 Jun 1761 David Morrill (SVR)
5. **NATHANIEL**, bpt 14 Feb 1748 (KChR): d Cornville, ME 20 Feb 1833: m Ruth Smith
6. **WILLIAM** (twin), bpt 7 Feb 1752 (KChR)
7. **PHEBE** (twin), bpt 7 Feb 1752 (KChR)
8. **PHEBE**, bpt 22 Apr 1753 (KChR)
9. **PHEBE**, bpt 3 Nov 1754 (KChR): m 28 Mar 1772 John Currier

ELISHA WINSLEY (WINSLOW), b Salisbury, MA 9 Jul 1703 son of Samuel & Catherine (Stevens) Winsley (SVR): d Kingston, NH (Est Adm) 21 May 1760 (PRNH 6:569): m Kingston, NH 4 Jan 1725 Mary Sleeper (KTR), b Kingston, NH 21 Feb 1705/6 dau of Aaron & Elizabeth (Shaw) Sleeper (KTR).

In 1730 Elisha signed a petition regarding the township of Kingston & in 1738 he signed a petition for a grant of land.

Children: born Kingston, NH (KTR)

1. **SAMUEL**, b 18 May 1726: m Kingston, NH 15 Feb 1749/50 Jean French (KTR)
2. **BENJAMIN**, b 10 Feb 1728: m Kingston, NH 7 May 1765 Mary Clough (KTR)
3. **JONATHAN**, b 14 Feb 1730: d Epping, NH 1810 (Greeley Gen p144): m Abigail ____
4. **MARY**, b 13 Dec 1732: (prob) m Kingston, NH 14 Jan 1755 Samuel Buswell (KTR)
5. **ZEBULON**, b 1 Jun 1734: d Kingston, NH 13 Nov 1736 (KTR)
6. **CATHERINE**, b 8 Nov 1738
7. **HANNAH**, b 5 Apr 1741
8. **ZEBULON**, b 30 Aug 1744: m 31 Mar 1766 Hannah Bagley
9. **ELIZABETH**, b 28 Aug 1747

SAMUEL WINSLEY (WINSLOW), b Salisbury, MA 21 Dec 1670 son of Ephraim & Mary (Greeley) Winsley (SVR): d Kingston, NH (killed by Indians) 22 Jul 1710 (KTR): m Salisbury, MA 29 Apr 1696 Catherine Stevens (SVR), b Salisbury, MA 2 Jan 1674 dau of Benjamin & Hannah (Barnard) Stevens (SVR), d Kingston, NH 18 Apr 1737 (KTR).

Samuel was granted 200 acres of land in Kingston at a meeting of the freeholders 30 Oct 1706.

Children: 1st 3 born Salisbury, MA (SVR)

1. **MARY**, b 26 May 1698
2. **SAMUEL**, b 26 Nov 1700: m(1) Kingston, NH 2 Jan 1723/4 Hulda Swett (KTR): m(2) ? Amesbury, MA 1 May 1739 Frances Tucker (AVR)
3. **ELISHA**, b 9 Jul 1703: m Kingston, NH 4 Jan 1725 Mary Sleeper (KTR)
4. **HANNAH**, b Kingston, NH 28 Nov 1710 (KTR): m Salisbury, MA 26 Dec 1728 Reuben Morrill (SVR)

SAMUEL WINSLEY (WINSLOW), b Salisbury, MA 26 Nov 1700 son of Samuel & Catherine (Stevens) Winsley (SVR): m(1) Kingston, NH 2 Jan 1723/4 Hulda Swett (KTR), b Hampton, NH 16 Jul 1699

dau of John & Bethia (Page) Swett (HmVR p69), d Kingston, NH 25 Sep 1738 (KTR): probably m(2) Amesbury, MA 1 May 1739 Frances Tucker (AVR).
Samuel's family belonged to Kingston in 1725 when Rev Clark took charge of the church.

Children: born Kingston, NH (KTR)
(by 1st wife)
1. **ELIZABETH**, b 8 Feb 1724/5: m Kingston, NH 27 Feb 1745/6 William Buswell (KTR)
2. **EPHRAIM**, b 25 Jun 1727: d abt 17 Jan 1810 (DAR 1:754): m Kingston, NH 27 Mar 1753 Hannah Colcord (KTR)
3. **JOHN**, b 10 Dec 1729: d 1816: m Kingston, NH 8 Dec 1763 Elizabeth French (NHGR 3: 129)
4. **JACOB**, b 27 Nov 1731: m 15 Oct 1778 Mrs Tryphena (Nichols) Severance
5. **SAMUEL**, b 31 Jun 1736: d Kingston, NH 31 Jun 1736 (KTR)
6. **CATHERINE**, b 30 Mar 1738: d Kingston, NH 15 Jun 1738 (KTR)

(by 2nd wife)
7. **SAMUEL**, b 6 Jan 1740: m Kingston, NH 9 Jun 1763 Phebe Buswell (KTR)
8. **HANNAH**, b 22 Apr 1743: m Kingston, NH 1 Aug 1768 Samuel Severance (KTR)

JOSEPH WORTH, b (prob) Hampton Falls, NH 6 Apr 1729 son of Joseph & Lydia (_) Worth (HFTR): m Kingston, NH 16 Apr 1752 Anne Stanyan (KTR).
Joseph was admitted to the Kingston Church 26 Jun 1756.

Children:
1. **LYDIA**, b Kingston, NH 9 Mar 1753 (KTR)

MOSES WORTHEN, b Haverhill, MA 4 Jul 1714 son of Samuel & Deliverance (Heath) Worthen (HvVR): d 1787 (DAR 1:763): m Abigail ___.
Abigail Worthen was dismissed from the 1st Church of Amesbury to the 2nd Kingston Church 2 Sep 1744.

Children: (SdTR)
1. **MARTHA**, bpt Kingston, NH 3 Feb 1744 (KChR)
2. **Martha**, b 12 Mar 1745: bpt Kingston, NH 12 May 1745 (KChR)
3. **MARY**, b 16 Mar 1747
4. **SAMUEL**, b 15 Jan 1748/9: d 29 Apr 1824 (DAR 1:763): m Hannah Ingalls

DANIEL YOUNG, b Kingston, NH 9 Jan 1710/11 son of Joseph & Elizabeth (Sleeper) Young (KTR): d Kingston, NH (Est Adm) 27 Mar 1751 (PRNH 4: 111): m Kingston, NH 23 Jan 1734/5 Hannah Lovering (KTR).

Daniel signed a petition in 1738 for a grant of land in Kingston. He & his wife were admitted to the Kingston Church 19 Feb 1738.

Children: born Kingston, NH (KTR)
1. **ANNA**, b 9 Nov 1735
2. **LOVE**, b 11 Jan 1736/7
3. **SAMUEL**, b 26 Nov 1738
4. **HANNAH**, b 25 Dec 1740
5. **DANIEL**, b 21 Jan 1742/3
6. **ELIZABETH**, b 21 Jan 1744/5
7. **DAVID**, b 13 Jul 1746
8. **ABIGAIL**, b 13 Jan 1747/8
9. **SARAH**, bpt 28 Oct 1750 (NHGR 5:159)

HEZEKIAH YOUNG, b Kingston, NH 18 Sep 1724 son of Joseph & Elizabeth (Sleeper) Young (KTR): d Unity, NH 17 Dec 1810 (UR p42): m Kingston, NH 19 Feb 1746/7 Anna Marthan (NHGR 3:43), b abt 1726, d Unity, NH 30 Apr 1801 a.74yrs (UR p42).

Hezekiah was admitted to the Kingston Church 23 May 1742 & his wife was admitted 2 May 1752.

Children:
1. **ELIZABETH** (adopted), bpt Kingston, NH 21 Sep 1755 (NHVR)

JOHN YOUNG, b Kingston, NH 11 Oct 1706 son of Joseph & Elizabeth (Sleeper) Young (KTR): d Kingston, NH 22 Aug 1758 (KTR); Est Adm 27 Sep

1758 (PRNH 6:318): m(1) Kingston, NH 13 Nov 1729 Sarah Burnham (KTR), d Kingston, NH 16 Mar 1749 (NHVR): m(2) Kingston, NH 25 May 1749 Dorothy (Brown) Sawyer (NHGR 3:44), b Newbury, MA 10 Aug 1712 dau of Thomas & Elizabeth (Berry) Brown (NVR). Dorothy m(1) Newbury, MA 1 Dec 1729 Joseph Sawyer (NVR). She m(3) Kingston, NH 12 Feb 1760 Thomas Thompson (NHGR 3:91).

In 1730 John signed a petition regarding the township of Kingston. Sarah Young, wife of John was admitted to the Kingston Church 2 Apr 1730.

Children: born Kingston, NH (KTR)
(by 1st wife)

1. **JOHN**, b 18 Dec 1730: m Kingston, NH Apr 1752 Meriam Sawyer (KTR)
2. **SARAH**, b 28 Feb 1732: d Kingston, NH 28 Mar 1732 (KTR)
3. **AARON** (twin), b 22 Feb 1733: d Kingston, NH 17 Dec 1733 (KTR)
4. **MOSES** (twin), b 22 Feb 1733: d Kingston, NH 19 May 1733 (KTR)
5. **GIDEON**, b 11 Oct 1734: d Kingston, NH 10 Jul 1735 (KTR)
6. **STEPHEN**, b 9 May 1736
7. **GIDEON**, b 29 Apr 1738
8. **MOSES**, b 5 Jan 1739
9. **SARAH**, b 1 Oct 1741: d Kingston, NH 25 Oct 1745 (KTR)
10. **AARON**, b 18 Aug 1743
11. **ISRAEL**, b 15 Sep 1744: d Kingston, NH 30 Sep 1745 (KTR)
12. **NATHANIEL**, b 22 Nov 1746: d Kingston, NH 8 Feb 1747 (KTR)

(by 2nd wife)

13. **RUTH**, b 18 Aug 1752
14. **HEZEKIAH**, b 3 Mar 1754
15. **MARTHA**, b 29 May 1756: d Kingston, NH 12 Jan 1758 (NHVR)

JONATHAN YOUNG, b Kingston, NH 6 Apr 1720 son of Joseph & Elizabeth (Sleeper) Young (KTR): m Kingston, NH 20 Oct 1741 Mary Lovering (KTR).

In 1738 Jonathan signed a petition for a

grant of land in Kingston. He & his wife were admitted to the Kingston Church 12 Sep 1742.

Children: born Kingston, NH (KTR)

1. **ABIGAIL**, b 29 May 1742: d Kingston, NH 25 Dec 1745 (KTR)
2. **NATHANIEL**, b 11 Apr 1744: d Kingston, NH 21 Dec 1745 (KTR)
3. **HEZEKIAH**, b 31 Oct 1746: d Kingston, NH 11 Oct 1748 (KTR)
4. **MARY**, b 6 Jan 1748/9
5. **DOROTHY**, b 27 Apr 1751
6. **JOANNA**, b 30 Nov 1753: d Kingston, NH 25 Apr 1756 (KTR)
7. **JOTHAM**, b 1 Oct 1756

JOSEPH YOUNG, son of John & Sarah (Wadleigh) Young (LND p776): d Kingston, NH 2 May 1756 (KTR): m Kingston, NH 24 Dec 1705 Elizabeth Sleeper (KTR), probably an unrecorded dau of Aaron & Elizabeth (Shaw) Sleeper (Hartford Times 7-19-41).

Joseph was granted 200 acres of land in Kingston at a meeting of the freeholders 30 Oct 1706. His family belonged to Kingston in 1725 when Rev Clark took charge of the church. In 1730 he signed a petition regarding the township of Kingston.

Children: born Kingston, NH (KTR)

1. **JOHN**, b 11 Oct 1706: d Kingston, NH 22 Aug 1758 (KTR): m(1) Kingston, NH 13 Nov 1729 Sarah Burnham (KTR): m(2) Kingston, NH 25 May 1749 Dorothy (Brown) Sawyer (NHGR 3:44)
2. **JOSEPH**, b 21 Dec 1708: d Kingston, NH 16 May 1749 (KTR): m Kingston, NH 9 Apr 1747 Sarah Brown (KTR)
3. **DANIEL**, b 9 Jan 1710/11: m Kingston, NH 23 Jan 1734/5 Hannah Lovering (KTR)
4. **AARON**, b 27 Oct 1714: m Kingston, NH 8 Nov 1737 Abigail Dudley (NHGR 3:39)
5. **ELIZABETH**, b 25 Oct 1717: d Kingston, NH 17 Oct 1756 (KTR): m Kingston, NH 1 Jan

1737/8 Joseph Fellows (KTR)

6. **JONATHAN**, b 6 Apr 1720: m Kingston, NH 20 Oct 1741 Mary Lovering (KTR)
7. **SARAH**, b 2 Aug 1722
8. **HEZEKIAH**, b 18 Sep 1724: m Kingston, NH 19 Feb 1746/7 Anna Marthan (NHGR 3:43)

JOSEPH YOUNG JR, b Kingston, NH 21 Dec 1708 son of Joseph & Elizabeth (Sleeper) Young (KTR): d Kingston, NH 16 May 1749 (KTR): m Kingston, NH 9 Apr 1747 Sarah Brown (KTR).

Joseph Jr signed a petition regarding the township of Kingston in 1730 & in 1738 he signed a petition for a grant of land.

Children: born Kingston, NH (KTR)

1. **JOANNA**, b 23 Dec 1747: m Kingston, NH 6 May 1779 Benjamin Clough (NHGR 3:130)
2. **JOSEPH**, b 20 Jun 1749

....

SECTION II

KINGSTON PATRIOTS & SOLDIERS

"Live Free or Die"

ASSOCIATION TEST

"WE, the SUBSCRIBERS, do hereby solemnly engage, and promise, that we will, to the utmost of our Power, at the Risque of our Lives and Fortunes, with ARMS, oppose the Hostile Proceedings of the British Fleets, and Armies, against the UNITED AMERICAN COLONIES."

KINGSTON

John Huntoon Jun
Willet Peterson
Benjamin Judkins
Philbrick Huntoon
Richard Hubbard
Simmons Seccomb
Thomas Elkins
Abraham Sanborn
Benjamin Huntoon
Josiah Bartlett
Ebenr Stevens
Abraham French
Richard Sleeper
Thomas Elkins Junr
Tristram Quinby
William Patten
Henry French
John Darling Sweat
John Calef
Jona Procter
Nathan Sweat
Daniel Colcord
Samuel Colcord
Ebenezer Eastmen
Joseph Calfe
William Saborn
Isaac Sanborn
James Procter
Elisha Sweat
John Pearson
Jacob Hook
Solomon Wheeler
Aaron Young Junr
Michll Carew
Joseph Nichols
Benjamin Sweat
Stephen Clifford
David Sambon

KINGSTON PATRIOTS

John Lad
John Judkins
John Judkins Junr
Amos Gale
Jethro Sanborn
Henry Judkins
Joseph Clafford
Samuel Fifield
Peter Fifield
David Kelly
Thomas Procter
John French
Joseph Woodman
Samll Buswell
Samuel Sweat
Joshua Bartlett Junr
Benja Cooper
Daniel Smith
David French
William Tande
Joseph Judkins
Samuel Woodman
Stephen Badger
William Sleeper
Jeremiah Bean
Stephen Tongue
Benjamin Lad
John Clifford Jr
Sanders Carr
John Thorn
Joshua Woodman
Benja Tucker
James Colbey
Samll Thompson
John Bartlet
Nathan Bartlet Junr
Thomas Sever Junr
Webster Davis
Jacob Carter Junr
Henery Hunt
Stephen Stuert
John Severance
Moses Hunt
John Stevens

Samul French
John Calef Juner
Ebenezer Long
Ebenezer Fifield
Caleb Judkins
Benjamin Stevens
Jonathan Sanborn
Saml Philbrick
Gorge Pitcher
Nathaniel Garland
Gideon George
Beainjman Sleeper
Ebenr Stevens Jr
Ebenezer Griffing
Edward Sleeper
Reuben Lowell
Jacob Webster
Benjamin Sanborn
Timothy Sanborn
Benjman _______
Jonathan Colens
Timothy Quimby
Jacob Smith
Peter Sanborn
Benjamin Lavrien
Joshua Bartlett
Stephen Sweat
Benjamin Clough
James Thorn
Corneliush Clough
Amos Burman
John Newton
Ralph Blasdel
Thomas Thompson
Ebenr Bartlet
Thomas Sever
Phillip Davis
Jacob Carter
Jeremiah Johnson
Jonathan Pallerd
Joseph Welch
Jonathan Sanborn Junr
Ebenezer Watson
Jonathan Sleeper

KINGSTON PATRIOTS

Moses Carter
Peaslee Hoyt
Benoni Eaton
Thomas Carter
Richard Hubbard Jr
Jacob Pesly
Calec Sever
John B Sleeper
Jacob Thorn
Timothy Bartlet
John Singleton
Bennet Greenfield
Daniel Busel
Samll Winslow
William Collins
Wellam Challes
Aaron Young
Benjamin Webster
James Nase (Noyes)
Joseph Fellows
John Sleeper
John Winslow
Samll Davis
William Calfe
Biley Hardie
John Noyes
Jacob Winsle

Agreeable to the Directions of the Hon'ble Committee of Safety of this Colony we have Requested Each Inhabitant of This Town to Sign to the within Declaration & hereunto Return the Names of those that have Sign'd as within also those that have not & Refuse to Sign who are as follows viz..

James Caruth a Scotch man Declines obliging himselfe to take up Arms against his Native Country but Declares he will neaver take up Arms against America & is willing to bear his Proportion of the publick taxes with his Town-men.

Moses Welch Refuses to take up arms & pleads Concience for an Excuse.

Hezekiah Beedy
John Clefford Fifield
John Webster
Samll Severance
John Tucker
John Eastman
John Sanborn
Ens Isaac Webster
Reuben Davise
Thomas Merrill
Ephraim Winslow
John Gilman

KINGSTON PATRIOTS

these persons Appear to be fearful that the Signing this Declaration would in some measure be an Infringement on their Just Rights & Libertys but they Appear to be Friendly to their Country & Several of them have Ventured their Lives in the American Cause & the 3 last named Persons are now in the Army.

Sept ye 23d 1776

Ebenr Eastmen } Selectmen
Richard Hubbard } of
Simmons Seccomb } Kingston

(New Hampshire State Papers vol. 30)

PETER ABBOTT, b Andover, MA 22 Jun 1758 son of Peter & Elizabeth (Damon) Abbott (AndVR): d Chester, NH Nov 1828 (PP 35:27): m Kingston, NH Mar 1782 Phebe Spratt of Deerfield, NH (PP 35: 27), d 1846.

Peter, of Kingston, enlisted 27 Jan 1777 & served as a pvt in Capt Zachariah Beal's Co, Col Alexander Scammel's NH Rgt #W16091 (NHSP 14:585,647; PP 35:27).

Children: (Boston Trans 19 Jan 1931-857)

1. **EDMOND**, b Kingston, NH 11 Nov 1782 (IGI)
2. **PETER GRAGG**, b Kingston, NH 5 Dec 1785 (IGI)
3. **GEORGE**
4. **HANNAH**
5. **CALVIN**
6. **JOHN**, b 3 May 1797: m Deborah Wiggin
7. **HENRY**, d (prob) Kingston, NH 24 Sep 1803 (NHVR)

WINBORN ADAMS, son of Samuel & Phebe (_) Adams (NHGR 6:5): d 17 Sep 1777 at the Battle of Stillwater: m Sarah Bartlett (EA 7:9), b Nottingham, NH 25 Nov 1741 dau of Israel & Love (Hall) Bartlett, d aft 1823. Sarah m(2) Exeter, NH 16 Oct 1784 Col Samuel Hobart (HE p80g).

In a petition dated Kingston 20 Nov 1797, Sarah Hobart "late widow of Col Winborn Adams" who was killed at Stillwater 19 Sep 1777 asked to have some interest, which she claimed to be due her, allowed & paid.

Children:

1. **SAMUEL**, b 1761: d Portsmouth, NH 2 Aug 1802 (HE p4g): m Exeter, NH (int) 1 May 1784 Elizabeth Parker (HE p79g)

STEPHEN BADGER, bpt Amesbury, MA 24 Jul 1748 son of Jonathan & Sarah (Currier) Badger (AVR): d Kingston, NH 16 Feb 1833 a.84yrs (GI p1): m Danville, NH 5 Apr 1770 Dorothy Webster (NEHGR 58:122), b (prob) Kingston, NH 30 Oct 1750 dau of Benjamin & Mary (Stanyan) Webster (KTR), d

Kingston, NH 18 Apr 1815 a.64yrs (GI p1).
Stephen signed the Association Test in Kingston, NH (NHSP 30:77). He served in Capt David Quimby's Co, Col Jacob Gale's Rgt (RW roll-50).

Children: born Kingston, NH
1. **HANNAH**, b Jul 1770: d Kingston, NH 30 Jan 1843 a.72yrs (NHVR): m Kingston, NH 16 Aug 1794 Elisha Quimby (NHGR 3:135)
2. **BENJAMIN** (twin), b 15 Mar 1774: d Kingston, NH 10 Mar 1859 (GI p1): m Kingston, NH 4 Apr 1799 Sarah Wadleigh (NHGR 3:169)
3. **JONATHAN** (twin), b 15 Mar 1774: m (prob) Hampstead, NH 21 Jan 1799 Sally Calef (HmstR)
4. **STEPHEN**, b 2 Apr 1777: m 3 Nov 1818 Polly Heeper (Badger Gen p24)
5. **SARAH**, b 6 Mar 1779: d Kingston, NH 23 Nov 1812 (NHVR): m Kingston, NH 21 Nov 1811 Amos Page (NHGR 4:179)
6. **JOSEPH**, b 28 Aug 1783: d Kingston, NH 18 Nov 1814 a.32yrs (GI p1)
7. **WILLIAM**, b 26 Dec 1786: d Kingston, NH 25 Dec 1855 (GI p1): m Kingston, NH 7 Jun 1812 Elizabeth Dearborn (NHGR 4: 179)
8. **MOLLY**, b 1 Apr 1791: d Kingston, NH (bur) 21 May 1810 (NHVR)

ENOCH BAGLEY, b Amesbury, MA 4 Feb 1758 son of Thomas & Ruth (Webster) Bagley (AVR): d Troy ME 30 Nov 1842 (RG 1:24): m So Hampton, NH 5 Apr 1781 Miriam Hoit (SHVR), b 1762, d Troy, ME 19 Jul 1844 (Bagley Gen p38).
Enoch lived in Kingston when he enlisted Apr 1775 as a Sgt under Capt Josiah Bachelder NH Line, served 6 months at Kittery Point. He reenlisted Jul 1780 as a Sgt under Capt Butler from Loudon, NH. (NHPR 2:34)

Children:
1. **JONATHAN**, b 8 Jun 1782: d Troy, ME 28 Feb 1881: m 4 Oct 1804 Eunice Reed
2. **ENOCH**, b 8 Jan 1788: d Troy, ME 16 Feb 1864: m(1) 2 Apr 1811 Rachel Reed: m(2)

26 Jul 1835 Mahala Myrick

3. **RUTH**, b 1790: d 19 Dec 1831: m John Work
4. **ISRAEL**, b 1 Jul 1793: d Troy, ME 28 Mar 1868: m(1) Cynthia Rogers (DAR LB 128: 81): m(2) 8 May 1844 Zuba Gerrish
5. **THOMAS H.**, b 1797: d 18 Oct 1877: m _____ Fairbanks
6. **MOSES**, b 1798: d 12 Sep 1869: m(1) Kezia Getchell: m(2) Charlotte Spencer
7. **REUBEN**, b 21 Sep or Oct 1802: d Wakefield, MA 11 May 1892: m 8 Mar 1830 Sarah Campbell
8. **SARAH**, b 23 Feb 1805: d 24 Oct 1882: m Troy, ME 23 Feb 1827 Charles Smith

JOSHUA BAGLEY, b Amesbury, MA 17 Apr 1752 son of David & Mary (Huntington) Bagley (AVR): d (prob) Warner, NH 9 Apr 1809 (bur Newton, NH): m Judith ____, b abt 1751 d 28 Apr 1821 a.70 yrs, bur Newton, NH (Bagley Gen p32).

Joshua enlisted Dec 1776 & served in Capt Gordon's Co, David Gilman's Rgt, from 5 Jan to 15 Mar 1776 (RW roll-50).

Children: born Newton, NH (NwtTR)

1. **MARY** (Molly), b 17 Aug 1774:
2. **RUTH**, b 7 Mar 1778: d Newton, NH 13 May 1806: m Kingston, NH 20 Jan 1802 Bagley Carter (NHGR 3:171)
3. **LYDIA**, b 2 Oct 1780: d Newton, NH 31 May 1814 a.34yrs: m Amesbury, MA (int) 5 May 1804 Isaac Merrill (AVR)
4. **DOLLY**, b 20 Sep 1782: d Newton, NH 11 Apr 1847: m Amesbury, MA (int) 10 Feb 1815 Isaac Merrill (AVR)
5. **JUDITH**, b 17 Jan 1787: m Salisbury, MA (int) 18 Feb 1810 Bagley Carter (SVR)

JACOB BARKHARTH, was paid by the Town of Kingston for his hire in the Rev War 29 May 1778 (NHSP 16:709).

EBENEZER BARTLETT, b Kingston, NH 23 Apr 1750 son of Nathan & Joanna (Flanders) Bartlett

(KTR): d Kingston, NH 12 Mar 1838 a.88yrs (NHVR): m ____, d Kingston, NH 17 Nov 1840 (NHVR).
Ebenezer signed the Association Test in Kingston, NH (NHSP 30:78).

JEREMIAH BARTLETT, b Kingston 6 Dec 1757 son of Nathan & Joanna (Flanders) Bartlett (KTR). He was living in Guildford, NH 1833 (NHPR 3:7).
Jeremiah enlisted at Kingston as a Militia Man in 1778 under Capt French & marched to Portsmouth. He enlisted again under Capt Ezra Currier's Co, Col Jacob Gale's NH Militia. (NH PR 3:7). After the War he moved to Deerfield then to Northwood & Guilford, NH.

JOHN BARTLETT, b (poss) Haverhill, MA 24 Nov 1708 son of Christopher & Susanna (Griffin) Bartlett (HvVR): m Kingston, NH 12 Jan 1742/3 Mary Quimby (KTR).
Possibly the John who signed the Association Test in Kingston, NH (NHSP 30:78).

Children:

1. **ELIZABETH**, b Kingston, NH 12 Jan 1743/4 (KTR): bpt 18 Mar 1743/4 (NHGR 5:111)
2. **CHRISTOPHER**, b Plaistow, NH 4 Apr 1747 (PlVR)
3. **HANNAH**, b Kingston, NH 30 Dec 1749 (KTR): bpt 31 Dec 1749 (NHGR 5:158)
4. **NATHANIEL**, bpt Kingston, NH 7 Jun 1752 (NHGR 6:27)

JOSHUA BARTLETT, b Newbury, MA 31 Aug 1707 son of Samuel & Abigail (Wells) Bartlett (NVR): d Kingston, NH 25 Apr 1792 (NHVR): m 16 Sep 1736 Priscilla Jacobs (MGFH 2:823), bpt 9 Nov 1718 dau of George & Hannah (Cousins) Jacobs (Anc of Lydia Harmon p52).
Joshua signed the Association Test in Kingston, NH (NHSP 30:77).

Children: last 4 born Amesbury, MA (AVR)

1. **JOSHUA**, b Wells, ME 29 Mar 1736: d 23 Jul 1823 (DAR 1:41): m Kingston, NH Feb 1760

Sarah Badger (KTR)

2. **GEORGE**, b abt 1739: d.y.
3. **PRISCILLA**, b abt 1740: d 1807: m Amesbury, MA 15 Dec 1761 Reuben Lowell (AVR)
4. **GEORGE**, b abt 1741: d 18 Jan 1819: m Amesbury, MA 7 Jan 1762 Priscilla Tewksbury (AVR)
5. **DAVID**
6. **MATHIAS**, b abt 1743
7. **HANNAH**, b abt 1746: m Amesbury, MA 17 Oct 1771 Mathias Merrill (AVR)
8. **SAMUEL**, b 3 Feb 1748: d 4 Feb 1813 (DAR 1:41): m(1) 1773 Lois Hix: m(2) Eleanor Martin Kimball
9. **ABIGAIL**, b 18 Mar 1750
10. **TIMOTHY**, b 18 Feb 1752
11. **LYDIA**, b 20 Jul 1754: m(1) Samuel Coffin: m(2) Samuel Cooper

JOSHUA BARTLETT JR, b Wells, ME 29 Mar 1736 (DAR #449905) son of Joshua & Priscilla (Jacobs) Bartlett: d Unity, NH 23 Jul 1823: m Kingston, NH Feb 1760 Sarah Badger (KTR), b Amesbury, MA 25 Jul 1739 dau of Jonathan & Sarah (Currier) Badger (AVR), d Unity, NH 6 Mar 1821.

Joshua Jr signed the Association Test in Kingston, NH (NHSP 30:77).

Children: (DAR #449905)

1. **HANNAH**, b Kingston, NH 1 Jul 1760 (KTR): m Uriah Wilcox
2. **JONATHAN**, b Kingston, NH 12 Apr 1762 (KTR)
3. **JACOB**, b 8 Jul 1764: m(1) Unity, NH 8 Mar 1786 Lucretia Marshall (UR p54): m(2) Polly Chase
4. **EDMUND**, b 3 Jun 1766: d 19 Jun 1766
5. **JONATHAN**, b 12 Jun 1768
6. **JOHN**, b 25 Nov 1770
7. **JOSHUA**, b 24 Aug 1772: m(1) Maria Barker: m(2) Mrs Lanna Spicer
8. **STEPHEN**, b 9 Jul 1774: m Emma Nourse
9. **SARAH**, b 21 Jun 1780: m Jacob Glidden

JOSIAH BARTLETT, b Amesbury, MA 21 Nov 1729 son of Stephen & Hannah (Webster) Bartlett (AVR): d Kingston, NH 19 May 1795 (KTR): m Kingston, NH 15 Jan 1754 Mary Bartlett (KTR), b Amesbury, MA 27 Dec 1730 dau of Joseph & Sarah (Hoyt) Bartlett (AVR), d Kingston, NH (bur) 16 Jul 1789 (NHVR).

Josiah signed the Association Test in Kingston, NH (NHSP 30:76). He was a signer of the Declaration of Independance & a Col in the NH Militia 1777-79 (DAR LB 153:154).

Children: born Kingston, NH (KTR)

1. **MARY**, b 28 Dec 1754: d E. Kingston, NH 7 Jul 1826 (CR): m Kingston, NH 12 Mar 1780 Jonathan Greeley (NHGR 3:131)
2. **SALLY**, b 1755
3. **LOIS**, b 2 Jun 1756
4. **MIRIAM**, b 19 Jun 1758: d Kingston, NH 27 Aug 1785 (GI p4): m Kingston, NH 28 Jun 1781 Joseph Calef (NHGR 3:131)
5. **RHODA**, b 22 May 1760: m Reuben True (Emery Gen p96)
6. **HANNAH**, b 31 Aug 1762: d Kingston, NH 7 Sep 1762 (KTR)
7. **LEVI**, b 2 Sep 1763: d Kingston, NH Jan 1828 (NHVR): m(1) 6 Nov 1791 Sally Hook (NEHGR 1:97): m(2) Kingston, NH 18 Apr 1807 Abigail Stevens (NHGR 4:176)
8. **JOSIAH**, b 20 Aug 1765: d Kingston, NH 30 Dec 1765 (KTR)
9. **JOSIAH**, b 29 Aug 1768: m(1) ___ Wingate: m (2) Apr 1812 Hannah Weeks (Emery Gen p50)
10. **EZRA**, b 13 Sep 1770: d 1848 (DAR LB 153:154): m Kingston, NH 30 Jan 1799 Hannah Gale (NHGR 3:169)
11. **SARAH**, b 29 Jul 1773: d Kingston, NH 19 Oct 1847 (GI p13): m Kingston, NH 24 Apr 1796 Amos Gale (NHGR 3:167)
12. **HANNAH**, b 13 Dec 1776: d Kingston, NH 17 Apr 1777 (KTR)

NATHAN BARTLETT JR., b Kingston, NH 25 Feb 1752 son of Nathan & Joanna (Flanders) Bartlett

(KTR): d Andover, NH: m Kingston, NH 9 Sep 1772 Mary Blaisdell (HA p18).
Nathan Jr signed the Association Test in Kingston, NH (NHSP 30:78).

Children: (HA p18)
1. **JOANNAH (HANNAH)**, b 3 Mar 1773: m Andover, NH 16 Aug 1793 John Keniston (NEHGR 58:17)
2. **NATHAN**, m 15 Jul 1829 Louisa Davis
3. **SALLY**, b Kingston, NH 22 Mar 1777
4. **MIRIAM**, b Northwood, NH 10 Jan 1780: m Andover, NH 25 Apr 1798 Jonathan Davis (NEHGR 58:18)
5. **ABIAH**, b Kingston, NH 1783: d 20 Mar 1851
6. **JEREMIAH**, b Northwood, NH 1789: d Andover, NH 23 Apr 1872: m 8 Feb 1818 Fanny Stearns

TIMOTHY BARTLETT, b (prob) Amesbury, MA 18 Feb 1752 son of Joshua & Priscilla (Jacobs) Bartlett (AVR).
Timothy signed the Association Test in Kingston, NH (NHSP 30:78).

Children:
1. **(INFANT)**, d Kingston, NH 21 Feb 1780 (NHVR)

NATHANIEL BATCHELDER, b abt 1757 probably son of Nathaniel & Mary (Longfellow) Batchelder of Deerfield, NH: d 20 Aug 1808 (NHPR 3:39): m(1) Rye, NH 10 Jun 1781 Mary Libby (Rye VR), bpt Rye, NH 20 Mar 1763 dau of Joseph & Mary (_) Libby (Rye VR): m(2) Loudon, NH Apr 1789 Mary Perkins (NHPR 3:39), dau of Stephen Perkins. Mary m(2) Loudon, NH 8 Mar 1817 Dodovah Bunker (NHPR 3:40).
Nathaniel, of Deerfield (a.22yrs), was mustered for Kingston to serve in the Continental Army for 1 year 4 May 1779 (NHSP 15:623). He served as a Cpl in the 5th NH troops under Col Joseph Cilley #W24634 (NHPR 3:40).

Children: (DAR #143887A103)
1. **MARY**, b 1783: d Apr 1855: m Samuel Dearborn
2. **SALLY**, b 1784: d 1809: m Deerfield, NH John Butler
3. **GREENLEAF CILLEY**, b 1810: d Boston, MA 1855 m Boston, MA Elizabeth Clesby
4. **PERKINS**
5. **TRUE**
6. **JONATHAN**
7. **NATHANIEL**
8. **NANCY**
9. **COMFORT**

PHINEAS BATCHELDER, b Kingston, NH 1762 (PRNH 3:43) probably son of Nathan & Margaret (Bean) Batchelder (Batchelder Gen p147).

Phineas deposed 1 May 1833 that he enlisted in the winter of 1777 from Loudon under Capt Shephard & served 2 months at Winter Hill. He re-enlisted May 1777 under Capt Sias for 2 months serving at Great Island near Portsmouth, NH & enlisted again in the same Co serving 3 months in Stark's Bridgade. At the time of his deposition, he was living at Garland, ME.

THEOPHILUS BATCHELDER, b Kingston, NH 1742 (MSSP p27) son of Theophilus & Maria (Blake) Batchelder: d Phippenburg, ME 1807: m Kensington, NH 9 May 1763 Ann Sleeper (NHVR), b 1742, d Phippenburg, ME 9 May 1821.

Theophilus served as a Cpl & as a 2nd Lt under Capt Parker, Col McCobb's MA Militia (DAR LB 165:93).

Children: (Batchelder Gen p148)
1. **JORDAN**, m(1) Mehitable Batchelder: m(2) Susan Bracket
2. **LYDIA**, b 1774: m 1807 Reuben Carleton (DAR LB 165:93)
3. **JOSIAH**, b 1765: m Hannah ___
4. **THEOPHILUS**, b 1766: d 3 Oct 1845

WILLIAM BATCHELDER, b abt 1754 deposed on 11

Jun 1818 that he enlisted at Kingston Jan 1777 for 3 years & served in Capt Hutchins Co, Col Joseph Cilley's Rgt. He was mustered Feb 1778 #S45236 (NHSP 15:717 & NHPR 2:25). After the War he lived in Jay & Weld, ME. In 1825 he was living in Chilliothe, OH.

JOSHUA BAYLEY, b Salem, NH 1 Aug 1747 son of Joshua & Sarah (Davis) Bayley (HSlm): m Bradford, MA 17 Mar 1774 Mary Clough (BdVR), b Salem, NH 11 Jan 1750 dau of Josiah & Abigail (Hastings) Clough (HSlm).

Probably the Joshua who was mustered in Capt Gordon's Co, Col David Gilman's Rgt Dec 1776 (RW roll-50).

Children: born Salem, NH (HSlm)

1. **PHINEAS**, b 22 Jan 1776
2. **JOSHUA**, b 20 Jun 1777

THOMAS BEAL, of Kingston (a.30yrs), served as a Sgt in Capt Philip Tilton' Co, Col Enoch Poor's Rgt Aug 1775 (RW roll-51 & NHSP 14:146).

JEREMIAH BEAN, b Exeter, NH 13 Feb 1753 son of Jeremiah & Abigail (Prescott) Bean (DnTR): d Danville, NH 17 Dec 1835 (NHPR 3:87): m Danville, NH 17 Mar 1778 Lydia Sanborn (DnTR), b Brentwood, NH 30 Oct 1755 dau of Daniel & Abigail (Prescott) Sanborn (BtTR), d aft 13 Jul 1837.

Jeremiah, of Kingston (a.21yrs), served in Capt Philip Tilton's Co, Col Enoch Poor's Rgt 1775 (RW roll-51). He enlisted again 1 Jun 1776 under Capt David Quimby, Col Wingate NH Militia. In 1781 he was hired by the Town of Newbury, MA for 9 months, serving under Capt Jenkins, Col Poor's MA Line #15580 (NHPR 3:86). Probably he is the Jeremiah who signed the Association Test in Kingston, NH (NHSP 30:77).

Children: (NHPR 3:90,91)

1. **HULDAH**, b Kingston, NH 19 Jun 1778
2. **LYDIA**, b Kingston, NH 10 Sep 1780

3. **ABIGAIL**, b Danville, NH 25 Jul 1782
4. **JEREMIAH**, b Danville, NH 2 Mar 1785
5. **NATHANIEL**, b Danville, NH 16 Jun 1787
6. **ELIZABETH**, b Danville, NH 31 Oct 1789: m Jesse Smith (NHPR 3:88)
7. **SUSANNA**, b Danville, NH 3 Apr 1792
8. **GILMAN**, b Danville, NH 14 Sep 1794
9. **JAMES**, b Danville, NH 3 May 1797
10. **EZRA SANBORN**, b Danville, NH 16 Oct 1801 (DnTR)

JONATHAN BEAN, b Kingston, NH 1720 (RG 1:43) son of Daniel & Ann (Sanborn) Bean (TAG 16: 168): d E. Bethel, ME 1800 (RG 1:43): m Kingston, NH 14 Sep 1744/5 Abigail Gordon (NHGR 3:42), d Bethel, ME 1821 (Hist of Bethel p478).
Jonathan served at Kittery & Portsmouth (Hist of Bethel p84 & MSSP p47).

Children:

1. **DANIEL**, bpt Kingston, NH 8 Jun 1746 (NHGR 5:154)
2. **JOSIAH**, bpt Kingston, NH 17 Apr 1748 (NHGR 5:156): m Mary Crocker (Hartford Times 11 Mar 1950-993)
3. **ABIGAIL**, bpt Kingston, NH 1 Jul 1750 (NHGR 5:159): d Bethel, ME 1827: m abt 1771 Col John York (ME Fam 2:283)
4. **ANNA**, b Chester, NH 19 Mar 1753: d Newry, ME 19 Dec 1821: m (int) Gorham, ME 17 Jul 1779 Ithiel Smith (ME Fam 2:264)
5. **JONATHAN**, b 1754: d Bethel, ME 19 Nov 1826: m(1) Standish, ME (int) 22 Oct 1774 Abigail York (ME Fam 2:283): m(2) Ann McGill
6. **DANIEL**, b 10 Mar 1757: d W. Bethel, ME 16 Mar 1834: m Pearsontown, ME 26 Apr 1781 Margaret Shaw (ME Fam 2:20)
7. **DOLLY**, d bef 1818: m Luther Toppin
8. **LOIS**, d 1840: m John Mareau
9. **EUNICE**, b 1767: d 18 Aug 1833 (HH p960): m Joseph Shaw (DAR 1:608)

NATHANIEL BEAN, b 21 Nov 1761 son of Sinkler &

Shuah (Fifield) Bean (TAG 16:167): d Alba, NY 11 Jun 1829: m Mary ____ (DAR #704996).

Probably the Nathaniel who is listed on the Kingston Town Records Returns for the Rev War (NHSP 16:510). He enlisted 13 Jul 1778 under Capt Nathan Dix in the 9th Rgt MA Line. On 29 Mar 1780 he enlisted under Capt Benjamin Ellis, Col Joseph Cilley 1st NH (NHPR 3:102).

Children: (DAR #704996)

1. **NATHANIEL**, b 15 Aug 1791: d Jackson Co, MI 24 Aug 1860: m 1809 Abigail Bean
2. **SINKLER**, b 16 Dec 1793: m Betsey Haynes
3. **MARY**, b 20 Nov 1794: m Leander McCain
4. **MEHITABLE**, m Jeremiah Cranmore
5. **PRUDENCE**
6. **SALLY**, a.12yrs in 1820 (NHPR 3:103): m John Gray
7. **MOSES**, a.9yrs in 1820 (NHPR 3:103): m Lydia Perry

BEZABEEL BEEDE, b Kingston, NH 22 Aug 1759 son of Hezekiah & Hepsibah (Smith) Beede (KTR): m Kingston, NH 18 Dec 1782 Judith Morgan (NHGR 3:131).

Bezabeel enlisted at Kingston 1 Aug 1776 under Capt John Calef, Col Tash (NHPR 39:68). He is also listed on the muster roll of Col Josiah Bartlett for Col Abraham Drake's Rgt Oct 1777 & served in Capt Ezra Currier's Co 8 Sep to 16 Dec 1777 (RW roll-49).

Children:

1. **BEZABEEL**

JOSIAH BEEDE, of Kingston, served in Capt Livermore's Co in the Continental Army (NHSP 16:709).

REZIAH BEEDE, b Kingston, NH 6 Jul 1764 son of Hezekiah & Hepsibah (Smith) Beede (KTR): d Keene, NY 24 Nov 1841: m 11 Apr 1785 Mary Ann Stroud (DAR #592708).

Reziah was placed on the pension roll, 1818

of Orange County, VT for service 1780, in Capt Nathaniel Hutchins Co, Col Joseph Cilley's 1st NH Rgt #S39185 (DAR LB 73:73 & NHPR 3:136).

Children: (DAR #592708)
1. **WILLIAM**
2. **DAVID**
3. **HYPSIA**
4. **AARON**, b 17 Nov 1797: d 1872: m 1815 Clarissa Smith

DANIEL BICKFORD, b 19 Jan 1760 (DAR 1:58) son of Daniel & Sarah (Hodgdon) Bickford: d 28 Mar 1815: m Pembroke, NH 28 Dec 1786 Martha Mann (NHPR 4:25), b 5 Jul 1759, d aft 1848 of Henniker, NH.

Daniel enlisted as a pvt 8 Sep 1777 in Capt Zebulon Gilman's Co, Col Stephen Evans Rgt (RW roll-50). He was one of the six months men raised by the State of NH for the Continental Army at West Point; mustered 31 Jul 1781; discharged 24 Dec 1781; time of service 4 months 25 days #W21671 (NHSP 16:256 & NHPR 4:24).

Children: (NHPR 4:25)
1. **WILLIAM MANN**, b 9 Oct 1787
2. **ABRAM**, b 4 Mar 1789: d 13 Mar 1789
3. **ABRAM**, b 1 Apr 1790
4. **DANIEL JR**, b 19 Jun 1792
5. **SALLY FITS**, b 1 Sep 1794
6. **JAMES D.**, b 12 Aug 1796
7. **POLLY MANN**, b 1 Oct 1798

JOHN BLAISDELL, bpt Kingston, NH 8 Jun 1760 son of Moses & Mary (Prescott) Blaisdell (KChR): d E. Kingston, NH 4 Feb 1835 (DAR #470899): m Newton, NH 9 Mar 1781 Dorothy Carter (NHPR 4:170), d aft 27 Sep 1848 of Haverhill, MA.

John, of Kingston (a.17yrs), enlisted in Capt F.M. Bell's Co 3 Feb 1777 #W21679 (NHSP 14:623 & NHPR 4:169).

Children: (DAR #470899)
1. **NANCY**, b 25 May 1783: m Kingston, NH

18 Aug 1805 Samuel Pierce (NHGR 4:175)

2. **ABIGAIL**, b 8 Feb 1785: d Shrewsbury, VT 5 Jun 1864: m bef 1805 Simon Gilman
3. **JEREMIAH**, b 14 May 1787
4. **LEVI**, b 26 Nov 1788: d a.19yrs
5. **MOSES**, b 25 May 1792: d E. Kingston, NH 22 Mar 1850
6. **DOROTHY**, b 28 May 1794
7. **JOHN**, b 14 Dec 1796
8. **SAMUEL CARTER**, b 18 Jul 1798
9. **SARAH**, b 28 Jan 1802
10. **MARY**, b 31 Oct 1807

PHILIP BLAIDELL, b 6 May 1753 (NHPR 4:176) son of Thomas & Sarah (Clough) Blaisdell: d Fairfax, VT 5 Mar 1823: m New Salisbury, NH 13 Apr 1782 Hannah Jameson (NHPR 4:177), b Kingston, NH 1755 dau of John Jameson and sister of Elizabeth Ladd & Jane Morrill. He lived in Kingston at the time of his marriage & later resided in Fairfax Co, VT.

Philip, of Kingston (a.21yrs), served in Col Enoch Poor's Rgt, Capt Philip Tilton's Co (RW roll-51). He enlisted again 1776 at Mt Independence & served under Capt Benjamin Titcomb, Col Hale until Jun 1783. He was at the Battles of Burgoyne, Monmouth & at the surrender of Cornwallis #W17319 (NHPR 4:176).

Children: (Blaisdell Papers 2:18)

1. **THOMAS**
2. **JOHN**
3. **JOSIAH**
4. **HANNAH**, a.26yrs in 1820 (NHPR 4:177)
5. **JAMES**

RALPH BLAISDELL, b Amesbury, MA 6 Jan 1717/8 son of Ralph & Mary (Davis) Blaisdell (AVR): d Kingston, NH 13 Apr 1806 a.89yrs (NHVR): m Kingston, NH 18 Oct 1748 Miriam Rowell (KTR), b abt 1719, d Kingston, NH 24 Jun 1800 a.81yrs (NHVR).

Ralph signed the Association Test in Kingston, NH (NHSP 30:78).

Children: 1st 4 born Kingston, NH (KTR)
1. **JUDITH**, b 21 Nov 1749: m 1776 Thomas Thompson (Blaisdel Papers 2:14)
2. **SAMUEL**, b 6 Mar 1750/1: m E. Kingston, NH 24 Jul 1781 Abigail Osgood
3. **MARY**, b 13 Feb 1753: m Samuel Thompson
4. **NEHEMIAH**, b 28 Feb 1756
5. **HANNAH**, b 1758: m 12 Nov 1776 Joshua Woodman (Blaisdell Papers 2:14)

THOMAS BLAISDELL, b abt 1759 son of Thomas & Dorothy (Clough) Blaisdell: d 1824: m Olive Hayes.

Thomas, of Kingston (a.18yrs) enlisted in Capt Bell's Co 3 Feb 1777 (NHSP 14:623). He lived in Kingston & Deerfield, NH & in Allenstown, NY.

Children: (Blaisdell Papers 2:18)
1. **THOMAS**
2. **BENJAMIN F.**
3. **GEORGE F.**
4. **BETTY**
5. **SALLY**
6. **NANCY**
7. **RHODA**
8. **LUCY**

ELIJAH BLAKE, bpt Kingston, NH 12 Oct 1755 son of Jonathan & Mary (Sanborn) Blake (NHVR): d Chelsea, VT 17 Nov 1839 (NHPR 4:117): m Strafford, Vt 4 Nov 1784 Sarah Preston (NHPR 4:118), b Winchester, NH 3 Feb 1766, d aft 1 Sep 1848.

Elijah, of Kingston, enlisted at Mystic, MA in Mar or Apr 1775 under Col John Stark, Capt Samuel Richards. He was in the Battles of Lexington & Bunker Hill. In 1777, he volunteered at Kingston in the NH Militia under Capt Collins & served as a pvt & as a waiter to his brother Lt Blake #W15586 (NHPR 4:115).

Child: (NHPR 4:118,119)
1. **SARAH**, b 28 Sep 1785: m 13 May 1802 Thomas Minard

AMOS BOOTMAN (BUTMAN), b Beverly, MA 5 Jan 1717/8 son of Joseph & Rebecca (Stone?) Bootman (BvVR): d Kingston, NH (bur) 1786 (NHVR): m Kingston, NH 11 Jul 1745 Sarah Webster (KTR), b Kingston, NH 31 Mar 1719 dau of Thomas & Mary (Greeley) Webster (KTR), d aft 1790.
Amos signed the Association Test in Kingston, NH (NHSP 30:77 - surely a misprint in NHSP - Amos Burman).

Children: born Kingston, NH
1. **THOMAS**, bpt 28 Jun 1747 (NHGR 5:155): d Kingston, NH 10 Sep 1749 (NHVR)
2. **(CHILD)**, d Kingston, NH 29 Oct 1749 (NH VR)
3. **MARY**, b 11 Nov 1750 (KTR)
4. **(INFANT)**, d Kingston, NH 6 Jan 1754 (NH VR)
5. **WEBSTER**, b 3 Feb 1755 (KTR): d (poss) Kingston, NH 22 Oct 1758 (NHVR)
6. **THOMAS**, b 25 Sep 1758 (KTR): d 29 Mar 1843 (NHPR 5:77): m Anna Hunt

THOMAS BOOTMAN (BUTMAN), b Kingston, NH 25 Sep 1758 son of Amos & Sarah (Webster) Bootman (KTR): d 29 Mar 1843 (NHPR 5:77): m Anna Hunt, dau of Henry & Hannah (Eastman) Hunt, d 1 Apr 1848 (NHPR 5:77).
Thomas enlisted in Kingston & served in the NH Line. After the war he lived in Hampton Falls & Enfield, NH #R1025 (NHPR 5:75).

Children:
1. **STEPHEN**, living 1852
2. **(SON)**, d Kingston, NH (bur) 25 Sep 1801 (NHVR)
3. **(DAU)**, living 1839
4. **(DAU)**, living 1839

PHILIP BOSDEL, of Kingston served in Capt Jeremiah Fogg's Co in the 2nd NH Rgt 6th Co (NHSP 16:230).

JAMES BOWLES, of Kingston, enlisted for the 7th

Rgt NH Militia in the Continental Army 1777, Capt Hutchin's Co (NHSP 14:585)

JAMES BOWLEY, of Kingston, served in Capt Dustin's Co in the Continental Army (NHSP 16:709).

EZEKIEL BROWN, b Kingston, NH 10 Aug 1756 son of Daniel & Ruth (Morrill) Brown (KTR): d Brunswick, ME 4 Jun 1798 (RG 1:85): m 3 Feb 1780 Elizabeth Mallet (DAR #426696), b Salisbury, MA abt 1763. Elizabeth m(2) Aaron Toothaker.

Ezekiel served as a drummer in Capt Curtis's Co, Col Jonathan Mitchell's MA Rgt (MSSP p90 & DAR #426696). MEHGR 9:202 has Ezekiel's wife as Elizabeth Wilson.

Children: (DAR #426696)

1. **LYDIA**, b 29 Aug 1780
2. **EZEKIEL MORRILL**, b 7 Apr 1782: m(1) Emma Nowell: m(2) Dorcas Preble: m(3) ___ Toothaker
3. **JOHN**, b 31 Mar 1784
4. **EPHRAIM**, b 26 Jan 1786
5. **SAMUEL W.**, b 18 Dec 1787
6. **ELIZABETH**, b Brunswick, ME 17 Feb 1790: d Lisbon, ME 20 Feb 1875: m 11 Jan 1811 James Woodard (MEHGR 9:202)
7. **MARTHA**, b 1 Jun 1792: m Samuel Hall
8. **ISAAC**, b 25 Nov 1794
9. **WILLIAM**, b 30 Apr 1796

JOSEPH BROWN, b Kingston, NH 31 Mar 1759 son of Joseph & Elizabeth (Sawyer) Brown (KTR): d Andover, NH 29 Jul 1843: m So Hampton, NH 5 Sep 1780 Abigail Towle (SHVR), b Danville, NH 24 Mar 1763 dau of Caleb & Ruth (Page) Towle (Dn TR), d Andover, NH 28 Oct 1831 (HA p32).

Joseph enlisted at Kingston 1 Aug 1776 under Capt John Calef (NHPR 39:68 & NHSP 14:405).

Children: (HA p32)

1. **RUTH**, b Hawke, NH 14 Apr 1781: m William Emery

2. **DOROTHY**, b Andover, NH 28 Jul 1783: m Caleb Marston
3. **REUBEN**, b Andover, NH 24 Jun 1785: d Andover, NH 17 Jun 1846: m 1807 Lydia Simonds
4. **LOIS**, b Andover, NH 15 Oct 1792: d 22 Jan 1861

NATHANIEL BROWN, b Kingston, NH 28 Oct 1748 son of Joshua & Joanna (Morrill) Brown (KTR): d Danville, NH 9 Apr 18_2 (DnTR): m Danville, NH 17 Nov 1771 Mary Clifford (DnTR).

Nathaniel enlisted at Kingston 1 Aug 1776 under Capt John Calef (NHSP 14:104 & NHPR 39:68).

Children: born Danville, NH (DnTR)

1. **HANNAH**, b 12 Dec 1772
2. **JEREMIAH**, b 30 Jan 1775
3. **JOSEPH**, b 4 Apr 1777
4. **MARY**, b 6 Aug 1779
5. **JACOB**, b 27 Jun 1781
6. **SARAH**, b 28 Jan 1784
7. **NATHANIEL**, b 18 May 1789

SCIPIO BROWN, of Kingston, enlisted for the 7th Rgt NH Militia in the Continental Army 1777, Emerson's Co (NHSP 14:585).

DANIEL BUSWELL, b Kingston, NH 3 May 1746 son of William & Abigail (Thorn) Buswell (KTR): d Kingston, NH 15 Dec 1820 a.82yrs (GI p3): m 4 Jul 1776 Hannah Runnels (Buswell Gen 1:25), b abt 1757, d Kingston, NH 2 Jan 1844 a.87yrs (GI p3).

Daniel signed the Association Test in Kingston, NH (NHSP 30:78).

Children: (Boswell-Buswell Gen 1:25)

1. **ABIGAIL**, b 5 May 1777: d Knox, ME 15 Oct 1871: m Kingston, NH 18 Jan 1806 Samuel Tilton (NHGR 4:175)
2. **STEPHEN**, b 21 Sep 1778
3. **HANNAH**, b 3 Jan 1781

4. **LYDIA**, b 25 Jul 1782: d 31 Dec 1783
5. **PHEBE**, b 13 Jul 1785
6. **WILLIAM**, b 21 Aug 1786
7. **DANIEL**, b 22 Nov 1788
8. **LYDIA**, b 21 Nov 1790
9. **JOHN**, b 16 Feb 1793
10. **POLLY**, b 9 Aug 1795: d 18 Dec 1795
11. **JAMES**, b 31 May 1798
12. **TRUE**, b 31 Jan 1802: d Kingston, NH 31 Mar 1881 a.79yrs (GI p3)

DAVID BUSWELL (BUSSELL), m Salem, NH 8 Mar 1781 Elizabeth Merrill (HSlm).

David was mustered in the 7th Rgt under Col David Gilman 1776 & in Oct 1777 he was mustered at Kingston in Col Bartlett's Militia Rgt for Col Drake's Rgt. He also enlisted in the 7th Rgt for the defense of RI Jul 1779 (NHSP 14: 453; 15:343,691).

JAMES BUSWELL, b Kingston, NH 10 Apr 1740 son of William & Abigail (Thorn) Buswell (KTR): m Kingston, NH 3 Feb 1761 Elizabeth Clough (KTR), b Kingston, NH 18 Sep 1741 dau of Elisha & Mary (Welch) Clough (KTR).

James served in Capt Gordon's Co, Col David Gilman's Rgt (RW roll-50).

Children: born Kingston, NH (KTR)

1. **ELIZABETH**, b 4 Sep 1761
2. **MARY**, b 9 Nov 1763
3. **ABIGAIL**, b 2 Feb 1765
4. **SARAH**, b 17 Feb 1767

SAMUEL BUSWELL, b Kingston, NH 14 Apr 1729 son of William & Judith (Davis) Buswell (KTR): d 26 Oct 1781 (DAR 1:106): m Kingston, NH 14 Jan 1755 Mary Winsley (KTR), b Kingston, NH 13 Dec 1732 dau of Elisha & Mary (Sleeper) Winsley (KTR), d 17 Feb 1809 (DAR #488067).

Samuel signed the Association Test in Kingston, NH (NHSP 30:77).

Children: born Kingston, NH (KTR)

1. **SARAH**, b 20 Nov 1755
2. **ELISHA**, b 10 Nov 1757
3. **CORNELIUS**, b 18 Nov 1759
4. **MARY**, b 8 Feb 1762: d Kingston, NH 17 Dec 1771 (KTR)
5. **JUDITH**, b 8 Oct 1763: d Kingston, NH 27 Sep 1765 (KTR)
6. **SAMUEL**, b 1 Mar 1766
7. **JUDITH**, b 14 Jun 1768
8. **MEHITABLE**, b 15 Jan 1771
9. **EBENEZER**, bpt 13 Jun 1773 (NHVR): d Hallowell, ME 13 Mar 1857: m abt 1799 Abigail Myrick (DAR #488067)
10. **MARY**, b 8 Jan 1776

JOHN CALEF, b Newbury, MA 14 Jun 1731 son of William & Sarah (Cheney) Calef (NVR): d Kingston, NH 28 May 1806 (KTR): m(1) Hannah Emerson: m(2) Kingston, NH 24 Dec 1754 Judith Challis (KTR), b Amesbury, MA 27 Jun 1732 dau of Joseph & Mary (Rowell) Challis (AVR), d Kingston, NH 5 May 1821 a.89yrs (GI p4).

John signed the Association Test in Kingston, NH (NHSP 30:77).

Children: born Kingston, NH (KTR)

1. **JOSEPH**, b 5 May 1756: d Kingston, NH 22 Oct 1836 (GI p4): m(1) Kingston, NH 28 Jun 1781 Miriam Bartlett (NHGR 3:131): m(2) Kingston, NH 23 Sep 1789 Mary Hook (NHGR 3:134): m(3) 18 Jul 1792 Susanna Batchelder
2. **MARY**, b 19 Jan 1758: m Kingston, NH 11 Dec 1780 Rev Zaccheus Colby (NHGR 3:131)
3. **HANNAH**, b 4 Mar 1760: m Danville, NH 28 Dec 1780 Rev Elihu Thayer (NEHGR 58:125)
4. **JOHN**, b 23 Sep 1762: d Goshen, NH 20 Aug 1841: m 27 Nov 1788 Abigail Bartlett
5. **SAMUEL**, b 11 Dec 1764: d Kingston, NH Nov 1809 a.45yrs (NHVR)
6. **AMOS**, b 1 Jul 1769: d Gloucester, MA 1 Jul 1856: m Mar 1803 Phebe Bartlett
7. **ROBERT**, b 26 Feb 1772: d Kingston, NH 20 Oct 1838 (GI p4): m Kingston, NH 26 May

1802 Polly Sleeper (NHGR 3:171)

JOHN CALEF, bpt Haverhill, MA 6 Jul 1746 son of James & Abigail (Jewett) Calef (HvVR): d Kingston, NH 26 Jul 1806 a.60yrs (NHVR): m ______, d Kingston, NH 27 Jul 1800 (NHVR).

John, of Kingston, volunteered in Capt Jacob Gale's Rgt, Capt Quimby's Co Aug 1778 (RW roll-50). Possibly the John Calef Jr who signed the Association Test in Kingston, NH (NHSP 30:77). He may have been known as John Jr to distinquish him from John son of William who also lived in Kingston.

JOSEPH CALEF, b Kingston, NH 12 Dec 1742 son of William & Lois (Sawyer) Calef (KTR): d 19 May 1823 (DAR 2:32): m(1) 30 Oct 1765 Hannah (Joanna) Pettingill (Calef Gen p18), b Plaistow, NH 17 Jan 1747 dau of Benjamin & Elizabeth (Stickney) Pettingill (PlVR), d Salisbury, NH 5 Dec 1793: m(2) Sarah Cushing (DAR 2:32).

Joseph signed the Association Test in Kingston, NH NHSP 30:76).

Children: (DAR #528573)
(by 1st wife)

1. **ELIZABETH**, b 1 Oct 1767
2. **NATHANIEL**, b 26 Oct 1769: m 1790 Elizabeth Hall
3. **LOIS**, b 4 Dec 1770: m Samuel Martin
4. **JOSEPH**, bpt Kingston, NH 13 Jun 1773 (NH VR): d Salisbury, NH 24 Jul 1824: m 12 Nov 1795 Esther Stevens
5. **HANNAH**, b 4 Nov 1774: bpt Kingston,NH 20 Jul 1777 (NHVR)
6. **JUDITH**, b 3 Jan 1777: bpt Kingston, NH 20 Jul 1777 (NHVR): m Jesse Worthley
7. **REBECCA**, b 26 Jan 1779: bpt Kingston, NH 13 Jun 1779 (NHVR): m 25 Oct 1798 John Huntoon
8. **DOROTHY**, b 24 Apr 1781: bpt Kingston, NH 15 Jul 1781 (NHVR): m 5 May 1803 Asa Sargent
9. **BENJAMIN**, b 22 Jun 1783: d 22 Jul 1783

10. **BENJAMIN**, b 13 Jul 1786: bpt Kingston, NH 30 May 1787 (NHVR): d Salisbury, NH 19 May 1854: m 13 Jul 1815 Rachel Blaisdell

JOSEPH CALEF, b Kingston, NH 5 May 1756 son of John & Judith (Challis) Calef (KTR): d Kingston, NH 22 Oct 1836 (GI p4): m(1) Kingston, NH 28 Jun 1781 Miriam Bartlett (NHGR 3:131), b Kingston, NH 19 Jun 1758 dau of Josiah & Mary (Bartlett) Bartlett (KTR), d Kingston, NH 27 Aug 1785 (GI p4): m(2) Kingston, NH 23 Sep 1789 Mary Hook (NHGR 3:134), b Sandown, NH 11 Oct 1762 dau Moses & Hannah (Huse) Hook (SdTR), d Kingston, NH 9 Oct 1790 (GI p4): m(3) 18 Jul 1792 Susanna Batchelder (Calef Gen p23), b 17 Jan 1766 dau of Nathaniel & Susanna (Gale) Batchelder.

Joseph, of Kingston (a.19yrs), served in Capt Philip Tilton's Co, Col Enoch Poor's Rgt 1775 (RW roll-51) & in Capt David Quimby's Co, Col Gale's Rgt (RW roll-50). He moved to Hallowell, ME in 1805 then moved back to Kingston #S9127 (NHPR 8:18).

Children: born Kingston, NH

1. **JOSIAH**, b 21 May 1782: d Saco, ME 2 Mar 1863: m(1) Susan Hussey: m(2) Sarah Philips Gale
2. **MIRIAM**, b 20 May 1784: d 18 May 1863: m Kingston, NH 8 May 1810 Dr Joseph Eastman (NHGR 4:178)
3. **JUDITH**
4. **MOSES HOOK**, b 9 Apr 1798: d Kingston, NH (bur) 30 Oct 1803 (NHVR)
5. **JOHN PIERCE BARNARD**, b 15 Sep 1801: d Salem, MA Dec 1880: m Salem, MA 25 Apr 1825 Rebecca Shreve (SlmVR)

WILLIAM CALEF, b Newbury, MA 17 Jul 1706 son of John & Deborah (King) Calef (NVR): d Kingston, NH 14 Nov 1784 (NHVR): m(1) Newbury, MA 5 Nov 1728 Sarah Cheney (NVR), b Newbury, MA 25 Jan 1708 dau of Daniel & Hannah (_) Cheney (NVR): m(2) Newbury, MA Nov 1736 Lois Sawyer (NVR), b

Newbury, MA 21 Jul 1718 dau of John & Sarah (Wells-Sibley) Sawyer (NVR), d Kingston, NH (bur) 29 Jul 1799 a.82yrs (NHVR).

William signed the Association Test in Kingston, NH (NHSP 30:78).

Children: last 8 born Kingston, NH (KTR)
(by 1st wife)

1. **SARAH**, b Newbury, MA 19 Aug 1729 (NVR)
2. **JOHN**, b Newbury, MA 14 Jun 1731: d Kingston, NH 28 May 1806 (KTR): m(1) Hannah Emerson: m(2) Kingston, NH 24 Dec 1754 Judith Challis (KTR)
3. **HANNAH**, b Newbury, MA 26 Jul 1733 (NVR)

(by 2nd wife)

4. **WILLIAM**, b Newbury, MA 26 Oct 1737 (NVR): d Kingston, NH 10 Jun 1812: m Kingston, NH (int) 16 Nov 1759 Anna Rowell (Calef Gen p17)
5. **LOIS**, b 4 Jan 1739/40: d Hampstead, NH: m Kingston, NH 23 Sep 1762 John Calef (NHGR 3:91)
6. **SAMUEL**, bpt 7 Feb 1741/2 (NHGR 5:108)
7. **JOSEPH**, b 12 Dec 1742: d Salisbury, NH 19 May 1823: m(1) 30 Oct 1765 Hannah Pettingill: m(2) Sarah Cushing (DAR 2:32)
8. **LYDIA**, b 30 Jul 1745: m Michael Sargent
9. **SARAH**, b 15 Sep 1749: m James Calef (DAR 1:109)
10. **MARY**, d Kingston, NH 15 Nov 1756 (NHVR)
11. **HANNAH**, bpt 29 Dec 1754 (NHGR 6:31): d Kingston, NH 25 Mar 1757 (NHVR)
12. **MARY**, b 22 Sep 1758: m Kingston, NH 19 Oct 1779 Charles Chase (NHGR 3:131)
13. **DOLLY**, b 20 Jun 1762: m ___ Dow

SAMUEL CAMMET, b Sandown, NH 11 May 1756 son of Silas & Catherine (Judkins) Cammet (SdTR): d Waterloo, ME 11 Jun 1825: m Elizabeth Sleeper (RG 1:105), b Kingston, NH 7 Apr 1760 dau of William & Dorothy (Rowell-Blaisdell) Sleeper (KTR), d aft 1820.

Samuel, of Kingston, served as a private in Capt Hutchins Co, Col Cilley's NH Rgt #S36950

(NHPR 8:31).

Children: (NHPR 8:31)
1. **SAMUEL**
2. **WILLIAM**
3. **SALLY**, a.18yrs in 1820

THOMAS CAMMET, b Sandown, NH 17 Aug 1760 son of Silas & Catherine (Judkins) Cammet (SdTR): d Cortlandt, NY 3 Aug 1835 (NHPR 8:35): m Cordlandt, NY 2 Mar 1786 Belinda Taylor (NHPR 8: 36).

Thomas, of Kingston, enlisted for the 7th Rgt of NH Militia in the Continental Army 1777, Hutchins's Co (NHSP 14:585). He enlisted again in the winter of 1782 at Exeter, NH & served under Capt Rowell; was transfered to Capt Senter's Co & served for 3 years (NHPR 8:35).

Children: (NHPR 8:35,36)
1. **THOMAS**, b 23 Mar 1798
2. **JOSEPH**, a.16yrs in 1820
3. **(DAU)**, a.15yrs in 1820

JAMES CAMPBELL, b Windham, NH 1 May 1754 son of Samuel & Mary (Robinson) Campbell (Hist of Windham p358): d 1834 (DAR 1:111): m(1) Rachel Gregg: m(2) Amherst, NH 18 Jun 1795 Agnes Kilpatrick (NEHGR 61:239), b Bedford, NH 15 Mar 1763 dau of Samuel & Agnes (Taggert) Kilpatrick (DAR #469489).

Probably the James Campbell, of Londonderry, NH, who served for the Town of Kingston in the Continental Army at West Point 25 Jul to 21 Dec 1781 (NHSP 16:255).

Children: born Bedford, NH (DAR #469489)
(by 1st wife)
1. **POLLY**, b 15 Jul 1786
2. **ANNE**, b 16 Aug 1788
3. **ANNE**, b 3 Sep 1790
4. **PHINEAS**, b 16 Mar 1793

(by 2nd wife)

5. **SAMUEL**, b 8 Mar 1796

6. **ABNER**, b 15 Sep 1797: d.y.
7. **BETSEY**, b 27 Oct 1799: m Hiram Bisbee
8. **HENRY**, b 4 Dec 1801: d Manchester, NH 5 Apr 1852: m Manchester, NH 21 Dec 1826 Sophia Lund
9. **NANCY**, b 26 Oct 1803: m Alva Wilkins
10. **THERON**, b 12 Feb 1806
11. **HIRAM**, b 12 Feb 1808: m Louisa Beard

MICHAEL CAREW signed the Association Test in Kingston, NH (NHSP 30:76).

ELIAS CARR, b Kingston, NH 26 Feb 1761 son of Sanders & Elizabeth (Pike) Carr (KTR): d Kingston, NH (bur) 15 Mar 1783 (NHVR).

Elias, of Kingston, served in Col Alexander Scammel's Rgt, Capt James Gray's Co 19 Apr 1777 (NHSP 14:585,659).

SANDERS CARR, b Salisbury, MA 5 Apr 1712 son of Sanders & Mary (Purington) Carr (SVR): m Salisbury, MA 21 Dec 1738 Elizabeth Pike (SVR), b Salisbury, MA 4 Dec 1718 dau of Elias & Joanna (Allen) Pike (SVR).

Sanders signed the Association Test in Kingston, NH (NHSP 30:77).

Children: born Kingston, NH (KTR)

1. **JOANNA**, b 4 Nov 1739
2. **BETTY**, b 14 Nov 1741
3. **SOLOMON**, b 20 Feb 1743
4. **LYDIA**, b 9 Jul 1745
5. **PRISCILLA**, b 9 Sep 1747
6. **ANNE**, b 19 Sep 1749
7. **SARAH**, b 13 May 1754
8. **ELIAS**, b 17 May 1757: d Kingston, NH 17 May 1757 (KTR)
9. **MARY**, b 27 Jun 1758
10. **ELIAS**, b 26 Feb 1761: d Kingston, NH (bur) 15 Mar 1783 (NHVR)
11. **ELIJAH**, b 27 Feb 1761: d Kingston, NH 27 Feb 1761 (KTR)

JACOB CARTER, m Kingston, NH 13 Sep 1742/3

Elizabeth Webster (NHGR 3:41), bpt Kingston, NH 11 Dec 1725 dau of John & Sarah (Stewart) Webster (NHGR 2:46).
Jacob signed the Association Test in Kingston, NH (NHSP 30:78).

Children:
1. **MERCY**, d Kingston, NH 16 Aug 1745 (NHVR)
2. **JACOB**, d Kingston, NH 2 Sep 1749 (NHVR)
3. **JACOB** (prob), b abt 1753

JACOB CARTER JR, b abt 1753 probably son of Jacob & Elizabeth (Webster) Carter: m (poss) Exeter, NH 13 Jan 1777 Abigail Steele (HE p51g).
Jacob Jr signed the Association Test in Kingston, NH (NHSP 30:78). On 10 Aug 1832, Jacob Carter of Exeter (a.79yrs) deposed that he lived in Kingston before & during the Revolution, but has since moved to Exeter. He was enlisted in Jul or Aug 1777 by Robert Stuart for Hale's Rgt NH Line (NHPR 8:153).

MOSES CARTER, b Kingston, NH 2 Oct 1739 son of Thomas & Mary (Webster) Carter: d New Hampton, NH 7 May 1831 (HL p110): m Anna Hoyt (Hoyt Gen p59), b 25 Nov 1745 dau of Eliphalet & Mary (Peaslee) Hoyt, d New Hampton, NH 30 May 1806.
Moses signed the Association Test in Kingston, NH (NHSP 30:78). He moved from Kingston Nov 1784 to New Hampton, NH.

Children: (HL p110-12)
1. **MOSES**, b Kingston, NH 1 Apr 1767: d Littleton, NH 22 May 1835 a.68yrs (CG p78): m Hannah Fuller
2. **ELIPHALET**, b Kingston, NH: d Littleton, NH 1829: m(1) int 2 Aug 1818 Abigail Wiggin: m(2) Abigail Sanborn
3. **THOMAS**, b Kingston, NH 1770: d Peacham, Vt 22 Feb 1847: m Sarah Gordon
4. **DANIEL**, b Kingston, NH 6 Mar 1773: d Littleton, NH 26 Sep 1861: m(1) Unity, NH 14 Nov 1797 Jemima Huntoon: m(2) Littleton,

NH 5 Dec 1823 Nancy Huntoon
5. **EBENEZER**, d Lyman, NH: m Abigail Sanborn
6. **PHILIP**, m(1) 18 Aug 1808 Mercy Swan: m(2) Rachel Swan (Greeley Gen p173)
7. **LEVI**, b New Hampton, NH 16 May 1788: d 16 Jun 1885: m(1) Sanbornton, NH 9 Jul 1812 Polly Mason: m(2) New Hampton, NH 2 Oct 1842 Melinda Dow: m(3) Bristol, NH 13 Sep 1855 Mary P. Mason
8. **MARY**, b New Hampton, NH: d 20 Apr 1835: m 4 Oct 1796 John Huse
9. **SALLY**, m Nathaniel Pearson
10. **NANCY**
11. **MIRIAM**, m ____ Blake

THOMAS CARTER, b Salisbury, MA 29 Oct 1713 son of John & Judith (Bagley) Carter (SVR): d bef 30 Oct 1782 (Greeley Gen p91): m Kingston, NH 25 Jan 1738/9 Mary Webster (NHGR 3:40), b Kingston, NH 31 Mar 1719 dau of Thomas & Mary (Greeley) Webster (KTR).

Thomas signed the Association Test in Kingston, NH (NHSP 30:78).

Children:
1. **MOSES**, b Kingston, NH 2 Oct 1739: d New Hampton, NH 7 May 1831: m Anna Hoyt
2. **SARAH**, b So Hampton, NH 21 Jul 1743 (SH VR)
3. **LEVI**, bpt Kingston, NH 2 Jan 1745 (NHGR 5:112)
4. **MARY**, b So Hampton, NH 2 Jul 1745 (SHVR)
5. **MIRIAM**, b Kingston, NH 3 Mar 1760 (KTR)

JONATHAN CASS, b Salisbury, MA 29 Oct 1753 son of Joseph & Sarah (Flanders) Cass (SVR): d Dresden, OH 9 Aug 1830 (DAR 1:119): m(1) ____: m(2) Exeter, NH 20 Dec 1781 Mary Gilman (HE p51g), bpt Exeter, NH 12 Aug 1759 dau of Theophilus & Deborah (_) Gilman (HE p70g), d Aug 1836.

Jonathan, of Kingston (a.25yrs) served as a pvt in Capt Philip Tilton's Co, Col Enoch Poor's Rgt (RW roll-51). At the close of the war he held the rank of Captain. He was in the Battles of Saratoga, Princeton, Germantown & in the Stillwater expedition 1779 (DAR LB 38:53)

Children: born Exeter, NH (HE p5g)

1. **LEWIS**, b 9 Oct 1782: d Detriot MI 17 Jun 1866: m 1806 Elizabeth Spencer
2. **DEBORAH WEBSTER**, b 16 Apr 1784
3. **GEORGE**, b 25 Jan 1786: d 1873
4. **CHARLES LEE**, b 15 Aug 1787: d Ohio 4 Jan 1842: m Josephine Mount (DAR LB 38:53)
5. **POLLY**, b 12 Aug 1788
6. **JOHN JAY**, b 28 Feb 1791: d 29 Apr 1792

CHRISTOPHER CHALLIS, b abt 1757 son of Gideon & Hannah (Blaisdell) Challis: d aft 1820 (NHPR 9:5): m Kingston, NH 6 Dec 1781 Lydia Blaisdell (NHGR 3:131), bpt Kingston, NH 8 May 1757 dau of Moses & Mary (Prescott) Blaisdell (KChR).

Christopher, of Kingston, enlisted 29 Apr 1777 in Capt Caleb Robinson's Co, Col Nathan Hale's Rgt. He also served under Capt Currier, Col Frye in 1775 (NHSP 14:628 & NHPR 9:5).

Children:

1. **LYDIA**, unmd in 1820
2. **HANNAH**

ENOS CHALLIS, b Amesbury, MA 25 Nov 1752 son of John & Miriam (Sargent) Challis (AVR): d Holland, NY Jun 1815 (DAR #455185): m bef 1797 Joannah Chase (DAR 1:122), b Kingston, NH 11 May 1764 dau of Ebenezer & Hepzibah (Sargeant) Chase (KTR), d Erie Co, NY 1813.

Enos enlisted for the 1st NH Rgt 14 Feb 1781, Capt Josiah Munroe's Co (NHSP 16:224).

Children: (DAR #455185)

1. **JOHANNA**, b Goshen, NH 3 Apr 1797 (IGI): m Joseph Hall
2. **EZEKIEL**
3. **SAMUEL**, b 7 Nov 1800: m Betsey Payne
4. **EBENEZER** (twin), b 3 Sep 1808: m Charlotte Gookins

5. **JOHN** (twin), b 3 Sep 1808

EPHRAIM CHALLIS, bpt Amesbury, MA 30 Sep 1753 son of William & Hannah (Weed) Challis (AVR): d 1 May 1827 (Pen Roll of 1835 p514): m(1) Amesbury, MA 26 Sep 1782 Anne Harvey (AVR), b Amesbury, MA 15 Aug 1754 dau of Joseph & Sarah (Sargent) Harvey (AVR), d Amesbury, MA 26 Oct 1792 (AVR): m(2) Amesbury, MA 26 Feb 1793 Hannah Nichols (AVR), b abt 1746.

11 Jul 1820, Ephraim Challis, of Kingston a.68yrs, testified that he was at the surrender of Burgoyne, Fort Stanwix. He enlisted in 1775 & served under Capt John Currier, Col Frye. He enlisted again about 1 Jan 1776 for 1 year under Capt James Norris, Col Poor NH Rgt & in Feb 1777 enlisted for 3 years under Capt Oliver, Col John Graton MA Line (NHPR 9:7).

Children: born Amesbury, MA (AVR)

1. **POLLY**, b 15 Oct 1781
2. **DOLLY**, b 21 Feb 1784
3. **HANNAH**, b 17 Jul 1786
4. **JOSEPH**, b 15 Feb 1790: d Danville, NH 22 Jan 1862: m 10 Dec 1812 Dorothy Blake

THOMAS CHALLIS, b Amesbury, MA 6 Jul 1749 son of John & Miriam (Sargent) Challis (AVR): d 1 Feb 1835 (DAR 1:122): m Danville, NH 5 Nov 1771 Molly French (NEHGR 58:122), b Danville, NH 9 Feb 1750 dau of Jonathan & Ann (Bagley) French (DnTR).

Thomas enlisted at Kingston abt 1 Oct 1775 & served in the NH Line at Winter Hill. He enlisted again abt 1 Jun 1776 & served under Capt Quimby, Col Wingate's Rgt at Independence. In the fall of 1777, he volunteered at Kingston & served under Lt French. He was residing in Plainfield, NH when he applied for a pension #S16704 (NHPR 9:11).

Children: (HS p524)

1. **ANNA**, b 3 Mar 1772; bpt Danville, NH 7 Apr 1776: d aft 1855: m Salisbury, NH 18

Jul 1787 Thomas Watson (NHPR 90:135)
2. **ENOCH**, b 22 Jan 1774; bpt Danville, NH 7 Apr 1776
3. **LYDIA**, bpt Danville, NH 7 Apr 1776 (NEHGR 58:45)
4. **MOLLY**, b 6 Apr 1779; bpt Danville, NH 9 May 1779 m ____ Puddleford
5. **LYDIA**, b 10 Jun 1781 (IGI): m ____ Baker
6. **THOMAS**, b 24 Mar 1784: m 25 Jun 1809 Abigail Morgan
7. **SAMUEL FRENCH**, b 3 Aug 1786: d Newport, NH
8. **MOSES**, b 11 Apr 1788: d Plainfield, NH
9. **AMOS**, b 7 Sep 1790: d Plainfield, NH
10. **JOHN**, b 6 Apr 1793: d Natchez, MS

THOMAS CHALLIS, b So Hampton, NH 25 May 1757 son of Enoch & Dorothy (Hoyt) Challis (SHVR): d Newton, NH 1 Aug 1796 a.40yrs (CG p109): m Newton, NH 26 Mar 1780 Elizabeth Bartlett (NHPR 9:9), b Newton, NH 19 Aug 1759 (NHPR 9:8) dau of Joseph & Elizabeth (Webster) Bartlett, d Kingston, NH 8 Jul 1840 a.81yrs (CG p109).
Thomas, of Newton, NH enlisted at Kingston 1 Mar 1777 & served in Capt Robinson's Co, Col Nathan Hale's Rgt (NHSP 14:627).

Children: born Newton, NH (NwtTR)
1. **NATHANIEL**, b 19 Dec 1779 ?: living Troy, NY 23 Mar 1837
2. **LYDIA**, bpt Kingston, NH 12 Aug 1781 (NHVR)
2. **ELIZABETH**, b 11 Feb 1782
3. **ENOCH**, b 6 Aug 1786

WILLIAM CHALLIS, probably m(1) Kingston, NH 12 Nov 1747 Hannah Dent (NHGR 3:43): m(2) Molly (Tuxbury) Colby, widow of Ezekiel Colby who died in Amesbury, MA 1762.
William signed the Association Test in Kingston, NH (NHSP 30:78).

Children: bpt Kingston, NH (NHGR & NHVR)
(by 1st wife)

1. **MARTHA**, bpt 17 Jul 1748
2. **MARGARET**, bpt 3 Mar 1750/1
3. **THOMAS DENT**, bpt 8 Aug 1756
4. **HANNAH**, bpt 29 Apr 1759
5. **WILLIAM**, bpt 30 Oct 1762

(by 2nd wife)

6. **EZEKIEL**, b 22 Jul 1765
7. **NANNE**, b 14 Apr 1767
8. **DAVID**, b 16 Jun 1769
9. **SARAH**, b 1 Oct 1771; bpt 25 Oct 1772
10. **JUDITH**, b 3 Sep 1773; bpt 17 Oct 1773
11. **DOLLY**, b 31 Jan 1776; bpt 8 Sep 1776

ABRAHAM CHASE, b Plaistow, NH 8 Jul 1750 son of Abraham & Elizabeth (Colby) Chase (PlVR): d aft 1818 (living Weare, NH): m abt 1770 Margaret Challis (PlVR).

Abraham, of Plaistow, was mustered at Kingston for the Continental Army 7th Rgt of NH Militia commanded by Col Jacob Gale 1779 (RW roll-50).

Children: 1st 2 born Plaistow, NH (PlVR)

1. **HANNAH**, b 19 Dec 1771: m William Stevens
2. **ABRAHAM**, b 29 Aug 1773: m Haverhill, MA 22 Feb 1795 Abigail Cogswell (HvVR)
3. **GEORGE W.**, d bef 2 Feb 1818
4. **DOLLY**, m Weare, NH 18 Feb 1806 Samuel Scribner (Chase Gen p77)

BENJAMIN CHASE, b Concord, NH 27 Sep 1758 son of Daniel & Mary (Pratt) Chase (Chase Gen p166): living 1818 in Clinton, ME.

Benjamin, of Concord, enlisted for Kingston in the 7th Rgt NH Militia 20 May 1777, Capt James Gray's Co (NHSP 14:585,660). He also served under Capt John Hale, Col Stark 1776. He was at the bombardment of Boston & in the Battle at Fort Ann, NY at the taking of Burgogne. He then went into Indian country under General Sullivan #S36964 (NHPR 9:87).

CALEB CHASE, b Kingston, NH Apr 1761 son of Ebenezer & Hepzibah (Sargent) Chase (KTR): d

1835 (DAR 1:126): m(1) ______ Challis: m(2) Fishersfield, NH 16 Aug 1818 Mrs Joanna Babb: m(3) Mary Straw (DAR 1:126).

Caleb was mustered by Col Josiah Bartlett Oct 1777. He served as a pvt in Capt Ezra Currier's Co, Col Abraham Drake's Rgt 8 Sep to 16 Dec 1777 (RW roll-49). He also served as a Cpl in the NH Militia Capt Jacob Webster's Co, Col Daniel Reynold's Rgt Jul to Nov 1781 (RW roll-52).

Children: (Chase Gen p151)

1. **JOHN**
2. **PHEBE**, b 26 Nov 1783: m 17 Sep 1805 Israel Gillingham
3. **HEPZIBAH**, b abt 1790: m William Atwood
4. **SARAH**, m 21 Feb 1805 Moses Bailey
5. **EBENEZER**, b 29 Mar 1791: d Ticonderoga, NY 16 Jan 1831: m Newbury, NH 8 May 1815 Mrs Sarah Cheney
6. **MARY**, m Sep 1810 Richard Thistle
7. **SUSANNA**, m 22 Oct 1818 Samuel Quimby
8. **LYDIA**, b 27 Feb 1794: m 26 Feb 1824 Daniel Gillingham

JACOB CHASE, b Haverhill, MA 4 Aug 1754 son of Ebenezer & Hepzibah (Sargent) Chase (HvVR): d 1818 (DAR 1:126): m 21 Dec 1777 Constance Saunders (Chase Gen p150), b (poss) Haverhill, MA 17 Mar 1749/50 dau of Jacob & Ann (Barney) Saunders (HvVR).

Jacob, of Kingston (a.21yrs), enlisted in Capt Henry Dearborn's Co under the command of Col Benedict Arnold 1775 (NHSP 14:217).

Children: (Chase Gen p151)

1. **NANCY ANN**, b 4 May 1778: m 15 Aug 1802 Job Saunders
2. **BENJAMIN**, b 2 Jul 1782: m 1 Jan 1809 Abigail Mason
3. **MARY**, b 14 Jul 1784: d 27 Jan 1871: m Jan 1812 George Whaley
4. **JAMES**, b 28 Nov 1786: m Jan 1809 Miriam Challis

5. **SARAH**, b 7 Jul 1790: m Jan 1807 Edward Whaley
6. **JOANNA**, b 24 Jun 1795: d Shelden, NY 19 May 1838: m 22 Mar 1818 Matthew Burn Jr.

MOSES CHASE, bpt Newbury, MA 19 Jul 1761 son of Moses & Susanna (Kelly) Chase (NVR): d Deerfield, NH 18 Nov 1840 (NHPR 19:102): m(1) abt 1781 Theodate Sanborn (Chase Gen p130), b Brentwood, NH 23 Feb 1761 dau of Daniel & Elizabeth (Sanborn) Sanborn (BtTR), d Deerfield, NH 1824 (CG p40): m(2) Deerfield, NH 2 Jun 1830 Mehitable (Smith) Bean (NHPR 19:103), d aft 1855. Mehitable m(1) Brentwood, NH 17 Mar 1778 Loami Bean (NHPR 3:88).

Moses enlisted Jul 1777 from Deerfield, NH & served under Capt Simon Marston, Col Senter for 6 months, first at Portsmouth, NH & then at Rhode Island where he was verbally discharged at Warwick in January 1778. On 5 Apr 1855 Mehitable Chase of Kingston, widow of Moses, applied for Bounty land (NHPR 19:102).

Children: born Deerfield, NH (Chase Gen p131)
1. **JOANNA**, b 16 Jun 1783: m John M. Steele
2. **SARAH**, b 14 Feb 1786: m Nathan Steele
3. **ABIGAIL**, b 4 Jun 1790: m Jacob Libby
4. **SUSAN**, b 29 Jul 1792: m 21 Feb 1821 John Steele
5. **DAVID**, b 3 Feb 1794: m 23 Jan 1821 Polly Philbrick
6. **POLLY**, b 22 Feb 1797: m Joseph Philbrick
7. **THEODATE**, b 9 Apr 1800
8. **ELIZA**, b 22 Apr 1802
9. **LYDIA**, b 28 Feb 1806: m 18 Aug 1825 Joel Bean

SIMEON CHOATE, b Kingston, NH 14 Jan 1748 son of Benjamin & Ruth (Edwards) Choate (KTR): d 22 Sep 1829 (DAR 1:130): m(1) Salisbury, MA 29 May 1770 Ruth Thompson (SVR), d Salisbury, MA 12 May 1795 (SVR): m(2) Salisbury, MA 9 Apr 1797 Hannah Norton (SVR), b Seabrook, NH, d 23 Feb 1839.

Simeon, of Kingston (a.72yrs), applied for a pension 9 Apr 1818. He enlisted in 1775 & served at Bunker Hill. He enlisted again abt 1 Jan 1776 under Capt Popkin, Col Greatry afterward by Col Knox MA Line & served until Jan 1777 as a Sgt (PP 24:20).

Children: born Salisbury, NH

1. **BENJAMIN**, b 30 Dec 1770: d 15 Sep 1854: m 23 Apr 1796 Jane True
2. **RUTH**, b 9 Nov 1772: d 5 Jan 1865: m Salisbury, NH 7 Jun 1795 Enoch Morrill (IGI)
3. **RUHAMAH**, b 19 Oct 1774: d 21 Jul 1847: m Kensington, NH 1 Jan 1798 Asa Dearborn
4. **BURNHAM**, b 25 Sep 1779
5. **RHODA**, b 30 Mar 1781: m 10 Jun 1803 Atkins Todd
6. **BETSEY**, b 1786: d 16 Jun 1873: m 6 Apr 1808 James Dennett
7. **JUDITH**, b 15 Feb 1788: d 24 Aug 1852: m 5 May 1805 Micajah Peaslee
8. **JACOB THOMPSON**, b 5 Jan 1791: d 12 Jun 1867: m(1) Mrs Freeman: m(2) 5 Feb 1828 Susan Dilworth

DANIEL CLARK, of Kingston, enlisted 7 Mar 1777 in Capt Zachariah Beal's Co, Col Alexander Scammel's Rgt (NHSP 14:648).

DAVID CLIFFORD, b Kingston, NH 28 Nov 1761 son of Joseph & Mary (Healey) Clifford (KTR): d Bath, ME 4 Apr 1837 (PP 15:37): m(1) Bath, ME 28 Nov 1781 Lydia Jones, dau of Jonas Jones of Georgetown, ME, d 1814: m(2) Bath, ME Mar 1816 Mehitable (Tuttle) Hanson (PP 15:37).

David enlisted Jun 1777 at Kingston & served as a pvt under Lt Cass 1st Co, Col Scammell's 3rd NH Rgt #W1026 (PP 15:37).

Children:(New Eng Fam Hist 4:713 & PP 15:37)
(by 1st wife)

1. **WILLIAM**, b 27 Apr 1783
2. **HANNAH**, b 1785
3. **DAVID**, b 11 Sep 1787

4. **LYDIA**, b 1 Aug 1789
5. **SUSANNAH**, b 6 Jun 1791
6. **MARGARET**, b 11 Apr 1792
7. **JOSEPH**, b 22 Feb 1794
8. **CLARISSA**, b 14 Oct 1796: m 1816 Joseph Clifford (DAR LB 93:44)
9. **RUFUS K.**, b 19 Mar 1799
10. **DOROTHY**, b 11 Jul 1802: living 1820
11. **CHARLES**, b 2 Dec 1804: living 1820

(by 2nd wife)

12. **ABIGAIL**, b 1816: living 1820
13. **MARY ANN**, b 8 Jul 1817: m James Mills Mitchell (DAR LB 145:288)
14. **MEHITABLE**, b 25 Jul 1819
15. **JOHN**, b 25 Jul 1819

DAVID CLIFFORD JR., possibly son of David & Joanna (Moody) Clifford: d aft 1800.

David Jr., of Kingston, was one of 20 men acquired by Gilmanton as its quota for the Continental Army (Hist of Gilmanton, NH p89).

JOHN CLIFFORD, JR., son of John & Ann (_) Clifford: m Kingston 23 Aug 1744 Elizabeth Sleeper (KChR), dau of Ebenezer & Sarah (Ward) Sleeper (PRNH 7:91).

John Jr signed the Association Test in Kingston, NH (NHSP 30:77).

Children: bpt Kingston, NH (KChR)

1. **EBENEZER**, bpt 24 Feb 1745
2. **HULDA**, bpt 10 May 1747
3. **STEPHEN**, bpt 10 Dec 1749
4. **ELIZABETH**, bpt 24 Sep 1752
5. **SAMUEL**, bpt 13 Oct 1754
6. **ISAAC**, bpt 29 May 1757

JOSEPH CLIFFORD, b Kingston, NH 17 Jun 1718 son of Isaac & Sarah (Taylor) Clifford (KTR): d Kingston, NH 3 Feb 1783 (NHVR): m Kingston, NH 28 Dec 1737 Mary Healey (KTR), b (prob) 1720 dau of William & Mary (Sanborn) Healey (New Eng Fam 4:728)

Joseph signed the Association Test in Kingston, NH (NHSP 30:77).

Children: born Kingston, NH (KTR)
1. **BENJAMIN**, b 21 Oct 1738
2. **JOHN**, b 11 Sep 1743
3. **JOSEPH**, b 21 Mar 1745: d Kingston, NH 7 Jan 1747/8 (KTR)
4. **MARY**, b 7 Jan 1747/8
5. **JOSEPH**, b 11 Jun 1750: d Gilmanton, NH 31 Dec 1824: m 3 Jan 1771 Lydia Moody
6. **ISAAC**, b 3 Feb 1753
7. **JEREMIAH**, b 8 Jun 1755
8. **SARAH**, b 17 Nov 1757: m Kingston, NH 28 Oct 1777 Jonathan Young (NHGR 3:130)
9. **WILLIAM HEALY**, b 27 Nov 1759: bpt 2 Mar 1760 (KChR): d 3 Jan 1831 (NHPR 10:155)
10. **DAVID**, b 28 Nov 1761: d Bath, ME 4 Apr 1837: m(1) Bath, ME 28 Nov 1781 Lydia Jones: m(2) Bath, ME Mar 1816 Mehitable (Tuttle) Hanson (PP 15:37)
11. **HANNAH**, bpt 23 Feb 1762 (NHVR)

STEPHEN CLIFFORD, bpt Kingston, NH 10 Dec 1749 son of John & Elizabeth (Sleeper) Clifford (KChR).

Stephen signed the Association Test in Kingston, NH (NHSP 30:77).

WILLIAM CLIFFORD, b Kingston, NH 27 Nov 1759 son of Joseph & Mary (Healey) Clifford (KTR): d 3 Jan 1831 of Loudon, NH (NHPR 10:155): m ____, a.62yrs in 1820.

William, of Kingston (a.18yrs), enlisted 3 Feb 1777 in Capt F.M. Bell's Co (NHSP 14:623). He also served as a pvt in Capt Philip Tilton's Co, Col Enoch Poor Rgt #S45681 (NHPR 10:155).

Children: born Loudon, NH
1. **WILLIAM**, b 2 Jan 1783
2. **MARY**, b 24 Apr 1785: living 1820
3. **EBENEZER**, b 21 Sep 1789
4. **BETSEY**, b 2 Apr 1792: living 1820
5. **DAVID**, b 2 Apr 1794
6. **SARAH C.**, b 16 Jul 1796

7. **SUSAN**, b abt 1798 (a.22yrs in 1820)
8. **HANNAH**, b abt 1801 (a.19yrs in 1820)
9. **PERSIS**, b abt 1804 (a.16yrs in 1820): m (prob) Loudon, NH 4 Feb 1823 William Tuttle
10. **CALVIN**, b abt 1815 (a.5yrs in 1820)

BENJAMIN CLOUGH, b Kingston, NH 23 Apr 1716 son of Cornelius & Joanna (Sanborn) Clough (KTR): d Kingston, NH 4 Apr 1792 a.76yrs (GI p6): m(1) Kingston, NH 20 Mar 1747 Elizabeth Smith (KTR), d Kingston, NH 22 Jan 1753 (KTR): m(2) Kingston, NH 1 May 1753 Mary Sanborn (KTR), b 22 Jan 1724 dau of Richard & Elizabeth (Batchelder) Sanborn (NEHGR 10:278), d Kingston, NH 11 Aug 1767 (KTR): possibly m(3) Mary ____, d Kingston, NH 23 Nov 1794 a.60yrs (GI p6).

Benjamin signed the Association Test in Kingston, NH (NHSP 30:77).

Children: born Kingston, NH (KTR)
(by 1st wife)
1. **JOANNA**, b 5 Apr 1748: d Kingston, NH 21 Nov 1756 (NHVR)

(by 2nd wife)
2. **CORNELIUS**, b 19 Jan 1755: d Unity, NH 22 Apr 1831 (NHPR 10:162): m So Hampton, NH 16 Jan 1775 Mary Levitt (SHVR)
3. **BENJAMIN**, b 7 Jun 1757: d Genesee, NY 22 Jan 1823 (RWPF 1:680): m Kingston, NH 6 May 1779 Joanna Young (NHGR 3:130)
4. **ELIZABETH**, 1 Apr 1760
5. **MARY**, 13 Aug 1763: m Nehemiah Davis

BENJAMIN CLOUGH, b Kingston, NH 7 Jun 1757 son of Benjamin & Mary (Sanborn) Clough (KTR): d Genesee, NY 22 Jan 1823 (RWPF 1:680): m Kingston, NH 6 May 1779 Joanna Young (NHGR 3:130), b Kingston, NH 23 Dec 1747 dau of Joseph & Sarah (Brown) Young (KTR), d 8 Sep 1850 (RWPF 1:680).

Benjamin enlisted at Cambridge 17 May 1775 in Capt Wm H. Ballard's Co, Col Frye's Rgt. He enlisted again & was an Ensign in Capt Wm Prescott's Co, Col Tash's Rgt of Durham and was at Ticonderoga 27 Nov 1776 and discharged 17 Jun 1777 #W18916 (RWPF 1:680).

Children: (UR p49)

1. **JOSEPH**, b Kingston, NH 4 Mar 1780
2. **BENJAMIN**, b Unity, NH 19 Feb 1782
3. **ELIM**, b Unity, NH 8 Apr 1784
4. **MOLLY**, b Unity, NH 11 Aug 1786
5. **JOANNA**, b Unity, NH 7 Jul 1788
6. **BETTY**, b Unity, NH 22 Feb 1791: m ___ Doty (RWPF 1:680)
7. **DOROTHY**, b Unity, NH 12 Feb 1793
8. **JOEL**, a.15yrs in 1820
9. **WESLEY**, living 1850 Orleans Co, NY
10. **POLLY**, m _____ Weed (RWPF 1:680)

CORNELIUS CLOUGH, b Kingston, NH 19 Jan 1755 son of Benjamin & Mary (Sanborn) Clough (KTR): d Unity, NH 22 Apr 1831 (NHPR 10:162): m So Hampton NH 16 Jan 1775 Mary Levitt (SHVR), b abt 1756 a.81yrs in 1837.

Cornelius enlisted Apr 1775 under Capt John Calef & marched to Lexington. He enlisted again & served 3 months at Portsmouth, NH & Cambridge, MA; also served 8 months at NY #W15998 (NHPR 10:162). He signed the Association Test in Kingston, NH (NHSP 30:77).

Children: born Kingston, NH

1. **DOROTHY**, b 13 Mar 1775
2. **BENJAMIN**, b 26 May 1777
3. **SARAH**, b 22 Oct 1779
4. **BENJAMIN**, b 2 Mar 1782

PHINEAS CLOUGH, b Salem, NH 16 Apr 1749 son of Josiah & Abigail (Hastings) Clough (HSlm): d VT 24 Sep 1809: m Haverhill, MA 29 Dec 1778 Sarah Ladd (HvVR), b Haverhill, MA 24 Sep 1758 dau of Asa & Sarah (Merrill) Ladd (HvVR).

Phineas served in Capt Gordon's Co, Col David Gilman's Rgt 1776 (RW roll-50).

Children: (Clough Gen p208)

1. **(DAU)**, d bef 1800
2. **(DAU)**, b bef 1791: m Erasmus Orcutt

JAMES COLBY signed the Association Test in Kingston, NH (NHSP 30:78).

LEVI COLBY was mustered in the 7th Rgt Dec 1776 under the command of Col David Gilman, Capt Gordon's Co (RW roll-50).

THOMAS COLBY, b Kingston, NH 25 Dec 1757 son of Thomas Elliot & Susanna (Ring) Colby (KTR): d Danville, VT 12 Jun 1842 (PP 194:47): m Newton, NH Jul 1784 Lydia Webster (PP 194:46), b Kingston, NH 28 Aug 1764 dau of Isaac & Sarah (Downing) Webster.

Thomas enlisted at Kingston Jun 1778 & served under Capt John Eastman, Col Bartlett's Rgt. Enlisted again 5 Jul 1780 & served under Capt Thomas Migill, Col Nathaniel Wade's Rgt. He also enlisted at Newburyport, MA under Capt Moses Nowell, Col Titcomb's Rgt (MAS&S 3:750 & PP 194:46).

Children: (Colby Gen p152)
1. **PAGE**, b 1785: d Danville, VT 15 Sep 1835
2. **SUSAN**, b 1787
3. **MARY**, b 1789
4. **MARIE**, b 1792
5. **JOHN**, b 28 Mar 1793: living 1844 Danville, VT
6. **SYLVIA**, b 1797
7. **GIDEON**, b Danville, VT abt 1795
8. **IRA**, b Danville, VT 22 Dec 1803

DANIEL COLCORD, b Kingston, NH 16 Oct 1747 son of Samuel & Mehitable (Ladd) Colcord (KTR): d (Est Adm) 31 Dec 1795: m Kingston, NH 1 Feb 1770 Dolly Clifford (TAG 17:224), d aft 1796.

Daniel signed the Association Test in Kingston, NH (NHSP 30:76).

Children: born Kingston, NH (TAG 17:224)
1. **DOLLY CLIFFORD**, b 11 Jan 1771: d King-

ston, NH 8 Dec 1790 (NHVR): m Kingston, NH 28 Jun 1790 Jedediah Philbrook (NHGR 3:135)
2. **LOUIS**, b 21 Oct 1772
3. **HANNAH**, b 28 Mar 1774: d 21 Oct 1774
4. **PETER**, b 13 Aug 1775: d Kingston, NH 6 Oct 1844 (GI p8): m Epping, NH 15 May 1801 Lydia Sleeper (NHGR 4:89)
5. **DANIEL**, b 13 Jun 1781: d Kingston, NH 18 Apr 1851 (GI p7): m Kingston, NH 2 Jan 1812 Polly Woodman (NHGR 4:179)

SAMUEL COLCORD, b Kingston, NH 22 Aug 1710 son of Samuel & Elizabeth (Folsom) Colcord (KTR): d Kingston, NH 23 Jan 1783 (GI p8): m Kingston, NH 28 Dec 1732 Mehitable Ladd (KTR), b Kingston, NH 30 Jun 1713 dau of Daniel & Mehitable (Philbrick) Ladd (KTR), d Kingston, NH 1 Apr 1803 (GI p8).

Samuel signed the Association Test in Kingston, NH (NHSP 30:76).

Children: born Kingston, NH (KTR)
1. **ELIZABETH**, b 19 Dec 1733: d Kingston, NH 9 Aug 1735 (KTR)
2. **PETER**, b 20 Jun 1736: d Kingston, NH 5 Nov 1749 (KTR)
3. **ELIZABETH**, b 25 1739: m Kingston, NH 23 Nov 1758 Nathaniel French Jr (NHGR 3:90)
4. **SAMUEL**, b 23 Jul 1741: d Kingston, NH 26 Nov 1749 (KTR)
5. **MARY**, b 6 Feb 1744: d (bur) Kingston, NH 30 Nov 1789 (NHVR): m Kingston, NH 2 Jul 1761 Ebenezer Griffin (KTR)
6. **DANIEL**, b 16 Oct 1747: m Kingston, NH 1 Feb 1770 Dolly Clifford (TAG 17:224)
7. **SAMUEL**, b 30 Mar 1749: d Kingston, NH 15 Apr 1749 (KTR)
8. **MEHITABLE** (twin), b 28 Mar 1751: m Danville, NH 29 Sep 1774 William Patten (NEHGR 58:123)
9. **HANNAH** (twin), b 28 Mar 1751: d Kingston, NH 17 Apr 1751 (KTR)
10. **HANNAH**, b 13 Mar 1754: d 29 Aug 1837: m

Kingston, NH 16 Dec 1773 Dr Joseph Bartlett (TAG 17:220)
11. **SUSANNAH**, b 2 Apr 1758: m 24 Jun 1792 Jabez Eaton

DANIEL COLLINS, b Kingston, NH 1758 (MSSP p153): d Harmony, ME 2 Feb 1851 (RG 1:142): m So Hampton, NH 18 Mar 1779 Mary Tewksbury (SH VR), b abt 1760 (a.60yrs in 1820), d 1832.

Daniel enlisted Apr 1775 as a pvt under Capt Moses McFarland, Col John Nixon MA Line. He enlisted again Jan 1776 under Capt Jeremiah Gilman, Col John Nixon. In 1777 he enlisted under Capt Samuel McConnell, Col Stickney NH Co & in 1778 he served under Capt David Quimby, Col Jacob Gale. He was at the Battles of Bunker Hill, Harlem Height, White Plains, Trenton, Princeton & Bennington (DAR LB 89:293 & PP 11:26).

Children: (PP 11:26-27)
1. **MARY**, b abt 1780: m Sandwich, NH 28 Oct 1802 Johnson D. Quinby
2. **JOHN**, b abt 1797: d 1884: m Abigail Jewell (DAR LB 89:293)
3. **MARTHA** (Patty), a.20yrs in 1820
4. **WILLIAM**, lived in Harmony, ME 1841
5. **DOLLY**, d 1863: m Andrew Hall (DAR LB 100:276)

JONATHAN COLLINS, probably m(1) ____: m(2) Danville, NH 29 Apr 1767 Dorothy Webster (NEHGR 58:47).

Jonathan signed the Association Test in Kingston, NH (NHSP 30:77).

Children: b Kingston, NH (KTR)
(by 1st wife)
1. **SARAH**, b 23 Nov 1761
2. **MOSES**, bpt Danville, NH 15 Jul 1764 (NEHGR 58:42)
3. **JOSEPH**, b 3 May 1763: bpt Danville, NH 15 Jul 1764 (NEHGR 58:42)
4. **JACOB**, b 27 Jan 1765

5. **TABITHA**, b 30 Sep 1766

(by 2nd wife)

6. **JONATHAN**, b 26 Feb 1768
7. **ELIZABETH**, b 4 Jul 1769
8. **SAMUEL**, b Feb 1772: m Kingston, NH 24 Dec 1795 Polly Blake (NHGR 3:136)

JONATHAN COLLINS, b abt 1745: m Lydia Carr

Jonathan, of Kingston (a.30yrs), served in Capt Philip Tilton's Co, Col Enoch Poor's Rgt 1775 (RW roll-51).

Children: born Kingston, NH

1. **LEVI**, b 16 Feb 1772
2. **MARY**, b 7 May 1774
3. **SARAH**, b 9 Jan 1777
4. **ANNA**, b 19 Aug 1782
5. **JAMES**, b 19 Aug 1784

ROBERT COLLINS, b Kingston, NH 12 Mar 1733 son of Ebenezer & Apphia (Merrill) Collins (KTR): d Sandown, NH 1777 (DAR LB 23:329): m _____

Robert served as a Capt in the NH Militia in the Burgoyne campaign 1777 (DAR #22934).

Children:

1. **SAMUEL**, m Salisbury, MA 5 Jul 1781 Betsey Hacket (SVR)

ROBERT COLLINS, bpt Kingston, NH 15 Sep 1765 son of Benjamin Collins (KChR).

Robert (a.16yrs) enlisted 15 Jan 1782 in Isaac Farwell's Co, 1st NH Rgt (NHSP 16:935).

WILLIAM COLLINS, b abt 1754: d Kingston, NH Sep 1809 a.55yrs (NHVR):

William signed the Association Test in Kingston, NH (NHSP 30:78).

BENJAMIN COOPER, possibly b Newbury, MA 12 Jan 1756 son of Benjamin & Susanna (Butler) Cooper (NVR): d aft 1790: m Lydia Bartlett.

Benjamin signed the Association Test in Kingston, NH (NHSP 30:77).

Children: born Kingston, NH (IGI)
1. **LYDIA**, b 23 Nov 1778
2. **PRISCILLA**, b 2 Nov 1780
3. **BENJAMIN**, b 26 Feb 1783
4. **ABIGAIL**, b 15 Mar ? 1783
5. **WILLIAM**, b 2 Jan 1788: d Kingston, NH 19 Mar 1790 a.2yrs (NHVR)

ISAAC DAVIS, b Amesbury, MA 27 Mar 1728 son of Joseph & Sarah (Colby) Davis (AVR): d 1808 (DAR 1:179): m Kingston, NH 8 May 1760 Keturah (Woodward ?) Follinsby (NHGR 3:91).

Isaac, of Boscawen, enlisted for Kingston in the 7th Rgt of NH Militia in the Continental Army 1777, Capt James Gray's Co (NHSP 14:585, 659).

Children: (DAR #134081)
1. **BETSEY**, b 1760: m Stephen Ward
2. **MOLLY**, b 1762: m Abner Ward
3. **JAMES**, b 1764: m ____ Brown
4. **DANIEL**, b 1766: d Bradford, NH 8 Nov 1842 (CG p22): m Mary Brown
5. **JOHN**, b 1768
6. **SUSAN**, b 1770: m Moses Bailey
7. **SALLY**, b 1772
8. **JOHN**, b 1774: m Sally Ward

JOHN DAVIS, b Kingston, NH 16 Jul 1759 son of John & Hannah (Wadleigh) Davis (KTR): d Kingston, NH 22 Dec 1841 a.83yrs (NHVR).

John enlisted 1775 under Capt Abraham French & marched to Portsmouth. In 1776, he served in Capt Quimby's Co, Col Jacob Gale's Rgt (RW roll-50). In Jun 1777 he served as a Sgt under Capt Ezra Currier #S17921 (NHPR 13:172).

JONATHAN DAVIS, of Kingston (a.20yrs), served in Col Enoch Poor's Rgt, Capt Philip Tilton's Co 1775 (RW roll-51).

PHILIP DAVIS, b Amesbury, MA 14 Sep 1725 son of Francis & Joanna (Ordway) Davis (AVR): d Kingston, NH 4 Aug 1800 (NHVR): m Kingston, NH 15

Feb 1749/50 Miriam Webster (KTR), b Kingston, NH 8 Aug 1729 dau of Thomas & Mary (Greeley) Webster (KTR).

Philip signed the Association Test in Kingston, NH (NHSP 30:78).

Children: born Kingston, NH (KTR)

1. **WEBSTER**, b 27 Jul 1751: d Kingston, NH Jan 1833 (NHVR): m(1) ____ Miller: m(2) Betsey Pollard
2. **MARCY**, 20 Jul 1759

PHINEAS DAVIS, b Kingston, NH 25 Mar 1754 son of John & Hannah (Wadleigh) Davis (KTR): m ___, who d Kingston, NH Feb 1833 a.82yrs (NHVR).

Phineas, of Kingston, testified 7 Dec 1832 to service at Rhode Island in 1778 under Capt D. Quimby (NHPR 75:77).

SAMUEL DAVIS, b Amesbury, MA 13 Jun 1745 son of Timothy & Judith (Pettingill) Davis (AVR): d Freemont, NH bef 4 Mar 1822 (NEHGR 116:263): m(1) 8 Mar 1768 Joanna Quimby, d Kingston, NH 25 May 1775 (NEHGR 116:264): m(2) Danville, NH 30 Nov 1775 Mary Pressy (NEHGR 58:123).

Samuel signed the Association Test in Kingston, NH (NHSP 30:78). He was mustered by Col Josiah Bartlett Oct 1777 & served in Capt Ezra Currier's Co, Col Abraham Drake' Rgt 8 Sep to 16 Dec 1777 (RW-roll 49).

Children: born Kingston, NH (NEHGR 116:265)

1. **MARY**, b 29 Jul 1768
2. **BENJAMIN**, b 8 Jan 1770
3. **JOANNA**, b 25 Oct 1771: bpt 3 May 1772 (NHVR)
4. **SAMUEL**, b 11 Feb 1773: bpt 17 Oct 1773 (NHVR)
5. **ELI**, b 15 Mar 1775

WEBSTER DAVIS, b Kingston, NH 27 Jul 1751 son of Philip & Miriam (Webster) Davis (KTR): d Kingston, NH Jan 1833 (NHVR): m(1) _____ Miller: m(2) Betsey Pollard (Pollard Gen 1:97), b

Kingston, NH 22 Aug 1753 dau of Francis & Sarah (Webster) Pollard (KTR), d Kingston, NH 4 Jan 1827 (NHVR)

Webster signed the Association Test in Kingston, NH (NHSP 30:78). He served in Col Jacob Gale's Rgt, Capt David Quimby's Co (RW roll-50).

Children:

1. **SARAH**, m Newton, NH Mar 1813 Samuel Sleeper (NwtTR)

THOMAS DOLLOFF, b 17 Jun 1759 (DAR 1:197) son of Thomas Dolloff: d Meredith, NH 11 Jun 1840 (NHPR 15:46): m Raymond, NH 5 Oct 1780 Elice Leavitt (NHPR 15:46), b 1761 dau of Nehemiah Leavitt, d 1854.

Thomas, of Raymond, enlisted for Kingston in the 7th Rgt NH Militia 27 May 1777, Capt James Gray's Co (NHSP v14 p585 & 660). He was in the Battles at Fort Ann at Stillwater 1777 & at Newton 1779 #W2099 (NHPR 15:45).

Children: (NHPR 15:45 & IGI)

1. **AMOS**, b Raymond, NH 11 May 1784
2. **MARY**, b Raymond, NH 27 Sep 1786: m Meredith, NH 22 Sep 1808 Samuel Dolloff (Annals of Meredith, NH p182)
3. **ELICE**, b Meredith, NH 19 Mar 1789
4. **JOHN R.**, b Meredith, NH 7 Oct 1791
5. **NOAH**, b Meredith, NH 13 Jan 1797
6. **JESSE**, b Meredith, NH 16 Nov 1799: d 1878: m 1822 Nancy P Huckins
7. **JOSEPH**, b Meredith, NH 26 Apr 1802
8. **ABIGAIL**, b Meredith, NH 29 Nov 1804
9. **MAHALA**, b Meredith, NH 26 Apr 1807

DANIEL DOW, bpt Haverhill, MA 26 Feb 1758 son of Stephen & Hannah (Shephard) Dow (HvVR).

Probably the Daniel, of Plaistow, who was mustered by Col Jacob Gale Jul 1779 for Kingston & served in the 7th NH Militia Rgt (RW roll-51).

JABEZ DOW, b 25 Aug 1747 (DAR 1:200) son of Ezekiel & Elizabeth (Cram) Dow: d Deerfield, NH 19 Sep 1808 (RWPF 1:1014): m So Hampton, NH 13 Feb 1777 Ann Jewell (SHVR), b So Hampton, NH 25 Apr 1755 dau of Jonathan & Sarah (Barnard) Jewell (SHVR), d Laconia, NH 22 May 1840.

Jabez, of Kingston (a.31yrs), was mustered 5 Apr 1777 & served in Capt John Drew's Co #W14626 (NHSP 14:618).

Children: (Dow Book P86)

1. **LYDIA**, b 1 Dec 1777: d Laconia, NH 17 May 1870
2. **SARAH**, b 22 Mar 1781: d 31 Oct 1878: m Deerfield, NH 14 Apr 1801 Sewall Dearborn
3. **EZEKIEL**, b 21 Jun 1785: d 20 Nov 1849: m 27 Feb 1814 Sally Hill

SAMUEL DOWNING, b Kingston, NH 2 Dec 1748 son of Jonathan & Sarah (Day) Downing (KTR): d near Lake Champlain, NY (of Small Pox) Jul 1777 (NHPR 15:125): m Sandown, NH abt 1764 Mary Carter (NHPR 15:127), b (prob) So Hampton, NH 2 Jul 1745 dau of Thomas & Mary (Webster) Carter (SHVR). Mary m(2) Kingston, NH 22 Aug 1782 Thomas Corser (NHGR 3:131) who died at Boscawen, NH 11 Dec 1829.

Samuel, of Kingston, enlisted in the Spring of 1775 & joined the army at Winter Hill #W14503 (NHPR 15:123).

Children: (NHPR 15:128)

1. **THOMAS**
2. **JONATHAN**
3. **RICHARD**
4. **MARY**

JEREMIAH DUDLEY JR., b Raymond, NH 27 Aug 1753 son of Samuel & Mary (Ladd) Dudley (Dudley Gen p431): d 10 Nov 1838 (DAR 1:204): m 10 Dec 1780 Elizabeth Turner (Dudley Gen p432), b Milford, ME 7 Jan 1763, d Bath, NY 28 Aug 1834.

Jeremiah, of Kingston, enlisted 1775 & served in Capt William Ballard's Co, Col James Frye's

MA Rgt (NHSP 15:746 & NHPR 15:189).

Children: (Dudley Gen p432)

1. **MEHITABLE**, b Readfield, ME 6 Nov 1781: d Bath, NY 15 May 1870: m Pittston, ME 19 Dec 1799 Jonathan Fluent
2. **JEREMIAH**, b Readfield, ME 29 Nov 1783: d Savannah, GA Oct 1807
3. **POLLY**, b Readfield, ME 3 Feb 1786: d Dixon, IL 18 Mar 1852: m(1) 10 Oct 1808 James Murphy: m(2) 25 May 1820 Josiah Moores
4. **DAVID**, b Readfield, ME 5 Sep 1788: m Bangor, ME 15 May 1813 Elizabeth Watson
5. **ELIZABETH**, b Pittson, ME 15 Dec 1790: d Bath, NY 20 Oct 1842: m Bath, NY 25 Mar 1814 Samuel Legro
6. **LOIS**, b Pittson, ME 17 Mar 1793: d 2 Jul 1850
7. **JOHN**, b Pittson, ME 7 Jun 1795: m Bath, NY 22 Dec 1815 Mrs. Elizabeth Rowe Harris
8. **MOSES**, b Pittson, ME 13 Jul 1797: m Bath, NY 1 Apr 1819 Mary Atwood
9. **THOMAS JEFFERSON**, b Pittson, ME 2 Aug 1800: m Caroline Bull
10. **BENJAMIN FRANKLIN**, b Bangor, ME 16 Jun 1803

BENJAMIN EASTMAN, b (prob) Kingston, NH 12 Feb 1752 son of Timothy & Mary (Blaisdell) Eastman (KTR): d Plaistow, NH 6 Feb 1837 (NHPR 30:49): prob m(1) Martha Peaslee: m(2) Plaistow, NH 25 Mar 1832 Anna Kelly (NHPR 30:50), b Plaistow, NH Jun 1783 dau of John & Sarah (Noyes) Kelly (PlVR), d Plaistow, NH 24 Mar 1863 (PlVR).

Benjamin, of Kingston (a.80yrs), deposed 6 Aug 1832 that he enlisted Apr 1775 under Capt Moses McFarland at Haverhill, MA #W287 (NHPR 30:48).

Children: (Eastman Gen p229)

1. **JACOB PEASLEE**, b Kingston, NH 4 Apr 1809: d Canfield, IL 14 Oct 18__: m Plaistow, NH 13 Jul 1835 Eliza A. Calef (PlVR)

EBENEZER EASTMAN, b Kingston, NH 14 Jul 1729 son of Ebenezer & Mary (Colcord) Eastman (KTR): d Kingston, NH 4 Dec 1799 (KTR): m Kingston, NH 19 Jun 1758 Sarah Fifield (KTR), b Kingston, NH 5 Jan 1739 dau of Samuel & Joanna (Clifford) Fifield (KTR), d Kingston, NH 5 May 1794 (KTR).
Ebenezer signed the Association Test in Kingston, NH (NHSP 30:76).

Children: born Kingston, NH (KTR)
1. **EBENEZER**, b 25 Oct 1760: d Kingston, NH 25 Jun 1846 (GI p10): m Kingston, NH 22 Oct 1789 Sarah Stevens (NHGR 3:134)
2. **JONATHAN**, b 18 Apr 1765: d Kingston, NH 25 Jan 1842 a.76yrs (GI p10): m Mary ____
3. **PETER**, b 30 Sep 1768: d Kingston, NH 21 Nov 1842 a.74yrs (GI p10)

HENRY EASTMAN, b Kingston, NH 4 Jul 1763 son of Joseph & Jemima (Bean-Smith) Eastman (KTR): d Grantham, NH 1 Feb 1845 (NHPR 16:112): m(1) Sarah Bean (Bean Gen p139), dau of Jeremiah Bean: m(2) Grantham, NH 5 Feb 1838 wid Eleanor Holbrook (NHPR 16:113), a.82yrs in 1853.
Henry enlisted Apr 1781 & served under Capt Bedel (NHPR 16:111). During the Rev War he lived in Salisbury, Kingston, Rumney, Deerfield & Grantham, NH.

JOHN EASTMAN, b Kingston, NH 24 Feb 1741 son of Benjamin & Margaret (Graves) Eastman (KTR): d Kingston, NH 11 Sep 1804 a.64yrs (GI p10): m Danville, NH 17 Feb 1774 Joanna French (NEHGR 58:123), b Kingston, NH 14 Jan 1752 dau of Jonathan & Joanna (Elkins) French (KTR), d Kingston, NH 17 Apr 1839 a.83yrs (NHVR).
John served as a 2nd Lt & afterwards as a Capt in the NH Militia. He also served as a 2nd Lt in Capt David Quimby's Co, Col Joshua Wingate's Rgt #W14669 (NHPR 16:132).

Children: last 10 bpt Kingston, NH (NHVR)
1. **BENJAMIN**, bpt Danville, NH 11 Jun 1775 (NEHGR 58:45)

2. **JOANNA**, bpt 14 Jul 1776: d Kingston, NH 17 Oct 1778 (NHVR)
3. **JOHN**, bpt 7 Sep 1778: d Kingston, NH Sep 1803 (NHVR)
4. **JOANNA** (Hannah), bpt 2 Jul 1780: m Sanborn Fifield (NHPR 16:135)
5. **MARY**, bpt 1 Apr 1782
6. **SARAH**, bpt 28 May 1785
7. **JONATHAN**, bpt 17 Jun 1787: d Union, ME 27 Feb 1871: m 15 Jan 1817 Nancy Hills
8. **MEHITABLE**, bpt 29 Aug 1790
9. **ANNA**, bpt 21 Jul 1793: d 3 May 1869: m 7 Oct 1816 Daniel Clarke
10. **JOSEPH**, bpt 25 Sep 1796
11. **SAMUEL**, bpt 7 Jul 1799

JOSHUA EASTMAN, b Hampstead, NH 31 Aug 1754 son of Edmund & Hannah (Hills) Eastman (HmstR): d 1 Feb 1841 (Eastman Gen p207): m Hampstead, NH 21 Dec 1780 Sarah Tucker (HmstR), b Sandown, NH 13 Jan 1755 dau of Jacob & Lydia (Hoyt) Tucker (SdTR), d 22 Aug 1827.

Joshua served as a Cpl in Capt Gordon's Co, Col David Gilman's Rgt 1776 (RW roll-50).

Children: born Hampstead, NH (HmstR)

1. **JOSHUA**, b 24 Oct 1787: d Hampstead, NH 15 Jun 1859: m Hampstead, NH 10 Dec 1818 Susan Chase
2. **AMASSA**, b 11 Apr 1789: d Hampstead, NH 29 Nov 1853: m Hampstead, NH 19 Nov 1818 Betsey Edmunds
3. **TAPPAN**, b 23 Nov 1790: d 13 Sep 1864: m Hampstead, NH (int) 3 Apr 1813 Susan Boynton (HmstR)
4. **SALLY**, b 10 Jan 1797: m Hampstead, NH 18 Aug 1822 George Moore

PETER EASTMAN, bpt Kingston, NH 3 Nov 1754 son Timothy & Mary (Blaisdell) Eastman (NHGR 6:31): living 1832 Compton, Lower Canada.

Peter enlisted at Kingston & served under Capt Moses McFarland, Col Thomas Nixon's MA Rgt. In Mar 1776, he enlisted again while still a resident of Kingston, for 9 months under Capt John Calef, Col David Gilman Rgt NH Line #R3205 (NHPR 16:156). After the war he resided in Salisbury, NH & Fairfax, VT then moved to Compton, Lower Canada.

THOMAS EASTMAN, b 11 Oct 1740 (DAR 1:212) son of Roger & Rachel (Nichols) Eastman: d Newbury, VT 11 Oct 1828 (Hist of Newbury, VT p535): m 1767 Sarah Ann Sargent, b abt 1741, d Newbury, VT 25 Mar 1831 a.90yrs.

Thomas was mustered by Col Josiah Bartlett Oct 1777 & served as a pvt in Capt Ezra Currier's Co, Col Abraham Drake's Rgt 8 Sep to 16 Dec 1777 (RW roll-49).

Children: (Hist of Newbury, Vt p535)

1. **ROGER**, b 2 Jan 1769: d 1790: unmd
2. **DAVID**, m Susan Ordway
3. **ISAAC**, b 13 Apr 1775: d 16 Jun 1856: m(1) 21 Nov 1796 Mehitable George: m(2) Mary Conant
4. **DANIEL**, b 25 Feb 1777: d Newbury, VT 22 Mar 1840: m 6 Mar 1797 Mina Worthley

BENONI EATON (Benoni Long alias Eaton), bpt Salisbury, MA 16 Dec 1722 son of Susannah Long (SVR): m Kingston, NH 28 Nov 1754 Hannah Watson (NHGR 3:87).

Benoni son of Susannah Long had land voted to him in Kingston 14 Apr 1738. He signed the Association Test in Kingston, NH (NHSP 30:78).

JAMES EATON, bpt Kingston, NH 3 Jun 1755 son of Ezekiel & Mary (Campbell) Eaton (NHGR 6:32): m (prob) Danville, NH 22 Apr 1778 Jemima George (NEHGR 58:124).

James was mustered by Col Josiah Bartlett Oct 1777, Col Drake's Rgt & served under Capt Ezra Currier in 1777 (NHSP 15:342).

JOSEPH EATON, b Sandown, NH 17 Aug 1757 (NHPR 16:189): d Greenfield, NH 2 Dec 1844 (NHPR 16:190): m (prob) Haverhill, MA 13 Dec 1781 Elizabeth George (HvVR), d bef 1844.

Joseph was mustered at Kingston Oct 1777 by Col Josiah Bartlett for Col Drake's Rgt & served under Capt Currier. He also served under Capt John Calef in 1776 #S10604 (NHSP 15:342; 16:189).

Children: (NHPR 16:190)
1. **NATHANIEL A.**
2. **SOPHRONIA**, m ____ Burdick
3. **LYDIA**, m ___ Flint
4. **BETSEY**, m ___ Martin
5. **POLLY**, m ___ Rogers

JOSEPH TRUE EATON, b Danville, NH 3 Apr 1758 son of Joseph & Jane (True) Eaton (DnTR): d Marshfield, VT 22 Nov 1845 (NHPR 16:193): m Plaistow, NH 29 May 1791 Mehitable Eastman (NHPR 16:193), b Danville, NH Mar 1767 dau of Edward & Sarah (Wadley-Clough) Eastman (DnTR).

Joseph served under Capt John Calef in 1777 #W24101 (NHPR 16:191).

SAMUEL EATON, b Plaistow, NH 31 Dec 1756 son of John & Hannah (Stevens) Eaton (PlVR): d Salisbury, NH 7 Mar 1826 (HS p552): m Plaistow, NH 10 Oct 1780 Lydia Ladd (NHPR 16:201), b Kingston, NH 4 Jan 1759 dau of Trueworthy & Lydia (Harriman) Ladd (KTR), d Salisbury, NH 29 Mar 1839 (HS p552).

Samuel was mustered at Kingston 2 Oct 1777 by Col Josiah Bartlett for Col Drake's Rgt. He also served in 1775 under Capt Richard Davis at Great Island & at West Point, NY in 1781 (NHSP 15:343 & NHPR 16:201)

Children: (HS p552)
1. **HANNAH**, b 14 May 1781: d 8 Aug 1833: m 10 Mar 1803 Moses Greeley
2. **LYDIA**, b 25 Apr 1783: d 9 Jun 1880: m 4 Mar 1805 Peter Fifield
3. **SARAH**, b 7 Jan 1785: d 12 Jul 1836: m 22 Dec 1814 Silas Call
4. **SAMUEL**, b 19 Feb 1787: d 11 Aug 1792

5. **MEHITABLE**, b 2 May 1789: d 6 Jun 1864: m 30 Mar 1813 Caleb Smith
6. **ABIGAIL**, b 2 Sep 1791: d 4 Dec 1825: m 24 Dec 1815 Joseph Huntoon
7. **SAMUEL**, b 7 Dec 1793: d 11 Apr 1808
8. **JOHN**, b 29 Mar 1796: d 22 Sep 1797
9. **JOHN L.**, b 27 Jul 1798: m(1) 22 May 1825 Mary Morgan: m(2) Mar 1837 Lovey Bickford
10. **LUCY**, b 5 Aug 1800: m(1) 25 Jun 1822 William Jackman: m(2) 14 Feb 1835 Alstead Brownell
11. **JESSE**, b 13 May 1803

THOMAS ELKINS, b Hampton, NH 10 Oct 1711 son of Thomas & Hannah (Fogg) Elkins (HmVR p55): d aft 31 Mar 1785 (DAR 1:217): m Salisbury, MA 22 Dec 1737 Anna Brown (SVR), b Salisbury, MA 23 Nov 1717 dau of Abraham & Hannah (Morrill) Brown (SVR).

Thomas signed the Association Test in Kingston, NH (NHSP 30:76).

Children: bpt Kingston, NH (NHGR)

1. **HANNAH**, bpt 8 Jun 1739/40
2. **THOMAS**, bpt 5 Sep 1742: d Kingston, NH 15 May 1827 a.85yrs (GI p11): m Kingston, NH 21 Mar 1769 Joanna Fifield (KChR)
3. **MARY**, bpt 17 Mar 1744/5: d Danville, NH 19 Dec 1816 (CG p39): m Kingston, NH 11 Jul 1763 Thomas Page (NHGR 3:129)
4. **HENRY**, bpt 3 Apr 1748: d Kingston, NH 19 Feb 1749 (NHVR)
5. **ABEL**, bpt 16 Dec 1750
6. **HENRY**, bpt 16 Jun 1754
7. **JEREMIAH**, bpt 25 Feb 1759 (NHVR)

THOMAS ELKINS JR, bpt Kingston, NH 5 Sep 1742 son of Thomas & Anna (Brown) Elkins (NHGR 5:109): d Kingston, NH 15 May 1827 (GI p11): m Kingston, NH 21 Mar 1769 Joanna Fifield (KChR), b Kingston, NH 17 Feb 1744/5 dau of Samuel & Joanna (Clifford) Fifield (KTR), d Kingston, NH 7 Mar 1829 a.84yrs (GI p11).

Thomas Jr signed the Association Test in

Kingston, NH (NHSP 30:76).

BARNARD ELLIOT, b Newton, NH 16 Jul 1751 son of John & Hannah (Jones) Elliot (NwtTR): d Concord, NH 15 Jan 1828 (Hist of Concord, NH p654): m Elizabeth Carter (DAR #720875), b Newton, NH 16 Nov 1753 dau of John & Elizabeth (Webster) Carter (NwtTR).

Barnard was mustered by Col Josiah Bartlett Oct 1777, Col Drake's Rgt (NHSP 15:342).

Children: (DAR #720875)

1. **ELIZABETH**, b Newton, NH 4 Aug 1773 (NwtTR): m Jonathan Sleeper
2. **ABIGAIL**, b 5 Sep 1778
3. **EZRA**, b 20 May 1781: m Grata Welch
4. **BARNARD CARTER**, b 1 Apr 1784: d Concord, NH 7 Dec 1851: m 6 May 1806 Deborah Welch
5. **JAMES**, m Concord, NH 6 May 1800 Eleanor Colby (NHGR 6:106)

JACOB ELLIOT, b Chester, NH 5 Nov 1755 son of Edmund & Mehitable (Worthen) Elliot (HC p515): d Chester, NH 6 Dec 1841 (NHPR 17:65): m Kingston, NH 11 Apr 1798 Martha Sleeper (NHGR 3: 168), b Kingston, NH 16 May 1772 dau of Richard & Martha (Fifield) Sleeper (KTR), d 19 May 1850 (NHPR 17:65).

Jacob, of Kingston, deposed 10 Apr 1818 that he served as a pvt from the Battle of Bunker Hill in which he was engaged until a little before the Battle of Bennington in which he was wounded. He served as a 2nd Lt from 20 Jan 1778 at RI for 12 months & as a Lt from 30 Jun 1779 at RI. He also served as a Lt from 29 Jun 1780 until Jan 1781 in NH & Vt (NHPR 17:59). Jacob lived in Enfield & Kingston after the war.

Children: (HC p515)

1. **EDMUND**, lived Exeter, NH
2. **ELIZA**
3. **MARTHA**, b Chester, NH 30 Nov 1800
4. **JACOB**, b Chester, NH 16 Oct 1802: lived Raymond, NH

5. **JOHN S.**, d Chester, NH
6. **JAMES**, lived Chester, NH

BENJAMIN FELLOWS, b Kingston, NH 7 Oct 1760 son of Joseph & Margaret (Webster) Fellows (KTR): m 18 Jan 1792 Mary Blaisdell (DAR #107290A93), b 1768, d 1800.
Benjamin served in the Continental Army from Newburyport, MA (DAR LB 108:98)

Children: (DAR #107290A93)
1. **MARGARET**, b Jul 1793: d 1856: m 1811 Samuel Heath
2. **JOSEPH**, lived & died NY

JOSEPH FELLOWS, b Kingston, NH 27 Feb 1714 son of Samuel & Sarah (Webster) Fellows (KTR): d 1795: m(1) Kingston, NH 1 Jan 1737/8 Elizabeth Young (KTR), b Kingston, NH 25 Oct 1717 dau of Joseph & Elizabeth (Sleeper) Young (KTR), d Kingston, NH 17 Oct 1756 (KTR): m(2) Kingston, NH 7 Mar 1757 Sarah (Treadwell) Green (KTR). Sarah m(1) Hampton Falls, NH 29 Sep 1737 Abraham Green (HFTR).
Joseph signed the Association Test in Kingston, NH (NHSP 30:78).

Children: born Kingston, NH (KTR)
(by 1st wife)
1. **SAMUEL**, b 14 Aug 1738: d Kingston, NH 15 Sep 1778 (DAR 1:232): m Kingston, NH 13 May 1761 Mary Ring (KTR)
2. **JOSEPH**, b 13 Jul 1740: d Kingston, NH 18 May 1749 (KTR)
3. **SARAH**, b 3 Nov 1742
4. **ELIZABETH**, b 7 Jan 1744/5
5. **NATHANIEL**, b 2 Jun 1747
6. **ABIGAIL**, b 21 Aug 1749
7. **JOSEPH**, b 26 Jul 1752
8. **MARY**, b 12 Sep 1754
9. **ANNE**, b 16 Oct 1756

(by 2nd wife)

10. **ELIZABETH**, b 10 Dec 1757

JOSEPH FELLOWS, b Kingston, NH 7 Jan 1762 son of Samuel & Mary (Ring) Fellows (KTR): d 1847 (DAR 1:232): m Kingston, NH 5 Nov 1787 Sarah Quimby (NHGR 3:133), b Hampstead, NH 24 Oct 1768, d 28 Aug 1838.

Joseph enlisted at Kingston, Hawke parish & served as a pvt in Capt Ezekiel Giles Co, Col Peabody Rgt (PP 11:56).

Children:

1. **PERKINS**, b 5 Sep 1789: d 12 Feb 1860: m Eleanor Clement (DAR #392496)
2. **ALMENA**, b Piermont, NH 15 May 1808 (IGI)

SAMUEL FELLOWS, b Kingston, NH 14 Aug 1738 son of Joseph & Elizabeth (Young) Fellows (KTR): d Kingston, NH 15 Sep 1778 (DAR #470125): m Kingston, NH 13 May 1761 Mary Ring (KTR), b Salisbury, MA 27 Sep 1741 dau of Jonathan & Esther (Batchelder) Ring (SVR), d Kingston, NH

Samuel served as a pvt in the NH Line.

Children:

1. **JOSEPH**, b Kingston, NH 7 Jan 1762 (KTR): d 1847 (DAR 1:232): m Kingston, NH 5 Nov 1787 Sarah Quimby (NHGR 3:133)
2. **JONATHAN**, b Danville, NH 18 Oct 1764 (Dn TR): d Jun 1841 (NHPR 18:196): m Eleanor Weeks (DAR 1:232)
3. **SAMUEL**, b Danville, NH 30 Dec 1766 (Dn TR): m Hannah Merrill
4. **MOLLY**, b Danville, NH 10 May 1770 (DnTR)
5. **DAVID**, bpt Danville, NH 14 Mar 1773: m Polly Clarke
6. **THOMAS**, bpt Danville, NH 21 May 1775: m Martha Kalton
7. **ESTHER**, bpt Danville, NH 5 Oct 1777: m Kingston, NH 17 Nov 1796 Josiah Jones (NHGR 3:167)

MOSES FERRIN (FARREN), b Amesbury, MA 15 Mar 1726 son of Jonathan & Sarah (Wells) Ferrin (AVR): d (prob) Newton, NH: m Biddeford, ME 26 Sep 1748 Mary Shephard (Farren Gen p12).

Moses served in Capt Moses McFarland Co, Col John Nixon's Regt (NHSP 15:742).

Children: bpt Biddeford, ME

1. **JONATHAN**, b abt 1752: m(1) Arundel, ME 12 Dec 1779 Sarah Goodridge: m(2) 10 Jun 1802 Elizabeth Sargent (ME Fam 2:245)
2. **MARY**, bpt 1 Mar 1755: m Newton, NH Mar 1778 Ephraim Hadly (NwtTR)
3. **MOSES**, bpt 3 Jun 1759: d 15 Jan 1843 (DAR 1:233): m(1) 9 Sep 1777 Mary Dellan: m(2) Newmarket, NH 8 Sep 1784 Aseneah Robinson (NHGR 6:138): m(3) Parsonsfield, ME 25 Feb 1839 Jane Blazo (RWPF 2:1179)
4. **ANNA**, bpt 2 Jul 1758
5. **HANNAH**, bpt 18 Sep 1763: m Newton, NH 1 Oct 1788 Benjamin Hoit Jr (NwtTR)
6. **SARAH**, b Saco, ME; bpt 26 May 1765: m 21 Apr 1786 Stephen Colby
7. **JOSEPH**, b Saco, ME; bpt 18 Oct 1767: m(1) Judith Edgerly: m(2) 5 Jan 1840 Mercy Gilbert

EBENEZER FIFIELD, b Kingston, NH 10 Dec 1751 son of Samuel & Joanna (Clifford) Fifield (KTR): d Readfield, ME 3 Jun 1834 (RG 1:235): m Hampton Falls, NH 8 Apr 1773 Mary Sanborn (IGI), b Kingston, NH 13 Jan 1758 dau of William & Mary (Sleeper) Sanborn (KTR), d 27 Jan 1839 (TAG 19:100).

Ebenezer signed the Association Test in Kingston, NH (NHSP 30:77).

Children: (TAG 19:100)

1. **EBENEZER**
2. **NOAH**, b 22 Jul 1783
3. **WEAVER**, b abt 1780
4. **MARY**, b abt Aug 1787: d 3 Feb 1843
5. **DOROTHY**

EDWARD FIFIELD, b Kingston, NH 22 Jan 1748 son of John & Dorothy (Fifield) Fifield (KTR): d Plainfield, NH 19 Aug 1831 (CG p89): m Dorothy Sleeper (DAR 1:235), b abt 1748, d Plainfield,

NH 26 Aug 1827 (CG p89).
Edward served as a pvt in Capt Benjamin Emery's Co at the Battle of White Plains & at Bennington under Capt Ebenezer Webster (DAR LB 28:261).

Children: (TAG 19:93)
1. **DOROTHY**
2. **IRA**
3. **JOSIAH**, lived Irasburg, VT
4. **SUSAN**
5. **LYDIA**, m Oliver Taylor
6. **MEHITABLE G.**
7. **PHEBE**, m Enos Richard
8. **PERLY**, b abt 1788: m Miriam Morgan
9. **EDWARD**, d Wetherfield, VT
10. **JESSE**
11. **JAMES**, b abt 1794
12. **LUCINDA**, b Meridan, NH: m Cyrus Beckley

EDWARD FIFIELD, bpt Kingston, NH 21 Dec 1755 son of William & Anne (Sinkler) Fifield (KChR): d 21 Jun 1812 (DAR 1:235): m Andover, NH 19 Nov 1787 Elizabeth Rowe (NEHGR 58:16), dau of John & Susan (Scribner) Rowe (HA p157). Elizabeth m(2) Samuel Kimball.
Edward, of Kingston (a.20yrs), served in Capt Philip Tilton's Co, Col Enoch Poor's Rgt (NHSP 14:112).

Children: (HA p157)
1. **MARY** (Polly), b 20 Sep 1788: m Jeremiah Sanborn
2. **SALLY**, m Apr 1825 John Emery
3. **SUSAN**, b 31 Jan 1791: m Moses Fuller
4. **JACOB**, b 1795: m 10 Jul 1831 Ann Sanborn
5. **SAMUEL**
6. **HIRAM**, b 10 Aug 1807: d Franklin, NH 1 May 1875: m 25 Sep 1833 Louisa Sanborn
7. **JOHN CROCKET**, b 17 Dec 1811: m Ann Hills

JOHN FIFIELD, bpt (poss) Kingston, NH 24 Feb 1754 son of John & Elizabeth (Greeley) Fifield (KChR): d 18 Sep 1828 (NHPR 19:41): m Gilmanton, NH 8 Mar 1791 Hannah Folsom (NHPR 19:42), b 10 Oct 1756 dau of Peter & Hannah (Morrison) Folsom (Folsom Gen p136), d Parsonfield, ME 25 Mar 1844 (NHPR 19:42). Hannah m(2) 26 Aug 1829 Henry Proal. In 1820, John was a resident of Milton, NH & in 1826 of York Co, ME.

John, of Kingston (a.22yrs), served in Capt Philip Tilton' Co, Col Enoch Poor's Rgt 1775 (RW roll-51). He enlisted again at Rumney, NH & served under Capt George Everett, Col Bedel. In Oct 1779, he served in the Naval service on the US Sloop of War Ranger commanded by Capt Thomas Simpson #W17500 (MSSP p256 & NHPR 19:37).

PETER FIFIELD, b Kingston, NH 7 Aug 1740 son of Samuel & Joanna (Clifford) Fifield (KTR): d Kingston, NH (bur) 31 May 1807 (NHVR): m Danville, NH 5 Jul 1773 Sarah French (NEHGR 58: 123).

Peter signed the Association Test in Kingston, NH (NHSP 30:77).

Children: bpt Kingston, NH (NHVR)

1. **DAVID**, bpt 6 Jul 1777
2. **JOANNA**, bpt 6 Jul 1777: m Peter Stevens
3. **RUHAMAH**, bpt 28 Aug 1778: m Kingston, NH 13 Dec 1798 John Stevens (NHGR 3:168)
4. **MOSES FRENCH**, bpt 13 Oct 1782
5. **SALLY**, bpt 18 Jul 1784: m Peter Sanborn
6. **JOSIAH**, bpt 2 Jul 1789

SAMUEL FIFIELD, b Kingston, NH 25 Jul 1733 son of Samuel & Joanna (Clifford) Fifield (KTR): d Kingston, NH 16 Jul 1811 a.77yrs (GI p11): m Kingston, NH 21 Feb 1757 Mary Eastman (KTR), b abt 1734, d Kingston, NH 20 Feb 1806 a.72yrs (GI p11).

Samuel signed the Association Test in Kingston, NH (NHSP 30:77).

Children: born Kingston, NH (KTR)

1. **PETER**, b 9 Oct 1758: d Kingston, NH 19 Jul 1836 (GI p11): m bef Dec 1782 Sarah Judkins

2. **SAMUEL**, b 16 Jun 1765
3. **AMOS**, b 13 Jun 1770: m Kingston, NH 5 Mar 1795 Hannah Fifield (NHGR 3:136)

RICHARD FITTS, b Sandown, NH 8 Aug 1758 son of Daniel & Abigail (Currier) Fitts (SdTR): d Sandown, NH 9 Dec 1826 (NHPR 19:82): m Brentwood, NH 24 Feb 1786 Dorothy Kimball (NHPR 19:82), b Freemont, NH 1768 dau of John & Dorothy (__) Kimball, d Sandown, NH 4 Jan 1848.

Richard served in Capt Philip Tilton's Co, Col Enoch Poor's Rgt 12 Jun 1775 until Jan 1776. He enlisted again & served in Daniel Gordon's Co from 5 Dec 1776 to 15 Mar 1777 #W16255 (RW roll-51 & NHPR 19:82).

Children: born Sandown, NH (Greeley Gen p174)

1. **DANIEL**, b 7 Mar 1789: d Webster, NH 13 Jul 1865: m(1) Sandown, NH 12 Nov 1812 Abigail Mitchell: m(2) 17 Mar 1846 Sarah Ann Weeks
2. **RICHARD**, b 6 Dec 1790: d Boscawen, NH 10 Jan 1846: m(1) 25 Nov 1817 Mary Blanchard: m(2) Salisbury, NH 2 Jan 1827 Maria Stevens
3. **NANCY B.**, b 2 Mar 1792: m Charlestown, MA John Tibbets
4. **ABEL**, b 26 Oct 1793: d Somerville, MA 3 May 1856: m Lexington, MA Apr 1820 Sally Locke
5. **MARY**, b 29 May 1797: d Penacook, NH 3 Aug 1880: m Sandown, NH 3 Dec 1827 Nathaniel Abbott
6. **CYRUS**, b 24 Aug 1798: d Sandown, NH 24 Dec 1845
7. **NATHANIEL**, b 28 Sep 1800: d Sandown, NH 14 Mar 1867: m Epping, NH Rhoda Purington
8. **HIRAM**, b 30 Oct 1807: d Sandown, NH 18 Mar 1872: m Hampstead, NH 28 Jul 1842 Mary Jane Currier
9. **SALLY**, b 28 Jun 1808
10. **CYNTHIA**, b 11 Nov 1809: d Chester, NH 14 Nov 1880: m Sandown, NH 29 Jun 1839 David Lane

EZEKIEL FLANDERS, b Kingston, NH 1759 son of Ezekiel & Ann (Nichols) Flanders (Flanders Gen p185): d Hereford, Lower Canada 1846 (NHPR 19: 101): m Hampstead, NH (int) 7 Jul 1782 Betty Rowell (HmstR).

Ezekiel, of Plaistow, NH, served for Kingston in Col Gale's 7th NH Militia Rgt for the defense of RI (RW roll-51). In Apr 1782, he enlisted at Pembroke, NH under Capt Robinson, Col George Reid & served until 24 Mar 1784 #S21756 (NHPR 19:96). After the War, he lived in Canaan, Vt & Hereford, Lower Canada.

Children: (Flanders Gen p188)

1. **EZEKIEL**, d Cattaraugus Co, NY 1838: m(1) Lyman, NH 15 Nov 1804 Stella Moore: m(2) Lydia White
2. **FRANCIS**, b Sutton, NH 5 Apr 1792: d Fawn River MI 14 Sep 1861: m 1 Jan 1818 Elizabeth Chandler
3. **NANCY PILSBURY WORTHEN**, b Bridgewater, NH 17 Apr 1805

NATHANIEL FLANDERS, bpt Kingston, NH 8 Dec 1751 son of Ezekiel & Ann (Nichols) Flanders (NHGR 6:27): d Danbury, NH 4 Jan 1832 (NHPR 19:117): m Hampstead, NH 4 Jan 1774 Mary Goodwin (NHPR 19:118), b Hampstead, NH 18 Apr 1756 dau of Nathan & Rhoda (Colby) Goodwin (HmstR), d aft 12 Jul 1838 of Wilmot, NH.

Nathaniel resided in Kingston during the Rev War & served in 1775 under Capt Jacob Tilton, Lt Webster at Winter Hill. In 1776 he served under Capt French at Portsmouth, NH #R3597 (NHPR 19:115).

Children: (Flanders Gen p184)

1. **HESTER**, b Hampstead, NH 19 Feb 1775
2. **JOHN**, b Hampstead, NH 28 Jan 1779
3. **HENRY**
4. **TIMOTHY**, b Danbury, NH 1785: d (WP) 17 Jul 1849: m Andover, NH 29 Oct 1807 Abigail Robie

STEPHEN FLANDERS, bpt Kingston, NH 7 May 1758 son of Ezekiel & Ann (Nichols) Flanders (NHVR): d 8 Nov 1835 (DAR 1:240): m Danville, NH 11 Mar 1779 Sarah Ring (NEHGR 58:124).

Stephen enlisted 1775 under Capt McFarland, Col Nixon. Enlisted again Oct 1776 as a Sgt under Capt Benjamin Kimball, Col Enoch Poor & served at Ticonderoga; when he became ill, his brother Nathaniel served in his place #S10680 (NHPR 19:121,130).

Children: (Flanders Gen p185)

1. **JOSEPH BARTLETT**, b Manchester, NH 8 Nov 1794: d Tunbridge, Vt 6 Nov 1873 m Strafford, Vt 23 Jan 1817 Sophia Tyler
2. **JAMES**, d Lawrence, NY 17 Feb 1834
3. **SAMUEL**, m Harriet Durfey

JEREMIAH FOLSOM, b Exeter, NH 9 Feb 1759 (NHPR 20:92) son of Jeremiah & Anna (Louge) Folsom (Folsom Gen p216): d Farmington, NH 13 Nov 1835 (NHPR 20:94): m Newburyport, MA 23 Mar 1789 Olive Clark (NHPR 20:94), d Farmington, NH 3 Sep 1843 (NHPR 20:95).

Jeremiah enlisted in 1776 under Capt Simon Marston in the NH Militia for 2 months. Enlisted again for 6 months under Capt Quimby NH Militia. In 1778 he served under Capt Cilley at Portsmouth & in 1779 served under Capt Jonathan Parsons, Col Mooney at RI. In the Spring of 1780 he enlisted for 8 months in the Continental Army #W16117 (NHPR 20:91).

Child:

1. **JOHN CLARK**, b abt 1789: d 1810 a.21yrs

JEREMIAH FOSTER, b Plaistow, NH 6 Mar 1745 son of Benjamin & Sarah (Woodard) Foster (PlVR): d aft 4 Jul 1820 living Goffstown, NH (NHPR 20: 175): m Hampstead, NH 5 Jan 1768 Jemima Kent (HmstR).

Jeremiah (a.30yrs), served in Capt Hezekiah Hutchin's Co, Col James Read's Rgt 1775 (RW roll-52). He also served in Capt Gordon's Co,

Col David Gilman's Rgt 5 Jan to 15 Mar 1777 (RW roll-50). In 1782 he enlisted at Exeter under Capt Jeremiah Fogg & served in the 2nd NH, Col Dearborn, Capt Asa Senter's Co until Jul 1784 & then served under Capt Josiah Johnson, Col McIntosh MA Line. He was in the Battles of Bunker Hill & Monmouth (NHPR 20:175).

Children:
1. **JEREMIAH**, b 7 Feb 1773: m Sally Killam

ABNER FOWLER, b 17 Mar 1753 (DAR 1:248) son of Samuel Fowler: d New Chester NH 30 Apr 1833 a. 80yrs (NHPR 20:195): m Seabrook, NH 8 Dec 1774 Mary Mason (NHPR 20:195), bpt Hampton, NH 9 May 1756 dau of John & Mary (Sanborn) Mason (HH p855), d Hill, NH 21 May 1843 a.87yrs (CG p67).
Abner enlisted at Kingston Apr 1777 & served as a pvt for 3 years under Capt James Gray, Col Alexander Scammel until Apr 1780. He was in the Battles of Fort Ann 1777, Monmouth 1778 & Newton 1779 #W16017 (NHPR 20:194).

Children: (NHPR 20:195)
1. **HANNAH**, a.24yrs in 1820
2. **JOHN**, a.19yrs in 1820
3. **ABRAHAM**, living 1836
4. **(DAU)**, d bef 1820: m ___ Gordon

PHILIP FOWLER, bpt Kingston, NH 10 Jul 1757 son of Joseph & Margaret (_) Fowler (NHVR):
Philip of Sandown served as a drummer in Capt Gordon's Co, Col David Gilman's Rgt 5 Jan to 15 Mar 1777 (RW roll-50). Also served in Capt James Norris's Co 1777 (NHSP 14:616).

PETER FREEMAN (negro), listed in the Town Returns of the Rev War for Kingston (NHSP 16: 510). Possibly he is the Peter, servant of Josiah Bartlett, who enlisted for 3 years in Col Reed's Rgt (NHSP 16:709).

ABRAHAM FRENCH, b Kingston, NH 22 Apr 1733 son of Nathaniel & Abigail (Eastman) French (KTR):

d Kingston, NH 12 May 1800 a.68yrs (GI p12): m Kingston, NH 15 Jan 1756 Sarah Smith (KTR), bpt Kingston, NH 1 Jun 1735 dau of William & Elizabeth (Cilley) Smith (NHGR 2:69), d Kingston, NH 22 Jan 1806 a.70yrs (GI p12).

Abraham signed the Association Test in Kingston, NH (NHSP 30:76).

Children: born Kingston, NH (KTR)
1. **ELISE**, b 12 Jan 1759: d (bur) Gilmanton, NH 28 Feb 1827: m Kingston, NH 27 Mar 1783 Stephen Judkins (NHGR 3:132)
2. **ROBERT SMITH**, b 23 Mar 1761: d Kingston, NH 26 Aug 1801 a.41yrs (GI p12)
3. **SARAH**, b 9 Jul 1764
4. **LOIS**, b Aug 1767: d Kingston, NH 2 Jan 1832 (GI p29): m Kingston, NH 26 Aug 1794 Robert Smith (NHGR 3:135)
5. **ABIGAIL**, b 1 Jan 1770

DAVID FRENCH, b Kingston, NH 20 Aug 1719 son of Simon & Sarah (Heard) French (KTR): d Kingston, NH 20 Oct 1792 (NHVR): m Kingston, NH 15 Sep 1747 Ruhumah Choat (KTR), b Kingston, NH 22 Dec 1718 dau of Benjamin & Abigail (Burnum) Choat (KTR), d Kingston, NH 4 Jan 1808 a.90yrs (NHVR).

David signed the Association Test in Kingston, NH (NHSP 30:77).

Children: born Kingston, NH (KTR)
1. **RUHAMAH**, b 17 Feb 1748/9: m(1) 16 Feb 1773 Moses Judkins (Judkins Gen p11): m (2) Kingston, NH 11 Dec 1777 Joseph Fitts (NHGR 3:130)
2. **JOHN**, b 25 Jun 1751: d Kingston, NH 31 Jan 1843 (NHVR): m Newton, NH 1 Apr 1792 Nancy Peaslee (NwtTR)
3. **SARAH**, b 29 Aug 1754
4. **ABIGAIL**, b 10 Oct 1758

HENRY FRENCH, b Kingston, NH 25 Jan 1747 son of Jonathan & Joanna (Elkins) French (KTR): d Kingston, NH 19 Apr 1816 a.69yrs (GI p12): m(1)

Danville, NH 21 Dec 1769 Judith Sanborn (NEHGR 58:122), b Kingston, NH 30 Nov 1748 dau of Abraham & Abigail (Clifford) Sanborn (KTR), d Kingston, NH 25 Jan 1784 (NHVR): m(2) Anna Shephard, b abt 1757, d Kingston, NH 28 Nov 1850 a.93yrs (GI p12).

Henry signed the Association Test in Kingston, NH (NHSP 30:77).

Children: 1st 3 bpt Kingston, NH (NHVR)
(by 1st wife)
1. **HANNAH**, bpt 13 Jun 1773: d Kingston, NH 13 Sep 1777 (NHVR)
2. **HENRY**, bpt 25 Apr 1779
3. **ABRAHAM SANBORN**, bpt 22 Jul 1781
4. **SAMUEL**,

(by 2nd wife)

5. **PETER**, b abt 1788: d Kingston, NH 4 Jul 1870 a.82yrs (GI p12): m(1) Danville, NH 11 Nov 1813 Mary Stevens (DnTR): m(2) Apr 1840 Elizabeth Kimball

JOHN FRENCH, b Kingston, NH 25 Jun 1751 son of David & Ruhamah (Choat) French (KTR): d Kingston, NH 31 Jan 1843 a.91yrs (NHVR): m (1) ____, d (bur) Kingston, NH 21 Sep 1780 (NHVR): m(2) ____, d Kingston, NH Jul 1790 (NHVR): m(3) Anna (Alma?) Peaslee (Gove Gen p63), b 20 Jun 1764 dau of Moses & Mary (Gove) Peaslee, d Kingston, NH 28 Apr 1851 a.86yrs (GI p12).

John signed the Association Test in Kingston, NH (NHSP 30:77).

Children: (NHVR)
1. **(INFANT)**, d Kingston, NH 24 Jan 1795
2. **POLLY**, d Kingston, NH Nov 1802

JOSHUA FRENCH JR., bpt Kingston, NH 5 Nov 1752 son of Joshua & Sarah (Carr) French (KChR): d 28 Jul 1783 (DAR 1:252): m 28 Dec 1771 Elizabeth Collins, bpt Kingston, NH 27 Oct 1754 dau of Jonathan & Elizabeth (Prescott) Collins (KChR), d 6 Jan 1784.

Joshua, of Kingston (a.22yrs), served as a

Cpl in Capt Philip Tilton's Co., Col Enoch Poor Rgt, 1775 (DAR LB 108:98 & RW roll-51).

Children: born East Kingston, NH (IGI)
1. **JONATHAN**, b 1 Jun 1772
2. **ELIZABETH**, b 11 Dec 1774: d 1832: m 1790 Daniel Brown (DAR LB 108:98)
3. **SARAH**, b 5 Apr 1778
4. **JOANNA**, b 6 Oct 1780
5. **JOSHUA**, b 2 Jan 1784: d 13 Feb 1784

SAMUEL FRENCH, b Kingston, NH 24 Oct 1705 son of Nathaniel & Sarah (Judkins) French (KTR): d Kingston, NH 20 Sep 1790 a.87yrs (NHVR): m Kingston, NH 1 Apr 1736 Abigail Godfrey (KTR), b Hampton, NH 28 Apr 1715 dau of John & Abigail (Greeley) Godfrey (HH p728), d (prob) Kingston, NH 24 Feb 1798 (NHVR).

Samuel signed the Association Test in Kingston, NH (NHSP 30:77).

Children: born Kingston, NH (KTR & NHGR)
1. **SAMUEL**, b 6 Jun 1739: d Kingston, NH 25 Dec 1748 (NHVR)
2. **JOHN**, bpt 27 Sep 1741: d Kingston, NH 10 Dec 1741 (NHVR)
3. **JOHN**, bpt 2 Jan 1742/3: d Kingston, NH 7 Oct 1743 (NHVR)
4. **ABIGAIL**, bpt 4 Nov 1744: d (prob) Kingston, NH 29 Dec 1755 (NHVR)
5. **JOSEPH**, bpt 5 Apr 1747: d 1790 (DAR 2:77): m(1) Huldah Clifford: m(2) Mrs Abigail Clough (HA p161)
6. **ABIGAIL**, bpt 9 Apr 1749: d E. Kingston, NH 25 May 1833 a.84yrs (CR): m Kensington, NH 9 Oct 1778 Caleb Webster (NHVR)
7. **SARAH**, bpt 21 Jul 1751: m Danville, NH 31 Dec 1777 Edmond Sanborn (NEHGR 58:124)
8. **SAMUEL**, bpt 9 Sep 1753: d 9 Jan 1849: m 20 Oct 1775 Elizabeth Tilton

THOMAS FRENCH, was mustered Dec 1776 in the 7th Rgt under the command of Col David Gilman, Capt Gordon's Co (RW roll-50).

AMOS GALE, b Kingston, NH 9 Apr 1744 son of Jacob & Susannah (Collins) Gale (KTR): d Kingston, NH Jun 1813 (NHVR): m Kingston, NH 12 Nov 1765 Hannah Gilman (NHGR 3:130), b Kingston, NH 14 May 1749 dau of Daniel & Hannah (Colcord) Gilman (KTR), d 1826. Hannah m(2) at a.73yrs John Moody (DAR 1:476).

Amos signed the Association Test in Kingston, NH (NHSP 30:77).

Children: bpt Kingston, NH (NHVR)

1. **GILMAN**, b 13 Sep 1766
2. **AMOS**, b 15 Oct 1768: d Kingston, NH 7 Dec 1824 (GI p13): m Kingston, NH 24 Apr 1796 Sarah Bartlett (NHGR 3:167)
3. **BENJAMIN**, bpt 3 May 1772: m Sally Noyes
4. **JONATHAN**, bpt 6 Feb 1774
5. **HANNAH**, bpt 15 Jun 1777: d 1855: m Kingston, NH 30 Jan 1799 Ezra Bartlett (NHGR 3:169)
6. **NATHANIEL**, bpt 29 May 1780
7. **STEPHEN**, bpt 8 Jun 1783: d Kingston, NH Aug 1804 a.22yrs (NHVR)
8. **SUSANNA**, bpt 4 Aug 1786
9. **POLLY**
10. **SARAH**

NATHANIEL GARLAND, probably b Hampton Falls, NH 22 Jun 1740 son of Jacob & Jane (_) Garland (HFTR): d Kingston, NH 5 Apr 1820 a.79yrs (GI p13): m Elizabeth Woodman (Garland Gen p351), b abt 1747, d Kingston, NH 7 Feb 1824 a.77yrs (GI p13).

Nathaniel signed the Association Test in Kingston, NH (NHSP 30:77).

Children:

1. **NATHANIEL**, b 7 Jun 1771: d abt 1850: m 25 Dec 1796 Lydia Garland (Garland Gen p351)
2. **JOSEPH**, b abt 1774: d Kingston, NH 31 Dec 1862 a.88yrs (GI p13): m Kingston, NH 29 Jan 1822 Sarah Sanborn (NHGR 5:17)
3. **(SON)**, d Kingston, NH 26 Sep 1777 (NHVR)
4. **MOSES**, d Kingston, NH 1 Nov 1777 (NHVR)

5. **ELIZABETH**, b 1779: d 22 Nov 1822
6. **HANNAH**, b 1781: d Kingston, NH 10 Feb 1836 a.54yrs (GI p13)
7. **MARY**, d 25 Jul 1847: m Brentwood, NH 4 Jul 1809 Asa Sawyer (BtTR)
8. **SARAH**, b 26 Oct 1783: d Kingston, NH 3 Jul 1877 (GI p23): m Hampstead, NH (int) 2 Nov 1811 Joshua Rogers (HmstR)

GIDEON GEORGE, b 12 Sep 1740 (DAR 1:264): d 17 Sep 1822: m Haverhill, MA 26 Sep 1758 Deborah Stevens (HvVR), b Plaistow, NH 10 Oct 1740 dau of John & Sarah (Blaisdell) Stevens (PlVR), d (prob) Kingston, NH Sep 1831 (NHVR).

Gideon signed the Association in Kingston, NH (NHSP 30:77). He was mustered by Col Josiah Bartlett Oct 1777 & served as a Cpl in Capt Ezra Currier's Co, Col Abraham Drake's Rgt 8 Sep to 16 Dec 1777 (RW roll-49).

Children: born Kingston, NH (KTR)
1. **MARY**, b 8 Jul 1759
2. **GIDEON**, b 8 Nov 1760: d Bradford, VT 23 Feb 1817: m Apr 1782 Anna Chase
3. **DEBORAH**, b 8 Aug 1762
4. **JOHN**, b 7 Nov 1764
5. **JAMES**, 21 Mar 1767
6. **DOLLY**, b 2 Sep 1769
7. **STEPHEN**, b 17 Dec 1771: d 1853: m Kingston, NH 27 Jul 1797 Sarah Towle (NHGR 3:168)
8. **SARAH**, 8 Jul 1774
9. **SAMUEL**, b 25 Oct 1776
10. **HANNAH**, b 9 May 1779: d Danville, NH 4 Oct 1844: m Kingston, NH 21 Apr 1800 Stevens Blake (NHGR 3:170)
11. **EPHRAIM**, b 2 May 1781
12. **NATHANIEL**, b 6 Sep 1783: d Kingston, NH 12 Sep 1783 (NHVR)
13. **ELIZABETH**, b 12 Aug 1786: d Kingston, NH Sep 1789 (NHVR)

GIDEON GEORGE JR., b Kingston, NH 8 Nov 1760 son of Gideon & Deborah (Stevens) George (KTR):

d Bradford, VT 23 Feb 1817 (Bolton Sail & Sol p25): m Apr 1782 Anna Chase, bpt Newbury, MA 6 Jun 1756 dau of Ebenezer & Dorothy (Foot) Chase (NVR).

Gideon Jr was mustered by Col Josiah Bartlett Oct 1777 & served in Capt Ezra Currier's Co, Col Abraham Drake's Rgt 8 Sep to 16 Dec 1777 (RW roll-49).

Children: 1st 3 born Brentwood, NH (BtTR)

1. **SARAH**, b 13 Aug 1784: m Peter Cross
2. **SUSANNAH**, b 1 Aug 1786: m Timothy Heath
3. **JOHN**, b 9 Apr 1789: m Amanda Kaye
4. **GIDEON**, b 2 Jun 1791: d.y.
5. **STEPHEN**, b 15 Jun 1793: m Lydia Leighton
6. **DOROTHY**, b 10 Apr 1795: m Timothy Heath
7. **GIDEON**, b 11 May 1797: m Mart Highlands
8. **EBENEZER**, b 12 Jul 1802: d 10 Jul 1814

NATHAN GILE, b Haverhill, MA 5 Apr 1736 son of Daniel & Joanna (Heath) Gile (HvVR): m Ruth Dow (PlVR), b Haverhill, MA 24 Mar 1732 dau of Timothy & Judith (Worthen) Dow (HvVR).

Nathan served in Capt Gordon's Co, Col David Gilman's Rgt (RW roll-50).

Children:

1. **REUBEN**, b Plaistow, NH 29 Nov 1764 (PlVR)
2. **EZEKIEL**, b Plaistow, NH abt 1776: m Plymouth, NH 15 Aug 1807 Polly Phillips (HP 2:294)

CARTER GILMAN, of Hawke, enlisted for Kingston in the 7th Rgt of NH Militia 5 Jun 1777, Capt James Gray's Co, Col Alexander Scammel's Rgt (NHSP 14:585,661).

Possibly he was the son of Cartee Gilman Jr of Exeter, NH b abt 1736. If so, he also served in Capt John Drew's Co 19 Feb 1777 (NHSP 14: 618).

Children:

1. **ABIGAIL**, bpt Exeter, NH 3 Oct 1762 (HE p70g)

DANIEL GILMAN, b Kingston, NH 17 Aug 1705 son of Jacob & Mary (Ladd) Gilman (KTR): d Kingston, NH 14 Mar 1797 (NHVR): m Kingston, NH 22 Apr 1730 Hannah Colcord (KTR), b Kingston, NH 21 Dec 1708 dau of Jonathan & (_) Colcord (TAG 17:218), d Kingston, NH 13 May 1795 (NHVR).

Although an old man, Daniel volunteered in the defense of Portsmouth Harbor and aided in checking the advance of the enemy from Canada (DAR LB 116:99).

Children: born Kingston, NH (KTR)

1. **HANNAH**, b 14 May 1749: d 1826: m(1) Kingston, NH 12 Nov 1765 Amos Gale (NHGR 3:130): m(2) abt 1822 John Moody

DANIEL GILMAN, b Kingston, NH 1754 (NHPR 22:153): d Springfield, NH 27 Oct 1835 (NHPR 22:154): m Sandown, NH Apr 1777 Mehitable Judkins (NHPR 22:154), bpt Kingston, NH 30 Jul 1758 dau of Samuel & Sarah (Bohonon) Judkins (NHVR), d Springfield, NH 17 Feb 1846 a.88yrs (NEHGR 83:382).

Daniel enlisted May 1775 at Kingston; Capt Ballard's Co, Col Arnold's Rgt and marched to Cambridge & Boston. He was at Bunker Hill; served 8 months. He then enlisted May 1776 at Rowley, MA, Capt Peabody's Co and was at Ticonderoga. He ended his service in Albany, NY. Served 5 months. (NHPR 22:153).

Children: 1st 6 born Salisbury, NH

1. **JOEL**, b 31 Dec 1778: bpt Sandown, NH 26 Sep 1779: d aft 1820: m Lebanon, NH 20 Jan 1799 Molly Elliot (Town Clerk Rec)
2. **MARY**, b 28 Aug 1780
3. **DANIEL JR**, b 24 Aug 1782: d 2 Feb 1847 a.65yrs (NEHGR 83:382)
4. **SAMUEL**, b 3 Feb 1785: m Springfield, NH 12 Jul 1807 Lydia Clark (Town Clerk Rec)
5. **AMAH**, b 12 May 1787
6. **WILLIAM**, b 21 May 1789: lived Springfield, NH
7. **CALEB** (prob), b Springfield, NH 22 Aug

1795: m(1) Abigail Davis: m(2) 6 Oct 1844 Sarah (Noyes) Eastman (NEHGR 83:382)

DUDLEY GILMAN, bpt Exeter, NH 16 Nov 1755 son of Antipas & Joanna (Gilman) Gilman (HE p69g).

Probably the Dudley, of Kingston (a.19yrs), who served in Capt Philip Tilton's Co, Col Enoch Poor's Rgt 1775 (RW roll-51).

JOHN GILMAN, bpt Kingston, NH 12 May 1745 son of John & Sarah (Stevens) Gilman (NHGR 5:112): m (prob) Brentwood, NH 28 Feb 1777 Abigail Smith (BtTR).

John lived on the Kingston-Brentwood line. He refused to sign the Association Test but later served in the army. Possibly the John Gilman in Capt John Calef's Co (NHSP 30:79; 14:404).

Children: born Brentwood, NH (BtTR)

1. **SARAH**, b 19 Oct 1777
2. **PATIENCE**, b 27 Jul 1779
3. **EZEKIEL**, b 10 Dec 1781

CALEB GORDON, b Brentwood, NH 1757 (MSSP p304) son of Daniel & Abigail (Judkins) Gordon: d Kennebec Co, ME 8 Jul 1833 (Pen Roll of 1835 p193): m Jan 1777 Mary Ann Mapes (Gordon Gen p32), d Jan 1845.

Caleb, of Kingston served in Col James Frye's Rgt, Capt William Ballard's Co. He went to Quebec (NHSP 15:746). He also served in Capt Williams Co. (MSSP p304)

Children: (Gordon Gen p33)

1. **LYDIA**, b 2 Mar 1780
2. **LYDIA**, b 15 Aug 1781: d Nov 1858: m 1815 Joseph Gifford
3. **JESSE**, b 6 Aug 1783: d 26 Oct 1865: m Maria Morgan
4. **JOHN**, b 13 Aug 1785: m Jane Gustin
5. **MARY**, b 27 Mar 1788
6. **GILMAN**, b 18 Mar 1791: m(1) Abigail Clark: m(2) Eliza Butler
7. **DANIEL**, b 17 Feb 1793: d 1854: m Martha

Trask
8. **SARAH**, b 28 Mar 1795: d 15 Aug 1811
9. **CALEB**, b 22 Apr 1797: d 23 Mar 1872: m Mary Cressy
10. **SUSAN**, b 4 Nov 1800: d 1880: m(1) Benjamin Barnes: m(2) Daniel Sheridan
11. **CYRUS**, b 15 Oct 1803: d 30 Dec 1879: m Mar 1822 Ruth Randall

JONATHAN GORDON, b Salem, NH 5 Dec 1744 son of Alexander & Susanna (Pattee) Gordon (NEHGR 146: 323): d Bath, NH 9 Sep 1812 a.67yrs (CG p17): m Salem, NH 3 Sep 1767 Esther Sanders (TAG 16: 229), b Salem, NH 29 Dec 1748 dau of William & Esther (Peaslee) Sanders (HSlm), d Bath, NH 14 Jul 1839 (CG p17).

Jonathan was mustered at Kingston 2 Oct 1777 in Col Bartlett's Militia Rgt for Col Drake's Rgt (NHSP 15:344).

Children: born Salem, NH (HSlm)
1. **DAVID**, b 28 Jun 1768: m(1) Hannah Hurd: m(2) Roxana Sampson
2. **PHINEAS**, b 18 Apr 1770: d 7 Sep 1863: m (1) 17 Nov 1791 Joanna Pattee: m(2) Salem, NH 4 Oct 1829 Mary Balch (HSlm)
3. **PEASLEE**, b 12 May 1772: d Bath, NH 19 Aug 1854 (CG p17): m Elizabeth Hutchins
4. **JONATHAN**, b 29 Jun 1774: m Apr 1809 Jennie Bedel
5. **ALEXANDER**, b 29 Jul 1776
6. **JEREMIAH** (Gordon Gen p25), m Abigail (Bailey) Rowell
7. **ISAAC**, b 12 Oct 1780: d 25 Nov 1854: m 1808 Mary Ann (Wells) Bates
8. **ABIGAIL**, b 27 Oct 1782: d Feb 1862: m(1) Cyrus Dow: m(2) Joseph McMillen
9. **BETTY**, b 23 Feb 1785: d 10 Jun 1871: m 24 Oct 1807 Oliver Cory
10. **ESTHER**, b 31 Jan 1788: d 29 Nov 1879: m 24 Dec 1814 Isaac Miner
11. **JOHN**, b 13 May 1790
12. **MOLLY**, b 12 Nov 1792: m ___ Emerson

JOSEPH GORDON, b Exeter, NH 25 Aug 1759 son of James & Elizabeth (Dolloff) Gordon (HE p24g): d Searsport, ME 9 May 1849 (RG 1:279): m Exeter, NH 31 Oct 1790 Dorothy Smith (NHPR 23:172), b 30 Dec 1767: d 11 May 1853

Joseph, of Kingston, served in Capt Robinson's Co in the 7th Rgt NH Militia in the Continental Army 1777 (NHSP 14:585). He enlisted Aug 1775 & served under Capt Jeremiah Gilman, Col Nixon's MA Rgt (NHPR 23:169).

Children: (Gordon Gen p31)

1. **CHARLES**, b 2 Dec 1794: living 1823
2. **ELIZA**, b 18 Apr 1797: m 6 May 1832 Jeremiah Morithew
3. **MARY**, b Feb 1800: d 19 May 1847: m New Sharon, ME 1 Mar 1822 Samuel Saunders
4. **NANCY**, b 5 Feb 1805: m 4 Dec 1834 Amos H. Ellis
5. **JOHN L.**, b 17 May 1808: d 1 Oct 1841

EDWARD GREELEY, bpt Kingston, NH 14 Apr 1754 son of Jonathan & Martha (French) Greeley (KChR): d E. Kingston, NH 5 Nov 1817 a.64yrs (CR): unmd.

Edward enlisted at Kingston 1 Aug 1776 & served under Capt John Calef, Col Tash (NHPR 39:68).

ENOCH GREELEY, b Kingston, NH 1 Aug 1754 son of Andrew & Mary (Webster) Greeley (NHPR 24:121): d Hallowell, ME 28 Feb 1815 (RG 1:288): m Kingston, NH Mar 1780 Dorothy Batchelder (NHPR 24:120), bpt Kingston, NH 27 May 1753 dau of Ebenezer & Dorothy (Boynton) Batchelder (KChR), d Hallowell, ME aft 27 Mar 1843 (NHPR 24:122).

Enoch, of Kingston (a.21yrs), served as a pvt in Capt Philip Tilton's Co, Col Poor's NH Rgt 1775 #W24314 (NHPR 24:120 & RW roll-51).

Children: (Greeley Gen p119)

1. **DOROTHY**, b 24 Jun 1780: d Hallowell, ME 1 Oct 1845: unmd
2. **MARY**, b 30 Mar 1782: d Hallowell, ME 15

Oct 1867: m Hallowell, ME Joseph Smith

3. **EBENEZER BATCHELDER**, b 8 Oct 1783: m Susanna Davis
4. **WILLIAM**, b 29 Jan 1785: d Belfast, ME 13 Mar 1850: m(1) Belfast, ME 15 Apr 1808 Mary Davis: m(2) Belfast, ME 1830 Harriet White
5. **JOANNA**, b 2 Oct 1786: d Hallowell, ME 6 Oct 1801 (NHPR 24:121)
6. **ENOCH**, b 30 Jan 1789: d Hallowell, ME 14 Jan 1843: m Medway, MA Susan Livett
7. **BETSEY**, b 18 Feb 1791: m Cook Kimball
8. **NANCY**, b 18 Jun 1793: d Hallowell, ME 1 Nov 1795 (NHPR 24:121)

NOAH GREELEY, b Kingston, NH 29 Jul 1760 son of Joseph & Elizabeth (Dudley) Greeley (KTR): d Mt Vernon, ME 3 Aug 1836 (RG 1:288): m Kingston, NH 7 Jan 1783 Hannah Morrill (NHPR 24:119), b Brentwood, NH 17 Apr 1764 dau of Levi & Molly (Currier) Morrill (BtTR), d Mt Vernon, ME 15 Apr 1851 (NHPR 24:119).

Noah, of Brentwood, enlisted for Kingston 31 Dec 1780 for the Continental Army (NHSP 16:66). He served as a pvt under Capt Nathan Brown, Col Pierce Long NH Line; also served under Capt James Sinclair, Col Waldron #W23153 (NHPR 24: 118).

Children: born Mt Vernon, ME (Greeley Gen p122)

1. **MARY**, b 20 Jun 1783: d Mt Vernon, ME 2 Oct 1874: m Mt Vernon, ME James Carson
2. **JOSEPH**, b 28 Feb 1785: d Smithfield, ME 11 Nov 1845 m Mt Vernon, ME 16 Aug 1812 Nancy Hovey
3. **NOAH**, b 15 Jan 1787: d 24 Aug 1872: m Mt Vernon, ME Eliza Robinson
4. **LEVI**, b 30 Aug 1789: m(1) Jane Sanborn: m(2) Charlotte Rundlett
5. **HANNAH**, b 23 Sep 1791: d 1871: m Benjamin Philbrick
6. **SAMUEL**, b 6 Nov 1793: d Ellsworth, ME 22 Dec 1877: m Farmington, ME 1 Nov 1825 Desire Stinchfield

7. **SARAH**, b 30 Nov 1795: m Mt Vernon, ME Apr 1820 Nathaniel Cofren
8. **BETSEY**, b 4 Mar 1798: m Nathaniel Larabee
9. **AURELLA**, b 10 Mar 1800: m John R. Taylor
10. **DAVID M.**, b 25 Feb 1802: d Mt Vernon, ME 25 May 1850: m(1) Susan Philbrick: m(2) 1830 Mrs Prudence Hill Tibbets
11. **DUDLEY**, b 21 Jun 1803: d Roscoe, IL 15 Oct 1851: m Ann Greeley
12. **LUCINDA**, b 15 Nov 1805: d Mt Vernon, ME 29 Jul 1813
13. **JOHN**, b 11 Feb 1810: d Mt Vernon, ME unmd

BENNETT GREENFIELD, b Amesbury, MA 1 Sep 1714 son of Charles & Bethiah (Bennett) Greenfield (AVR): d Kingston, NH (bur) 24 Jun 1789 (NHVR): m Salisbury, MA 19 May 1737 Elizabeth Flanders (SVR), b Salisbury, MA 30 Dec 1716 dau of John & Sarah (Prince) Flanders (SVR), d Kingston, NH Oct 1808 (NHVR).

Bennett signed the Association Test in Kingston, NH (NHSP 30:78).

Children: born Salisbury, MA (SVR)
1. **TAMZIN**, b 1 Jan 1737/8: m Salisbury, MA Oct 1761 Benjamin Noyes (SVR)
2. **MEHITABLE**, b 19 Aug 1739
3. **ELIZABETH**, b 9 Mar 1741/2
4. **SARAH**, b 5 Jul 1744
5. **HANNAH**, b 3 Oct 1746
6. **MARY**, bpt 12 Mar 1749
7. **ABIGAIL**, b 20 Aug 1752: m Danville, NH 24 Oct 1775 Aaron Colby (NEHGR 58:123)
8. **SAMUEL**, b 5 Sep 1756
9. **ELIZABETH**, b 24 May 1761

ABRAHAM GREENWAY, of Kingston, was mustered 4 Apr 1777, Capt James Norris's Co, Col Enoch Poor's Rgt (NHSP 14:616).

WILLIAM GREGG, was mustered Dec 1776 in the 7th Rgt under the command of Col David Gilman, Capt Gordon's Co (RW roll-50).

EBENEZER GRIFFIN, d Kingston, NH 19 Oct 1790 (NHVR): m Kingston, NH 2 Jul 1761 Mary Colcord (KTR), b Kingston, NH 6 Feb 1744 dau of Samuel & Mehitable (Ladd) Colcord (KTR): d Kingston, NH (bur) 30 Nov 1789 (NHVR).

Ebenezer signed the Association Test in Kingston, NH (NHSP 30:77). He served as a Sgt in Capt Jeremiah Gilman's Co, Col John Nixon's Rgt (NHSP 15:743).

Children: born Kingston, NH (KTR)

1. **SAMUEL**, b 3 Jul 1762
2. **ELIZABETH**, b 5 Jan 1764
3. **EBENEZER**, b 7 Mar 1766: d Kingston, NH 14 Sep 1766 (KTR)
4. **MARY**, b 20 Oct 1767
5. **EBENEZER**, b 23 Sep (prob) 1768

RICHARD GRIFFIN, bpt Kingston, NH 3 Jun 1753 son of Isaac & Mary (Rowell) Griffin (KChR): d Auburn, NH 31 Oct 1833: m 1774 Sarah Batchelder (DAR 1:286), bpt Kingston, NH 13 Oct 1754 dau of Elisha & Theodate (Smith) Batchelder (NHGR 6:31), d 12 Jan 1834.

Richard served as a pvt in Capt Robert Crawford's Co at Great Island 5 Nov 1775. He also served in Capt Gordon's Co, Col David Gilman's Rgt (RW roll-50).

Children: (Batchelder Gen p142)

1. **DOLLY**, b 12 Jul 1774: d 10 Jan 1847: m Amos Rowell
2. **ISAAC**, b 1776: d.y.
3. **SARAH**, b 21 Mar 1779: d 28 Mar 1877: m Kingston, NH 24 Apr 1806 William Collins (NHGR 4:175)
4. **PEGGY**, b 30 May 1781: d 6 Feb 1856: m 1805 Webster Paige
5. **ISAAC**, b 3 Apr 1783: m Abigail Young
6. **POLLY**, b 4 Nov 1785: d 1864: m(1) 1808 Dyer Hook: m(2) 18 Sep 1816 Walter Foss
7. **NATHAN**, b 3 Oct 1788: d 30 Jun 1867: m 23 Jan 1820 Sally Evans
8. **BETSEY**, b 12 Mar 1791: d 13 Oct 1859:

m(1) Phineas Wheelock: m(2) Jeremiah Roy
9. **RICHARD**, b 11 Sep 1794: d 24 Mar 1872: m 1824 Linda Hutchinson

SAMUEL GRIFFIN, b Kingston, NH 10 Aug 1742 son of Ephraim & Mary (Elkins) Griffin (KTR): d 8 Jul 1797 (bur Freeport, ME): m No Yarmouth, ME (int) 23 Aug 1766 Priscilla Royal, b No Yarmouth, ME 10 Aug 1747 dau of Eliab & Bathsheba (Bayley) Royal (ME FAM 2:118).
Samuel served in Capt John Soule's Co (MSSP p318).

Children: born No. Yarmouth, ME (ME FAM 2:118)
1. **HANNAH**, b 21 Feb 1768
2. **THOMAS MILLET**, b 17 Jun 1770: d Levant, ME 22 Jun 1857: m 9 Aug 1796 Hannah Rollins
3. **MIRIAM**, bpt 8 Nov 1772
4. **SAMUEL**, b 14 Dec 1775: m No Yarmouth, ME 29 Jan 1801 Martha Worthley
5. **BATHSEBA**, b 10 Mar 1778: m New Gloucester, ME 29 Jan 1799 John Rollins
6. **JOHN**, b 13 May 1780
7. **REUBEN GAGE**, b 6 Aug 1782: m Mary _____
8. **MARTHA MERRILL**, b 24 Nov 1784

SAMUEL GRIFFIN, b Bradford, MA 3 Jun 1756 son of Nathaniel & Elizabeth (Fails) Griffin (Bd VR): d Nelson, NH 29 Jan 1811 (NHPR 24:199): m Nelson, NH 13 Aug 1783 Sophia Foster (NHPR 24:200), b Berwick, ME 19 May 1760 dau of Jacob & Hepzibah (Prentiss) Foster (Foster Gen p178), d Nelson, NH 6 Mar 1846 (CG p100). Sophia m(2) Apr 1822 Philip Atwood (NHPR 24:199) who died Nelson, NH 8 Oct 1841 (NHPR 24:200).
Samuel, of Kingston, served in Capt Jeremiah Gilman's Co, Col Nixon's Rgt 30 Sep 1775 #W20637 (NHSP 15:743 & NHPR 24:199).

Children: born Nelson, NH (IGI)
1. **SAMUEL**, b 30 May 1784: d 11 Dec 1867: m Silence Goodenow
2. **NATHAN**, b 25 Nov 1785: d 15 Apr 1872: m

Nelson, NH 11 Sep 1808 Sally Wright
3. **NATHANIEL**, b 11 Apr 1788: d 22 Dec 1789
4. **SOPHIA**, b 22 Dec 1789: d 17 Sep 1866: m Josiah Parker Jr
5. **SALLY**, b 24 Oct 1791: d 27 Jun 1872: m Simeon Goodenow
6. **HEPZIBAH**, b 23 Jun 1793: d 22 Jun 1839: m Nathaniel Abbott
7. **HANNAH**, b 30 Jun 1795: d 15 Nov 1870: m (1) Simeon Wilson: m(2) Rufus Atwood
8. **BETSEY**, b 19 May 1797: d 2 Aug 1872: m John Atwood
9. **PRISCILLA**, b 13 Jun 1800: d 7 Jan 1873: m Otis Grow
10. **REBECCA**, b 13 Dec 1801: d 3 Dec 1879: m Dexter Whitcomb
11. **LOIS**, b 9 Jul 1804: d 9 Oct 1839: m Samuel Osgood

BILEY HARDIE, b Brentwood, NH 13 Apr 1754 son of Biley & Mehitable (Graves) Hardie (BtTR).
Biley signed the Association Test in Kingston, NH (NHSP 30:78).

PETER HARRIMAN, b Haverhill, MA Apr 1727 possibly son of John & Sarah (Morrill) Harriman (Essex Gen 10:23): d Goffstown, NH 6 Oct 1815: m Plaistow, NH abt 1778 Lydia Jackman (DAR #47759), b Plaistow, NH 22 Jul 1747 dau of Moses & Rachel (Heath) Jackman (PlVR), d Goffstown, NH 9 Apr 1831 (Hist of Goffstown p207).
Peter served in Capt Gordon's Co, Col David Gilman's Rgt 5 Jan to 15 Mar 1777 (RW roll-50).

Children: born Plaistow, NH (PlVR)
1. **PETER**, b 25 Feb 1779
2. **ESTHER**, b 16 Sep 1780: d 1 Feb 1864: m John Parker
3. **AMOS**, b 10 May 1782: d Goffstown, NH 7 Mar 1864: m 29 Mar 1810 Betsey Saltmarsh
4. **JAMES**, b 31 Dec 1783
5. **WARREN**, b 6 Apr 1788: d Goffstown, NH 29 Mar 1872
6. **SARAH**, b 20 May 1789: d Goffstown, NH 27

Mar 1872
7. **JOHN**, b 13 Jun 1791: d 26 Jul 1837: unmd

DANIEL HEATH, b abt 1758 probably Plaistow, NH 21 Jan 1759 son of Jonathan & Hannah (Stevens) Heath (PlVR): d aft 1823 of Enfield, NH (NHPR 34:191): m ?(1) Sarah March (NH Gen Digest p125): m(2) Mary ___, a.55yrs in 1820.

Daniel was mustered at Kingston 2 Oct 1777 by Col Bartlett for Col Drake's Rgt (NHSP 15:343).

Children:

1. **JONATHAN**
2. **DANIEL**
3. **EBEN**
4. **DAVID**
5. **HOLLAND**
6. **ICHABOD**
7. **LYDIA**
8. **SARAH**
9. **DORSET**, a.19yrs in 1820 (NHPR 34:190)
10. **RHODA**, a.12yrs in 1820
11. **CHARLOTTE**, a.10yrs in 1820

SAMUEL HEATH, b abt 1755: d 15 Jul 1828 (NHPR 35:21): m ____, who was a.68yrs in 1820.

Samuel, of Kingston (a.63yrs), deposed 2 May 1818 that he enlisted in Plaistow Dec 1779 under Capt John Dennett, Col George Reid & served until Jun 1783 when he received his discharge #S44412 (NHPR 35:21).

Children:

1. **(DAU)**, a.15yrs in 1820

SAMUEL HEATH, b Plaistow, NH 22 Apr 1756 son of Daniel & Elizabeth (Call) Heath (PlVR): d Bristol, NH 11 Jun 1833 (PP 32:106): m Plymouth, NH 11 Apr 1782 Sarah Webster, b 8 Jul 1763 dau of Stephen & Hannah (Dolbear) Webster (HP p705), d Bristol, NH 14 Sep 1839 (PP 32:106).

Samuel enlisted at Kingston 3 Jun 1775 & served 8 months as a pvt under Capt Hezekiah Hutchins, Col George Reid NH Line. In 1776 he served under Capt Quinby, Col Wingate NH Line. He enlisted again May or June 1778 under Capt Pettingill, Col Weston MA Line. He was at the Battle of Bunker Hill. Daniel Heath, father of Samuel, substituted for him on account of illness in the summer of 1775 #W19764 (PP 32:106).

Children: (PP 32:106 & Hist of Bristol p231)

1. **SARAH**, b Plymouth, NH 3 Sep 1783
2. **SAMUEL**, b Plymouth, NH 22 Mar 1785: d 23 Jun 1874: m 1811 Margaret Fellows
3. **ROBERT**, b Bristol, NH Nov 1788: d Bristol, NH 8 Oct 1853: m(1) Hannah Nelson: m (2) Mrs Polly Dow
4. **MOSES**, b Bristol, NH 19 Sep 1791: d 31 Jul 1862: m 18 Mar 1819 Nancy Norris
5. **ELIZABETH**, b Bristol, NH 15 Mar 1795: d 30 Dec 1818: m 12 Oct 1813 Oliver Ballou
6. **HANNAH**, b Bristol, NH 1 May 1796: m Samuel Worthen
7. **LUCY**, b Bristol, NH 3 Nov 1799: d 19 Aug 1828
8. **WEBSTER**, b Bristol, NH 3 Dec 1801: d 18 Feb 1830
9. **LEWIS**, b Bristol, NH 15 Aug 1803: m 15 May 1832 Sarah Edwards

SAMUEL HEATH, b Kingston, NH 1760 (NHPR 35:19): d aft 8 Aug 1834 of Jefferson, ME.

Samuel was residing in Kingston when he first enlisted May 1775. He served as a fifer under Capt McFarland, Col Gerrish MA Line, Sep 1777. He enlisted as a pvt under Capt Quimby & was at the taking of Burgoyne. He enlisted again June 1780 as a pvt under Capt Eastman, Col Bartlett, NH Troops at West Point, NY #R4828 (NHPR 35: 19). He moved to Hampstead, NH & later to Jefferson, ME.

TIMOTHY HEATH, was mustered Dec 1776 in the 7th Rgt under the command of Col David Gilman, Capt Gordon's Co (RW roll-50).

JOSEPH HOMANS, bpt Newbury, MA 14 Dec 1765 son

of Joseph & Bette (Richardson) Homans (NVR): d Warren, NH 2 Feb 1830 (PP 27:86): m Kingston, NH 14 May 1789 Sarah Walton (NHGR 3:134), b abt 1761 (living Portland, ME a.83yrs in 1844).

Joseph (a.16yrs) was mustered for the Continental Army by Samuel Folsom 7 Apr 1781 & served under Capt Ellis, Col Alexander Scammel's Co #W23323 (NHSP 16:244,709 & PP 27:86).

Children: born Campton, NH (IGI)

1. **ELISHA THAYER**, b 28 Mar 1790
2. **SALLY CARTER PETERSON**, b 28 Dec 1791
3. **BETTY**, b 24 Jan 1794
4. **JOSEPH**, b 25 Nov 1799
5. **MARY**, b 21 Jun 1803
6. **SAMUEL WALTON**, b 13 Oct 1805
7. **JAMES W.**, b 20 Jun 1809: m Sarah Ann Flanders (DAR LB 36:328)

JACOB HOOK, b Salisbury, MA 29 Nov 1724 son of Jacob & Elizabeth (French) Hook (SVR): d Kingston, NH 14 Dec 1804 (GI p14): m Kingston, NH 15 Nov 1749 Mary Batchelder (KTR), b (prob) Kingston, NH 13 Apr 1729 dau of Phineas & Elizabeth (Gilman) Batchelder (KTR), d Kingston, NH 12 Jun 1813 a.85y (GI p14).

Jacob signed the Association Test in Kingston, NH (NHSP 30:76).

Children: 1st 4 born Kingston, NH (KTR)

1. **ELIZABETH**, b 25 Jun 1750: d Kingston, NH 22 Sep 1835 (GI p27): m Danville, NH 16 Jan 1771 John Sanborn (NEHGR 58:122)
2. **PHINEAS**, b 1 Jun 1753: d Kingston, NH 11 Jul 1753 (KTR)
3. **MARY**, b 16 Feb 1756: d Mt Vernon, NH 25 Jun 1842: m(1) Kingston, NH 15 Jun 1777 Rev Joseph Appleton (NHGR 3:130): m(2) Kingston, NH 15 Nov 1798 Daniel Gould (NHGR 3:168)
4. **SARAH**, b 26 Jun 1759: d Danville, NH 30 Nov 1764 (DnTR)
5. **ABIGAIL**, b Danville, NH 1 Aug 1761: d Danville, NH 18 Nov 1764 (DnTR)

6. **SARAH**, b Danville, NH 22 Dec 1765 (DnTR): d Kingston, NH 17 Feb 1793 (GI p2): m Dr Levi Bartlett

PEASLEE HOYT, b Kingston, NH 23 Oct 1749 (RG 2:361) son of Eliphalet & Mary (Peaslee) Hoyt: d Readfield, ME 27 Nov 1827 (RG 2:361): m 1774 Margaret Hubbard (Hoyt Gen p133), b Kingston, NH 2 Apr 1755 dau of John & Joanna (Davis) Hubbard (KTR).

Peaslee signed the Association Test in Kingston, NH (NHSP 30:78). He also served as a pvt in Capt John Calef's Co on Great Island (DAR LB 25:1 & MSSP p389 & RW roll-49).

Children: (Hoyt Gen p133)

1. **JOHN**, b 13 Jun 1775: d 10 Apr 1847: m Abigail Howes
2. **MARY**, b 9 Aug 1777: d unmd 1847
3. **ELIPHALET**, b 9 Jul 1779: d Readfield, ME 15 Aug 1856 m 22 Jan 1806 Sally Hoit
4. **NANCY (ANNA)**, b 13 Jun 1781: d Readfield, ME 17 Jul 1816
5. **PEASLEE**, b 4 Apr 1783: m Achsa Marrow
6. **SAMUEL**, b 23 Feb 1785: d Phillips, ME 5 Nov 1859: m Apr 1810 Elizabeth Tower
7. **JOANNA**, b 5 May 1787: m Eliphalet Hoyt
8. **MARGARET**, b 6 Oct 1788: m Mt Vernon, ME 10 May 1820 Daniel Kimball (IGI)
9. **SIMEON**, b 1 Jul 1791: d Fairfield, ME 1857 m Rachel Wheeler
10. **FRANCIS**, b 18 Jul 1793: d Winthrop, ME 11 Jun 1824 m Winthrop, ME 13 Aug 1818 Elizabeth Fowler (IGI)
11. **LEVI**, b 21 May 1795 Readfield, ME: m 27 May 1822 Lucy Wood
12. **LOIS**, b 1 Jun 1797: d Winthrop, ME: m Isaac Foster
13. **JOSHUA**, b 8 Feb 1799: d Corinna, ME 9 Aug 1823
14. **VELINA**, b 29 Jan 1805: d Hallowell, ME: m Benjamin Calden

RICHARD HOYT, b Amesbury, MA 30 Mar 1756 son of

Timothy & Hannah (_) Hoyt (AVR): d 14 Jan 1837 (PP v19): m(1) Salisbury, MA 9 Sep 1779 Mary Martin (SVR), d Salisbury, MA 16 Jul 1783 (SVR): m(2) Somersworth, NH (int) 24 Apr 1784 Mercy (Horne) Leighton (Leighton Gen p98), b (poss) Berwick, ME 14 Oct 1758 dau of William & Phebe (Heard) Horne. Mercy m(1) Dover, NH 23 Nov 1775 Thomas Leighton (Dv VR) whose estate was administered 12 Feb 1783 (Strafford Co Probate Rec).

Richard enlisted 1775 in Capt Caleb Robinson's Co, Col Laomi Baldwin MA Rgt for 1 year (PP v19). He enlisted again & served as a pvt in Capt Ezra Currier's Co, Col Abraham Drake's Rgt 1777 (RW roll-49).

Children:

1. **THOMAS**, m abt 1810 Susannah Demerit (DAR LB 83:367). He became his father's guardian as Richard became insane.

FRANCIS HUBBARD, b Kingston, NH 17 Dec 1761 son of John & Joanna (Davis) Hubbard (KTR): d Fayette, ME 22 Mar 1838 (RG 2:361): m(1) Kingston, NH 29 Oct 1785 Mehitable Judkins (NHGR 3:132), b Kingston, NH 7 Mar 1766 dau of John & Esther (Swett) Judkins (KTR), d Fayette, ME 7 Nov 1825 (Judkins Gen p7): m(2) Fayette, ME 10 May 1829 Mrs Ruth Cochran (IGI).

Francis served in Capt Eastman's Co & Capt Quimby's NH Co, Col Jacob Gale's Rgt Aug 1778 #W7831 (MSSP p389 & RW roll-50).

Children: born Fayette, ME (IGI)

1. **ELIZABETH**, b 9 Dec 178_
2. **JOANNE**, b 25 Jan 1789
3. **JOHN**, b 26 Jan 1791
4. **MEHITE**, b 19 May 1797
5. **FANNE**, b 11 Mar 1799
6. **SAMUEL**, b 6 May 1801
7. **JOANNE**, b 4 Nov 1805
8. **FRANCIS**, b 20 Mar 1808
9. **(SON)**, b 12 Feb 1809

JOHN HUBBARD, b Kingston, NH 28 Sep 1759 son of John & Joanna (Davis) Hubbard (KTR): d Readfield, ME 22 Apr 1838: m Olive Wilson (Hubbard Gen p91), b Brentwood, NH 23 Jan 1762 dau of John & Sheba (Pease) Wilson (BtTR), d Readfield, ME 20 Oct 1847.

John served in the NH Line. He enlisted as a fifer Aug 1776 & served at Fishkill, NY under Capt Calef (NHPR 38:118). He moved to Readfield, ME 1785 & applied for a pension 27 Mar 1833 #R5314.

Children: (Hubbard Gen p91-2)

1. **OLIVE**, b 1 Mar 1786: m Henry Carlton
2. **SOPHIA**, b 21 Feb 1788: d 14 Feb 17__
3. **MARY**, b 26 Apr 1790: d Monmouth, ME 28 Jul 1871: m Orchard Cook
4. **NANCY**, b 15 Jul 1792: d 25 Nov 1856: m Ichabod Rollins
5. **JOHN**, b 22 Mar 1794: d Hallowell, ME 6 Feb 1859: m Dresden, ME 12 Jul 1825 Sarah Hodge Barrett (MGFH 2:888-9)
6. **THOMAS**, b 23 Apr 1795: d 26 Aug 1827
7. **ELIZA**, b 16 Oct 1796: m(1) Dr William Case: m(2) Alexis Sappington
8. **VELINA**, 16 Sep 1798: d 16 Mar 1804
9. **CYRUS**, b 1800
10. **GREENLEAF**, 11 Mar 1801: d 24 Feb 1885
11. **JOANNA**, b 18 Oct 1802: d 2 Feb 1890: m Rev David Copeland
12. **SARAH**, b 7 Aug 1805: d 24 Sep 1805

RICHARD HUBBARD, b Salisbury, MA 27 Dec 1696 son of John & Jane (Follinsby) Hubbard (SVR): d Kingston, NH 26 Dec 1782 (GI p15): m(1) Haverhill, MA 27 Dec 1722 Abigail Davis (HvVR), b Haverhill, MA 11 Mar 1702/3 dau of Elisha & Grace (Shaw) Davis (HvVR), d Kingston, NH 25 Sep 1733 (KTR): m(2) Kingston, NH 16 Oct 1734 Abigail Taylor (KTR), dau of William & Margaret (Bean) Taylor (LND p676), d Kingston, NH 9 Dec 1768 (KTR): m(3) Dorcas _____, b abt 1712, d Kingston, NH 28 Jan 1774 a.62yrs (GI p15).

Richard signed the Association Test in Kingston, NH (NHSP 30:76).

Children: (See p110)

RICHARD HUBBARD JR., b Kingston, NH 3 Dec 1742 son of Richard & Abigail (Taylor) Hubbard (KTR): d Kingston, NH 11 Nov 1780 (KTR): m Kingston, NH 21 Dec 1762 Elizabeth Webster (KTR), b Kingston, NH 15 Jun 1740 dau of Benjamin & Mary (Stanyan) Webster (KTR).

Richard Jr signed the Association Test in Kingston, NH (NHSP 30:78). He served as a Lt in Capt David Quimby's Co, Col Jacob Gale's Rgt Aug 1778 (NHSP 15:560).

Children: born Kingston, NH (KTR)

1. **ABIGAIL**, b 10 Jul 1762
2. **BENJAMIN**, b 24 Oct 1766
3. **MARY**, b 24 Jul 1768
4. **DORCUS**, b 14 Feb 1772
5. **JOHN HILLS**, b 2 Nov 1773
6. **ELIZABETH**, b 12 Jul 1776
7. **RICHARD**, b Dec 1779

DANIEL HUNT, b Amesbury, MA 12 Apr 1723 son of Samuel & Elizabeth (Clough) Hunt (AVR): d Ryegate, VT (bur) 1807 (Hist of Ryegate, VT p391): m Mary Trussell (HmstR), b (prob) Amesbury, MA 12 Oct 1721 dau of Henry & Hannah (Weed) Trussell (AVR): d 1795.

Daniel lived in Newbury, Vt before the Revolution, but moved to Kingston & served in the War. In 1779 he moved to Ryegate, VT (Hist of Ryegate, VT p391).

Children: 1st 3 born Hampstead, NH (HmstR)

1. **SAMUEL**, b 15 Mar 1746
2. **NEHEMIAH**, b 15 Sep 1747: m Kingston, NH 27 Jun 1765 Sarah Carter (KChR)
3. **HANNAH**, b 17 Jul 1749
4. **HENRY**, m Elizabeth _____
5. **DANIEL**, lived Derry, NH
6. **ZEBULON**
7. **MARY**, m Danville, NH 15 Aug 1776 Abner

Hunt (NEHGR 58:124)

8. **MOSES**, b abt 1761: m (prob) Bath, NH May 1780 Ruth Dodge (NHPR 39:14)
9. **JOSHUA**, b abt 1766: d 3 Mar 1814/5 (DAR 1:356): m 1787 Elizabeth Whittlesey

HENRY HUNT, b abt 1726 son of Nathaniel & Hannah (Tuxbury) Hunt (Hunt Gen p11): d Kingston, NH 25 Oct 1794 (NHVR): m So Hampton, NH 5 Mar 1747 Hannah Eastman (SHVR), b Amesbury, MA 13 Aug 1731 dau of Roger & Rachel (Nichols) Eastman (AVR).

Henry signed the Association Test in Kingston, NH (NHSP 30:78).

Children: (Hunt Gen p12)

1. **ELIAKIM**, b Amesbury, MA 21 Nov 1747 (AVR)
2. **HENRY**, b Amesbury, MA 29 Aug 1749 (AVR): m Amesbury, MA (int) 27 Dec 1777 Mrs Rhoda Titcomb (AVR)
3. **ABNER**, lived Danville, VT: d 1828: m Danville, NH 15 Aug 1776 Mary Hunt
4. **MOSES**, b 19 Oct 1752: d Kingston, NH 26 Oct 1834 (GI p15): m(1) Mary Peasley: m (2) Lydia Johnson
5. **RACHEL**, d Weare, NH 22 Nov 1827: m Tristram Collins
6. **HANNAH**, m Newton, NH Nov 1777 Jonathan Peasley (NwtTR)
7. **ELIZABETH**, m _____ Pudington
8. **JUDITH**, m ____ Peasley
9. **MIRIAM**, m Kingston, NH 3 Feb 1789 Paul Quimby (NHGR 3:133)
10. **ANNA**, d 1 Apr 1848 (NHPR 5:77): m Thomas Bootman
11. **STEPHEN**, b 29 Jan 1766: d 12 Aug 1832: m(1) Kingston, NH 16 Jan 1793 Lois Welch (NHGR 3:135): m(2) Kingston, NH Feb 1796 Polly Woodman (NHGR 3:136)
12. **ELIPHALET**, d Kingston, NH 26 Oct 1834: m _____ Peasley

MOSES HUNT, b 19 Oct 1752 son of Henry & Hannah (Eastman) Hunt: d Kingston, NH 26 Oct 1834 (GI p15): m(1) Mary Peasley (Hist of Weare p962), dau of Nathaniel & Mary (Colby) Peasley: m(2) Lydia Johnson

Moses signed the Association Test in Kingston, NH (NHSP 30:78).

Children: (Hunt Gen p14)

1. **HENRY**, b Danville, NH 10 Nov 1782 (DnTR): d 9 May 1822: m 19 May 1805 Mercy Pollard
2. **JOHN**
3. **MOSES**
4. **JOHN**
5. **STEPHEN**
6. **MIRIAM**, m ____ Johnson

AARON HUNTOON, b Kingston, NH 9 Jun 1758 son of John & Elizabeth (Beede) Huntoon (KTR): d aft 20 Jun 1820 (DAR 1:357): m Kingston, NH 11 Jan 1781 Elizabeth Smith (NHGR 3:131), b 17 Jan 1762.

Aaron was mustered by Col Josiah Bartlett Oct 1777 & served in Capt Ezra Currier's Co, Col Abraham Drake's Rgt 8 Sep to 16 Dec 1777 (RW roll-49). He applied for a pension at Portsmouth, NH 25 Apr 1818 & was residing in Epping, NH at the time. #S44450 (NHPR 39:44).

Children: (DAR #306193)

1. **JACOB**
2. **SETH**
3. **NATHANIEL**
4. **POLLY**, b 22 Jul 1783: m George Poor

AMOS T. HUNTOON, b Kingston, NH 15 Mar 1768 (NHPR 39:46) son of Joseph & Sarah (Davis) Huntoon: d aft 23 Nov 1853, living Brownington, VT.

Amos enlisted May 1781 & served at Fort Washington near Portsmouth, NH under Capt Ebenezer Deering, Lt Joseph Huntoon in a Co of artillery until Dec 1781 #R5418 (NHPR 39:46).

BENJAMIN HUNTOON, b Kingston, NH 12 Sep 1729 son of Philip & Ann (Eastman) Huntoon (KTR): d

Franklin NH 6 Dec 1815 (CG p53): m(1) Kingston, NH 7 Feb 1751 Judith Clough (KTR), b Salisbury, MA 7 Oct 1735 dau of Zacheus & Sarah (Page) Clough (SVR), d Kingston, NH 17 Apr 1756 (KTR): m(2) Kingston, NH Jan 1757 Abigail Page (KTR), b Haverhill, MA 21 Mar 1734/5 dau of Joseph & Mary (Thompson) Page (HvVR): m(3) Kingston, NH 17 Jul 1758 Mrs Mercy (Dearborn) Quimby (KTR), b Hampton, NH 21 Aug 1732 dau of Nathaniel & Mary (Batchelder) Dearborn (HmVR p166), d 23 Oct 1791: m(4) Kingston, NH 21 Jun 1792 Mrs Hannah (James) Dearborn (DAR 1:357), d Franklin, NH 6 Oct 1803 (CG p53).

Benjamin signed the Association Test in Kingston, NH (NHSP 30:76).

Children: 1st 12 born Kingston, NH (KTR)
(by 1st wife)

1. **PHILIP**, b 28 Nov 1751: d 1780: m ____ Fellows
2. **JONATHAN**, b 4 Jan 1754: d 25 Mar 1815: m Sarah ____
3. **SARAH**, b 17 Mar 1756: d 28 Aug 1814: m Isaac Marston

(by 3rd wife)

4. **NATHANIEL**, b 16 Jun 1759: d 22 Jan 1793: m 10 Sep 1783 Hannah Webster
5. **MARY**, b 15 Dec 1761: d 29 Mar 1805: m Andover, NH 28 Nov 1782 Joseph Fellows (NEHGR 58:16)
6. **HANNAH**, b 13 Nov 1763: d 7 Mar 1858: m Andover, NH 13 Oct 1785 Jonathan Bartlett (NEHGR 58:16)
7. **BENJAMIN**, b 6 Apr 1765: d Franklin, NH 26 Jan 1855 a.91yrs (CG p53): m(1) 10 May 1792 Mehitable Page: m(2) 21 May 1805 Hannah Baker
8. **ANNA**, b 13 Aug 1766
9. **SAMUEL**, b 10 May 1768: d Franklin, NH 13 Dec 1835 (CG p53): m Salisbury, MA (int) 18 Mar 1801 Martha Tucker (SVR)
10. **REBECCA**, b 28 Nov 1770: d 28 May 1836: m David Webster
11. **ELIZABETH**, b 3 May 1771: d 9 Aug 1853: m

Andover, NH 22 Nov 1792 Jonathan Brown

12. **JOHN**, b 15 Jul 1773: d Andover, IL 26 Oct 1818: m 25 Oct 1798 Rebecca Calef
13. **MERCY**, b Salisbury, NH 18 Apr 1775: d May 1833: m 16 Jun 1796 David Chandler

JOHN HUNTOON JR., bpt Kingston, NH 1 Oct 1727 son of John & Mary (Rundlett) Huntoon (NHGR 2:47): d Canterbury, NH 14 Nov 1821 (HCnt p198): m Kingston, NH 7 Dec 1754 Elizabeth Beede (KTR), b Feb 1739 dau of Eli & Mehitable (Sleeper) Beede, d Canterbury, NH 18 Nov 1821

John Jr signed the Association Test in Kingston, NH (NHSP 30:76).

Children: born Kingston, NH (KTR)

1. **MOSES**, b 31 Aug 1755: d Whitefield, NH 5 Dec 1841 (CG p149): m Unity, NH 1 May 1777 Elizabeth Clifford (UR p50)
2. **AARON**, b 9 Jun 1758: d abt 1820: m Kingston, NH 11 Jan 1781 Elizabeth Smith (NHGR 3:131)
3. **STEPHEN**, 15 May 1761: m So Hampton, NH 10 Dec 1782 Abigail Proctor (SHVR)
4. **JOSHUA**, b 15 Jun 1763: d Gilmanton, NH 29 Mar 1815: m Gilmanton, NH 25 Jan 1790 Molly Winslow
5. **CALEB**, b 1 Aug 1765: d Kingston, NH 20 Aug 1765 (KTR)
6. **ELI**, b 20 Jul 1766
7. **ELIJAH**, b 20 Nov 1768: d 20 Dec 1860: m Hannah French
8. **MEHITABLE**, bpt Kingston, NH 6 Feb 1774 (NHVR): m Nathaniel Batchelder
9. **BETSEY** (HCnt p198), m Jacob Worthen

JOSEPH HUNTOON, bpt Kingston, NH 1 Nov 1741 son of John & Mary (Rundlett) Huntoon (NHGR 5:108): d Stanstead, Canada 8 Mar 1813 (NHPR 39:65): m Sarah Davis (DAR LB 23:153).

Joseph, of Kingston, served as a Lt in Capt James Gray's Co, Col Alexander Scammel's Rgt #R5419 (NHSP 14:661 & NHPR 39:65).

Children:

1. **REUBEN**, b abt 1761: d Clinton Co, NY 30 Mar 1844: m Milton, VT 21 Jan 1818 Mrs Mary (Woodard) Lawton (NHPR 39:72)
2. **AMOS T.**, b Kingston, NH 15 Mar 1768 (NHPR 39:46)
3. **BETSEY**, m Col John Stone (DAR LB 23:153)
4. **ANNE**, m ___ Stone: living Cabot, VT 1838
5. **JOSEPH**, bpt Kingston, NH 23 Oct 1774 (NH VR): m 1803 Esther Nichols (DAR LB 141: 214)
6. **MARY**, bpt Kingston, NH 23 Oct 1774 (NHVR)
7. **ENOCH P.**, bpt Kingston, NH 21 Apr 1776 (NHVR): living Palermo, ME 1838

JOSIAH HUNTOON, b Kingston, NH 1 May 1758 son of Charles & Meriah (Smith) Huntoon (KTR): d Lowell, MA 28 Feb 1794 (DAR #553131): m Hannah Glidden, b 1760, d ME.

Josiah enlisted at Kingston & marched for Winter Hill 18 Jun 1775 being just after the Battle of Bunker Hill (NHPR 78:90).

Children: born Unity, NH (DAR #553131 & IGI)

1. **JONATHAN**, b 14 Mar 1781
2. **CHARLES**, b 16 Jun 1783
3. **JOSIAH**, b 8 Feb 1785
4. **BEMSLEY**, b 28 Dec 1787
5. **RHODA**, b 5 Sep 1788: m Joseph Straw
6. **MARGARET**, b 23 Nov 1790: m Ira Ladd
7. **POLLY**, b 27 Nov 1792: m Levi Cram
8. **LEWIS**, b 2 Aug 1794: m Eliza Haines

MOSES HUNTOON, b Kingston, NH 31 Aug 1755 son of John & Elizabeth (Beede) Huntoon (KTR): d Whitefield, NH 5 Dec 1841 (CG p149): m Unity, NH 1 May 1777 Elizabeth Clifford (UR p50), b Kingston, NH 20 Jan 1756, d Whitefield, NH 4 Oct 1825 a.69yrs (CG p149).

Moses, of Kingston (a.20yrs), served in Col Enoch Poor's Rgt, Capt Philip Tilton's Co 1775 (RW roll-51). He enlisted again at Kingston 1 Aug 1776 under Capt John Calef, Col Tash & served at Fishkill, NY. He applied for a pension 19 Sep 1832 Whitefield, Coos, NH a.76yrs. He enlisted in Kingston & lived in Unity, NH. #S13470 (NHPR 39:68).

Children: (UR p50)
1. **ANNA**, b Kingston, NH 24 Nov 1777
2. **DAVID**, b Kingston, NH 9 Dec 1779
3. **SUSANNA**, b Kingston, NH 14 Aug 1783
4. **JAMES**, b Unity, NH 30 Nov 1785
5. **LOIS**, b Unity, NH 16 Nov 1787
6. **GEORGE**, b Unity, NH 2 Jan 1790

PHILBRICK HUNTOON (see Thomas Philbrick Huntoon)

REUBEN HUNTOON, b Kingston, NH abt 1761 son of Joseph & Sarah (Davis) Huntoon: d Clinton Co, NY 30 Mar 1844 (NHPR 39:72): m Milton, VT 21 Jan 1818 Mrs. Mary (Woodard) Lawton (NHPR 39:72), d aft 20 Mar 1855. Mary m(1) John Lawton who died Peacham, VT 24 Jul 1808.

Reuben, of Kingston, served in Col Scammel's Rgt, Capt James Gray's Co 1777 (NHSP 14:585, 660). He also enlisted Dec 1775 under his father Lt Joseph Huntoon, Capt Philip Tilton's Co, Col Enoch Poor #W25808 (NHPR 39:70).

Children:
1. **IRENA**, b abt 1814: m Daniel Loomis

SAMUEL HUNTOON, b Kingston, NH 18 Jan 1718 son of John & Mary (Rundlett) Huntoon (KTR): d May 1796 (DAR 1:357): m(1) Kingston, NH 6 May 1742 Hannah Ladd (KTR), b Kingston, NH 17 Apr 1720 dau of Daniel & Mehitable (Philbrick) Ladd (KTR): m(2) 1768 Widow Margaret Newly (DAR 1:357).

Samuel served in Capt Ballard's Co, Col Frye's Rgt, 1775 (DAR LB 143:156).

Children: born Kingston, NH (KTR)
1. **PETER**, b 10 Nov 1743: d Kingston, NH 15 Oct 1744 (KTR)
2. **PETER**, b 31 Jul 1745: d Kingston, NH 30

Sep 1747 (KTR)

3. **PETER**, b 4 Jan 1748
4. **SAMUEL**, b 12 Oct 1749: d Kingston, NH 25 Oct 1749 (KTR)
5. **SAMUEL**, b 12 Oct 1750
6. **THOMAS PHILBRICK**, b 2 Nov 1753: d Concord, OH 2 Jan 1831: m Charlestown, NH 9 Aug 1777 Elizabeth Huntoon (NHPR 39:77)
7. **CHARLES**, b 18 Mar 1755
8. **NATHANIEL**, b 6 May 1757
9. **JONATHAN**, bpt 13 May 1759 (NHVR)
10. **HANNAH**, bpt 18 Mar 1762 (NHVR)
11. **HANNAH**, bpt 2 Jan 1763 (NHVR)

THOMAS PHILBRICK HUNTOON, b Kingston, NH 2 Nov 1753 son of Samuel & Hannah (Ladd) Huntoon (KTR): d Concord, OH 2 Jan 1831 (NHPR 39:76): m Charlestown, NH 9 Aug 1777 Elizabeth Huntoon (NHPR 39:77), b abt 1759, d Concord, OH 3 Oct 1847 a.88yrs (NHPR 39:76).

Thomas, of Kingston (a.22yrs), served in Col Enoch Poor's Rgt, Capt Philip Tilton's Co (RW roll-51) & in Capt Uriah Wilcox's Co, Col Benjamin Bellows Rgt (RW roll-49). He signed the Association Test in Kingston, NH as Philbrick Huntoon (NHSP 30:75).

Children: (NHPR 39:75,76)

1. **SCRIBNER**, a.69yrs in 1853
2. **CORBIN**, b 1786: d 1873: m Jane Gage (DAR LB 103:199)
3. **BETSEY**, m Jonathan Whipple
4. **MAHALA**, m John Prentiss

SAMUEL HUSE, b abt 1762; possibly son of Samuel Huse: d Kingston, NH 1 Apr 1838 (NHVR); (W) 28 Feb 1838: m(1) ___: m(2) 24 Apr 1828 Sarah Lever (Huse Gen p124).

Samuel, of Kingston (a.75yrs), testified 15 Jul 1837 that in Jul 1776, he enlisted under Capt David Quimby & marched to NY where he joined Col Burnham's Rgt (NHPR 63:38).

Children:

1. **DANIEL**
2. **JOHN**, m Delia ___
3. **MARTHA**

JOHN JEFFERS JR., b abt 1753 (DAR 1:366): d 27 Sep 1827 a.74yrs: m Sybil Foster (PlVR), b Winchester, NH 11 Oct 1751 dau of Josiah & Submit (Wells ?) Foster (NEHGR 38:288), d 13 Aug 1805 a.54yrs.

John served in Col David Gilman's Rgt, Capt Gordon's Co (RW roll-50).

Children: born Plaistow, NH (PlVR)

1. **SUBMIT**, b 3 Jul 1777: m Haverhill, MA (int) 15 Jun 1798 Samuel Page (HvVR)
2. **JAMES**, b 13 Feb 1779: m Newbury, MA 15 Nov 1803 Judith Carr (NVR)
3. **ISIAH**, b 12 Dec 1781
4. **JOHN**, b 27 Dec 1782: d 5 Sep 1859: m(1) int 13 Apr 1807 Lydia Gould: m(2) Susan _____: m(3) 18 Apr 1834 Polly Royce
5. **SYBIL**, b 10 Jan 1785: m Hampstead, NH (int) 26 Nov 1807 William Roach (HmstR)
6. **STEPHEN**, b 10 Apr 1787: d E. Haverhill, NH 8 Jul 1870: m(1) 31 Dec 1810 Phebe Whitaker: m(2) abt 1844 Aschsah ____
7. **MAREY**, b 31 Jun 1789: m (prob) John Flanders
8. **JOSIAH**, b 19 Feb 1792: d E. Haverhill, NH 29 Dec 1862: m Hampstead, NH 28 Nov 1811 Lydia Goodwin
9. **LUCY**, b 29 Jan 1794: d E. Haverhill, NH 9 Nov 1850: m Joseph Hardy

JOB JENNESS, probably son of John & Mary (Jenness) Jenness of Rye, NH: d 7 Oct 1777 in the Battle at Stillwater (NHPR 40:63).

Job, of Kingston, served in Capt Beal's Co in the 7th Rgt NH Militia (NHSP 14:585). John Jenness of Pembroke, NH, brother of Job, applied for BLWT. On 20 Feb 1819 the BLWT was issued to John Jenness & other heirs for service of his brother Job who was slain in the Rev War (NHPR 40:63).

ABRAHAM JOHNSON, of Kingston (a.16yrs), was mustered by Maj Scott (NHSP 16:90). Probably this is the same Abraham of Hampstead who served for Kingston in Col Gale's 7th NH Militia Rgt for the defense of RI 1 Jul 1779 (RW roll-51).

JEREMIAH JOHNSON, b Plaistow, NH 6 Jun 1741 son of Thomas & Phoebe (Hardy) Johnson (PlVR): d Kingston, NH Jan 1803 (NHVR).

Probably the Jeremiah who signed the Association Test in Kingston, NH (NHSP 30:78).

BENJAMIN JUDKINS, b Kingston, NH 18 Apr 1749 son of Joel & Mehitable (Elkins) Judkins (KTR): d Brentwood, NH 18 May 1790 a.42yrs (CG p23): m Brentwood, NH 15 Oct 1771 Ruth Choat (BtTR), b Kingston, NH 1 Aug 1750 dau of Benjamin & Ruth (Edwards) Choat (KTR), d 7 Mar 1814 (Judkins Gen p12).

Benjamin signed the Association Test in Kingston, NH (NHSP 30:76)

Children: 1st 7 born Brentwood, NH (BtTR)

1. **PETER**, b 6 Aug 1772: d Palmyra, ME 10 Nov 1864: m Jun 1795 Alice Page
2. **EBENEZER HILLS**, b 6 Dec 1774: d Palmyra, ME 2 Dec 1852: m Brentwood, NH 17 Jan 1799 Betsey Shaw (BtTR)
3. **RHODA**, b 19 Nov 1776: d 4 Mar 1864: m 1 Jan 1801 Dr Coker Marble
4. **BENJAMIN**, b 9 Sep 1779: d Cornville, ME 7 May 1847: m 22 Apr 1804 Miriam Fowler
5. **MOSES**, b 24 May 1781: d Brentwood, NH Mar 1783 (BtTR)
6. **RUTH**, b 13 May 1783: d 3 Sep 1833: m 14 Nov 1808 Moses Fowler
7. **LEVI**, b 11 Nov 1785: m(1) 11 Dec 1811 Hannah Emery: m(2) Lucinda ___
8. **URSULA**, b 7 Mar 1789 (Judkins Gen p12): d 1860: m 17 Jan 1809 Ebenezer Stevens

CALEB JUDKINS, b Kingston, NH 16 Jan 1753 son of Joel & Mehitable (Elkins) Judkins (KTR): d

Salisbury, NH 25 Aug 1816 (HS p645): m 13 Jan 1777 Mary Huntoon (Judkins Gen p13), b 1759 dau of Josiah & Joanna (Ladd) Huntoon.

Caleb signed the Association Test in Kingston, NH (NHSP 30:77).

Children: born Salisbury, NH (Judkins Gen p13)

1. **ANNA**, b 27 Feb 1778: d 1826
2. **MOLLY**, b 18 Jul 1780: m 20 Feb 1799 Daniel True
3. **CALEB**, b 30 Mar 1783: d Claremont, NH 9 Nov 1861: m(1) 22 Nov 1841 Lucy Kelly: m(2) 4 Apr 1848 Susan Marshall
4. **HILTON**, b 25 May 1786
5. **MEHITABLE**, b 3 May 1788: d 27 Nov 1797
6. **BENJAMIN**, b 13 Mar 1791: m 9 May 1815 Betsey Thompson
7. **MOSES**, b 12 Jan 1794: d 24 Aug 1840: m 27 Jan 1829 Sally True
8. **LEVI**, b 20 Nov 1796: d Claremont, NH 9 May 1872: m Sophia Alden
9. **DANIEL**, b 11 Apr 1799
10. **JOEL**, b 13 Apr 1801: m(1) Apr 1826 Lois Field: m(2) 3 Dec 1831 Betsey Way
11. **JOSEPH H.**, b 11 May 1804: d Claremont, NH 15 Apr 1882: m(1) 29 Dec 1829 Polly Marshall: m(2) 16 Jul 1856 Rebecca Dinsmore

HENRY JUDKINS, b Kingston, NH 5 Dec 1750 son of Joel & Mehitable (Elkins) Judkins (KTR): d Kingston, NH 27 Sep 1825 (GI p16): m(1) Danville, NH 25 Apr 1776 Mary French (NEHGR 58:124), b Kingston, NH 18 Feb 1750 dau of Jonathan & Joanna (Elkins) French (KTR), d Kingston, NH 22 Dec 1778 (NHVR): m(2) Danville, NH 9 Nov 1780 Mary Barnard (NEHGR 58:125), b Kingston, NH 17 Apr 1753 dau of Stephen & Mary (Collins) Barnard (KTR), d Kingston, NH 12 Mar 1839 (GI p16).

Henry signed the Association Test in Kingston, NH (NHSP 30:77).

Children: born Kingston, NH (Judkins Gen p13)

(by 1st wife)

1. **HANNAH**, b 9 Sep 1777: d Kingston, NH 8 Sep 1800 (GI p16)
2. **(DAU)**, d Kingston, NH 15 Dec 1778 (NHVR)
3. **MARY**, b 12 Dec 1778: m Kingston, NH 21 Jul 1802 Reuben Sanborn (NHGR 3:171)

(by 2nd wife)

4. **ABIGAIL**, b 26 Aug 1781: d Kingston, NH (bur) 13 Nov 1782 (NHVR)
5. **JANE**, b abt Jun 1782: d Kingston, NH 17 Nov 1782 a.5mo (GI p16)
6. **HENRY**, b 27 Mar 1783: d Kingston, NH 25 Jun 1839 a.56yrs (GI p16): m 28 Nov 1811 Lydia Brown
7. **JOEL**, b 3 Jun 1785: d Kingston, NH 8 Apr 1833 (NHVR): m Kingston, NH 26 Nov 1807 Nancy Dudley (NHGR 4:176)
8. **ABIGAIL**, b 4 Aug 1787: d Brentwood, NH 8 Mar 1864: m 1 Jun 1826 Edward Thing
9. **ESTHER**, b 4 Mar 1790: m (int) Amesbury, MA 26 Apr 1840 Robert Hoyt (AVR)
10. **STEPHEN**, b 21 Jun 1792: d Kingston, NH 16 Dec 1794 (GI p16).
11. **MEHITABLE**, b 24 Nov 1794: d Brentwood 2 Jan 1867: m Epping, NH 6 Jul 1814 James Thing (NHGR 3:178)

JOHN JUDKINS, b Kingston, NH 8 Feb 1719 son of Samuel & Abigail (Harriman) Judkins (KTR): d Kingston, NH 29 May 1788 (NHVR): m(1) Kingston, NH 21 Nov 1744 Martha Hook (KTR), b Salisbury, MA 29 Mar 1727 dau of Jacob & Elizabeth (French) Hook (SVR), d Kingston, NH 12 Sep 1750 (KTR): m(2) Kingston, NH 7 Nov 1750 Esther Swett (KTR), bpt Kingston, NH 10 Jan 1730/1 dau of Elisha & Sarah (Tilton) Swett (NHGR 2:65), d Kingston, NH 30 Jun 1798 (NHVR).

John signed the Association Test in Kingston, NH (NHSP 30:77).

Children: 1st 9 born Kingston, NH (KTR)

(by 1st wife)

1. **WILLIAM**, b 29 Jan 1745/6: d Kingston, NH 20 Mar 1746/7 (KTR)

(by 2nd wife)
2. **MARTHA**, b 1 Aug 1751: m Kingston, NH 26 Aug 1789 Nathaniel Huntoon (NHGR 3:134)
3. **JOHN**, b 11 May 1753: d abt 1830: m Exeter, NH 12 Jan 1778 Abigail Swasey (HE p55g)
4. **STEPHEN**, b 2 Mar 1756: m Kingston, NH 27 Mar 1783 Lisa French (NHGR 3:132)
5. **ELISHA**, b 1 Jan 1758
6. **SAMUEL**, b 8 Jan 1760: d 11 Nov 1809: m Epping, NH 24 Mar 1785 Mary Cushing (NHGR 4:134)
7. **SARAH**, b 24 Sep 1762: d Kingston, NH 26 May 1845 (GI p11): m bef Dec 1782 Peter Fifield
8. **ELIZABETH**, b 14 Apr 1764: d New Sharon, ME 9 Dec 1839: m Kingston, NH 9 Sep 1790 Joseph Cram (NHGR 3:135)
9. **MEHITABLE**, b 7 Mar 1766: d Fayette, ME 7 Nov 1825: m Kingston, NH 29 Oct 1785 Francis Hubbard (NHGR 3:132)
10. **ANNA** (Judkins Gen p7), m (prob) Joseph Marston
11. **REUBEN** (Judkins Gen p7)
12. **MOSES**, bpt 10 Nov 1771 (NHVR): d (W) 6 Jun 1823 of Fayette, ME: m 20 Oct 1798 Mary Dudley

JOHN JUDKINS JR., b Kingston, NH 11 May 1753 son of John & Esther (Swett) Judkins (KTR): d abt 1830: m Exeter, NH 12 Jan 1778 Abigail Swasey (HE p55g), b Exeter, NH 14 Jan 1759 dau of John & Elizabeth (Newmarch) Swasey (HE p77g).

John signed the Association Test in Kingston, NH (NHSP v30 p77).

Children: born Exeter, NH (Judkins Gen p14))
1. **SAMUEL**, b abt 1781: d Litchfield, ME 5 Nov 1843: m(1) int 12 Oct 1801 Judith Springer: m(2) 13 Mar 1810 Zilpha (Hall) Babb: m(3) 9 Jul 1818 Lois Gray
2. **THOMAS**, b abt 1785: m bef 1814 Abigail Stevens: lived Norway, ME

3. **EBENEZER**, b abt 1790: m 19 Mar 1818 Abigail Eaton or Yeaton
4. **MARY**, b 13 Oct 1792: m Mar 1810 Asa Noyes
5. **JOSEPH PRESCOTT**, b abt 1791: d Norway, ME 23 Dec 1873 m(1) Barnstead, NH 20 Mar 1815 Hannah Hodge: m(2) int 13 Jul 1816 Mahalah Stevenson: m(3) 2 Jul 1846 Eliza beth Judkins

JOSEPH JUDKINS, b Kingston, NH 23 Aug 1743 son of Joel & Mehitable (Elkins) Judkins (KTR): d Kingston, NH 10 Jan 1804 (GI p16): m Kingston, NH 20 Apr 1766 Rebecca Sanborn (Judkins Gen p12), b Brentwood, NH 14 Mar 1747 dau of Daniel & Abigail (Prescott) Sanborn (BtTR), d abt 1826.

Joseph signed the Association Test in Kingston, NH (NHSP 30:77).

Children: born Kingston, NH

1. **LOUIS (LOIS)**, b 12 Sep 1769: m (prob) Kingston, NH 20 Dec 1792 Benjamin Stevens (NHGR 3:135)
2. **ELIZABETH**, bpt 3 Mar 1772 (NHVR): m (prob) Haverhill, MA (int) 23 Feb 1791 William Bryant Jr (HvVR)
3. **REBECCA**, bpt 14 Dec 1777 (NHVR): m Kingston, NH Apr 1805 Andrew Judkins (NHGR 4:174)
4. **MOSES**, b 28 Jun 1780

DAVID KELLY, b Amesbury, MA 9 Sep 1746 son of Samuel & Elizabeth (Heath) Kelley (AVR): d Kingston, NH 1 Apr 1813 (NHVR): m Kingston, NH 24 Dec 1767 Mary Greenfield (KChR).

David, of Kingston (a.28yrs) served as a Sgt Maj in Col Enoch Poor's Rgt, Capt Philip Tilton's Co Aug 1775 (RW roll-51). He signed the Association Test in Kingston, NH (NHSP 30:77).

Children: bpt Kingston, NH (NHVR)

1. **RUHAMAH**, b 17 Mar 1769
2. **BETTY**, bpt 10 Nov 1771: m John Cheney lived Utica, NY

3. **JAMES**, bpt 28 Aug 1774

JAMES KELLY, b Exeter, NH 1 Dec 1733 son of James & Deborah (Stiles) Kelley (Middlesex Co by Cutter p1642): m(1) Esther Folsom: m(2) Stratham, NH 11 Sep 1794 Anna Keniston (NHGR 3:126)

Probably the James of Kingston, who received from the Town of Hampton, NH 40 silver dollars & 3500 paper dollars for 6 months service in Rev War (HH p273). He was mustered at Kingston Dec 1780 for the Continental Army (NHSP 16:62).

Children: born Stratham, NH (NHGR 3:123)
1. **CATHERINE**, b 18 Feb 1762: d Stratham, NH 5 Jan 1845 (NHGR 3:123)
2. **DANIEL**, b 29 Jun 1767
3. **ADDI**, b 6 Mar 1769: d Fowler, NY 13 Jan 1849: m(1) 3 May 1794 Sally Hartford: m(2) 3 Feb 1799 Letty Ervin: m(3) Nancy Fowler
4. **LEVI**, b 23 Oct 1770: d abt 1820: m Sarah Snell
5. **JOSEPH**, b 14 Sep 1772: m Mehitable Thurston
6. **BENJAMIN**, b 14 Sep 1772: d 1839: m Stratham, NH 10 Apr 1794 Betsey Chase (NHGR 3:126)
7. **ESTHER**, b 12 Nov 1774: m John Blaisdell
8. **GEORGE WASHINGTON**, b 18 Jan 1776

NEHEMIAH KELLY, b Amesbury, MA 19 Mar 1760 son of Samuel & Elizabeth (Heath) Kelly (AVR): m Hampstead, NH (int) 15 Jul 1780 Lydia Dearborn (HmstR).

Nehemiah was mustered at Kingston 2 Oct 1777 in Col Bartlett's Militia Rgt for Col Drake's Rgt (NHSP 15:343).

Children: born Hampstead, NH (HmstR)
1. **BETTY**, b 12 Jul 1781
2. **JOSEPH DEARBORN**, b 15 Feb 1784
3. **RUHAMAH**, b 26 Sep 1786

SAMUEL KELLY, b Kingston, NH 25 Aug 1733 son of Darby & Sarah (Huntoon) Kelley (KTR): d 28 Jun 1813 (DAR 1:381): m Brentwood, NH 1 Oct 1756 Elizabeth Bowdoin (BtTR), b abt 1740 dau of William & Phebe (Murdock) Bowdoin.

Samuel served as a Lt in Capt Daniel Gordon's Co, Col David Gilman's Rgt Dec 1776 (RW roll-50).

Children: born Brentwood, NH (BtTR)

1. **BETSEY BOWDOIN**, b 6 Mar 1757: m Nathaniel Plummer
2. **SAMUEL**, b 12 Feb 1759
3. **HANNAH**, b 28 May 1761: d Brentwood, NH 5 Mar 1762 (BtTR)
4. **JOHN**, b 5 Mar 1763
5. **NATHANIEL**, b 7 Jul 1765
6. **WILLIAM BOWDOIN**, b 25 Dec 1767
7. **SARAH**, b (no date)
8. **JONATHAN FOLSOM**, b 10 Sep 1772
9. **DANIEL**, b 2 Nov 1774

CALEB KNIGHT, b Plaistow, NH 1 May 1758 son of Stephen & Susanna (Noyes) Knight (PlVR).

Caleb served in Capt Gordon's Co, Col David Gilman's Rgt (RW roll-50).

MOSES KNIGHT, b Plaistow, NH 24 Dec 1757 son of Ebenezer & Mehitable (Simmons) Knight (PlVR): d Landaff, NH 29 Feb 1828 (CG p73): m Atkinson, NH 13 Feb 1788 Abiah Page (NHPR 43:132), b Plaistow, NH 30 Jul 1766 dau of Asa & Susanna (Johnson) Page (PlVR), d Landaff, NH 26 Mar 1845 a.77yrs 9mos (CG p73).

Moses belonged with Col Bartlett's Rgt of Militia 1777 & served under Capt Benjamin Stone, Col Scammell's 3rd NH Rgt until Jan 1780 (NHSP 14:587 & NHPR 43:135).

Children: (NHPR 43:135)

1. **(STILLBORN)**, b 7 Jan 1791
2. **SUKEY**, 11 Oct 1793: d 1 Oct 1796
3. **RUTH**, b 31 Mar 1795: d 6 Oct 1796
4. **MOSES**, b Mar ____

5. **AARON**, b 10 Mar 1799: lived Coventry, NH 1838
6. **CALEB**, b 10 Jul 1801
7. **JOSHUA**, b 17 Oct 1804
8. **(DAU)**, m Kinsley Batchelor (NHPR 43:133)

BENJAMIN LADD, b Kingston, NH 25 Apr 1718 son of John & Elizabeth (Sanborn) Ladd (KTR): d Kingston, NH 6 Feb 1783 (NHVR): m Kingston, NH 11 Feb 1746 Mary French (KTR), b Salisbury, MA 28 Oct 1727 dau of Timothy & Mary (Pike) French (SVR), d Kingston, NH 9 Feb 1784 (NHVR).

Benjamin signed the Association Test in Kingston, NH (NHSP 30:77).

Children:

1. **MARY**, b Kingston, NH 20 Sep 1760: m Kingston, NH 6 Apr 1780 James Prince (NHGR 3:131)

BENJAMIN LADD, b Kingston, NH 25 Sep 1753 son of Nathaniel & Sarah (Clifford) Ladd (KTR): d Monteville, ME 12 Dec 1830: m(1) Deborah Allen dau of Jude Allen: m(2) Deborah ______: (DAR 1:397).

Benjamin served as a pvt in Capt Isaac Sherman's Co, Col Baldwin Rgt 1776 (MAS&S 9:406).

Children: (Ladd Gen p57)
(by 1st wife)

1. **DEBORAH**, b 1777: m 17 Aug 1799 Joseph Fisk
2. **BENJAMIN**, b 1779: d 1810: m Betsey Blaisdell
3. **SALOME**, b 1781: m 1 Aug 1802 Benjamin Seavey
4. **ELEAZER**, b 26 Mar 1783: m 15 Nov 1802 Betsey Rollins
5. **SALLY**, b 1785: m David Rollins

(by 2nd wife)

6. **BENJAMIN**, b 29 Nov 1814: m 17 Nov 1840 Joannah Field
7. **LAVINNA**, b 1817: m Charles Higgins
8. **HANNAH**, b 1819: m Royal Higgins

JOHN LADD, b Kingston, NH 7 May 1720 son of John & Elizabeth (Sanborn) Ladd (KTR): d Kingston NH (bur) 21 Oct 1802 a.82yrs (NHVR): m bef 1748 Alice Thing (LND p407), b Exeter, NH 14 Feb 1722/3 dau of Samuel & Abigail (Gilman) Thing (LND p678), d Kingston, NH (prob) 24 May 1788 (NHVR).

John signed the Association Test in Kingston, NH (NHSP 30:77).

BENJAMIN LEACH, of Kingston, served in Capt Jeremiah Fogg's Co in the 2nd NH Rgt 1781. (NHSP 16:230).

AMOS DOLLOFF LEAVITT, b Raymond, NH 21 Jan 1759 son of Nehemiah Leavitt (IGI): living New Hampton, NH 1832 (NHPR 45:53): m Dorothy Smith, a.54yrs in 1820.

Amos enlisted for 3 years in the Continental Army 23 May 1777 (NHSP 16:708). He lived in New Hampton, NH in 1820 a.61yrs, when he applied for a pension #S23761 (NHPR 45:52).

Children: born Meredith, NH (IGI)

1. **MEHITABLE**, b 25 Sep 1786
2. **ELIZABETH**, b 18 Jul 1788
3. **AMOS**, b 1790
4. **MERCY**, b 1792
5. **DOROTHY**, b 1796
6. **EZEKIEL**, b 1799
7. **POLLY**, a.16yrs in 1820 (NHPR 45:53)

JOSEPH DOLLOFF LEAVITT, of Raymond, NH, enlisted for Kingston in the 7th Rgt NH Militia 1777, Rowell's Co (NHSP 14:585).

EBENEZER LONG, b Kingston, NH 23 Oct 1727 son of William & Deborah (Tongue) Long (KTR): d Kingston, NH 2 Apr 1808 a.80yrs (NHVR): m Kingston, NH 12 Mar 1752 Anna Towle (NHGR 3: 86), b Kingston, NH 28 May 1728 dau of Caleb & Rebecca (Prescott) Towle (KTR), d Kingston, NH 26 Apr 1796 a.67yrs (GI p18).

Ebenezer signed the Association Test in

Kingston, NH (NHSP 30:77).

Children: bpt Kingston, NH (NHGR & NHVR)
1. **MARY**, bpt 11 Feb 1753
2. **MARIA**, bpt 8 Dec 1754
3. **EBENEZER**, bpt 15 Aug 1756: m abt 1780 Hannah Sanborn
4. **SARAH**, bpt 7 May 1758
5. **ANNA**, bpt 15 Jun 1760
6. **LUCY**, bpt 5 Sep 1762

BENJAMIN LOVERING, bpt Kingston, NH 16 Apr 1738 son of William & Comfort (Smith) Lovering (NHGR 5:103): m Kingston, NH Dec 1759 Jemima Thorn (KTR), b Kingston, NH 10 May 1737 dau of John & Elizabeth (Clough) Thorn (KTR).

Benjamin signed the Association Test in Kingston, NH (NHSP 30:77).

Children: born Kingston, NH (KTR)
1. **ELIZABETH**, b Nov 1760
2. **HANNAH**, b 9 Sep 1762

JOSEPH LOVERING, b Kingston, NH 1 Jan 1749 son of Samuel & Mary (Gooden) Lovering (KTR): m Sarah _____, d (poss) Kingston, NH 30 Jan 1822 a.62yrs (GI p18).

Joseph, of Kingston (a.25yrs), served in Capt Henry Dearborn's Co, Col Arnold's detachment 1775 (NHSP 14:211).

NATHANIEL LOVERING, bpt Exeter, NH 11 Jul 1762 son of John Lovering (HE p73g): d Winthrop, ME 30 Dec 1842 (RG 2:449): m Winthrop, ME (int) 11 Jul 1792 Jerusha (Brewster) Follet (NHPR 47:92), d aft 1855. Jerusha m(1) Jesse Follet.

Nathaniel enlisted 1779 under Capt Jonathan Leavitt, Col Hercules Mooney NH Militia. In Jun 1780 he enlisted as a pvt under Capt Robinson, Col George Reid & while at West Point was transferred to Capt Cherry's Co of Light Infantry. #W24593 (NHPR 47:91 & RW roll-51). Nathaniel moved to Kingston in 1774 and lived there until 1792 when he moved to Winthrop, ME.

Children: (NHPR 47:93)
1. **NATHANIEL**, b 23 Feb 1793
2. **JERUSHA**, b 31 Oct 1795
3. **JOHN**, b 4 Jan 1799
4. **RICHARD**, b 16 Apr 1805

RICHARD LOVERING, bpt Exeter, NH 18 Jan 1761 son of John Lovering (HE p73g): d Newburyport, MA 18 Aug 1829 (NHPR 47:98): m Newbury, MA 24 Feb 1784 Anna Coffin (NVR), b abt 1760, d Newburyport, MA 1 Nov 1843 a.83yrs (NptVR).

Richard, of Exeter, NH, served for Kingston in the Continental Army at West Point 3 Jul to 12 Dec 1781 #W15039 (NHSP 16:256).

Children: 1st 2 born Newbury, MA (NVR)
1. **JOHN**, b 17 Feb 1784
2. **ANNA**, b 27 Apr 1786
3. **FRANCIS**, d Newburyport, MA 17 Sep 1790 (NptVR)
4. **NANCY**, d Newburyport, MA 14 Oct 1828 (NptVR)

REUBEN LOWELL, b 29 Jun 1739 (DAR 1:427) son of Stephen & Miriam (Collins) Lowell: d Chesterville, ME 1 Jun 1824; bur Farmington, ME (RG 2:451): m(1) Amesbury, MA 15 Dec 1761 Priscilla Bartlett (AVR), b abt 1740 dau of Joshua & Priscilla (Jacobs) Bartlett, d 1807: m(2) 2 Nov 1807 Sally Williams (DAR 1:427).

Reuben signed the Association Test in Kingston, NH (NHSP 30:77).

Children: (Lowell Gen p346-8)
(by 1st wife)
1. **ROSSAMUS**, b Kingston, NH 17 Jul 1762: d Thomaston, ME 27 Jul 1829: m 24 Jan 1786 Debora Keen
2. **PERSIS**, b Kingston, NH 30 Jun 1764: d Feb 1839: m 1789 John Mitchell (ME Fam 2:198)
3. **SARAH**, b Kingston, NH 5 Jan 1767: m Haverhill, MA (int) 20 Nov 1786 Samuel Eames Jr (HvVR)
4. **JOSHUA BARTLETT**, b Brunswick, ME 23 Mar

1769: d 12 Mar 1821: m 25 Jan 1795 Elizabeth Heath
5. **HANNAH**, b Brunswick, ME 9 May 1771: d 9 Jul 1789
6. **REUBEN JR**, b Brunswick, ME 16 Sep 1773: d Abbott, ME 20 Sep 1841: m(1) 1795 Betsey Smith: m(2) 25 Apr 1830 Sally Willard
7. **SAMUEL**, b Kingston, NH 4 Jan 1776: d Abbott, ME 5 Sep 1862: m(1) int 22 Dec 1803 Elizabeth Bartlett: m(2) int 23 Dec 1816 Miriam Sherburn
8. **JOHN**, b Kingston, NH 22 Aug 1778: d 5 Apr 1868: m 20 Apr 1802 Lois Bartlett

DAVID LUCE, (a.22yrs), served for Kingston in the Continental Army for the NH Rgt 1781. He was mustered by Samuel Folsom 23 Mar 1781 (NHSP 16:243,709).

ANDREW MACE, b Hampton Falls, NH Dec 1757 (NHPR 48:163) bpt Hampton, NH 25 Dec 1757 son of Richard Mace (HH p831): d Readfield, ME 6 Apr 1845 (RG 2:455): m(1) Kensington, NH 15 Mar 1779 Jenny Hale (NHVR): m (2) Sarah ____ (MSSP p498).

Andrew lived in Kingston during the War. He enlisted Sep 1775 under Capt Quimby & served at Kittery & Great Island. He enlisted again Jun 1776 & served under Capt David Quimby, Col Wingate NH Line. 1 Jul 1777, he enlisted under Capt Ezra Currier, Col Drake NH Troops & was at the Battle of Bennington under General Stark. In Jul 1780, he enlisted under Capt John Eastman, Col Runnels NH Troops & in Jul 1781 he served as a Sgt under Capt Jacob Webster, Col Runnels NH Troops #17566 (NHPR 48:163).

Children: born East Kingston, NH
1. **MARY** (Polly), b 15 Aug 1779: d 1862: m John Young (DAR LB 68:139)
2. **RICHARD**, b 27 Jul 1781
3. **ANNE**, b 25 Jan 1783
4. **ANDREW**, b 8 Dec 1784
5. **ISAAC**, b 25 Feb 1786

6. **JANE**, b 16 Jul 1789
7. **BETTY**, b 1 Jun 1791

EDWARD MAGOON, bpt Exeter, NH 26 Sep 1756 son of Benjamin Magoon Jr (HE p74g): d aft 11 Mar 1846 (NHPR 49:113): m Kingston, NH 14 Aug 1782 Jehoshea Beede (NHGR 3:131), b Kingston, NH 15 Jan 1762 dau of Hezekiah & Hephsibah (Smith) Beede (KTR).

Edward, of Kingston (a.20yrs), served in Col Enoch Poor's Rgt, Capt Philip Tilton's Co (RW roll-51). He applied 20 Jun 1820 while living at Wheelock, VT, a.63yrs for a pension. At that time he was living with a wife Joshoshaba a.58 yrs and a grandson Eli Magoon a.5yrs #S40962 (NHPR 49:112)

JOSEPH MAGOON, b Kingston, NH 1752 (NHPR 49: 115) bpt Exeter, NH 18 Sep 1757 son of Joseph & Hannah (Moulton) Magoon (HE p74g): d aft 1832.

Joseph enlisted abt 1 Nov 1775 under Capt James Shephard & served as a Sgt (NHPR 49:115). He enlisted again as a pvt to go to RI under Capt Benjamin Sias, Col Moses Nichols Rgt (RW roll-51). He lived in the province of Stanstead, Lower Canada when applying for a pension & had a brother Ephraim Magoon #S13881 (NHPR 49:115).

JOSIAH MAGOON, b Kingston, NH 1758 (NHPR 49: 119), bpt Exeter, NH 25 Jun 1758 son of Benjamin Magoon Jr (HE p74g): living New Hampton, NH in 1840 (NHPR 49:120): m Ann Sleeper (DAR 1: 433).

Josiah enlisted at Kingston 1776 in NH Militia under Capt Simon Marston. He enlisted again Apr 1776 at Kingston & served as a pvt under Capt Nathan Brown, Col Gilman NH troops where he served until 1 Aug 1776, assisting in building a fort in Portsmouth Harbor; then he enlisted under Capt Brown, Col Long, for one year & served until 6 Aug 1777 (NHPR 49:118).

Children: (IGI)

1. **STEPHEN SLEEPER**, b Poplin, NH 2 Jun 1782
2. **MEHITABLE**, b New Hampton, NH 21 Apr 1793
3. **JOHN CALVAN**, b New Hampton, NH 11 Dec 1797
4. **MARTIN LUTHER**, b New Hampton, NH 24 Mar 1801

SAMUEL MARCH, b Kingston, NH 15 Oct 1734 son of John & Margaret (Bean) March (KTR): m Kingston, NH 17 Feb 1756 Mary Derby (NHGR 3:88).

Samuel enlisted 1 Aug 1776 at Kingston under Capt John Calef, Col Tash (NHPR 39:68).

Children:

1. **(SON)**, d Kingston, NH 20 Jan 1757 (NHVR)

JAMES MARSTON, b Brentwood, NH abt 1758 son of Winthrop Marston (NHPR 50:95): d Newport, KY 16 Jan 1828 (NHPR 50:96).

James is listed on the Town Returns of the Rev War for Kingston where he was mustered 10 Jul 1780 by Josiah Bartlett (NHSP 16:510). He enlisted May 1775 under Capt Daniel Moore NH Troops. Enlisted again in the spring of 1776 & served under Capt James Gray, 3rd NH until 1783 when his Co was commanded by Capt Benjamin Ellis, Col Dearborn's Rgt #S36071 (NHPR 50:94).

DANIEL MCCARTY, of Derry, NH, was enlisted for Kingston by Josiah Bartlett for the Continental Army 1780 (NHSP 16:64).

THOMAS MERRILL, b Newbury, MA 4 Jun 1746 son of Thomas & Hannah (Bagley) Merrill (NVR): d Raymond, NH 15 Nov 1790 (Merrill Memorial p279).

Probably the Thomas who refused to sign the Association Test in 1776, but later went into the army (NHSP 30:79).

NATHANIEL MORRILL, b Danville, NH 1 Nov 1762 (NHPR 45:__) son of Henry & Susanna (Folsom) Morrill: d 20 Jan 1844 (DAR 1:480): m(1) June 1783 Elizabeth Eastman (NHPR 54:_), bpt Kingston, NH 13 Jun 1762 dau of Edward & Sarah

(Wadley-Clough) Eastman (NHVR), d Sanbornton, NH 15 Nov 1841 (Hist of Sanbornton p489): m(2) Franklin, NH 24 May 1842 Sally (Johnson) Flanders (NHPR 54: _), b Sanbornton, NH 6 May 1790 dau of John & Mary (Smith) Johnson. Sally m(1) 14 Dec 1815 Eliphalet Flanders (Flanders Gen p202).

Nathaniel was mustered at Kingston in 1780 (NHSP 16:65) & served at West Point under Col Alexander Scammell, 3rd NH Troops #W9210 (NHPR 54:__).

Children: (Hist of Sanbornton, NH p490-93)

1. **HENRY**, b 5 May 1784: m(1) 27 Nov 1806 Nancy Calley: m(2) Elizabeth Hunkins: m (3) Sally Cate
2. **SARAH**, b 5 Jul 1786: m David Shaw
3. **SUSANNA**, b 14 Dec 1788: m 8 Oct 1807 Samuel George
4. **EDWARD**, b 21 Jun 1790: m 14 Oct 1813 Rachel Shaw
5. **NANCY**, b 9 May 1793: d Franklin, NH 1 Feb 1879: m 31 May 1819 John Colby Jr
6. **OBEDIAH EASTMAN**, b 21 Mar 1796: d NY 22 Feb 1863: m Nancy Dalson
7. **FOLSOM**, b 9 Dec 1798: m 10 Mar 1825 Rosilla Morrison
8. **BETSEY**, b 1 Mar 1801: m John Simonds
9. **HULDA WEEKS**, b 3 Oct 1804: m 23 Sep 1827 Joseph Fellows
10. **NATHANIEL**, b 13 Dec 1807: m(1) 14 Jun 1829 Nancy Quimby: m(2) 14 Jun 1853 Clarissa White

JOHN NEWTON, son of John & Judith (_) Newton (PRNH 6:17): m ____

John signed the Association Test in Kingston, NH (NHSP 30:77).

Children: bpt Kingston, NH (NHGR)

1. **ESTHER**, bpt 7 Jan 1738/9
2. **MARGARET**, bpt 26 Oct 1739/40
3. **WILLIAM**, bpt 6 Nov 1743
4. **THOMAS**, bpt 27 Apr 1746

THOMAS NEWTON, bpt Kingston, NH 27 Apr 1746 son of John Newton (NHGR 5:153).

Thomas, of Kingston, enlisted 17 Feb 1777 in Zachariah Beal's Co, Col Alexander Scammel's Rgt (NHSP 14:648).

JOSEPH NICHOLS, b Amesbury, MA 25 Nov 1730 son of William & Mary (Davis) Nichols (AVR): possibly m Amesbury, MA 6 Jun 1754 Hannah Lancaster (AVR).

Joseph signed the Association Test in Kingston, NH (NHSP 30:76). The wife of Joseph Nichols was dismissed from the Amesbury 2nd Church 12 Sep 1762 & received into the Kingston 1st Church 3 Oct 1762.

Children: bpt Amesbury, MA (AVR)

1. **JOSIAH**, bpt 18 Jul 1756
2. **MARY**, bpt 3 Jul 1757

JAMES NOYES, bpt Haverhill, MA 21 May 1738 son of Timothy & Sarah (Richards) Noyes (HvVR): d Kingston, NH (bur) 26 May 1790 (NHVR): m Newbury, MA 2 Jul 1761 Jane Noyes (NVR), b 1725.

James signed the Association Test in Kingston, NH (NHSP 30:78). He served as a pvt in Capt Richard Dawes Co, Col John Wingate's MA Rgt 1775 (DAR LB 101:235).

Children: (Noyes Gen p316)

1. **JANE**, b Newbury, MA 30 Apr 1763
2. **JAMES**, b 30 Apr 1764: d Kingston, NH 7 Mar 1814 a.50yrs (NHVR): m Hampstead, NH 1 May 1794 Mary Webster (HmstR)
3. **JOHN**, b Kingston, NH: d 1847: m Hampstead, NH (int) 13 Jan 1788 Elizabeth Webster (HmstR)
4. **DANIEL**, b Kingston, NH 1771: d 5 Aug 1812: m Nancy Weare
5. **EBENEZER**, m 1798 Lydia Sawyer
6. **SAMUEL**, m 1807 Hannah P. Dow
7. **CALEB**, b 13 Oct 1774: d Feb 1850 lived in Woodbury, VT: m 1803 Polly Sweet

JOHN NOYES, b Newbury, MA 15 Nov 1749 son of Joseph & Elizabeth (Woodman) Noyes (NVR): d 17 Aug 1819 (Noyes Gen p72): m 1771 Diana Cockran
 Possibly the John who signed the Association Test in Kingston, NH (NHSP 30:78).

Children:
1. **JOHN C.**, b Kingston, NH 22 Sep 1772 (IGI)
2. **LEMUEL**, b Kingston, NH 28 Sep 1773 (IGI)
3. **ANNA**, b 10 Feb 1785
4. **DIANA C.**, d 1847

OLIVER NOYES, b Plaistow, NH 12 May 1759 son of Ebenezer & Elizabeth (Greenleaf) Noyes (Noyes Gen p326): d 24 Oct 1842 (DAR 1:501): m 1783 Mehitable Eaton (Hist of Henniker, NH p662)
 Oliver was mustered at Kingston 2 Oct 1777 in Col Bartlett's Militia Rgt for Col Drake's Rgt #8921 (NHPR 57:86 & NHSP 15:343).

Children: born Henniker, NH
1. **HANNAH**, b 2 Oct 1783: m William Cressy
2. **SALLY**, b 2 Apr 1786: m John Campbell
3. **BETSEY**, b 28 Apr 1789: m 8 Jul 1812 James Howe
4. **JAMES**, b 4 Sep 1791: d 7 Nov 1838
5. **NATHANIEL**, b 11 Oct 1793: m Bathsheba Sargent
6. **BENJAMIN FRANKLIN**, b 16 Feb 1802: m 20 Dec 1826 Sally Temple

ROBERT PAGE (Col), b Kingston, NH abt 1747: d Readfield, ME 6 Sep 1825 (RG 2:527): m Abigail ______
 Robert served as a Col & PS (MSSP p594)

Children:
1. **ROBERT**

JOSHUA PALMER, b abt 1762 (NHPR 16:134): m Rhoda ____.
 Joshua, of Kingston, testified 24 Mar 1837 that he enlisted Jul 1780 for 3 months under Capt John Eastman & marched to West Point, NY

(NHPR 16:134).

Children:
1. **MOLLY**, b Sandown, NH 25 Feb 1788 (SdTR)

TRUEWORTHY PALMER, b 20 Jul 1749 son of Jonathan & Anna (Brown) Palmer (NEHGR 68:261): d Conway, NH 25 Jun 1830: m(1) So Hampton, NH 27 Apr 1772 Joanna Webster (SHVR), bpt Kingston, NH 24 Sep 1749 dau of Thomas & Judith (Noyes) Webster (KChR), d 14 Feb 1794 (NEHGR 68:261): m(2) 14 Jun 1795 Love Perkins.

Trueworthy, of Kingston (a.26yrs), served in Col Enoch Poor's Rgt, Capt Philip Tilton's Co (RW roll-51). He also served in Capt Calef's Co, Col T Bartlett's Rgt which reinforced the Continental Army at NY 1776 (NHSP 14:404).

Children: (NEHGR 68:261)
(by 1st wife)
1. **SARAH**, b 23 Apr 1773; bpt E. Kingston, NH 27 Nov 1773 (NHVR): m 27 Oct 1796 Benning Adams
2. **JUDITH**, b 22 Apr 1775
3. **JAMES**, b 17 Jun 1777
4. **LOIS**, b 11 Jul 1779
5. **JONATHAN**, b Loudon, NH 25 Apr 1782: d Exeter Mills, ME 24 Nov 1866: m(1) Gilmanton, NH 15 Mar 1807 Anna Osgood: m(2) 22 Apr 1810 Martha Prescott
6. **MOLLY**, b 16 Jun 1784
7. **WILLIAM**, b 17 Jul 1786
8. **ENOCH**, b 21 Apr 1789
9. **ANNA**, b 15 Aug 1791

(by 2nd wife)
10. **TRUEWORTHY**, b 27 Aug 1797
11. **STEPHEN**, b 19 Aug 1799

WILLIAM PATTEN, b Newbury, MA 29 Jan 1748/9 son of Aaron & Jane (Ordway) Patten (NVR): d Kingston, NH 16 Dec 1824 a.75yrs (GI p20): m Danville, NH 29 Sep 1774 Mehitable Colcord (NEHGR 58:123), b Kingston, NH 28 Mar 1751 dau of Samuel & Mehitable (Ladd) Colcord (KTR).

William signed the Association Test in Kingston, NH (NHSP 30:76).

Children: born Kingston, NH (Patten Gen p91)
1. **AARON**, b 1 Sep 1775: d Kingston, NH 6 Jun 1823 (GI p20): m Kingston, NH 1 Jan 1807 Sally Chase (NHGR 4:176)
2. **SUSANNA**, b 30 Jun 1777: d Gilmanton, NH 19 May 1856 a.80yrs (GI p3): m Kingston, NH 18 May 1802 George Burroughs (NHGR 3:171)
3. **LOIS**, b 15 Oct 1779: m Kingston, NH 22 Feb 1801 Stephen Gale (NHGR 3:170)
4. **MEHITABLE**, b 21 Jan 1782: d Kingston, NH 8 Sep 1830 (GI p20)
5. **HANNAH**, b 3 May 1785: d Kingston, NH 24 Jul 1830 (GI p20)
6. **ISAAC**, b 18 Jun 1787: d Kingston, NH 10 Sep 1836 a.46yrs (NHVR): m Kingston, NH 23 Jun 1832 Nancy Bean (NHGR 5:21)
7. **COLCORD**, b 21 Sep 1789: m Kingston, NH 8 Jul 1818 Maria Fletcher (NHGR 4:180)

DOLE PEARSON (PARSONS), b Exeter, NH abt 1754 son of Taylor Pearson: d St Albans, VT aft 1790: m Exeter, NH 30 Nov 1773 Hannah Fogg (DAR #608393A703), bpt Exeter, NH 14 Sep 1755 dau of David & Hannah (Folsom) Fogg (HE p68g).

Dole of Kingston, NH received from the Town of Hampton, NH 40 silver dollars & 1600 paper dollars for 6 months service (HH p273). He served as a pvt in Col Tash's Rgt, Capt Daniel Gordon's Co 20 Sep 1776 (RW roll-52). Enlisted again 28 Jun 1780 to serve until the last day of 1780 in the 2nd NH Rgt under Lt Col George Reid. He was mustered at Kingston & stationed at West Point (DAR #608393A703).

Children: (Hist of Sanbornton, NH p548)
1. **JETHRO**, b 1778
2. **DAVID**, b 1780: lived Beverly, MA
3. **HANNAH**, b 1782: m 7 Nov 1799 Jonathan Foss
4. **DOLE JR**, b 1784

5. **SALLY**, b Exeter, NH 1786: m Sanbornton, NH 13 Oct 1807 Reuben Morgan Jr
6. **SAMUEL**, b 1788: d St Albans, Vt abt 1875: m(1) Ruth Hayes: m(2) Mrs Keniston
7. **JONATHAN**, b 8 Sep 1790: d 21 Jan 1879: m 11 Nov 1813 Dorothy Johnson
8. **MARY**, b 17 Nov 1795: m Jeremiah Sanborn

JOHN PEARSON, b (prob) Andover, MA 9 Aug 1744 son of John & Rebecca (Osgood) Pearson (AndVR): m Andover, MA 3 Aug 1769 Abigail Tyler (AndVR).

John signed the Association Test in Kingston, NH (NHSP 30:76). He served in Capt Quimby's Co, Col Jacob Gale's Rgt (RW roll-50).

Children:

1. **REBECCA**, b Andover, MA 4 Jan 1770 (AndVR)
2. **JAMES**, bpt Kingston, NH 1 Sep 1771 (NHVR)
3. **ELIZABETH GARISH**, bpt Kingston, NH 5 Dec 1773 (NHVR)

DAVID PEASLEY, b Sandown, NH 6 Mar 1751 son of David & Rachel (Straw) Peasley (SdTR).

David, of Sandown (a.28yrs), served in Col Jacob Gale's 7th Rgt of NH Militia. He was mustered in Kingston 28 Oct 1779 (RW roll-50).

JACOB PEASLEY, b Newton, NH 17 Nov 1748 son of Nathan & Lydia (Gove) Peasley (NwtTR): d Kingston, NH 2 Mar 1833 a.87yrs (GI p21): m(1) Martha Challis (NH Gen Digest p193), b abt 1749, d Kingston, NH 26 Oct 1824 a.75yrs (GI p21): possibly m(2) Mrs Mary Clement, d Kingston, NH 31 May 1830 a.50yrs (GI p21).

Jacob signed the Association Test in Kingston, NH (NHSP 30:78).

Children: (NH Gen Digest p193)

1. **LYDIA**, b abt 1770: d Kingston, NH 5 Dec 1834 a.64yrs (GI p30): m Kingston, NH 18 Jun 1797 Samuel Spofford (NHGR 3:168)
2. **DANIEL**, b abt 1777: d Kingston, NH 10 Apr 1832 a.55yrs (GI p21): m Kingston, NH Feb 1805 Elizabeth Secombe (NHGR 4:174)

3. **MARTHA**, b abt 1780: m Benjamin? Eastman
4. **JOHN**, d Kingston, NH 6 Sep 1784 (NHVR)
5. **JOHN**, m Hannah Peaslee
6. **HANNAH**, m Jonathan Bartlett
7. **MOSES**, b abt 1789: d Kingston, NH 14 May 1826 a.37yrs (GI p21)

WILET PETERSON, b Newbury, MA 19 Feb 1722 son of Daniel & Elizabeth (Willet) Peterson (NVR): m Newbury, MA 19 Feb 1746/7 Hannah Ordway (NVR).

Willet signed the Association Test in Kingston, NH (NHSP 30:76).

Children: born Newbury, MA (NVR)
1. **DANIEL**, b 11 Nov 1750
2. **JOHN**, b 15 Feb 1754
3. **HANNAH**, bpt 15 Feb 1756
4. **JAMES**, bpt 1 Mar 1761

SAMUEL PHILBRICK, b Kingston, NH 11 Feb 1739/40 son of Jedediah & Mary (Taylor) Philbrick (KTR): d Kingston, NH 4 Apr 1779 (NHVR) m 9 Feb 1767 Sarah Sanborn (NEHGR 38:284), b Kingston, NH 1 Mar 1742 dau of Peter & Mary (Sanborn) Sanborn (KTR).

Samuel signed the Association Test in Kingston, NH (NHSP 30:77).

Children: born Kingston, NH (IGI)
1. **JEDEDIAH**, b 5 Nov 1767
2. **JEREMIAH**, b 13 Mar 1769
3. **ABRAHAM**, b 16 May 1771: d Springfield, NH 23 Apr 1852: m 1797 Hitty Lovering
4. **JOHN**, b 13 Sep 1774
5. **SARAH**, b 22 Aug 1776
6. **SAMUEL**, b 3 Feb 1779: bpt 1 Apr 1779: d Kingston, NH 30 Jul 1779 (NHVR)

GEORGE PITCHER signed the Association Test in Kingston, NH (NHSP 30:77).

BARTON POLLARD, b Gloucester, MA 28 Jul 1734 son of John & Mary (Pope) Pollard (GlVR): d bef

24 Feb 1800 (Pollard Gen 1:99): m Kingston, NH 22 May 1754 Elizabeth Smith (NHGR 3:87).

Barton, of Raymond, served for Kingston 1 Jul 1779 in Col Gale's 7th NH Militia. He served as a pvt in Col Hercules Mooney's Rgt, Capt Jonathan Leavitt's Co for the defense of RI 1779 (RW roll-51).

Children: 1st 5 born Plaistow, NH (PlVR)

1. **HANNAH**, b 2 Feb 1755: m (prob) Joseph Peavy
2. **BARTON**, b 22 May 1756: d Albion, ME 10 Sep 1828 (RG 2:557): m Mary Phillips
3. **THOMAS**, b abt 1758: m Elizabeth Woodman
4. **EZEKIEL**, b 22 Mar 1759
5. **ELIJAH**, b 9 Jun 1761: m (int) 24 Apr 1785 Nancy Fitch
6. **HEZEKIAH**, b Raymond, NH 22 May 1763
7. **JOHN**, b Raymond, NH 10 Jan 1765
8. **MOLLY**, b Raymond, NH 27 Mar 1768: m (int) 9 Jun 1789 Joshua Sargent
9. **ASA**, b Raymond, NH 5 Mar 1770

FRANCIS POLLARD, b Chebacco, MA abt 1723 son of John & Mary (Pope) Pollard (Pollard Gen 1:94): d aft 1790: m(1) Kingston, NH 6 Sep 1747 Sarah Webster (KTR), bpt Kingston, NH 11 Dec 1725 dau of John & Sarah (Stewart) Webster (NHGR 2:46): m(2) Eleanor Whitney, b Dunstable, MA 23 Jul 1740 dau of James & Eleanor (Robbins) Whitney (Founders of Dunstable by Stearns p63).

Francis served in the Rev War as a priviteer under James Barret. He was mustered into service in 1777 (Middlesex Co by Wm Cutter 4:1661).

Children: 1st 6 born Kingston, NH (KTR)
(by 1st wife)

1. **JOHN**, b 11 Apr 1748: m Molly Flanders
2. **JONATHAN**, b 9 Aug 1749: m Danville, NH 16 Nov 1775 Sarah Webster (NEHGR 58:123)
3. **MOLLY**, b 28 Jul 1751: m Benjamin Eastman
4. **BETSEY**, b 22 Aug 1753: m Webster Davis
5. **MERCY**, b 11 Feb 1756: d Kingston, NH 10 Jul 1818 (NHVR) m Caleb Seaver

6. **ISAAC**, b 1 Mar 1758: d Plaistow, NH 20 Jan 1836: m 28 Apr 1797 Lucy Smith

(by 2nd wife)

7. **ABIGAIL**, b Dunstable, MA 9 Mar 1773
8. **FRANCIS JR**, b Winchendon, MA 20 Jul 1775
9. **RUFUS**, b 16 May 1782

JOHN POLLARD, b Kingston, NH 11 Apr 1748 son of Francis & Sarah (Webster) Pollard (KTR): d abt 1776: m Molly Flanders who m(2) Benjamin Colby (NHPR 63:41).

John enlisted May 1775 & served under Jacob Quimby at Bunker Hill (NHPR 63:41).

JONATHAN POLLARD, b Kingston, NH 9 Aug 1749 son of Francis & Sarah (Webster) Pollard (KTR): d Kingston, NH 24 Mar 1823 a.74yrs (NHVR): m Danville, NH 16 Nov 1775 Sarah Webster (NEHGR 58:123), b Kingston, NH 1 May 1754 dau of Benjamin & Mary (Stanyan) Webster (KTR), d Kingston, NH 26 Mar 1840 a.86yrs (NHVR).

Jonathan signed the Association Test in Kingston, NH (NHSP 30:78). He was a volunteer in Col Jacob Gale's Rgt, Capt Quimby's Co (RW roll-50).He served in the Battle at Bunker Hill #W15267 (NHPR 63:36).

Children: (NHPR 63:47)

1. **MARY**, b 12 Apr 1776: d Kingston, NH 22 Dec 1851 (NHVR): m Kingston, NH Apr 1804 Israel Collins (NHGR 4:173)
2. **SARAH**, b 10 Dec 1778
3. **SARAH**, b 12 Nov 1779: d 8 Apr 1813
4. **JACOB** (Pollard Gen), b 1780: m Kingston, NH 28 Nov 1805 Sally Secomb (NHGR 4:175)
5. **JOHN**, b 25 Oct 1781: d 15 Apr 1788
6. **BETSEY**, b 10 Sep 1783: d 8 Apr 1803 or 1813: m Kingston, NH 4 Sep 1800 Peltiah Peaslee (NHGR 3:170)
7. **MERCY**, b 30 Mar 1786: d 24 Jun 1867: m 19 May 1805 Henry Hunt
8. **DOROTHY**, b 22 Nov 1789: d 18 Oct 1873: m Jacob Quimby
9. **ISAAC**, b 3 Jul 1792: d Kingston, NH 1 Apr

1833 a.40yrs (NHVR): m Plaistow, NH 2 Feb 1817 Hannah Hunt (PlVR)

EBENEZER PROCTOR, b Kingston, NH 5 Mar 1757 son of James & Abigail (Whittemore) Proctor (KTR): d Kingston, NH 2 Jul 1813 (NHPR 65:15): m Kensington, NH 24 Sep 1781 Sarah George (NHVR), b abt 1762, living Kingston, NH 1840 a.78yrs.

Ebenezer, of Kingston (a.18yrs), served in Col Enoch Poor's Rgt, Capt Philip Tilton's Co #W16379 (RW roll-51 & NHPR 65:15).

Children: (Proctor Gen p44)

1. **JOHN**
2. **BETSEY**
3. **SARAH**
4. **FANNIE** one dau m ___ Gale
5. **JUDITH** " " m ___ Wescott
6. **POLLY**

JAMES PROCTOR, b Woburn, MA 18 Jun 1722 son of James & Judith (Nichols) Proctor (WoVR): d 11 Nov 1776 (DAR 1:549) on his way from Ticonderoga: m 1743 Abigail Whittemore, b 7 Jun 1722, d 3 May 1812 (Proctor Gen p23).

James signed the Association Test in Kingston, NH (NHSP 30:76). He enlisted as a pvt in Capt David Quinby's Co, Col Joshua Wingate's Rgt & served at Ticonderoga, 1776 (DAR LB 119: 152).

Children: last 8 born Kingston, NH (KTR)

1. **JAMES**, b Woburn, MA 19 Jan 1743 (WoVR): d 31 Jan 1772: m Lydia Myrick
2. **JOHN**, b Woburn, MA 1 Jun 1746 (WoVR): d Kingston, NH 11 Aug 1764 a.19yrs (KTR)
3. **THOMAS**, b Woburn, MA 28 Jun 1748 (WoVR): d Loudon, NH 28 Mar 1836: m Danville, NH 21 May 1776 Fanny Kimball (NEHGR 58:124)
4. **JONATHAN**, b Salisbury, MA 1 Oct 1751 (SVR): d Unity, NH 3 Aug 1820: m So Hampton, NH 20 Feb 1777 Martha Graves (SHVR)
5. **ELIZABETH**, b 3 Sep 1753: d Andover, NH 5 Nov 1819 (HA p278)

6. **EBENEZER**, b 1 Mar 1756: d Kingston, NH 10 Apr 1756 (KTR)
7. **EBENEZER**, b 5 Mar 1757: d Kingston, NH 2 Jul 1813 (NHPR 65:15): m Kensington, NH 24 Sep 1781 Sarah George (NHVR)
8. **JUDITH**, b 2 Jan 1760: m Bradford, MA 27 Jun 1785 Ebenezer Griffin (BdVR)
9. **ESTHER** (twin), b 13 Jun 1762: m Kingston, NH Mar 1785 John Nichols (NHPR 56:181)
10. **MEHITABLE** (twin), b 13 Jun 1762: d Bridgewater, NH: m Richard Batchelder
11. **JOHN**, b 7 Apr 1767: d 3 Aug 1795
12. **WILLIAM**, b 8 Apr 1767: d Andover, NH 29 Oct 1848 (HA p278): m Salisbury, MA 7 Jan 1793 Rhoda Bagley (SVR)

JONATHAN PROCTOR, b Salisbury, MA 1 Oct 1751 son of James & Abigail (Whitemore) Proctor (SVR): d Unity, NH 3 Aug 1820 (UR p49): m So Hampton, NH 20 Feb 1777 Martha Graves (SHVR), b 20 Dec 1757, d Franklin, NH 6 Sep 1836 (CG p53).

Jonathan signed the Association Test in Kingston, NH (NHSP 30:76).

Children: (UR p49)

1. **JAMES**, b Kingston, NH 13 Sep 1777: d Franklin, NH 1 Feb 1847: m Unity, NH 3 Jun 1804 Abigail Ladd
2. **AMOS**, b Kingston, NH 16 Oct 1778: d Kingston, NH 21 Jul 1783 (NHVR)
3. **AMOS**, b Kingston, NH 25 Sep 1783: d NY 3 May 1844: m Kensington, NH 31 Dec 1805 Elizabeth Fellows (NHVR)
4. **LUCY**, b Unity, NH 10 Oct 1785: d 25 Mar 1860: m 25 Sep 1828 Nathaniel Huntoon
5. **LEMUEL**, b Unity, NH 15 Mar 1788
6. **JONATHAN**, b Unity, NH 9 Dec 1789: d NY City 11 Jun 1861 (Proctor Gen p90): m Sanbornton, NH 13 Apr 1815 Ruth Carter
7. **BENJAMIN CLOUGH**, b Unity, NH 7 Sep 1793: d Appleton, WI 5 Sep 1867: m(1) Unity, NH 10 May 1818 Sally Huntoon: m(2) Lebanon, NH 15 Jun 1824 Julia Post (IGI)

THOMAS PROCTOR, b Woburn, MA 28 Jun 1748 son of James & Abigail (Whittemore) Proctor (WoVR): d Loudon, NH 28 Mar 1836 (Proctor Gen p43): m Danville, NH 21 May 1776 Fanny Kimball (NEHGR 58:124), b Bradford, MA 4 Feb 1755 dau of Solomon & Martha (Graves) Kimball (BdVR), d 1 Jun 1830.

Thomas signed the Association Test in Kingston, NH 1776 (NHSP 30:77).

Children: last 9 born Loudon, NH

1. **LYDIA**, b Kingston, NH 24 Oct 1776: d Conneaut OH 14 Jul 1828: m 1793 Avery Moulton
2. **FANNY**, b Kingston, NH 9 Nov 1778: d 2 Apr 1857: m Barnstead, NH Sep 1801 Nathaniel Wilson
3. **SALLY**, 31 Dec 1780: d 16 Oct 1870: m Ezekiel Gilman
4. **THOMAS**, b 12 Jun 1783: d Barnstead, NH 25 Jun 1856: m(1) 1807 Martha Drew: m(2) 1831 Comfort Ayers: m(3) 1848 Betsey (Priest) Clark
5. **REBECCA**, b 20 Nov 1785: m Barnstead, NH 29 Apr 1812 Andrew Bunker (IGI)
6. **PETER**, b 7 Jul 1788: d Linesville, PA 23 Oct 1863: m 1815 Abigail Bunker
7. **JOSEPH**, b 31 Dec 1790: d New Sharon, ME 14 Aug 1867: m Pittsfield, NH 16 Mar 1816 Betsey Shaw (IGI)
8. **WILLIAM**, b 19 Feb 1793: d Hillsdale, MI 18 Jul 1862: m Loudon, NH 4 Sep 1823 Betsey Dyer (IGI)
9. **JAMES**, b 18 May 1795: d Lowell, MA 28 Sep 1862: m 20 Nov 1816 Joan Boynton
10. **BENJAMIN**, b 18 Nov 1797: d 13 Aug 1803
11. **PRISCILLA**, b 4 Feb 1800: d Haverhill, MA 6 Dec 1876: m Loudon, NH 19 May 1823 John Tucker

MARK PURMOT, b Exeter, NH 29 May 1755 son of John & Hannah (Sinclair) Purmot (HE p38g): d 12 Jul 1776 (Purmort Gen p53).

Mark, of Kingston (a.20yrs) served in Col

Enoch Poor's Rgt, Capt Philip Tilton's Co Aug 1775 (RW roll-51).

AARON QUIMBY, b 22 Jul 1733 son of William & Hannah (Barnard) Quimby (Quimby Gen 2:118): d Sandwich, NH Dec 1810: m(1) Anne Hadley (DAR 1:553), b 6 Apr 1738: m(2) Hampstead, NH 20 Mar 1766 Mary Johnson (HmstR), b Haverhill, MA 19 Apr 1744 dau of Samuel & Susanna (Black) Johnson (HvVR), d Sandwich, NH 25 Aug 1825.

Possibly the Aaron Quimby Jr who served in Col David Gilman's Rgt, Capt Gordon's Co 5 Jan to 15 Mar 1777 (RW roll-50). Perhaps, he was called Aaron Jr to distinquish him from his relative Aaron Quimby son of Jeremiah.

Children: (Quimby Gen 2:121-2)
(by 1st wife)

1. **SARAH**, b Manchester, NH 6 Apr 1758: d Sandwich, NH 22 Sep 1803: m Sandwich, NH Hugh Bean
2. **JOSEPH**, b Weare, NH 1 Sep 1761: m 26 Sep 1780 Molly Colby

(by 2nd wife)

3. **MOSES**, b Weare, NH 12 Feb 1767: m Sandwich, NH 16 May 1791 Dolly Atkins
4. **ENOCH**, b Weare, NH 23 Mar 1769: d Sandwich, NH 22 Mar 1831: m 22 Jul 1792 Sarah Libby
5. **SAMUEL**, b Weare, NH 23 Sep 1770: m Chester, NH 4 Feb 1795 Lydia Currier
6. **JAMES**, b Weare, NH 5 Apr 1772
7. **DANIEL**, b Weare, NH 26 Dec 1773: d 29 Nov 1850: m(1) Sandwich, NH 1 Feb 1798 Dorothy Burley: m(2) Sandwich, NH 22 May 1803 Lydia Gilman
8. **ANNA**, b Weare, NH 13 Dec 1775: m John Bean
9. **AARON**, b Weare, NH 27 Sep 1777: m Tamworth, NH 27 Sep 1798 Elizabeth Wells
10. **SUSAN**, b Weare, NH 6 Apr 1780
11. **BENJAMIN**, b Sandwich, NH 17 Apr 1782 (Changed his name to **JOHNSON DAVIS QUIMBY**): d 23 Feb 1855: m Sandwich, NH 28 Oct

1802 Mary Collins
12. **MARY**, b 22 Jul 1784: m 24 Feb 1803 Jonathan Bean

BENJAMIN QUIMBY, b Kingston, NH 7 Jan 1757 son of David & Mary (Wadleigh) Quimby (KTR).
Benjamin, of Hawke, enlisted for Kingston in the 7th Rgt NH Militia 1777, Capt James Gray's Co (NHSP 14:585).

BENJAMIN QUIMBY, b Kingston, NH 1763 (MSSP p644) son of Col John Quimby (NHPR 65:148): d Greene, ME 27 Mar 1840 (NHPR 65:149): m Kingston, NH 18 Jul 1787 Mary Critchet (NHGR 3: 133), b abt 1761, d 4 Jun 1842 (NHPR 65:149).
Benjamin enlisted at Exeter, NH Jul 1782 for 3 years under Capt Cherry, Col George Reid's NH Rgt (NHPR 65:147).

Children: (Hist of Greene, ME p407)
1. **DAVID**, b 2 Jun 1788
2. **SALLY**, b 12 Nov 1789: d 9 Sep 1830: m Greene, ME (int) Sep 1813 Reuben Robbins
3. **POLLY**, b 11 Sep 1791: m Greene, ME (int) Mar 1814 Luther Robbins
4. **BENJAMIN**, b 13 May 1793
5. **JOHN**, b 16 Aug 1795: d 21 Apr 1864
6. **SAMUEL**, b 29 Jun 1797
7. **HENRY**, b 6 Oct 1799
8. **AARON**, b 28 Apr 1802: living in 1820
9. **DANIEL**, b 19 Jun 1805: living in 1820

DANIEL QUIMBY, b Kingston, NH 3 Nov 1755 son of Tristram & Susanna (Blaisdell) Quimby (KTR): d Jun 1836 of Waterford, VT (NHPR 65:155): m Kingston, NH 17 Jan 1782 Abigail Hubbard (NHGR 3:131).
Daniel, of Kingston (a.18yrs) served as a Cpl in Capt Philip Tilton's Co, Col Enoch Poor's Rgt Jun 1775 to Jan 1777. He also served 9 months under Capt John Kilby Smith, Col Ebenezer Sprout MA Line (NHPR 65:153 & RW roll-51).

Children: (Hist of Barnet, VT p584)

1. **DANIEL**, d a.17yrs
2. **RICHARD**, d 1857: m Mary Bedel
3. **BENJAMIN**, d.y.
4. **SUSANNA**, m Luther Knight
5. **HUBBARD**, b 1792: m Mehitable Hazelton
6. **ABIGAIL**, m Wentworth Blake
7. **IRA**, m Elmira Russell
8. **SALMA DAVIS**, m Mary Johnston

DAVID QUIMBY, b Kingston, NH 4 Dec 1731 son of David & Abigail (Webster) Quimby (KTR): d Danville, NH 19 Dec 1794 a.63yrs (CG p40): m Kingston, NH 19 Nov 1755 Mary Wadleigh (KTR), b Kingston, NH abt 1732 dau of Benjamin & Judith (Clough) Wadleigh (Pillsbury Gen 1:235), d Danville, NH 31 Oct 1814 (CG p40)

David served as a Lt in Capt Ezra Currier's Co, Col Abraham Drake Rgt 8 Sep to 16 Dec 1777 (RW roll-49).

Children: last 5 born Danville, NH (DnTR)

1. **BENJAMIN**, b Kingston, NH 7 Jan 1757 (KTR)
2. **MARY**, b Kingston, NH 6 Nov 1760 (KTR)
3. **DAVID**, b 13 Mar 1762
4. **PAUL**, b 29 Jun 1764
5. **LUCY**, b 28 Jan 1766
6. **RHODA**, b 1 Jan 1770
7. **THOMAS**, b 27 Oct 1771

EBENEZER QUIMBY, b Kingston, NH 31 Aug 1755 (RG 2:569) son of Joseph & Patience (Thompson) Quimby: d Exeter, ME 19 May 1821 (RG 2:569): m Hannah Colby (DAR 1:553).

Ebenezer served in Col Timothy Bedell Rgt, Capt John Parker's Co (RW roll-49).

Children: (Quimby Gen 2:136)

1. **HANNAH**, b 8 Dec 1779: m Lisbon, NH 8 Jul 1801 Dr Aldrich
2. **MOLLY**, b 8 Dec 1781
3. **JOSEPH**, b 21 Dec 1783: d Littleton, NH 4 May 1860: m Ruth Richardson
4. **SARAH**, b 5 Feb 1788: d 23 Feb 1878
5. **EBEN E.**, b 20 Jun 1789: m(1) Sebec, ME 25

Mar 1822 Charlotte Bunker: m(2) Sebec, ME 29 May 1831 Rhoda Packard

6. **THOMAS**, b abt 1790: m Maria Mathews
7. **PATIENCE**, d 14 Jan 1830: m __ Woodard
8. **JOHN**, b 6 Feb 1791: d 2 Sep 1890: m Exeter, ME Feb 1819 Ruby Townsend
9. **JOANNA**, b 17 May 1797: m 1 Jul 1815 Rickman Chamberlain
10. **CHARLOTTE**, b 27 Feb 1803
11. **RHODA**, d 23 May 1821 or 1827: m ___ Southard

ELIPHALET QUIMBY, b Kingston, NH 11 May 1758 son of Tristram & Susanna (Blaisdell) Quimby (KTR).

Eliphalet, of Kingston (a.18yrs), served in Col Enoch Poor's Rgt, Capt Philip Tilton's Co 1775 (RW roll-51). He also enlisted for the 7th NH Rgt of NH Militia in the Continental Army 1777, Capt Hutchins Co (NHSP 14:585).

JACOB QUIMBY, b abt 1760 son of Jacob Quimby (NHPR 65:159): d Hampstead, NH 23 Mar 1833 (NHPR 65:160): m Kingston, NH 16 Dec 1787 Anna Plummer (NHGR 3:133), b abt 1772, d aft 1855.

Jacob served Apr 1775 in Capt Moses McFarland's Co of Haverhill, MA. He also enlisted for a year in the same Co in which his father Jacob Quimby was a Lt & served at Winter Hill until Feb 1776. On 26 Apr 1855 Anna Quimby, of Kingston, a.84yrs applied for bounty land #W24714 (NHPR 65:160).

Children: born Hampstead, NH (HmstR)

1. **JACOB**, b 16 Oct 1789
2. **SAMUEL**, b 2 Jan 1795
3. **NATHAN**, b 11 Oct 1796
4. **ANNA**, b 28 Nov 1803

MOSES QUIMBY, b Kingston, NH 1757 (NHPR 65: 174). Probably the Moses b Kingston, NH 29 Sep 1755 son of John & Martha (Sargent) Quimby (KTR): d Lunenburg, Vt 1840.

Moses enlisted at Hampstead May 1775 & served

under Capt Hezekiah Hutchins, Col James Reed NH Line & was in the Battle of Bunker Hill. In Apr 1778, he enlisted at Northhumberland, NH into a Co commanded by Capt Luther Richardson, Col Timothy Bedel's NH Troops. He move to Lunenburg, Vt in 1781 (NHPR 65:173).

Children: (DAR #13458)
  1. **REBECCA**, m John Cobleigh

SAMUEL QUIMBY, b Kingston, NH 10 Apr 1729 son of David & Abigail (Webster) Quimby (KTR): d aft 1794 (DAR 2:171): m Kingston, NH May 1757 Ann Young (KTR).
  Samuel is listed in the DAR Patriot Index as having performed Civil Service during the Rev War (DAR 2:171).

Children: last 9 born Danville, NH (DnTR)
  1. **MARY**, b Kingston, NH 1 Dec 1756 (KTR)
  2. **SAMUEL**, b Kingston, NH 28 Jan 1759 (KTR): d Essex, MA 29 Jun 1833: m(1) 1783 Sarah Allen: m(2) Elizabeth Andrews
  3. **ANNE**, b Kingston, NH 22 Sep 1760 (KTR): (a.92yrs in 1852 living in Danville, NH)
  4. **BENJAMIN**, b 7 Jul 1763
  5. **ELIZABETH**, b 2 Apr 1765
  6. **DANIEL**, b 2 Nov 1767
  7. **SARAH**, b 20 Aug 1769
  8. **DAVID**, b 3 Mar 1771
  9. **ABIGAIL**, b 7 Feb 1773
  10. **JOHN**, b 25 Dec 1774
  11. **TIMOTHY** (Quimby Gen 1:162)
  12. **HANNAH**, b 17 Feb 1779: m ____ Hardy of Newburyport, MA (PP v182)

SAMUEL QUIMBY, b Kingston, NH 28 Jan 1759 son of Samuel & Ann (Young) Quimby (KTR): d Essex, MA 1 Jul 1833 (ExVR): m(1) abt 1783 Sarah Allen (DAR 1:553), dau of Azariah & Sarah (Leach) Allen, d 1796: m(2) Ipswich, MA 15 Sep 1796 Elizabeth Andrews (IpVR), d Essex, MA 19 Mar 1841 (ExVR).
  Samuel served in Capt William Ballard's Co,

Col James Frye's Rgt 1775 #S30050 (PP v182 & NHSP 15:746).

Children:
(by 1st wife)
1. **SALLY**, b 17 Jul 1784: d 1867: m Chester, NH 23 Oct 1804 Abel Currier: lived Norwich, VT
2. **SAMUEL**, bpt 13 Nov 1785
3. **AZARIAH ALLEN**, b 23 Nov 1787
4. **NANCY**, bpt 3 Jan 1790: m ____ Lee of NY City, NY (PP v182)
5. **JOHN**, bpt 23 Nov 1791
6. **ABIGAIL**, b 1 Apr 1793: d unmd 1852
7. **DANIEL**, b 17 Sep 1795: d Oct 1814

(by 2nd wife)
8. **CALEB**, b 15 Jul 1797: d 2 Sep 1804
9. **(CHILD)**, b Mar 1799
10. **MARY**, b 22 Jul 1807: m Abraham Jones
11. **HANNAH**, b 2 Mar 1803: m ___ Smith: lived Boston, MA (PP v182)

TIMOTHY QUIMBY, b Kingston, NH 16 Apr 1750 son of David & Abigail (Webster) Quimby (KTR).
Timothy, of Kingston (a.25yrs), served in Col Enoch Poor's Rgt, Capt Philip Tilton's Co (RW roll-51). He also served as a Cpl in Capt David Quimby's Co, Col Jacob Gale's Rgt (NHSP 15:560).
Timothy signed the association Test in Kingston, NH 1776 (NHSP 30:77).

TRISTAM QUIMBY, probably son of Jeremiah & Hannah (George) Quimby: m Kingston, NH 26 Nov 1753 Susanna Blaisdell (KTR), d Kingston, NH 5 Mar 1765 (KTR).
Tristram signed the Association Test in Kingston, NH 1776 (NHSP 30:76).

Children: born Kingston, NH (KTR)
1. **MARY**, b 7 Dec 1754
2. **DANIEL**, b 3 Nov 1755: d Jun 1836: m Kingston, NH 1782 Abigail Hubbard (NHGR)
3. **ELIPHALET**, b 11 May 1758

4. **HANNAH**, b 4 Jan 1761
5. **SUSANNA**, b 12 Dec 1762
6. **BETTY**, b 25 Feb 1765

JOHN RENDAL, of Lee (a.18yrs), was mustered for Kingston & served in Col Jacob Gale's 7th Rgt of NH Militia for the defense of RI Jul 1779 (RW roll-50).

WILLIAM RICHARDSON, b Newbury, MA 8 Mar 1746 son of William & Elizabeth (Sawyer) Richardson (NVR): d Canaan, NH 25 Feb 1829 (Hist of Canaan p632): m(1) Haverhill, MA 24 Oct 1771 Prudence Morse (HvVR), d Hampstead, NH 3 Apr 1774 (Hm stR): m(2) Hampstead, NH 23 Mar 1775 Esther Sawyer, d 11 May 1840 a.85yrs.

William was mustered in the 7th Rgt 16 or 17 Dec 1776 to be under the command of Col David Gilman to recruit the American army (NHSP 14: 453). He also served as a Cpl in Hezekiah Hutchins Co of volunteers & as a 2nd Lt in Capt Ezekiel Giles Co, Col Stephen Peabody.

Children: 1st 4 born Hampstead, NH (HmstR)
(by 1st wife)

1. **JACOB**, b 15 Feb 1772: d 30 Jun 1864: m Mary Morse
2. **EDNA**, b 29 Jul 1773: d 16 Apr 1800: m Robert Wilson

(by 2nd wife)

3. **RUHAMAH**, b 10 May 1775
4. **NATHANIEL**, b 3 Jan 1779: d 15 Nov 1849: m Hannah Tucker
5. **JOSHUA**, b 25 Feb 1785: m(1) 12 Feb 1812 Lois Hoyt: m(2) 7 Jun 1859 Mary Jackson
6. **AMOS**, b 21 Dec 1796: m 24 Feb 1820 Elsa Eldridge

JAMES RUSSELL was mustered in the 7th Rgt under the command of Col David Gilman, Capt Gordon's Co (RW roll 50).

DANIEL SAMPSON (SAMSON), b Newbury, MA 10 Nov 1758 son of William & Judith (Merrill) Sampson

(NVR): d Barre, NY 27 May 1842: m(1) Cornwall, Vt 31 Oct 1787 Betsey Gilbert (DAR #582698 A561), b Woodbury, Ct Feb 1768: m(2) Cornwall, Vt 2 Apr 1797 Polly Wooster: m(3) 21 Dec 1802 wid Polly Lane.

Daniel enlisted at Kingston 1780 where he resided & served under Capt Penniman, Col Scammell's NH Troops in the Continental Army (NHSP 16:67 & NHPR 72:103).

Children: (DAR #582698A561)

1. **ASHLEY**, b 8 Mar 1790: m Emma Gregory
2. **DANIEL**, 15 Mar 1792: d 21 Mar 1792
3. **FLORA**, b 27 Jul 1793: m 10 Jan 1817 Alvin Bateman
4. **BETSEY**, b 12 Jan 1799: m Horace Linsley
5. **POLLY** (Mary), b 27 Apr 1800: m John Francisco
6. **THANKFUL**, b 18 Mar 1802
7. **GILBERT**, b 20 Apr 1804: m(1) Harriet Bentley: m(2) Sophronia Eells

ABRAHAM SANBORN, b Kingston, NH 2 Mar 1716/7 son of Tristram & Margaret (Taylor) Sanborn (KTR): d Kingston, NH 21 Feb 1780 (NHVR): m Kingston, NH 6 Jan 1736/7 Abigail Clifford (KTR), b Kingston, NH 18 Aug 1713 dau of Joseph & Sarah (French) Clifford (KTR), d Kingston, NH 19 Feb 1797 (NHVR).

Abraham signed the Association Test in Kingston, NH 1776 (NHSP 30:76).

Children: born Kingston, NH (KTR)

1. **JOSEPH CLIFFORD**, b 30 Nov 1737: d Danville, NH 13 Apr 1810 (CG p40): m(1) Danville, NH 4 Dec 1761 Elizabeth French (DnTR): m(2) Danville, NH 26 Feb 1777 Miriam (Fifield) Batchelder (DnTR)
2. **SARAH**, b 26 Mar 1739: d Kingston, NH 28 Dec 1743 (KTR)
3. **JOHN**, b 19 Feb 1740/1: d Chester, NH 3 Dec 1828 a.90yrs (HC p624): m Elizabeth Sargent
4. **DEBORAH**, b 8 Jan 1742/3

5. **SARAH**, b 2 Jul 1745: d Kingston, NH 28 Jul 1746 (KTR)
6. **SARAH**, b 8 Feb 1746/7
7. **JUDITH**, b 30 Nov 1748
8. **SHUAH**, b 11 Feb 1750/1
9. **ISAAC**, b 6 Mar 1752: d Kingston, NH 24 Sep 1803 (NHVR): m Kingston, NH 4 Apr 1782 Abigail French (NHGR 3:131)
10. **ABRAHAM**, bpt 22 Mar 1756 (NHVR): d Kingston, NH 14 Dec 1846: m Hannah Quimby

ABRAHAM SANBORN JR., bpt Kingston, NH 22 Mar 1756 son of Abraham & Abigail (Clifford) Sanborn (NHVR): d Kingston, NH 14 Dec 1846 a.91yrs (GI p25): m Hannah Quimby (Sanborn Gen p108), d Kingston, NH 16 Feb 1849 a.88yrs (GI p25).

Possibly the Abraham Jr who served in Col David Gilman's Rgt, Capt Daniel Gordon's Co (RW roll-50).

BENJAMIN SANBORN, b Kingston, NH 20 May 1719 son of Samuel & Elizabeth (Folsom) Sanborn (KTR): d Salisbury, NH 7 Jan 1806: m(1) Kingston, NH 3 Apr 1746 Dorothy Ladd (KTR), b Kingston, NH 2 Nov 1730 dau of John & Elizabeth (Sanborn) Ladd (KTR): d 27 Jul 1784: m(2) Rebecca ___ (Sanborn Gen p129), b 1737, d 6 Apr 1825 a.88yrs.

Benjamin signed the Association Test in Kingston, NH 1776 (NHSP 30:77).

Children: 1st 7 born Kingston, NH (KTR)

1. **ELIZABETH**, b 15 Nov 1746
2. **LUCY**, b 20 Nov 1748 (Elee in KTR)
3. **BENJAMIN**, b 1750: d 14 May 1756
4. **DOROTHY**, b 29 Jan 1756: m John Call
5. **LYDIA**, b 10 Apr 1758
6. **BENJAMIN**, b 7 Nov 1760: lived in Salisbury, NH
7. **SAMUEL**, b 25 Dec 1762: d Fort Covington, NH 1840: m abt 1785-7 Polly Rolf
8. **SARAH**, m ____ Marston
9. **JOHN**, b 1770: d Salisbury, NH 5 May 1853: m(1) Dorcas Nelson: m(2) 1831 Sarah

Pepperal Ayers (HS p726)
10. **PETER**, m 9 May 1795 Abigail Morrill

DAVID SANBORN, b Kingston, NH 24 May 1753 son of Timothy & Alice (Quimby) Sanborn (KTR): d Kingston, NH 22 Sep 1817 (GI p23): m Kingston, NH 25 Mar 1779 Dorothy Gilman (NHGR 3:130), bpt Kingston, NH 24 Aug 1755 dau of John & Sarah (Stevens) Gilman (NHGR 6:32): d Kingston, NH 2 Oct 1849 (GI p23).

David signed the Association Test in Kingston, NH 1776 (NHSP 30:77).

Children: (Sanborn Gen p192)
1. **DAVID**, b 3 Jul 1780: d Kingston, NH 26 Jun 1866 (GI p23)
2. **BENJAMIN**, b 10 Mar 1782
3. **JOHN GILMAN**, b 26 Jun 1784
4. **DOROTHY**, b 9 Mar 1788: m Kingston, NH 20 Feb 1812 John Page (NHGR 4:179)
5. **JOSEPH CALEF**, b 27 Aug 1794: d Kingston, NH 27 Apr 1820 a.25yrs (GI p23)
6. **SARAH**, b 8 Sep 1797: m Kingston, NH 29 Jan 1822 Joseph Garland (NHGR 5:17)

ENOS SANBORN, bpt Kingston, NH 7 Jun 1752 son of Peter & Mary (Sanborn) Sanborn (NHGR 6:27): d 5 Jan 1824: m Kingston, NH 14 Dec 1772 Sarah Lyford (IGI), b Brentwood, NH 22 Feb 1757 dau of Byley & Judith (Wilson) Lyford (BtTR), d 2 Aug 1810 (MGFH 3:1479).

Enos served as a pvt in Capt Abram French's Co at Great Island for the defense of Piscataqua Harbor (NHSP 14:226).

Children: (Sanborn Gen p141)
1. **SALLY**, b 18 Jun 1779: d 15 Jan 1857: m 4 Feb 1796 Peter Sanborn
2. **ENOS**, b 16 Dec 1785
3. **BETSEY**, b 3 May 1795: m 26 Sep 1814 Francis D. Randall

ISAAC SANBORN, b Kingston, NH 6 Mar 1752 son of Abraham & Abigail (Clifford) Sanborn (KTR): d

Kingston, NH 24 Sep 1803 (NHVR): m Kingston, NH 4 Apr 1782 Abigail French (NHGR 3:131).

Isaac signed the Association Test in Kingston, NH 1776 (NHSP 30:76).

Children: (Sanborn Gen p142-3)

1. **ELIZA**, b 29 Mar 1783: m 20 Sep 1804 John Sanborn
2. **JULIA**, b 21 Oct 1785: d unmd 1809
3. **ABRAHAM**, b 25 Dec 1787: d Kingston, NH 1 Feb 1833 (NHVR): m Epping, NH 16 Sep 1812 Rebecca Lyford (NHGR 3:177)
4. **MOSES**, b 31 Dec 1789: d 1 Oct 1818: m Kingston, NH 3 May 1818 Deborah Hoyt (NHGR 4:179)
5. **SEWELL**, b 5 Nov 1791: d 1828: m Sebec, ME Anna Sands
6. **ISAAC**, b 29 Nov 1793: d Kingston, NH 1 Oct 1862 (GI p26): m 25 Nov 1834 Plooma Stevens
7. **TAPPAN**, b 31 May 1796
8. **WENDALL**, b 4 Jun 1798: d.y.
9. **ARAMINTA**, b 7 Jun 1801: m Kingston, NH 2 May 1819 Robert French Smith (NHGR 4:180)

JETHRO SANBORN, b Kingston, NH 15 Nov 1755 son of William & Mary (Sleeper) Sanborn (KTR): d 22 Jan 1829 (DAR 1:591): m 1779 Elizabeth Rand (Sanborn Gen p144), bpt Hampton, NH 30 Mar 1760 dau of Thomas & Elizabeth (Chapman) Rand (HH p931), d 16 Mar 1836. He lived in Sandwich, NH & Sutton, VT.

Jethro signed the Association Test in Kingston, NH 1776 (NHSP 30:77). He served as a pvt in Capt Ezra Currier's Co, Col Abraham Drake's Rgt 8 Sep to 16 Dec 1777 (RW roll-49).

Children: (Sanborn Gen p144)

1. **MARY**, b 7 Sep 1782: m(1) 1798 Daniel George: m(2) 18 Apr 1830 Leonard Walter
2. **THOMAS**, b 4 Nov 1784: m 1806 Polly Grover
3. **BETSEY**, b 7 Sep 1786: d 3 Nov 1836: m Benjamin Bowlar
4. **DOLLY**, b 23 May 1787: m Daniel Goodell

5. **WILLIAM**, b 30 May 1788: d Sandwich, NH 14 Sep 1854: m 3 Apr 1817 Mary Wilder
6. **NOAH**, b 5 May 1792: d Charlestown, MA 10 Jun 1851: m 1821 Hannah Clark
7. **PETER**, b 5 Jul 1794: d Charlestown, MA Oct 1863: m 13 Sep 1818 Sarah Proctor Whitney
8. **RUTH**, b 7 Dec 1797: d 30 Nov 1843
9. **JOHN**, b 2 Mar 1799: m Deborah Clark
10. **AZEL**, b 14 Jul 1802: d Boston, MA 21 Apr 1877: m 14 Oct 1826 Abigail Lovejoy
11. **PEACE**, b 4 Sep 1804: d 16 Nov 1837

JOHN SANBORN, b Kingston, NH 28 Dec 1743 son of Paul & Mary (Fifield) Sanborn (KTR): d Baldwin or Sebago, ME 1828 (RG 2:608): m(1) Jane Deban: m(2) Susannah ____ (DAR 1:591).

John served as a pvt in Capt Gray's Co, Col Mitchell's MA Rgt (DAR LB 55:120).

Children:

1. **MEHITABLE**, b 1771
2. **JONATHAN**, b 1773
3. **LYDIA**, b 1775
4. **BENJAMIN**, b 1777: m Abigail Hobbs
5. **MARY**, b 1779
6. **WILLIAM**, b 1781: d Sebago, ME 25 Jan 1834: m Miriam Hobbs

JONATHAN SANBORN, bpt Kingston, NH 4 Feb 1738/9 son of Paul & Mary (Fifield) Sanborn (NHGR 5:104): d Kingston, NH 23 May 1809 (GI p27): m Kingston, NH 19 Sep 1758 Lydia Severance (NHGR 3:90), b abt 1739 (bpt as an adult - Kingston, NH 5 Aug 1758) dau of Jonathan & Catherine (Tucker) Severance, d Kingston, NH 1 Apr 1827 a.88yrs (GI p27).

Jonathan signed the Association Test in Kingston, NH 1776 (NHSP 30:77). He was mustered by Col Josiah Bartlett Oct 1777 & served in Capt Ezra Currier's Co, Col Abraham Drake's Rgt 8 Sep to 16 Dec 1777 (RW roll-49).

Children:

1. **CATHERINE**, b 14 May 1768: d Kingston, NH 13 Jun 1816 (GI p20): m Kingston, NH Jan 1786 Nicholas Nichols (NHGR 3:132)

JONATHAN SANBORN JR, b Kingston, NH 23 Nov 1738 son of Jonathan & Theodate (Sanborn) Sanborn (KTR): d Kingston, NH Mar 1782 (NHVR): m(1) Kingston, NH 15 Dec 1761 Sarah James (KTR), b Kensington, NH 31 Mar 1740 dau of Israel & Ruth (Marston) James (NHVR), d 27 May 1767: m(2) Kingston, NH 26 Jan 1768 Mary Swett (KTR), b Kingston, NH 26 Mar 1737 dau of Nathan & Mary (Dearborn) Swett (KTR), d 3 Jun 1817 (Sanborn Gen p130).

Jonathan Jr signed the Association Test in Kingston, NH 1776 (NHSP 30:78).

Children: born Kingston, NH (KTR)
(by 1st wife)

1. **JONATHAN**, b 8 Mar 1764: d 28 Jun 1843: m Kingston, NH 25 Apr 1787 Mary Morrill (NHGR 3:132)
2. **ISRAEL**, b 3 Feb 1767: d 19 Dec 1843: m 11 Nov 1788 Patta Morgan

(by 2nd wife)

3. **JOSEPH**, b 3 Aug 1770: d 7 Mar 1836: m 27 Oct 1794 Sally Thing

MOSES SANBORN, b Kingston, NH 17 Jul 1742 son of Tristram & Abigail (Blake) Sanborn (KTR): d Salisbury, NH 27 Jun 1821 (NHPR 73:29): m Deliverance ____, a.73yrs in 1820.

Moses, of Kingston, was mustered 30 Sep 1776 & served in Capt Mark Wiggin's Co, Col Pierce Long's Rgt at Portsmouth (NHSP 14:370,377). He also enlisted Apr 1777 under Capt Robinson & served until after the Battle at Monmouth, NJ at which time he was under Capt Hutchins, Col Cilley 1st NH Rgt (NHPR 73:28).

Children: (HG p727)

1. **ABIGAIL**, m ___ Clay
2. **SARAH**, m John Barber
3. **LYDIA**, m ___ Colby

4. **DELIVERANCE**, m ___ Bean
5. **MARY**, m ___ Mills
6. **BETSEY**, m ___ George
7. **MEHITABLE**
8. **HANNAH**, m Samuel Tandy

PETER SANBORN, b Kingston, NH 25 May 1713 son of Tristram & Margaret (Taylor) Sanborn (KTR): d Kingston, NH 15 Jan 1810 (NHVR): m Kingston, NH 14 Dec 1732 Mary Sanborn (KTR), b Kingston, NH 7 Dec 1713 dau of Jonathan & Elizabeth (Sherburne) Sanborn (KTR): d Kingston, NH 5 Oct 1782 (NHVR).

Peter signed the Association Test in Kingston, NH 1776 (NHSP 30:77).

Children: born Kingston, NH (KTR)

1. **(DAU)**, d Kingston, NH 19 Apr 1733 (NHGR 2:133)
2. **JOHN**, b 10 Mar 1733/4: d Kingston, NH 11 Feb 1734/5 (KTR)
3. **PETER**, b 1 Jun 1735: d Kingston, NH 21 Dec 1735 (KTR)
4. **JOHN**, b 20 Sep 1736: d Kingston, NH 6 May 1737 (KTR)
5. **MARY**, b 10 Mar 1738: m 12 Jul 1756 Joseph Kimball
6. **BENJAMIN**, b 26 Dec 1739: d 18 Nov 1824: m Kensington, NH 17 Dec 1761 Theodate Batchelder (NHVR)
7. **SARAH**, b 1 Mar 1742: m 9 Feb 1767 Samuel Philbrick
8. **TRISTRAM**, bpt 20 Apr 1746 (NHGR 5:153): d Enfield, NH: m(1) Sally Clifford: m(2) Molly Lyford
9. **PETER**, b 27 Jan 1747/8: d 11 Dec 1818: m Anna Scribner
10. **JOHN**, b 22 Mar 1749/50: d 1788: m Alice Lyford
11. **ENOS**, bpt 7 Jun 1752 (NHGR 6:27): d 5 Jan 1824: m Kingston, NH 14 Dec 1772 Sarah Lyford

TIMOTHY SANBORN, b Kingston, NH 15 Aug 1720 son

of Jonathan & Theodate (Sanborn) Sanborn (KTR): d Kingston, NH (bur) 22 Mar 1794 (NHVR): m Kingston, NH 8 May 1745/6 Alice Quimby (NHGR 3:42), b Kingston, NH 17 Nov 1726 dau of David & Abigail (Webster) Quimby (KTR).

Timothy signed the Association Test in Kingston, NH 1776 (NHSP 30:77).

Children: born Kingston, NH (KTR)

1. **BENJAMIN**, b 27 May 1747: d 1782: m Danville, NH 25 Aug 1772 Hannah Thorn (NEHGR 58:122)
2. **ABIGAIL**, b 10 Sep 1749: m Danville, NH 10 Jan 1778 James Thorn (NHPR 86:33)
3. **DAVID**, b 24 May 1753: d Kingston, NH 22 Sep 1817: m Kingston, NH 25 Mar 1779 Dorothy Gilman (NHGR 3:130)
4. **SAMUEL**, b 8 Nov 1755: m Abigail Hobbs
5. **ALICE** (Ellas), b 23 Dec 1758: m Kingston, NH 5 Nov 1787 Joseph Tucker (NHGR 3:133)
6. **MARY**, b 28 Mar 1761: d Kingston, NH 11 Jul 1839 (NHVR)
7. **SARAH**, b 1 Oct 1763: m Kingston, NH 29 Apr 1795 David Buzzell (NHGR 3:136)
8. **JOHN QUIMBY**, b 9 Jul 1766: d Kingston, NH 13 Jun 1840 (GI p24): m 30 Jun 1785 Elizabeth Kimball

WILLIAM SANBORN, b Kingston, NH 1 May 1723 son of Tristram & Margaret (Taylor) Sanborn (KTR): d Kingston, NH (bur) 25 May 1810 (NHVR): m(1) Kingston, NH 6 Nov 1750 Mary Sleeper (KTR), b Kingston, NH 9 Mar 1729 dau of Moses & Margaret (Sanborn) Sleeper (KTR), d Kingston, NH 17 Oct 1773 (KTR): m(2) Kingston, NH 3 Jun 1774 Mrs Elizabeth Weare (KTR): m(3) Kingston, NH Oct 1788 Widow Elizabeth Chase (NHGR 3:133), d Chester, NH 19 Dec 1811 (Sanborn Gen p109).

William signed the Association Test in Kingston, NH 1776 (NHSP 30:76).

Children: born Kingston, NH (KTR)

1. **MARGARET**, b 2 Nov 1751: d 30 Nov 1835: m Stephen Fifield (TAG 19:100)

2. **HULDAH**, b 15 Dec 1752: d Kingston, NH 23 Feb 1838 a.85yrs (GI p14): m Kingston, NH 29 Jan 1778 Joseph Hoit (NHGR 3:130)
3. **JETHRO**, b 15 Nov 1755: d 22 Jan 1829: m 1779 Elizabeth Rand
4. **MARY**, b 13 Jan 1758: d 27 Jan 1839 (TAG 19:100): m Hampton Falls, NH 8 Apr 1773 Ebenezer Fifield
5. **TRISTRAM**, b 13 Oct 1759: d 28 Oct 1834: m Kingston, NH 31 Dec 1782 Patience Page (NHGR 3:131)
6. **NOAH**, b 15 Oct 1761: d Kingston, NH 4 Apr 1838 a.78yrs (GI p25): m Hampstead, NH 30 Apr 1793 Hannah Shaw (HmstR)
7. **DOROTHY**, b 12 Nov 1763: d Kingston, NH 19 Feb 1847: unmd
8. **JOSEPH** (twin), b 3 Apr 1765
9. **BENJAMIN** (twin), b 3 Apr 1765: d Kingston, NH 13 Sep 1830 (GI p25): m(1) Kingston, NH 14 Mar 1802 Rebecca Smith (NHGR 3:171): m(2) Kingston, NH 21 Aug 1810 Hannah Fifield (NHGR 4:178)
10. **PETER**, b 13 Aug 1767: d 8 Aug 1857: m(1) 26 May 1798 Polly Simpson: m(2) 10 Nov 1819 Martha Wakefield
11. **WILLIAM**, b 13 Mar 1769: d Falmouth, ME 13 Mar 1847: m 21 Feb 1847 Nancy Merrill

MATHEW SCALES, of Boscawen, NH, enlisted for Kingston in the 7th Rgt of NH Militia in the Continental Army 1777, Capt James Gray's Co (NHSP 14:585).

SIMMONS SECOMBE, b Derryfield, NH 1 Dec 1740 son of Simmons & Elizabeth (Rand) Secombe (IGI): d Kingston, NH 10 Jun 1810 (GI p28): m So Hampton, NH 10 Oct 1770 Mary Toppan (SHVR), b Newbury, MA 27 Sep 1742 dau of Samuel & Dorothy (Moody) Toppan (NVR), d Kingston, NH 21 Mar 1813 a.70yrs (GI p28).

Simmons signed the Association Test in Kingston, NH 1776 (NHSP 30:76).

Children: born Kingston, NH

1. **DOROTHY**, b 9 Jul 1771: d Kingston, NH 19 Oct 1777 (NHVR)
2. **ELIZABETH**, b 10 Feb 1773: d Kingston, NH 7 Sep 1777 (NHVR)
3. **MARY**, b 11 Jul 1775
4. **MEHITABLE**, b 15 Mar 1779
5. **DOROTHY**, b 15 Mar 1779: d Kingston, NH 25 Oct 1837 a.58yrs (GI p28)
6. **ELIZABETH**, b 9 Feb 1781: d Kingston, NH 13 Feb 1869 (GI p21): m Kingston, NH Feb 1805 Daniel Peaslee (NHGR 4:174)
7. **SARAH**, b 12 Jun 1783: d Tamworth, NH 26 Aug 1855 m Kingston, NH 28 Nov 1805 Jacob Pollard (NHGR 4:175)
8. **JOSEPH TOPPAN**, b 2 Mar 1786

CALEB SEVER, b Kingston, NH 12 Sep 1746 son of Thomas & Martha (Webster) Sever (KTR): d Kingston, NH 18 Mar 1821 (NHVR): m Mercy Pollard (Pollard Gen 1:97), b Kingston, NH 11 Feb 1756 dau of Francis & Sarah (Webster) Pollard (KTR), d Kingston, NH 10 Jul 1818 a.66yrs (NHVR)

Caleb signed the Association Test in Kingston, NH 1776 (NHSP 30:78). He served in Capt John Calef's Co (NHSP 14:405).

ELIJAH SEVER, b Kingston, NH 19 Dec 1762 son of Thomas & Martha (Webster) Sever (KTR): d Kingston, NH 23 Jan 1822 (GI p28): m Sarah ___, b abt 1755: d Kingston, NH 14 Oct 1847 a.91yrs (GI p28).

Elijah served as a pvt in the NH Militia Capt Jacob Webster's Co, Col Daniel Reynold's Rgt Jul to Nov 1781 (RW roll-52).

THOMAS SEVER, b 30 Mar 1716 son of Thomas & Elizabeth (Greeley) Sever (NEHGR 26:307): d aft 1790: m Kingston, NH 10 Dec 1745 Martha Webster (KTR), b Kingston, NH 16 Jun 1722 dau of Thomas & Mary (Greeley) Webster (KTR).

Thomas signed the Association Test in Kingston, NH 1776 (NHSP 30:78).

Children: born Kingston, NH (KTR)

1. **CALEB**, b 12 Sep 1746: d Kingston, NH 18 Mar 1821: m Mercy Pollard
2. **(CHILD)**, d Kingston, NH 24 Apr 1749 (NH VR)
3. **ELIZABETH**, b 19 Apr 1750
4. **THOMAS**, b 19 Nov 1752
5. **MARY**, b 24 Mar 1756
6. **ELIJAH**, b 19 Dec 1762: d Kingston, NH 23 Jan 1822 (GI p28): m Sarah ____
7. **ELISHA**, b 20 Aug 1767: d Kingston, NH Dec 1803 (NHVR): m Patience Carter

THOMAS SEVER JR, b Kingston, NH 19 Nov 1752 son of Thomas & Martha (Webster) Sever (KTR).
Thomas Jr. signed the Association Test in Kingston, NH 1776 (NHSP 30:78).

EPHRAIM SEVERANCE, b 1759 (RG 2:619): d Knox, ME 6 Mar 1825 (NHPR 75:74): m Rye, NH 30 Oct 1785 Ruth Gould (Rye VR), b May 1764 (NHPR 75:74) possibly dau of Christopher & Elizabeth (Waters) Gould, d 18 Apr 1836 (DAR #181958A193)
Ephraim enlisted in Kingston 1775 & served as a pvt in Capt Gilman's Co, Col John Nixon's 5th Rgt MA Line. He also served in Capt John Winslow's Co 1777 #W25172 (NHPR 75:73 & MAS&S 13:1009).

Children: (DAR #181958A193)
1. **(DAU)**, m ____ Mulhoon
2. **JAMES**, b 18 Mar 1786
3. **JACOB**, b 1788: d 1859: m Aug 1813 Susanna (Haskell) Severance
4. **EPHRAIM**, a.21yrs in 1820 (NHPR 75:74)

JOHN SEVERANCE, bpt Kingston, NH 9 Sep 1750 son of Ephraim Jr & Elizabeth (Swett) Severance (NHGR 5:159): m ____
John who signed the Association Test in Kingston, NH 1776 (NHSP 30:78).

Children:
1. **(INFANT)**, d Kingston, NH 11 May 1778 (NHVR)

JONATHAN SEVERANCE, b Kingston, NH 31 Jul 1757 son of Jonathan & Tryphene (Nichols) Severance (KTR): d Tuftonborough, NH 5 Mar 1835 (NHPR 75: 78): m Kingston, NH 18 Jan 1781 Mehitable Brown (NHPR 75:78), d Tuftonborough, NH aft 1840.

Jonathan enlisted 1775 in the NH Militia under Capt Gilman, Col Poor. He was mustered by Col Josiah Bartlett Oct 1777 & served in Capt Ezra Currier's Co, Col Abraham Drake's Rgt (NH PR 75:76 & RW roll-49).

Children: born Belmont, NH (IGI)
1. **JONATHAN**, b 4 Jul 1781
2. **SARAH**, b 10 Sep 1784
3. **SAMUEL**, b 1 May 1793

PETER SEVERANCE, b Kingston, NH 6 Mar 1754 son of Ephraim & Elizabeth (Swett) Severance (KTR): d Bradford, VT 31 Jul 1835: m Salisbury, NH 20 Sep 1779 Abigail (Greeley) Pettengill (Greeley Gen p102), b Salisbury, MA 9 Sep 1749 dau of Benjamin & Ruth (Eastman) Greeley (SVR), d Bradford, VT 5 Feb 1819. Abigail m(1) Salisbury, MA 23 Apr 1769 Andrew Pettengill (SVR).

Peter enlisted 1775 under Capt Henry Dearborn, Col John Stark. In 1776, he enlisted at Deerfield, NH & came to Kingston to visit his mother. After staying only one night, he left to join the American Army where he served under Capt Joseph Dearborn, Col Isaac Wyman. He enlisted again in 1777 under Capt Ebenezer Webster, Col Stickney & was in the Battle of Bennington at the taking of Burgoyne #S19077 (NHPR 75:92).

Children: born Salisbury, NH (Greeley Gen p102)
1. **BETSEY**, b 27 Jul 1780: m(1) ___ Lyon: m (2) ___ Hoyt
2. **ANDREW P.**, b 9 Jul 1782: d 6 Apr 1803
3. **REUBEN G.**, b 6 Jun 1784: m(1) Bradford, VT 1809 Hadanah Smith: m(2) Bradford, VT Dec 1829 Anna Smith (Greeley Gen p199)
4. **RUTH**, b 8 Aug 1786: d Bradford, VT 28 Aug 1833: m Bradford, VT 6 Mar 1806 Moses

Smith
5. **PETER**, b 25 Dec 1788: d 6 Apr 1819
6. **MOSES**, b 30 Sep 1792: d Bradford, VT 10 May 1871: m Bradford, VT 11 Sep 1814 Lydia Stevens

SAMUEL SEVERANCE, b abt 1741: d aft 1832 (NHPR 75:77): m Kingston, NH 1 Aug 1768 Hannah Winslow (KTR), b Kingston, NH 22 Apr 1743 dau of Samuel & Frances (?Tucker) Winslow (KTR).
Samuel, of Kingston (a.34yrs), served in Col Enoch Poor's Rgt, Capt Philip Tilton's Co 1775 (RW roll-51).

Children: born Kingston, NH (KTR)
1. **HANNAH**, b 3 Jul 1769: d Newburyport, MA 15 Mar 1855: m Newbury, MA (int) 25 Mar 1799 Henry Adams (NVR)
2. **PHEBE**, b 31 Aug 1771
3. **ELIZABETH**, b 5 Aug 1773
4. **SAMUEL**, b 25 Aug 1775: d Kingston, NH 26 Aug 1836 a.61yrs (NHVR): m Kingston, NH 6 Jan 1802 Judith Towle (NHGR 3:171)
5. **KATHERINE**, b 9 May 1778

THOMAS SEVERANCE, of Kingston, served in Capt Hutchin's Co, Col Joseph Cilley's Rgt Feb 1777 (NHSP 14:611). He also served as a Cpl in NH Militia Col Daniel Reynold's Rgt, Capt J. Webster's Co Jul to Nov 1781 (RW roll-52).

LEVI SHAW, bpt Hampton, NH 18 Feb 1759 son of Edward & Ruth (Fellows) Shaw (HH p970): d Minot, ME 8 Nov 1834 (Shaw Rec p61): m(1) Betty ___, d 30 Sep 1803: m(2) Salisbury, MA (int) 18 Sep 1804 Sarah Fellows (SVR), d Minot, ME 20 Sep 1808: m(3) 15 Mar 1810 Dorcas Millet, d 6 Jun 1832.
Levi enlisted at Kingston latter part of summer (no year given) & served under Capt Kiah, Col Drake at the taking of Burgoyne. He enlisted again 1780 & served as a Cpl under Capt Butler (NHPR 75:176).

Children: (Shaw Records by H. Farwell p61)

1. **LEVI**, b 25 May 1811: m Charlotte Wyatt
2. **MARY**, b 7 Oct 1812: d 13 Aug 1893: m Gloucester, MA (int) 29 May 1836 Lemuel Gott (GlVR)
3. **LYDIA**, b 26 Jun 1814: d 12 Aug 1843
4. **DAVID**, b 16 Jun 1816: d Carson City, NV 3 Aug 1863
5. **SIMEON**, b 7 Apr 1819: d NY City
6. **JOHN**, b 22 Feb 1821: d Stuart, IA 26 Sep 1876
7. **DORCAS**, b 14 Feb 1823: m Joel Worthing
8. **SARAH**, b 8 Nov 1825: d 27 Aug 1840

WILLIAM SHAW, was mustered Dec 1776 in the 7th Rgt under the command of Col David Gilman, Capt Gordon's Co (RW roll-50).

BENJAMIN WEBSTER SILLOWAY, b Kingston, NH 21 Sep 1752 son of Jacob & Alice (Webster) Silloway (KTR): d aft 1800: m Mary Severance, d Kingston, NH 23 Dec 1812 a.59yrs (GI p29).

Benjamin was a volunteer in Col Jacob Gale's Rgt, Capt Quimby's Co Aug 1778 (RW roll-50).

Children: born Kingston, NH

1. **SARAH**, b 27 Feb 1775: d Kingston, NH 29 Sep 1778 (NHVR)
2. **ALICE**, b 21 Sep 1777: d Kingston, NH 7 Oct 1778 (NHVR)
3. **JACOB**, b 7 Jul 1779
4. **SARAH**, b 26 Dec 1781
5. **BENJAMIN**, b 27 Aug 1784: d Kingston, NH 23 Jan 1870 (GI p29): m Kingston, NH 30 Oct 1809 Polly Davis (NHGR 4:177)
6. **GEORGE**, b 4 Mar 1787: d (prob bur) Kingston, NH 7 Mar 1787 (NHVR)

GREELEY SILLOWAY, b Kingston, NH 11 Aug 1759 son of Jacob & Alice (Webster) Silloway (KTR): d aft 1800.

Greeley went as a volunteer to join the Army at Winter Hill after the news of the Battle of Lexington reached Kingston (NHPR 15:128).

JACOB SILLOWAY, b Kingston, NH 11 Dec 1755 son of Jacob & Alice (Webster) Silloway (KTR).
Jacob, of Kingston (a.20yrs), served in Col Enoch Poor's Rgt, Capt Philip Tilton's Co 1775 (RW roll-51).

JOHN SINGLETON, d Kingston, NH 20 Jul 1796 (NHVR).
John signed the Association Test in Kingston, NH 1776 (NHSP 30:78).

BENJAMIN SLEEPER, b Kingston, NH 14 Feb 1733 son of Moses & Margaret (Sanborn) Sleeper (KTR): m(1) 9 Apr 1750 Hannah Hersey (DAR manuscript): m(2) Kingston, NH 11 Apr 1759 Hannah Lovering (KTR).
Benjamin signed the Association Test in Kingston, NH 1776 (NHSP 30:77).

Children: born Kingston, NH (KTR)
1. **MARY**, b 4 May 1759
2. **HANNAH**, b 21 Jan 1761
3. **SARAH**, b 5 May 1763
4. **ANNE**, b 10 Oct 1765
5. **BENJAMIN**, b 3 Dec 1767

EDWARD SLEEPER, b Kingston, NH 26 Oct 1719 son of Aaron & Sarah (_) Sleeper (KTR): d Kingston, NH 16 Mar 1811 (GI p29): m Kingston, NH 15 Sep 1746 Ann Clough (KTR), b Kingston, NH 3 Jan 1723/4 dau of Cornelius & Ann (Evans) Clough (KTR), d Kingston, NH 16 Jan 1815 a.93yrs (GI p29).
Edward signed the Association Test in Kingston, NH 1776 (NHSP 30:77).

Children: born Kingston, NH (KTR)
1. **JOHN**, b 21 Mar 1746/7: m Danville, NH 2 Apr 1772 Judith Badger (NEHGR 58:122)
2. **SARAH**, b 9 Oct 1750
3. **JONATHAN**, b 28 Feb 1754: d Kingston, NH 4 Sep 1811 (GI p29): m 24 Mar 1785 Mary Clark
4. **ANN**, b 17 Sep 1757

5. **ABIGAIL**, b 27 Jul 1762
6. **HANNAH**, b 1 Nov 1767: d Loudon, NH 4 Nov 1859: m Bartholow Winslow

JOHN SLEEPER, b Kingston, NH 21 Mar 1746/7 son of Edward & Ann (Clough) Sleeper (KTR): m Danville, NH 2 Apr 1772 Judith Badger (NEHGR 58: 122), bpt Amesbury, MA 23 Sep 1750 dau of Jonathan & Sarah (Currier) Badger (AVR).

John signed the Association Test in Kingston, NH 1776 (NHSP 30:78).

Children: (UR p49)

1. **JONATHAN**, b Kingston, NH 25 Jun 1775
2. **AARON**, b Kingston, NH 10 Mar 1779
3. **JOHN**, b Kingston, NH 13 Jul 1783
4. **EDWARD**, b Unity, NH 12 Jun 1787

JOHN BLAISDEL SLEEPER, b Kingston, NH 31 Aug 1752 son of William & Dorothy (Rowell) Sleeper (KTR): d Kingston, NH 7 Aug 1830 (GI p29): m 30 Jan 1776 Mary Burbank (DAR manuscript), b Rowley, MA 7 Feb 1757 dau of Eleazer & Mercy (Bailey) Burbank (RwVR).

John signed the Association Test in Kingston, NH 1776 (NHSP 30:78). He was mustered by Col Josiah Bartlett Oct 1777 & served in Capt Ezra Currier's Co, Col Abraham Drake's Rgt 8 Sep to 16 Dec 1777 (RW roll-49).

Children: (DAR manuscript)

1. **WILLIAM**, b 19 Nov 1776: m Kingston, NH 17 Nov 1801 Betsey Hubbard (NHGR 3:170)
2. **MOLLY**, b 14 Mar 1780
3. **SAMUEL**, b 15 Oct 1786: m Sarah Webster
4. **JOHN**, b 28 Apr 1791: m Betsey Jones
5. **HANNAH**, b 15 Dec 1794
6. **DAVID**, b 5 Mar 1799

JONATHAN SLEEPER, b Kingston, NH 6 Dec 1716 son of Moses & Margaret (Sanborn) Sleeper (KTR): m Kingston, NH 4 Nov 1740 Lydia Huntoon (NHGR 3: 40), b abt 1723, bpt Kingston, NH 8 May 1726 dau of John & Mary (Rundlett) Huntoon (NHGR 2:

46).
Jonathan signed the Association Test in Kingston, NH 1776 (NHSP 30:78).

Children: bpt Kingston, NH (NHGR)
1. **HANNAH**, bpt 8 Mar 1740/1
2. **JONATHAN**, bpt 3 Nov 1742
3. **MEHITABLE**, bpt 11 Nov 1744
4. **DOROTHY**, bpt 12 Oct 1746: d Kingston, NH 2 Oct 1747 (NHVR)
5. **DOROTHY**, bpt 17 Jul 1748
6. **SANBORN**, bpt 27 Jan 1750/51: m (prob) Danville, NH 28 Apr 1774 Dorcas Graves (NEHGR 58:123)

JONATHAN SLEEPER, b Kingston, NH 28 Feb 1754 son of Edward & Ann (Clough) Sleeper (KTR): d Kingston, NH 4 Sep 1811 a.57yrs (GI p29): m 24 Mar 1785 Mary Clark, d Kingston, NH 29 Nov 1832 a.74yrs (GI p1). Mary m(2) ____ Badger.
Jonathan served in Col Enoch Poor's Rgt, Capt Philip Tilton's Co (NHSP 14:147).

Children:
1. **ANNA**, b 1 Oct 1798: m Joseph Wadleigh

RICHARD SLEEPER, b Kingston, NH 17 Apr 1738 son of Moses & Margaret (Sanborn) Sleeper (KTR): d Kingston, NH 1 Apr 1813 (NHVR): m Kingston, NH 22 Apr 1762 Martha Fifield (KTR), b abt 1744 dau of Jonathan & Miriam (Veasey) Fifield (TAG 19:105).
Richard signed the Association Test in Kingston, NH 1776 (NHSP 30:76). He was a Lt in Capt Abraham French's Co of Kingston (DAR LB 54:333).

Children: born Kingston, NH (KTR)
1. **ELIZABETH**, b 15 Feb 1763: m Kingston, NH Nov 1783 Samuel Stevens (NHGR 3:132)
2. **MIRIAM**, b 12 Dec 1764
3. **JONATHAN FIFIELD**, b 1 Jun 1767: d 16 Dec 1805: m Exeter, NH 20 Nov 1791 Dorothy Tilton (HE p42g)

4. **DOROTHY** (Dolly), b 25 Nov 1769: m Kingston, NH 17 Apr 1787 Benjamin Batchelder (NHGR 3:132)
5. **MARTHA**, b 16 May 1772: m Kingston, NH 11 Apr 1798 Jacob Elliot (NHGR 3:168)
6. **LEVI**, b 22 Apr 1777: m Kingston, NH 23 Feb 1800 Elizabeth Lovering (NHGR 3:169)
7. **ANNAH**, bpt 7 May 1780 (NHVR)
8. **MOLLY**, b 19 Oct 1781: d Kingston, NH 15 Jul 1855 a.74yrs (GI p4): m Kingston, NH 26 May 1802 Robert Calef (NHGR 3:171)
9. **SHERBURN**, b 4 May 1784
10. **RICHARD**, b 31 Aug 1786

WILLIAM SLEEPER, bpt Kingston, NH 11 Sep 1726 son of Joseph & Sarah (Hutchins) Sleeper (NHGR 2:47): d (w) 20 Jun 1787: m(1) Kingston, NH 14 Mar 1745 Dorothy (Rowell) Blaisdel (KTR), b Amesbury, MA 20 Jan 1720/1 dau of Philip & Sarah (Davis) Rowell (AVR): m(2) Ruth Choate (PRNH 6:300).

William signed the Association Test in Kingston, NH 1776 (NHSP 30:77).

Children: born Kingston, NH (KTR)

1. **DOROTHY**, b 1 Apr 1746: d Kingston, NH 3 Dec 1749 (KTR)
2. **ANNE**, b 2 Sep 1748: d Kingston, NH 22 Apr 1749 (KTR)
3. **DOROTHY**, b 6 Apr 1750: m Danville, NH 26 Apr 1770 John Challis (NEHGR 58:122)
4. **JOHN BLAISDEL**, b 31 Aug 1752: d Kingston, NH 7 Aug 1830 (GI p29): m 30 Jan 1776 Mary Burbank
5. **ANNA**, b 29 Jan 1755: m Danville, NH 9 Jun 1774 Jeremy Webster (NEHGR 58:123)
6. **ELIZABETH**, b 27 Jun 1757: d Kingston, NH 28 Nov 1758 (KTR)
7. **ELIZABETH**, b 7 Apr 1760: m Samuel Cammet (RG 1:105)

DANIEL SMITH, b Exeter, NH 13 Apr 1730 son of Nathaniel & Elizabeth (Stone) Smith (HE p43g): d Kingston, NH (bur) 2 Nov 1803 a.74yrs (NHVR):

m Kingston, NH 30 Aug 1757 Hannah Colby (NHGR 3:89).

Daniel Signed the Association Test in Kingston, NH 1776 (NHSP 30:77).

Children: bpt Kingston, NH

1. **BETTY**, bpt 16 Jul 1758 (NHVR)
2. **PATIENCE**, bpt 18 May 1760 (NHVR)
3. **DANIEL**, bpt 22 Aug 1762 (KChR)

DANIEL SMITH, d 11 Mar 1847 (NHPR 78:17): m Machias, ME 28 Jul 1798 Phebe Larabee (NHPR 78:17) dau of Moses & Sarah (Sanborn) Larabee (Saco Valley p847), living Machiasport, ME in 1853.

Daniel resided in Kingston during the Rev War & served as a Sgt in Capt Parsons's NH Co, Col David Gilman's Rgt (RW roll-50). He also served under Capt Kimball & was at Saratoga and Ticonderoga, marching in the NH Militia to the Northern Continental Army (NHPR 78:17).

Children: b Machias, ME

1. **PHEBE**, b 17 May 1806
2. **DANIEL**, b 17 Feb 1810
3. **SALLY**, m William Larabee

ISRAEL SMITH, d 15 Nov 1775 of camp fever while still in the service: m Poplin, NH 3 Sep 1770 Hannah Colby (NHPR 78:89), living Claremont, NH 1838 a.83yrs.

Israel enlisted at Kingston May 1775 & served as a pvt under Capt Philip Tilton, Col Poor NH Militia (NHPR 78:89).

ITHIEL SMITH, bpt Kingston, NH 22 Mar 1740/1 son of Ithiel & Catherine (_) Smith (NHGR 5:107): d Newry, ME 18 Jun 1821 (RG 2:637): m(1) Bathsheba Foot: m(2) Gorham ME (int) 17 Jul 1779 Anna Bean, b Chester, NH 19 Mar 1753 dau of Jonathan & Abigail (Gordon) Bean (ME Fam 2:264), d Newry, ME 19 Dec 1821.

Probably the Ithiel who enlisted 19 Jul 1775 & served as a drummer in Capt David Stout's Co

(MAS&S 14:421).

Children: (Hist of Limington, ME p307-08)
(by 1st wife)
1. **BETSEY**, b 11 Sep 1765: d Parsonfield, ME 10 Nov 1849: m John Lougee
2. **ITHIEL JR**, b Oct 1767: d Newry, ME 26 Dec 1838: m abt 1792/3 Lucy Littlehale
3. **POLLY**, m 4 May 1794 Simeon Lougee
4. **SALLY**, b 20 Aug 1775: d Jan 1769: m Bethel, ME 29 Jan 1793 Aaron Barton
5. **JAMES YOUNG**, b 1776: d Parsonsfield, ME 14 Sep 1842
6. **CATHERINE**, m Stephen Bowers & moved to NY

(by 2nd wife)
7. **JONATHAN**, b 1780: d Bethel, ME 1 Aug 1859: m (int) Newry, ME 14 Nov 1808 Lydia Brown (ME Fam 2:264)
8. **JESSE**, b abt 1788: living Grafton, 1860
9. **DAVID**, b 1789: d 18 Feb 1856: m (int) Newry, ME 2 Feb 1807 Hannah Brown
10. **JOSIAH**, b 1791: d Newry, ME 19 Jan 1880
11. **ANNA**, m Sargent Bean of Bethel, ME
12. **PETER GILMAN**, b Newry, ME 11 Feb 1795: d Bethel, ME 25 Dec 1875: m Polly Brown

JACOB SMITH, b (prob) Brentwood, NH 20 Oct 1755 son of Jacob & Jemima (Bean) Smith (BtTR): m Danville, NH 21 Apr 1777 Mary Gilman (NEHGR 58:124).

Jacob signed the Association Test in Kingston, NH 1776 (NHSP 30:77).

JOHN SMITH, d 1 Mar 1778 (NHPR 78:137).

John, of Boscawen, NH, enlisted for Kingston in the 7th Rgt of NH Militia in the Continental Army 1777. Served in Capt James Gray's Co (NHSP 14:585,659).

SAMUEL SPOFFORD, b Andover, MA 26 Apr 1757 son of Thomas & Roxbee (Moody) Spofford (AndVR): d Kingston, NH 1 Mar 1835 a.78yrs (GI p30): m Kingston, NH 18 Jun 1797 Lydia Peaslee (NHGR 3: 168), b abt 1770 dau of Jacob & Martha (Challis) Peaslee (NH Gen Digest p193), d Kingston, NH 5 Dec 1834 (GI p30).

Samuel Spofford of Kingston, NH a.75yrs deposed 17 Aug 1832,that he enlisted 15 Dec 1776 under Capt Gage, Col Pinckney & that in Sep or Oct 1777, he volunteered under Capt John Adams to march against Burgoyne. He then enlisted into a Co of Artificers under Capt Boynton (NHPR 79:132).

Children: (Spofford Gen p86)

1. **JAMES**, b 12 Jul 1797: m Haverhill, MA 16 Dec 1824 Martha Johnson (HvVR)
2. **ORIN**, b 19 May 1800: d Kingston, NH Apr 1803 (NHVR)
3. **ORIN P.**, b 4 Jun 1804: d Kingston, NH 25 Oct 1856 (GI p30): m Kingston, NH 23 Jul 1829 Susan Clement (NHGR 5:19)
4. **MERINDA**, b 11 May 1808: m Kingston, NH 30 Dec 1828 Thomas Bassett (NHGR 5:19)
5. **ROXBEE**, b 15 Nov 1810: d Kingston, NH 23 Jun 1834 (GI p30)

BENJAMIN STEVENS, b Kingston, NH 2 Oct 1737 son of Benjamin & Sarah (Fifield) Stevens (KTR): m Kingston, NH 15 Sep 1760 Ann Colcord (KTR), b abt 1735 dau of Edward & Mary (Gordon) Colcord (TAG 17:219).

Benajmin signed the Association Test in Kingston, NH 1776 (NHSP 30:77).

Children: born Kingston, NH (KTR)

1. **SAMUEL**, b 28 Jul 1761
2. **ELIZABETH**, b 23 Apr 1763
3. **SARAH**, b 13 Nov 1765
4. **BENJAMIN**, b 13 Nov 1767
5. **EDWARD**, d Kingston, NH 9 Oct 1772 a.10mo (GI p30)

CESAR STEVENS was mustered by Col Josiah Bartlett Oct 1777. He served in Capt Ezra Currier's Co, Col Abraham Drake's Rgt 8 Sep to 16 Dec 1777 (RW roll-49).

EBENEZER STEVENS, b Kingston, NH 14 Jun 1715 son of Ebenezer & Elizabeth (Colcord) Stevens (KTR): d Kingston, NH (bur) 19 Jul 1800 (NHVR): m(1) Kingston, NH 21 Oct 1736 Mary Colcord (KTR), b Kingston, NH 1 Jan 1714/5 dau of Samuel & Elizabeth (Folsom) Colcord (KTR), d Kingston, NH 16 Aug 1768 (KTR): m(2) Kingston, NH 19 Dec 1768 Mrs Dolly Stevens (KTR), d Kingston, NH (bur) 10 Dec 1811 a.over 70yrs (NHVR).
Ebenezer signed the Association Test in Kingston, NH 1776 (NHSP 30:76).

Children: born Kingston, NH (KTR)
(by 1st wife)
1. **EBENEZER**, b 18 Feb 1739: m(1) Kingston, NH 10 Jan 1760 Sarah Emerson (KTR): m(2) Kingston, NH 27 Feb 1783 Sarah Stevens (KTR)

(by 2nd wife)
2. **JOHN**, b 3 Mar 1770: m Kingston, NH 13 Dec 1798 Ruhamah Fifield (NHGR 3:168)
3. **MOSES**, b 5 Sep 1771
4. **PETER COLCORD**, b 27 Jun 1773
5. **PAUL**, b 1 May 1775: m Epping, NH 17 Mar 1796 Sally Howe (NHGR 3:181)

EBENEZER STEVENS JR, b Kingston, NH 18 Feb 1739 son of Ebenezer & Mary (Colcord) Stevens (KTR): m(1) Kingston, NH 10 Jan 1760 Sarah Emerson (KTR), b (prob) 17 Oct 1739 dau of Samuel & Sarah (Ayer) Emerson (HC p517), d Kingston, NH 16 Sep 1768 (KTR): m(2) Kingston, NH 27 Feb 1783 Sarah Stevens (KTR).
Ebenezer Jr signed the Association Test in Kingston, NH 1776 (NHSP 30:77).

Children: born Kingston, NH (KTR)
(by 1st wife)
1. **SAMUEL**, b 2 Apr 1761
2. **EBENEZER**, b 10 Feb 1763
3. **MARY**, b 23 Nov 1764: d Kingston, NH 6 Sep 1782 (KTR)
4. **SARAH**, b 30 Mar 1766
5. **ELIZABETH**, b 20 Aug 1768

(by 2nd wife)
6. **PETER**, b 25 May 1785
7. **JOHN**, b 15 Apr 1787
8. **BENJAMIN**, b 8 Nov 1790: d Kingston, NH 24 Sep 1794 (KTR)
9. **HANNAH**, b 12 May 1792
10. **BENJAMIN**, b 21 Nov 1794
11. **MARY**, b Jun 1796
12. **JOANNA**, b 17 Jan 1805

ISAAC STEVENS, b Hampstead, NH 1 Dec 1751 (NHPR 81:149) son of Joseph & Ruth (Heath) Stevens: d aft 29 May 1833 of Stratford, NH (NHPR 81:147): m(1) Henniker, NH 20 Sep 1777 Elizabeth (Rich) Stone, b 28 Feb 1756 dau of John & Catherine (Whiteman) Rich, d Stratford, NH 27 Oct 1813: m (2) 1 Jan 1815 Lydia (Brainard) Osburn, b 1783 dau of David Brainard: m(3) Sally (Bowker) Curtis, b 16 Sep 1774, d Jan 1851 (Hist of Stratford, NH p450 & 455).

Isaac was mustered at Kingston in the 7th Rgt Dec 1776 by Col Bartlett & served as a Cpl in Capt Gordon's Co #S11460 (NHSP 14:453).

Children: (Hist of Stratford, NH p450)
(by 1st wife)
1. **JOSEPH**, b 13 Mar 1781: m Abigail Crouch
2. **RICH**, b 24 Jun 1782: d 1851: m 10 Apr 1805 Fanny Schoff
3. **ISAAC**, b 10 Nov 1784: m Sally Dole
4. **BETSEY**, b 20 Nov 1786
5. **DANIEL**, b 23 Apr 1788: m Eunice Barlow
6. **RUTH**, b 23 Mar 1791: m Barney Tortelotte
7. **JOHN**, b 22 Apr 1793: m Samantha Fuller
8. **ELIZABETH**, b 1 May 1797: m Elisha Barlow

(by 2nd wife)
9. **CATHERINE**, b 6 Apr 1816: m Nelson Gamsby
10. **LYDIA**, m Roberson Marshall

JOHN STEVENS, b Kingston, NH 9 Mar 1729 son of Ebenezer & Elizabeth (Colcord) Stevens (KTR): m Kingston, NH 15 Apr 1756 Mary Hubbard (KTR), b Kingston, NH 21 May 1735 dau of Richard & Abigail (Taylor) Hubbard (KTR).

John signed the Association Test in Kingston, NH 1776 (NHSP 30:78).

Children: born Kingston, NH (KTR & NHVR)
1. **ELIZABETH**, b 20 Mar 1757
2. **JOHN**, b 17 Sep 1758
3. **MARY**, bpt 30 Mar 1760
4. **ANNA**, bpt 26 Dec 1762

OTHO STEVENS, b Hampstead, NH 4 Feb 1762 son of Samuel & Susanna (Griffin) Stevens (HmstR).
Otho, of Sandown (a.17yrs), was mustered by Kingston & served in Col Jacob Gale's 7th Rgt of NH Militia 1779 (RW roll-50).

SAMUEL STEWART, b Kingston, NH 10 Sep 1761 son of Samuel & Grace (Hubbard) Stewart (KTR): d Newport, ME 12 Jul 1832 (RG 2:673): m Danville, NH 28 Jun 1781 Hannah Brown (NEHGR 58:125), b Freemont, NH 5 Sep 1763 dau of Daniel & Ruth (Whicher) Brown, d 1848.
Samuel enlisted Aug 1776 for 1 year under Capt Nathan Brown, Col Pierce Long NH Rgt & marched to Ticonderoga (NHPR 82:47).

Children:
1. **NATHANIEL**, b abt 1785: living Newport, ME in 1832
2. **ROBERT**, d 1868: m Abigail Eastman (DAR LB 160:186)

STEPHEN STEWART, bpt Amesbury, MA 5 Jan 1745/6 son of Robert & Ann (Adams) Stewart (AVR): d (Est Adm) 18 Aug 1817: m Kingston, NH 5 Apr 1775 Sarah Peaslee (Early Settlers of Rowley p362), b Newton, NH 15 Jan 1759 dau of James & Abigail (Johnson) Peaslee (NwtTR).
Stephen signed the Association Test in Kingston, NH 1776 (NHSP 30:78).

Children: born Kingston, NH
1. **ANNA**, b 8 May 1776
2. **STEPHEN**, b 25 Dec 1779
3. **JAMES**, b 5 Apr 1782

4. **MOSES**, b 12 Oct 1784: living 1817
5. **SARAH**, b 5 Jan 1787
6. **ABIGAIL**, b 26 Mar 1792
7. **EBENEZER**, b 7 Dec 1794
8. **BETSEY**, b 29 Sep 1797

MOSES STRAW, m Kingston, NH 27 Jul 1771 Hannah French (KChR)

Moses served as a pvt in the NH Militia Capt Jacob Webster's Co, Col Daniel Reynold's Rgt Jul to Nov 1781 (RW roll-52).

ABRAHAM TITCOMB SWETT, b Newbury, MA 18 Mar 1760 son of Benjamin & Rebecca (Pierce) Swett (NVR): d Bradford, NH 1850 (NHPR 84:43): m 1781 Priscilla Eastman (Swett Gen p71), b Boscawen, NH 2 May 1763 dau of Timothy & Hannah (Richardson) Eastman (Eastman Gen p104), d 5 Jun 1849

Abraham, of Boscawen, enlisted for Kingston in the 7th Rgt of NH Militia in the Continental Army 1777. Served in Capt James Gray's Co #43190 (NHSP 14:585,659).

Children:

1. **SAMUEL P.**, b Boscawen, NH 11 Jun 1783: m Henniker, NH 16 Feb 1804 Abigail Shattuck
2. **SILAS**, b 2 Jan 1786: m Polly _____
3. **HANNAH**, b 29 Jul 1790
4. **JUDITH**, b 2 Jun 1792: d 3 Jun 1878: m 17 May 1810 Peter Ayers Cook
5. **SARAH**, b 19 Feb 1795
6. **REBECCA**, b 12 Apr 1797
7. **ENOCH**, b 17 Dec 1801: living Baltimore, MD in 1830 (NHPR 84:43)

BENJAMIN SWETT, b Hampton, NH 17 Oct 1707 son of John & Bethiah (Page) Swett (HmVR p36): d Kingston, NH (bur) 26 Jun 1787 (NHVR): m Kingston, NH 20 Feb 1728/9 Abigail Darling (KTR), b Salisbury, MA 4 Oct 1709 dau of John & Mary (Page) Darling (SVR), d Concord, NH.

Benjamin signed the Association Test in Kingston, NH 1776 (NHSP 30:77).

Children: born Kingston, NH (KTR)

1. **MOSES**, b 3 Dec 1729: d Kingston, NH 17 Oct 1730 (NHGR 2:132)
2. **BENJAMIN**, b 31 Dec 1736: d aft 1777 (DAR 1:662) m Kingston, NH 13 Mar 1760 Mary Elliot (KTR)
3. **NAOMI**, b 13 Mar 1739: m Kingston, NH 18 Sep 1764 Jonathan Elliot (KTR)
4. **JOHN**, b 10 Jun 1741: d Kingston, NH 18 Aug 1746 (NHVR)
5. **SAMUEL**, b 15 Dec 1744: d Boston, MA 21 Sep 1792: m Kingston, NH 28 Aug 1766 Mary Jones (NHGR 3:130)
6. **JOHN DARLING**, b 7 Jun 1750: d Andover, NH 1793 (DAR 2:205): m Kingston, NH 28 May 1771 Elizabeth Clifford (NHGR 3:130)
7. **MOSES**, b 23 Dec 1754: d So Sanford, ME 30 Aug 1822 (RG 2:676): m 21 Oct 1783 Hannah Eastman

DANIEL SWETT, b Hampton Falls, NH 23 Apr 1763 son of Moses & Eunice (Rogers) Swett (Swett Gen p58): d Gilmanton, NH 24 Aug 1837 (NHPR 84:51): m 1788 St Stephens, New Brunswick Jane McNeil, b 3 Jun 1768. Lived Perry, ME.

Daniel & Jane separated, having lived unhappily together for several years & Daniel went to Gilmanton, NH to live where he told people that his wife had died. There was no divorce, but a paper was drawn up dividing the property. Daniel married (illegally) abt 1814 widow Sally (Gunnison) Brown of Epping (NHPR 84:54). He then m(3) 30 Dec 1829 Sally (Sanborn) Nelson (Swett Gen p58).

Daniel, of Gilmanton (a.55yrs), deposed 23 Apr 1818 that he was enlisted Jul 1779 by John Morrill, a recruiting officer; was mustered by Col Gale, 16 Jul in the town of Epping, for the lower part of Kingston; & in the fall of 1779 he joined at Danbury the Co commanded by Capt Carr, Col George Reid 2nd NH Rgt; before he joined Capt Carr's Co to which he really belonged, he was under Capt Caleb Robinson at Fishkill, NY. He served until 16 Jul 1780

#W22361 (NHPR 84:47).

Children: (NHPR 84:47-60)

1. **LYDIA**, b 25 Apr 1789: d 23 Sep 1791
2. **JANE**,, b 14 May 1791: m Samuel Norwood
3. **DANIEL**, b 3 Dec 1792: d Boston, MA 1827: m Rachel Loring
4. **ELIZABETH**, b 19 Mar 1794: m Eliphalet Olmstead
5. **SARAH**, b 24 Jan 1796: m John Dudley
6. **NANCY**, b 19 Dec 1797: m Peter Folsom
7. **MARY ANN**, b 19 Sep 1799
8. **SUSANNA**, b 18 Aug 1801
9. **LYDIA**, b 21 Jun 1803: m ___ Gibson
10. **BENJAMIN**, b Perry, ME 5 Feb 1805: m Elsie Shannon
11. **(DAU)**, b 1 Jan 1808: d Jan 1808
12. **EUNICE**, b 13 Aug 1809: m ____ Lincoln
13. **ELMIRA**, b 24 Jun 1811: m ____ Johnson
14. **IZETTE**, b 24 Jun 1811: d 18 Jan 1812

ELISHA SWETT, b Hampton, NH 13 Aug 1705 son of John & Bethiah (Page) Swett (HmVR p32): d Kingston, NH 1 Apr 1788 (NHVR): m(1) Kingston, NH 11 Nov 1729 Sarah Tilton (KTR), b Hampton, NH 25 Jan 1705 dau of Joseph & Margaret (Sherburne) Tilton (HmVR p38), d Kingston, NH 10 Oct 1735 (KTR): m(2) Kingston, NH 10 Feb 1735/6 Abigail Sanborn (KTR), b Kingston, NH 6 May 1713 dau of John & Mehitable (Fifield) Sanborn (KTR), d Kingston, NH 10 Mar 1802 a.89yrs (NHVR).

Elisha signed the Association Test in Kingston, NH 1776 (NHSP 30:76).

Children: born Kingston, NH (KTR)
(by 1st wife)

1. **ESTHER**, b 7 Aug 1730: m Kingston, NH 7 Nov 1750 John Judkins (KTR)
2. **JOSEPH**, b 9 Jan 1732/3: d 25 Sep 1806: m Kingston, NH 6 Nov 1755 Hannah Sleeper (NHGR 3:88)
3. **STEPHEN**, b 18 Dec 1734: d Kingston, NH 8 Apr 1736 (KTR)

(by 2nd wife)
4. **STEPHEN**, b 21 May 1739: d Kingston, NH Oct 1807 (NHVR): m Kingston, NH 25 Feb 1761 Sarah Garland (KTR)
5. **SARAH**, b 4 Jan 1741/2
6. **ABIGAIL**, b 18 Jul 1744: m Gilmanton, NH 1 Nov 1764 John Moody
7. **HANNAH**, b 13 Apr 1747: m Thomas Swett
8. **ELISHA**, b 2 Dec 1751: m 10 Oct 1782 Hannah Sanborn

JOHN DARLING SWETT, b Kingston, NH 7 Jun 1750 son of Benjamin & Abigail (Darling) Swett (KTR): d Andover, NH 1793 (DAR 2:205): m Kingston, NH 28 May 1771 Elizabeth Clifford (NHGR 3:130).

John, of Kingston (a.22yrs), served in Capt Philip Tilton's Co, Col Enoch Poor's Rgt 1775 (RW roll-51). He signed the Association Test in Kingston, NH 1776 (NHSP 30:77).

Children: born Kingston, NH
1. **TIMOTHY**, b 21 Jan 1772: d Andover, NH 22 Oct 1852: m 1795 Molly Thorn
2. **STEPHEN DECATUR**, b 4 Oct 1775: m Sep 1796 Experience Stevens
3. **JOHN**, b 6 Oct 1779: m 4 Feb 1801 Elizabeth Evans (HA p347)
4. **ELIZABETH**, b 15 Oct 1787
5. **POLLY**, b 24 Oct 1791

MOSES SWETT, b Kingston, NH 28 Mar 1740 son of John & Judith (Young) Swett (KTR): d Sanford, ME 6 Jan 1827: m Wells, ME 15 Mar 1770 Priscilla Hatch (RWFP 3:3403), b abt 1750, d aft 1836.

Moses served as an Ensign in Capt Bragdon's MA Co (MSSP p769).

Children:
1. **MOSES**, m(1) Mary Connor: m(2) Eunice ____
2. **HULDAH**, m 5 Aug 1807 Mark Wiggin
3. **SIMEON**, m Alfred, ME 26 Jul 1796 Susanna Goodwin
4. **JOHN**, m(1) Tuftonboro, NH 27 Nov 1806

Eunice Harford: m(2) Moultonboro, NH 3 Nov 1811 Sarah Pierce

5. **SAMUEL**, b 1788: d Tuftonboro, NH 1 Aug 1867 m Wolfeboro, NH 23 May 1813 Mehitable Neal
6. **ROBERT**, m Wolfeboro, NH 11 Dec 1812 Polly Wiggin

MOSES SWETT (Rev), b Kingston, NH 23 Dec 1754 son of Benjamin & Abigail (Darling) Swett (KTR): d So Sanford, ME 30 Aug 1822 (RG 2:676): m 21 Oct 1783 Hannah Eastman (Swett Gen p37), b Danville, NH 6 Feb 1759 dau of Edward & Sarah (Wadley-Clough) Eastman (DnTR).

Moses is listed in "Soldiers, Sailors & Patriots of Maine" as having performed patriot service (MSSP p767).

Children:

1. **HOMER**, bpt Kingston, NH 5 Dec 1784 (NH VR): m Sanford, ME 16 Nov 1809 Isabella Shaw (MHGR 2:110)
2. **HANNAH**, b 6 May 1789: m Sanford, ME 22 Jun 1817 Jeremiah Moulton Jr (MHGR 2:111)
3. **MOSES**, b 9 Jul 1792
4. **SARAH**, b 23 Jan 1795: m Sanford, ME 2 Nov 1817 James Furbush (MHGR 2:111)
5. **BENJAMIN**, b 26 Jan 1799: m Kittery, ME 7 Oct 1824 Harriet McIntire (KitVR p276)

NATHAN SWETT, b Kingston, NH 9 Jun 1711 son of John & Bethiah (Page) Swett (KTR): d Kingston, NH (WP) 3 Feb 1796: m(1) Kingston, NH 6 Jan 1731 Mary Dearborn (KTR), dau of Thomas & Mary (Garland) Dearborn (Swett Gen p21), d Kingston, NH 1 May 1750 (KTR): m(2) aft 1746 Mrs Jane Garland (PRNH 3:364).

Nathan signed the Association Test in Kingston, NH 1776 (NHSP 30:76).

Children: born Kingston,NH (KTR)
(by 1st wife)

1. **BETHIA**, b 27 Sep 1731: m(1) Kingston, NH 8 Nov 1750 John Morrill (KTR): m(2) Ste-

phen Ladd

2. **DEARBORN**, b 16 Oct 1733: d Kingston, NH 17 Mar 1736 (KTR)
3. **MARY**, b 26 Mar 1737: d 3 Jun 1817: m Kingston, NH 26 Jan 1768 Jonathan Sanborn (KTR)
4. **NATHAN**, b 11 May 1739: m Haverhill, MA 16 Apr 1765 Sarah Frye (HvVR)
5. **HULDAH**, b 29 Jul 1741
6. **DEARBORN**, b 29 Dec 1744: m(1) Mary Grendall: m(2) Elizabeth _____
7. **THOMAS**, b 11 May 1747: m Hannah Swett

(by 2nd wife)

8. **JOHN**, bpt Kingston, NH 1 Apr 1750 (NHGR 5:158): d Kingston, NH 4 Apr 1750 (NHVR)
9. **JANE**, b Hampton Falls, NH 26 Jul 1751 (HFTR): d Seabrook, NH 11 Mar 1833 a.81 yrs (CG p127): m So Hampton, NH 8 Feb 1792 John Janvrain (SHVR)
10. **JOHN**, b Hampton Falls, NH 26 Nov 1752 (HF TR): m 4 Nov 1779 Hannah Peterson
11. **WILLIAM**, bpt Kingston, NH 12 Jun 1757 (NH VR): m Hampton, NH 16 Feb 1789 Elizabeth Javrain (HmVR p211)
12. **MOSES**, b Kingston, NH 3 May 1757 (KTR)

SAMUEL SWETT, b Kingston, NH 15 Dec 1744 son of Benjamin & Abigail (Darling) Swett (KTR): d Boston, MA 21 Sep 1792 (Swett Gen p36): m Kingston, NH 28 Aug 1766 Mary Jones (NHGR 3:130), dau of Samuel Jones.

Samuel signed the Association Test in Kingston, NH 1776 (NHSP 30:77). He served as an Ensign in Capt Nathaniel Hutchin's Co, Col Cilley's Rgt (NHSP 14:610).

Children: last 4 bpt Kingston, NH (NHVR)

1. **SAMUEL JONES**, b 26 Aug 1767
2. **MARY**, b 9 Sep 1768
3. **JAMES JONES**, m Boston, MA 30 May 1805 Christiana Cecilia Vonhagen
4. **ELIZABETH**, m 30 Jan 1806 John Flagner
5. **SARAH**
6. **ABIGAIL**, bpt 26 Mar 1777: m Boston, MA 18

Dec 1800 John Bodge
7. **BENJAMIN**, bpt 26 Mar 1777: m Boston, MA 27 Jun 1796 Nabby Benson
8. **MARK PERMONT**, bpt 26 Mar 1777: d Roxbury, MA 9 Mar 1808: m Boston, MA 6 Jun 1802 Abigail Wood Tower
9. **ZEBULON**, bpt 21 May 1781

STEPHEN SWETT, b Kingston, NH 21 May 1739 son of Elisha & Abigail (Sanborn) Swett (KTR): d Kingston, NH Oct 1807 (NHVR): m Kingston, NH 25 Feb 1761 Sarah Garland (KTR), bpt Hampton Falls, NH 18 Apr 1742 dau of Joseph & Jane (Stickney) Garland (Swett Gen p34), d (prob) Kingston, NH 4 Apr 1797 (NHVR).

Stephen signed the Association Test in Kingston, NH 1776 (NHSP 30:77).

Children: born Kingston, NH (KTR)
1. **JOSEPH**, b 30 Jan 1762: m Plaistow, NH 18 May 1795 Sally Severance
2. **JOHN**, b 9 Feb 1763: m Pittsfield, NH 15 Jul 1790 Mary Leavitt
3. **SARAH**, b 8 May 1766: d 14 Feb 1830
4. **NATHANIEL**, b 9 May 1768: m Kingston, NH 23 Nov 1801 Sarah Bartlett (NHGR 3:171)
5. **STEPHEN**, b 20 May 1770: d 14 May 1864: m Gilmanton, NH 26 Dec 1793 Keziah Clarke
6. **ABIGAIL**, b 28 Aug 1772: m 21 Nov 1793 Moses Shephard
7. **PAUL**, bpt 23 Oct 1774 (NHVR): m(1) Gilmanton, NH 18 Dec 1813 Judith Currier: m (2) Elizabeth (Evans) Piper
8. **HANNAH**, b 27 Mar 1776
9. **NOAH**, b 8 Apr 1778: m Gilmanton, NH 31 May 1803 Sally Morrill
10. **ELISHA**, b 28 Jul 1780: m Sally Currier
11. **JANE**, b 17 Jun 1782: d Kingston, NH 29 Aug 1838 (NHVR) m Joseph Secomb

WILLIAM TANDY, b Gloucester, MA 6 Aug 1725 son of Richard & Rachel (Allen) Tandy (GlVR): d Kingston, NH 1 Jan 1800 (NHVR): m Kingston, NH 29 May 1746 Mary Morgan (KTR), b Hampton Falls,

NH 11 Nov 1725 dau of John & Mary (Dearborn) Morgan (HFTR).

William signed the Association Test in Kingston, NH 1776 (NHSP 30:77).

Children: born Kingston, NH (KTR)

1. **ELIZABETH**, b 2 Mar 1746/7: d Kingston, NH (prob) 5 Jan 1749 (NHVR)
2. **MARY**, b 4 Nov 1749: d Kingston, NH 22 Nov 1749 (KTR)
3. **ABIGAIL**, b 29 Dec 1750
4. **MARY**, b 2 Nov 1752: d Kingston, NH 19 Nov 1752 (KTR)
5. **(INFANT)**, d Kingston, NH 9 Nov 1753 (NH VR)
6. **WILLIAM**, b 24 Dec 1754
7. **PARKER**, b 18 Feb 1758: d 1823: m Danville, NH 15 Sep 1777 Mary Thorn (NEHGR 58:124)
8. **MARY**, b 28 Apr 1762

WILLIAM TANDY JR., b Kingston, NH 24 Dec 1754 son of William & Mary (Morgan) Tandy (KTR).

William Jr, of Kingston (a.19yrs), served in Col Enoch Poor's Rgt, Capt Philip Tilton's Co 1775 (RW roll-51).

SAMUEL THOMPSON, b Amesbury, MA 5 Jun 1729 son of Samuel & Mary (Bartlett) Thompson (AVR): d Kingston, NH Feb 1802 (NHVR): m Kingston, NH 26 May 1757 Catherine Tucker (KTR), b Amesbury, MA 15 May 1734 dau of Ezra & Bathsheba (Sargent) Tucker (AVR), d Kingston, NH 26 Mar 1813 (NHVR).

Samuel signed the Association Test in Kingston, NH 1776 (NHSP 30:78).

Children: born Kingston, NH (KTR)

1. **JOHN**, b 14 Mar 1758
2. **PHEBE**, b 23 May 1760
3. **MOSES**, b 20 Feb 1763
4. **MEHITABLE**, b 13 Feb 1765: m Newbury, MA (int) 3 May 1788 Jacob Hoyt (NVR)
5. **EZRA**, b 4 Jun 1771

6. **BARSHEBA**, b 4 Mar 1774: d Kingston, NH 30 May 1803 (NHVR)
7. **SAMUEL**, b 5 Aug 1777: d Kingston, NH 3 Feb 1856 a.78yrs (GI p32): m Polly ___

THOMAS THOMPSON, bpt Kingston, NH 26 Dec 1742 son of Samuel & Mary (Bartlett) Thompson (KChR): d aft 1796: m 1776 Judith Blaisdell (Blaisdell Papers 2:14), b Kingston, NH 21 Nov 1749 dau of Ralph & Miriam (Rowell) Blaisdell (KTR).

Thomas signed the Association Test in Kingston, NH 1776 (NHSP 30:78).

Children: born Kingston, NH

1. **Hannah**, b 10 Jun 1776: m 1793 Bitfield Sawyer of Newton, NH (Virkus 5:472)
2. **MOLLY**, b 16 Jul 1779
3. **SARAH**, b 22 Sep 1786
4. **RALPH**, b 11 Apr 1789
5. **THOMAS**, b 22 Dec 1791

BARNET (BARNARD) THORN, b Salisbury, MA 22 Jul 1740 son of Samuel & Abigail (Sanborn) Thorn (SVR): m Salisbury, MA 14 Dec 1769 Apphia Norton (SVR).

Probably the Barnard who served in Col Hercules Mooney's Rgt, Capt Jonathan Leavitt's Co for the defense of RI 1779 (RW roll-51). He also served in Capt J. Webster's Co, Col Reynold's Rgt 1781 (RW roll-52).

Children:

1. **MOSES**, b Salisbury, MA 25 Dec 1771 (SVR)

JACOB THORN, b Kingston, NH 27 Oct 1747 son of John & Elizabeth (Brown) Thorn (KTR): d Kingston, NH 9 Apr 1829 (GI p32): m Sarah ____, d Kingston, NH 17 Oct 1839 (GI p32).

Jacob signed the Association Test in Kingston, NH 1776 (NHSP 30:78).

Children:

1. **MOLLY**, b 2 Jun 1772: d Andover, NH 21 Sep

1852 (HA p347): m 1795 Timothy Swett

JAMES THORN, b Salisbury, MA 6 Jan 1715/6 son of James & Hannah (Brown) Thorn (SVR): d Kingston, NH Jun 1796 (NHVR): m Kingston, NH 12 Jan 1748/9 Hannah Brown (KTR), b Salisbury, MA 7 Jul 1725 dau of George & Elizabeth (Eastman) Brown (SVR).

James signed the Association Test in Kingston, NH 1776 (NHSP 30:77).

Children: born Kingston, NH (KTR)

1. **HANNAH**, b 15 Oct 1749
2. **SARAH**, b 15 Sep 1751
3. **JAMES**, b 9 Aug 1755: d Kingston, NH 18 Dec 1813 a.60yrs (GI p32): m Danville, NH 10 Dec 1778 Abigail Sanborn (NHPR 86:33)
4. **MARY**, b 20 Jan 1757
5. **NATHAN**, b 17 Jul 1759: d E. Candia, NH 9 Apr 1851 a.91yrs (CG p31): m 13 Apr 178_ Elizabeth James (DAR #317715)
6. **BETTY**, b 24 Apr 1764
7. **ABIGAIL**, b 14 Jun 1766

JAMES THORN, b Kingston, NH 9 Aug 1755 son of James & Hannah (Brown) Thorn (KTR): d Kingston, NH 18 Dec 1813 (GI p32): m Danville, NH 10 Dec 1778 Abigail Sanborn (NHPR 86:33), b Kingston, NH 10 Sep 1749 dau of Timothy & Alice (Quimby) Sanborn (KTR), d Kingston, NH 24 Jul 1843 a.94 yrs (GI p32).

James enlisted 1775 & served under Capt Philip Tilton at Winter Hill. He enlisted again Jul 1776 & served under Capt Quimby. Also served in 1777 under Capt Currier, Col Drake for 6 months (NHPR 86:33).

Children: (DnTR)

1. **EZEKIEL**, b Danville, NH 2 Mar 1779
2. **LOIS**, b Candia, NH 24 May 1782: m Atkinson, NH 8 Feb 1815 John Sanborn
3. **ABIGAIL**, b Candia, NH 18 Dec 1785: m James Prescott
4. **MIRIAM**, b Danville, NH 26 Feb 1789: bpt

Kingston, NH 20 Sep 1789 (NHVR): d bef 1843

5. **JOHANNA**, b Danville, NH 2 Sep 1793: bpt Kingston, NH 12 Oct 1793 (NHVR): m (prob) Epping, NH 18 Dec 1812 Jacob Tucker (NHGR 3:177)

JOHN THORN, b Salisbury, MA 13 Jul 1710 son of James & Hannah (Brown) Thorn (SVR): d Kingston, NH 1 Nov 1790 a.81yrs (NHVR): m(1) Salisbury, MA 13 Feb 1734/5 Elizabeth Clough (SVR), d Kingston, NH 22 Nov 1741 (KTR): m(2) Salisbury, MA 21 Oct 1742 Elizabeth Brown (SVR), b Salisbury, MA 16 Sep 1715 dau of George & Elizabeth (Eastman) Brown (SVR).

John signed the Association Test in Kingston, NH 1776 (NHSP 30:77).

Children: born Kingston, NH (KTR)
(by 1st wife)

1. **JOHN**, b 18 May 1736: d Tilton, NH Sep 1807: m Danville, NH 5 Dec 1762 Mary Cilley (DnTR)
2. **JEMIMA**, b 10 May 1737: m Kingston, NH 13 Dec 1759 Benjamin Lovering (NHGR 3:91)

(by 2nd wife)

3. **(CHILD)**, d Kingston, NH 27 Sep 1743 (NH VR)
4. **JACOB**, b 27 Oct 1747: d Kingston, NH 9 Apr 1829: m Sarah ____
5. **ELIZABETH**, b 26 May 1751
6. **ABRAHAM**, b 20 May 1754: d Kingston, NH 20 Sep 1754 (KTR)
7. **ABRAHAM**, b 31 Jan 1757

JOHN THORN, b Kingston, NH 18 May 1736 son of John & Elizabeth (Clough) Thorn (KTR): d Tilton, NH Sep 1807 (CG p139): m Danville, NH 5 Dec 1762 Mary Cilley (DnTR), d (prob) Sanbornton, NH 16 Aug 1812 (Hist of Sanbornton p792).

John is listed in Maine Soldiers, Sailors & Patriots p786.

Children: 1st 4 born Danville, NH (DnTR)

1. **PHINEAS**, b 27 Feb 1764: d Tilton, NH 1853 (CG p139): m Concord, NH 21 May 1795 Miriam Lovejoy (NHGR 6:58)
2. **MERCY**, b 7 Nov 1766: d 15 Mar 1862: m Nov 1789 Samuel Dudley
3. **MARY**, b 29 Nov 1768
4. **HENRY**, b 22 Oct 1770: d Sanbornton, NH 1854: m 14 Mar 1793 Betsey Sanborn
5. **ABRAHAM**, b 22 Dec 1772: d 20 Aug 1818: m Mary Calef
6. **MARY**, d Sanbornton, NH
7. **JOHN**, d Concord, NH abt 1808: m Concord, NH 29 Nov 1804 Sarah Lovejoy (NHGR 6:109)
8. **JEREMIAH**, lived in ME

NATHAN THORN, b Kingston, NH 17 Jul 1759 son of James & Hannah (Brown) Thorn (KTR): d E. Candia, NH 9 Apr 1851 (CG p31): m 13 Apr 178_ Elizabeth James (DAR #317715), b 1761, d Candia, NH 12 Sep 1843.

Nathan enlisted in 1775 & served as a pvt under Capt Webster. He also served in Capt Quimby's Co, Col Jacob Gale's Rgt (RW roll-50).

Children: (DAR #317715)

1. **JAMES**, b 26 Sep 1784: m Mary ___
2. **AMOS**, b 11 Apr 1786: m Hannah Martin
3. **BETTY**, b 9 Jul 1791
4. **SALLY**, b 3 Mar 1794
5. **POLLY**, b 28 May 1796
6. **NATHAN JR**, b Candia, NH 17 Jul 1797: d Holland, Vt 3 Feb 1877: m(1) Hampton, NH 13 Feb 1822 Lois Rowell (HmVR p243): m(2) Lucy Chaplin

JOSIAH TILTON, b Kingston, NH 22 Oct 1743 son of Josiah & Sarah (Flanders) Tilton (KTR): d Cornville, ME 13 Feb 1820 (RG 2:693): m(1) Sarah True (DAR 1:680), dau of Abraham True: m(2) Kensington, NH 25 Aug 1789 Abigail Nudd (NHVR).

Josiah served as an Ensign in Capt Stephen Clark's NH Co (MSSP p791 & DAR LB 126:10).

Children: (Essex Gen 10:95)
(by 1st wife)

1. **SAMUEL**, b 1771: m 30 Sep 1795 Sarah Batchelder
2. **MERIBAH**, b abt 1775: m Deerfield, NH 6 Jan 1795 Daniel Currier
3. **JOSIAH**, b 28 Feb 1778: d 1860: m Kensington, NH 5 May 1800 Sarah Dearborn (NHVR)
4. **SALLY**
5. **HULDA**

(by 2nd wife)

6. **ABRAHAM TRUE**, m Boxford, MA 16 Feb 1816 Sally Bixby (BxVR)
7. **DANIEL**
8. **HORATIO GATES**, m (prob) China, ME 19 Nov 1826 Fanny Dow (ME Fam 1:86)

PHILIP TILTON, b Kingston, NH 10 Apr 1741 son of Josiah & Sarah (Flanders) Tilton (KTR): d 26 Jan 1835 (DAR 1:680): m(1) So Hampton, NH 11 Sep 1766 Mary Batchelder (SHVR), b abt 1750, d E. Kingston, NH 27 Aug 1817 a.67yrs (CR): m(2) 4 Oct 1809 Eunice Dodge (Essex Gen 10:94).

Philip was appointed & commissioned a Capt of the 11th Rgt by Col Enoch Poor 1 Jul 1775 & served as such until Nov or Dec 1776 (NHPR 86: 150 & DAR LB 54:332).

Children: bpt E. Kingston, NH (NHVR)

1. **NATHANIEL**, bpt 19 Sep 1773
2. **MOLLY**, bpt 19 Sep 1773: d E. Kingston, NH 25 Jul 1776 (CR)
3. **NATHAN**, bpt 19 Sep 1773
4. **JOSEPH**, bpt 30 Oct 1774
5. **LEVI**, bpt Jun 1778: d 1847: m(1) Kensington, NH 23 Feb 1801 Anna Shaw (NHVR) m(2) Kensington, NH 8 Sep 1817 Betsey Wadleigh
6. **MOLLY**, bpt 7 Oct 1781: d E. Kingston, NH 13 Jul 1828 a.47yrs (CR)

STEPHEN TONGUE, b Amesbury, Ma 18 Jan 1725/6 son of James & Elizabeth (Davis) Tongue (AVR): d Kingston, NH (bur) 21 Mar 1785 (NHVR): m Kingston, NH Nov 1752 Dorothy Blaisdell (KTR), b abt 1732, bpt Kingston, NH 22 Apr 1744 dau of Ralph & Mary (Davis) Blaisdell (KChR).

Stephen signed the Association Test in Kingston, NH 1776 (NHSP 30:77).

Children: born Kingston, NH (KTR)

1. **SARAH**, b 5 Mar 1754
2. **MARY**, b 1 Aug 1756
3. **STEPHEN**, b 9 May 1761

BENJAMIN TRUE, b 6 May 1762 (DAR 1:689) son of Benjamin & Mehitable (Osgood) True: d Chester, NH 6 Dec 1843 a.81yrs (HC p626): m 1783 Mary Locke (Locke Gen p120), b Chester, NH 27 Oct 1769 dau of William & Christian (Paine) Locke (Locke Gen p53).

Benjamin enlisted Jun 1780 & was mustered at Kingston. He served in the 2nd NH Rgt #S18255 (NHPR 87:151).

Children: (Locke Gen p120)

1. **HANNAH**, b 24 May 1784: d Hatley, Canada 1 Jan 1864: m 25 Nov 1802 Isaac Worthen (NHPR 87:153)
2. **SARAH**, b 22 Aug 1788: d 30 Sep 1859: m 9 Apr 1808 Samuel Poor
3. **MARY**, b 10 Aug 1791: d Epping, NH 24 Nov 1857: m(1) Joseph Norris: m(2) Levi Blake
4. **JUDITH**, b 3 Nov 1796: m 1 Jul 1817 Joseph Stevenson
5. **OSGOOD**, b 25 Dec 1799: m Betsey True
6. **ALMIRA**, b 5 Jan 1804: m 24 Jul 1845 Daniel Sanborn
7. **LYDIA**, b 27 May 1806: d 5 Apr 1810
8. **WILLIAM STEPHEN**, b 16 Jan 1808: d 8 Jul 1879: m Chester, NH 17 Nov 1836 Mary Prescott

BENJAMIN TUCKER, b Kingston, NH 25 Sep 1727 son of Samuel & Mary (Elkins) Tucker (KTR): d Kingston, NH 13 Jul 1791 (KTR): m Kingston, NH Sep 1748 Judith Thuriel (KTR), b (prob) Newbury, MA 24 Mar 1724 dau of Thomas & Joannah (_) Thuriel (NVR), d Kingston, NH 12 Dec 1786 (KTR).

Benjamin signed the Association Test in Kingston, NH 1776 (NHSP 30:77).

Children: born Kingston, NH (KTR)
1. **THOMAS**, b 21 Aug 1749
2. **JONATHAN**, b 29 Jul 1751: d 13 Jul 1822: m Abigail ____
3. **HANNAH**, b 4 Jan 1754: d Kingston, NH 18 Dec 1755 (KTR)
4. **MARY**, b 27 Sep 1756
5. **HANNAH THURLA**, b Sep 1762

JONATHAN TUCKER, b Kingston, NH 29 Jul 1751 son of Benjamin & Judith (Thuriel) Tucker (KTR): d Auburn, NY 13 Jul 1822 (NHPR 88:28): m Abigail ____, d St Lawrence Co, NY 15 Nov 1827.

Jonathan enlisted Jun 1779 & served as a pvt under Major Wait, Col Scammell 3rd NH. He was then transferred to the 2nd NH & served in Capt Enoch Chase's Co commanded by George Reid (NHPR 88:27 & NHSP 16:231).

Children: (NHPR 88:28)
1. **(SON)**
2. **(SON)**
3. **(SON)**
4. **EBEN L.**, of Hartland, NY in 1851
5. **(DAU)**

JOSEPH TUCKER, b Kingston, NH 9 Jun 1753 (Hist of Hartford, VT p471): d Norwich, VT 1841 (DAR 1:690): m Andover, NH 11 Dec 1783 Elizabeth Rollins (NEHGR 58:16), b Exeter, NH 1 Aug 1759.

Joseph enlisted 1778 for 3 years. He was at Valley Forge and was placed on the pension roll of Windsor, Vt, 1818 for service in NH line (DAR LB 26:111). He lived in Kingston and was mustered 24 Jul 1781 to serve at West Point. He served for the Town of Andover, NH #S43206 (NHPR 88:30 & NHSP 16:251).

Children: (Hist of Hartford, VT p472)
1. **BETSEY**, b Andover, NH 3 Oct 1784: d Albion, ME Oct 1868

2. **JOSEPH**, b Andover, NH 8 Jul 1786: d Norwich, VT 4 Jul 1808
3. **NATHANIEL**, b Norwich, VT 8 Oct 1788: d Boston, MA 10 Apr 1847
4. **HANNAH**, b Norwich, VT 26 Jan 1791: d West Hartford, VT 4 Aug 1878
5. **LYDIA**, b Norwich, VT 9 Oct 1793: d Danville, VT 6 Jun 1846
6. **DAVID**, b Norwich, VT 14 Feb 1796: d Waterbury, CT 9 Jan 1842
7. **JAMES**, b Norwich, VT 6 Mar 1798
8. **KETURAH**, b Norwich, VT 25 May 1800: d West Hartford, VT 19 Apr 1851
9. **ALVAN**, b Norwich, VT 12 Jan 1803: d Elkhart, IN Nov 1878: m Sharon, VT 14 Aug 1825 Abigail Tossey
10. **JASPER**, b Norwich, VT 3 Apr 1805: d Worcester, MA 4 Sep 1854

JOSIAH TUCKER, b Salisbury, NH 5 Aug 1766 (NHPR 88:32), brother of Dr John Tucker: d Granby, NY 9 Nov 1845 (NHPR 88:34): m Deerfield, NY 31 Jan 1794 Lucy Dougherty (NHPR 88:34).

Probably the Josiah, of Kingston, who served in the Continental Army at West Point 1781 for the town of Weare (NHSP 16:253). He also enlisted Jul 1779 & served under Capt Ezekiel Worthen, Col Mooney. In 1782, he served under Capt Ebenezer Webster in Newbury, command of Gen Bailey & scouted for Indians (NHPR 88:32).

Children: (NHPR 88:35,37)

1. **LAVINIA**, a.51yrs in 1849: m ___ Kingsley
2. **HENRY D.**, living Albany, NH in 1850
3. **JULIA**, m Nicholas White

THOMAS WADLEIGH, b Hampstead, NH 29 Mar 1755 (HmstR): bpt Kingston NH 29 Jun 1755 son of Thomas & Margaret (Rowen) Wadleigh (NHGR 6:32): d 25 Feb 1827 (DAR 1:708): m Hampstead, NH (int) 9 Dec 1783 Merriam Atwood (HmstR), b Hampstead, NH 18 Jan 1763 dau of John & Ruth (Whitaker) Atwood (HmstR), d 1843 (HSt p967).

Thomas was mustered in Capt Gordon's Co, Col

David Gilman's Rgt Dec 1776 (NHSP 14:453). He served in Capt Hezekiah Hutchin's Co, Col Reed's Rgt 9 Jun 1775 (RW roll-50).

Children: (HSt p979)

1. **RUTH**, b 23 Nov 1784: d 17 Jan 1871: m Jonathan Harvey
2. **MIRIAM**, b 30 Mar 1786: d 26 Jun 1830: m Joseph Pillsbury
3. **DANIEL**, b 1 Sep 1788: m Apr 1811 Nancy Champlin
4. **ELIZABETH**, b 18 Jun 1790: d 1841: m 31 Jan 1811 Asa Nelson
5. **LUCRETIA**, b 19 Jun 1792: d 29 Nov 1794
6. **POLLY**, b 1 Jul 1794: m 8 Oct 1816 Edward Dodge
7. **SARAH**, b 25 Apr 1796: d 1 May 1876: m Moses Harvey
8. **MEHITABLE**, b 29 Oct 1798: d 13 Aug 1824: m 15 Jun 1820 Thomas Cheney
9. **PATTY**, b 2 Aug 1800: d 22 Aug 1827: m 28 Nov 1822 Sumner Fowler
10. **THOMAS**, b 9 Dec 1802: d 13 Nov 1847: m(1) 1824 Hannah Roby: m(2) 14 Jan 1838 Lavina Roby: m(3) 30 Apr 1839 Mary Kimball
11. **SUSANNA**, b 12 Apr 1806: d 2 Oct 1836: m John Burnham
12. **JAMES MADISON**, b 17 Apr 1809: d 12 Feb 1830

EBENEZER WATSON, m Kingston, NH 25 Jul 1758 Elizabeth (Swett) Severance (KTR), b Kingston, NH 24 Dec 1724 dau of John & Judith (Young) Swett (KTR). Elizabeth m(1) 25 Oct 1749 Ephraim Severance (KTR).

Ebenezer signed the Association Test in Kingston, NH 1776 (NHSP 30:78).

Children: born Kingston, NH (KTR)

1. **BETTY**, b 11 or 17 Apr 1759
2. **HULDA**, bpt 19 Apr 1761 (NHVR)
3. **THOMAS**, b Aug 1763: d 25 Aug 1841: m Salisbury, NH 18 Jul 1787 Anna Challis
4. **ANNE**, b 2 Feb 1768

THOMAS WATSON, b Kingston, NH Aug 1763 son of Ebenezer & Elizabeth (Swett-Severance) Watson (KTR): d Plainfield, NH 25 Aug 1841 (NHPR 90:135): m Salisbury, NH 18 Jul 1787 Anna Challis (NHPR 90:135), b Salisbury, NH 3 Mar 1772 dau of Thomas & Molly (French) Challis (HS p524), d aft 1855.

Thomas, of Kingston, enlisted Mar 1780 & joined the Army at West Point in Apr. He served until he was discharged 7 Jun 1783 #W22507 (NHPR 90:133).

Children: (NHPR 90:135)
1. **ANNA**, a.19yrs in 1820
2. **(CHILD)**, b abt 1805: d Plainfield, NH Mar 1820
3. **SOPHIA**, a.6yrs in 1820

BENJAMIN WEBSTER, b Kingston, NH 24 Aug 1701 son of Thomas & Sarah (Godfrey) Webster (KTR): d Kingston, NH 5 Feb 1781 (NHVR): m(1) Kingston, NH Feb 1725 Elizabeth Stewart (KTR), dau of Ebenezer & Elizabeth (Johnson) Stewart, d Kingston, NH 20 Apr 1737 (NHVR): m(2) Kingston, NH 1 Dec 1737 Mary Stanyan (KTR), b Hampton, NH 15 Jul 1712 dau of Jacob & Dorothy (_) Stanyan (HmVR p45), d Kingston, NH (bur) 11 Dec 1789 (NHVR).

Benjamin signed the Association Test in Kingston, NH 1776 (NHSP 30:78).

Children: born Kingston, NH (KTR)
(by 1st wife)
1. **(CHILD)**, d Kingston, NH 26 Oct 1726 (NHGR 2:131)
2. **ANNA**, b 17 Oct 1728: d (prob) 29 Nov 1728
3. **ANNE**, b abt 1729: bpt 15 Jun 1735: m Kingston, NH 19 Sep 1749 John Page (KTR)
4. **BENJAMIN**, b 18 Dec 1732: bpt 15 Jun 1735: d Kingston, NH 22 Nov 1745 (KTR)
5. **(CHILD)**, d Kingston, NH 11 Jul 1736 (NHGR 3:39)

(by 2nd wife)
6. **WILLIAM**, b 22 May 1738: d Kingston, NH 11

Nov 1745 (KTR)

7. **ELIZABETH**, b 15 Jun 1740: m Kingston, NH 21 Dec 1762 Richard Hubbard (KTR)
8. **JACOB**, b 3 Sep 1742: d Kingston, NH 6 Feb 1744/5 (KTR)
9. **JACOB**, b 15 Feb 1744/5: d Kingston, NH 21 Apr 1836 (GI p33): m 13 Feb 1767 Elizabeth George (DAR LB 153:80)
10. **MARY**, b 30 Sep 1747
11. **DOROTHY**, b 30 Oct 1750: d Kingston, NH 18 Apr 1815 (GI p1): m Danville, NH 5 Apr 1770 Stephen Badger (NEHGR 58:122)
12. **SARAH**, b 1 May 1754: d Kingston, NH 26 Mar 1840 a.86yrs (NHVR): m Danville, NH 16 Nov 1775 Jonathan Pollard (NEHGR 58: 123)

ISAAC WEBSTER, bpt Kingston, NH 23 Apr 1727 son of John & Sarah (Stewart) Webster (NHGR 2:47): d Kingston, NH 2 Jan 1792 (NHVR): m Kingston, NH 29 Dec 1747 Sarah Downing (NHGR 3:43), b Gloucester, MA 11 Dec 1729 dau of Jonathan & Sarah (?Day) Downing (GlVR).

Isaac served in Capt Caleb Robinson's Co, Col Nathan Hale's Rgt (NHSP 14:629).

Children: born Kingston, NH

1. **DAVID**, b 13 Nov 1748
2. **DANIEL**, b 5 Feb 1750
3. **JOHN**, b 8 Jan 1752: d Kingston, NH 8 Sep 1835 a.84yrs (NHVR): m Martha ____
4. **ENOS**, b 10 May 1755
5. **GIDEON**, b 7 Jun 1758: d 4 Jun 1823: m(1) Danville, NH 1 Aug 1776 Sarah Carter (NEH GR 58:124): m(2) Haverhill, MA 29 Oct 1805 Joanna Bryant (HvVR)
6. **MARY**, b 30 Oct 1760
7. **JONATHAN**, b 15 Apr 1762
8. **LYDIA**, b 28 Aug 1764: m Newton, NH Jun 1784 Thomas Colby
9. **JOSEPH**, b 22 Mar 1767
10. **HOPE**, b 23 Jul 1769
11. **LOVE**, b 15 Nov 1773

ISRAEL WEBSTER, b Kingston, NH abt 1756 (NHPR 91:6) son of John & Susanna (Snow) Webster: d 11 Sep 1835 (NHPR 91:7): m Salisbury, NH 25 Oct 1772 Elizabeth Rolfe (NHPR 91:7)

Israel enlisted Mar 1776 as a Sgt under Capt James Osgood, Col Bedel NH Line #W22550 (NHPR 91:6). Israel lived in Readfield, Belgrave, ME & Salisbury, NH.

Children: (HS p845)

1. **RUTH**, b May 1773: d Salisbury, NH 17 Sep 1859
2. **ISRAEL**, b 10 Oct 1775: d 22 Jun 1851
3. **JOHN**, b 20 Jun 1777
4. **SARAH**, b 27 Oct 1779
5. **HUMPHREY**, b 1 Feb 1781: m Clarissa Greeley (DAR LB 17:86
6. **SAMUEL**, b 15 Jan 1783: d Salisbury, NH 2 Mar 1784
7. **CHARLOTTE**, b 4 Mar 1785
8. **BETSEY**, b 20 Apr 1788

JACOB WEBSTER, b Kingston, NH 15 Feb 1744/5 son of Benjamin & Mary (Stanyan) Webster (KTR): d Kingston, NH 21 Apr 1836 a.91yrs (GI p33): m 13 Feb 1767 Elizabeth George (DAR #339690), d Kingston, NH 13 Mar 1824 a.71yrs (GI p33).

Jacob signed the Association Test in Kingston, NH 1776 (NHSP 30:77). He served as a Lt in Col Enoch Poor's Rgt, Capt Philip Tilton's Co (RW roll-51). In Aug 1778, he enlisted as an Orderly Sgt under Capt David Quimby, Col John Calef Rgt (NHPR 91:10). He also served as a Capt in the NH Militia Col Daniel Reynold's Rgt Jul to Nov 1781 (RW roll-52).

Children: born Kingston, NH (DAR #339690)

1. **BENJAMIN**, b 14 Aug 1767: m Kingston, NH 28 Apr 1785 Sarah Page (NHGR 3:132)
2. **SARAH**, b 5 Jan 1770: m Kingston, NH 29 Jun 1789 Nathaniel Dearborn (NHGR 3:134)
3. **MARY**, b 11 Dec 1772: m Kingston, NH 14 Apr 1796 John Winslow Jr (NHGR 3:167)
4. **SUSANNA**, b 18 Mar 1775: d Kingston, NH 12

Apr 1847 (GI p20): m(1) Samuel Winslow: m(2) Benjamin Norris
5. **LUCY**, b 22 Mar 1777
6. **WILLIAM**, b 25 Sep 1779: d Kingston, NH 23 Jun 1868: m(1) Kingston, NH 26 Dec 1798 Polly Davis (NHGR 3:169): m(2) Martha Winslow
7. **JOHN**, b 14 Apr 1782: d Kingston, NH 28 Jun 1871 (GI p33): m Kingston, NH 16 Dec 1807 Hannah Swett (NHGR 4:176)
8. **NANCY** (Anne), b 25 Jun 1787
9. **JACOB**, b 26 Jun 1791

JONATHAN WEBSTER, b Kingston, NH 15 Apr 1762 son of Isaac & Sarah (Downing) Webster.
Probably the Jonathan, of Kingston, who enlisted for the 7th NH Rgt of Militia in the Continental Army 1777, Capt Hutchin's Co (NHSP 14:585).

JOSEPH WEBSTER, b Kingston, NH 4 Apr 1754 (NHPR 91:13) son of Samuel & Dorothy (Stanyan) Webster. He later lived in Allenstown, NH.
Joseph enlisted May 1775 under Capt Gordon Hutchins, Col John Stark & was in the Battle of Bunker Hill. He enlisted again Jan 1776 under Capt Andrew Buntin, Col Waldron. In May 1776, he served under Capt Joshua Tyler & in Jun 1777, he enlisted under Capt Martin #S14810 (NHPR 91:12).

JOSEPH WELCH, b Haverhill, MA 28 Feb 1702/3 son of Samuel & Mary (Judkins) Welch (HvVR): m Kingston, NH 29 Dec 1726 Deborah Scribner (KTR), b Kingston, NH 7 Sep 1705 dau of Thomas & Sarah (Clifford) Scribner (KTR).
Possibly the Joseph who signed the Association Test in Kingston, NH 1776 (NHSP 30:78).

Children: born Kingston, NH (KTR)
1. **THOMAS**, b 13 Oct 1727: m Kingston, NH 26 Jun 1752 Elizabeth Pressey (KTR)
2. **JOHN**, b 7 Aug 1729: d 1811: m So Hampton, NH 5 Dec 1751 Abra Flanders (SHVR)

3. **MOSES**, b 7 Jun 1731: d Kingston, NH 3 Nov 1820 (GI p34): m Kingston, NH 18 Jun 1755 Judith Worcester (KTR)
4. **JOSEPH**, b 20 Feb 1733: d Plaistow, NH 8 Jul 1829 (PlVR): m Kingston, NH 12 Oct 1756 Hannah Chase (NHGR 3:88)
5. **BENJAMIN**, b 20 Nov 1735: d Kingston, NH Sep 1737 (KTR)
6. **BENJAMIN**, b 20 Sep 1739: d Kingston, NH 26 Dec 1750 (NHVR)
7. **SAMUEL**, b 26 Jun 1742: d 14 Sep 1817 a.75yrs (NEHGR 23:420): m(1) abt 1768 Elizabeth Cheney: m(2) 1777 Anna (Chase) Cheney: m(3) 19 Dec 1797 Susanna Cheney
8. **DEBORAH**, bpt 13 Jul 1745 (NHGR 5:112): d Kingston, NH 10 Jun 1746 (NHVR)

JOSEPH WELCH, b E. Kingston, NH 20 Oct 1761 (NH PR 91:124) son of John & Abra (Flanders) Welch: d Aug 1850 (NHPR 91:125): m Unity, NH 25 Feb 1784 Elizabeth Huntoon (UR p54), b Kingston, NH 1 Apr 1765 dau of Benjamin & Deliverance (Goss) Huntoon (UR p45).

Joseph enlisted 1 Jul 1779 & served under Capt Leavit, Col Mooney. In 1780, he was mustered at Kingston & served under Capt Caleb Robinson, Col Reid #S11707 (NHPR 91:123). He lived in Unity, NH abt 21 years & then moved to Stansted, Lower Canada where he was residing in 1832.

Children: (Welch Gen p168-9)

1. **JOSEPH**, b 9 Jun 1786: m Weare, NH Nov 1832 Mary Richardson
2. **DELIVERANCE**, b 20 Jun 1788: d Lempster, NH May 1790
3. **DELIVERANCE**, b 25 Mar 1791
4. **RACHEL**, b 2 May 1793: m 3 Mar 1813 Joseph Prescott: of Moor, NY 1855 (NHPR 91:126)
5. **JEMIMA**, b 2 Jun 1795
6. **BENJAMIN**, b 5 May 1798
7. **BETSEY**, b 29 Jun 1800
8. **ARRETHUSA**, b 10 Apr 1803
9. **HILLS HUNTOON**, b 21 Feb 1805: d Weare, NH

23 Aug 1896: m(1)____: m(2) 22 Sep 1886 Ruth (Perkins) Philbrick

10. **TRIPHENA**, m 30 Jan 1834 Hosea Hyde: living Albany, VT in 1853 (NHPR 91:125)

TIMOTHY WELLS, b Sandown, NH 2 Dec 1755 son of Jacob & Ruth (Sargent) Wells (SdTR): m Danville, NH 14 Jul 1774 Sarah Williams (NEHGR 58:123).

Timothy enlisted at Kingston abt 1 Jun 1775 under Capt Philip Tilton, Col Enoch Poor. He enlisted again 1 Sep 1777 at Sandown under Lt David Quimby, Capt Ezra Currier, Col Drake's NH Militia. He was in the Battles of Saratoga & Stillwater and was at the surrender of the British Army under General Burgoyne #S18277 (NHPR 92:36).

Children: born Sandown, NH

1. **RUTH**, bpt 16 Jun 1776
2. **JEMIMA**, bpt 25 Oct 1778

JOHN WEST, m Kingston, NH 9 May 1779 Mary Jacobs (NHGR 3:131)

Probably the John who was enlisted for the town of Kingston by Josiah Bartlett for the Continental Army 1780 (NHSP 16:64).

SILAS WHEELER, b Salem, NH 26 Feb 1749 son of Stephen & Hannah (Heath) Wheeler (HSlm).

Silas served in Col David Gilman's Rgt, Capt Daniel Gordon's Co Dec 1776 (RW roll-50).

SOLOMON WHEELER, b (prob) Weston, MA 3 Feb 1740 son of Abijah & Tabitha (_) Wheeler (see NEXUS Feb 1985 p23): m Concord, MA 29 Nov 1764 Abigail Straton, b Concord, MA 13 Aug 1737 dau of Joseph & Rachel (Wooley) Straton (Book of Straton 1:174).

Solomon signed the Association Test in Kingston, NH 1776 (NHSP 30:76). His name appears on the roll of men raised for Canada belonging to Col Josiah Bartlett's Rgt 1776 (NHSP 14:341).

BENJAMIN WHITTIER, b Salisbury, MA 24 Oct 1737? son of Nathaniel & Hannah (Clough) Whittier (SVR): d Chesterville, ME 11 Nov 1822 (RG 2: 751): m Salisbury, MA (int) 24 May 1755 Mary Joy (SVR), b Salisbury, MA 17 Oct 1736 dau of Benjamin & Sarah (Sawyer) Joy (SVR), d Farmington, ME 5 Jul 1822.

Benjamin, of Raymond, enlisted for Kingston in the 7th Rgt NH Militia 1777 & served in Capt James Gray's Co (NHSP 14:585,660 & DAR LB 164: 250).

Children: last 9 born Raymond, NH

1. **ANNA**, b 3 Dec 1757: d Chester, NH 3 May 1759
2. **BETSEY**, b Chester, NH 24 Apr 1759: m Samuel Prescott
3. **BENJAMIN**, b Chester, NH 26 Apr 1760: d Salisbury, MA 24 Apr 1782
4. **MARY**, b 17 Jan 1763: m Jesse Prescott
5. **MOSES**, b 14 Sep 1764: m Betsey Flint
6. **ANNA**, b 2 Jul 1766: m Joseph Hutchins
7. **MIRIAM**, b 20 Jun 1768: m Richard Maddocks
8. **SARAH**, b 20 Jul 1771: m Amos Weathern
9. **WILLIAM**, b 22 Feb 1774: m Nancy Butterfield (DAR LB 164:250)
10. **RUTH**, b 18 Sep 1775: m Jedidiah Whittier
11. **HANNAH**, b 26 Apr 1777: m Simeon Norris
12. **NATHANIEL**, b 14 Jun 1779: m Alice Sears

DANIEL WHITTIER, b Methuen, MA 13 Jan 1763 (PP 63:183) son of John & Eleanor (Emery) Whittier (MthVR): d Haverhill, MA 9 Mar 1831 (HvVR): m Haverhill, MA 9 Mar 1784 Hepzibah Black (HvVR), b Haverhill, MA 31 Dec 1759 dau of Edmund & Sarah (Lufkin) Black (HvVR).

Evidently the Daniel, of Kingston (a.63yrs), who deposed 11 Jul 1820 that he was in the Battles of Springfield, Morrysinia, Knightbridge & Readhooke. He enlisted 28 Jul 1777 under Capt Ezra Lunt, Col D. Handley MA Line & served as a Sgt. About Jan 1779, he enlisted under Capt Thomas Turner & in the Fall of 1782 was transferred to a Co commanded by Capt Larnard #S43322 (NHPR 94:108 & PP 63:182).

Children: Born Haverhill, MA (HvVR)

1. **POLLY**, b 6 Oct 1782: d Danvers, MA 10 Feb 1839: m Danvers, MA 3 Apr 1806 Noah Whittier
2. **JONATHAN**, b 23 Jan 1785: m (poss) Kingston, NH 12 Dec 1805 Polly Webster (NHGR 4:175)
3. **EDMOND**, b 19 Mar 1787: m Haverhill, MA 28 Sep 1807 Abigail P. Moody (HvVR)
4. **JAMES**, b 17 Aug 1789
5. **DANIEL**, b 28 Dec 1791: m(1) Haverhill, MA Jul 1812 Mary M. Knight (HvVR): m(2) Haverhill, MA 24 Nov 1842 Mary Noyes (HvVR)
6. **MOSES**, b 4 Apr 1794: d Newton, NH 22 Aug 1875: m Newton, NH Feb 1817 Miriam Goodwin (NwtTR)
7. **THOMAS**, b 12 Aug 1796: m Boxford, MA 3 May 1819 Tryphena Hovey (BxVR)
8. **SUSANNAH** (Sukey), b abt 1798: d Haverhill, MA 2 Sep 1801 a.3yrs (HvVR)
9. **BAILEY**, b 3 Jun 1804: living 1820

BENJAMIN WILLIAMS, bpt Newbury, MA 17 Jul 1757 son of Benjamin & Jemima (Robinson) Williams (NVR).

Benjamin, of Hawke, enlisted for Kingston in the 7th Rgt of NH Militia 1777, served in Capt Stone's Co (NHSP 14:585).

JOHN WILLIAMS, of Kingston, was mustered by Col Josiah Bartlett Oct 1777 & served in Capt Ezra Currier's Co, Col Abraham Drake's Rgt 8 Sep to 16 Dec 1777 (RW roll-49).

JOHN WIMOND, of Kingston, served in Capt William Ballard's Co, Col James Frye's Rgt (NHSP 15:746).

EPHRAIM WINSLOW, b Kingston, NH 25 Jun 1727 son of Samuel & Huldah (Swett) Winslow (KTR): d abt 17 Jan 1810 (DAR 1:754): m Kingston, NH 27 Mar 1753 Hannah Colcord (KTR), b abt 1727 dau of

Edward & Mary (Gordon) Colcord (TAG 17:219).
Ephraim refused to signed the Association Test 23 Sep 1776, but later went into the army (NHSP 30:79).

Children: born Kingston, NH (KTR)
1. **ANNA**, bpt 23 Sep 1754 (NHVR)
2. **HITTY**, b 18 Apr 1755
3. **BARTHOLOMEW**, b 4 Oct 1757: d Loudon, NH 26 Feb 1838: m Hannah Sleeper
4. **ANNA**, b 17 Sep 1759: d Strafford, VT 6 Apr 1851: m Loudon, NH 12 Dec 1799 Harvey Blaisdell
5. **MERIAH**, b 4 Mar 1762
6. **LYDIA**, b 7 Mar 1766: d Deerfield, NH: m Kingston, NH 28 Jun 1792 Elisha Winslow
7. **MARY COLCORD**, b 10 Jan 1771
8. **ELISHA** (Greeley Gen p142)

JACOB WINSLOW, b Kingston, NH 27 Nov 1731 son of Samuel & Huldah (Swett) Winslow (KTR): d (WP) Exeter, NH 18 May 1801: m 15 Oct 1778 Tryphena (Nichols) Severance (Greeley Gen p143), b Amesbury, MA 27 Mar 1737 dau of Jonathan & Mary (Challis) Nichols (AVR). Tryphena m(1) Kingston, NH 5 Sep 1754 Jonathan Severance (KTR).

Jacob signed the Association Test in Kingston, NH 1776 (NHSP 30:78). He was mustered by Col Josiah Bartlett Oct 1777 & served in Capt Ezra Currier's Co, Col Abraham Drake's Rgt 8 Sep to 16 Dec 1777 (RW roll-49).

Children:
1. **JACOB**, b Kingston, NH 24 Sep 1779

JOHN WINSLOW, b Kingston, NH 10 Dec 1729 son of Samuel & Huldah (Swett) Winslow (KTR): d Kingston, NH 15 May 1816 a.87yrs (GI p35): m Kingston, NH 8 Dec 1763 Elizabeth French (NHGR 3:139), d Kingston, NH 30 Oct 1823 a.82yrs (GI p35).

John signed the Association Test in Kingston, NH 1776 (NHSP 30:78).

Children: born Kingston, NH
1. **ELIZABETH**, b 14 Sep 1764: d unmd
2. **MARTHA** (twin), b 11 Feb 1766
3. **MARY C.** (twin), b 11 Feb 1766: d 28 Aug 1849: m Gilmanton, NH 25 Jan 1790 Joshua Huntoon
4. **HANNAH**, b 8 Jul 1768
5. **SARAH**, b 20 Dec 1770: m Simon Page
6. **JOHN**, b 28 Oct 1774: d Kingston, NH 26 Nov 1848: m Mary Webster
7. **NATHANIEL**, b 8 Sep 1778

SAMUEL WINSLOW, b Salisbury, MA 26 Nov 1700 son of Samuel & Catherine (Stevens) Winslow (SVR): m(1) Kingston, NH 2 Jan 1723/4 Huldah Swett (KTR), b Hampton, NH 16 Jul 1699 dau of John & Bethia (Page) Swett (HmVR p69), d Kingston, NH 25 Sep 1738 (KTR): m(2) Amesbury, MA 1 May 1739 Frances Tucker (AVR).

Samuel signed the Association Test in Kingston, NH 1776 (NHSP 30:78).

Children: (See p218)

SIMON WINSLOW, probably son of Jonathan & Abigail (_) Winslow of Epping.

Simon, of Kingston (a.18yrs), was mustered by Major William Scott (NHSP 16:98).

ZACHARIAH WOODBURY, b Beverly, MA 29 Jun 1730 son of William & Martha (_) Woodbury (BvVR): d 8 Feb 1815 (DAR 1:759): m(1) Salem, NH 15 Jun 1757 Hannah Corning (TAG 16:119), b Beverly, MA 26 May 1733 dau of Benjamin & Judith (Reynolds) Corning (BvVR): m(2) Louisa Chandler (DAR 1:759).

Zachariah served as a Sgt in Capt Daniel Gorden's Co, Col David Gilman's Rgt 1777 (RW roll-50).

Children: born Salem, NH (HSlm)
1. **WILLIAM**, b 24 Nov 1758: m Salem, NH 4 Mar 1784 Hannah Kelly (TAG 16:232)
2. **LOIS**, b 26 Jan 1759

3. **ZACHARIAH**, b 28 Aug 1762: m Salem, NH 2 Oct 1783 Hannah Vining (HSlm)
4. **HANNAH**, b 19 Feb 1769

DANIEL WOODMAN, b Kingston, NH 10 Dec 1752 son of Daniel Woodman (IGI).

Daniel, of Kingston (a.22yrs), served in Col Enoch Poor's Rgt, Capt Philip Tilton's Co (RW roll-51)

JOHN WOODMAN (Capt), b Kingston, NH 24 Apr 1740 son of Joshua & Eunice (Sawyer) Woodman (KTR): d New Gloucester, ME 21 Mar 1808 (RG 2:768): m Hampstead, NH 21 Oct 1762 Sarah Page (HmstR), b Salisbury, MA 17 Oct 1737 dau of Nehemiah & Mary (True) Page (SVR), d 13 Feb 1809 (Page Gen p30).

John served on War Committees in New Gloucester, ME (DAR LB 28:225 & MSSP p879).

Children: born New Gloucester, ME
1. **JOHN**, b 15 Aug 1767: d Minot, ME: m(2) Hannah Bates
2. **SARAH**, b 4 Jan 1771
3. **JABEZ**, b 20 Apr 1776 m Damaris Howard (DAR LB 28:225)

JOSEPH WOODMAN, b abt 1747: d Brentwood, NH 6 Apr 1829 a.82yrs (CG p24): m Kingston, NH 24 May 1779 Anna Wadleigh (NHGR 3:131), b 17 Jan 1745/6 dau of Joseph & Anna (Swaine) Wadleigh (NEHGR 132:218), d Brentwood, NH 25 Apr 1830 (CG p24).

Joseph signed the Association Test in Kingston, NH 1776 (NHSP 30:77).

JOSEPH WOODMAN, b Kingston, NH 27 Mar 1749 son of Joshua & Eunice (Sawyer) Woodman (KTR): d Freeport, ME 1835: m Love ____, d Kingston, NH 23 Dec 1776 (NHVR). A Joseph Woodman m So Hampton, NH 23 Apr 1767 Loughea Brown (SHVR).

Joseph, while living with his father at Kingston, enlisted Dec 1776 in a Co of Militia commanded by Capt Gordon, Col Gilman & Major

Coffin of Exeter. He also served in a Co of Militia commanded by Moses Merrill of New Gloucester in May or June 1775 (NHPR 97:112).

JOSHUA WOODMAN, b Newbury, MA 6 Jun 1708 son of Archelaus & Hannah (_) Woodman (NVR): d Kingston, NH 4 Apr 1791 (KTR): m Newbury, MA Mar 1735/6 Eunice Sawyer (NVR), b Newbury, MA 21 Jan 1714 dau of John & Sarah (Wells) Sawyer (NVR), d Kingston, NH (bur) 31 Jul 1803 a.87yrs (NHVR).

Joshua signed the Association Test in Kingston, NH 1776 (NHSP 30:77).

Children: born Kingston, NH (KTR)

1. **JOSHUA**, b 14 Dec 1736: m(1) Newbury, MA 26 May 1772 Judith Woodman (NVR): m(2) E. Kingston, NH 12 Nov 1776 Hannah Blaisdell
2. **EUNICE**, b 18 May 1738: m Kingston, NH 26 Oct 1758 Daniel Watson (NHGR 3:90)
3. **JOHN**, b 24 Apr 1740: d New Gloucester, ME 21 Mar 1808 (RG 2:768): m Hampstead, NH 21 Oct 1762 Sarah Page (HmstR)
4. **MOSES**, d Kingston, NH 23 Sep 1742 (NHVR)
5. **MOSES**, b 25 Mar 1743: d Danville, NH 1824: m Kingston, NH 8 Jul 1777 Hannah (Pierce) Eaton (NHGR 3:130)
6. **SAMUEL**, b 19 Nov 1744: d Kingston, NH 10 Jun 1825 (GI p35): m So Hampton, NH 3 Sep 1776 Judith French (SHVR)
7. **JONATHAN**, b 25 Jul 1746: m(1) Danville, NH 27 Aug 1772 Mary Elkins (NEHGR 58: 122): m(2) Kingston, NH 13 Nov 1782 Abigail Morse (NHGR 3:131)
8. **DAVID**, b 4 Dec 1747
9. **JOSEPH**, b 27 Mar 1749: d Freeport, ME 1835: m Love ____
10. **HANNAH**, b 8 Oct 1750: d Amesbury, MA 10 May 1830 (AVR): m Amesbury, MA 1 Sep 1782 William Bagley (AVR)
11. **SARAH**, b 28 Jun 1752: m Kingston, NH 14 Oct 1783 John Emmons (NHGR 3:132)
12. **MARY**, b 30 Mar 1755: m Eliphalet Haskell
13. **ELIZABETH**, b 4 Dec 1756: d Kingston, NH 1

Sep 1758 (NHVR)
14. **Dolly**, d Kingston, NH 24 Aug 1758 (NHVR)
15. **BENJAMIN**, b 18 Oct 1759: d 6 Oct 1835: m 25 Jun 1782 Sarah Magoon

MOSES WOODMAN, b Kingston, NH 25 Mar 1743 son of Joshua & Eunice (Sawyer) Woodman (KTR): d Danville, NH 1824: m Kingston, NH 8 Jul 1777 Hannah (Pierce) Eaton (NHGR 3:130), b abt 1751, d Aug 1850 a.99yrs (Hist of Raymond, NH p296).

Moses, of Kingston (a.32yrs), served in Col Enoch Poor's Rgt, Capt Philip Tilton's Co 1775 (RW roll-51).

Children:
1. **POLLY**, b Salisbury, NH 25 Sep 1778
2. **ELIZABETH GERRISH**, b Salisbury, NH 15 Apr 1781
3. **BENJAMIN**, b Salisbury, NH 9 Sep 1783: m Rachel Eaton. He lived in Sweden, ME
4. **MOSES**, b Danville, NH 7 Oct 1785 (DnTR)
5. **JOHN**, b Danville, NH 19 Jun 1792 (DnTR)

SAMUEL WOODMAN, b Kingston, NH 19 Nov 1744 son of Joshua & Eunice (Sawyer) Woodman (KTR): d Kingston, NH 10 Jun 1825 a.80yrs (GI p35): m So Hampton, NH 3 Sep 1776 Judith French (SHVR), b (prob) So Hampton, NH 14 Apr 1753 dau of Daniel & Sarah (Gould) French (SHVR), d Kingston, NH 28 Sep 1846 a.93yrs (GI p35).

Samuel signed the Association Test in Kingston, NH 1776 (NHSP 30:78).

Children: born Kingston, NH
1. **JOSHUA**, b 18 Aug 1777
2. **DANIEL**, b 19 Aug 1779
3. **SARAH**, b 25 Jul 1782: d Kingston, NH 26 Dec 1858: m Kingston, NH 28 Feb 1810 Morris Whitcher (NHGR 4:177)
4. **NAHAN**, b 7 Dec 1789
5. **JUDITH**, b 16 Sep 1794
6. **ELIHU**, b 20 Jun 1797

AARON YOUNG, b Kingston, NH 27 Oct 1714 son of

Joseph & Elizabeth (Sleeper) Young (KTR): d 1 Apr 1789: m Kingston, NH 8 Nov 1737 Abigail Dudley (NHGR 3:39), b 31 Oct 1716 dau of James & Mary (Folsom) Dudley (Dudley Gen p283), d Boston, MA 18 Nov 1802

Aaron signed the Association Test in Kingston, NH 1776 (NHSP 30:78).

Children: 1st 3 bpt Kingston, NH (NHGR)

1. **DUDLEY**, bpt 25 Feb 1738/9: m Kingston, NH 19 Oct 1758 Jenne Smith (NHGR 3:91)
2. **DAVID**, bpt 3 Jan 1741/2: d Kingston, NH 4 Nov 1745 (NHVR)
3. **AARON**, bpt 17 Jun 1744: d Kingston, NH 1 Dec 1745 (NHVR)
4. **AARON**, b 3 Aug 1746: d Union, ME 1814 (RG 2: 775): m 1769 Dorothy Young
5. **DAVID**, b 1 May 1753: d Pittson, ME 15 Feb 1826: m 1779 Elizabeth Clark (RG 2: 776)

AARON YOUNG JR, b Kingston, NH 3 Aug 1746 (RG 2:775) son of Aaron & Abigail (Dudley) Young: d Union, ME 1814: m 1769 Dorothy Young (DAR LB 89:149).

Aaron Jr signed the Association Test in Kingston, NH 1776 (NHSP 30:76). He served as a Lt in Capt Ezra Currier's Co, Col Abraham Drake's Rgt 8 Sep to 16 Dec 1777 (RW roll-49).

Children:

1. **JOHN**, b 1775: d 1840: m 1801 Polly Mace (DAR LB 89:149)
2. **DOROTHY**, b 12 Nov 1785: m 30 May 1804 David Bartlett
3. **SALLY**, m Isaac Bartlett

DAVID YOUNG, b Kingston, NH 1 May 1753 (RG 2: 776) son of Aaron & Abigail (Dudley) Young: d Pittston, ME 15 Feb 1826: m 1779 Elizabeth Clark (RG 2:776).

David served in the defense of Boston & at Ticonderoga under Capt Wm Ballard, Col James Frye's Rgt of NH Militia (DAR LB 21:335 & MSSP

p889).

Children: born Pittston, ME (ME Fam 1:298)
1. **DAVID**, b 24 Jul 1779: d 11 Jun 1848: m Pittston, ME (int) 9 Sep 1802 Sally Colburn
2. **BETSEY**, b 18 Mar 1781: m Abiather Kendall
3. **AARON**, b 12 May 1783: m Pittston, ME 19 Feb 1803 Mary Colburn
4. **ABIGAIL**, b 30 Jan 1785: m Pittston, ME 24 Oct 1802 James Johnson
5. **ELI**, b 26 Feb 1787: d 15 Feb 1839: m Pittston, ME 18 Oct 1813 Eleanor Blinn
6. **JOSEPH**, b 29 Jan 1789: m Eliza Hatch
7. **JOANNA**, b 5 Feb 1791: m Eliakim Scammon
8. **JONATHAN**, b 31 May 1793: m Pittston, ME 14 May 1815 Mary Morris
9. **DUDLEY**, b 26 Apr 1795: m Pittston, ME 29 Sep 1817 Rebecca Reed
10. **STEPHEN**, b 21 Mar 1797: m(1) Mary Smith: m(2) Pittston, ME 21 Nov 1822 Betsey Jewett
11. **JOHN**, b 22 Aug 1799: m Pittston, ME 23 Mar 1820 Emma Presman
12. **MARY**, b 22 Mar 1802: m Pittston, ME 20 Nov 1822 Zenas Hatch

JONATHAN YOUNG, b 12 Jan 1756 (DAR #316099): d 27 Mar 1807 (DAR 1:769): m Kingston, NH 28 Oct 1777 Sarah Clifford (NHGR 3:130), b Kingston, NH 17 Nov 1757 dau of Joseph & Mary (Healey) Clifford (KTR), d 9 Nov 1816.

Jonathan served in Capt William Ballard's Co, Col James Frye's Rgt (NHSP 15:746).

Children: (DAR #316099)
1. **DAVID**, b 14 Apr 1778: d May 1800
2. **PHINEAS**, b 14 Mar 1780
3. **JONATHAN**, b 25 Jul 1788: m Phebe Towle
4. **AARON**, b 12 Jan 1794: d 1 Mar 1846: m 8 Dec 1816 Betsey Bickford

....

REFERENCES

AbVR.... Vital Records of Abington, MA 2 vols. (New Eng. Hist. & Gen. Soc. 1912)

AndVR... Vital Records of Andover, MA 2 vols. (Topsfield Hist. Soc. 1912)

AVR..... Vital Records of Amesbury, MA (Topsfield Hist. Soc. 1913)

BdVR.... Vital Records of Bradford, MA (Topsfield Hist. Soc. 1907)

BtTR.... Town Records of Brentwood, NH (microfilm of original records)

BvVR.... Vital Records of Beverly, MA 2 vols. (Topsfield Hist. Soc. 1906-1907)

CG...... Colonial Gravestone Inscriptions by Mrs. C. Goss (Clearfield Co. 1989)

CR...... Old Cemetery Records, East Kingston, NH by Mrs W.B. Folsom (DAR Lib. 1930)

DAR..... DAR Patriot Index 2 vols. (DAR Lib. 1966 & 1980)

DAR LB.. DAR Lineage Book, 166 vols. (Washington, D.C. 1890-1939)

DnTR.... Town Records of Danville, NH (microfilm of original records)

DvVR.... Vital Records of Dover, NH (Heritage Books, Inc. 1977)

ExA..... Essex Antiquarian: A Quart. Mag. Devoted to the Bio., Gen., Hist. & Ant. of Essex Co. MA (Salem, MA 1897-1909)

ExVR.... Vital Records of Essex, MA (Essex Institute, 1908)

GI...... Gravestone Inscriptions of Kingston, NH (DAR Lib. 1929)

GlVR.... Vital Records of Gloucester, MA (Topsfield Hist. Soc. 1917-1924)

HA...... History of Andover, NH 1751-1906 by J. Eastman (Concord 1910)

HC...... History of Old Chester, NH by Benjamin Chase (Heritage Books, Inc. 1992)

HCnt.... History of the Town of Canterbury, NH 1727-1912 by James Lyford (Rumford Press 1912)

HE...... History of Exeter, NH by Charles Bell (Heritage Books, Inc. 1979)

REFERENCES

HFTR.... Town Records of Hampton Falls, NH (microfilm of original records)

HH...... History of Hampton, NH by Joseph Dow (N.H. Pub. Co. 1970)

HL...... History of Littleton, NH by J. Jackson 3 vols. (Cambridge, MA 1905)

HmstR... Records of Hampstead, NH by Harriet Noyes (Hunterdon House 1984)

HmVR.... Vital Records of Hampton, NH by G. & M. Sanborn (New Eng. Hist. & Gen. Soc. 1992)

HP...... History of Plymouth, NH by Ezra Stearns (University Press 1906)

HS...... History of Salisbury, NH by John Dearborn (Manchester, NH 1890)

HSlm.... History of Salem, NH by E. Gilbert (Rumford Print. Co. 1907)

HSt..... History of Sutton, NH by A.H. Worthen (New Eng. Hist. Press 1974)

HvVR.... Vital Records of Haverhill, MA 2 vols. (Topsfield Hist. Soc. 1910-1911)

IGI..... International Genealogical Index

IpVR.... Vital Records of Ipswich, MA 3 vols. (Essex Institute 1910-1919)

KChR.... Church Records of Kingston 2nd Church of Christ (DAR Lib. 1930)

KitVR... Vital Records of Kittery, ME by ME Hist. Soc. (Picton Press 1991)

KTR..... Town Records of Kingston, NH (microfilm of original records)

LND..... Gen. Dict. of ME & NH by Libby, Noyes & Davis (Gen. Pub. Inc. 1988)

LndVR... Vital Records of Londonderry, NH by D. Annis (Heritage Books, Inc. 1989)

MAS&S... Mass. Soldiers & Sailors of the Rev War, 17 vols. (Boston 1896-1908)

ME Fam.. Maine Families in 1790 3 vols. edited by Ruth Gray (Picton Press 1988-1992)

MEHGR... Maine Hist. & Gen. Recorder 9 vols. (Gen. Pub. Inc. 1973)

MGFH.... Gen. & Family History of the State of ME by G. Little 4 vols. (Lewis Hist. Pub. Co. 1909)

MthVR... Vital Records of Methuen, MA

(Topsfield Hist. Soc. 1909)
MSSP.... Maine Soldiers, Sailors & Patriots of the Rev. War by C. & S. Fisher (Sons of the Amer. Rev. 1982)
NEHGR... New England Hist. & Gen. Register
NEM..... New England Marriages by C. Torrey (Gen. Pub. Inc. 1985)
NHGR.... The New Hampshire Genealogical Record 7 vols. (Heritage Books, Inc. 1988)
NHPR.... New Hampshire Pension Records by Mrs. Amos Draper 101 vols. (DAR Lib 1918-1933)
NHSP.... New Hampshire Provincial & State Papers (Concord, 1867-1943)
NHVR.... Vital Records of various New Hampshire towns (microfilmed transcripts)
NptVR... Vital Records of Newburyport, MA 2 vols. (Essex Institute, 1911)
NVR..... Vitals Records of Newbury, MA 2 vols. (Essex Institute 1911)
NwtTR... Town Records of Newton, NH (microfilm of original records)
OF...... Old Families of Salisbury & Amesbury, MA by David Hoyt (Gen. Pub. Co. 1982)
PlVR.... Vital Records of Plaistow, NH by Priscilla Hammond (DAR Lib. 1937)
PP...... Pension Papers/ NSDAR Reg. General 234 vols. (DAR Lib. 1925-1965)
PRNH.... Probate Records of the Province of N.H. 9 vols. (Heritage Books, Inc. 1990)
RG...... Revolutionary Graves in ME/ME Old Cem. Assoc. 2 vols. (DAR Lib. 1981)
RW...... Revolutionary War Rolls/m246 Series (microfilm at National Archives)
RWPF.... Revolutionary War Pension File Abstracts 3 vols. by Virgil White (National Hist. Pub. Co. 1990-1992)
RwVR.... Vital Records of Rowley, MA 2 vols. (Essex Institute, 1928)
SdTR.... Town Records of Sandown, NH (microfilm of original records)
SHVR.... Vital Records of South Hampton, NH (Hist. Com. of So. Hampton 1970)

REFERENCES

SlmVR... Vital Records of Salem, MA 6 vols. (Essex Institute, 1916-1925)
SVR..... Vital Records of Salisbury, MA (Topsfield Hist. Soc. 1915)
TAG..... The American Genealogist
TwkVR... Vital Records of Tewksbury, MA (Essex Institute 1912)
UR...... Miscellaneous Records of the Town of Unity, NH (DAR Lib. 1987)
WoVR.... Vital Records of Woburn, MA (Andrew Cutler & Co. 1890-1918)

....

KINGSTON, NH

CORRECTIONS & ADDITIONS

Page 57 - **AMASSA DOW**, b abt 1704 was the son of Joseph & Hannah (Challis) Dow (NHGR 7:181)

Page 193 - **JAMES TOWLE**, b 31 Dec 1747 married ABIGAIL COLBY 13 Sep 1768 (DnTR)

Page 326 - **JOHN LADD** married Alice Thing 2 Dec 1742 (Town Records of East Kingston)

Page 337 - **JOHN PEARSON** who signed the Association Test was probably John PEARSON Sr.

JOHN PEARSON, b Lynn, MA 10 Mar 1709/10 son of James & Hepzebeth (Swaine) Pearson (Lynn VR): m Andover, MA 16 Jun 1732 Rebecca Osgood (AndVR), b abt 1714 probably dau of Ebenezer & Rebecca (Symmes) Osgood (Osgood Gen).

Children: born Andover, MA (AndVR)
1. JOHN, b 29 Feb 1735/6: m Abigail Tyler
2. SUSANNA, b 13 Jul 1740: m William Ingalls
3. SAMUEL, b 19 Dec 1743
4. ELIZABETH, b 31 Jul 1748
5. HANNAH, b 7 Nov 1751: m(2) Moses Woodman
6. DORCAS, b 31 Dec 1753: m Jonathan Fifield

Page 362 - **JONATHAN SEVERANCE**
Additional Children: born Belmont, NH (IGI)
MOLLEY, b 3 Feb 1788
BENJAMIN, b 26 Jul 1790
STEPHEN, b 26 Jul 1796
ELIZABETH, b 26 Jul 1796

Page 404 - **HANNAH EATON** wife of MOSES WOODMAN was the dau of John & Rebecca (Osgood) Pear son. She was born in Andover, MA 7 Nov 1751 (AndVR)

www.ingramcontent.com/pod-product-compliance
Lightning Source LLC
Chambersburg PA
CBHW071825270326
41929CB00013B/1903

* 9 7 8 1 5 5 6 1 3 9 0 9 3 *